List of Symbols and Their Meanings (more or less in the o...)

Symbol	Meaning
N	total number of all observations of variable values; total number of units of analysis included in the study or number of ranks in a set of ranks
n	number of observations (units of analysis) in a sample; sample size
n_1	the number of observations (units of analysis) in Sample 1; size of Sample 1; similar interpretations for n_2, n_3, etc.
Σ	find the sum (of)
$\Sigma\Sigma$	find the sum of the sums of
$\sqrt{}$	square root (of)
x	a variable; in bivariate and multivariate analysis, an independent variable
x^*	standardized value(s) of x [z-score equivalent(s) of x]
$\bar{x}$	the mean of x
y	a variable; in bivariate and multivariate analysis, a dependent variable
y^*	standardized value(s) of y [z-score equivalent(s) of y]
$\bar{y}$	the mean of y
s	standard deviation
s^2	variance
z	standard normal (curve or distribution) score
p	probability (of)
q	$1-p$
$p(H)$	probability of heads in one trial or coin flip
$p(T)$	probability of tails in one trial or coin flip
$p(S)$	probability of a success (e.g., a head) in a single trial (e.g., coin flip)
$p(F)$	probability of a failure (e.g., a tail) in a single trial (e.g., coin flip)
$p(K)$	probability of K successes in a series of trials
T	number of trials in a series of trials (in probability calculations)
K	number of successes in T trials (in probability calculations)
O	an observed cell frequency in chi-square analysis
E	an expected cell frequency in chi-square analysis

Symbol	Meaning
χ^2	the chi-square test statistic
α	significance level; probability of rejecting a true null hypothesis
tf	test factor variable in elaboration analysis
μ	population mean
$\hat{\mu}$	estimate of the population mean
$\hat{\mu}_{\bar{x}}$	estimate of a mean of a sampling distribution for means
σ	population standard deviation
$\hat{\sigma}$	estimate of a population standard deviation
t	Student's t-test statistic for the difference between two means
$\hat{\sigma}_{\bar{x}}$	estimate of the standard error of a sampling distribution for means
$\sigma_{\bar{y}-\bar{y}}$	variance of the sampling distribution for difference between means of y
$\hat{\sigma}^2_{\bar{y}-\bar{y}}$	estimate of the variance of the sampling distribution for difference between means of y
$\sigma_{\bar{y}-\bar{y}}$	standard error of the sampling distribution for difference between means of y
$\hat{\sigma}_{\bar{y}-\bar{y}}$	estimate of the standard error of the sampling distribution for difference between means of y
D	difference score for the t test for two dependent samples
$\bar{D}$	mean of difference scores for the t test for dependent samples
$\sigma_{\bar{D}}$	standard error of the sampling distribution for $\bar{D}$
$\hat{\sigma}_{\bar{D}}$	estimate of the standard error of the sampling distribution for $\bar{D}$
σ_D	standard deviation of D in the population
$\hat{\sigma}_D$	estimate of the standard deviation of D in the population
y_i	an individual variable value (score) without regard to the particular sample of which it is a part
y_{ik}	an individual variable value (score) in a particular sample (k)
$\bar{y}_k$	mean of a particular sample or group
$\bar{Y}$	grand mean
k	the number of groups [samples, categories (values) of the independent variable]
F	the test statistic for analysis of variance (ANOVA)

Symbol	Meaning
TSS	total sum of squares (in ANOVA)
BSS	between-group sum of squares (in ANOVA)
WSS	within-group sum of squares (in ANOVA)
MSB	mean (sum of) squares between (in ANOVA)
MSW	mean (sum of) squares within (in ANOVA)
Q	Tukey's Honest Significant Difference test statistic
a	the y intercept in a least squares regression equation
b	beta; the slope of a least squares regression line; the amount of change in y for every unit change in x in a linear equation
b^*	standardized beta (beta weight) in a least squares regression equation
r	Pearson's coefficient of correlation (or the correlation coefficient)
r^2	Pearson's coefficient of determination
x, y	the coordinates of a data point in a scattergram
$y.x$	the least squares regression of y on x
$x.y$	the least squares regression of x on y
$b_{y.x}$	the least squares regression coefficient (slope of the regression line) for $y.x$
$b_{x.y}$	the least squares regression coefficient (slope of the regression line) for $x.y$
T	test variable in a least squares partial regression and correlation analysis
$r_{xy.T}$	the least squares correlation between x and y, controlling for T; the partial correlation of x and y, taking T into account
A	the Y intercept in a logistic regression equation
β	probability of a type II error; also, beta in a logistic regression equation
β^*	standardized beta in logistic regression
b_{yx}	the coefficient of regression of the dependent variable y on independent variable x
$b_{yx_1.x_2}$	the coefficient of regression of the dependent variable y on independent variable 1 (x_1), controlling for or taking into account independent variable 2 (x_2); parallel interpretations for other combinations of subscripts
$\log_e$	the natural log (2.7182)
R	Pearson's coefficient of multiple correlation
R^2	Pearson's coefficient of multiple determination

Symbol	Meaning
$\mathrm{Exp}(\beta)$	the odds ratio of the effect of an independent variable on a dependent variable, which is $\log_e$ raised to the power of β
r_{xy}	the correlation between x and y
$r_{yx_1.x_2}$	the least squares partial correlation of independent variable 1 (x_1) and the dependent variable (y), controlling for or taking independent variable 2 (x_2) into account; parallel interpretations for other combinations of subscripts
n_1	the number of ranks in Sample 1 (the size of Sample 1 in M-W U and K-W H analyses)
n_2	the number of ranks in Sample 2 (the size of Sample 2 in M-W U and K-W H analyses)
N_T	the total number of observations (ranks) in both samples ($N_T = n_1 + n_2$) in M-W U analysis
ΣR_1	the sum of the n_1 ranks in Sample 1 after Samples 1 and 2 have been combined, ranked, and then separated again (in M-W U and K-W H analysis)
ΣR_2	the sum of the n_2 ranks in Sample 2 after Samples 1 and 2 have been combined, ranked, and then separated again (in M-W U and K-W H analysis)
ΣR_T	the sum of the N_T ranks after Samples 1 and 2 have been combined (in M-W U and K-W H analysis)
σ_u	the standard deviation of M-W U in the population
μ_u	the mean of the sampling distribution for M-W U (which is the value of U in the population)
μ_{pop}	the mean of M-W U in the population
$\bar{R}_1$	the mean of the ranks in Sample 1 (in K-W H analysis)
$\bar{R}_2$	the mean of the ranks in Sample 2 (in K-W H analysis)
$\bar{R}_T$	the mean of all ranks in all samples (in K-W H analysis)
U	the Mann-Whitney (M-W) test statistic
U_1	a M-W statistic calculated from Sample 1 data after Samples 1 and 2 have been combined, ranked, and then separated again
U_2	a M-W statistic calculated from Sample 2 data after Samples 1 and 2 have been combined, ranked, and then separated again
U_{obs}	M-W U calculated from sample data; the smaller of U_1 and U_2
K-W BSS$_{obs}$	the observed between-group sum of squares in K-W H analysis
$\bar{X}_{K\text{-W BSS}}$	the mean of the sampling distribution of K-WBSS (in K-W H analysis)
H	the test statistic in Kruskal-Wallis analysis of variance for ranks
ρ	Spearman's rho correlation coefficient for ranks
ρ^2	Spearman's rho coefficient of determination for ranks
D_ρ	difference score in Spearman's rho calulations

STATISTICS for Criminal Justice and Criminology in Practice and Research

An Introduction

JACK FITZGERALD
JERRY FITZGERALD

Los Angeles | London | New Delhi
Singapore | Washington DC

Los Angeles | London | New Delhi
Singapore | Washington DC

FOR INFORMATION:

SAGE Publications, Inc.
2455 Teller Road
Thousand Oaks, California 91320
E-mail: order@sagepub.com

SAGE Publications Ltd.
1 Oliver's Yard
55 City Road
London, EC1Y 1SP
United Kingdom

SAGE Publications India Pvt. Ltd.
B 1/I 1 Mohan Cooperative Industrial Area
Mathura Road, New Delhi 110 044
India

SAGE Publications Asia-Pacific Pte. Ltd.
3 Church Street
#10-04 Samsung Hub
Singapore 049483

Acquisitions Editor: Jerry Westby
Publishing Associate: MaryAnn Vail
Production Editor: Eric Garner
Copy Editor: Liann Lech
Typesetter: C&M Digitals (Ltd.)
Proofreader: Wendy Jo Dymond
Indexer: Jeanne Busemeyer
Cover Designer: Anupama Krishnan
Marketing Manager: Terra Schultz
Permissions Editor: Karen Ehrmann

Copyright © 2014 by SAGE Publications, Inc.

All rights reserved. No part of this book may be reproduced or utilized in any form or by any means, electronic or mechanical, including photocopying, recording, or by any information storage and retrieval system, without permission in writing from the publisher.

Library of Congress Cataloging-in-Publication Data

Fitzgerald, Jack D.
 Statistics for criminal justice and criminology in practice and research: an introduction / Jack Fitzgerald, Jerry Fitzgerald.
  pages cm
 Includes bibliographical references and index.

 ISBN 978-1-4129-9368-5 (pbk.)

 1. Criminal statistics. I. Fitzgerald, Jerry. II. Title.

HV7415.F58 2014
519.5024'364—dc23   2012043932

13 14 15 16 17 10 9 8 7 6 5 4 3 2 1

Contents

Preface   xv

Chapter 1: The Study of Statistics in Criminal Justice   1
- Learning Objectives   1
- Introduction   1
- What Are Statistics?   2
  - Quantitative Raw Data or Compilations of Nonquantitative Raw Data as Statistics   3
  - The Results of Mathematical Calculations as Statistics   4
  - The Application of Probability Theory as Statistics   4
- Where Do Statistics Come From?   5
  - Categorizing and Counting   5
  - Measuring   5
  - Applying Probability Theory   6
- How Are Statistics Used in Criminal Justice?   6
  - Description   6
  - Estimation   7
  - Explanation   7
  - Prediction   8
- Major Sources of Statistical Data in Criminal Justice   8
- Why Study Statistics?   9
  - The Sometimes Contrasting Views of Researchers and Practitioners About Quantitative Research   9
  - Professionalization of Criminal Justice Careers   12
  - Statistics-Based Initiatives for Improving Criminal Justice Agency Policies and Practices   13
- Tips for Succeeding in This Course   15
- Summary   17
- Concepts to Master   18
- Review Questions   18
- Exercises and Discussion Questions   19

Chapter 2: Scientific Research and Statistical Analysis   21
- Learning Objectives   21
- Introduction   22
- Units of Analysis and Variables   22
- Mutually Exclusive and Exhaustive Variable Values   23
- Discrete and Continuous Variable Values   23
- Levels of Measurement   24
  - Nominal-Level Measurements   24
  - Ordinal-Level Measurements   24
  - Interval-Level Measurements   25
  - Ratio-Level Measurements   26
  - Some Additional Considerations Regarding Levels of Measurement   26

Hypotheses	27
Hypotheses as Proposed Causal Explanations	27
Research Hypotheses and Null Hypotheses	29
The Conditions for Causality	30
Sampling	32
Simple Random Sampling	33
Research Design	34
Before-After Design	34
Before-After With Control Group Design	35
Quasi-Experimental Research Designs	38
Ethical Integrity in Data Analysis	38
Plagiarism	39
Due Diligence in Data Management and Analysis	39
Garbage In-Garbage Out	40
Summary	40
Concepts to Master	41
Review Questions	41
Exercises and Discussion Questions	43

Chapter 3: Basic Descriptive Univariate Analysis — 45

Learning Objectives	45
Introduction	46
Some Basic Types of Statistical Analysis	46
Univariate, Bivariate, and Multivariate Statistics	46
Descriptive and Inferential Statistics	47
Univariate Descriptive Analysis	47
Frequency Counts	48
Ratios, Fractions, Proportions, and Decimals	48
Percents	49
Rates	51
Odds	53
Creating Data Distributions	53
Frequency Distribution Tables	53
Frequency Distribution Bar and Line Graphs	55
Percent Distribution Tables and Graphs	63
Cumulative Distributions	67
More About Graphs	71
The Power of Graphs	72
Some Additional Kinds of Graphs	73
Titling and Labeling Tables and Graphs	80
Cautions With Graphs	80
Summary	87
Concepts to Master	87
Review Questions	88
Exercises and Discussion Questions	89

Chapter 4: Describing Univariate Distributions — 93

Learning Objectives	93
Introduction	94
Different Distribution Shapes, Skewness, and Kurtosis	94
Bell-Shaped and Normal Distributions	94
Skewness	96
Kurtosis	97
Measures of Central Tendency	97
Mean	97
Median	99
Mode	102
Collapsing Variable Values	103
Finding a Mode, Median, and Mean for Distributions of Grouped Scores	105
Selecting Appropriate Measures of Central Tendency	108
Measures of Dispersion	112
Range	112

Average Deviation	112	**Chapter 6: An Introduction to Probability Theory and Probability Distributions**	**167**
Variance and Standard Deviation	113		
Selecting Appropriate Measures of Dispersion	117	Learning Objectives	167
		Introduction	168
A Special Property of the Mean	118	Probability Theory	168
Measures of Location in a Distribution	120	Some Rules of Probability Theory	169
Quartile, Decile, and Percentile Analyses	120	Rules for Outcomes of a Single Trial	170
Selecting Appropriate Measures of Location	123	Independent and Dependent Events	172
Dealing With Missing Data	124	Rules for Outcomes of Multiple Trials	173
Some Other Cautions in the Uses and Interpretations of Univariate Descriptive Statistics	125	Probability Distributions	176
		Binomial Distributions and Binomial Probability Distributions	177
Summary	128		
Concepts to Master	128	Normal Curve Approximations of Binomial Probability Distributions	180
Review Questions	128		
Exercises and Discussion Questions	129	Some Concluding Comments About Binomial Distributions	184
Chapter 5: Distributions: Normal and Otherwise	**133**	Probabilities and Random Sampling	184
Learning Objectives	133	Summary	185
Introduction	133	Concepts to Master	185
Proportional Area Graphs	134	Review Questions	185
Normal Distributions and Normal Curves Revisited	140	Exercises and Discussion Questions	186
The Special Characteristics of the Theoretical Normal Curve	140	**Chapter 7: Univariate Inferential Statistics: Sampling Distributions and Population Parameter Estimation**	**189**
Means, Standard Deviations, and Areas Under the Normal Curve	141		
The Theoretical Standard Normal Curve and z Scores	144	Learning Objectives	189
		Introduction	190
The z-Score Table	150	Sampling Distributions and Their Role in Inferential Statistics	191
Using the z-Score Table	150		
A Note About Tests for Normality	160	A Simple Illustration: Who'll Buy the Coffee?	192
Summary	161		
Concepts to Master	162		
Review Questions	162		
Exercises and Discussion Questions	163		

Constructing a Sampling
   Distribution Empirically   193
Describing Sampling
   Distributions: Means and
   Standard Errors   196
Constructing Sampling
   Distributions Mathematically   197
   Binomial Distributions as
      Sampling Distributions   197
Point and Interval Estimates of
   Population Means   202
   Sampling Distributions for
      Sample Means   204
   Two Provisions of the
      Central Limit Theorem   205
   Point Estimates of
      Population Means   205
   Interval Estimates of
      Population Means   206
Estimating Population
   Proportions Revisited   217
Parametric and Nonparametric
   Inferential Statistics   221
Assumptions and Cautions   221
Summary   222
Concepts to Master   223
Review Questions   223
Exercises and Discussion
   Questions   224

Chapter 8: Bivariate Hypothesis Testing With Nominal and Ordinal Variables   227

Learning Objectives   227
Introduction   228
Some Basics of Hypothesis
   Testing   228
   Type I and Type II Errors   230
Comparing Frequency
   Distributions   231
   Both Variables at the
      Nominal Level   232
   One Variable at the
      Nominal Level and One
      Variable at the Ordinal
      Level   234
   Both Variables at the
      Ordinal Level   236
Fundamentals of Cross-
   Tabulation   236
   Constructing a
      Contingency Table   236
   Titling and Labeling the
      Contingency Table   239
   Collapsing Categories   240
   Using Percents in
      Contingency Tables   242
   Reading the Diagonals in
      Contingency Tables   243
Elaboration Analysis   245
   Replication   248
   Explanation   249
   Interpretation   249
   Specification   250
   No Apparent Relationship
      in the Zero-Order Table   251
   Some Examples of
      Elaboration Analysis   251
Chi-Square Analysis   258
   Assumptions   258
   The Basic Ideas Underlying
      Chi-Square Analysis for
      Contingency Tables   259
   Calculating Expected Cell
      Frequencies   261
   Calculating Chi Square   264
   Using the Chi-Square Table   265
   Statistical Significance and
      Rejection Regions   266
   Chi Square as a Univariate
      Goodness-of-Fit Test   268
   How to Present Results   268
Assumptions and Cautions   270
Summary   272
Concepts to Master   273
Review Questions   273
Exercises and Discussion
   Questions   275

Chapter 9: Bivariate Hypothesis Testing for the Difference Between Two Means — 279

Learning Objectives — 279
Introduction — 280
Independent and Dependent Random Samples — 282
  Independence and Dependence Within a Random Sample — 282
  Independence and Dependence Between Random Samples — 282
A t Test for the Difference Between Two Independent Random Sample Means — 285
  Assumptions and Hypotheses — 286
  Directional and Nondirectional Hypotheses — 287
  Heteroscedasticity and Homoscedasticity — 287
  The Basic Ideas Underlying the Independent Random Samples Version of the t Test — 289
  The Theoretical Formulas for the Independent Random Samples Version of the t Test — 291
  The Sampling Distributions for the Difference Between Two Independent Random Sample Means — 293
  Calculating t for the Independent Random Samples Version of the t Test — 298
  Testing t for Statistical Significance — 298
  One- and Two-Tailed Tests of Significance — 301
Some Reflections on Statistical Significance Tests — 305
A t Test for the Difference Between Two Dependent Random Sample Means — 306
  Assumptions and Hypotheses — 308
  The Basic Ideas Underlying the Dependent Random Samples Version of the t Test — 309
  The Theoretical Formula for the Dependent Random Samples Version of the t Test — 310
  The Sampling Distribution for $\bar{D}$ — 311
  Calculating t for the Dependent Random Samples Version of the t Test — 313
  Calculating Degrees of Freedom — 313
  Interpreting the Results — 314
  Presenting Results for t Tests — 314
The Relationship Between t and z — 316
Confidence Limits and Intervals for the Difference Between Means — 316
Assumptions and Cautions — 318
Summary — 320
Concepts to Master — 321
Review Questions — 321
Exercises and Discussion Questions — 322

Chapter 10: Bivariate Hypothesis Testing With One-Way Analysis of Variance — 325

Learning Objectives — 325

Introduction	326
Analysis of Variance (One-Way)	327
Assumptions and Hypotheses	327
The Basic Ideas Underlying ANOVA	331
The Theoretical ANOVA Test Statistic F	337
Estimating Population Variances	338
Calculating the Population Variance Estimates	338
Calculating F	345
The Sampling Distributions for F	346
Using the F Tables	347
Presenting ANOVA Results	347
Follow-Up Analysis After a Significant F	348
Tukey's HSD Test	349
The Relationship Between F and t	352
Assumptions and Cautions	352
Summary	352
Concepts to Master	353
Review Questions	353
Exercises and Discussion Questions	354

Chapter 11: Bivariate Linear Regression and Correlation and Linear Partial Regression and Correlation   357

Learning Objectives	357
Introduction	358
The Basic Ideas Underlying Linear Correlation and (Regression) Analyses	359
Scattergrams	360
Linear Bivariate Regression Analysis	365
Calculating the Best Fitting (Regression) Line Constants a and b	368
Best Fitting Lines and the Means of x and y	370
Designating y as the Dependent Variable	372
Positive, Negative, and No Relationship	373
Linear and Nonlinear Relationships	376
Standardized Betas	378
Cautions With Predictions From Linear Regression Equations	379
Linear Bivariate Correlation Analysis	379
Correlation Matrixes	383
The Problem of Outliers	383
Comparing r and b	386
The Coefficient of Determination r^2	388
Calculating r, r^2, and the Constants (a and b) for a Best Fitting Line	390
Other Statistical Measures of Strength of Relationship	393
Correlation and Cross-Tabulation	393
Test of Statistical Significance for r and b	395
Linear Partial Regression and Correlation Analysis	397
Calculating $r_{xy.T}$	398
Assumptions and Cautions	400
Summary	401
Concepts to Master	402
Review Questions	402
Exercises and Discussion Questions	404

Chapter 12: Multivariate Linear Regression and Correlation Analysis and Logistic Regression: An Introduction   407

Learning Objectives	407
Introduction	408

Dealing With Missing Data — 411
Assumptions of Linear Multiple Regression and Correlation Analyses — 413
Linear Multiple Regression Analysis — 413
    The Basic Ideas Underlying Linear Multiple Regession Analysis — 414
    The General Linear Multiple Regression Equation — 418
    Standardized Betas — 420
    Stepwise Regression — 421
Linear Multiple Correlation — 422
    The Basic Ideas Underlying Linear Multiple Correlation Analysis — 422
Dummy Variables in Multiple Regression and Correlation Analyses — 423
Models — 425
Main Effects and Interaction Effects — 427
The Problem of Multicollinearity — 429
Tests of Statistical Significance for Linear Multiple Regression and Correlation Analyses — 430
    Reporting the Results of Multiple Regression and Correlation Analyses — 430
Logarithm-Based Analyses — 436
    Logistic Regression — 437
    Reporting the Results of Logistic Regression — 448
Assumptions and Cautions — 454
Summary — 455
Concepts to Master — 456
Review Questions — 456
Exercises and Discussion Questions — 458

Chapter 13: Nonparametric Statistics — 461

Learning Objectives — 461
Introduction — 462
Choosing Between Parametric and Nonparametric Inferential Statistics Revisited — 462
General Assumptions of Nonparametric Inferential Statistics — 464
The Mann-Whitney U Test for Two Independent Random Samples — 465
    Asssumptions of the M-W U Test — 465
    The Basic Ideas Underlying the M-W U Test — 465
    Preparing Data for M-W U Analysis — 466
    Calculating M-W U — 471
    The Sampling Distribution for U — 475
    Testing U for Statistical Significance — 476
    Reporting the Results of M-W U Analysis — 479
    Concluding Remarks Regarding M-W U Analysis — 479
The Kruskal-Wallis H Test for Three or More Independent Random Samples — 479
    Assumptions of the K-W H Test — 488
    The Basic Ideas Underlying the K-W H Test — 488
    Preparing Data for K-W H Analysis — 489
    Calculating K-W H — 492
    Testing K-W H for Statistical Significance — 494

Reporting the Results of K-W H Analysis	495	**Chapter 14: Real-Life Adventures of Statistics Users**	**517**
Concluding Remarks About K-W H Analysis	495	Statistics: A Practitioner's View By John H. Schlaf, Director of Campus Safety, Knox College, and Former Chief of Police, Galesburg, Illinois	517
Spearman's ρ Analysis	498		
Assumptions of Spearman's ρ Analysis	499		
The Basic Ideas Underlying Spearman's ρ Analysis	499	Statistics: A Researcher's View By Jerry Fitzgerald, Former Alcohol and Drug Abuse Researcher, Department of Psychiatry, University of Iowa, and Co-Author of This Text	529
Preparing Data for Spearman's ρ Analysis	500		
Calculating Spearman's ρ	502		
Testing ρ for Statistical Significance	503	**Chapter 15: Summary and Conclusions**	**539**
Reporting the Results of ρ Analysis	504	**Glossary**	**545**
		Answers to Questions	**555**
Concluding Remarks Regarding Spearman's ρ Analysis	504	**Bibliography**	**571**
		Index	**573**
Some Final Cautions About Nonparametric Statistics	510	**List of Key Formulas**	**583**
		About the Authors	**587**
Summary	511		
Concepts to Master	512	Appendices A–H are included on the open-access Student Study Site: www.sagepub.com/fitzgerald	
Review Questions	512		
Exercises and Discussion Questions	513		

Acknowledgments

Many involved with us in this project deserve our profound gratitude. The many positive comments from our reviewers encouraged us enough to carry on. The less favorable comments led us to take out some materials and add others and forced us to rethink and clarify our treatment of various topics. We didn't always agree with our reviewers, but the quality of the book is clearly better as a result of their encouragement and critiques. Included among the reviewers were Lori Anderson, Jeb Booth, Evita Bynum, Noelle Fearn, Shannon Fowler, Lori Guevara, John Hazy, Matthew Hickman, Wendy Hicks, Beth Huebner, Connie Ireland, Anthony Hoskin, Suman Kakar, Gini Mann-Deibert, Carlos Posadas, Brian Stults, Angela Taylor, Barbara Warner, Richard Whaley, and Kevin Wright.

We also owe a great debt of gratitude to Jerry Westby, Publisher, at SAGE and his staff, especially Denise Simon and MaryAnn Vail, all of whom provided much need guidance, advice, and encouragement. Our production editor, Eric Garner, and copy editor, Liann Lech, made the book a much better "read" and otherwise helped put the finishing touches on the manuscript. It has been a real pleasure working with the entire crew at SAGE.

To all of these folks, we say thank you very much! Of course, the final responsibility for the contents of the text is ours.

J.D.F & J.L.F.

We dedicate this book to our parents, Mildred and Donald Fitzgerald, two remarkable people of very modest means who, in addition to all the things really good parents do, worked hard and sacrificed so that their two sons could get a first-class higher education. We are profoundly grateful for all they did for us.

Preface

Both of us brothers attended graduate school at the University of Iowa, though not at the same time. Jerry has devoted most of his professional career to research, primarily about alcohol and drug use and abuse, in the Department of Psychiatry at the University of Iowa. Jack taught for many years at Knox College in Galesburg, Illinois. Each of us has written and published alone and with others, but this is our first collaboration. It has not been all sweetness and harmony, but we are glad to say our filial relationship remains basically intact. In fact, it turns out we can work together pretty well—most of the time. In any event, the book is no doubt much better than either of us alone could have written.

Although we present many formulas, as well as describe and illustrate how various basic statistics are calculated, we wanted our text to be more than a basic statistics "cookbook" or step-by-step manual. We have made a major effort to help students understand the basic ideas underlying the statistics we discuss. We have also emphasized some of the major problems that can arise when using and interpreting the various kinds of statistics.

We have tried to produce a text that is accessible yet challenging to students with varying degrees of academic talent, preparation, and proclivity. Furthermore, we know that instructors teach in a wide variety of settings, have different ideas about what should and should not be included in an introductory statistics text, and work with students who are diverse in many ways. It is, of course, impossible to satisfy all instructors' desires and meet all students' needs. We hope, however, to have written a text that will serve many teachers well and encourage a variety of students, whether future researchers or practitioners, to appreciate what knowledge of statistical analysis can contribute to the empirical knowledge base in their fields, advancement in their careers, and the quality of their public service.

The text has been structured so that materials can be selected to match students' abilities and the instructional time available, as well as the instructor's ideas of what a text like this should include. For example, Chapter 6 on probability theory can be skipped with only a little fill-in from the instructor. Chapter 12 on multivariate, including logistic, analysis can simply be omitted from the reading list. The section on elaboration analysis in Chapter 8 and the section on partial regression and correlation in Chapter 11 can also be skipped. In these and other ways, instructors can shape the text to suit their own particular courses.

We know all too well that many students approach the study of statistics with trepidation. With the intent of easing some of this math anxiety, we present formulas in different ways. We include formulas that make clearer the relationship between the ideas underlying a procedure or test and the calculations to be performed—we call them the easier-to-understand formulas. We also offer the mathematically equivalent formulas that are easier to calculate. And in many instances, we translate the formulas into step-by-step narratives. Students are thus provided with more than one way of understanding the formulas.

With the help of our publisher, editors, and staff, as well as our reviewers, we have tried to write in these and other ways with struggling students in mind. Whether or not we have succeeded, of course, remains to be seen. We know from our own experiences, as well as those reported by many of our reviewers and others, that those planning careers as criminal justice practitioners are often skeptical of the value of a course in statistics. We acknowledge and address at least some of their concerns directly. Materials and examples from the professional literature relevant to both researchers and practitioners are included. Many learning aids have been incorporated into the text. We offer some advice on how to manage math anxiety when it exists and some other tips for achieving success in the course in Chapter 1 and occasionally in other chapters. Concepts to master are printed in bold in the text near where they are defined, listed again at the end of each chapter, and defined in a glossary at the end of the book. A list of symbols and their meanings is included with several chapters; a complete list is located in the beginning of the book, as is a list of key formulas in the back of the book. "Pause, Think, and Explore" boxes, usually closely following the introduction of formulas, invite students to play with the formulas, helping them understand what the formula is doing with the data. Review questions as well as discussion questions and exercises are included with all but the last two chapters.

We know the price of college texts has increased steadily, placing increasing burdens on students whose financial resources are limited. And we know many instructors are very concerned about these costs to their students as well. We wholeheartedly support SAGE Publications' effort to offer the text at a more affordable price point than many other such texts.

Finally, we know the book is far from perfect. We welcome the feedback of instructors and students alike as you gain experience with our text.

Some Special Notes to Instructors

We wish to call your attention to a few of the less obvious pedagogical elements we have incorporated into the text. First, some reviewers of the text in the early stage of its development objected that there was too much of what they regarded as "research methods" materials in the early chapters of the book. The amount of such material in this final version of the text has been greatly reduced as a result. But there are still some materials of this nature, especially in Chapter 2, and brief discussions scattered in other chapters as well. You can skip Chapter 2 if you wish, of course, but we think students need this material to make sense of the statistical analysis examples in the rest of the book. You might think your students already know this stuff from their research methods class, assuming they have had one. They should, of course, and perhaps they do—but our experience leads us to seriously doubt it in almost all cases. If you don't believe us, try giving your class a little quiz on these matters the first day of class and let the results be your guide.

Second, we have included a questionnaire in Appendix J on the study site (www.sagepub.com/fitzgerald) that you may use "as is" or modify as you wish to establish a database for purposes of illustrating some of the statistical analyses discussed in the book. When it is feasible, we found this attracts and involves students in the course's subject matter—always a good instructional strategy. In addition, the questionnaire, as well as the review questions, exercises, and discussion questions for each chapter, will be on the text's website, available for download and modification in any way you wish.

Third, we have also included a random numbers table (Appendix B) on the study site (**www.sagepub.com/fitzgerald**) that can be used to illustrate the principles of random sampling. It can also be used to demonstrate the pattern of variable values (e.g., for mean ages) that emerges from a number of random samples of the same size from a population (perhaps students in your class) and the relationship between this pattern and the corresponding population parameter.

Fourth, we urge you to urge your students to make use of the "Pause, Think, and Explore" boxes following the mathematical formulas. They are intended to help students develop an understanding of how the formula works, gain confidence in working with the mathematics, and develop better insight about what the formulas are revealing about the data being analyzed.

Fifth, the "From the Literature" boxes in each of the first 13 chapters provide good opportunities for reviewing many of the statistics and statistical analyses discussed in those chapters. In addition, those in the later chapters, especially the ones in the non-parametric statistics chapter (Chapter 13), offer the chance to review various statistics and statistical analyses covered in earlier chapters. We encourage you to make use of them in these ways.

Finally, we believe in a pedagogy that might be described as spiraling toward complexity. We first introduce key concepts and statistical procedures in simple and basic ways. As the text moves along, the treatment of the same concepts becomes increasingly detailed and complex. We have found this way of presenting the materials tends to reduce student anxiety about the more difficult aspects of the course and builds an increasingly sophisticated understanding of them. This strategy inevitably involves some repetition, but we think it is more than worth it. We hope you do too.

Instructor Teaching Site

A password-protected site, available at **www.sagepub.com/fitzgerald**, features resources that have been designed to help you plan and teach your courses. These resources include an extensive test bank, chapter-specific PowerPoint presentations, sample syllabi, answers to the end-of-chapter exercises, and links to recent, relevant SAGE journal articles as well as audio, video, and web resources.

Student Study Site

An open-access student study site is available at **www.sagepub.com/fitzgerald**. This site provides access to several study tools including eFlashcards, web quizzes, and additional appendices as well as links to SAGE journal articles and audio, video, and web resources.

To all students and instructors: We wish you as happy an experience as possible with our text! Again, we welcome your feedback.

Jack Fitzgerald
Jerry Fitzgerald
June 30, 2012

The Study of Statistics in Criminal Justice

Learning Objectives

What you are expected not only to learn but to master in this chapter:

- What statistics are
- Where statistics come from
- How statistics are used in criminal justice
- Some major sources of criminal justice statistics
- Why the study of statistics is important for all criminal justice professionals, whether they practice, teach, or do research
- Tips for succeeding in this course, even if you have "math anxiety"

Introduction

This book is about statistics and statistical analysis in criminal justice, including criminology. For brevity's sake, we usually refer only to criminal justice with the understanding that criminology is included. We discuss in considerable detail the nature and uses of several basic statistical tools and procedures for describing and analyzing quantitative data in criminal justice.

We should note at the outset, however, that research in criminal justice is not limited to quantitative methods; qualitative research also has a long and distinguished history in criminal justice. Qualitative research reports are usually presented in narrative form; typically include few, if any, numbers beyond simple frequency counts; and may be presented in a variety of media. Very important qualitative research has been and will continue to be done in criminal justice. (For some classic qualitative research, see Goffman, 1961; Manning & Van Maanen, 1999; Skolnick, 1967; and Van Maanen 1978.) Furthermore, in our view, some of the best research combines qualitative and quantitative methods. Nevertheless, you will have to look elsewhere for a presentation and discussion of qualitative research (e.g., Bailey, 2006; Cresswell, 2007). From here forward, unless indicated otherwise, whenever we use the word *research* in this text, we are referring to quantitative research with its emphasis on counting, measuring, and statistical analyses.

Also, before we begin our detailed discussion of these matters, it is important to recognize that statistical analysis is only one of several steps in carrying out a criminal justice research project. Furthermore, what happens in the preceding steps has important implications for statistical analysis. More specifically, we can neither choose the appropriate statistical procedure(s) to apply nor make good sense of the results we calculate without knowing what hypotheses are being tested; how the variables were defined and measured; the nature of the research design; and how the persons, objects, or events being studied were chosen. Therefore, in this and the following chapter, in addition to introducing some basic statistical concepts, we review a number of closely related topics, often referred to as research methods, with important implications for statistical analysis.

In the remainder of this chapter, we (a) review three common uses of the term *statistics*, (b) consider the basic origins of all types of statistics, (c) discuss the general ways in which statistics are used in criminal justice research, (d) identify some major sources of statistical data in criminal justice, and (e) consider some reasons why those students wishing to become criminal justice practitioners, as well as those pursuing careers as policymakers and researchers, should study statistics. The chapter concludes with some suggestions for how you might best approach your study of criminal justice statistics, including ways to deal with math anxiety. Our aim, of course, is to help you master the text's contents and achieve success in this course.

What Are Statistics?

Any number may qualify as a statistic. If we are referring to a single number, it is referred to as a **datum**. Examples include the number of sworn personnel in a city's police department, the number of inmates in a particular cell block, the number of traffic accidents at a particular intersection, and the annual caseload of a criminal court judge. If we are referencing more than one such number, we use the plural of datum, which is **data**. Thus, two or more crime statistics, traffic accident statistics, employment statistics, and so on, are data. Three different, but somewhat overlapping, uses of the term **statistic(s)** may be distinguished: (a) quantitative raw data or numerical summaries of compilations of nonquantitative raw data, (b) the results of mathematical calculations, and (c) the application of probability theory.

Quantitative Raw Data or Compilations of Nonquantitative Raw Data as Statistics

To illustrate statistics of this first type, consider a dispatcher's log in a law enforcement or emergency response center. In the log, the dispatcher records a variety of information (data) about each call received. Some of the data may be quantitative (for example, the date and time of the call), and some may be nonquantitative (for example, the name of the caller, the town from which the call was made). Entries in the dispatchers' logs would be the **raw data** (i.e., the information contained in the original source files or documents).

Among other entries, the raw data in a department's dispatcher's log might include the year, month, day, and time of the call; the location of the reported incident; and the kind of service being requested. Each of these types of entries in the log may be considered a variable pertaining to the call. A **variable** is an aspect, characteristic, or feature of the person, group, place, event, or object whose "value" may vary or change from one object of study to the next. In our example, the objects of study are the calls to dispatch, and they may vary in the characteristics listed from one dispatch call to another.

Raw data from sources such as those described above are often compiled and arranged in a **table**. In the most basic sense, a table is a two-dimensional rectangular grid within which data are compiled, organized, and displayed in an easy-to-understand way. An example is in Table 1.1. The data in the table are taken from an annual "Calls for Service" report prepared by the Cass County, Minnesota, Sheriff's Department. These data, in turn, were compiled from the department's dispatcher's log. The table includes frequency counts (i.e., the number) of calls for service logged by the department dispatchers from different townships in the county over several recent years.

Two of the log entry variables were selected to construct Table 1.1. The "township" variable has seven **variable values**. That is, each particular township (Meadow Brook, Moose Lake, Pine Lake, etc.) is a value of the township variable. Each of these variable values was used to define a row of the table. "Year of the call" is the other variable used to construct Table 1.1. Its values (the years 2004, 2005, 2006, etc.) were used to define the columns of the table. To fill in the table, the number of calls for service for each township in each year was counted and entered. These data are called frequency counts. **Frequency counts** are numbers indicating how many observations fell into a particular category or how often something was observed.

Of course, different variables could be selected from the raw data logs, and the data pertaining to those variables could be compiled in tables in different ways for different purposes, such as assisting the sheriff in decisions about allocating law

Table 1.1 Number of Calls for Service From Selected Townships, Cass County, MN Sheriff's Office, by Year

Townships	Years					
	2004	2005	2006	2007	2008	2009
Meadow Brook	91	83	165	135	98	90
Moose Lake	16	22	27	24	26	19
Ottertail Peninsula	8	9	14	18	22	23
Pike Bay	1,715	1,790	2,485	2,001	1,650	1,913
Pine Lake	114	93	118	124	130	147
Pine River	396	379	520	424	402	377
Ponto Lake	164	170	191	172	166	177

enforcement resources, launching crime prevention programs where they are most needed, or supporting a request for a budget increase.

The Results of Mathematical Calculations as Statistics

A second use of the term *statistic(s)* refers to the quantities arrived at by applying mathematical formulas to data, usually frequency counts or variable values. Such formulas and the statistics they produce provide summaries and analyses of data on the variables included in the study. For example, we might calculate the township from which the most and least calls originate and the average time it takes for a police officer to respond to a call for assistance, as well as identify the shortest and longest response times that appear in our data set. We discuss these kinds of summary statistics and analyses in Chapter 3.

The Application of Probability Theory as Statistics

Statistics of the third type come in part from the application of mathematical theory, especially a branch of mathematics called probability theory. We provide an introduction to probabilities at an appropriate point later in the book. For now, we will simply note that you know you are dealing with statistics in this third sense when you read or hear statements such as "Based on our sample data, the mean number of offenses for this population of offenders is estimated to be nine," or "The margin of error for this poll was plus or minus four percentage points," or "The difference between the average ages of the two groups of offenders was statistically significant at the .05 level." By the time you finish this course, you will understand what these statements and others like them mean.

Where Do Statistics Come From?

As we noted above, statistics of whatever type are numerical quantities. For our purposes here, we can say that in the most basic sense, they come from four human activities: categorizing, counting, measuring, and applying probability theory.

Referring to these as human activities calls to our attention that they do not appear if we sit back and wait; they demand some sort of intervention in the world—they require that we do something, such as creating categories, counting the number of observations that fall into each category, and/or developing and applying measuring devices. Although categorizing, counting, and measuring are essential elements of scientific research and data analysis, calling them *human* activities reminds us that they are subject to the biases, fumbles, and foibles to which all human endeavors may fall prey.

Categorizing and Counting

Counting may be defined as the process of determining "how many" or "how often." A little reflection should convince you that counting depends on our capacity for **categorizing**—that is, sorting persons, places, events, or objects into different groups according to some specified criteria. In short, before we can count, we have to decide exactly who or what we are counting. Furthermore, to make our counting meaningful, we need to have clear definitions of the categories so that we "know one when we see one." For example, we could define, categorize, and then count the number of first-, second-, and third-degree assaults occurring in a particular jurisdiction. Doing so would produce statistics in the form of frequency counts such as those we saw in Table 1.1.

Measuring

Measuring may be defined as the process of determining "how much" or to what degree or extent. Like counting, meaningful measurement depends on identifying and defining some aspect, feature, or characteristic of the persons, groups, events, or objects we are studying that is worth measuring. Measuring also depends on having a "good" measuring device; that is, a device that yields numbers reflecting the degree or extent to which that aspect, feature, or characteristic is present or is occurring. For example, yardsticks measure length, width, and height (of a jail cell, for example); clocks, stopwatches, and calendars measure time (length of sentence, for example); bathroom scales measure weight (of a convict on entrance to a jail, for example) and breathalyzers measure blood alcohol as manifested in a person's exhaled breath. IQ tests and certain personality inventories, as well as some types of questions and answers in interviews or on questionnaires, may also serve as measuring devices.

Applying Probability Theory

Probability theory permits us to determine the likelihood (probability) that some estimate we make is accurate or some hypothesis we are testing is true. It is applied to statistics derived from frequency counts or variable measurements in samples. It allows us to make inferences about the corresponding statistics for the population from which the sample was drawn. For example, applying probability theory to data on the ages of a sample of first-time drug users, including their average age, may yield a very good statistical estimate of the average age of the population of first-time drug offenders from which the sample was drawn. We will have much more to say about probability theory and its applications in criminal justice studies in later chapters.

Categorizing, counting, measuring, and probability theory applications can be used in various combinations, of course. We can, for example, count the number of OWI (operating a motor vehicle while intoxicated) arrestees who "blew" (measured) more than .3 blood alcohol on the breathalyzer. We can also calculate how many convicts were given more than a 7-year sentence and determine the probability that a convict will get a sentence of more than 7 years.

Every type of statistic and statistical analysis we discuss in this book rests on the human activities of categorizing, counting, measuring, and applying probability theory. Although the details are beyond the scope of this text, you should also always keep in mind that the *quality* of those categorizations, counts, measurements, and applications determines to a large extent the meaningfulness and usefulness of any statistical analysis we perform on them.

How Are Statistics Used in Criminal Justice?

Statistics are used by criminal justice researchers and practitioners in four basic ways: description, estimation, explanation, and prediction. These uses are related, sometimes overlap a great deal, and may be quite complex. Our purpose here is just to convey some general ideas about them. We give them detailed consideration in later chapters.

Description

Statistics may be used to describe phenomena of interest to criminal justice researchers and practitioners. **Description** consists of identifying and reporting on selected features or aspects (that is, variables and their values) of the persons, groups, places, objects, or events we are studying, as well as changes in variable values over time. The reported height, weight, and age of a wanted person; the number of nonnegligent homicides in the United States in 2009; the percentage of female officers in Police Department A; the rate of domestic assaults in City B; the capacity of cell block or pod Alpha in Correctional Facility C; and the client case load of a public defender in Jurisdiction D exemplify description. So does observing and reporting changes in these numbers from year to year.

Criminal justice agency administrators may use such descriptive statistics to monitor various aspects of their agencies' operations or the types of criminal justice-related activities occurring in their jurisdictions. They may be used, for example, to evaluate some aspects of personnel performance, identify crime hot spots, and/or facilitate fiscal and human resource allocation decisions.

Estimation

Researchers and administrators may also use statistics for the purposes of **estimation**. Usually, estimation involves the application of probability theory to statistical descriptions of a sample in order to say something about the corresponding statistics for the population from which the sample was drawn. Perhaps a sheriff's candidate wants to know how much support she has among the voters in the county she serves or a police chief wants to know what the reputation of his officers is among citizens in a particular neighborhood. The candidate could select and interview a sample of county voters and use the sample data to estimate her support among the entire population in the county. The chief could select a sample of neighborhood citizens and use their opinions to estimate the opinions of all citizens in the neighborhood. Such estimations involve statistics in all three common uses of the term discussed earlier, including the application of probability theory.

Explanation

When statistics are used for **explanation**, they are typically part of a process for testing a causal hypothesis. Both researchers and administrators use statistics in this way. In its simplest form, a causal hypothesis asserts a connection between two variables such that a change in the values of one variable will "cause" or "explain" a change in the values of another variable. We might hypothesize, for example, that a longer prison sentence reduces subsequent offenses by the same offender (a specific deterrence hypothesis) or that longer prison sentences reduce crime rates (a general deterrence hypothesis). Or, we might claim that plea bargains increase recidivism rates, that arresting alleged perpetrators of domestic violence reduces the number of subsequent domestic assaults, or that gun buy-backs reduce assaults with guns. We could then gather and analyze statistical data to determine whether or not our proposed explanation is supported by the data. For example, recidivism rates for those who served longer and those who served shorter sentences could be compared. The recidivism rate for those who were given plea bargains could be compared with those who were not. The number of firearms-related assaults before and after a gun buy-back could be compared. Differences in the direction we hypothesize (that is, we observe that more of those with shorter sentences or plea bargains recidivated than those with longer sentences or no plea bargains, or we find fewer gun assaults after a buy-back) would indicate support for our hypothesis. If our research involved appropriate sampling from a population, we could also apply probability theory to test our explanations for the population. In practice, of course, as we will see, things are more complicated than indicated here, but these brief examples serve to illustrate the uses of statistics in explanation.

Prediction

Statistics may also be used for **prediction**. If we understand some of the descriptive characteristics of current juvenile delinquents or some of the reasons they became delinquent, for example, we can use statistics pertaining to those factors to predict which juveniles are likely to become delinquent in the future. We might then design a program to intervene early in the most vulnerable juveniles' lives with the aim of preventing any subsequent delinquency. Similarly, we might use statistics on former probationers who are incarcerated to predict which future probationers are likely to fail and take steps to prevent their failure. Or we might use data on auto accident rates for intersections of a particular type to predict the rates for new intersections of the same design. Obviously, the use of statistics for prediction is closely related to the other uses we have discussed previously, relying as it often does on description, estimation, and explanation.

Major Sources of Statistical Data in Criminal Justice

Criminal justice data in the form of counts and measurements may come from a wide variety of sources. At the most basic level, data may originate in incident reports filled out by dispatchers or responding officers, or in probation or parole supervisors' written reports of conferences with those under their supervision, for example. Data may also come from completed interview or questionnaire forms (whether administered in person, online, or by paper and pencil) or video surveillance records. Public records of various kinds, such as court records, may also serve as data sources. These are sources of what we referred to earlier as raw data—the basic information that is assembled, sorted, counted, and sometimes entered into statistical tables, graphs, or formulas.

Often, selected data from these kinds of raw data records are compiled into periodic reports for a criminal justice agency's internal purposes and/or for public distribution (the media, political bodies with an interest in the subject matter, etc.). For example, the calls for service data in Table 1.1 were derived from dispatchers' log entries and compiled into weekly, monthly, and annual reports that were released to local newspapers and used by the county sheriff in resource allocation decisions.

Compilations of such data are called **databases**. Databases may be compiled for any group of persons, events, locations, and so on. Crime statistics, for example, may be compiled for major cities, states, nations, and larger geopolitical units. Some of the major criminal justice databases, which are drawn from three major sources, are accessible to anyone over the Internet. Law enforcement agencies are one source, and some of the data they gather are compiled in the Uniform Crime Reporting System (UCR) and the National Incident-Based Reporting System. (Go to www.fbi.gov and search for UCR and NIBRS.) General surveys of citizens, such as the National Crime Victimization Survey (go to www.icpsr.umich.edu and search for NCVS) and the National Youth Survey-Family Study (go to www.colorado.edu and search for NYSFS), are a second source. The third major source is offenders themselves, as gathered in self-report surveys, such as the Drug Use Forecasting (go to www.ncjrs.gov and search for DUF) and the Arrestee Drug Abuse Monitoring program (go to www.ojp.usdoj.gov and search for Arrestee Drug Abuse Monitoring). The University of Michigan is the home of two very large archives of criminal justice data, the National Archive of Criminal Justice Data and the Inter-University Consortium for Political and Social Research (go to www.umich.edu and search for NACJD and ICPSR). These archives contain some of the data sets mentioned above, and several others as well. As a criminal justice practitioner or a researcher, you are quite likely to provide and/or use the data contained in at least some of these databases, so you should become familiar with how they are compiled and what data they contain. You should also inform yourself about their different strengths and weaknesses as sources of potentially useful criminal justice data.

Why Study Statistics?

Students planning for a career in criminal justice policy making or research, whether in a university, government, law enforcement, court, correctional, or some other institutional setting, don't need to be persuaded that they must master at least the basics of statistical analysis. They recognize this knowledge will be required in order to do the research necessary to formulate sensible goals, policies, and procedures; implement them successfully; test their effectiveness in achieving the goals; and revise the policies and procedures if necessary in light of what the evidence from the research shows. At the very least, critiquing others' research and keeping up-to-date with the latest developments in their chosen field will require statistical competence.

Those planning to be criminal justice practitioners, however, sometimes doubt the usefulness of the course of study included in this book. For those who do have their doubts, we hope to make clear in the next few pages that all who are pursuing careers in criminal justice, including practitioners, will find themselves more and more in need of this knowledge, especially if they hope to advance in their careers.

The Sometimes Contrasting Views of Researchers and Practitioners About Quantitative Research

Let's begin by acknowledging that practitioners and researchers do sometimes have very different perspectives on the usefulness of quantitative research and analysis. Frontline police or juvenile officers, prison guards or officials, and prosecuting or defense attorneys, of course, have lots of firsthand experience on the ground, where the action is. They often regard themselves—and believe that they should be regarded by others—as the experts when it comes to understanding what's going on in their bailiwicks and how best to do their jobs. They sometimes doubt that the statistics produced by department statisticians, government agencies, private think tanks, or university professors can offer anything useful regarding how frontline personnel like themselves might improve their individual performances or better achieve their agencies' objectives. They may well resist such research-driven mandates for change, especially when those recommendations challenge their personal, experience-based views and suggest they should change their own behaviors.

Consider a couple of examples from law enforcement. On a PoliceOne.com article posted on January 17, 2010, about a California police department's adoption of computer analysis of crime data in order to improve performance, "derb79" commented,

> What a bunch of "crap." . . . If you want to really fight crime, just listen to the cops that are out there, on the streets, everyday [sic]. That's where the wealth of information is, not a computer. Most of the time these highly sophisticated, very expensive computer programs do nothing more than simply verify what the street cop already knows. (Comment on Gill, 2010)

Frontline officers are not the only ones skeptical about and/or critical of some researchers and some types of quantitative research. William Bratton, the former chief of the Los Angeles Police Department and well known for his willingness to speak frankly, has some thoughts about these matters, too. According to Chief Bratton,

> For the last half of the 20th century, the relationship between police practitioners and researchers was, at best, one of agreeing to disagree on the causes of crime and the best ways to respond to and prevent crime. At worst we talked past each other and didn't connect at all. . . . (Ritter, 2007)

There are some good reasons for practitioners to be skeptical of the statistical analyses that inform researchers' conclusions. Academic theorists and theories do sometimes conflict with each other. Different studies aimed at testing a particular theory or evaluating particular programs or procedures do sometimes yield apparently contradictory results. Furthermore, scientific research is indeed often a painfully slow process. Almost all major academic research projects require a good deal of time—sometimes years—to plan, obtain the approval of human subjects review committees, secure funding, gather and analyze the data, specify action implications, and prepare reports for dissemination. Although such research may ultimately yield actionable results, it often does not do so quickly enough for practitioners faced with immediate dilemmas about how best to carry out their missions. In addition, academic research often involves variables, such as socioeconomic status, age, or gender, over which practitioners have little or no control, making the results largely irrelevant to practitioners' ongoing, day-to-day decisions as they struggle to fulfill their missions.

Yet these indictments of research and researchers are arguably too broad and, at least to some extent, unfair. After all, practitioners often disagree among themselves, too, about the best approaches to address criminal justice issues and problems. Witness their differing takes on gun control, for example. It is also undeniable that research, including statistical analysis, has clearly led to significant changes for the better in criminal justice agency policies and practices. Among the research projects that have been very influential are those of Sherman and his colleagues (Sherman, Schmidt, &

Rogan, 1992) on police responses to domestic violence and Kelling and colleagues (Kelling, Pate, Dieckman, & Brown, 1974) on different patrol practices in Kansas City. More recent examples would include Logan's research on protective orders in domestic abuse cases (reported in Hawkins, 2010), the Memphis police department's Blue Crush initiative for reducing crime (go to www.memphispolice.org and http://nucleus research.com and search for Memphis Police), and Weisburd's large body of work (Braga & Weisburd, 2010; Curtis, 2010; Eck, Chainey, Cameron, Leitner, & Wilson, 2005). Then, too, some data gathering and statistical analyses do produce quick and actionable results. Examples would include crime mapping, hot-spot policing, shots fired technology, surveillance video analysis, and Computer Statistics or Comparative Statistics (usually called COMPSTAT) crime reduction initiatives.

Furthermore, many researchers would applaud some of derb79's and Bratton's assertions. Few would doubt the need for taking seriously the views and experiences of frontline practitioners on at least some kinds of research questions. In the same statement as that quoted from above, Chief Bratton goes on to say,

> I'm a proponent of more intimate partnerships and collaboration between practitioners and academics. I'm convinced that these partnerships are particularly important as we enter the new paradigm of the 21st century. . . .
>
> We need more ideas and more research into what works, especially on how the police can make a difference. . . .
>
> I'm asking that more researchers begin to work with us and among us in the real-world laboratories of our departments and cities to help us prove or disprove the beliefs and practices that I, as a practitioner, and most of my colleagues deeply believe, espouse, and practice. (Ritter, 2007)

Most researchers would welcome Bratton's call for more studies evaluating the effectiveness of various criminal justice policies and practices. Many would also endorse his call for more studies in the field closer to the action, whether in police departments, courts, or correctional facilities.

In any event, whether you plan to be a researcher or a practitioner (or perhaps both!), it is worth remembering these differences in perspective and working toward mitigating them when possible. Researchers often depend on the honest cooperation of practitioners for the successful execution of their research plan. Furthermore, the cooperation of practitioners is essential for the successful implementation of any research-based policy or practice recommendations that may increase the efficiency or effectiveness of practitioners' efforts—a result researchers and practitioners alike would surely applaud.

Often, too, if practitioners have not taken a course like this, their capacity to understand and assess quantitative research is limited. This lack of knowledge puts them at a significant disadvantage. Why? Because like it or not, statistics are going to directly affect their lives and careers—how they are expected to do their jobs, how they are evaluated, and their chances of advancement. Without at least a basic knowledge of statistics, they are less able to participate in the dialogue and debate about the results of research, including statistical analyses, in informed and effective ways. Let's be clear. It is a fundamental part of the scientific credo that the results of scientific research, including statistical analyses, are always tentative and subject to rejection or revision in the light of additional research. They are also always partial—that is, it is not possible in any particular research project to identify and measure all of the variables that may influence the phenomenon being studied. And even if accurate, informative, and actionable in some situations, the results may not be generalizable to other situations where different variables may be at work. So, there is nothing certain, complete, or automatically generalizable about the results of scientific research and statistical analyses. The results must be judged not by their certainty, completeness, or generalizability, but rather by whether they are derived from a procedure that, over the long run, represents a better way of figuring out what is going on than other methods available. History clearly suggests that, for many important questions, scientific research procedures, including statistical analysis, and the results they produce are clearly superior.

The increasing importance of research and statistical analyses in criminal justice is reflected in some major recent trends in the field. Among them are the professionalization of all criminal justice careers and a number of statistics-based initiatives aimed at improving the efficiency and effectiveness of frontline professionals.

Professionalization of Criminal Justice Careers

Over the past 25 years or so, criminal justice has become increasingly professionalized. One of the hallmarks of professionals is that they have specialized education and training. They are required to contribute, if they can, to the growth of expertise and knowledge in their profession or, at the very least, to keep up-to-date on the latest developments in their fields. Usually that involves research, whether they are doing it themselves, cooperating in research projects organized by others, or reading about and incorporating research results into their professional practice. In this sense, this course is an important part of your professional preparation and growth.

If you do research yourself, or are asked to help others with a research project, this course (together with your research methods course) provides some of the tools you will need to understand how knowledge in your profession may be advanced, how data may be gathered and analyzed, and which statistical procedures are appropriate in particular research situations. It will also alert you to the strengths and weaknesses of various types of statistical analyses and data presentations.

Even if you do not plan to do research yourself, you need to know what is taught in this course for a variety of reasons. The knowledge you gain will help you critically assess the data presented as a routine part of many daily briefings and training sessions. Furthermore, what you are expected to do in practicing your profession has been and will increasingly be impacted by research and statistical analysis. What you learn from this course and text will help you understand the research you read as you fulfill your professional obligation, whether as a practitioner or researcher, to keep up with the advancing knowledge in your field.

Statistics-Based Initiatives for Improving Criminal Justice Agency Policies and Practices

A number of closely related, often overlapping, statistics-based approaches to improving performance have gained wide acceptance in criminal justice agencies in recent years. Here we mention only two: efforts to identify evidence-based best practices and what we call predictive analysis, including crime mapping.

Evidence-Based Best Practices

Perhaps you recall the old saying that runs something like, continuing to do the same things and expecting different results is a sign of insanity. Criminal justice practitioners are constantly confronted with choosing the most effective ways of responding to problematic situations; protecting their own safety; achieving their immediate, situation-specific objectives; and accomplishing their agencies' goals. How should police officers respond to domestic abuse situations to maximize the chances that a battered spouse will not be battered again? How should judges respond to parole violations to maximize the chances of the parolee's future success on parole? Which juveniles might profit most from drug courts? Research can help determine what works in achieving individual practitioner and agency goals and what doesn't. Clear evidence of policy or program failure can bring about a change in the ways things are done and, perhaps, improve results. **Evidence-based best practices** are those policies and procedures that have proven through scientific research most likely to produce the desired results.

Predictive Analysis

Predictive analysis combines information pertaining to past and current events of interest (e.g., particular kinds of crime, prison disturbances, recidivism, civil disturbances, court loads, etc.) with data on the context within which the events occur (e.g., neighborhoods, institutional populations, etc.) to create statistical models practitioners can use to assess the probability of the events recurring. Action may then be taken to prevent their recurrence or to prepare better to respond if they do. Reliance on predictive analysis signals a change in agency orientation and priorities from reactive responses to proactive interventions. We will use predictive policing as a specific example, but the basic ideas apply to all criminal justice agencies.

As Beth Pearsall (2010) explains, "Predictive policing . . . is taking data from disparate sources, analyzing them and then using the results to anticipate, prevent and respond more effectively to future crime. Predictive policing entails becoming less reactive" (pp. 16–17). Currently, two of the most prominent uses of predictive policing are crime mapping and hot spot intervention. Both involve an ongoing process of gathering and analyzing statistical data pertaining to the location and types of past and current criminal activity. These data are used to predict (estimate the probability of) future criminal activity in various locations and to mobilize law enforcement resources with the aim of deterring further criminal activity in these or similar locations or to increase the likelihood of apprehending offenders.

Carl J. Jensen of the FBI Academy summarizes well the significance of these statistics-based initiatives for improving criminal justice agency practices. He notes the growing interest among U.S. law enforcement professionals in evidence-based policing (which he refers to as EBP), predictive policing, and establishing best practices guidance. He goes on to say,

> There are many good reasons why successful law enforcement executives will have to be consumers and appliers of research. . . . [T]hey must use research in their everyday work. . . . We often do not know whether what we do works at all. In many cases, even after research has shown that something doesn't work, we continue to do it as a result of political pressure, inertia, or ignorance. . . . Using the EBP model . . . an agency determines the best practices as identified in the relevant literature. A great deal of cutting edge research is already available. (Jensen, 2006)

Although a detailed consideration is beyond the scope of this text, another type of predictive analysis has been widely adopted, especially among major urban police departments. *Crime mapping* combines data for many variables pertaining to past crimes with sophisticated statistical analyses. The results of these analyses identify crime hot spots, predict the locations and timing of future crimes, and locate perpetrators. With such results in hand, always-limited police resources can be allocated in more efficient and effective ways. Some of those resources may be directed to crime prevention, whereas others may focus on locating and apprehending offenders, sometimes in the act of offending.

As we noted previously, there is often some tension between researchers and practitioners concerning the value of quantitative research in shaping criminal justice policies and practices. Nevertheless, it seems clear that the extent and importance of research leading to evidence-based best practices and predictive policing, including crime mapping, will almost certainly grow as the law enforcement, judicial, and correctional agencies evolve through the 21st century.

It seems clear, too, that the further you advance in your profession, the more important it is for you to know about research methods and statistical analysis. Your responsibility for formulating effective policies and procedures will increase. If you achieve positions of advanced leadership in your profession, the knowledge you gain from this course will be essential.

Finally, it's worth noting that the different types of statistical analyses we will be discussing are not unique to criminology and criminal justice. In fact, they are basic tools used by practitioners and researchers in a wide variety of professions and fields of study, including medicine, genetics, nursing, forensics, social work, biology, economics, political science, sociology, pharmacology, archaeology, and anthropology, just to name a few. They inform our understanding of many vital issues and help shape many of the decisions that influence our day-to-day lives in a direct way. Some of these are, literally, life-and-death decisions. In short, you will be learning about some widely used and consequential analytic strategies in this course. Your ability to understand them and assess their strengths and weaknesses will not only contribute significantly to your professional skills and opportunities to advance in your career, but will also help you arrive at better decisions in your personal life and make you a more informed and effective community citizen.

Tips for Succeeding in This Course

Let's face it: Statistics is a tough subject. The concepts and procedures you are expected to learn in this course are not easily grasped by most of us. For some students, a fear of anything mathematical, often referred to as math anxiety, complicates the situation. Perhaps you are one of them. When confronted by a mathematical formula, your brain begins to freeze, a little (maybe a lot of) panic sets in, and your sweat glands open. You begin to read and study but get frustrated almost immediately and say to yourself, "I can't do this!" But the truth is that with some patience, persistence, and hard work, almost everyone—including you—can master the contents of this text and succeed in this course.

We know, of course, this is much easier said than done. And we wish it were otherwise, but we have no sure-fire suggestions for conquering math anxiety. We offer instead just a few observations and suggestions based on our years of experience in working with a variety of students and our reading of the research literature about human learning. Whether you are subject to math anxiety or not, we hope you find the following tips for mastering the subject matter in this text useful. Go to www.mathacademy.com/pr/minitext/anxiety/index.asp and explore some additional suggestions.

Consider the statistical concepts and ways of analyzing data we will be discussing simply as tools for making sense of quantitative data—for figuring out what the data can tell you. Whether you are a statistical analyst or consumer of quantitative research, you need to know (a) what statistical tools are available, (b) what the underlying principles and assumptions of those tools are, (c) how to select and use the appropriate tools, (d) what the limitations of those tools are, and (e) how to interpret and critique the results of the statistical analyses those tools produce. The materials in this text and course will provide you with this requisite knowledge.

If you are subject to math anxiety, our first suggestion is to acknowledge to yourself that math anxiety can be self-defeating, tempting you to give up before you even begin. We urge you to resist the temptation to surrender and give yourself a chance to succeed. Some students, especially those who experience some degree of math anxiety, may be tempted to try to memorize their way through a course like this. Memorization has its place in learning about statistics and statistical analysis, but try not to let memorization become a substitute for striving to really grasp the basic ideas underlying the statistical procedures you are learning about and the calculations you are performing. Rise to the challenge of really understanding what statistics and statistical analyses can do for you. You may well find that doing so will actually make the course easier and more interesting now and much more valuable to you in the future.

Some of the materials in this course will likely be difficult for almost every student, not just those with math anxiety. Don't assume you can casually glance over the text—or even read it once slowly, word for word, and "get it." You almost certainly won't. Read slowly and carefully, yes—but you will probably need to do much more. We recommend that you read each chapter once through quickly to get a general idea of where you are headed. Then read each one slowly at least twice, pausing occasionally to ask yourself whether you have understood what you just read. If your answer is no, read again. Chances are, you will need to be proactive, too—that is, you will need to actively engage with and think about what you are reading, to work it through in your mind in various ways. Use the "Pause, Think, and Explore" questions inserted at various points within the text and the end-of-chapter list of key concepts and review questions, as well as the discussion questions and exercises, to build and test your knowledge of the chapter's contents.

We move through the new subject matter in this course gradually, pointing out the links between what you have already learned and the new ideas and statistics being introduced. In many cases, we introduce concepts in a general way in one chapter and then consider them in more detail in a later chapter. In fact, we have already begun this process in this chapter.

The content in later chapters builds on your understanding of what has been covered in the earlier chapters. For this reason, and because difficult subject matter is usually best mastered by a gradual progression from the more basic to the more complex, approach the material one chapter at a time and be sure you understand the content in each before you move on to the next. You will almost certainly be confused and at a loss if you don't understand the more basic concepts and analytic procedures before you tackle the more complex ones. In later chapters, we provide suggestions for rereading some sections of earlier chapters when doing so might help you understand topics you are currently studying.

Master the specialized vocabulary to which you will be introduced in this course. It is the key to understanding statistical analysis. Learn the definitions of these special terms and how to use them correctly in written reports and face-to-face discussions. In short, learn to speak and write the lingo of statistical analysis. If you can become fluent in this specialized language, you are well on your way to understanding statistics and succeeding in this course. Learning the language is learning statistics!

We provide many statistical formulas and ask you to do many calculations, but this is not just a "cookbook" of statistical applications. Meaningful statistical analysis involves more than plugging numbers into formulas. Frankly, the formulas don't care what numbers are plugged into them. But you as an analyst must care about the quality of those numbers and what the formulas can and can't do for you as you use them to help figure out what the data tell you. Thus, in our view, it is essential that you work toward not just knowing how to "crunch numbers," but *understanding* what you and the formulas are doing when you perform a statistical analysis. We will be urging you to think—and think critically—about what you are doing as you perform these analyses.

Because we think doing calculations can, in some instances, enhance your understanding of what the data analysis is designed to reveal about the data, we take you step-by-step through several of them. We spare you at least some of the long, complex (and boring) mathematical exercises, though. Computers can apply a specified formula to a set of quantitative data much faster and with many fewer errors than can any of us humans. In general, we think it is best to leave those long and complicated tasks to the machines. We know it is a pain, but take notes in class and on your reading. There is something about physically transferring information and ideas you are hearing or reading to paper (or to your computer, but it seems to be more effective if you take the notes by hand) that makes understanding and remembering easier for many of us.

Ask questions in class or in online forums—even if you fear your questions may make you look dumb. We'll bet that others in the class have the same questions, but don't dare ask them.

If it fits your style (and maybe even if it doesn't), have discussions or study sessions in person or online regularly with others taking the course. Try explaining or teaching the course materials to each other; this is one of the best ways of learning new subject matter.

Insist on getting help outside of class from your instructor and/or teaching assistant when you need it. Attend/log in to discussion/review sessions led by your teachers if they are available.

Remember to be patient with yourself, as well as disciplined and persistent, in your approach to the materials in this course. Perhaps most important is that you find a way to study that works for you. If you do, your chances of success will be greatly enhanced.

Finally, we recognize we have an important role to play in your chances for success in this course as well. To help you get up to speed, we will provide a review of selected topics from your course in research methods in the next chapter. (For a more thorough discussion, see Fitzgerald & Cox, 2002.) We also pledge, with the help of our reviewers and editors, to write with as much clarity as we can muster, always keeping in mind the struggles many students have—and we ourselves had—with the study of statistics.

Summary

In this chapter, we have discussed uses of the term *statistics* in criminal justice. We have explored the nature and origin of statistics as well as their general uses in criminal justice. Some major sources of statistical data in criminal justice were identified. Several reasons for criminal justice researchers and practitioners to study statistics and statistical analyses were discussed. The sometimes contrasting views of researchers and practitioners about the usefulness of research and statistical analysis were discussed, and some ways in which practitioners may profit from the study of criminal justice statistics were suggested. Some recent statistics-based initiatives for improving the performance of criminal justice agencies were identified. Finally, some tips for succeeding in this course were offered, including some suggestions for overcoming some potential barriers, such as math anxiety.

Concepts to Master

Categorizing	Evidence-based best practices	Probability theory
Counting	Explanation	Raw data
Databases	Frequency counts	Statistic(s)
Datum/data	Measuring	Table
Description	Prediction	Variable
Estimation	Predictive analysis	Variable values

Review Questions

1. What are some of the common uses of the term *statistics*?
2. Distinguish between datum and data. Give three examples of each.
3. What is a table?
4. Where do statistics come from?
5. What are raw data?
6. What is a variable? What are variable values?
7. What is categorizing?
8. What is counting?
9. What is measuring?
10. What is applying probability theory?
11. What are the four ways statistics are used in criminal justice?
12. Compare and contrast description, estimation, explanation, and prediction.
13. What is a database? Give examples.
14. Describe two archives of criminal justice data.
15. Why should criminal justice practitioners as well as researchers study statistics?
16. In what ways do researchers' and practitioners' perspectives on research differ? When they disagree, what are the main critiques each makes of the other's perspective?
17. What are "evidence-based best practices," and how are statistics related to establishing them?
18. What is predictive analysis? How are statistics related to establishing it?

19. What is math anxiety, and what are some of the strategies for managing it?
20. What are some of the ways a student might best approach the study of statistics in order to achieve mastery of the material?
21. Define and use in three different sentences each of the terms in the "Concepts to Master" list.

Exercises and Discussion Questions

1. Keep your eye out for criminal justice statistics and quantitative analysis in your other textbooks, the mass media, and online throughout your studies in this course. Bring copies of examples to class for review and discussion in light of what you are learning as you make your way through this text.
2. Is it either wise or practical to establish evidence-based best practices and/or predictive analysis in criminal justice? Why or why not? If they may be helpful, how should they be established? Do statistics and statistical analysis have a role to play in establishing them? What kind of role?
3. Go to www.ojp.usdoj.gov/nij/journals/258/police-lineups.html and http://en.wikipedia.org/wiki/eyewitness_identification to learn about the impact of research on police lineups and best practices for lineups. Have you participated in or directly observed a police lineup? Have you seen any on TV or in the movies or online? Did they conform to best practices? Why or why not?
4. Have you participated in or observed closely a criminal justice research project? If so, what role did you play? What did you observe about the relationships between researchers and practitioners? What are the main issues or problems in researcher-practitioner relationships? Do you think collaboration between researchers and practitioners is important? Why or why not? If it is important, how can it be improved? Were any statistics from the study reported? If so, did you find them credible? Why or why not?
5. What is your attitude toward research in criminal justice? Do you agree with "derb79"? Why or why not? Do you agree with Chief Bratton? Why or why not?
6. What if well-educated practitioners decided to do some research on criminal justice researchers? Would the attitudes of either about criminal justice research in general, and about researcher-practitioner collaboration in particular, change? Why or why not?
7. If you are a practitioner (or plan to be one), do (would) you use statistics in your day-to-day activities? If you do (would), what kinds do (would) you use and how do (would) you use them? Are there statistics you would like to have available to you, but don't? If so, which kinds? How would they be helpful to you in your day-to-day professional activities?
8. If you are a practitioner (or plan to be one), do you think past research has played a role in how you (do/would) fulfill your professional obligations? If it has played a role, how has it

influenced you? Do you think future research is likely to play a role? Do you think you will be gathering any statistics to help inform your professional activities? Why or why not?

9. If you are a practitioner (or plan to be one), would you participate in a research project in your agency or institution? Why or why not? What kinds of research would be appropriate?

10. If you are a practitioner (or plan to be one), would you conduct a research project in your agency? Why or why not?

11. Go to www.ojp.usdoj.gov/nij/events/research-real-world.htm and listen to some of the seminars on how research has changed criminal justice policy and practice.

12. Go to www.ojp.usdoj.gov/nij/events/expert-chats/welcome.htm and listen to experts talk about criminal justice research and its implications for policy and practice.

13. Go to www.ojp.usdoj.gov/nij/multimedia/welcome.htm and watch presentations of your choice related to criminal justice research.

14. Go to www.ncjrs.gov/pdffiles1/nij/178240.pdf and look in Appendix A to learn about recommendations for best practices in working with eyewitnesses.

15. Follow the links in the text to the UCR, NIBRS, NCVS, NYSFS, DUF, and ADAM (Arrestee Drug Abuse Monitoring Program) as well as the NACJD and ICPSR to learn more about their specific content, strengths, and weaknesses. Drawing on your knowledge of the databases, which source of crime statistics (UCR, NIBRS, or NCVS) do you think gives the most accurate general picture of crime in the United States? Why?

Student Study Site

Visit the open-access student study site at **www.sagepub.com/fitzgerald** for access to several study tools including eFlashcards, web quizzes, and additional appendices as well as links to SAGE journal articles and audio, video and web resources.

Scientific Research and Statistical Analysis

Learning Objectives

What you are expected not only to learn but to master in this chapter:

- What units of analysis and variables are
- What mutually exclusive and exhaustive variables are
- The four levels of variable measurement (nominal, ordinal, interval, and ratio)
- The three conditions for a causal argument
- The nature of samples, especially simple random samples
- What a research design is
- What before-after, before-after with control group, and quasi-experimental designs are
- Principles of ethical integrity in data management and analysis
- The principle of garbage in-garbage out

Introduction

As we noted at the beginning of the first chapter, statistical analysis is just one of several steps in the scientific research process. Whether you are choosing an appropriate kind of statistical analysis, interpreting the results of that analysis, or evaluating others' choices and interpretations, you have to know something about other aspects of the research project.

We might summarize the steps in the research process as follows: (a) Decide on a research topic; (b) identify the appropriate units of analysis (the persons, places, objects, or events that are of interest); (c) specify, define, and develop measures for the relevant variables pertaining to those units of analysis; (d) construct one or more hypotheses about the relationship(s) among the variables; (e) develop an appropriate research design; (f) select the particular units of analysis to be studied, which often involves sampling; (g) gather the data; (h) analyze the data; (i) interpret the results of the analysis; and (j) write the research report.

Although performing statistical analyses and interpreting the results occur late in this process, it would be a serious mistake to think of these steps as entirely independent of those preceding them. In fact, what happens in each of the preceding steps has at least some implications for the statistical analysis to come. We focus here, however, on a few key concepts associated with earlier stages that have direct implications for statistical analysis. You need to be familiar with these concepts in order to understand our discussion of the different types of statistical analysis in the chapters that follow. In particular, we discuss units of analysis, variables and levels of variable measurement, hypotheses, causality, sampling, and research design. We refer back to these matters in subsequent chapters. The chapter concludes with a discussion of garbage in-garbage out and ethical integrity in data management, analysis, and reporting.

Units of Analysis and Variables

The **units of analysis** for a research project are the persons, places, objects, or events being studied. In one study, judges may be the units of analysis, whereas in another, the units of analysis may be trials. One research project might be concerned with inmates, and another may have cell blocks or entire correctional facilities as the units of analysis. A researcher may choose to study events, such as traffic stops, the persons driving the stopped vehicles, or the officers doing the stops. Variables appropriate for each unit of analysis must be selected, and conclusions drawn must be limited to those and not some other units of analysis. That is, the conclusions drawn from a study of variables pertaining to trials (events) should not be applied to the judges presiding at the trials (persons).

As we noted in Chapter 1, a variable is a characteristic, feature, or attribute that differs (varies) from one unit of analysis to another. The researcher identifies and defines the variables in which she or he is interested, specifies each variable's possible values, and determines how the variables will be measured—that is, how the variable value for each unit of analysis will be established. How a variable is actually measured is often referred to as the **operational definition** of the variable.

Researchers often refer to the operational definition of a variable as how the variable has been operationalized.

Knowing the definitions of variables, including their operational definitions, is important for a number of reasons. Among the more important is that a variable with the same label can be defined and operationalized in different ways. For example, a variable labeled "sex" might be defined as a biological variable, assigned two values (male and female), and operationalized (measured) by a survey question asking the respondent's sex or by performing a chromosomal analysis. Sex may also be defined as a conjugal relationship, and its quality might be measured by a survey respondent's answer to a question with the answer choices: "awesome," "so-so," and "awful." One researcher may assign the variable "crime" the possible values misdemeanor and felony, whereas another might assign the possible values murder, robbery, breaking and entering, and theft. One may operationalize the definition of crime using official court records and another by asking questionnaire respondents to indicate which offenses he or she has committed. To make sense of any statistical analysis, you need to know how the variables are defined and operationalized.

Mutually Exclusive and Exhaustive Variable Values

To be useful for statistical analyses, the possible values of a variable must be mutually exclusive and exhaustive. Variable values are **mutually exclusive** if there is one and only one response category/measurement value appropriate for each unit of analysis. Measurements that overlap are not mutually exclusive. For example, the possible age ranges "less than 15 years," "15-18 years," "18-21 years," and "more than 21 years" are not mutually exclusive because a respondent who is 18 years old could be placed in either the second or the third category.

Variable values are **exhaustive** if there is a category/measurement for every unit of analysis. For example, a researcher might specify the possible values of a "political party affiliation" variable as Republican and Democrat. If the study group also included members of the Libertarian party, the categories available would not be exhaustive because there is no category for those respondents. Adding an "other" category is a frequently used strategy for ensuring that the available variable value categories/measurements are exhaustive.

Categories/measurements that overlap (i.e., that are not mutually exclusive) or omit possible variable values (i.e., that are not exhaustive) make even the most sophisticated statistical analyses meaningless.

Discrete and Continuous Variable Values

Whether variable values are, in principle, continuous or discrete depends on the number of possible values the variables can have. **Continuous variable values** can, in principle at least, be infinite. Suppose we were interested in the variable "length of a preliminary court hearing." Time is a variable whose values are continuous because, no matter what units of time we use for its measurement, we can always use a smaller unit of time. That is, we could measure the length of the hearing in hours, minutes, seconds, fractions of second, fractions of a fraction of seconds, and so on. Other examples of continuous variable values include measurements of physical distance, age, and time served, as well as, in most cases, percents, proportions, and rates.

In contrast, **discrete variable values** are finite in number and usually consist of whole number values. Examples include biological sex (with values of male and female); political party affiliation (with values of Democrat, Republican, Independent, and so on); number of crimes committed by a person (values of 0, 1, 2, ... but not 1.6); and type of crime (with values "misdemeanor" and "felony").

Understanding whether the variable values under investigation are continuous or discrete is important because many kinds of statistical analyses assume we are working with continuous measurement. As we will see, however, relatively minor modifications of the calculation formulas for many of these statistics (referred to as corrections for continuity) make them applicable in the analysis of discrete variable values as well.

Levels of Measurement

Variables may be measured at four levels: nominal, ordinal, interval, and ratio. We briefly discuss the nature, strengths, and weaknesses of each.

Nominal-Level Measurements

The most basic level of variable measurement is called nominal. A variable measured at the **nominal** level has possible values consisting of a set of mutually exclusive, exhaustive categories. Every unit of analysis included in the study can be placed in one and only one of the nominal-level measurement categories. Neither the categories (variable values) nor the units of analysis placed in them on the basis of their variable values can be ordered—that is, they can't be arranged from higher to lower, or ranked. Examples of variables measured at the nominal level include responses to a statement on a questionnaire with possible responses of true or false; religious affiliation categorized as Protestant, Catholic, Jewish, and other; and ethnic affiliation categorized as Irish, Dutch, English, and so on. Nominal variable values are always discrete.

Ordinal-Level Measurements

Ordinal-level measurements consist of measurement categories (variable values) that are not only mutually exclusive and exhaustive, but also may be ranked in ascending or descending order. The possible variable values might represent the different degrees to which a certain attribute is present, for example. Suppose we asked people to respond to the following attitude questionnaire item:

> The death penalty is an effective deterrent to crime. (Circle the answer corresponding to your degree of agreement or disagreement with this statement.)
>
> strongly agree   agree   neutral   disagree   strongly disagree

These response categories (variable values) can be arranged according to the degree of agreement they represent. Once a group of respondents answered the question, we could rank order the respondents according to their degree of agreement (or disagreement) with the statement.

Note that we cannot say how much more one of these categories of measurement differs from another, or how much more one person (unit of analysis) agrees with the statement than with another. Why? Because with an ordinal measurement, the difference or distance between ranks (that is, for example, the difference between one person circling "disagree" and another circling "strongly disagree") has no precise quantitative value or meaning. That is, it would make no sense to say the second person disagrees two times as much as the first person on the basis of this ordinal measurement of the variable, but we can say that the second person disagrees more than the first person.

Are ordinal measures discrete or continuous? Although there is some disagreement among researchers and statisticians, and many treat them as continuous in their statistical analyses, we suggest they are best treated as discrete in most cases.

Interval-Level Measurements

With **interval-level measurements** (sometimes referred to as equal-interval-level measurement), the possible variable values are not only mutually exclusive and exhaustive categories (as in nominal-level measurement) that can be ranked (as in ordinal-level measurement), but we can specify the *quantity* of variation between points on the measurement scale. An interval measurement scale has measurement units of equal size, but an arbitrary zero point. Because the units are the same size, the difference between any two adjacent points on the measurement scale is the same as the difference between any other two adjacent points on the same scale. Heat, as measured in degrees centigrade (C) or Fahrenheit (F), are examples of interval-level measurements. Within each of the scales, the units of measurement (degrees) are the same size. Therefore, we can say that the difference (interval) in heat between 50°C and 25°C is quantitatively the same as the difference (interval) between 40°C and 15°C. Note, however, that the size of a centigrade degree does not equal the size of a Fahrenheit degree.

Note also that the location of the zero point on each of these two temperature scales is arbitrary and does not indicate an absence of heat. The temperature at which water freezes is arbitrarily set at 32° on the Fahrenheit scale and 0° on the centigrade scale. To understand the effects of an arbitrary zero point on some mathematical operations, suppose we have two measurements, 20°C and 40°C. Note that in this case, 40°C is twice 20°C. Now consider what would happen if we moved the arbitrary zero point on the centigrade thermometer up 10° units. The point on the scale that was originally 20°C would now read 10°C, and the point that was originally 40°C would now be 30°C. Obviously, 30°C is not twice 10°C. Nevertheless, the differences between 15°C and 40°C and between 25°C and 50°C remain 25°C, reflecting the equal interval nature of the centigrade temperature scale. Variables measured at the interval level may be discrete or continuous.

Ratio-Level Measurements

Ratio-level measurements have all the properties of nominal, ordinal, and interval measurements and, in addition, have an absolute zero point representing a complete absence of whatever is being measured. The Kelvin (K) heat scale, for example, is a ratio-level measurement with a nonarbitrary zero point. That is, 0°K indicates the complete absence of heat. Therefore, it makes sense to say 40°K is twice as warm as 20°K. Age, time, proportions, rates, number of offenses, length, the number of days in office (or jail), number of contacts between parole officer and parolee, frequency of coffee breaks, blood alcohol level, and number of court cases are all examples of ratio-level data. Variables measured at the ratio level may be discrete or continuous.

Some Additional Considerations Regarding Levels of Measurement

Before we leave the subject of measurement level, it should be noted that different ways of operationalizing the same variable will often produce different results. For example, it is widely (and correctly) recognized that how a pollster phrases a question soliciting respondents' opinions about some issue (i.e., how a variable is operationalized) influences the answers respondents give.

It should also be noted that the same variable can sometimes be measured at different levels. For example, we might ask respondents to tell us about their shoplifting activities. In one operationalization of the "shoplifting activities" variable, we might ask if they have ever shoplifted and offer "yes" and "no" as the possible variable value alternatives. This is, at best, a discrete ordinal-level measurement. We might also ask respondents how many times, if at all, they have shoplifted and invite them to give us a number of times, beginning with zero. This would be a discrete ratio-level measurement of the variable.

It is also true that variables measured at the nominal level for one unit of analysis (such as a correctional officer) can usually serve as the basis for measurements of another variable at the ratio level for a different unit of analysis (such as a group of correctional officers). For example, although male is a nominal value of the discrete biological variable sex pertaining to a particular correctional officer, proportion of males is a continuous variable measured at the ratio level pertaining to a group of correctional officers. Table 2.1 illustrates this point.

Be alert for possible confusion regarding the language referring to variables and their levels of measurement. Sometimes, authors refer to variables measured at, say, the ordinal level simply as ordinal variables. Just remember that when we or others refer to an ordinal variable, what we really mean is a variable that is measured at the ordinal level. Finally, we should note that data sets often contain two very different kinds of numbers. It is important not to confuse them. One kind consists of mathematical *quantities* such as frequency counts and variable measurements. Numbers such as 12 females, 12% females, and a reading of .12 on a blood alcohol test are

Table 2.1 Units of Analysis and Levels of Measurement for a Criminal Justice Methods Class

Sex as a Nominal Variable Pertaining to Persons as Units of Analysis	Sex as a Ratio Variable Pertaining to Groups as Units of Analysis
Males: 6	Proportion of male: 6/10 = .60
Females: 4	Proportion of female: 4/10 = .40
Total: 10	Total: 1.00

numbers representing quantities. Such quantities can be subjected to mathematical calculations (addition, subtraction, multiplication, division).

Another kind is comprised of numerical *codes* used to represent variable values. Numbers used as computer codes are simply numerical labels or names for particular variable values, usually of nominal-level measurements. Recording a "1" in the data set if the survey respondent is male and "2" if female is an example of numbers used as codes. These numerical codes are not quantities and cannot be subjected to mathematical calculations.

Of course, we or the computer can count the number of 1s and 2s in the data set, which would yield a frequency count of males and females. As we noted earlier, frequency counts are examples of numbers that are quantities and can be subjected to mathematical calculations.

In any event, knowing the levels at which variables are measured is important because, as we will see in later chapters, it determines, among other things, the types of mathematical and statistical procedures we can use in analyzing our data.

Hypotheses

Theories, which are made up of related hypotheses, may be about abstract issues, such as the causes of crime, or about the pragmatic concerns of a practitioner, such as how best to protect his or her safety during a traffic stop. Much of criminal justice research is devoted to testing (that is, determining if the evidence does or does not support) hypotheses.

Hypotheses as Proposed Causal Explanations

A **research hypothesis** typically asserts a causal relationship between two or more variables. That is, it asserts that changes in the values of one variable, referred to as the **independent** (or causal) **variable**, produce (cause) changes in another variable, referred to as the **dependent** (or effect) **variable**.

Suppose we believe that as cities' populations grow, their crime rates increase. Cities are the units of analysis in this case and the research hypothesis (the proposed causal relationship) might be diagrammed as follows:

Time →

Cause	→	Effect
Change in the independent variable	→	Change in the dependent variable
Growing city populations	→	Increase in cities' crime rate

Of course, many of the phenomena of interest to criminal justice researchers and practitioners are much more complex than can be understood or explained by a single variable. Rather, such variables as crime, recidivism, prison riots, and plea bargaining outcomes are considered to be the result of many different variables, which is referred to as **multiple causation**. For example, we might hypothesize that income, perceived ethnic or racial equality, and age are causally related to crime. More specifically, we might say the lower the income, the greater the racial discrimination, and the younger the age, the higher the likelihood of a criminal offense.

Increasingly sophisticated statistical procedures have been developed to examine the contributions of several different possible causes to some particular effect. The classic examples of these procedures are multiple correlation and regression analyses, which we discuss later in the book.

Cause is often thought of as a unidirectional concept. We can easily imagine a research hypothesis asserting a **causal chain** in which a causes b and b causes c, and which may be diagrammed as follows:

Time →

$a \to b \to c$

In explanatory research, a variable that comes between two other variables in such chains of causation is referred to as an **intervening variable**. "Between" in this case refers to the occurrence of changes in the variable values in a time sequence. In the chain illustrated above, variable b might be called an intervening variable between variables a and c, if changes in it occurred after a changed and before c changed. Suppose we hypothesize that persons who are poor and then begin to associate with others who commit crimes are likely to commit a criminal offense. We might diagram this set of variable relationships as follows:

Time →

Independent Variable → Intervening Variable → Dependent Variable

Income → Criminal associations → Criminal offense

In this research hypothesis, the "criminal associations" variable intervenes between the poverty and crime variables in the causal chain.

Statistical analysis helps us determine whether a good argument can be made for a causal relationship of any kind between or among variables.

Research Hypotheses and Null Hypotheses

We began our discussion of hypotheses by saying that much of criminal justice research is devoted to testing a research hypothesis. It turns out, however, that in most statistical analyses, a research hypothesis is not tested directly. Instead, for reasons we discuss later in the book, research hypotheses are tested *indirectly* by testing directly what is called a **null hypothesis**, which asserts that there is no causal relationship between the variables.

Note that null hypotheses can be true or false. That is, in the real world, either there is a relationship between the two variables as asserted in the research hypothesis (in which case the null hypothesis is false) or there is not such a relationship (in which case the null hypothesis is true). As statistical analysts, we must decide, on the basis of the available statistical evidence, whether we believe the null hypothesis is true or false—that is, whether we will accept or reject the null hypothesis.

Note also that when we make a decision about a null hypothesis, it can be correct or incorrect. That is, we can decide that a null hypothesis is true when it is, in fact, true, which would be a correct decision. But we can also decide it is true even though it is, in fact, false, which would be an incorrect decision. And, we can decide that a null hypothesis is false when it is, in fact, false (correct) or when it is, in fact, true (incorrect).

The four possible combinations regarding null hypotheses and our decisions about them can be diagrammed as in Table 2.2.

Two of the four possible results in Table 2.2 present no problem. If we decide that the null hypothesis is true and it is, in fact, true—that is, there is, in fact, no relationship between the variables—we made a correct decision. Similarly, if we decide the null hypothesis is false and it is, in fact, false, our decision was correct.

The remaining two decision/fact combinations, however, can be quite problematic. If we decide that the null hypothesis is false and it is, in fact, true—that is, there really is no relationship between the variables—we have made an error. We have

Table 2.2 Decisions About and Realities of the Null Hypothesis

		In Reality	
		Null Hypothesis Is True	Null Hypothesis Is False
Decision About the Null Hypothesis	It's True	Correct decision	Type II error (accept a false null)
	It's False	Type I error (reject a true null)	Correct decision

rejected a null hypothesis that is true. In statistical parlance, this is referred to as a **Type I error**. If we decide that the null hypothesis is true and it is, in fact, false—that is, there really is a relationship between the variables—we have made a different kind of error. We have accepted a null hypothesis that is false. In statistical analysis, this mistake is referred to as a **Type II error**. As we will see later in the book, some kinds of statistical analysis permit us to determine the probability that we have committed a Type I or a Type II error.

Finally, note that whatever decision we make regarding the null hypothesis has important implications for the research hypothesis. If we decide the null hypothesis is true, then we must conclude that the research hypothesis is false. If we decide the null hypothesis is false, then the truth of the research hypothesis is supported. We can't quite say the research hypothesis is definitely true if we decide the null hypothesis is false, because what looks like a causal relationship may not be, for reasons we will discuss in the next section. In any event, if the statistical analysis indicates that we should reject the null hypothesis, we can claim at least indirect and tentative support for our research hypothesis.

The Conditions for Causality

A preliminary note about our use of the terms *cause* and *causality* is in order. Some researchers and statisticians recommend against using these terms at all in scientific discourse because we can never be absolutely certain we have discovered a causal relationship between variables. Instead, we should speak or write only of relationships, not causal relationships, between variables. Although we agree that scientific methods, including statistical analysis, can never definitively establish a causal relationship between variables (for reasons we will discuss later), we think avoiding the concept of cause entirely is not the most honest way to talk about what we are seeking when we do scientific research. After all, what kind of "relationships" between variables are we hoping to find? Whether we are theorists or practitioners, we are looking for relationships that demonstrate strength and repeatability. In practical terms, we hope to discover relationships such that doing x "makes" y occur reliably—and the best available term for that is a causal relationship between variables x and y. Even if we can't ever be certain we have conclusively demonstrated a causal relationship between variables, we often have to *act* as if we have when we implement evidence-based policies and procedures. Furthermore, it is useful to establish criteria necessary for establishing a causal relationship, even if we acknowledge that the goal is, in principle, unattainable. The criteria can be used to evaluate the strengths and weaknesses of the evidence and arguments that there is a causal relationship between variables. So long as we constantly bear in mind ourselves, and remind others about, the tentativeness of any assertion about causality, we think using causal language is being more honest about what all scientists are seeking.

Generally, three criteria must be satisfied to justify claiming a causal relationship between or among variables: concomitant variation, the right time sequence, and the elimination of other possible causal variables.

Concomitant Variation

The first requirement is that of **concomitant variation**, also known as **correlation**—that is, when a change occurs in variable x, a change also occurs in variable y. When we observe that the values of the two variables change together, we say that x is correlated with y. The changes must vary systematically with each other. If we contend that greater alienation causes more frequent participation in radical political activities, then the data must show that those people who are more alienated participate in radical political activities more frequently than those who are less alienated. If the data reveal coordinated changes among the variables, the concomitant variation requirement for making a causal inference has been met.

Establishing strong evidence of concomitant variation is the objective of most statistical analyses in explanatory research. Bivariate and multivariate correlation analyses are the most obvious examples. These and other ways of testing for concomitant variation between or among variables are discussed in later chapters.

Appropriate Time Sequence

The second requirement is one of **appropriate time sequence**. If changes in x cause changes in y, then the changes in x must occur with or before the changes in y. If x changes after y changes, the change in x cannot be the cause of the change in y. To return to our example, if more frequent participation in radical activities precedes increasing feelings of alienation, the feelings of alienation cannot be a cause of the participation. The investigator demonstrates that he or she has satisfied this requirement by observing that the appropriate temporal sequence of conditions has occurred. Usually, appropriate time sequence is established by the structure of the research design. We consider this aspect of research design later in this chapter.

Elimination of Other Possible Causal Variables

The third requirement is to **eliminate other possible causes**. In practice, this requirement, unlike the two preceding ones, can never be fully satisfied because there is always the possibility of other unidentified and/or unmeasured causal variables. What looks like a causal relationship between two variables may, in fact, be caused by a relationship between each of these two variables and a third variable. When this is the case, the apparent, but false, relationship between the original two variables is called a **spurious relationship**.

Remember, then, that statistical analysis never, in and of itself, establishes causality. Statistical analysis does permit us to determine if the evidence indicates concomitant variation. But concomitant variation is only one of the three requirements for a causal argument. Research design may help us establish evidence of an appropriate time sequence, and some kinds of statistical analyses help us eliminate at least some other possible causes. In the final analysis, however, we simply can't ever be sure that we have established a causal relationship between variables. A spurious relationship remains an ever-present possibility because we may have failed to identify one or more variables that really caused the changes we observed in the dependent variable.

Sampling

Sometimes, we gather data from the entire set of units of analysis we are interested in learning about. In these cases, the data we gather are referred to collectively as a **census** and the entire set of units of analysis is called a **population**. In other cases, we select and gather data on only a portion of a population, but nevertheless still desire to learn something about that population. The process of selecting the portion of the population for study is called **sampling**, and the subset of the population selected for study is called a **sample**.

For example, to determine whether the 400 registered voters in Hitsville would support a tax increase to fund a drug court and associated counseling, we might interview every registered voter—that is, take a census of the population of Hitsville on this question. Or, if we were short of funds or had limited time, we might identify a small subgroup of the 400 registered voters (that is, we might select a sample of, say, 50) and ask them about their support for such a proposal, with the intent of using their responses to learn something about the views of the population.

Because the sample will represent the population for our research purposes, we need to be concerned about the quality of that representation. Our goal is to select a "good" sample—one whose characteristics accurately represent the characteristics of the population. To the extent that the sample is, in fact, representative, we can use data from the sample to make accurate inferences about the population.

Sampling, however, is inevitably a risky business. Some samples are good representatives of their populations (that is, the samples have the same characteristics as the populations from which they were drawn), whereas others are not. Furthermore, even a good sample may not mirror *exactly* the characteristics of the population from which it was drawn. Any differences between the characteristics of the sample and those of the population are said to be the result of **sampling error**. We can expect that any sampling procedure will result in some sampling error. To complicate matters further, we don't usually know the characteristics of the population. So, it would appear we have no way of knowing how good a sample drawn from it is (that is, we don't know how much sampling error has occurred).

Given this situation, the procedures researchers use to select a sample become critical. Some sampling techniques are more likely than others to produce "good" samples, samples whose characteristics match pretty well those of the population from which they are drawn. Fortunately, these same sampling procedures permit us to estimate the amount of the sampling error that is likely to have occurred. That is, they allow us to estimate the probability of making a Type I error by rejecting a true null hypothesis. These sampling procedures are clearly preferable to those that do not permit such estimates. Here we discuss the sampling procedure that, in the absence of other information about the population, produces the "best" sample—that is, a sample whose characteristics are most likely to be representative of the population from which it was drawn: the simple random sample. It turns out that, in addition to providing the best sample as we defined it above, random sampling also gives us a way of estimating the amount of sampling error that is likely to occur. For these reasons (and for others we won't discuss now), simple random sampling is required in order to apply many of the statistical procedures we describe in later chapters.

Simple Random Sampling

Many statistical analyses are based on the assumption that the data being analyzed are from a sample selected "at random" from a population. The most basic type of random sample is called a simple random sample. For our present purposes, we can define a **simple random sample** as a sample selected in such a way that each unit of analysis (which, for brevity's sake, we will refer to here as an element) in the population has an equal chance of being selected for the sample. For example, to draw a simple random sample of the 400 Hitsville registered voters, each voter must have a 1 in 400 chance of being drawn for the sample. Ideally, drawing a simple random sample requires a complete and accurate **sampling frame**—that is, a complete list of all elements in the population. In our Hitsville example, the sampling frame would be the list of 400 registered voters. Furthermore, the sampling would be done with replacement. That is, after an element is drawn for the sample, it would be placed back in the sampling frame before the next draw. Why? Because if a drawn element is not returned to the population before the next draw, the probability of selecting one of the remaining elements for the sample has gone up due to the fact that there are now fewer elements in the population. For example, if you drew at random one of the Hitsville voters for your sample and didn't replace her, the probability of drawing any one of the remaining voters for the sample has gone up from 1 in 400 to 1 in 399.

When selecting relatively small samples from large populations, most statisticians say the differences in probabilities associated with selecting elements from such samples without replacement are small enough to be ignored for the purposes of statistical analysis. For small populations, though, sampling without replacement can be important because, without replacement, the probabilities of selecting elements go up substantially as the sampling proceeds, thereby violating the defining principle of a simple random sample that all elements of a population have an equal chance of being drawn for the sample.

You may wonder—we know you did—what you should do if, when sampling *with* replacement, you draw the same population element again. The answer, for most practical purposes, is that you can return the duplicate to the population and either draw again or count him or her twice in the data you are gathering. Either way preserves the equal probability principle of the simple random sample.

As you can imagine, getting a complete and accurate list of population elements may be very difficult to obtain in many instances, for a variety of reasons. No such list may be available and, even if one were available today, it may not be accurate or complete tomorrow. Incomplete or inaccurate lists threaten the randomness of the sample. To the degree that samples are not random, they jeopardize the validity of statistical analyses based on that assumption.

If you have a complete sampling frame, you or the computer can assign a unique number to each element in the population and use a random numbers table or ask the computer to use a random number generator to select a simple random sample. These tables or digital generators produce numbers, each of which has an equal chance of appearing next in a numerical sequence. Random numbers are matched with the unique numbers assigned to the population elements in order to select the random sample.

For your information and use, Appendix B on the study site (www.sagepub.com/fitzgerald) contains a random numbers table and instructions for using it to draw a simple random sample. A project you might undertake to explore random sampling and sampling error is included in the end-of-chapter exercises.

Research Design

A **research design** is a plan for carrying out a research project to test a research hypothesis. It specifies who or what will be measured, how many times it will be measured, and when (i.e., at what points during the research process) the measurements will occur. Properly executed research designs help determine if the evidence supports the existence of concomitant variation and the appropriate time sequence required for an argument that a causal relationship exists between or among the variables being analyzed. Some also help in eliminating other possible causal variables from consideration.

Research designs may be classified in a number of different ways. In this section, we briefly review three types of causal research designs: before-after, before-after with control group, and quasi-experimental designs. We discuss the strengths and weaknesses of these designs and suggest their implications for statistical analysis. All have the objective of determining if the evidence gathered while executing the plan supports a causal argument. Assuming the evidence supports the research hypothesis, they differ in the strength of the evidence and argument they produce.

Before-After Design

If the researcher is able to anticipate a change in the independent variable, or to induce it in a research situation, she can use a **before-after research design**. Such a design is often used to evaluate the impact of a new program or procedure. Suppose a statistics teacher wants to know if her statistics course causes a change in her students' knowledge of statistics. To find out, she could give her students a test the first day of class (i.e., before the students take the class) and the last day of class (i.e., after the students take the class). Comparing the students' scores on the two tests would provide evidence of whether taking the class (the change in the independent variable) was associated with an increase in test scores (change in the dependent variable). Or, suppose a state policymaker wanted to know if a change in the self-defense law led to a reduction in violent crime. She could compare the violent crime rate for, say, the 3 years before and the 3 years after the law changed. In a before-after design, the dependent variable of interest is measured before the change in the independent variable occurs and again after it has occurred.

Let's explore this design in a little more detail. Suppose we let y be our dependent variable and y_{m1} represent our observation (measurement) of the value of the dependent variable y at a given point in time (T_1). We let y_{m2} represent a second observation (measurement) of the same variable at a later point in time (T_3). Finally, we let x be our independent variable and "x changes" represent our observation of a change in the values of the independent variable, the variable that we think explains changes in y, the dependent variable. We could then represent a before-after research design as follows:

$$\text{Time} \rightarrow \quad T_1 \quad T_2 \quad T_3$$
$$\quad\quad\quad y_{m1} \quad x \text{ changes} \quad y_{m2}$$

In the diagram, T_1, T_2, and T_3 are different points in time. The first measurement of the dependent variable (y_{m1}) occurs at time T_1, before the change in the independent variable (x) occurs. Change in the value of the independent variable (x) occurs at T_2. The second measurement of the dependent variable (y_{m2}) occurs at time T_3. Here, the investigator measures y before x occurs (a premeasurement of the dependent variable). Then, x changes and y is measured again (postmeasurement of the dependent variable). Now, suppose we compare our two measurements of y—that is, we compare y_{m1} and y_{m2}. There are two possibilities: y either changed or did not change in value. If no change in y is observed, there is presumably nothing to explain, and it appears that x has no effect on y. If y did change, then there may be something to explain, and it is at least possible that the change in x caused the change in y.

In a before-after design, statistical analyses are often used to determine how much, if any, change in y has occurred and, if the study group is a random sample from a population, whether an observed change is "statistically significant." As we will see, that phrase has a special and precise meaning in statistical analysis, and we discuss it in great detail later in the book. For now, we simply note that if our analysis indicates a change in y, we *could* infer that our independent variable x caused the change because the before-after design provides reasonably clear evidence of both concomitant variation and appropriate time sequence. Remember, however, that, as we noted previously, any apparent relationship between x and y may be spurious, so caution about inferring a causal relationship is in order.

Before-After With Control Group Design

Although the before-after design can help establish two of the conditions for a causal relationship (concomitant variation and appropriate time sequence), it has a substantial flaw that seriously weakens the argument that changes in variable x cause changes in variable y. The basic problem is satisfying the third condition for a causal inference—the elimination of other possible causes for changes in the dependent variable.

Assuming the data show an appropriate time sequence and concomitant variation, the evidence for a causal relationship between the variables is greatly strengthened if the research design includes a control group. The basic structure and underlying ideas that distinguish the before-after research design from the before-after with control group design can be summarized as follows. In the before-after with control group design, two separate study groups are included. One is called the **experimental group**, and it, like the single study group in the before-after design, is exposed to a change in the values of an independent variable (x). The other study group in this design is called a control group. A **control group** is as similar as possible to the experimental group, but it is *not* exposed to the change in the independent variable. The dependent variable (y) is measured twice in both groups and changes in the measurements of y for the two groups are compared to determine if there is strong evidence for a causal relationship between x and y.

Research that follows this design is the only research properly referred to as an experiment, and the design is referred to as the classic experimental design, usually shortened to experimental design. When rigorously conducted, experiments are the gold standard of scientific research, for reasons that we discuss below. We can diagram the **before-after with control group** research design, often referred to as the **classic experimental design**, as follows:

Time →	T_1	T_2	T_3
Experimental Group (E)	y_{em1}	x changes	y_{em2}
Control Group (C)	y_{cm1}		y_{cm2}

In the diagram, y_{em1} and y_{em2} stand for the before and after measurements of y for the experimental group, respectively, and y_{cm1} and y_{cm2} stand for the first and second measurements of y for the control group, respectively.

Let's explore this design in a little more detail. As a simple illustration, suppose our instructor, who is interested in determining how much her statistics students learn in her class, added a control group to her research design. The control group would be a group of students as similar as possible to the students about to take her class, but who will not be taking her class. Both the students who are going to take the class (the experimental group) and those who aren't (the control group) would complete a statistical knowledge test twice, once before the class starts (T_1) and once at a particular time after it is over (T_3). The differences between the before and after test scores for each group would then be compared to determine if the evidence supports a causal relationship between x and y. We'll discuss exactly how they might be compared in just a bit.

Why is the argument for a causal relationship between x and y strengthened in this design as compared with the before-after research design? Because the inclusion of the control group, in which the value of x does not change, makes it possible to measure the combined effects of at least some possible causal variables other than x. The difference between the values of the dependent variable observed at T_1 and T_3 in the control group is a measure of any effects of those other varaibles. And remarkably, we don't even have to know exactly what these other possible causal variables are!

Note that the difference in the measurements of y for the experimental group also includes a measurement of the effects of these other possible causal variables. But it includes something else as well—something *not* included in the differences in y for the control group: the effects, if any, of the change in the independent variable x on changes in y.

Therefore, we can isolate the effects of x on y by subtracting the differences between y_{cm1} and y_{cm2} (in the control group) from the differences between y_{em1} and

y_{em2}—that is, the differences that include the effect, if any, of x in the experimental group. Any difference that remains after this subtraction can be attributed to the effects of the independent variable x. We might represent this subtraction as follows:

Experimental Group   Control Group
change in y –   change in y
$(y_{em1} - y_{em2})$ – $(y_{cm1} - y_{cm2})$ = Net effect of changes in x on changes in y

We can call any change in y remaining after this subtraction the net effect of changes in x on changes in y.

As you can see, using an experimental research design (i.e., a before-after with control group design) goes a long way toward satisfying all three requirements for a causal argument. It gives us clear evidence of concomitant variation and appropriate time sequence. It also gives us strong reason to believe that the net change in y is caused by the change in x because we have eliminated many, but not necessarily all, other possible causes of a change in y. Hence, it is clearly preferable to a before-after design and should be used whenever possible to assess the effectiveness of, for example, new training programs or other innovations in procedures.

Note that an alternative to the subtraction just described is to subtract y_{cm2} from y_{em2}. Assuming that y_{cm1} is approximately equal to y_{em1}, any effects of the independent variable would be reflected in the difference between y_{cm2} and y_{em2}.

Scientists prefer to conduct experiments in laboratories. Why? Because laboratories provide the researcher complete control, more or less, over many aspects of the research situation and therefore over many possible causal variables in addition to the one they are studying. More specifically, when doing laboratory experiments, the researcher controls (a) the setting in which the research occurs. (b) the selection of subjects for the experimental and control groups, and (c) the occurrence of the change in the independent variable. When these controls are exercised, the researcher is able to keep many possible causal variables from varying (that is, to hold them constant; constants, by definition, don't change and therefore can't explain any change in the dependent variable). These controls, as well as the ability to use the control group to measure the effects of still other possible causal variables that may vary, makes a very rigorous test of a causal hypothesis possible. Both help isolate the effects, if any, of changes in x on changes in y.

As we have suggested above, experimental research designs—even those conducted in laboratories—cannot be executed perfectly and, hence, the results of even the most rigorous experiments cannot demonstrate a causal argument with complete certainty. Researchers can't, in fact, control everything that happens even in a laboratory (remember the inevitable biases, fumbles, and foibles of human researchers). Furthermore, the experimental design introduces a new problem that has no perfect solution: the possibility that the experimental and control groups initially differ in some important but unknown way. If they are different, the benefits afforded by this design are partly negated, because any such differences are also variables that may cause any observed changes in our dependent variable. In short, the relationship we observe between x and y may be spurious. Strategies for selecting members of the experimental and control groups that make them as comparable as possible are discussed later in this book.

Quasi-Experimental Research Designs

Although exercising rigorous control over the three aspects of the research situation identified earlier is maximized in a laboratory, it is often impossible to do so in criminal justice research because much of the research takes place in the field—that is, in natural, real-world settings. In such settings, the researcher has limited control, and difficult ethical issues often arise. For practical, ethical, and methodological reasons, then, criminal justice researchers must often resort to **quasi-experimental designs**, with features that depart from the most rigorous requirements of causal hypothesis tests using the before-after with control group research design. For example, criminal justice researchers can't create two identical neighborhoods, one to serve as an experimental group and one as a control group, to study the effects of a drug use prevention program. Instead, they have to find two existing neighborhoods that are as similar as possible for their study. Similarly, it would be unethical for a researcher to require a judge to randomly assign different sentences for the same offense in order to test the effects of length of sentence on recidivism or some other dependent variable of interest. So, the criminal justice researcher has to resort to studying defendants who are as similar as possible in other respects, but have already been assigned different sentences for the same offense. It would also be unethical to encourage a drug use spike in a neighborhood in order to investigate why such spikes might occur. The investigator will have to be content with finding a neighborhood as similar as possible to the one in which a spike has already occurred to serve as a control group and measure the "before" conditions in both groups in retrospect. Remember that control over the three basic aspects of the before-after with control group design is important because that control plays a crucial role in eliminating possible causal variables other than the hypothesized causal variable from consideration. Hence, any quasi-experimental research design compromises ultimately weaken the evidence and argument for a hypothesized causal relationship. The importance of the nature and quality of research design for meaningful statistical analysis and causal arguments should not be underestimated. Even the most complex and sophisticated statistical analyses cannot compensate for design compromises, however necessary those compromises may be.

Ethical Integrity in Data Analysis

We have granted the topic of ethical integrity its own special section. We do this because it is often given little attention, especially in texts like this one, and because various kinds of data manipulation and falsification are simply too prevalent and dangerous to ignore. Principles of ethical integrity covering all the stages of the research process are spelled out in the ethical standards developed and enforced by professional associations such as the Academy of Criminal Justice Sciences (ACJS—www.acjs.org), the American Society of Criminology (ASC—www.asc41.com), the American Sociological Association (www.asanet.org), and the American Psychological Association (ww.apa.org). We focus here on those principles pertaining specifically to research reports, data management, and statistical analysis: plagiarism and due diligence in managing and analyzing data.

Plagiarism

Plagiarism is quoting or using someone else's work without proper acknowledgment or citation. Failure to provide proper citation leaves the impression that the work is that of the reporters/authors. Direct quotations and close paraphrases of other texts, whether digital or in hard copy, as well as any statistics and statistical analyses, must always be cited. Also required is giving credit for coworkers' and collaborators' contributions to a research project in the research report and elsewhere.

When concepts become part of the "common language" of a profession or academic discipline (as have many we discuss in this book), citation is usually not required. It is not always easy to determine if this is the case, however, especially for students new to the discipline. The general rule we recommend is, if you have the slightest doubt, cite the source.

Due Diligence in Data Management and Analysis

We have an ethical obligation to manage data and their analyses with **due diligence**. Due diligence in this case means acting with ethical integrity and professional competence, as well as careful attention to detail and accuracy. Deliberately biasing the selection of a study group or sample, selectively dropping data from the database, and manipulating data analyses in order to suggest the data support an outcome favored by the researcher are unethical. (Some exceptions might apply here. For example, dropping a few extreme scores, called outliers, from a data set before the statistical analysis is performed is sometimes justified because of their disproportionate impact on the results of our statistical calculations. But if this is done, it must be clearly acknowledged and justified in the research report.)

We must select statistical analyses appropriate for the type of sample, if any, we have selected and for the levels at which the variables are measured. We must perform our analyses as accurately as possible. Doing so requires checks for respondent dishonesty, inaccurate data entry (data cleaning), incorrect computer instructions, and verification of results in whatever ways are available. We must report missing data and discuss how we adjusted our analysis accordingly. We must also present our results completely and honestly and inform our readers/audience of any peculiarities in the data or the analysis that we are aware of and that may bear on the results we calculate or their appropriate interpretation.

In research, as in other human activities, we often try to curry favor with those who hold social, political, or economic power. Hiding any of our own data or attempting to suppress the publication of others' data that challenge or disconfirm our own or our benefactors' preferred results is unethical. Contracts that give other interested parties—especially the politically powerful and/or those providing funds (whether private individuals, corporations, government agencies, etc.)—control over data gathering, statistical analyses, research report contents (including language used), or the dissemination of results (through publication or otherwise) pose very significant challenges to maintaining the ethical integrity of scientific research.

When researchers and research are paid for by those with a strong political or economic interest in the results, difficult ethical issues are almost certain to arise. Such arrangements do not *necessarily* lead to unethical research, but skepticism is justified and careful scrutiny is required.

In Appendix C on the study site (**www.sagepub.com/fitzgerald**), you will find excerpts from the codes of ethics of the Academy of Criminal Justice Sciences and the American Sociological Association pertaining to data management and analysis. We suggest you familiarize yourself with them now.

Garbage In-Garbage Out

You have perhaps heard the expression **garbage in-garbage out**. In general, it means that if you subject bad data (garbage in) to statistical analysis, you will get, at best, meaningless and, at worst, seriously misleading results (garbage out). Bad data can derive from several sources. It should be clear from our discussions in this and the previous chapter that uncooperative relationships between researchers and practitioners participating in the research, careless definitions and measurements of variables, inadequate research designs, improperly drawn samples, failure to exercise due diligence in data management, and mistakes in computer instructions will yield garbage too.

Summary

In this chapter, we have discussed some key concepts and processes important in statistical analysis. Among them were units of analysis, variables, hypotheses, levels of measurement, sampling, causality, and research design. We also discussed the principle of garbage in-garbage out and ethical guidelines for managing and analyzing data and writing research reports. Knowledge of these basic concepts and processes is necessary if you are to understand the discussions of particular statistical analysis procedures to which we turn in the remaining chapters of this book.

The list of concepts to master is admittedly long, but most of the terms on the list should already be familiar to you. Remember that mastering the language (terminology) of any field of study is essentially equivalent to mastering that field of study. So, really learning these concepts and those introduced in other chapters is essential to your mastery of the materials in this course.

Concepts to Master

Appropriate time sequence

Before-after research design

Before-after with control group design (classic experimental design)

Causal chain

Causal relationship

Census

Concomitant variation (correlation)

Continuous variable values

Control group

Dependent variable/effect

Discrete variable values

Due diligence

Eliminate (control for) other possible causes

Exhaustive variable values

Experimental group

Garbage in-garbage out

Independent variable/cause

Interval-level measurement

Intervening variable

Multiple causation

Mutually exclusive variable values

Nominal-level measurement

Null hypothesis

Operational definition

Ordinal-level measurement

Plagiarism

Population

Quasi-experimental design

Ratio-level measurement

Research design

Research hypothesis

Sample

Sampling

Sampling error

Sampling frame

Simple random sample

Spurious relationship

Type I error

Type II error

Units of analysis

Review Questions

1. What are the basic stages of the research process? In what ways, if any, do the earlier stages have implications for statistical analysis?
2. What is a unit of analysis? Give two examples of different units of analysis.
3. What are variables, and how are they connected to units of analysis?
4. What are mutually exclusive variable values? Give two examples.
5. What are exhaustive variable values? Give two examples.
6. Distinguish between discrete and continuous variables. Give two examples of each.
7. Define nominal-, ordinal-, interval-, and ratio-level measurements, and give two examples of each.
8. Distinguish among numbers used as codes, numbers as frequency counts, and numbers as measured quantities. Give two examples of each.

9. What is a research hypothesis? What is a null hypothesis? Give two examples of each.

10. What are independent and dependent variables? Give two examples of each. Discuss what makes a variable independent or dependent. Can the same variable be both independent and dependent?

11. Distinguish between Type I and Type II errors. Give examples of each.

12. Why do some researchers say the term *cause* should not be used in science? Why do the authors disagree?

13. What are the three conditions that must be met to justify claiming a causal relationship between two variables?

14. Why is eliminating other possible causal variables so difficult to achieve?

15. What is a spurious relationship between two variables?

16. What is the difference between a population and a sample? Why would a researcher want to sample? What is a census?

17. What is a simple random sample?

18. What is a sampling frame?

19. What is a research design, and why is it important for statistical analysis?

20. Describe the before-after research design.

21. Describe the before-after with control group research design.

22. What is the difference between the experimental and control group?

23. How do quasi-experimental designs differ from before-after with control group designs?

24. What three basic aspects of the research situation do laboratory researchers control? How is control of these aspects related to the strength of a causal argument provided by the before-after with control group (experimental) research design? Why do criminal justice researchers often have to compromise on these controls? What strategies can they use to match the experimental research design as closely as possible?

25. What is plagiarism, and why is it unethical?

26. What are the due diligence obligations of statistical analysts in managing data?

27. What are the major issues in maintaining ethical integrity in statistical analysis?

28. What is meant by the expression "garbage in-garbage out"?

29. If you haven't already done so, define each term in the "Concepts to Master" list and use the term in three different sentences.

Exercises and Discussion Questions

1. For the following items, consider any criminal justice issue, problem, or theory that especially interests you.
   a. Identify at least two different units of analysis implicated in the topic you have chosen.
   b. Identify at least two discrete and two continuous variables pertaining to each of the units of analysis.
   c. Identify at least one variable pertaining to each of the units of analysis for each level of the four levels of measurement.
   d. Give an operational definition of each of the variables you identified in b and c, specifying the possible values of each variable and how they will be measured.
   e. Formulate at least six hypotheses using any of the variables you identified in b and c.
2. Consider the members of your statistics class as units of analysis. Suppose you wish to explain (or predict) the grades the students will earn in the class.
   a. Identify a discrete and a continuous variable you think may help explain grades earned. Discuss why you chose the variables you did.
   b. Identify a nominal, an ordinal, an interval, and a ratio variable you think may help explain grades students will earn. Explain why the variables qualify as being measured at these levels.
   c. Develop mutually exclusive and exhaustive measurements for each of the four variables you identified in b, as well as a measurement for the grades earned variable.
   d. Formulate a research and a corresponding null hypothesis for each of the four variables you identified in b and the grades earned variable.
3. Suppose you wanted to test whether participating in a weekly discussion session with a teaching assistant would improve the grades students earned.
   a. Describe a before-after and a before-after with control group research design to test this hypothesis.
   b. Describe how you would determine who was in the experimental and control groups in the before-after with control design.
   c. Discuss the difficulties you might have executing a before-after with control group design and how you might try to overcome them. Discuss why, even with those difficulties, the before-after with control group research design would be a better test of your hypothesis than a before-after design.
4. Discuss your views about the use of causal language in science.
5. Why is causation so difficult to establish? Why isn't concomitant variation (correlation) enough to establish causation?
6. What roles do research design and statistical analysis play in establishing causality?

7. You often read or hear in the mass media statements like, pollsters asked 545 randomly selected people about their views on some issue, such as how safe they feel in their city. Suppose the city has a population of 750,000. We know you don't have the information yet to answer this question statistically, so for now we'll just ask you to tell us what your gut feelings tell you. Do you think a sample that size can yield valid statistics about how the city as a whole views the issue? Why or why not? What is the smallest sample you think would be adequate? How would you know?

8. Suppose you wanted to know something about drug use among adolescents in your community and you chose to study a random sample. What specific population would you sample? How would you construct your sampling frame? (Think carefully; this is not as easy as it might sound!) If you had to leave some members of the population out of your sampling frame, who would they be? Would their absence undermine the representativeness of your sample and the validity of your statistics? Do these issues relate in any way to garbage in-garbage out?

9. Create a complete sampling frame for your class and assign a unique number to each class member (unit of analysis). Using the random numbers table in Appendix B (**www.sagepub.com/fitzgerald**), draw a simple random sample of, say, 10 from your class. Calculate the percent female for the sample and for the class. Would you expect the percent female from the sample to be close to the percent female in the class? Why or why not? Compare the percent of females in your sample with the percent in your class. How close are they? Now draw four other simple random samples of the same size, comparing the percent female in each sample with the class percent female. Calculate the average of the five sample percents female and compare this average with the class percent female. Describe what you observe about the relationship between samples and populations on percent female. Does anything surprise you about the results? If yes, what? Why?

10. What is plagiarism, and why is it important? Do the Internet and other electronic media pose any special issues concerning plagiarism? How might these issues be best managed? Do the Internet and other electronic media offer any potential solutions?

11. Identify and discuss ways due diligence may be exercised in gathering, recording, analyzing, and reporting data. When you read a research report, do you have any way of determining whether due diligence has been exercised?

12. Have you ever participated in or had a chance to observe closely a research project? Describe and critique your experiences. What role did you play? What were the relationships between the researchers and the researched? Were there any ethical neutrality or integrity issues? Any bias issues? Any due diligence with data issues? How could the research project have been improved?

Student Study Site

Visit the open-access student study site at **www.sagepub.com/fitzgerald** for access to several study tools including eFlashcards, web quizzes, and additional appendices as well as links to SAGE journal articles and audio, video and web resources.

Basic Descriptive Univariate Analysis

Learning Objectives

What you are expected not only to learn but to master in this chapter:

- How to distinguish between descriptive and inferential statistics
- The basics of univariate descriptive analysis (frequency counts, ratios, fractions, proportions, decimals, percents, rates, and odds)
- How data distributions such as frequency tables, bar and line graphs, and cumulative distributions are created
- The power of graphs to help us understand and communicate quantitative data, shape impressions and interpretation of data, and mislead
- How to title and label tables and graphs
- Cautions to be observed when creating or interpreting graphs

Introduction

In the first two chapters, you have been introduced to a number of basic concepts used in statistical analyses and to the research process within which these analyses must be placed in order to make sense of their results. In this chapter, we discuss a few more basic concepts, as well as some elementary procedures for analyzing data. We begin with two important distinctions. One is among univariate, bivariate, and multivariate (i.e., one, two, and many variable) statistical analyses. The other is between descriptive and inferential statistics. This chapter and the next are devoted primarily to univariate descriptive (one-variable population) statistics.

In particular, we focus here on the basics of data description and depiction pertaining to a single variable and its values. You have already been introduced to or are already familiar in a general way with some of the statistics used in many analyses, including univariate descriptive analysis (e.g., frequency counts, percents, rates, etc.). We discuss these in a more complete, organized, and detailed way. We also describe the construction of tables as well as bar, line, and selected other types of graphs, and illustrate their uses in analyzing and presenting univariate data. Some potentially misleading aspects of different types of graphs are identified. Finally, statistics used for describing a *distribution's* variable values using measures of central tendency (means, medians, and modes) and dispersion (ranges, average and standard deviations from the mean, and quantiles) are considered.

This chapter has quite a few pages, but there are lots of pictures—here they are called figures. Unfortunately, though, you are going to have to pay close attention to the figures if you are to understand these statistics in a more sophisticated way.

Some Basic Types of Statistical Analysis

Statistical analyses may be divided up in a number of different ways. We discuss two such divisions here, one based on the number of variables being considered and one on the purposes of the analysis.

Univariate, Bivariate, and Multivariate Statistics

Statisticians distinguish among types of statistical analysis on the basis of the number of variables being analyzed. Three categories are frequently applied: univariate, bivariate, and multivariate statistical analysis. **Univariate** (think uni = one) **analysis** pertains to the analysis of a single variable and its values. We could investigate the ages of inmates in a prison or the political affiliations of public defenders in a state, for example. **Bivariate** (think bi = two) **analysis** typically looks for evidence of a causal relationship between two variables. We could analyze our data to see if there was a relationship between the political affiliations of public defenders and their ages, for example. In **multivariate** (think multi = many) **analysis**, the relationships among three or more variables are examined. We might analyze our data to determine if there were relationships among public defenders' political affiliations, ages, and sexes, for example. In this chapter, we will be concerned only with univariate statistics.

Descriptive and Inferential Statistics

Statisticians also distinguish between two types of statistical analysis based on their uses or purposes. Here the categories are descriptive and inferential. **Descriptive statistics** are used to characterize (i.e., describe) the values of a particular variable and the distributions of those values in some population or sample.

Inferential statistics always begin with descriptive statistics for sample data, but go beyond this description in one of two sometimes overlapping ways. First, they may be used to estimate (infer—hence the name) the value of a particular variable in a population based on data for that variable obtained from a sample drawn at random from the population. In this case, a descriptive sample statistic (such as mean variable value or percent of survey respondents who answered a question in a particular way) and some principles of probability theory are used to estimate the corresponding statistic (e.g., the mean or percent) in the population from which the sample was drawn. We might use the mean income of a random sample of criminal justice assistant professors in the United States to estimate the mean income of the population consisting of all criminal justice assistant professors in the United States. This use of inferential statistics is referred to as parameter estimation.

Second, inferential statistics may be used to test hypotheses. Some hypotheses are about the distribution of the values of a single variable. Such a test might be used to determine if the distribution of a variable's values is random or nonrandom. We might wish to know, for example, if the number of juvenile offenders residing in each of several blocks in a neighborhood is random or whether there is a pattern such that the number residing in some blocks is significantly higher than in others. Inferential statistics are also used to test causal hypotheses about relationships among two or more variables. For example, we might use them to test the difference between the mean salaries of judges from two random samples (say, one from the northern United States and one from the southern United States) to determine if there is a significant difference between judges' salaries in the two populations. The results would help us decide if there was a relationship between area of the United States and judges' salaries.

As we will see, these uses of inferential statistics are closely related. Testing causal hypotheses involves parameter estimation, for example. We discuss these applications of inferential statistics in detail in later chapters. Here we are concerned only with descriptive statistics.

Univariate Descriptive Analysis

Univariate descriptive statistics are concerned with describing the data pertaining to the variable values that have been gathered on one variable. Once the appropriate units of analysis have been determined, a variable of interest pertaining to them has been defined, and the variable has been measured for each unit of analysis, our next challenge is making sense of the data we have assembled. We could, of course, proceed on a case-by-case basis, noting the particular variable value associated with each unit of analysis chosen for study. But this doesn't offer any way of discovering interesting *patterns* in the way a variable's values are distributed among the units of analysis or of summarizing the data we have gathered for the study group as a whole. We need some other procedure for making sense of the data we have gathered. Univariate description and analysis begin when we compile and organize our data, look for any patterns that may reveal themselves, and think about what the patterns might tell us about this particular variable in our study group. As we noted in Chapter 1, statistics provide some tools for accomplishing these tasks. Among the tools available to us are frequency counts, ratios, fractions, proportions, decimals, percents, rates, and odds.

Frequency Counts

The most basic kind of statistical analysis is the frequency count. A **frequency count** indicates how many times each of the values of a particular variable appears in the data. Many other statistical analyses are based on frequency counts.

Suppose, as a project for a criminal justice class, we asked a number of people who passed by on a street corner if they thought the courts in their city were basically fair. After collecting their answers, we might report the results of our informal survey in several ways. We could say that 100 people considered them fair and 25 people thought they were not fair. In this case, the frequency counts, or the number of people who answered our question in each of the two ways, were reported.

Statistical descriptions should always include frequency counts and totals, or at the very least the data should be presented in a way that enables a reader to derive them. If you read a statistical report that does not include the frequency counts and totals upon which the other statistics, such as proportions or percents, were based, be very suspicious. Statistical data presented without them can be very misleading, as we will see in the next paragraph and a bit later in this chapter.

Let's add a further, related caution here regarding frequency counts. Returning to the data from the court survey, note that the description includes only the responses of those people who answered the question in one of two ways. We said nothing about the number of people who might have refused to answer, or who answered "don't know." In short, the possible variable values we specified are not exhaustive. Perhaps no one fit into these other categories, but unless the presentation of the data indicates that, we can't be sure. Maybe the total number of people interviewed was really equal to 575, and 450 people said they did not know whether the courts were fair or not. Knowing this would surely change our interpretation of the data. Whether the data are presented in frequency counts or in any of the other forms we discuss, it pays to think about other variable values (response categories or other variable measurements) for which data may not have been presented. As with all descriptions, what is left out of a statistical description may be more important than what is included!

Ratios, Fractions, Proportions, and Decimals

Frequency counts are often converted into other mathematical expressions, such as **ratios, fractions, proportions,** and **decimals**. You probably recall how these statistics are calculated and that each can be converted into any of the others as well as into percents.

Thus, for example, the ratio of 1 out of 5 equals the fraction 1/5, and the equivalent proportion, often written as a decimal, is .20. Recall that we convert a proportion or decimal to a percent by multiplying a decimal such as .20 by 100, which is accomplished by moving the decimal point two places to the right and adding the percent sign, giving us, in this case, 20%. We have more to say about percents in the next section.

The data from our survey about courts could be presented using any of these descriptive statistics. Recall that 100 of 125 respondents said the courts were fair. We could record these data as a ratio of 100 out of 125 or as a fraction: 100/125. We could reduce the fraction by dividing the numerator (the number on the top of the fraction) and the denominator (the number on the bottom of the fraction) each by 25 resulting in the fraction 4/5. Or, we could divide the denominator into the numerator of this or the original fraction, yielding the proportion (decimal) .80. Multiplying the proportion .80 by 100 in this case yields the percent 80%. Hence, we could report that 4 out of 5 (or 4/5, or .80, or 80%) of the respondents said the courts were fair, whereas 1 out of 5 (or 1/5, or .20, or 20%) said they were not.

Note that by examining the ratios, fractions, or percents alone, you know that considerably more respondents thought courts were fair than did not, but you would not know *how many* people responded in a particular way. We might have talked to 5 people or 5,000. Consider the following statements: "Two out of three doctors recommend..."; "One out of four marriages ends in divorce"; "Statistics professors are right at least 50% of the time." Although they may appear precise and scientific at first glance, they are, in fact, almost meaningless. To make sense of them, we must know, among other things, the frequency counts and totals involved.

Although frequency counts, ratios, fractions, proportions, and percents are very important in assessing the variables in a data set, there are other matters to attend to as well. In general, for example, the method used to identify or select the cases for study (sampling) is just as important in the assessment of the data. Furthermore, a well-planned study—especially one conforming to the before-after with control group design and reporting on a relatively small number of cases—should elicit greater confidence than a poorly designed one reporting on a larger number of cases. In any event, assuming that the frequency counts have been provided or can be derived from the data presented, ratios, fractions, proportions, and percents are very useful statistical tools.

Other frequently used descriptive statistics include rates and odds. Because percents are perhaps the most frequently used descriptive statistics and rates and odds are more complex statistical expressions, we discuss each of these in more detail in the following sections.

Percents

Percents are standardized fractions with a base of 100. They are called standardized because they convert all fractions to their equivalents with a denominator (the bottom number in a fraction) of 100. Because the common denominator is understood (percent means "for each 100"), only the numerator (the top number in a fraction) is given, followed by the percent sign. Thus, 80/100 = 80%. Given the fraction $x/100$ and any other fraction connected by an equal sign (=), you can solve the equation for x. The solution for x is the percent that the numerator (the top number of a fraction) is of the denominator in the second fraction. For example, consider the equation $x/100 = 1/5$. As you will recall, to solve for x in this equation, we first cross-multiply—that is, we multiply the denominator of each fraction by the numerator of the other fraction. In our example, this would yield $5x = 100$. Next, to solve the equation for x, we divide both sides of the equation by the same number, in this case by 5, which yields $x = 100/5$ or $x = 20$.

Thus, the equivalent of 1/5, when converted to a base of 100 (i.e., to a percent), is 20% and, therefore, 1 is 20% of 5. In practice, we can simply divide the numerator by the denominator and multiply the result by 100 to calculate the percent: $1 \div 5 = .20$ and $.20 \times 100 = 20\%$. Given the frequency count of responses for a specific response category and the total number of responses for all response categories, we can calculate the percent for that response category. The sum of all the percentages for all of the response categories should, of course, equal 100%, or the whole. Percents are sometimes referred to as **relative frequencies**. They express frequencies relative to the whole when the whole is defined as 100%.

Confusion is sometimes created when percentages are used to describe increases or decreases. For example, if a county's jail population of 36 experiences a 100% increase, the new population is 72. In short, a 100% increase results in a *doubling* of the original quantity. A 200% increase yields a *tripling* of the original count (in our example, to 108); and a 50% increase means that the count is now one and one-half times as large as it was (in our example, 54).

A percent of less than 1% is expressed as a *decimal percent*, as in .2% or .01%, each of which represents a proportion of a percent. Whenever decimals (proportions) are converted to percents, confusion in interpretation and serious data reporting errors may occur. Thus, the decimal or proportion .20 is equivalent to 20%, but .20% and 0.2% are decimal percents equaling two tenths of 1%. Note also that $.25 = 25/100 = 25\%$ and that $.0025 = 25/10,000 = .25\%$ (i.e., one fourth of 1%). Care must be taken in the placement of decimal points in expressions of percents, as well as in their interpretation.

When should you go beyond the presentation of frequency counts to the calculation and presentation of percents? Because percents are standardized to a base of 100, they may make results for data on very large groups easier to understand. Perhaps most important, they facilitate *comparisons* among the results of analyses when the study groups or subgroups being compared are very different in size.

Suppose that instead of 125 people, we had asked 38,400 people whether they regarded the courts as fair, and 24,576 said they did. It's easier to grasp the meaning of these data by saying that 64% of the persons we talked to thought the courts were fair. Now let us further suppose that we had taken a similar survey a year ago, obtaining responses from 12,400 people, 7,936 of whom said they regarded the courts as fair. Has the tendency to regard the courts as fair changed? It is difficult to tell simply by comparing the raw numbers, but if we compare the two results in terms of percents, we discover that in both cases, 64% of the people surveyed felt the courts were fair. Because percents are standardized forms of numerical expressions, they should be used in addition to frequency counts when frequency counts alone would be hard to interpret or when comparing results from studies of different-sized populations.

Note, however, that conversion of frequency counts to percents can be misleading when the frequency counts are either very large or very small. When frequency counts are small, a conversion to percents may give the impression of large differences. For example, if the total number of cases is 10, converting to percents magnifies the differences in the numbers reported by a factor of 10. If there are four cases in one category of response and six in another, the frequency count difference is two, whereas the percent difference is 60% − 40% = 20%. This magnification of differences in small samples may well distort the impression of the data conveyed to the reader.

Just as the conversion of very small frequency counts to percents magnifies apparent differences, the conversion of very large frequency counts to percents diminishes apparent differences. If 1,000,000 votes were cast in an election with a 490,000-to-510,000 candidate count, a frequency count difference of 20,000 yields a percentage difference of 51% − 49% = 2%. The impression created by such conversions is more dramatic if we consider another example. Suppose two different surgical procedures are available for repairing a damaged heart valve. One group of 50,000 patients is operated on using one procedure, and another group of 50,000 patients receives the other procedure. Suppose further that 9,500 patients (19%) in the first group and 9,000 patients (18%) in the second group died during surgery. Saying that the outcome of the two procedures differs by 19% − 18% = 1% may give the impression that there is very little difference between them, but stating that 500 more people survived the second procedure than the first provides quite a different impression. Still, statistically, these two presentations of the data are equally correct. There is no simple rule of thumb indicating the maximum number of cases for which the conversion of frequency counts to percents is appropriate. To be on the safe side, we recommend always reporting both the frequency counts and the percents derived from them.

Finally, we should note that probabilities are often expressed as percents, as in there is a 10% probability that the difference between the average grade points of two student samples is due to chance. We discuss probabilities in detail in later chapters.

Rates

Another statistical expression we may read or hear about often is rate—the crime rate, the conviction rate, the incarceration rate, and so forth. **Rates** express the frequency of an event in relation to a fixed base, which may be a frequency count or a measurement. Time is often one of the fixed bases. A rate of speed, for example, is expressed in number of miles per hour. A crime rate is the number of crimes of a particular kind per fixed unit of population (say, 100,000), per some specified unit of time (say, 1 year).

Calculating a Crime Rate

We can illustrate some significant features of rates and their calculation through an examination of crime rates. Let's begin with a basic rate calculation by dividing the number of offenses of a particular type (e.g., robbery, sexual assault, DUI, etc.) by the total in the population. So, if we have a population of 160,000 in a city and 2,475 robberies were recorded in the city for last year, the per person rate of robberies for the city population would be 2,475/160,000 for that year. We could convert this fraction to a proportion, which equals .0155 (rounded). That is, there were approximately .0155 robberies per person in that population. As a check on our calculations, if we multiply this proportion (.0155) by the total population (160,000), we get back to 2,480, which is equivalent (within rounding error) to the number of offenses in the population (2,475).

As a general rule, though, crime rates are computed not per person in the population, but per some base population number, such as per 1,000 or 10,000 or 100,000 persons in the population. We will refer to these as base population units. How do we calculate such rates? The first two steps are to select a population base unit and to determine how many of these base units there are in the total population. Suppose we choose a population base unit of 10,000. To determine how many of these base units there are in our population, we divide the population (160,000) by the chosen base population unit (10,000). 160,000/10,000 = 16. Thus, there are 16 base units of 10,000 in the population. The final step is to divide the number of offenses by this result: 2,475/16 = 154.69 (rounded). Thus, the robbery rate for this city is 154.69 (rounded) per 10,000 persons. Again, as a check on our calculations, we can multiply the number of 10,000 population base units (16) times the robbery rate per 10,000 (154.69), which yields 2,475 (rounded) offenses.

Like percents, rates can be very useful statistics for comparative purposes. When used in this way, however, the size of the base units (e.g., per 100,000) must be specified and they must be equal from one rate calculation and comparison to another. For example, crime rates for different societies or for different periods in the same society can be compared as long as the definitions of criminal offenses are the same and the same population base unit as well as the same period are used (e.g., per 100,000 population, per year).

Note that all of our discussion and calculations so far have referenced a population. The assumption has been that by population we meant all of the persons, from infants to elders, in a population. One could choose to calculate rates based on the population of adults (defined as, say, ages 18 and over) or on the population of adult females, for example. The choice of the population for which rates are to be calculated is important, of course, and may be especially so when comparing across time or society. For example, comparing crime rates based on total population may be misleading if one population has a much larger proportion of children than another.

In addition to expressing the frequency with which something occurs per some base, we can calculate a rate at which a rate is changing, that is, increasing or decreasing. We can also express rate changes as percent changes. For example, there was a 15% increase in the rate of felonies this year as compared to last. Again, these are useful expressions, as long as you do not get tangled up in them. Consider, for example, the following statement: "The rate of increase in the nation's crime rate is decreasing." This means that although the crime rate is still going up, it is not going up as fast as it had been. The statement does make sense, but you must interpret such statements carefully to avoid being misled.

Finally, because rates are also standardized forms of statistical expression, all of the cautions we raised about percents apply here as well.

Odds

The word **odds** is used in a number of different contexts and in some slightly different ways. We are perhaps most familiar with it in the contexts of lotteries or making wagers. If I buy a lottery ticket, I might be interested in knowing what my odds are of winning. Here, "odds" means chances or probability, and the odds rest on the assumption that each of the possible combinations of numbers in the draw has an equal chance of being selected. My chances or probability of winning the lottery may be one in several million, depending on the number of numbers and the number of possible unique combinations in the lottery draw.

Sports wagers are also often expressed in odds. In this case, though, they are not necessarily based on the assumption that the possible outcomes are equally likely and are expressed in a somewhat different way. Suppose our horse racing tip sheet says the odds of Seabiscuit winning in the fourth race against eight other horses are 3 to 2. If every horse had an equal chance of winning, the odds of a Seabiscuit win would be 1 in 8. But the concept of odds used in sports wagers combines information derived from many different sources. Odds of 3 to 2 for a Seabiscuit win mean there are 3 in 5 chances of a Seabiscuit win and 2 in 5 chances he will not finish first. That is, to convert the odds in this second use of the term into percents or probabilities, we first must add the odds for and against a particular outcome (in our example, 3 for a Seabiscuit win + 2 against a Seabiscuit win = 5). We can then convert these odds for and against to percents using this sum as the denominator or divisor. Thus, we have 3 divided by 5 = .60 = 60%. There is a 60% chance or probability that Seabiscuit comes in first and a 40% chance or probability he does not.

Statisticians use odds in this second sense in the context of more sophisticated kinds of statistical analyses, such as logistic regression. We discuss these analyses in Chapter 12.

Creating Data Distributions

Additional tools in our statistical toolkit for making sense of data use the frequency counts, percents, and other statistics we have just described to construct data distributions of various kinds that help us get a sense of how the variable values "behave" in our data set. In this section, we discuss frequency distribution tables and corresponding bar and line graphs, as well as percent distributions in these same forms. We also discuss cumulative frequency and percent distribution tables, bar graphs, and line graphs.

Frequency Distribution Tables

In a **frequency distribution table**, variable values are ordered from lowest to highest (or highest to lowest), if appropriate, and the frequency of each variable value is counted. Suppose you have defined the nominal variable *sex* as having two categories, male and female, and gathered data about the sex of shoplifters. (See Chapter 2, pp. 24–27 for a review of levels of measurement.) You could begin your analysis by making two columns on a sheet of paper, one labeled "male shoplifters," the other labeled "female shoplifters," and listing the names of the shoplifters under the appropriate heading. Suppose your lists looked like the ones in Table 3.1.

Table 3.1 List of Shoplifters by Sex

Male Shoplifters	Female Shoplifters
Bob	Sally
George	Matilda
Tom	Joan
Ricardo	Francine
Henry	
Alphonso	
Beauregard	

By counting the number of names in each list, you would find the frequency distribution of the shoplifters' sex to be seven males and four females. To convert this expression into a frequency distribution table, you would list the values (in this case, the categories) of the sex variable in one vertical column and the corresponding frequencies in a parallel vertical column, as in Table 3.2. When frequency counts for subgroups within a larger group are presented in statistical tables they are typically designated by the letter f. The total number in all subgroups combined is usually designated by n or N. When a sample is being used to represent a population and/or the analysis involves two or more subgroups, the lowercase letter n is typically used for the sample or subgroup size and the capital letter N for the size of the population or the total number of observations included in the analysis. In our previous example of opinions regarding the fairness of courts, $f = 100$ for the number that thought the courts were fair, and the total of the frequency counts for our population is N (or n) = 125.

Table 3.2 is a frequency distribution table describing our data on shoplifters' sex in quantitative terms.

Note that for nominal variables, the order in which the variable values are listed in the left column of the frequency table is arbitrary. Variables measured at the other

Table 3.2 Frequency Distribution Table for Sex of Shoplifters

Sex of Shoplifters	Frequency (f)
Male	7
Female	4
Total	$N = 11$

three levels (ordinal, interval, or ratio) have values that can be ordered from highest to lowest (or lowest to highest) and they would be listed in the appropriate order in the left column.

Frequency Distribution Bar and Line Graphs

As an alternative to frequency distribution tables like the one in Table 3.2, we could describe and analyze our data using graphs. Graphs translate numerical data into visual images. These images attract more attention than tables and can facilitate understanding of the data used to construct the graph. Therefore, the appropriate use of graphs is highly recommended.

There are many different kinds of graphs, and each kind can be drawn by hand in many different ways. Graphing software is also widely available, making it easy to convert frequency counts and percents into a variety of graph types. In this chapter, we discuss the basics of several types of graphs.

Frequency Distribution Bar Graphs

To convert the data in Table 3.2 into a frequency distribution bar graph, we would first create a two-dimensional space defined by horizontal and vertical axes that are perpendicular (i.e., at right angles) to each other. Then, along the horizontal axis, we would assign an equal space for each of the possible variable values (in our example, male and female). The vertical axis would also be marked off in equal-size spatial units. The number of these units corresponds to the number of possible frequencies with which the possible variable values arrayed along the horizontal axis may occur in our data set. The sizes of the spatial units on the two axes may be different, but the sizes of the spatial units on any one of the axes must be the same.

The size of the units selected for constructing the graph is called the **scale** of the graph. Changing the size of the units on one or both of the axes changes the scale of the graph. As we will see, changing its scale can produce a graph dramatically different in appearance from the original and, as a result, may mislead the viewer about the quantitative data used to construct the graph.

Next, for each of the possible variable values, we would create a rectangular space (a bar) inside the graph space representing the frequency with which that variable value occurs in our data set. We would do so by raising the bar from the space on the horizontal axis corresponding to each possible variable value to the height corresponding to the frequency with which that variable value appears in the data. Figure 3.1 shows what a **frequency distribution bar graph** of the data from Table 3.2 might look like. Note that the zero frequency category is located at the point where the horizontal axis meets the vertical axis. As with frequency tables, the level at which a variable is measured matters in constructing the graph. For all nominal variables, such as sex (as a biological category), political affiliation, religion, or type of crime committed, the order in which the variable values are listed on the horizontal axis is arbitrary. When bar graphing an ordinal-, interval-, or ratio-level variable, the variable's values are arranged in ascending order beginning with the lowest value at the left end of the axis.

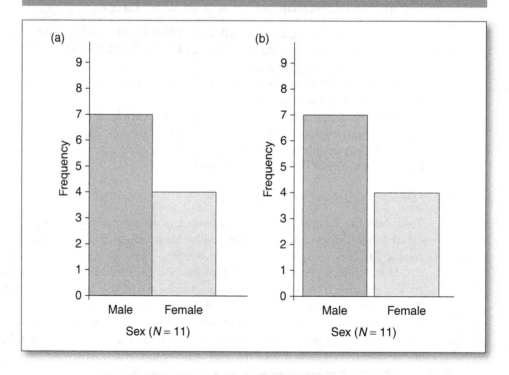

Figure 3.1 Frequency Distribution Bar Graphs of Sex of Shoplifters

When graphing variables measured at the nominal level, some statisticians recommend that the bars be separated by a space—that is, the bars should not touch each other. Figure 3.1b shows such a bar graph for the same data as in Figure 3.1a. This graphing style for nominal variables has the advantage of signaling clearly that the variable is nominal and that no significance should be attached to the order in which the variable values are arranged along the axis.

Let's consider another example of converting frequencies to a bar graph. Suppose we have data on the ages of inmates in Hitsville state prison, a ratio-level variable. Suppose also that we have decided to group the possible variable values as indicated in the left column of Table 3.3, with corresponding frequencies in the second column.

Table 3.3 Frequency Distribution Table for Ages of Hitsville Inmates

Age	Frequency (f)
18–19	120
20–21	105
22–24	75
25–30	55
31–40	30
Over 40	15
Total	$N = 400$

To convert the age group frequency data from Table 3.3 into a bar graph, we would proceed essentially in the same way as with our shoplifter sex data, with one exception. When the variables being graphed are measured at the ordinal, interval, or ratio level, the possible variable values would still be allocated equal spaces, but they would be listed in ascending order along the horizontal axis. The frequency units would be marked off and labeled in ascending order along the vertical axis. The resulting bar graph might look like the one in Figure 3.2.

Note that the bars in the graph in Figure 3.2 are adjacent to each other. As a general rule, bar graphs representing ordinal-, interval-, or ratio-level data would be constructed in this way. Such bar graphs are sometimes called **histograms.**

Let's explore another example. Suppose that a test has been given to a class of 36 police recruits and that a perfect score on the test is 20. After scoring the exams, the tester might use a frequency distribution to provide herself and the recruits with a picture of the class's performance. To construct the frequency distribution, the tester must count the number of people who received each particular score on the examination. Suppose the results are as indicated in the frequency distribution table in Figure 3.3a. To convert this frequency distribution table to a frequency distribution bar graph, the possible examination scores—in this case, 0 to 20—is arranged in ascending order along the horizontal axis, beginning at the left. The possible frequencies—in this case, 0 to 9, because no more than nine officers had the same score—is arranged in ascending order along the vertical axis. Remember that each bar in the graph represents the frequency with which the corresponding score occurs in the distribution. Suppose our

Figure 3.2 Frequency Distribution Bar Graph of Hitsville Inmates' Ages

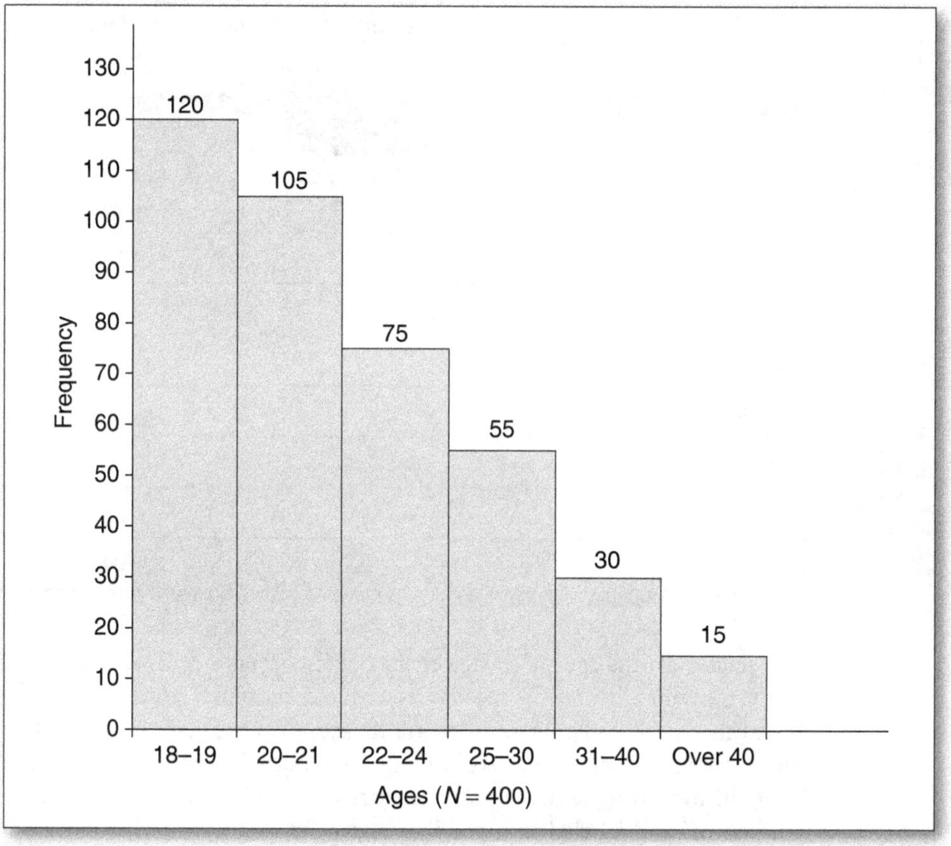

[Bar graph showing frequency on y-axis (0–130) and Ages on x-axis (N = 400):
- 18–19: 120
- 20–21: 105
- 22–24: 75
- 25–30: 55
- 31–40: 30
- Over 40: 15]

bar graph looked like the one in Figure 3.3b. Like the frequency distribution table, the bar graph indicates that no one in the class scored lower than 8, that one person scored 8, two scored 9, six scored 13, three scored 16, and so on.

Frequency Distribution Line Graphs

Line graphs are constructed only for variables measured at the ordinal, interval, or ratio levels; they are not appropriate for nominal-level variables. They communicate essentially the same information as bar graphs, but in a slightly different way. In contrast to frequency distribution bar graphs, **frequency distribution line graphs** (sometimes called **frequency polygons**) are constructed by assigning each of the possible variable values (in our police recruit example, the possible scores on the test) a point, rather than a space, on the horizontal axis. Each of the possible frequencies is also assigned a point rather than a space on the vertical axis. A point is also used inside the graph space to represent the intersection of a variable value and its corresponding frequency.

Figure 3.3 Frequency Distribution Table and Frequency Distribution Bar Graph of Police Recruit Test Scores

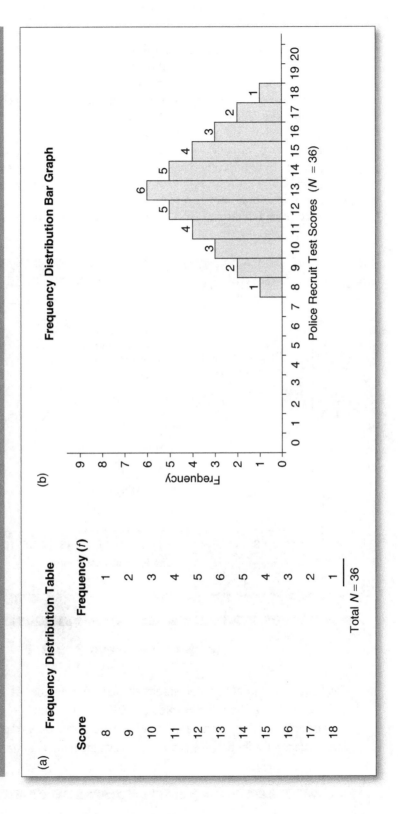

To locate this point in the graph, we draw an imaginary line perpendicular to the horizontal axis beginning at the point on the horizontal axis representing the variable value, and another imaginary line perpendicular to the vertical axis beginning at the point on the vertical axis representing the frequency with which that variable value appears in the data. The point where these two imaginary lines intersect represents the frequency with which the selected variable value appears in the data. We repeat this procedure for each variable value and its corresponding frequency. The line in the graph is created by connecting the points we have located with a series of straight lines.

The line graph corresponding to the bar graph of police recruit test scores in Figure 3.3b might look like the one in Figure 3.4.

The From the Literature Box 3.1 provides examples of frequency distribution bar and line graphs.

Figure 3.4 Frequency Distribution Line Graph for Police Recruit Test Scores

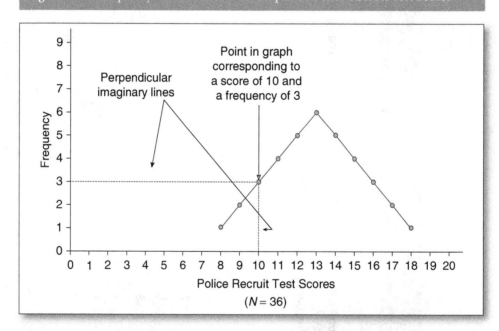

From the Literature Box 3.1

The frequency distribution bar graphs indicate the number of injury accidents recorded each year from 2006 through 2011 and the number of different citations issued in 2011 by the Champlin, Minnesota, Police Department's patrol unit. The frequency distribution line graph represents the number of traffic citations the

(Continued)

(Continued)

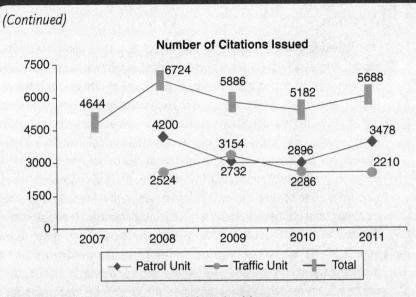

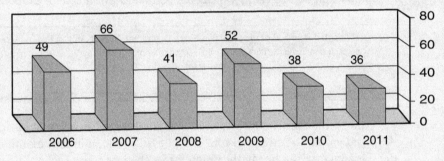

Average number of injury accidents:
52 – 2006 through 2008
42 – 2009 through 2011

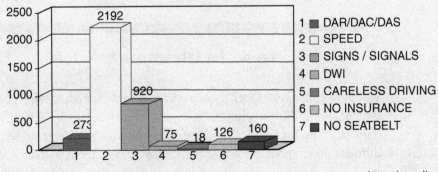

(Continued)

(Continued)

unit issued in 2011. These graphs were a page in the department's 2011 annual report. Almost all police departments in the United States prepare and distribute such annual reports to their members, government officials, and the public both in print and online. Many include bar and other types of graphs to illustrate various aspects of their operations and activities, as well as criminal activity within their jurisdictions. The graphs, often presented in color and in apparent three dimensions as this one was, are usually produced by graphing software. Variations on these graph styles, including the addition of color, contrasting shadings, and so on, are quite common in police department annual reports and other communications from police and other criminal justice agencies, especially when they are directed to outside audiences. Note that the bars in the graph are drawn to appear three-dimensional. When data are presented in this way and color and other enhancements are added, their dramatic appearance attracts the attention of the viewer/reader. We have modified the citations-issued graph for non-color reproduction here to clarify which bars pertain to which type of citation.

Source: Adapted from p. 8 of the Champlin Police Department's 2011 Annual Report. Accessed online at www.ci.champlin.mn.us/documents/2011AnnualReportpdf on May 23, 2012. Reprinted with the permission of the Champlin Police Department.

Among the most frequently used line graph types in criminal justice statistics is the trend graph. In a **trend graph**, units of time (e.g., minutes, months, years) form the horizontal axis. A line in the graph traces changes over time in the frequency, percent, or rate of some variable (e.g., caseloads, percent of juvenile offenders younger than 16 years of age, incarceration rates, etc.) whose possible values are marked on the vertical axis. From the Literature Box 3.2 provides an example of a trend graph. Note that the line graph in the From the Literature Box 3.1 is also a trend graph.

From the Literature Box 3.2

This trend graph represents changes in the size of four adult correctional populations from 1980 through 2008. It was prepared for the Bureau of Justice Statistics "Key Facts at a Glance" report, using different colored lines for the different populations. Note that the source of the numerical data is identified.

(Continued)

(Continued)

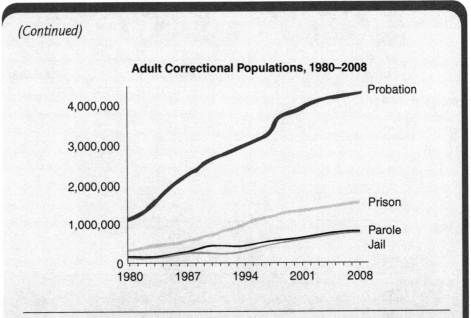

Source: Bureau of Justice Statistics Correctional Surveys (The Annual Probation Survey, National Prisoner Statistics Program, Annual Survey of Jails, and Annual Parole Survey) as presented in Correctional Populations in the United States, anuual, Prisoners in 2008, and Probation and Parole in the United States, 2008.

Source: "Key Facts at a Glance," Bureau of Justice Statistics Correctional Populations Trends Chart, Bureau of Justice Statistics, accessed online at http://bjs.ojp.usdoj.gov/content/glance/corr2.cfm on October 14, 2010.

Percent Distribution Tables and Graphs

So far, we have discussed using frequency count distributions in table, as well as bar and line graph, forms to help us make sense of the data. As we noted earlier in this chapter, frequencies can be converted to percents, and doing so is often advisable. Just as we can construct frequency distributions based on frequency counts, we can create percent (relative frequency) distributions based on those frequencies.

To construct percent distributions in table and graph forms, the first task is to calculate the percents corresponding to the frequencies. Then, we can create tables or graphs using the percents we have calculated.

To make a percent distribution table of our recruit test scores, we would first calculate what percent of all the scores ($N = 36$) each score or group of tied scores represents. (Tied scores are scores with the same value; there are three scores of 10, for example.) For the purposes of illustration, we will round our results to the nearest tenth of a percent (.1%). There is one score of eight. This one score out of the total of 36 scores = $1/36 = .028 = 2.8\%$. So that score represents 2.8% of the total number of scores in the distribution. There were two scores of 9, or $2/36 = 5.6\%$ of the total; and three scores of 10 for 8.3%, one score of 18 for 2.8%, four scores of 15 for 11.1%, and so on. The frequencies and corresponding percents are presented in Table 3.4.

Table 3.4 Frequency and Percent Distribution Table for Police Recruit Test Scores

Scores	Frequencies (f)	Percents (%)
8	1	2.8
9	2	5.6
10	3	8.3
11	4	11.1
12	5	13.9
13	6	16.7
14	5	13.9
15	4	11.1
16	3	8.3
17	2	5.6
18	1	2.8
Totals	$N = 36$	100.1

A percent distribution table should always indicate at least the total number of observations (in our test score example, $N = 36$) included in the table. It is not a bad idea to include the frequency counts for each variable value as well. However, if all we have is the total number of observations (N), we can use the percent corresponding to each variable value to calculate the corresponding frequency count. We do this by multiplying each of the variable value percents by the total number of observations in the data set. To calculate the frequency for the test score of 13, for example, we take .167 (the decimal equivalent of 16.7%, the percent corresponding to the score 13 in the third [percent] column of Table 3.4) times 36. The result equals 6 (rounded to the nearest whole number), which is the frequency associated with the score of 13 in the second (frequency count) column in Table 3.4. Note that in such reconstructions of frequency data from percent data, rounding percents may yield some inexact corresponding frequency results.

To construct our percent bar graph for these data, we arrange the possible variable values (in this case, the possible test scores) on the horizontal axis, as we did with the frequency counts distribution. On the vertical axis, we list not the possible frequency counts, but the possible percents, beginning with 0% at the point where the

Figure 3.5 Percent Distribution Bar Graph for Police Recruit Test Scores With Line Graph Superimposed

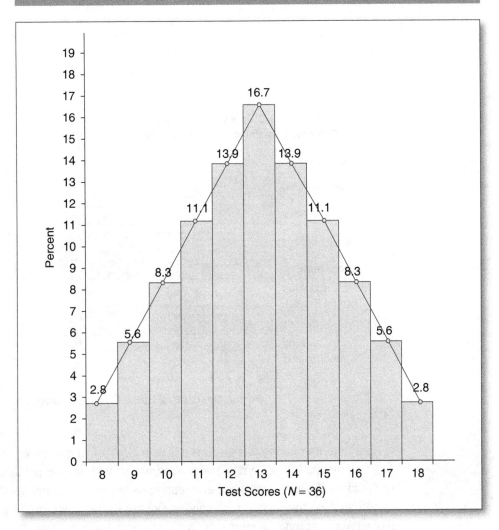

horizontal axis intersects with the vertical axis. Figure 3.5 is the percent bar graph distribution of the police recruit test scores. In this figure, we have also superimposed the corresponding line graph, using the midpoints in the space allocated for the possible scores in the bar graph to locate the required points for drawing the lines.

Note that the general profile of the distribution in Figure 3.5 is the same as that in Figure 3.3b. The difference is that the percents in Figure 3.5 are standardized quantities, which, as we noted in our discussion of percents earlier in this chapter, would greatly facilitate comparisons, for example, among study groups of different sizes who took the same test.

From the Literature Box 3.3

This percent bar graph represents the percent of local police officers employed in departments with special policies pertaining to appropriate actions when dealing with selected special populations or situations in 2007.

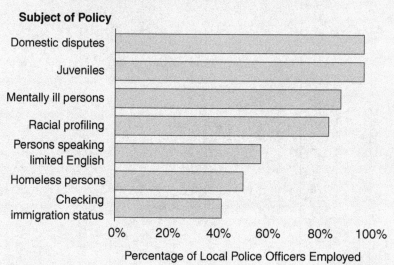

Local Police Officers Employed by a Department With Selected Special Population/situation Policies, 2007

Note that interpreting this graph is a little tricky. At first glance, you might think it represents the percent of *police departments* with special policies. But if you read carefully, you will see that it represents the percent of *police officers employed in departments* with such policies. Does that change your understanding of what the graph is saying? Why would the data analyst create this graph rather than one pertaining to police departments? Note also that this percent bar graph is different in two important respects from the others we have been discussing. First, the possible percents are arrayed along the horizontal rather than the vertical axis. Almost any bar graph can be drawn in this way, and when they are, they are referred to as horizontal bar or percent graphs. Second, this is not a percent *distribution* bar graph like the ones we have been discussing. A particular police department may have policies for dealing with two of these

(Continued)

> *(Continued)*
>
> special populations/situations, whereas another may have policies dealing with four of them. Each bar represents the percent of all police officers who are employed in a department with a special policy for dealing with the specified special population/situation. So, the bars do not represent the mutually exclusive possible values of a single variable. We should not expect, therefore, that the sum of the percents will be 100%, as it obviously is not.
>
> *Source:* Reaves, Brian A., Local Police Departments, 2007. USDOJ, OJP, BJS (NCJ 231174). December 2010. Figure 10, p. 16 accessed online at http://bjs.ojp.usdoj.gov/content/pub/pdf/lpd07.pdf on March 5, 2011.

Cumulative Distributions

We can also create cumulative distribution tables and bar and line graphs for frequencies and percents. They are appropriate for variables measured at the ordinal, interval, or ratio level. With measurements at these levels, variable values can be arranged from lowest to highest. Cumulative distributions are constructed by beginning with distributions like those we have discussed above.

Cumulative Frequency Distribution Tables

To construct a **cumulative frequency distribution table**, we begin with a base frequency, usually the frequency associated with the lowest variable value in the data set, and add the frequencies associated with each increase in variable value in succession, recording the cumulating totals as we go.

We'll use our Hitsville inmate age data (see Table 3.3) to illustrate the process. To create a cumulative frequency (which we symbolize as cf) table for these data, we would begin with the frequency ($f = 120$) for the lowest age group (ages 18–19) and record it in the row opposite this age group in the table. For the entry in our cumulative frequency table opposite the next highest age group (ages 20–21), we would add the frequency for the lowest age group ($f = 120$) and the frequency for this 20–21 age group ($f = 105$), yielding $cf = 225$. This total would be entered in the table opposite the ages 20–21 category. Then, we take this total and add the frequency for the next highest age group ($f = 75$ for age group 22–24), yielding $cf = 300$. We proceed in this way successively through all the age groups and their corresponding frequencies, producing the entries in the third (cf) column in Table 3.5.

The cumulative frequency distribution table for the police recruit test scores would look like the one in Table 3.6.

Cumulative frequency distribution tables such as the one for inmates' ages tell us how many inmates have ages from the lowest age group to any other age group we choose. Thus, looking at the cf column in Table 3.5, we can say 300 of the inmates are ages 22 to 24 or younger. Similarly, the cumulative frequency distribution for police

Table 3.5 Frequency and Cumulative Frequency Distribution Table for Ages of Hitsville Inmates

Ages	Frequencies (f)	Cumulative Frequencies (cf)
18–19	120	120
20–21	105	225
22–24	75	300
25–30	55	355
31–40	30	385
Over 40	15	400
Total	400	

Table 3.6 Frequency and Cumulative Frequency Distribution Table for Police Recruit Test Scores

Scores	Frequencies (f)	Cumulative Frequencies (cf)
8	1	1
9	2	3
10	3	6
11	4	10
12	5	15
13	6	21
14	5	26
15	4	30
16	3	33
17	2	35
18	1	36
Total	36	

recruit test score data in Table 3.6 indicates that 21 of the recruits scored 13 or lower on the test. Note that the cumulative frequency associated with the oldest age group of Hitsville inmates is $cf = 400$, corresponding to the total number of inmates' ages in our data set. Likewise, the cumulative frequency associated with the highest police recruit test score is $cf = 36$, the total number of recruit test scores in the distribution.

Cumulative Frequency Distribution Bar and Line Graphs

The cumulative frequency tables can be used to create **cumulative frequency bar and line graphs,** following the same basic procedures we used in converting frequency distribution tables to bar and line graphs. We'll use the police recruit test score data (see Table 3.6) for purposes of illustration.

The cumulative frequency bar and line graphs for these test data would look like the ones in Figure 3.6. We have superimposed the corresponding line graph over the bar graph in this illustration.

Cumulative Percent Distribution Tables, Bar Graphs, and Line Graphs

We can also construct **cumulative percent distribution tables** and **cumulative percent distribution bar and line graphs** following the same general procedures we used in constructing the cumulative frequency distributions. We'll use our recruit test score data again to illustrate. Table 3.7 shows the possible scores, with their corresponding

Table 3.7 Frequency, Percent, and Cumulative Percent Distribution Table for Police Recruit Test Scores

Scores	Frequencies (*f*)	Percents (%)	Cumulative Percents (%)
8	1	2.8	2.8
9	2	5.6	8.4
10	3	8.3	16.7
11	4	11.1	27.8
12	5	13.9	41.7
13	6	16.7	58.4
14	5	13.9	72.3
15	4	11.1	83.4
16	3	8.3	91.7
17	2	5.6	97.3
18	1	2.8	100.1
Totals	$N = 36$		100.1

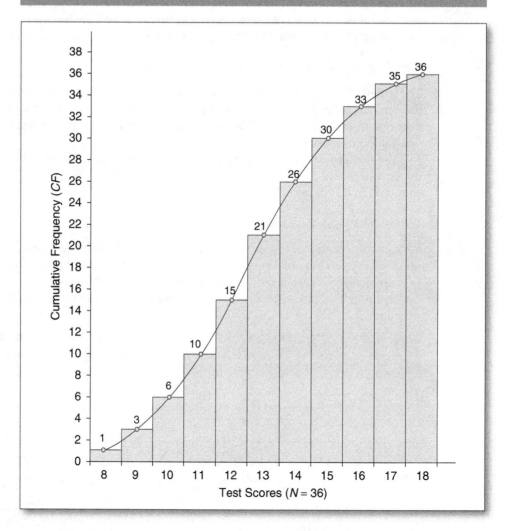

Figure 3.6 Cumulative Frequency Distribution Bar and Line Graphs for Police Recruit Test Scores

frequencies and percents, in the first three columns. In the far right column is the corresponding cumulative percent distribution.

As with the cumulative frequency distribution, we begin with the percent corresponding to the lowest score and add the percent corresponding to the next highest, ending with the addition of the percent corresponding to the highest score. The cumulative percent entry corresponding to the highest score is, of course, 100%. (In our example, the sum is actually 100.1% due to rounding error.)

We can use our cumulative percent distribution to report what percent of the recruits got a particular score or lower. Thus, 72.3% of our police recruits scored 14 or lower on the test. Subtracting that percent from 100% gives us the percent of recruits who scored higher than that particular score—in our example, 27.8%.

We can also construct cumulative percent bar and line graphs using the same data. Remember that the cumulative percent distribution is in the far right column of Table 3.7. The corresponding cumulative percent bar and line graphs are presented in Figure 3.7.

Note that cumulative frequency and percent bar and line graphs may also be said to have a shape (see Figures 3.6 and 3.7, for example). They have a profile like a stretched lazy "s," without the turn downward at the top end and the upward turn at the bottom end. The length of the sections at the ends of the cumulative frequency "curve" (these end sections of curves are often called the "tails" of the curve), the length and angle of the center section's rise, and the sharpness of the curves at the bottom and top may all vary. We'll ask you to draw some of these graphs in the exercises and think about how the shapes of the cumulative line graphs change as the corresponding frequency or percent bar and line graph distributions change.

Note also that the profile of a nominal variable bar or line graph of whatever type is meaningless because the order in which the variable values are listed on the horizontal axis is arbitrary. Hence, the profile of the graph can be changed simply by changing the order in which the variable values are listed. Ordinal, interval, or ratio variables, on the other hand, have values that ascend (or descend) on the horizontal axis. The ordered listing of the possible variable values lends meaning to the shape of the graph.

More About Graphs

Now that we have discussed some basics of graphs, graph construction, and a few graph types, we can consider the general nature and appeal of graphs in a little more detail. Graphs (also sometimes called charts) may perhaps best be defined as visual displays of quantitative information. Such graphs may be said to convert or translate numerical quantities into visual images in a two-dimensional graphic space. There are many ways of accomplishing this translation. We have already discussed the basics of two of the available options, univariate bar and line graphs. But there are many variations on these two graph types, and many other types as well, from which graph constructors may choose.

Many graphs based on quantitative data are relatively simple in their construction and portray information about just one variable, like those we have discussed in this chapter. They can be quite complex, however, displaying multivariate information and requiring great creativity on the part of the graph designer. Tufte (1997, 2001) offers an interesting discussion of the history of graphic displays of quantitative information and some examples of various complex and remarkably informative graphs.

Figure 3.7 Cumulative Percent Distribution Bar and Line Graphs for Police Recruit Test Scores

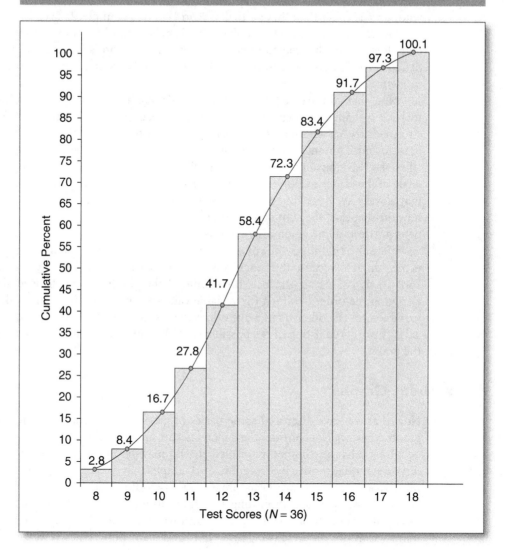

The Power of Graphs

Whatever their type or complexity, at their best, graphs catch our attention in ways that no list or table of numbers can, and they can convey quantitative data in ways easily comprehensible to other professionals and the general public as well. But graphs also have great potential to induce distinctly false impressions of the data on which they are based. Sometimes, unfortunately, these false impressions are conveyed quite deliberately. As a result, graphs must be constructed, used, and interpreted with great care.

The power of graphs to influence our understanding and interpretation of quantitative data lies mainly in their reliance on the sense most humans depend on and trust most for getting information about the world—the sense of sight and the visual images or the pictures of the world it provides. Looking at a graph gives us a picture of the data being analyzed. And who wouldn't prefer to look at graphs—especially multicolored ones with interesting shapes, shadings, and apparent three-dimensional depths—rather than read and try to make sense of a bunch of numbers presented in a narrative or table? Furthermore, graphs appeal to us, in part, because they seem to make understanding numbers easy, almost intuitive. We think we comprehend what the numbers mean because we can comprehend the various parts of the image that represent the quantities on which the graph is based. In a sense, then, we are, as a species, suckers for a graph's visual appeal and ease of interpretation—so much so, in fact, that we may not pay any attention to the numbers on which the graph is based. As we will see later in this chapter, ignoring those numbers could be a serious mistake!

Be aware, however, that interpreting visual images engages a different part of our brain than does understanding numbers. And, just as numbers should never be regarded as speaking for themselves, neither should graphs. Graphs are always produced by particular humans (with or without computer assistance) and for a particular purpose. How a graph is constructed may reflect consciously or unconsciously the points of view or biases of the grapher. As we will see, the same data can be graphically depicted in ways that present very different visual images and, therefore, if we are not careful, very different impressions of what the underlying quantitative data indicate. Statisticians' failure to communicate clearly with the person or computer creating the graph and/or failure to double-check the graphs produced are the sources of many incorrectly drawn and misleading graphs.

Some Additional Kinds of Graphs

Graphs come in a variety of types beyond the simple bar and line graphs we have discussed so far. Here we will discuss briefly three additional types of graphs found frequently in the criminal justice literature and used by both researchers and practitioners, often, for example, in agency annual reports intended for other professionals and the general public. One is a variation on the basic bar graph, called a segmented bar graph. The other two are the pie graph and the pictograph.

Segmented Bar Graphs

In a **segmented bar graph**, the values of more than one variable can be represented in the bars. Consider a basic bar graph depicting the number of first-time arrestees in various districts of a large city, as in Figure 3.8a. The total length of each bar in the graph is determined by the total number of first-time arrestees in the corresponding district.

Now suppose we wished to indicate the sex distribution of our first-time arrestees. We could do so by dividing each bar in the basic bar graph into two segments, one representing the number of male first-time arrestees and the other representing the

Figure 3.8 A Basic and a Segmented Bar Graph

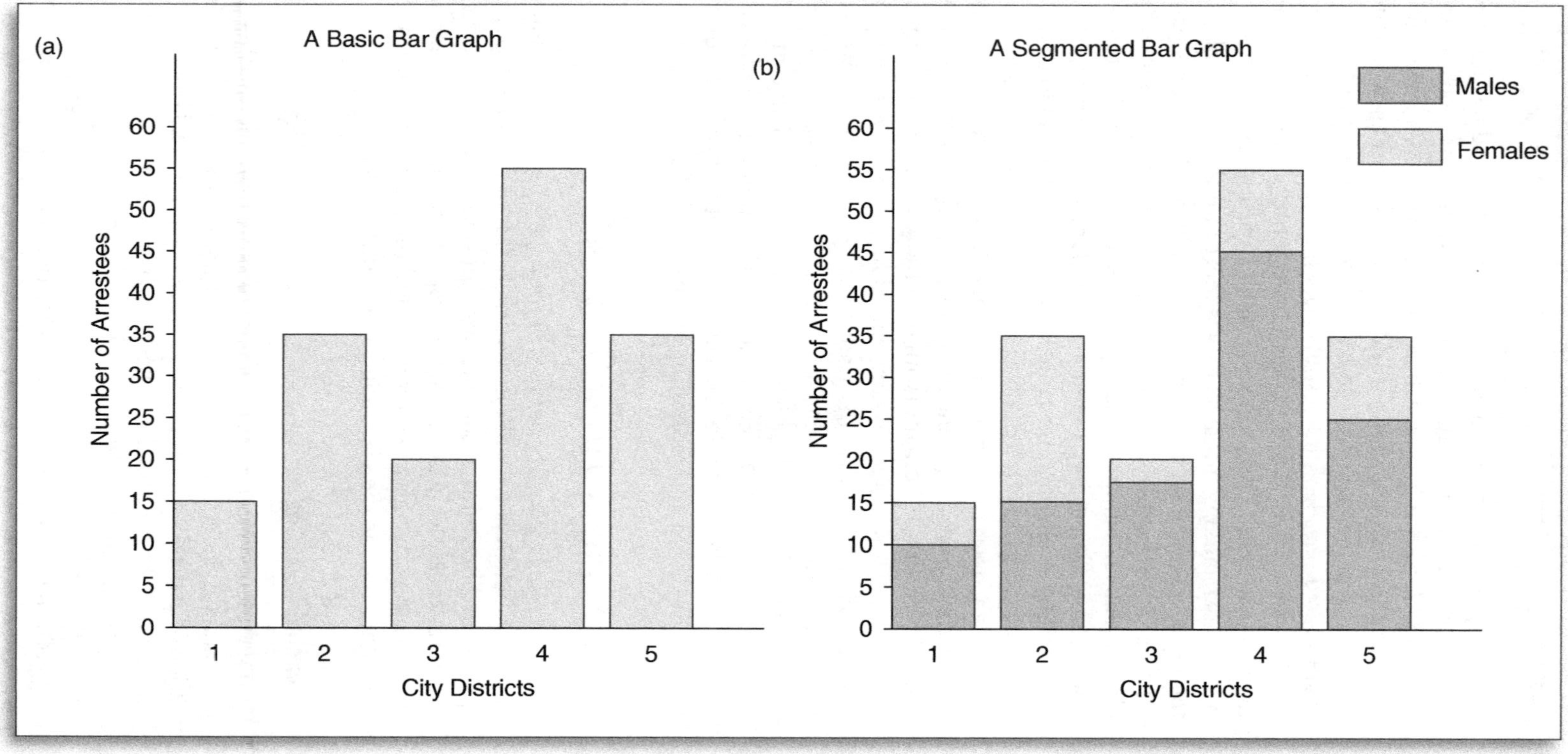

number of female first-time arrestees in the corresponding district. To make the bars representing the two variables pertaining to first-time arrestees (district and sex) easier to read, the two segments in each bar could be distinguished by color or hashing pattern. It might look like the one in Figure 3.8b.

Theoretically, we could divide each of the two segments based on sex into two additional segments based on age—say, those 21 and under and those over 21. We would then have a segmented bar graph representing three variables pertaining to first-time arrestees (district, sex, and age). In practice, segmented bar graphs representing data for more than three variables are rarely employed. As you might imagine, adding more variables makes the graphs very difficult to read.

In effect, drawing the graph in this way stacks the bar segments representing the frequency of the sexes on top of one another, producing one bar with two parts. As an alternative, we could put the segments side by side over the corresponding variable value, assigning appropriate labels to the bars, as exemplified in the From the Literature Box 3.4. Technically speaking, this would not be a segmented bar graph, but the principle is the same. In this case, the segments of what could be a segmented bar graph are instead placed side by side.

Pie Graphs

A **pie graph** (also called a pie chart) is a circle (think pie) subdivided into segments (think slices of a pie). The circle (pie) is divided into as many segments (slices) as there are possible values of the variable being represented in the pie graph. As with a bar in a bar graph, the size of each segment of the circle corresponds to the number or proportion (percent) of observations for the corresponding variable value. To do this, recall that the radius of any circle has 360 degrees of possible rotation. The area of the

---

From the Literature Box 3.4

As a part of their 2011 annual report to their community, the Vernon Hills (IL) Police Department prepared this frequency distribution bar graph. It represents the number of Part I and Part II crimes (as classified in the FBI's Uniform Crime Reporting System) recorded in the city from 2005 through 2011. The bars in the original were presented in red and blue. Note that the bars for the two types of crime have been drawn side by side for each year. Alternatively, they could have been stacked on top of each other so that the height of each bar represented the total number of Part I and Part II crimes and the height of each segment represented the number of that particular type within that total.

(Continued)

(Continued)

Part I Crimes

Homicide	Burglary	Criminal Sexual Assault
Burglary to Auto	Robbery	Motor Vehicle Theft
Aggravated Battery	Theft	Aggravated Assault
Arson		

Part II Crimes

Simple Assault	Controlled Substances Act	Simple Battery
Hypo-Syringes/Needles Act	Criminal Damage	Deceptive Practice
Liquor Control Act	Interference With Officers	Disorderly Conduct
Criminal Trespass	Sex Offenses	Weapons Offenses
Kidnapping	Fireworks	Cannabis Control Act
Warrant Arrests	Violation Order of Protection	Offenses Involving Children

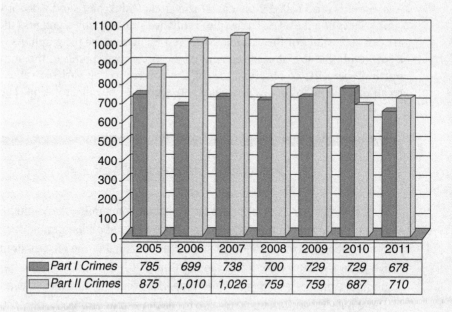

	2005	2006	2007	2008	2009	2010	2011
Part I Crimes	785	699	738	700	729	729	678
Part II Crimes	875	1,010	1,026	759	759	687	710

Source: Vernon Hills Police Department. In Service of Others, 2011 Annual Report, p. 33. Accessed online at www.vernonhills.org/userfiles/file/PD_Documents/2011_annual_report.pdf on April 24, 2012.

Table 3.8 Citizens' Views of a Community Policing Initiative

View	Frequencies	Percents	Decimals	Degrees
Strongly approve	33	15%	.15	54
Approve	99	45%	.45	162
No opinion	11	5%	.05	18
Disapprove	55	25%	.25	90
Strongly disapprove	22	10%	.10	36
Totals	$N = 220$	100%	1.00	360

circle is divided into the appropriately sized segments by dividing these 360 degrees into proportions corresponding to the frequencies or percents with which the different variable values occur in the data.

Suppose we have asked a sample of citizens about their views of a new community policing initiative. The possible answers provided were "strongly approve," "approve," "no opinion," "disapprove," and "strongly disapprove." This variable then has five ordinal values and the circle will be divided into five sections or slices. Suppose the citizens' responses were distributed as in Table 3.8. The first column in Table 3.8 lists the possible responses (the variable values). The second column includes the frequency count for each of the possible responses.

To determine the appropriate size of the pie graph slices required to represent these data, we need to convert the raw frequencies into their corresponding proportions. This permits us to determine the number of degrees of rotation to allocate for each slice. A simple way of accomplishing this is to convert the raw frequencies to percents, as we have done in the third column. Then, we convert the percents to decimals, as we have done in the fourth column. (Remember that to convert percents to decimals, we remove the percent sign and move the decimal point two places to the left. So, for example, 15% is equal to .15. These conversions are found in column 4 of the table.) Finally, we multiply each of these decimals by 360 degrees to determine the number of degrees of rotation that determines the size of each slice. The results of those calculations are in the fifth column of Table 3.8.

As indicated in the third and fourth columns of Table 3.8, "strongly approve" comprises 15% or .15 of the responses. As indicated in column 5, .15 of the 360 degrees of rotation of a circle's radius is 54 degrees (.15 × 360 = 54). Beginning with a circle of any size we choose, we first draw a radius in the circle, which, as you will recall, is a straight line from the center of the circle to its circumference. Next, using that radius as a baseline, we mark the point on the circle's circumference corresponding to 54 degrees on a protractor. Drawing another radius from that point to the center of the

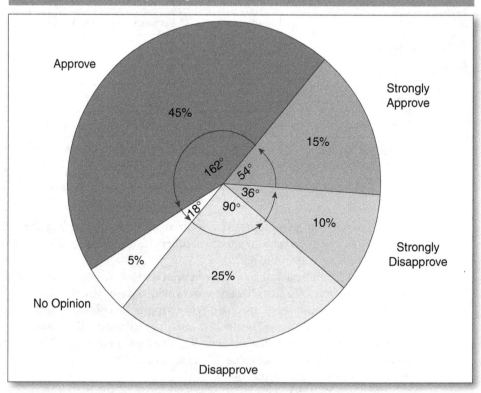

Figure 3.9 A Pie Graph Showing Degrees of Rotation for Each Variable Value and Corresponding Slice ($N = 220$)

circle would define the slice of the pie graph corresponding to the 15% of the total responses that were "strongly approve."

The "approve" responses are 45% of the responses and 45% of 360 degrees is 162 degrees. Beginning with the new radius we just drew as the baseline, we would use the protractor to mark the point on the circle's circumference corresponding to 162 degrees. This would define the slice of the pie graph corresponding to the "approve" response. We would proceed in the same way for each of the remaining responses, eventually dividing the circle into five slices. The result might look like Figure 3.9.

As with bar graphs, we can assess the relative frequencies of the various variable values by comparing the areas of the segments of the circle to which they correspond. Also as with bar graphs, the appearance of pie graphs can be enhanced by using contrasting colors and/or shadings for the different slices. They may also be drawn to appear three-dimensional. See the From the Literature Box 3.5 for an example.

Pictographs

Pictographs provide still another alternative for graphing data. They are perhaps the most eye-catching of all the graphs and can be used most effectively for illustrating the frequencies or percents corresponding to the different values of a single nominal or ordinal variable.

From the Literature Box 3.5

This percent distribution pie graph divides the 2010 Vernon Hills (IL) Police Department's 2010 budget into three categories. (We think they meant to indicate it was their 2011 budget.) The original pie graph featured three colors (red, white, and blue). Note that the numerical data on which the graph is based are also reported with the graph.

Vernon Hills Police Department 2010 Budget

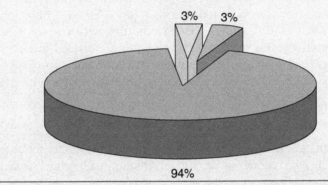

■ Personnel ■ Contractual Services ☐ Equipment and Commodities

Expenditure	Amount
Personnel	$ 8,037,917
Contractual Services	$ 293,122
Equipment & Commodities	$ 300,579
Total	$ 8,631,618

Source: Vernon Hills Police Department, op. cit, p. 32. Accessed online at www.vernonhills.org/userfiles/file/PD_Documents/2011_annual_report.pdf on April 24, 2012.

We call the basic type of **pictograph** the **standardized size multiple icon pictograph**. We'll call them SSMIPs to save ink as well as lip, tongue, and jaw muscles. They can be thought of as modified versions of bar graphs. In an SSMIP, an icon of a particular, fixed size is chosen to represent a specified number (or percent) of observations for each variable value—hence, the designation as an SSMIP.

Rather than using a simple rectangular bar, pictograph creators typically construct their graphs using an interesting, eye-catching, and widely recognized icon associated with the variable whose values are being represented in the graph. Thus, for example, a human figure of a particular size in black-and-white-striped clothes might represent a specified number of inmates in a graph of the number of inmates being held in several county jails. If each of the icons stood for 5 inmates and if there were 28 inmates in a particular county jail, five of the icons plus three fifths of another would be lined up to represent that jail's total. Another jail might have 10 inmates and that frequency would be represented by 2 of the striped icons. Or, a gavel of a particular size might be chosen to represent 10 judges in a pictograph representing the number of such judges in each of two jurisdictions. Differences in frequencies (or percents) are indicated by differences in the number of icons lined up above (in a vertical pictograph) or beside (in a horizontal pictograph) the corresponding variable values. Fictitious examples of these pictographs are included in Figure 3.10.

Note that a key is included in each of the Figure 3.10 pictographs. A key should always be provided with an SSMIP, indicating what frequency or percent each of the standardized icons represents. When icons are divided to represent fractions of the standardized quantity, they should be divided in one dimension only (either horizontally or vertically). This preserves the appropriate spatial proportions.

Titling and Labeling Tables and Graphs

Regardless of their type, careful titling and clear labels for tables and graphs are essential. The basic contents of a table or graph must be clearly indicated by its title. The rows and columns of a table and the axes of a graph, as well as the units into which they are divided, must be clearly labeled. If we don't know what the table or graph is about, we don't know how to "read" what it is telling us.

Percent tables and all graphs must be accompanied by the quantities used to construct them. At a minimum, at least the total number of observations included in the table or graph should be reported. For graphs depicting raw frequencies, the frequency (f) of each variable value should be clear. Although relative differences in frequencies or percents may be apparent in the different sizes of the areas (bars or icons) in the graph space, if we don't know what those relative differences represent, the graph may be very misleading. In a relative frequency (percent) graph, the relationships among the areas of the bars would look the same whether it is based on 15 or 150,000 observations, for example.

Finally, if a statistician is not reporting on her own data, the source of the data being depicted in tables or graphs should be cited. This permits the viewer to consult the original data source to verify the accuracy of the information on which the table or graph is based.

Cautions With Graphs

The bar graph's simplicity and ease of interpretation makes it among the most frequently used devices for communicating simple quantitative data, especially to nonprofessional audiences. In some ways, however, their production is more complex

Figure 3.10 Standardized Size Multiple Icon Pictographs (SSMIPs)

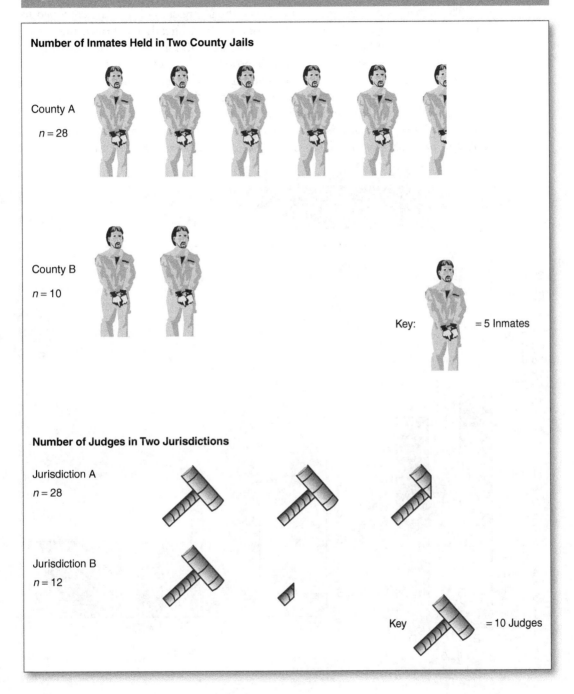

than it appears, and interpreting them appropriately requires some careful thought and attention to detail.

The appearance of the graph, and hence the impression of the data conveyed to the viewer, depends on a number of factors. We have already mentioned the use of color or hashing, and apparent three-dimensional drafting. Perhaps the most impact on the viewers' impressions left by a graph, however, is the scale on which the graph is drawn. As we noted earlier, the scale of a graph is determined by the size of the spatial units on the two axes of the graph. By manipulating the scale, the graph producer can create very different visual impressions of the data.

As an illustration of this point, in Figure 3.11 we have produced a number of different basic bar graphs, *all of which represent exactly the same quantitative data*.

Figure 3.11 Frequency Distribution Bar Graphs of the Same Data Drawn to Different Scales and With Different Shadings and Spacings

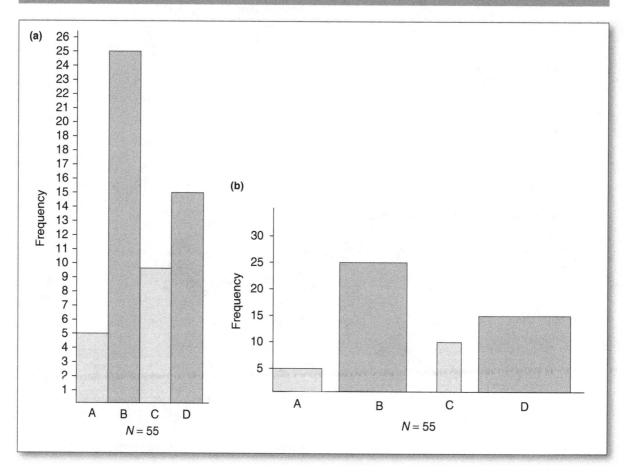

(Continued)

Figure 3.11 (Continued)

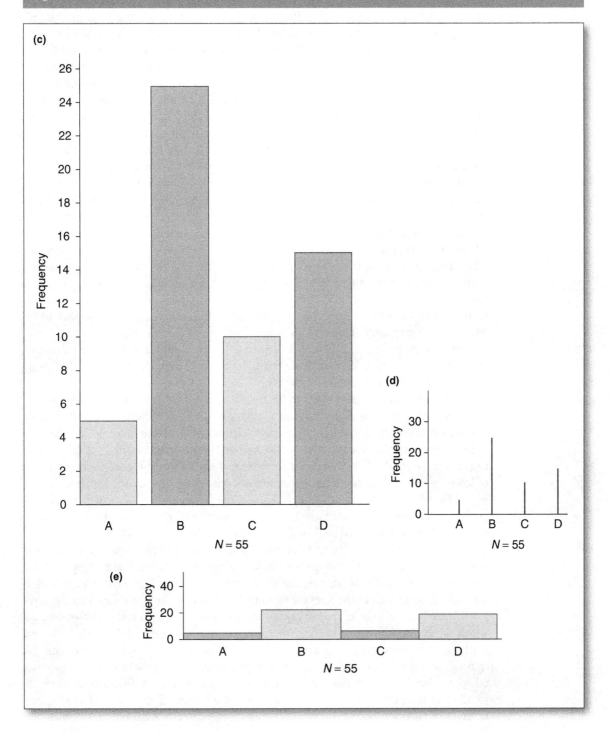

As you can readily see in Figure 3.11, changing the scale on the frequency (or percent) axis (i.e., allocating more or less space for each possible frequency or percent) can make any differences in these quantities among the variable values appear large or small. Though perhaps not as dramatic in visual effect, changing the scale on the variable value axis also alters the appearance and hence the impression of the data conveyed by the graph. Manipulating both scales at the same time magnifies the changes in appearance. Differences in color, shading, and spacing also influence the visual impact of the graphs.

Line graphs are subject to the same potential difficulties as bar graphs. Changing the scale of line graphs representing the same data yields graphs with very different visual appearances. Hence, the viewers' impression of the data on which the graphs are based may be altered as well. The graphs in Figure 3.12 both illustrate exactly the same changes in the same crime rate (that is, they are both based on exactly the same quantitative data). Both are, in that sense, accurate representations of the data, but the scales on the horizontal and vertical axes have been changed. Viewers who don't pay attention to the scales and the numbers on which the graph is based might come away with very different impressions of what is happening to the crime rate, depending on which graph they see. One viewer may see the crime rate as relatively unchanging while another may see it as changing both markedly and rapidly. Imagining the bar graphs in Figure 3.11 converted to line graphs further illustrates the variety of appearances that might be produced using the same quantitative data. At the very least, as with bar graphs, when several line graphs are included in a report, they should be constructed using approximately the same scale, in so far as possible.

Because they are basically modified versions of bar graphs, SSMIPs are subject to the same pitfalls as bar graphs. Scale changes can yield very different visual impressions of the underlying data.

Perhaps the graph most likely to be drawn in a misleading way is a type of pictograph we will call a size changing icon pictograph (SCIP, for short). Recall that in an SSMIP, variations in frequency (or percent) from one variable value to another are reflected in changes in the number of standardized (same sized) icons. In a **size changing icon pictograph**, these variations are represented, not by differences in the number of icons, but by differences in the *size* of single icons. Thus, one figure in striped clothes would be twice as tall as another such figure if the frequency (or percent) represented by the former were twice that of the latter. Two examples of SCIPs, using the inmate data in Figure 3.10, are included in Figures 3.13a and 3.13b.

SCIPs are especially subject to conveying a misleading impression. The reason is related to the necessity to change the size of a single icon. Look again at Figure 3.13. Even though it is correctly drawn, does the icon for County B in Figure 3.13a look a little weird, compared to the icon for County A? Most would say yes. Can you see why?

Unlike bars in a bar graph, many icons have what we might call expected length/width proportionate dimensions. We expect a human figure, whether in striped clothes or not, for example, to have certain height-to-width proportional dimensions in order to appear "normal" or "correct." Suppose we need to make one icon twice as tall as another in order to represent a corresponding difference in frequencies. In order to preserve the expected "normal" appearance of a human figure, we will be required to make the former icon about twice as wide as the latter as well. When we do so, the

Figure 3.12 Frequency Distribution Line Graphs Representing the Same Data but Drawn to Different Scales

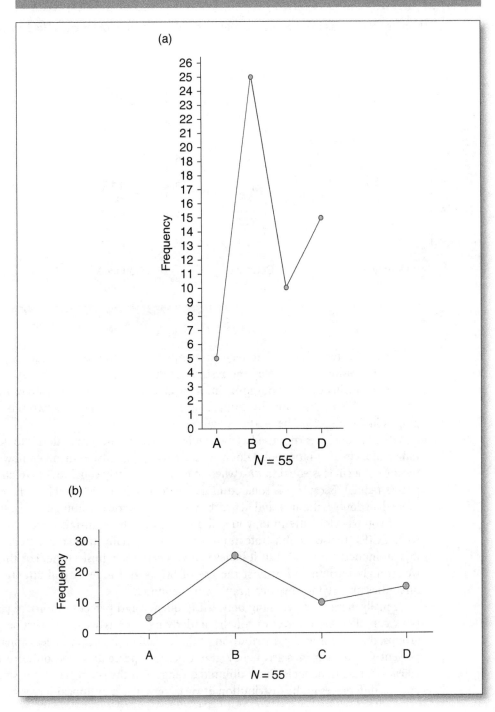

Figure 3.13 Size Changing Icon Pictographs (SCIPs)

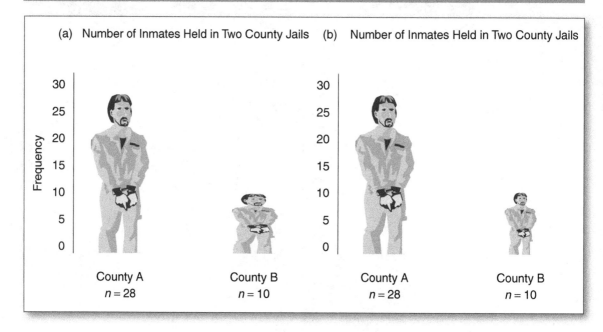

height of the two icons accurately represents the differences in frequency, but the visual impression conveyed by the resulting figures does not. Roughly speaking, the former icon will occupy about four times the area of the latter. This kind of mistake in drawing SCIPs is illustrated by comparing the icons in each of the two sets of pictographs in Figure 3.13. The SCIPs in Figure 3.13b are incorrect.

Be wary of circles (not used as pie graphs) as SCIPs. The temptation is to double the radius of a circle to represent a doubled underlying quantity. Remember, however, that the area of a circle is equal to πr^2 (where π is approximately equal to 3.1416 and r is the circle's radius). Because r is squared in the circle area formula, doubling the radius far more than doubles the area, and hence the visual impression communicated by the graph.

If you pay close attention, you will discover that these mistakes occur quite often when SCIPs are used to illustrate numerical data, especially in the mass media. Usually, it is an innocent mistake, but it is nevertheless extremely misleading. For this reason, we strongly recommend against the use of SCIPs and urge careful attention to the quantities underlying any such graph you encounter.

Finally, note that switching between frequency and percent graphs, regardless of type, can alter the impression of the underlying data as well. For very large study groups, differences in the distribution of the variable values may be less apparent in a percent graph than in a frequency graph because percents range only from 0% to 100% whereas frequencies have unlimited range. On the other hand, for small study groups, differences in the distribution of variable values may appear larger in a percent graph than in a frequency graph. Of course, changes in graph scales can exaggerate or mitigate these differences in appearance.

Summary

In this chapter, we began our discussion of making sense of the data we have using basic univariate descriptive statistical data analysis. We distinguished among univariate, bivariate, and multivariate analysis and between descriptive and inferential statistics. We defined and discussed several of the most basic tools for univariate (single variable) descriptive analysis, including frequency counts, ratios, fractions, proportions, decimals, percents, rates, and odds. Ways of calculating crime rates were outlined and critiqued. We described the construction of frequency distributions in the forms of tables, bar graphs, and line graphs. Such distributions may present frequency count data as well as measures derived from them, including percents. Cumulative frequency and percent distributions in the form of tables and bar and line graphs were also discussed. The analysis of data for a single variable almost always begins with at least some of the statistics we have considered in this chapter. Finally, we considered some other kinds of graphs, as well as some cautions that should be observed in constructing and reading graphs, lest one be misled by graphic images.

In the next chapter, we explore data distributions in more detail, focusing on how the distributions themselves may be described and what they may tell us about our data.

Concepts to Master

Bivariate analysis
Cumulative frequency bar graph
Cumulative frequency distribution table
Cumulative frequency distribution line graph
Cumulative percent distribution bar graph
Cumulative percent distribution line graph
Cumulative percent distribution table
Decimal
Descriptive statistics
Fractions

Frequency count
Frequency distribution bar graph
Frequency distribution line graph
Frequency distribution table
Frequency polygon
Histogram
Inferential statistics
Multivariate analysis
Odds
Percent
Pictograph
Pie graph

Proportion
Rate
Ratio
Relative frequencies
Scale of a graph
Segmented bar graph
Size changing icon pictograph (SCIP)
Standardized size multiple icon pictograph (SSMIP)
Trend graph
Univariate analysis
Univariate descriptive statistics

Review Questions

1. What are the differences among univariate, bivariate, and multivariate statistics?
2. What are the principal differences between descriptive and inferential statistics?
3. What is a frequency count?
4. What are ratios, fractions, and decimals?
5. What are percents, and why are they especially useful?
6. How are decimals or proportions converted to percents?
7. What is a relative frequency?
8. What is a rate? How does it differ from a percent?
9. How are crime rates calculated?
10. What are odds, and how are they converted to ratios, decimals, and percents?
11. What is a frequency distribution?
12. What are the different types of frequency distributions?
13. How is each type of frequency distribution constructed?
14. What is a bar graph? How is it constructed?
15. What is a line graph? How is it constructed?
16. How is a frequency distribution table converted to a bar graph? How is a bar graph converted to a line graph? What is a trend graph?
17. What are cumulative frequency distribution tables and cumulative frequency bar and line graphs, and how are they constructed?
18. What is the general shape of a cumulative line graph distribution?
19. What two features of all tables and graphs are essential? Why are they important?
20. What is the power of graphs? How and why do they catch our eye?
21. What is a pie graph? How is it constructed? In what ways are pie graphs similar to and different from bar graphs?
22. What is a pictograph? How is it constructed? Distinguish between an SCIP and an SSMIP. How and why are SCIPs likely to be constructed incorrectly?
23. What is the scale of a graph? Why is the scale in which a graph is drawn important?
24. If you haven't already done so, define each of the terms in the Concepts to Master list and use each in three sentences. (You have to learn the lingo!)

Exercises and Discussion Questions

1. Use the following hypothetical data for Exercises 1a through 1l below.

Subject	Sex	Number of Arrests	Highest Level of Education Achieved*
1	M	2	3
2	M	4	1
3	F	5	1
4	F	3	4
5	M	1	4
6	F	3	1
7	M	2	4
8	F	0	6
9	M	3	2
10	F	4	2
11	M	5	4
12	F	3	6
13	M	2	5
14	M	1	1
15	F	4	1
16	M	6	1
17	F	3	3
18	M	4	5
19	F	2	4
20	M	3	4

*Category (variable value) codes: 1 = grade school or less; 2 = junior high school; 3 = high school; 4 = community college; 5 = 4-year college; 6 = more than 4-year college.

a. At what level of measurement is each of the variables measured? Discuss why you have designated each variable's level of measurement as you have.

b. Are the variables discrete or continuous? Are the variable values mutually exclusive and exhaustive? Explain your answers.

c. What is the frequency count for each of the variable values? What is the ratio of males to females? What is the percent female? Convert the percent female to a decimal. What are the odds of being arrested exactly four times? What are the odds of being arrested four or more times? What is the rate of having at least a high school education? What is the rate of being arrested at least once?

  d. Construct a frequency distribution table and bar graph for each of the variables.
  e. Construct a percent (relative frequency) distribution table and percent bar graph for each of the variables.
  f. Change the scale of the percent distribution bar graph you drew for the "highest level of education" variable by doubling the size of the units on the percent axis and cutting the size of the units on the highest level of education achieved axis by half. Compare the two graphs. Is one more accurate than the other? Why or why not? Is one more misleading than the other? Why or why not?
  g. Convert the bar graphs you have drawn to line graphs.
  h. Construct a cumulative frequency distribution table and cumulative frequency bar and line graphs for all appropriate variables.
  i. Critique the measurement of the highest level of education achieved. Could it be improved? How would you improve it? How would any changes you make in the measurement of this variable influence the analysis of this variable?
  j. Construct a pie graph for the number of arrests variable.
  k. Construct an SSMIP for the number of arrests variable. Use handcuffs or some other appropriate icon.
  l. Construct an SCIP for the number of arrests variable using the same icon. Discuss the precautions you took to not draw a misleading pictograph.

2. Find at least two examples of bar, line, or pie graphs or pictographs in newspapers, magazines, or textbooks other than this one. Are you given the information necessary to make sense of them? What else would you like to know about the data represented? (Pay especially close attention to such data presentations in advertising!)

3. Use the data in Table 3.5 to construct cumulative frequency and cumulative percent bar and line graphs. Compare the line graphs with those in Figures 3.6 and 3.7. Think about the differences in the shapes of these graphs. How do the shapes of cumulative frequency line graphs change as the underlying frequency distribution line graphs change? Can you tell what the shape of a frequency distribution is by looking at the shape of its cumulative frequency line graph?

4. Suppose you have a population of 1,350,000 and 14,200 OMVI offenses in the past year. What is the rate of OMVIs per 1,000? What is the rate per 100,000?

5. Look at the bar graphs in From the Literature Box 3.1. Do you trust these data? Why or why not?

6. Construct a frequency distribution table and draw a two-dimensional bar graph (like the one in Figure 3.1b) using the data in From the Literature Box 3.1. Which presentation of these data would you prefer to look at? Why?

7. Look at the percent bar graph in From the Literature Box 3.3. Answer the two questions in the paragraph below the graph.

8. Look at the line graph in From the Literature Box 3.2. How would you describe in words what the graph says? Identify another way of graphing these data. Which would be the better graph? Why?

9. Go to www.fbi.gov/stats-services/crimestats and explore links to examples of basic descriptive statistics.

10. Go to www.ojjdp.ncjrs.org/ojstatbb/ and follow the links to statistical reports that interest you.

Student Study Site

Visit the open-access student study site at **www.sagepub.com/fitzgerald** for access to several study tools including eFlashcards, web quizzes, and additional appendices as well as links to SAGE journal articles and audio, video and web resources.

Describing Univariate Distributions

Learning Objectives

What you are expected not only to learn but to master in this chapter:

- How to describe univariate distributions
- The different shapes of distributions and ways statisticians characterize the different shapes
- Skewness and kurtosis
- Some of the differences among bell-shaped, normal, and other distributions
- Three measures of a distribution's central tendency (mean, median, and mode) from ungrouped and grouped scores
- Three measures of a distribution's dispersion (range, standard deviation, and variance)
- A special property of the mean
- Three measures of location in a distribution (quartiles, deciles, and percentiles)
- What missing data are and the problems they create for analysis

Introduction

In addition to calculating basic descriptive statistics such as frequency counts, percents, rates, and so on, and presenting these data in tables and graphs, statisticians often find it useful to characterize univariate data distributions as a whole. In particular, they describe and distinguish among univariate distributions on the basis of their general shapes, their "typical" variable values, and the extent to which those variable values tend to be close to each other or spread out—that is, their dispersion. The tools statisticians use for these tasks include bar and line graphs, classifications of distributions according to their shape (including degree of skewness and/or kurtosis); and measures of central tendency, dispersion, and location. These tools are essential in making sense of almost all statistical data and analyses.

Remember that it makes no sense to speak of the shape of a distribution of variable values measured at the nominal level because the location of the possible variable values on the horizontal axis is arbitrary. So, unless otherwise specified, we will be referring in this chapter to distributions of ordinal-, interval-, or ratio-level variables. For the sake of brevity, we often refer to variable values as scores in our discussion.

Different Distribution Shapes, Skewness, and Kurtosis

As you can see from Figures 3.2, 3.3b, and 3.4 in the previous chapter (see pp. 58–60), bar and line graphs can be said to have a shape. Figure 3.4 has the profile of a pyramid, for example. As you can imagine, the number of different shapes a frequency or relative frequency (percent) distribution might take is very large. Statisticians categorize distributions on the basis of their general shapes. Consider the distributions in Figure 4.1. Figure 4.1a illustrates several different types of bell-shaped curves, including one we have labeled a normal distribution. They are called **bell shaped** because, as you can see, they are shaped like bells. (How's that for clever labeling! Who said statisticians are devoid of common sense?!) The distributions in Figures 4.1b and 4.1c look like someone leaned on one side or the other of a bell-shaped distribution. As we will see later in this and subsequent chapters, knowing the shape of a distribution is very important in statistical analysis.

Note that we have identified areas on the left and right ends of the distributions in Figure 4.1 as the **tails of the distributions**. In frequency or percent distributions, these areas typically (though not always) correspond to the frequencies or percents of the lower and higher scores in the distributions.

Bell-Shaped and Normal Distributions

As we noted earlier, some distributions are bell shaped, like those in Figure 4.1a. Bell-shaped distributions are described as **symmetric** (think symmetry—"same shaped") **distributions** because if we were to divide the distribution in half vertically, the shape of the curve on one side of the distribution would be the mirror image of the curve's shape on the other side.

Figure 4.1 Types of Distribution With Tails Indicated

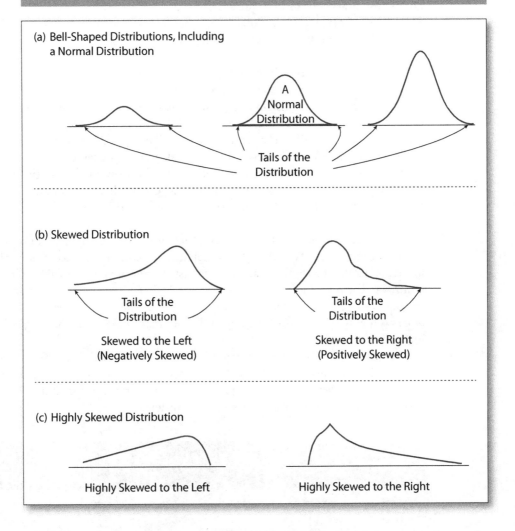

Some bell-shaped (symmetric) distributions have special properties that make them very useful in statistical analysis. In statistical parlance, they are called normal distributions or normal curves. The distribution in the middle of the three in Figure 4.1a is a normal distribution. For now, we define a **normal distribution** as a particular kind of bell-shaped (symmetric) distribution. We will have a great deal more to say about the special properties and varied uses of normal distributions in statistical analysis in the chapters that follow. The other two distributions, although symmetric, have shapes somewhat different from that of the normal distribution. The shapes of the distributions in Figures 4.1b and 4.1c also differ from the normal distribution. In the following two sections, we discuss two general ways in which statisticians differentiate between normal and non-normal distributions.

Skewness

Distributions like those in Figures 4.1b and 4.1c are called **skewed distributions**. They are not normal distributions, in part because they are not symmetric. The shape of a skewed distribution appears unbalanced, having a longer tail on one or the other of its ends.

Skewed distributions differ in the direction of their skewness—that is, distributions are said to be skewed to the left or the right. The direction of skewness is determined by which of the distribution's two tails is longer. If the longest tail is on the right side of the distribution, the distribution is said to be skewed to the right or **positively skewed** (think "skewed toward the higher variable values"). If the longest tail is on the left side, it is described as being skewed to the left or **negatively skewed** (think "skewed toward the lower variable values"). Skewed distributions can vary according to their degree (or amount) of skewness, as illustrated in Figures 4.1b and 4.1c. Basically, the longer the longest tail of a skewed distribution, the greater the degree of skewness.

Suppose we have scores on a different test for recruits, this time a group of correctional officer recruits, and the line graph distribution for their scores looks like that in Figure 4.2. Compare the shape of this distribution with that of the police recruit scores we discussed in Chapter 3 (see Figure 3.3b, p. 59). The distribution of police recruits' test scores is symmetric, whereas that of the correctional officer recruits' scores is highly skewed negatively, or to the left, made evident by the long tail extending to the left in Figure 4.2.

Skewness, then, is one way distributions may be classified and differentiated from normal distributions. Normal distributions are symmetric, not skewed. We will note in passing that there are ways of quantifying (measuring) a distribution's degree of skewness, but they are beyond the scope of this text.

Figure 4.2 Frequency Distribution Line Graph for Correctional Officer Recruit Test Scores

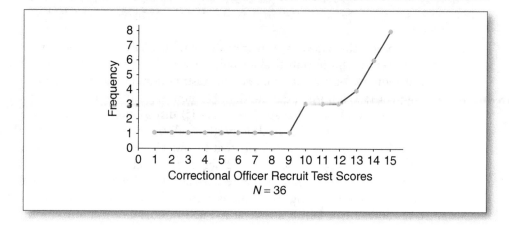

Kurtosis

Compare the three symmetric distributions in Figure 4.1a. Note, in particular, that in comparison with the normal distribution in the middle, the one on the far left is flatter and the one on the far right is more peaked. This dimension of a distribution is referred to as its **kurtosis**. Distributions that are flatter than a normal distribution are called **platykurtic** (platy—think flat, like a plate) and those that have sharper peaks are called **leptokurtic** (lepto—think tall and thin). As with skewness, a distribution's kurtosis may vary in degree or amount. In general, the more platykurtic (flat) is a distribution, the more spread out are the scores (i.e., the greater is the variation among the scores) and the more leptokurtic (peaked) is a distribution, the closer to each other are the scores in it (i.e., the less variation [dispersion] there is among the scores).

Normal distributions are said to have moderate kurtosis. They differ from other bell-shaped distributions because they are neither platykurtic nor leptokurtic, but, like Baby Bear's porridge, are just right kurtic—sometimes referred to as **mesokurtic** (meso—think moderately kurtic).

As with skewness, there are formulas for quantifying the degree of a distribution's kurtosis, but we will spare you a discussion of them, as well as the controversies that surround them.

Skewness and kurtosis, then, are features of distribution shapes that differentiate them from a normal distribution. We can now sharpen our definition of normal distributions a bit by saying they are symmetric, not skewed, and have moderate kurtosis. As we will see in this and later chapters, whether a distribution is normal or departs from normality in skewness or kurtosis is important information for many kinds of statistical analyses.

We turn now to a discussion of other ways of describing distributions as a whole, using measures of their central tendencies and dispersions.

Measures of Central Tendency

There are three basic **measures of the central tendency** of a distribution: the mean, the median, and the mode.

Mean

The **mean** is the arithmetic average of the individual numerical scores that make up a distribution of a variable measured at the interval or ratio level. It is calculated by summing all the scores and dividing by the number of scores that were included in the sum. Formula 4.1 gives us a distribution's mean score ($\bar{x}$).

$$\bar{x} = \frac{\Sigma x}{n} \qquad (4.1)$$

In the formula, x is a score (such as one person's exam score or one convict's sentence length or one department's annual budget, etc.), the Greek letter sigma Σ is a summation sign and n is the number of scores summed. So, Σx tells us to sum all the individual scores in the distribution. Dividing this sum by the number of scores (n) gives us the mean score ($\bar{x}$).

Let's use the police recruit exam scores we considered in Chapter 3 to illustrate the calculation of a mean. The frequency distribution table for these data is reproduced in column 2 of Table 4.1. (Ignore column 3 in Table 4.1 for now.) Instead of presenting the scores in a frequency distribution table, however, we will list all 36 scores individually in ascending order, beginning with the lowest score. The list would look like this: 8, 9, 9, 10, 10, 10, 11, 11, 11, 11, 12, 12, 12, 12, 12, 13, 13, 13, 13, 13, 13, 14, 14, 14, 14, 14, 15, 15, 15, 15, 16, 16, 16, 17, 17, 18. You should verify that this list accurately reproduces the data in Table 4.1 now.

We calculate the mean by adding the 36 scores in the distribution and dividing by 36, the number of scores. Thus, we would have

$$\Sigma x = 8 + 9 + 9 + 10 + 10 + 10 + \cdots + 16 + 16 + 16 + 17 + 17 + 18 = 468.$$

The sum of the 36 scores (Σx), then, is 468. The mean score for this distribution is the sum of scores ($\Sigma x = 468$) divided by the number of scores ($n = 36$).

$$\bar{x} = \frac{\Sigma x}{n} = \frac{468}{36} = 13$$

Hence, the mean or arithmetic average score on the test for the police recruits is 13.

Table 4.1 Frequency and Cumulative Frequency Distributions for Police Recruit Test Scores

Scores	Frequencies (f)	Cumulative Frequencies (cf)
8	1	1
9	2	3
10	3	6
11	4	10
12	5	15
13	6	21
14	5	26
15	4	30
16	3	33
17	2	35
18	1	36
Total	$N = 36$	

PAUSE, THINK, AND EXPLORE THE MEAN

In Formula 4.1, what happens to the value of $\bar{x}$ if the numerator (Σx) stays the same and n goes up? If n goes down? What happens to the value of $\bar{x}$ if the denominator (n) stays the same and the numerator goes up? If the numerator goes down? Can you tell anything about the shape of a distribution by knowing its mean?

For a little more practice, let's calculate the mean score for the 36 correctional officer recruits' test score distribution displayed in Figure 4.2's line graph. The corresponding frequency distribution is presented in column 2 of Table 4.2. (Ignore column 3 in this table for now.) Before proceeding, you should satisfy yourself that the line graph in Figure 4.2 and the frequency distribution in column 2 of Table 4.2 represent the same exam score data. This time, instead of summing the individual scores in the distribution to calculate the mean, we will first multiply each of the scores by its corresponding frequency as indicated in column 2 of Table 4.2 and then sum the results of these multiplications. This achieves the same mathematical result as listing the 36 scores individually and adding them. Then, we will divide the sum by the number of scores (36). To find the mean score for this distribution of correctional officer test scores, we would have the following calculations:

$$\begin{aligned}\bar{x}=\frac{\Sigma x}{n} &= [(1 \times 1) + (2 \times 1) + (3 \times 1) + (4 \times 1) + (5 \times 1) + (6 \times 1) \\ &\quad + (7 \times 1) + (8 \times 1) + (9 \times 1) + (10 \times 3) + (11 \times 3) + (12 \times 3) \\ &\quad + (13 \times 4) + (14 \times 6) + (15 \times 8)]/36 \\ &= [1 + 2 + 3 + 4 + 5 + 6 + 7 + 8 + 9 + 30 + 33 + 36 + 52 + 84 + 120]/36 \\ &= 400/36 \\ &= 11.11\end{aligned}$$

So, the mean for this distribution is 11.11 (rounded to the nearest hundredth).

Note that when we calculate a mean, the numerical values of the scores are included in the calculations. Means are appropriate measures of central tendency for variables measured at the interval or ratio level, but not for ordinal or nominal variables.

Median

The median is another way of gauging the central tendency of a distribution for variables measured at the ratio and interval level. It is also appropriate for ordinal-level variables. The **median** of a distribution is the score that divides the distribution of scores in such a way that half of the scores in the distribution are equal to or lower than that score and half are equal to or higher than that score. We can also express the location of a distribution's median score in terms of percents by noting that 50% of the scores in the distribution are equal to or less than the median score and 50% are equal

Table 4.2 Frequency and Cumulative Frequency Distributions for Correctional Officer Recruit Scores

Scores	Frequencies	Cumulative Frequencies (cf)
1	1	1
2	1	2
3	1	3
4	1	4
5	1	5
6	1	6
7	1	7
8	1	8
9	1	9
10	3	12
11	3	15
12	3	18
13	4	22
14	6	28
15	8	36
Total	N = 36	

to or greater than the median score. We say "equal to or . . ." here because of the possibility that the median score may fall somewhere in the midst of a group of equal (tied) scores in the distribution, a subject to which we will return later.

As its definition indicates, one way to find a distribution's median score is to arrange all of the scores in numerical order from lowest to highest and find the score that is located in the center (at the midpoint) of this array—that is, the score that has as many scores to its left as to its right in the array. Let's use the group of 36 police recruit test scores again to illustrate. Here's the array of these 36 test scores again: 8, 9, 9, 10, 10, 10, 11, 11, 11, 11, 12, 12, 12, 12, 12, 13, 13, 13, 13, 13, 13, 14, 14, 14, 14, 14, 15, 15, 15, 15, 16, 16, 16, 17, 17, 18. The location of the score at the center (midpoint) of any array of scores can be determined by first dividing the number of scores in the array by two (i.e., finding $n/2$, which tells us how many scores make up half of the scores in the distribution) and then counting in from either end to locate it. Because there are 36 scores ($n = 36$) in the distribution, the score located at the center or midpoint of the array must be located $n/2$ or $36/2 = 18$ scores in from either end. We invite you to count 18 scores in from either end of the array of scores immediately above now. When you do so, you will discover that, because there is an even number of scores, the midpoint of the array falls between two scores, in this case between two of the 13s. When the division point falls between scores, the statistical convention is to take the arithmetic average of these two scores—in this case, $13 + 13 = 26$ and $26/2 = 13$. The median of this distribution, then, is 13.

Now consider the correctional officer recruits' scores in Table 4.2. If we arrayed these 36 scores as we did for the police recruit scores, they would be as follows: 1, 2, 3, 4, 5, 6, 7, 8, 9, 10, 10, 10, 11, 11, 11, 12, 12, 12, 13, 13, 13, 14, 14, 14, 14, 14, 15, 15, 15, 15, 15, 15, 15, 15. You should satisfy yourself that this array is an accurate duplication of the scores and their frequencies in Table 4.2 and in the line graph in Figure 4.2. You can discover for yourself that the median score for this distribution falls between 12 and 13. So, to find the median score, we have $12 + 13 = 25$ and $25/2 = 12.5$. The median exam score for the distribution of correctional officer recruits, then, is 12.5.

Note that if the number of scores in a distribution is odd, a single score occupies the location in the array equidistant from the ends of the array. In such cases, that score would be the distribution's median score.

Of course, we don't actually have to array and count each of the scores in the way we just described to determine a distribution's median score. Instead, we can use a frequency distribution or, even better, a cumulative frequency distribution table like those we discussed in Chapter 3 to locate and determine the value of a distribution's median score.

For this illustration, let's return to the police recruit test score data. As we noted above, the frequency distribution table for these data is reproduced in column 2 of Table 4.1. The corresponding cumulative frequency distribution is in column 3 of that table. We know there are 36 scores in the distribution, and we know that the median score lies 18 scores from either end of the array. To determine the median score for the data in Table 4.1, we simply add the frequencies in column 1 in order (beginning with the frequency of the lowest score) until we arrive at a cumulative sum of 18 and note the score associated with that sum of frequencies. In this case, the 18th score would be one of the six scores of 13, so the median score for this distribution is 13. In a cumulative frequency distribution, as in column 3 of Table 4.1, this task is already done for us. We simply look for the *lowest* cumulative frequency that is *at least* 18 and identify the test score corresponding with that cumulative frequency. The score corresponding to this cumulative frequency is 13. Therefore, 13 is the median score of this distribution—the same result for this distribution that we arrived at earlier in the chapter using the array of 36 scores.

For a second illustration using cumulative frequencies to determine a median score, let's consider again the distribution of correctional officers' test score data. We would proceed in the same way as we did with the police recruit scores. Again, there are 36 scores, which means half the scores ($n/2 = 36/2$) equals 18. Looking at the cumulative frequency distribution in column 3 of Table 4.2, we see that a cumulative frequency of exactly 18 corresponds with a test score of 12. This means that 18 of the scores are 12 or lower and that, in turn, means 18 of the scores are higher than 12. You can confirm that, in this case, there are 18 scores equal to or lower than 12 and 18 scores higher than 12 by looking at the array of scores. Hence, the midpoint of the array of scores lies between 12 and 13. So, the median score for this distribution is $(12 + 13)/2 = 12.5$—again, the same result for this distribution we achieved previously.

PAUSE, THINK, AND EXPLORE THE MEDIAN

Considering how the median is determined, do you think the value of the median would change if a few very high scores were added to the distribution? Many very high scores? A few very low scores? Many low scores? A few high and many low scores? A few with the same value in the middle of the distribution? Does it make sense to determine a median for a nominal-level variable? Why or why not? Can you tell anything about the shape of a distribution by knowing its median? By knowing its mean and its median?

Note that in identifying the median of a distribution, the numerical values of the scores are taken into consideration, but only in a limited way. That is, a score's quantity is used only to rank it as higher or lower than or the same as another score. How much higher or lower is not important.

Mode

A distribution's **mode** is the score (variable value) that occurs most frequently in a distribution. Modes may be used to describe distributions of scores regardless of their level of measurement. That is, because the mode does not depend on the numerical value of the scores, only on their frequencies, a mode is an appropriate measure of central tendency even for nominal-level variable distributions.

By inspecting column 2 in the frequency distribution table for the police recruits' test scores in Table 4.1, it's easy to locate the mode. Because the score 13 appears six times, and no other score appears more than five times, the mode of this distribution is 13. Similarly, a quick look at column 2 in Table 4.2 tells you that this distribution's mode is 15 because 15 is the score that occurs with the greatest frequency in this distribution.

It is easy to find the modes of distributions presented as line graphs as well. We simply look for the highest point(s) on the line and determine the corresponding score. Why? Because the highest point(s) in a line graph correspond to the scores with the highest frequency in the distribution. You can satisfy yourself that this yields the same results as we just achieved immediately above by looking at the line graph distributions in Figure 3.4 (p. 60) for the police officer recruits' test score data and in Figure 4.2 for the correctional officer recruits' test score data.

> **PAUSE, THINK, AND EXPLORE THE MODE**
>
> Considering how the mode is determined, what changes in the shape of a distribution would likely change the value of its mode? Would adding a few low scores? A few high scores? Many low scores? Many high scores? A few high scores and a few low scores? A few high scores and many low scores? Can you tell anything about the shape of a distribution by knowing its mode? Its mean, median, and mode (where appropriate)?

Distributions have only one mean and median score, but they may have more than one mode. Those with one mode are called **unimodal** (think uni = one) **distributions**. Those with two modes are called **bimodal** (think bi = two) **distributions** and those with more than two are called **multimodal** (think multi = many) **distributions**. In practice, a distribution does not have to have scores with exactly the same frequency to be called bimodal or multimodal. What counts is the number of "humps" or high spots in a distribution's line graph, as indicated in Figure 4.3c. Examples of these different types of distributions are found in Figure 4.3.

Collapsing Variable Values

Sometimes, instead of including each possible variable value (score) in a distribution, adjacent variable values are combined to form groups of variable values. This procedure is referred to as **collapsing variable values**, or sometimes as collapsing categories, and the result is a set of **grouped scores**. Frequencies, percents, cumulative frequencies, or cumulative percents can be determined for the scores included in each of the groups and entered in a distribution table or graph. For example, the police recruit scores (see Table 4.1) might be combined into groups consisting of exam scores ranging from 8–10, 11–13, 14–16, and 17–18. Now, in effect and for the purposes of presentation and analysis, the test score variable has 4 instead of 11 possible values. As you can determine from Table 4.1, the frequencies corresponding to these four groups of scores would be 6, 15, 12, and 3, for a total of 36.

Collapsing variable values simplifies data presentation and analysis and is perhaps most useful in some circumstances when a variable has a very large number of possible values. For example, if we have data on the annual salaries of a few hundred court

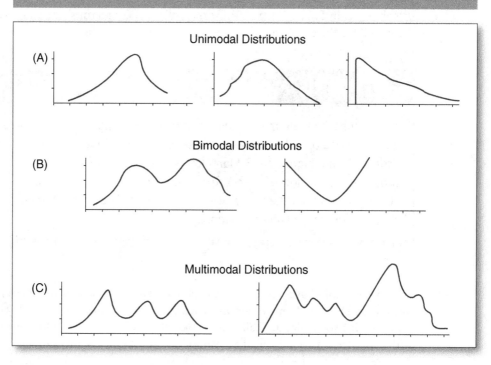

Figure 4.3 Unimodal, Bimodal, and Multimodal Distributions

administrators, the number of different possible salaries would likely be large and the frequency for any one of them might be quite small. So, it would be appropriate to combine the salary variable values into groups consisting of nonoverlapping salary ranges for purposes of presenting and analyzing the salary data. Variables measured at any level may be collapsed, but those at the interval or ratio level are collapsed most often for some data presentations and analyses, simply because they are likely to have a large number of different possible values with small frequencies.

Like the list of all possible scores, the groups into which they are combined must be mutually exclusive and exhaustive. (For a review of these concepts see Chapter 2, p. 23.)

What is at stake in deciding whether or not to collapse categories? Obviously, some possibly important detail is sacrificed if our variable is originally measured with a larger number of possible values and the data are analyzed and presented with fewer values. Although there is no point in measuring a variable with greater detail and precision than is justified by the purposes at hand, it is also true that, short of doing another study, the researcher will never have a greater level of detail available for analysis than that recorded originally. In analyzing the data, the researcher can always reduce the number of categories, but it is very difficult to increase the number of categories beyond those with which the data for a particular variable were recorded in the first place. Within reason, then, the original raw data deliberately might be collected in more detail than the researcher expects to use for the analysis. In analyzing the data, if the researcher encounters unexpected or otherwise intriguing results, the more detailed data may come in handy as she pursues these leads.

How do you decide how many groups to create and which adjacent scores to collapse into each group? A number of factors might be considered in deciding which categories to collapse. First, a variable may have more or less "natural" divisions. For example, an age variable might be broken down into categories corresponding roughly to infancy, childhood, adolescence, adulthood, and old age—assuming those divisions make sense with respect to the problem being investigated. Second, divisions could be based on the categories, natural or not, included in a hypothesis, such as "Middle-class people are more likely to support the police than are upper-class or working-class people." If the social class variable were operationalized in terms of annual income, it would be reasonable to break these data into three income categories corresponding to the three social classes mentioned in the hypothesis. Finally, by examining the frequency distribution of the variable, the original categories could be combined so that a sufficiently large number of cases is represented in each category to permit meaningful analysis. Caution is in order here, however. Categories should not be collapsed in a way that violates the theoretical basis underlying the study, even though it may be expedient to do so. Some or all of these considerations must be weighed in any decision to collapse categories in a particular way. You should remember, however, that the way data are collapsed almost certainly will influence the results of the analysis. Consequently, the procedure and criteria used in collapsing categories should always be reported.

Finding a Mode, a Median, and a Mean for Distributions of Grouped Scores

As we noted earlier, when scores (possible variable values) are collapsed and grouped, information is lost. We cannot determine the mode for the scores in a grouped score distribution, for example, but only the group of scores qualifying as the modal group. Note that the score occurring with the highest frequency in the corresponding ungrouped distribution may not even be included in the modal group of collapsed scores. Similarly, we cannot determine the median score for a grouped distribution, but only the group of scores within which the median falls. Finding the mean for a distribution of grouped scores raises additional issues, as we will see.

Suppose we have data on court administrators' beginning salaries in 260 jurisdictions as indicated in Table 4.3. The data are said to be grouped because each value of the salary variable consists not of a specific salary, but of a range of salaries. Table 4.3 includes frequencies and cumulative frequencies corresponding with each of the salary categories. (Ignore column 4 in the table for now.)

To determine the modal category for grouped salaries, we simply search for the highest group frequency. In Table 4.3, column 2, the highest frequency is 46, and it is associated with the salary group $30,001–$34,000. So, $30,001–$34,000 is the modal group of salaries in this distribution.

Table 4.3 Beginning Salaries of Court Administrators

Beginning Salaries ($)	Frequencies (f)	Cumulative Frequencies (cf)	Cumulative Percents (cp)
5,000–10,000	10	10	3.85
10,001–14,000	14	24	9.23
14,001–18,000	18	42	16.15
18,001–22,000	25	67	25.77
22,001–26,000	29	96	36.92
26,001–30,000	32	128	49.23
30,001–34,000	46	174	66.92
34,001–38,000	39	213	81.92
38,001–42,000	21	234	90.00
42,001–46,000	15	249	95.77
46,001–50,000	11	260	100.00
Total	N = 260		

To determine the median of this distribution, we begin in basically the same way as for finding the modal group—by examining the cumulative frequencies. The salary group that must include the median salary is determined as follows: Recall that we identify a median by dividing the array of scores in half. In this case, $n = 260$ and $n/2 = 130$. We begin with the frequency corresponding to the lowest salary category (which is a frequency of 10 corresponding to the $5,000–$10,000 category). We successively add frequencies until we reach the salary category with a cumulative frequency of at least 130, which is 174 and it corresponds to the $30,001–$34,000 group of salaries. Again, the cumulative frequencies in column 3 of Table 4.3 take care of this task for us. The lowest cumulative frequency of at least 130 is the $30,001–$34,000 category. So, we can say that the median category of salaries in this distribution is $30,001–$34,000.

The median score can also be expressed in terms of percents and cumulative percents. Consider column 4 of Table 4.3, which is the cumulative percent distribution for the grouped salaries. Because 50% (one half) of the scores are equal to or lower than the median score, we look for the cumulative percent that is lowest but at least 50%. That cumulative percent is 66.92, which, again, corresponds to the $30,001–$34,000 salary category.

The procedure for determining the mode for grouped scores yields a category or group of scores with the highest frequency, although the mode for the ungrouped distribution may not fall within the modal group. The procedure for determining the median yields the group of scores within which it must fall. In contrast, the procedure for determining the mean of a grouped score distribution produces a single value, but as we will see, it is not likely to be accurate.

To find the mean of the grouped scores distribution in Table 4.3, the first step is to *find the midpoint of the range of each group of scores* in the distribution. The lowest salary group has a range of $5,000–$10,000. The difference between the lowest and highest salaries in this group is $10,000 − $5,000 = $5,000, which is another way of expressing what the range of salaries in this group is. To find the midpoint of the salary group, we need to know what half of this difference is. Half of this difference is $5,000/2 = $2,500. To find the midpoint of the $5,000–$10,000 salary group, we add the $2,500 to the lowest salary in the group, which is $5,000 + $2,500 = $7,500. So, the midpoint of the salary group $5,000–$10,000 is $7,500.

We'll do one more for practice. In the case of the salary group $10, 001–$14,000, the difference between the highest and lowest salaries in the group $14,000 − $10,001 = $3,999. Next, we find one half of this difference, which is $3,999/2 = $1,999.50. Finally, we add this difference to the lowest salary in the group, which is $10,001 + $1,999. 50 = $12,000.50. So, $12,000.50 is the midpoint of the range of salaries in the salary group $10,001–$14,000. This procedure is repeated for each salary group in the distribution. The midpoint for each salary group is in column 1 of Table 4.4. Once we have calculated the midpoints of the salary ranges for each salary group, we are ready to take the next steps in calculating a mean salary for this grouped score distribution.

Once the midpoints have been determined, we multiply each salary group's midpoint salary by its frequency (see columns 1 and 2 in Table 4.4). In effect, this treats each salary in a salary group as if it were equivalent to the midpoint salary we calculated for the group. We've listed the results of these calculations for each of the salary groups in column 3 of Table 4.4.

The final steps are to add these products and divide by the total number of salaries in the distribution. Those calculations are included at the bottom of Table 4.4. So, the mean we have arrived at for this distribution of grouped scores is $28,950.48 (rounded).

In the absence of other information, the single value for any mean we calculate using these procedures must be regarded as an *estimate* of the mean salary for a grouped score distribution. For it to be accurate, the actual mean of the salaries in each group would have to equal the mean we arrived at by finding the midpoint of the range of salaries in each group. Although this is possible, it is extremely unlikely. As a result, our estimate is likely to be in error and, depending on the distribution of actual salaries within the groups, may, in fact, be quite a bit in error. For this reason, we strongly recommend using the actual scores (salaries or whatever the variable values are) to calculate a mean whenever possible. We also recommend being very skeptical about the accuracy of means calculated according to the procedures we have described. Finally,

Table 4.4 Salary Group Midpoints, Frequencies, and Calculations for the Mean

Salary Group Midpoints ($)	Frequencies (f)	Midpoints × Frequencies ($)
7,500.00	10	75,000.00
12,000.50	14	168,007.00
16,000.50	18	288,009.00
20,000.50	25	500,012.50
24,000.50	29	696,014.50
28,000.50	32	896,016.00
32,000.50	46	1,472,023.00
36,000.50	39	1,404,019.50
40,000.50	21	840,010.50
44,000.50	15	660,007.50
48,000.50	11	528,005.50
Totals	N = 260	7,527,125.00

Note: Mean = $\Sigma x/n$ = $7,527,125/260 = $28,950.48 (rounded).

note that the procedures we have described for estimating a grouped data mean should be used only when the mean is an appropriate measure of central tendency—that is, for variables measured at the interval or ratio level.

Selecting Appropriate Measures of Central Tendency

Selecting appropriate measures of central tendency depends on a number of considerations. Among the most important are (a) the shape of the distribution, (b) the level at which a variable is measured, and (c) whether the variable is discrete or continuous.

First, selecting appropriate measures of central tendency for distributions should be guided by their shapes. As we discovered earlier in the chapter, for bell-shaped distributions like the one for police recruit test scores in Figure 3.3b, the mean, the median, and the mode all have the same value. In our police recruit example, that score was 13. Because they all have the same value, a statistician could report any one of the measures of central tendency without misleading herself or a reader. For skewed distributions, the values of the different measures of central tendency almost certainly are not equal—in fact, they are sometimes quite different. For the correctional officer recruits' test score data, for example, we found that the distribution had a mean score of 11.11, a median score of 12.5, and a mode of 15.

In general, if a unimodal distribution is skewed to the left (negatively), the value of the mean will be less than that of the median and the median less than the mode. If the distribution is skewed to the right (positively), the value of the mode will be less than the median and the median less than the mean.

Figure 4.4a displays three bell-shaped distributions (I, II, and III), each with a different kurtosis. Figure 4.4b includes two skewed distributions, one positively skewed and one negatively skewed, showing the relationships among the values of the mean, median, and mode for the different types of distributions.

Why should these relationships among the three measures of central tendency hold for these types of distributions? Take another look at the skewed distributions in Figure 4.4b. Recall that when we calculate a mean, we add the numerical scores—that is, we take the *quantitative values* of the scores into account. A few extreme scores would, therefore, "move" the mean in their direction—that is, toward the tail in which they are located in the distribution. A few high scores (relative to the other scores in the distribution) would increase the mean score, whereas a few low scores (relative to the other scores in the distribution) would decrease the mean score. The median score is influenced by the scores' quantitative values *only* to the extent that they determine the rank order of the scores. The quantitative differences among them are not taken into account.

The annual income distribution in the United States is an example of a positively skewed distribution. Because a few persons have extremely large incomes, the mean annual income in the United States is considerably larger than the median income. As another example, recall that we found the mean of the distribution of correctional officer recruits' test scores (a negatively skewed distribution) was 11.11, the median was 12.5, and the mode was 15. Note also that the more skewed a distribution, the larger the differences among these measures of central tendency.

Finally, the mode is not influenced at all by the quantitative values of the scores, but only by the frequencies with which they occur in the distribution. For unimodal distributions like those in Figure 4.4b, then, it makes sense that the relationships among the measures of central tendency would be as illustrated.

Clearly, the measures of central tendency for skewed distributions, especially highly skewed ones, that are selected for reporting can produce substantial differences in the impression given of the data included in the distribution. If a tester wanted to brag about how well the correctional officer recruits performed (see Table 4.2), he might choose to report the modal score, 15. On the other hand, if the tester wanted to play down the group's performance, she might report the mean score, 11.11. Choosing a particular measure of central tendency for skewed distributions, then, requires special caution, because the choice influences the interpretation of the data. In the absence of other information (such as a statement that the distribution is normal or otherwise bell shaped), the safest and most honest way to describe the central tendency of a distribution is to report all three measures. In doing so, there is less chance of misleading or being misled.

Figure 4.4 Means, Medians, and Modes for Bell Shaped and Skewed Distributions

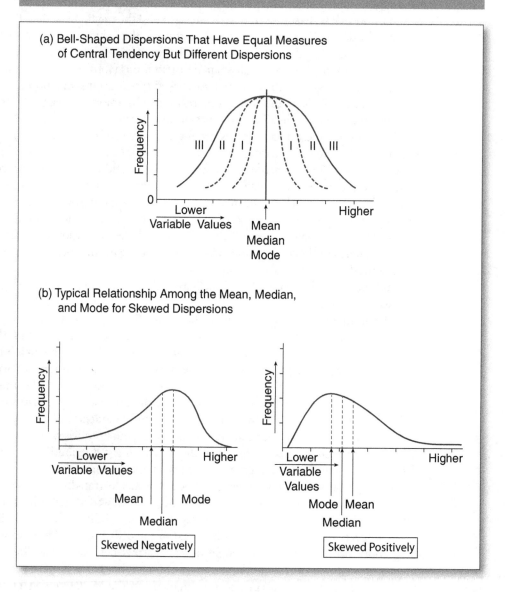

Note that we can turn the knowledge we have just gained about the relationships between the shapes of distributions and measures of central tendency around. That is, if we know all three of a unimodal distribution's measures of central tendency, we know quite a bit about its general shape. Substantial differences among the reported mean, median, and mode of a distribution are a sure sign that the distribution is highly skewed in one direction or another. And, because of the relationships between the relative sizes among the three measures of central tendency and the shape of a skewed distribution, we can usually tell if the distribution is positively or negatively skewed and roughly to what degree it is skewed. If, on the other hand, the measures of central tendency all have about the same value, we can be pretty sure it is at least an approximately symmetrical distribution. Furthermore, one or more of the measures of central tendency may not be appropriate for the level at which the data are measured. A variable such as sex measured at the nominal level has only one appropriate measure of central tendency: the mode. It makes no sense to speak of "mean sex" (except in another context, of course) or "median sex." For ordinal-level data—data that permit the ranking of variable values—both median and mode are appropriate but the mean is not. In the case of interval or ratio levels of measurement, all three of the measures of central tendency, including the mean, may be used.

Finally, the selection of an appropriate measure of central tendency also depends on whether the variable investigated is discrete or continuous. (See Chapter 2, pp. 23–24.) Modes and medians can be used with either discrete or continuous variables. Strictly speaking, a mean should be used only when the variable is continuous. In practice, though, statisticians do calculate means for discrete data, telling us, for example, that the average American family has 2.3 children—which, of course, is impossible unless you count the gestation time of a fetus at the time family size is measured. A mode for discrete data cannot assume a fractional value, and a median can do so only when the distribution contains an even number of scores.

A few additional concerns are in order when considering measures of central tendency. You may hear or read in the mass media that the median score is higher (or lower) than half of the scores in a distribution. This is, at best, an imprecise characterization and, at worst, a seriously misleading one. Remember that because of the way we arrive at a median score, we can say only that approximately half of the test scores were above the median and approximately half were below the median. The "approximately" is required because, as we noted in our earlier discussion of the median, the median score may be located among tied scores. The larger the number of such scores tied with the median score, the more inaccurate is a statement that half the scores lie above and half are below the median. That's why it is always advisable to say that a median score is equal to or higher than half the scores in the distribution and equal to or lower than half the scores in the distribution.

For the reasons cited previously, we strongly recommend looking at a frequency distribution in graph form before choosing measures of central tendency. A quick glance can tell you if the distribution is approximately bell shaped, if there are extreme scores, and so on. We also strongly recommend reporting all three measures of central tendency in most cases.

We conclude our discussion of measures of central tendency by observing that the terms *average* and *typical* are often used imprecisely. Any one of the measures of central tendency may be referenced by such terms. Be sure to specify in your own work—and insist that others specify in their work—which measure is being used, and remember that measures of central tendency for skewed distributions, or distributions with extreme scores even if they are not skewed, can be misleading.

Measures of Dispersion

A more complete description of a frequency distribution can be provided if, in addition to its central tendency, we know something about its dispersion.

A distribution's **measure of dispersion** indicates how spread out the variable's values are in the distribution. Consider again Figure 4.4a, where several bell-shaped distributions have been drawn on the same scale. Although all of these distributions are bell shaped and have the same mean, median, and mode, they represent quite different arrays, one spanning most of the possible scores (III), and one encompassing only a small portion of them (I). Measures of dispersion quantify these differences.

Range

The **range** of a distribution is indicated by the largest and the smallest variable values that appear in the distribution. For the distribution of police recruit test scores in Table 4.1, the lowest score was 8 and the highest was 18; therefore, one way of reporting the distribution's range is to say that scores range from 8 through 18. Sometimes, the range is indicated as a single number, arrived at by subtracting the smallest score from the largest one (in our example, 18 – 8 for a range of 10). Note, however, that when the range is reported only as a single number, the reader has no way of knowing what the highest and lowest scores obtained were, and it is, to some extent, inaccurate because 11 possible scores, not 10, are included in the range. If the range is reported in the latter way, it is best, therefore, to report the former as well.

In addition, it can be helpful to put the *observed* range of variable values in the context of the range of *possible* variable values. Doing so may well influence the interpretation of the data. For example, if the possible range of test scores was from 0 to 100, but the range of observed scores was 8 to 18, this contrast provides potentially important information about the recruits' exam performance.

Average Deviation

The average deviation from the mean is seldom used in statistical analysis. We discuss it briefly here, however, as a step toward understanding the next two measures of dispersion to be considered: the variance and standard deviation.

In statistical lingo, the word *deviation* refers to how much a score in a distribution differs (deviates) from the distribution's mean score. That is, it refers to the arithmetic difference between the score and the distribution's mean score. If a distribution has a mean score of 25 and a particular score in the distribution is 12, the deviation from the mean for that score is 25 – 12 = 13.

The **average deviation** from the mean is the mean of the differences between a distribution's mean score and each of the individual scores in the distribution. To find the average deviation from the mean, the first step is to calculate the mean and then subtract each of the scores in the distribution from it. The absolute value of the differences (that is, the value without regard to a plus or minus sign) is used in these calculations. Why? Because it is a special mathematical characteristic of the mean that, if we take the signs into account, the sum of the signed deviations from the mean is always zero. The absolute value differences are then added and the total is divided by the number of scores in the distribution.

We can use the set of police recruit test scores in Table 4.5 to illustrate. (These are the same data as in Table 4.1, except that we have listed all the scores individually in Table 4.5. You should satisfy yourself that the two tables contain the same data.) Recall that we found the mean score was 13. Ignoring the signs, subtracting 13 from each of the 36 scores in column 1 gives us the absolute values of the differences (deviations) shown in column 4 of Table 4.5. (Ignore columns 2 and 5 in Table 4.5 for now.) The sum of the absolute values of the differences (column 4) is 70, and because there are 36 scores, the average difference, or deviation, is 70/36 = 1.9 (rounded to the nearest tenth). In general, the greater the average deviation of the scores from the distribution's mean score, the more spread out the scores and the larger the range of scores in the distribution.

Variance and Standard Deviation

The variance (symbolized as s^2) and the standard deviation (symbolized as s) are the most frequently used and reported measures of dispersion. They are closely related to the average deviation from the mean. As its name suggests, the standard deviation for a distribution expresses the differences between the scores and the mean in standardized units (i.e., units of equal size) for that particular distribution. The standard deviation of a distribution is the square root of its variance, so we need to calculate the variance first.

To calculate the **variance** (s^2), we begin with the absolute differences between the mean and each of the scores in the distribution that we calculated to find the average deviation from the mean. (See column 4 of Table 4.5). Then, we square each of these differences (i.e., multiply the deviation times the deviation—see column 5 of Table 4.5) and add the results. Finally, the sum of these squared deviations is divided by the number of scores in the distribution as in Formula 4.2.

$$s^2 = \frac{\Sigma(\bar{x}-x)^2}{n} \qquad (4.2)$$

In Formula 4.2, s^2 is the variance of the scores in the distribution, n is the number of scores in the distribution, and $\Sigma(\bar{x} - x)^2$ indicates the sum of the squared deviations of each individual score from the mean score. In statistical lingo, the **sum of squared deviations from the mean** is often shortened to the **sum of squares.** We will follow this convention from time to time in the following chapters. Recall that, in discussing average deviation, we took absolute values of the deviations in order to avoid the problem that arises from the fact that if we pay attention to the sign, the sum of deviations from the mean is always zero. Squaring the deviations from the mean also solves the problem of signed deviations because when we multiply signed numbers, a plus times a plus is a plus and a minus times a minus is also a plus. Furthermore, it turns out that squared deviations have some properties especially useful in statistical analyses, as we will see in later chapters.

Table 4.5 Deviations and Other Calculations for Police Recruit Test Scores ($N = 36$)

Scores (x)	Square of Scores (x^2)	(Mean) ($\bar{x}$)	Difference (Absolute Values) From Mean $|(\bar{x} - x)|$	Squared Difference or Deviation From Mean $(\bar{x} - x)^2$
8	64	13	5	25
9	81	13	4	16
9	81	13	4	16
10	100	13	3	9
10	100	13	3	9
10	100	13	3	9
11	121	13	2	4
11	121	13	2	4
11	121	13	2	4
11	121	13	2	4
12	144	13	1	1
12	144	13	1	1
12	144	13	1	1
12	144	13	1	1
12	144	13	1	1
13	169	13	0	0
13	169	13	0	0
13	169	13	0	0
13	169	13	0	0
13	169	13	0	0
13	169	13	0	0
14	196	13	1	1
14	196	13	1	1
14	196	13	1	1

Scores (x)	Square of Scores (x^2)	(Mean) ($\bar{x}$)	Difference (Absolute Values) From Mean $|(\bar{x} - x)|$	Squared Difference or Deviation From Mean $(\bar{x} - x)^2$
14	196	13	1	1
14	196	13	1	1
15	225	13	2	4
15	225	13	2	4
15	225	13	2	4
15	225	13	2	4
16	256	13	3	9
16	256	13	3	9
16	256	13	3	9
17	289	13	4	16
17	289	13	4	16
18	324	13	5	25
$\Sigma x = 468$	$\Sigma x^2 = 6{,}294$		$\Sigma(|\bar{x} - x|) = 70$	$\Sigma(\bar{x} - x)^2 = 210$

PAUSE, THINK, AND EXPLORE THE VARIANCE

What would happen to the value of s^2 if the range or average deviation of the scores was increased? If the range or average deviation was decreased? If the numerator stayed the same, but n increased? Or decreased? Which has the greater impact on s^2—changing n or changing $\Sigma(\bar{x} - x)^2$? Can you tell anything about the shape of a distribution if you know its variance?

To calculate the **standard deviation**, we take the square root of the variance. This calculation is given by Formula 4.3.

$$s = \sqrt{\frac{\Sigma(\bar{x} - x)^2}{n}} \qquad (4.3)$$

Applying Formula 4.3 to the data from Table 4.5, we have the following:

$$s = \sqrt{\frac{\Sigma(\bar{x}-x)^2}{n}}$$

$$= \sqrt{\frac{(13-8)^2+(13-9)^2+(13-9)^2+\cdots+(13-17)^2+(13-17)^2+(13-18)^2}{36}}$$

$$= \sqrt{\frac{(+5)^2+(+4)^2+(+4)^2+\cdots+(-4)^2+(-4)^2+(-5)^2}{36}}$$

$$= \sqrt{\frac{25+16+16+\cdots+16+16+25}{36}}$$

$$= \sqrt{\frac{210}{36}}$$

$$= \sqrt{5.8}$$

$$= 2.4$$

PAUSE, THINK, AND EXPLORE THE STANDARD DEVIATION

What would happen to the value of s if the range or average deviation of scores was increased? If the range or average deviation was decreased? If the numerator stayed the same, but n increased? Or decreased? Which has the greater impact on s—changing n or changing $\Sigma(\bar{x} - x)^2$? Can you tell anything about the shape of a distribution if you know its standard deviation? If s^2 doubles, how much does s change? If s^2 triples, how much does s change? If it quadruples, how much does s change? Do you see a pattern? Can you tell anything about the shape of a distribution by knowing its standard deviation?

As with the average deviation from the mean, the greater the dispersion of the scores in the distribution, the larger the variance and standard deviation. Because it is easier to use, Formula 4.4 (which is algebraically equivalent to Formula 4.3) is usually preferred for calculating the standard deviation by hand.

$$s = \sqrt{\frac{\Sigma x^2}{n} - \left(\frac{\Sigma x}{n}\right)^2} \qquad (4.4)$$

The term on the left side of the minus sign under the square root tells us to square each of the scores in the distribution, sum these squares, and divide that sum by n. The term on the right side of the minus sign under the square root tells us to sum the scores in the distribution, divide that sum by n, and square the result. To find the value of s, we subtract the latter from the former and take the square root of the result.

Applying Formula 4.4 to our data from Table 4.5, rounding to the nearest tenth, we have the following:

$$\begin{aligned} s &= \sqrt{\frac{\sum x^2}{n} - \left(\frac{\sum x}{n}\right)^2} \\ &= \sqrt{\frac{6{,}294}{36} - \left(\frac{468}{36}\right)^2} \\ &= \sqrt{\frac{6{,}294}{36} - (13)^2} \\ &= \sqrt{174.8 - 169} \\ &= \sqrt{5.8} \\ &= 2.4 \end{aligned}$$

In our calculations, we have plugged the sums of columns 1 and 2 of Table 4.5 and $n = 36$ into the appropriate places in our formula. We find in the final stages of our calculations that $s = \sqrt{174.8 - 169} = \sqrt{5.8} = 2.4$. The variance of the scores (s^2) is, of course, 5.8. As expected, these values for the standard deviation and variance are the same as those we found applying Formulas 4.3 and 4.2, respectively.

What use can be made of standard deviations and variances beyond being a measure of a distribution's dispersion? It turns out that they are very useful in many different kinds of statistical analysis, as we shall see beginning with Chapter 5. For now, we will just note that, as their names indicate, standard deviations, like percents, are *standardized* quantities and can be used to facilitate comparisons among different distributions.

Selecting Appropriate Measures of Dispersion

Each measure of dispersion has its own strengths and limitations. Choosing the most appropriate one depends largely on the level at which the variable is measured and the characteristics of the distribution.

The range is most affected by relatively large and relatively small variable values that would fall on the far left or far right (the tails) of a frequency distribution graph. For example, if all of a distribution's variable values fell between 35 and 50 except one that was 10, reporting the range as 10 to 50 does not describe the actual dispersion of the distribution's variable values very well. Also, the possible range of scores should be reported along with the observed range.

As we noted earlier, the average deviation is seldom used in statistical analysis. The variance and the standard deviation from the mean express how far, on average, variable values differ from the mean variable value, but they do not in themselves tell us what the range of the variable values is. These measures are also greatly influenced by extreme variable values, though less so than the range. Because extreme scores have a disproportionate influence on means and especially on variances and standard deviations (remember deviations are squared in calculating these measures of dispersion), a case can be made in some situations for eliminating extreme variable values from a descriptive analysis, but doing so should always be reported.

Although a range can appropriately be used with either discrete or continuous data measured at the ordinal level or above, both the variance and the standard deviation assume that the data are continuous and measured at least at the interval level. Again, as in the case of measures of central tendency, in practice these measures of dispersion are often used with discrete data. Doing so often yields quantitatively nonsensical but interpretable results, similar to 2.3 for the mean family size in the United States. When done cautiously and explicitly, little harm is done in this compromise with statistical rules.

As with measures of central tendency, we strongly recommend looking at the distribution in bar or line graph form before selecting measures of dispersion. For bell-shaped distributions, including normal distributions, the standard deviation (or variance) gives us a pretty good picture of the dispersion of a distribution's scores. As we will see in Chapter 5, however, the standard deviations of skewed distributions may be misleading.

Of course, a more complete summary of a data distribution is provided by reporting both its measure(s) of central tendency and its measures of dispersion. Taken together, these quantities indicate important aspects of the distribution's shape and other characteristics. The From the Literature Box 4.1 illustrates how measures of central tendency and dispersion combine to present a summary description of a distribution.

We conclude this part of our discussion of measures of central tendency and dispersion by noting that, although the same cannot be said of all distributions, if we know the mean and standard deviation (or variance) of a *normal* distribution, we can reconstruct it in its entirety. We have more to say about normal distributions in the next chapter.

A Special Property of the Mean

A distribution's mean score has a special property in relation to the rest of the scores in the distribution that we will find useful in coming chapters. In particular, *the mean score of a distribution is the score that minimizes the sum of the deviations and of the squared deviations (and, hence, of the standard deviation and variance) for that distribution.* That is, if you picked any score in the distribution other than one equivalent to the mean score, calculated the squared deviation of each of the scores in the distribution from it, and summed those deviations, this sum would be larger than the sum of the squared deviations from the mean score. In this sense, the mean score is the best representative of all the scores in a distribution because the differences between it and the other scores are the smallest possible. We might also say that we could use the mean score as the best *estimate* of the scores in the distribution. We make use of this and other special properties of means, sums of squares, standard deviations, and variances on many occasions throughout the remainder of this book.

From the Literature Box 4.1

John L. Worrall and Robert G. Morris were interested in the relationship between certain prison-level variables, especially custody level, and inmate violations of prison rules. They analyzed Texas Department of Corrections data from more than 7,000 Texas inmates in 47 Texas penal institutions on April 28, 2008. As part of their preliminary analysis, they prepared a table that included lists of their dependent and independent variables divided into what they term "dichotomous variables" and "continuous variables." For the dichotomous variables (a nominal-level "yes" or "no" categorization), they give frequencies and percents. For the continuous variables (ratio-level measures), they give means, standard deviations, and minimum and maximum values (range). Part of the table in which these data are included is reproduced in the following.

	Dichotomous variables			Continuous variables			
	Obs.	Freq.[a]	Pct.	M	SD	Minimum	Maximum
GS	71,203	2,667	3.75	—	—	—	—
Good time lost	71,203	32,767	46.02	—	—	—	—
Prison-level variables							
Staff to inmate ratio	47[5]	—	—	0.18	0.03	0.12	0.32
Percentage with Prior incarc.	47	—	—	0.34	0.09	0.16	0.56
Racial Integration index	47	—	—	0.87	0.02	0.75	0.90
Percentage gang member	47	—	—	0.10	0.08	0.00	0.27
Percentage GS	47	—	—	0.03	0.04	0.00	0.16

a. Frequency refers to the number of "yes" responses, or responses coded with a 1.

b. Data are from the same institution over the past five years.

c. There were a handful of missing observations for this and the next variable.

d. White served as the reference category. There were 20.932 white inmates.

e. The observations were constant across 47 prisons.

Source: From Worrall, John L. & Morris, Robert G. (2011). Inmate Custody Levels and Prison Rule Violations. *The Prison Journal* 91:131–157. Retrieved June 13, 2012 from http://tpj.sagepub.com/content/91/2/131.

Measures of Location in a Distribution

Suppose that you have just received a report on the results of a scholastic achievement test that you and 267,598 other students have taken, and your score on the test was 575. This information would not be very helpful to you, would it? In order to make sense of your score, it would be useful to know the mean, the median, and the mode, as well as the range and standard deviation or variance of the scores' distribution. These measures of central tendency and dispersion would give you some sense of where you stood in relation to others who took the test.

There are other ways, however, of locating a score in a distribution of scores that would be of more help in locating your score in a distribution of scores. One such procedure is to calculate what are referred to as **measures of location** in a distribution. We discuss three such measures of the location of a score in a distribution: quartiles, deciles, and percentiles.

Quartile, Decile, and Percentile Analyses

The median score of a distribution, you will recall, is found by dividing the distribution's scores arrayed in ascending numerical order into two groups, each of which contains the same number of scores. What if, by extending the procedure used to determine the value of the median, the scores were divided into more than two groups? In principle, we could divide the scores into any number of groups, each containing the same number of scores, as long as the number of scores is equal to or greater than the number of groups we chose to create. In practice, statisticians often use three different subdivisions of the array of scores in a distribution: quartiles, deciles, and percentiles. **Quartiles** are arrived at by dividing the scores into four groups, **deciles** are based on a division of the scores into 10 groups, and whole **percentiles** are determined by dividing the scores into 100 groups. Collectively, these descriptive statistics are called **quantiles**. As in locating the median, the scores must be arranged in ascending numerical order before the values of these various measures can be determined.

Although there is only one median for a particular distribution, there are three quartiles, nine deciles, and 99 whole percentiles. Identifying labels are assigned to the various quantiles, beginning with the first division point that occurs in the array. Examples would be first quartile, third decile, and 75th percentile.

Of course, depending on the number of scores and the number of quantiles involved, division points between groups of scores may fall between two scores in the array. In such instances, as we did in identifying the median score in a distribution, we take the mean of those two adjacent scores in the array as the value of the particular quantile. These difficulties may be exacerbated when n is small, so it is best to restrict the use of quartiles, deciles, and percentiles to distributions that contain both a large number of scores and a broad range of scores. Because the scores must be arranged from lowest to highest, variables measured at the nominal level are not suited to quantile analysis.

Imagine that the horizontal string of dots at the top of Figure 4.5 represents an array of scores listed from left to right in ascending numerical order, each dot

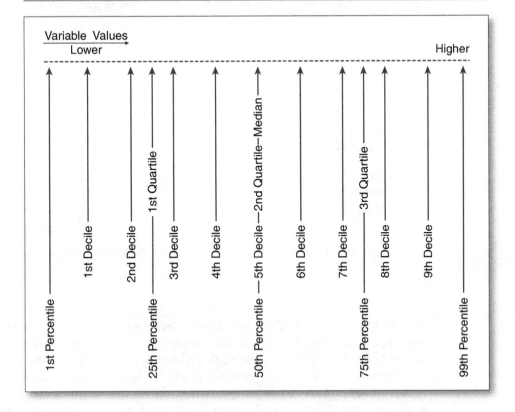

Figure 4.5 Illustration of Quantiles

representing an individual's score. The array of dots can be divided into various numbers of segments or groups, each containing the same number of dots (scores). The boundary points of these divisions correspond to the scores that are used to determine the values of the various types of quantiles (quartiles, deciles, and percentiles). To find the quartile division points, we would divide the scores (the dots) into four groups of (approximately) equal size and label the first division point from the left the first quartile, the second division point the second quartile, and so on. For deciles, the scores would be divided into 10 equal-sized groups; for whole percentiles, into 100 equal-sized groups.

Let's use a simple example to illustrate quartiles and deciles. In Figure 4.6, we have 20 scores arranged in ascending order from values 1 to 9. Quartiles divide the scores into four equal-sized groups of scores, so 20/4 = 5. To locate the quartiles, beginning with the lowest score we would count off five scores. In our example, the first quartile falls between the scores 2 and 3. We follow the same procedure here as we did with the median: We sum the two scores and divide by 2, giving us (3 + 2)/2 = 2.5 as the value of our first quartile. Then we count off the next five scores, ending in a division point that falls between a score of 3 and a score of 4. The value of the second quartile, then, is 3.5. Counting five scores again locates the third quartile, which has a value of 5.

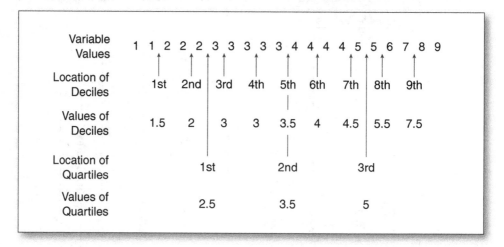

Figure 4.6 A Series of 20 Variable Values With Quartile and Decile Locations and Values

The procedure for finding the values of deciles and percentiles is essentially the same. For deciles, we divide the scores into 10 equal-sized groups. In our Figure 4.5 data, for example, 20/10 = 2, so we would divide the 20 scores into groups of two each. Nine division points would be established, and the value of each decile score would be determined as discussed above for quartiles. For whole percentiles, the scores would be divided into 100 equal-sized groups, the 99 division points would be located, and the values of each percentile would be determined as above. There are too few scores in our Figure 4.6 example to illustrate percentile locations.

Note that the values of the second quartile, median, fifth decile, and the 50th percentile are all equal. Similarly, the first quartile and the 25th percentile would have the same value, and so on.

If we know both the values of the various quantiles for a given distribution and a particular individual's score, we can locate that score approximately, relative to the other scores in the distribution, by saying it is less than, equivalent to, or greater than a particular quartile, decile, or percentile. Because percentiles provide more reference points in the distribution, they permit a more precise location of a particular score than do quartiles or deciles and are, therefore, the most frequently used quantiles, especially when both the number of scores in the distribution and their range are very large.

When we say, for example, that a particular score falls at the 36th percentile, we are referring to the percentage of scores in the distribution that are either equal to or less than the value of the given percentile. For example, if you are told that your score on a promotional test is equivalent to the 76th percentile, your score was higher than or equal to 76% of the scores, but 24% of the scores were equal to or higher than yours.

Furthermore, in contrast to quartiles and deciles, percentiles are often expressed, not just as whole numbers, but as decimal numbers, as in your score was located at the 65.6th percentile. Such expressions are interpreted in the conventional way. That is, a score at the 65.6th percentile is equal to or greater than 65.6% of the scores in the distribution.

Selecting Appropriate Measures of Location

Selecting appropriate measures of the location of scores in a distribution depends largely on the size of the study group and the precision with which one wants to locate a particular score. For large study groups (say, a few thousand), percentiles are perhaps the best choice because they offer more precision than the other quantiles we have discussed. Quartiles and deciles would also be appropriate, however. For smaller study groups (say, less than 250), it's probably best to stick with quartiles and deciles.

Although quantiles are useful as indicators of location, we must be careful not to misinterpret them. First, the smaller the number of quantiles used as reference points in locating a particular score, the less apparent may be the differences in the scores reported by referring to their quantile values alone. For example, two scores may be reported as "below the first quartile," but one may also be below the first decile, whereas the other is above the second decile. Furthermore, one may be equivalent to the second percentile, and the other may be equivalent to the 24th percentile. To put the same point in another way, percentiles provide the more precise indicator of location in a distribution. Obviously, the nature of the particular quantiles being used is critical when interpreting reports of scores made in terms of quantiles alone.

Other difficulties can be illustrated by examining a particular distribution of deciles, but the difficulties discussed apply to the use of quartiles and percentiles as well. Consider the 20 scores ranging from 1 to 9 and the deciles for the distribution illustrated in Figure 4.6 again. At the outset, we see that the third and fourth deciles have the same value: 3.

Now, suppose that your score on this test is 3. How would you report your score by referencing decile values? You must resist the temptation to identify the last 3 in the distribution as yours and contend that your score was above the fourth decile, because for the purposes of determining the decile values, it is irrelevant which of the 3s is yours. It would not be fair to a friend who also scored 3 to designate the first 3 as his and say it fell below the third decile; after all, you both received the same score on the test. To be honest, you would have to say that your score (and your friend's) was equivalent to the value of the third and fourth deciles.

Using the same distribution for illustrative purposes, suppose that your score is 4. What would be a conventional interpretation of a report indicating that your score is equivalent to the sixth decile? Your score would apparently be equivalent to or higher than 60% of the scores, but when we observe the actual distribution, your score is, in fact, equivalent to or higher than 70% of the scores. We hasten to note that the use of percents here violates the rule of thumb about having at least 30 scores before using percentages, but the general point is valid nonetheless: There is a margin—sometimes a large margin—of imprecision in the conventional interpretation of quantiles.

This imprecision arises because the procedures used to determine the values of the quantiles involve dividing the scores into groups that contain equal numbers of scores. Hence, it is true, for example, that 50% of the scores in the distribution fall below the fifth decile (and the second quartile and the 50th percentile). But this procedure, as we have already seen with the median, takes into account only the number and rank order of the scores; it ignores the scores' values. Hence, the relationship between the quantiles' values and the scores' values is imperfect. A number of scores that have the same value (that is, they are tied scores) may overlap quantile division points. When this happens, the conventional interpretation in terms of the percentage of scores equivalent to or below a particular quantile must be regarded as an approximation rather than a precise statement.

We've used a very small data set to illustrate these potential problems in interpreting quantiles, but the problems would also arise in a large data set with many tied scores.

For large study groups without large numbers of tied scores, some of the imprecision can be eliminated by using whole and fractional percentiles, which are expressed as percentiles with decimals (e.g., the score was equivalent to the 35.61 percentile). As we will see later in our discussion of areas under the normal curve, such percentiles are used commonly in statistical analyses.

Note also that the range of values of scores encompassed between a pair of adjacent quantiles and any other adjacent pair of quantiles in a distribution can vary greatly. This is most apparent in highly skewed distributions. Quantiles, then, are most useful and least misleading as indicators of location when both the number of cases and the range of score values are large, and the frequency distribution of the scores is at least approximately bell shaped.

Finally, arrays of variable values (e.g., scores) often cannot be divided exactly evenly into 4 or 10 or 100 equal-sized groups. An array of 135 scores, for example can't be evenly divided into 4 or 10 or 100 equal-sized groups. There are no hard-and-fast rules to guide us here. The general rule is just to do the best you can to keep the numbers in each group equal. For example, if we wanted to divide the 135 scores into four groups of scores with an approximately equal number of scores in each group (for determining the distributions' quartile values), we might divide them so that the first three groups contains 34 scores and the last group contains 33.

Dealing With Missing Data

It is not unusual for data sets to be incomplete in one way or another. For one reason or another (the respondent forgot to answer a question, the observer forgot to record an observation, the record was lost or can't be read, etc.), one or more of the units of analysis in the study group was not measured on one or more variables, resulting in **missing data**. Suppose, for example, that there are 45 newly graduated paralegals in a study group, but the data set contains information on the college GPAs for only 42 of them. Data are missing on this variable for three graduates.

Missing data pose a dilemma for statistical analysts because in order to calculate accurate measures of central tendency, dispersion, or location, the total N is required.

Which N should you use for your calculations, the $N = 45$ of the total group or the $N = 42$ for whom we have complete information? You can see the problem. If you use $N = 45$ to calculate the group's mean GPA without doing anything else, you are, in effect, treating the missing GPAs as equal to zero, thereby lowering the group's mean GPA. If you use $N = 42$, you are then calculating the mean GPA not for all the graduates in the study, but only for those for whom you have complete data.

If the study group is large and the number of missing measurements is small, either approach is acceptable because the difference in results is likely to be quite small. But when data are missing for small study groups or the number of missing measurements is large in larger study groups, either approach can be misleading. At the very least, the analyst's chosen strategy should be reported and the missing data counts should be provided, as they are in the output of almost all computerized statistical analysis packages. If you use a statistical analysis package, be sure you know how the analysis program treats missing data.

The occurrence of missing data presents problems not just for the relatively simple descriptive statistical analyses we have discussed in this and the previous chapter, but also for the more complex procedures we take up in later chapters. As you can imagine, when doing multivariate analysis (i.e., analysis involving two or more variables at the same time), the problem can grow rapidly. You should be aware that statisticians have developed some procedures for dealing with the problem of missing data. They include such strategies as "imputing" for each missing variable value the mean value of the available scores for that variable so that units of analysis with missing data can be included in the statistical analysis. Discussion of these strategies, as well as their advantages and risks, are beyond the scope of this text, but we do need to be aware as practitioners and researchers of the dilemma posed by missing data and the possibly misleading results they can produce in statistical analysis.

Some Other Cautions in the Uses and Interpretations of Univariate Descriptive Statistics

We can use crime data to illustrate how complex and tricky things can get even with the relatively simple descriptive statistics we have discussed so far. Doing so will help reinforce our discussion of garbage in-garbage out in Chapter 2.

If someone tells you that the crime rate for City A was 4 per 1,000 in 1986, can any sense be made of such a report? For reasons that will become obvious, the answer is no. We need to know a great deal more about how that rate was calculated before we have any idea of what it really means.

The first thing that we need to ask is, What was the population base used—per 1,000 of what? The rate may have been calculated on the basis of

- the total population in the city,
- only adults in the city (defined how?),
- adults and juveniles (defined how?),

- only males,
- and so on.

The rate means very different things depending on what "per 1,000" is involved.

Furthermore, when and how was the population counted? During the previous census? If it was some years ago, has the population in the city changed very much? How do we know? If it has, was the population count used for the base adjusted? How and on what basis was the adjustment made? Was the count of crimes made in at least roughly the same period as the count for the population base? A rate calculated on the basis of a 1980 population census and a count of crimes in 1985 may be seriously misleading.

We also need to know exactly what was counted as a crime. How was crime defined? Felonies only? Misdemeanors and felonies?

Finally, consider the following possible ways of counting crimes during a specified period:

- Crimes actually committed (the "real" crime rate)
- Crimes observed by others (perpetrators, victims, witnesses)
- Crimes reported to the police
- Crimes recorded by the police (the basis for most official crime statistics)
- Crimes for which someone was arrested
- Crimes for which someone was prosecuted
- Crimes for which someone was convicted

Any of these could be used to arrive at the "4" of the 4 per 1,000, and a reasonable argument could be made that any one of them would be useful for some purpose. In any event, it should be obvious that the definition of crime used is quite important in making sense of the reported crime rate. Likewise, meaningful comparisons of crime rates are possible only when they are defined according to the same criteria and calculated using the same population base.

In addition to crime rates, we might want to consider other crime statistics that are potentially useful, but susceptible to ambiguities and other complications that might affect their interpretation. The same or similar concerns about rates would pertain to the proportion of crimes cleared by arrest; the mean, the median, and the mode of the distribution of length of sentences handed down by courts in a given jurisdiction; and the standard deviation of the distribution of the number of months persons convicted of felonies in your state actually spend in confinement. All such descriptive statistics require the kinds of clarification indicated earlier before they can be meaningfully interpreted. As we noted in Chapter 2, garbage can get into a statistical analysis in many ways. If it does, the result is garbage out, even if an appropriate descriptive statistic has been chosen and the calculations are correct.

Table 4.6 summarizes our discussion of measures of univariate descriptive statistics in this chapter.

Table 4.6 Measures of Central Tendency, Dispersion, and Location, With Appropriate Levels of Measurement and Formula Definition

		Appropriate Levels of Measurement	Formula/Definition
Measures of central tendency	Mode	Nominal Ordinal Interval Ratio	Variable value with highest frequency
	Median	Ordinal Interval Ratio	Variable value at the midpoint in the array of scores
	Mean	Interval Ratio	$\bar{x} = \dfrac{\sum x}{n}$
Measures of dispersion	Range	Ordinal Interval Ratio	Lowest and highest variable values that occur in the data set
	Standard deviation	Interval Ratio	$s = \sqrt{s^2} = \sqrt{\dfrac{\sum (x-\bar{x})^2}{n}}$
	Variance	Interval Ratio	s^2 (square of the standard deviation)
Indicators of location in a distribution	Quartiles	Ordinal Interval Ratio	Variable values that lie at the three division points when the array of variable values is divided into four equal-sized groups
	Deciles	Ordinal Interval Ratio	Variable values that lie at the nine division points when the array of variable values is divided into 10 equal-sized groups
	Percentiles	Ordinal Interval Ratio	Variable values that lie at the 99 division points when the array of variable values is divided into 100 equal-sized groups

Summary

In this chapter, we discussed some of the ways in which statisticians characterize distributions as a whole. One way is by distinguishing among the general shapes of distributions, in particular between bell-shaped and skewed distributions and between leptokurtic and platykurtic distributions. Another way is by calculating measures of central tendency and dispersion, as well as location. The uses and potential misuses of these measures were discussed. A special property of the mean—namely, that it is the variable value that minimizes the difference between it and the other scores in the distribution—was identified. We also explored some of the ways in which basic descriptive statistics such as percents and rates as well as measures of central tendency and dispersion can be misleading.

In Chapter 5, we discuss in more detail the uses of graphs in data analysis and presentation. After a brief discussion of probability in Chapter 6, we discuss additional aspects of distributions and explore some of the special properties of normal distributions in Chapter 7.

Concepts to Master

Average deviation	Median	Quartile
Bell-shaped distribution	Mesokurtic distribution	Range
Bimodal distribution	Missing data	Skewed distribution (skewness)
Collapsing variable values	Mode	
Decile	Multimodal distribution	Standard deviation
Grouped scores	Negatively skewed (skewed to the left)	Sum of squared deviations from the mean
Kurtosis	Normal distribution	Sum of squares
Leptokurtic distribution	Percentile	Symmetric distribution
Mean	Platykurtic distribution	Tails of a distribution
Measures of central tendency	Positively skewed (skewed to the right)	Unimodal distribution
Measures of dispersion		
Measures of location	Quantile	Variance

Review Questions

1. How does a normal distribution differ from a skewed one?

2. What are the tails of a distribution?

3. What is the difference between a distribution skewed to the left (negative skew) and one skewed to the right (positive skew)?
4. How does a normal distribution differ from a platykurtic and a leptokurtic distribution?
5. What does a measure of central tendency tell us about a distribution?
6. What are the mean, the median, and the mode of a distribution? How are their values determined?
7. Compare and contrast the measures of central tendency. What are the strengths and weaknesses of each of these measures?
8. What is collapsing categories (variable values)? How is it done, and when is it most appropriate? What are some concerns to keep in mind when doing so?
9. In the United States, mean income is quite a bit larger than the median income. What does this suggest about the shape of the income distribution?
10. What is a special property of the mean?
11. What do measures of dispersion tell us about a distribution?
12. What are the range, the average deviation, the variance, and the standard deviation of a distribution? How are their values determined?
13. Why is the average deviation from the mean not used in statistical analysis?
14. What is the relationship between the standard deviation and the variance?
15. Compare and contrast the measures of dispersion. What are the strengths and weaknesses of each of these measures.
16. Which measures of central tendency and dispersion are appropriate for distributions of nominal data? Of ordinal data? Of interval data? Of ratio data?
17. What are the three types of quantiles discussed in the text? How do they differ, and how is the value of each determined?
18. How might quantiles be used to locate a person's score in a distribution?
19. What are missing data? Why are they a problem? What are some alternatives for dealing with missing data?
20. Define each of the terms in the "Concepts to Master" list and use each in three different sentences.

Exercises and Discussion Questions

1. If you haven't already done so, answer the questions in all of the "Pause, Think, and Explore" boxes in this chapter.

2. It is appropriate to calculate a mean for a ratio-level variable, such as a test score. Does it make sense to calculate a mean for an ordinal-level variable? Why or why not? To calculate a mean for an interval-level variable? For a nominal-level variable?

3. Use the following hypothetical data for Exercises 3a through 3d.

Subject	Sex	Number of Arrests	Highest Level of Education Achieved*
1	M	2	3
2	M	4	1
3	F	5	1
4	F	3	4
5	M	1	4
6	F	3	1
7	M	2	4
8	F	0	6
9	M	3	2
10	F	4	2
11	M	5	4
12	F	3	6
13	M	2	5
14	M	1	1
15	F	4	1
16	M	6	1
17	F	3	3
18	M	4	5
19	F	2	4
20	M	3	4

*Category (variable value) codes: 1 = grade school or less; 2 = junior high school; 3 = high school; 4 = community college; 5 = 4-year college; 6 = more than 4-year college

a. Calculate appropriate measures of central tendency, dispersion, and location for the distributions of each variable.
b. Are any of the distributions approximately bell shaped?
c. Do any of the distributions appear skewed? How would you describe their kurtosis?
d. Calculate quartile and decile values for the number-of-arrests variable.

4. How would you describe the following distributions? Be as specific as you can.

Figure 4.7 A Variety of Line Graphs

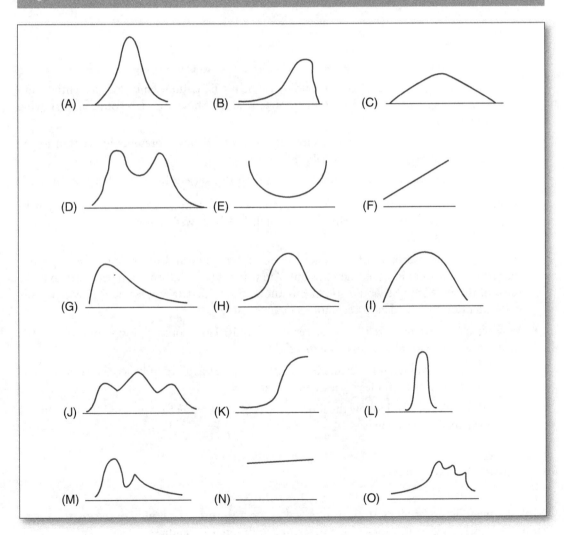

5. Use the data in the table below to answer Exercises 5a through 5c.

Length of Sentence (in days)	Frequency (f)
1–7	15
8–14	18
15–22	22
23–30	35
31–45	52
46–60	31
61–90	25
91–120	16
121–150	13
n = 227	

   a. Find the sentence category corresponding to the median, mode, and 78th percentile. Find the mean length of sentence for these grouped values. Show the steps you take in arriving at your results.

   b. Describe what each of these measures of central tendency represents in relation to the other sentence lengths in the distribution.

   c. What shape does the distribution have? (Bell shaped? Skewed? Kurtotic?) How can you tell?

6. Is the frequency distribution of salaries in Table 4.3 (see column 2) an approximately bell-shaped or skewed distribution? How can you tell? If it is skewed, is it positively or negatively skewed? How can you tell?

7. Find at least two examples of measures of central tendency and dispersion in newspapers, magazines, or textbooks other than this one. Are you given the information necessary to make sense of them? What else would you like to know about the data represented? (Pay especially close attention to such data presentations in advertising!)

8. Why are missing data a problem in statistical analysis? How could choosing one way or the other of dealing with missing data be misleading?

9. Go to www.fbi.gov, search for crime in the US 2011, and explore links to city, county, state, and national data as examples of descriptive statistics.

10. Go to www.ncjrs.gov and follow the links in the upper left panel to topics and then to statistical reports that interest you.

Student Study Site

Visit the open-access student study site at **www.sagepub.com/fitzgerald** for access to several study tools including eFlashcards, web quizzes, and additional appendices as well as links to SAGE journal articles and audio, video and web resources.

Distributions

Normal and Otherwise

Learning Objectives

What you are expected not only to learn but to master in this chapter:

- The nature of proportional area bar and line graphs, as well as normal distributions and curves.
- The special characteristics of normal distributions and curves that complete their definition
- The relationships between the mean and units of standard deviation from the mean in normal distributions and curves, including standard normal distributions and curves, and areas in the distributions and under the normal curves
- The nature of standard normal scores (z scores) and how to calculate them
- The relationships among z scores, areas under the normal curve, and probabilities
- How to use a z-score table to find various areas under the standard normal curve and to interpret them as frequencies, proportions, and probabilities

Introduction

As we have seen in Chapters 3 and 4, distributions come in a variety of shapes and sizes. In this chapter, our discussion of different distribution types continues, paying special attention to the characteristics of normal distributions and their theoretical counterparts, called normal curves. We begin with a discussion of all properly drawn bar and line graphs, whether normal or not, as proportional area displays of data.

Then, we describe some special characteristics of normal distributions as proportional area bar and line graphs. Building on what we have learned about normal distributions, we explore the features of two types of theoretical normal distributions—theoretical normal curves and theoretical standard normal (z-score) curves that are used to approximate normal distributions. You will learn how to use a z-score table to determine areas under a normal curve and to answer a number of questions about proportions, percentages, and probabilities of scores in a normal distribution. As we will see in subsequent chapters, theoretical normal and theoretical standard normal curves are tools statisticians find especially useful in many kinds of descriptive and inferential statistical analyses.

Be sure you have mastered the contents of this chapter before moving on to the next chapters. Ask for help if you need to, lest you get lost as we explore later in the book more complex statistical analyses, many of which rely heavily on concepts discussed in this chapter.

Proportional Area Graphs

In Chapter 3, we described the proper construction of frequency and percent bar and line graphs. (See pp. 54–65 to review that discussion.) All properly drawn frequency and percent bar and line graphs may be regarded as proportional area graphs.

Let's explore this idea of proportional area graphs in some detail. We'll use the 36 police recruit test scores first presented and discussed in Chapter 3 for purposes of illustration, but our discussion would apply to any ratio- or interval-level variable values, such as ages, months of sentence, number of sworn personnel, and so on. The frequency distribution bar graph of these 36 test scores is reproduced in Figure 5.1. Note that for the figures in this chapter, we have truncated the horizontal axis of the graph, presenting only those possible variable values (scores) that we actually observed in our data set (scores 8 through 18). (Compare Figure 3.3b, p. 59 with Figure 5.1.) This truncation does not affect the arguments we make about proportional area graphs in this chapter.

Suppose that we calculated the area of each of the bars in this bar graph by multiplying its width by its length. We could then add the areas of all the bars and determine the total area encompassed by all the bars in the graph. We could also express the area encompassed by any given bar in the graph as a proportion of the total area of all the bars. In a **proportional area bar graph**, the proportion of the total area represented by a particular bar corresponds with the proportion or percent of times the variable value represented by that bar occurs in the distribution.

For purposes of illustration, let's suppose that, when we added the area of all of the bars in a proportional area bar graph, we found a total area of 5 square inches. Obviously, the total square inches for any particular proportional area bar graph would vary depending on the scale on which the graph is drawn. As long as it is a proportional area bar graph, however, the basic relationship between areas in a graph and corresponding proportions of frequencies or percents will still hold. Why? Because proportions and percents are standardized quantities. They are derived by converting the frequencies of

Figure 5.1 Area Bar Graph of Police Recruit Test Scores (Same Data as Figure 3.3b)

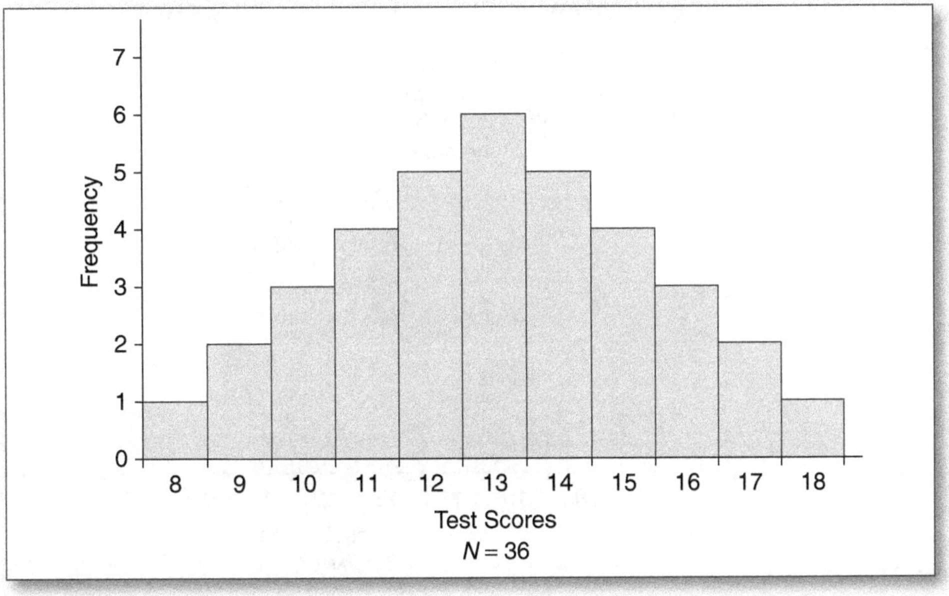

raw scores into fractions with a common base. Recall that, in the case of percents, the raw score frequencies are converted into a fraction with a base of 100.

Now suppose we want to calculate the proportion of the total area of all the bars in the graph represented by *one* of the 36 scores in the distribution. We can calculate that proportion in two different ways, but they will yield the same result. We'll round our decimals to the nearest ten thousandth and our percents to the nearest hundredth here for these calculations; we can expect some small differences due to rounding error.

On one hand, we could say that because we have 36 scores in the distribution, each of the 36 scores is represented by .1389 square inches—that is, five square inches (total area) divided by 36 test scores = 5 sq. in./36 scores = .1389 sq. in. of the total graph area per test score in the graph. The same proportion of the total graph area would be taken up by each of the 36 scores in the distribution, regardless of its particular numerical value—that is, whether it is a score of 8 or 12 or 17. Together, the 36 scores, each taking up .1389 sq. in., would comprise the 5 sq. in. total graph area (36 × .1389 sq. in. = 5.0004 sq. in.). What proportion and percent of the graph's total area does the .1389 sq. in. for each score represent? To find out, we divide this area (.1389 sq. in.) by the total graph area (5 sq. in.): .1389/5 = .0278. So, each score takes up .0278 or 2.78% of the total area of 5 square inches, as illustrated in Figure 5.2.

Alternatively, we could say that any single score represents 1/36th of the scores in the distribution. Note that 1/36th of the scores is 1 ÷ 36 = .0278 or 2.78% of the scores

Figure 5.2 Proportional Area Bar Graph of Police Recruit Test Scores (Same Data as Figure 5.1)

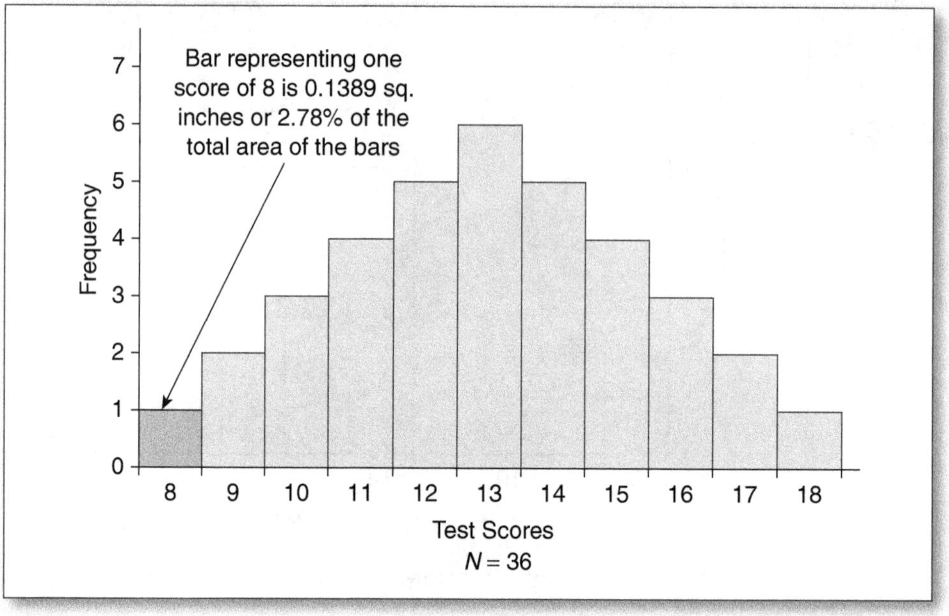

[Bar graph showing frequency distribution of test scores from 8 to 18, with N = 36. Annotation: "Bar representing one score of 8 is 0.1389 sq. inches or 2.78% of the total area of the bars"]

in the distribution. Every score in the distribution, then, is represented by 2.78% of the total area of all the bars in the graph (5 sq. in.), the same result we achieved in the previous paragraph.

Using either of the general procedures described earlier, we can determine what proportion of the total bar graph area represents those who received any particular score, those who scored from 10 through 12, or those who scored 16 or more on the test. The calculations are pretty straightforward if we remember that each score is represented by 2.78% of the area of all the bars in the graph. For the areas of the bars pertaining to those who scored from 10 through 12, we would add the areas of the bars corresponding to each score's frequency. There are three scores of 10. If each of these three scores is represented by 2.78% of the total area, then these three scores are represented by 3 × 2.78% = 8.34% of the total area of the bars. The four scores of 11 are represented by 4 × 2.78% = 11.12% of the total area, and the five scores of 12 are represented by 13.90% of the total area of the bars. So, for the proportion of the area in the graph representing scores 10 through 12, we would have 8.34% + 11.12% + 13.90% = 33.36% of the total area of the bars. Hence, we can say that 33.36% of the recruits scored from 10 through 12 on the test.

Using the alternative method, we have 3 + 4 + 5 = 12 scores, which is 12/36 or 1/3 or 33.33% of the scores in the distribution, the same result as the calculations above, allowing for rounding error, as illustrated in Figure 5.3. Finally, recall we found that each score occupies .1389 sq. in. in the area of the graph. So, the area of the graph

Figure 5.3 Proportional Area Bar Graph of Police Recruit Test Scores (Same Data as Figure 5.1)

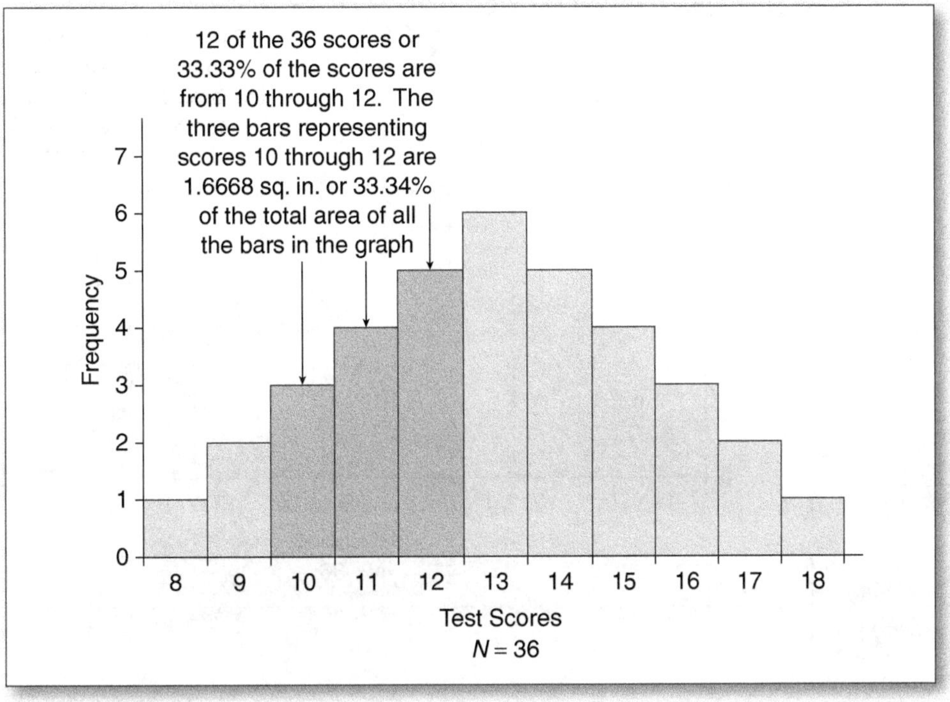

12 of the 36 scores or 33.33% of the scores are from 10 through 12. The three bars representing scores 10 through 12 are 1.6668 sq. in. or 33.34% of the total area of all the bars in the graph

Test Scores
$N = 36$

occupied by the 12 scores in the distribution whose values are from 10 through 12 is 12 × .1389 sq. in. = 1.6668 sq. in. To get the proportion of the total area (5 sq. in.) represented by the area of these bars, we would have 1.6668/5 = .3334 or 33.34% of the total area, again the same result (within rounding error) we achieved above using the first method.

For the percent of those scoring 16 or higher, we have three scores of 16, or 8.34%; two scores of 17, or 5.56%; and one score of 18, or 2.78%. The total is 8.34% + 5.56% + 2.78% = 16.68%. This total is the percent of the total bar area corresponding to those scores and the percent of recruits who scored 16 or higher on the test. Based on square inches, we have six scores of 16 or higher, so 6 × .1389 sq. in. = .8334 sq. in., the area of the graph representing these six scores. Finally, .8334/5 = .1667 or 16.67% of the total area is occupied by these six scores.

Alternatively, we have 3 + 2 + 1 = 6 scores of 16 or higher, and 6/36 = 16.67% of all the scores in the distribution, as illustrated in Figure 5.4.

Remember that when we calculate percents, we are calculating standardized quantities. Instead of considering the total area of the graph as 5 square inches and dividing the area into square-inch portions, we are considering the total area of the graph, no matter what the actual area in square inches, as 100% and dividing the area into fractions with a base of 100—that is, into proportions that we can convert to percents.

Figure 5.4 Proportional Area Bar Graph of Police Recruit Test Scores (Same Data as Figure 5.1)

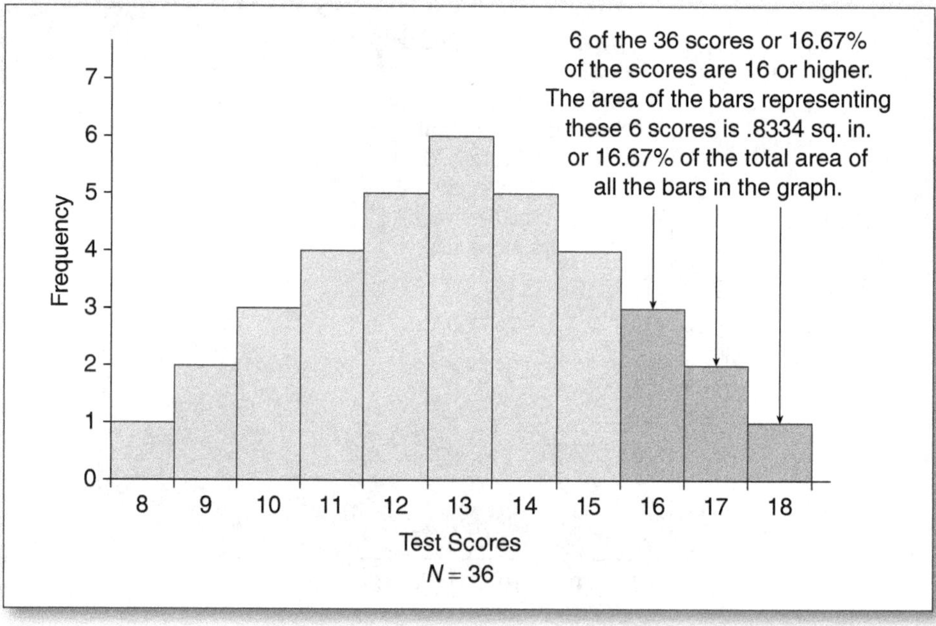

6 of the 36 scores or 16.67% of the scores are 16 or higher. The area of the bars representing these 6 scores is .8334 sq. in. or 16.67% of the total area of all the bars in the graph.

Frequency vs. Test Scores, N = 36

Now suppose we superimposed a line graph over the bar graph for these test score data, as we have in Figure 5.5. Remember that the bar graph and the line graph represent the same data. Note that the area under the line is essentially the same as the area encompassed by the bars. We can, therefore, speak of the equivalence between the proportion of area under the line and the proportion of times a particular variable value (score) occurs in the data set, just as we did when we referred to the areas of the bars. We can say, for example, that the area under the line corresponding to the one test score of 8 is about 2.78% of the total area under the line, as illustrated in Figure 5.5.

Similar to what we did with bar areas, we can say that 33.34% of the area under the line corresponds to those who scored 10 through 12. For those who scored 16 or higher, we can say that they are represented by 16.67% of the area under the curve, as illustrated in Figure 5.6.

Note that in both of these illustrations, we could use the cumulative frequencies or percents to do calculations for the scores in the distribution. (You might wish to review the discussion of cumulative frequencies in Chapter 3, pp. 67–71 now to refresh your memory.) In the case of those scoring from 10 through 12, the cumulative frequencies are 3 + 4 = 7; 7 + 5 = 12. The cumulative percents are 8.34% + 11.12% = 19.46% and 19.46% + 13.90% = 33.36%. So, the cumulative frequency for these scores results in a total of 12 scores and 12/36 = 33.33%. In the case of those scoring 16 or higher, we have 3 + 2 = 5; 5 + 1 = 6. The cumulative frequency of these scores, then, is 6 and 6/36 = 16.67%. For the cumulative percents, we have 8.34% + 5.56% = 13.90% and 13.90% + 2.78% = 16.68%, again the same except for rounding error.

Distributions: Normal and Otherwise ❖ 139

Figure 5.5 Proportional Area Bar and Line Graph of Police Recruit Test Scores (Same Data as Figure 5.1)

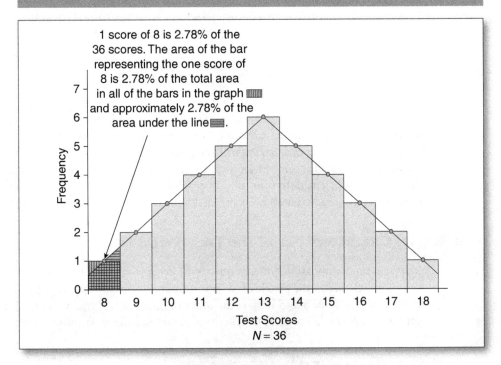

Figure 5.6 Line Graph of Police Recruit Test Scores Showing Different Areas Under the Line and Corresponding Proportion of Scores Within Specified Ranges

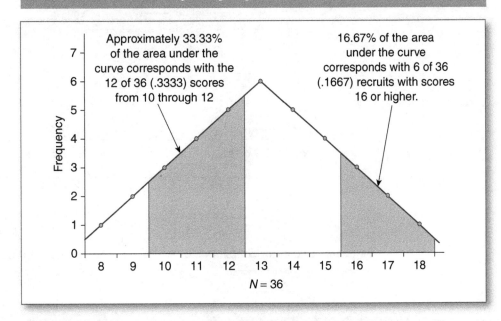

Note also that, if we squint a bit, the police recruit test score distribution we have used for illustrative purposes roughly approximates the bell shape of the normal curve as we discussed it in Chapter 4. Whether approximately normal or not, though, all proportional area graphs are characterized by this proportional relationship between areas in the graph and corresponding frequencies or percents.

Normal Distributions and Normal Curves Revisited

In Chapter 4, we described a normal distribution or curve as bell shaped (unimodal and symmetric about its mean), with mean, median, and mode of equal value. But as we also learned in Chapter 4, not all bell-shaped distributions or curves with these characteristics are normal. Saying a distribution or curve is bell-shaped, unimodal, and symmetric about its mean, with a mean, a median, and a mode of equal value, then, is not quite a sufficient definition of a normal distribution. Normal distributions have other special characteristics, however, that will give us a complete definition.

The Special Characteristics of the Theoretical Normal Curve

It is practically impossible for a frequency or percent line graph distribution of actual data to exactly match the profile of the normal curve's smooth bell shape (see Figure 5.7). In part for this reason and in part for other reasons we will discuss in Chapter 6, this smooth curve is referred to as the **theoretical normal curve** or, more simply, as we will

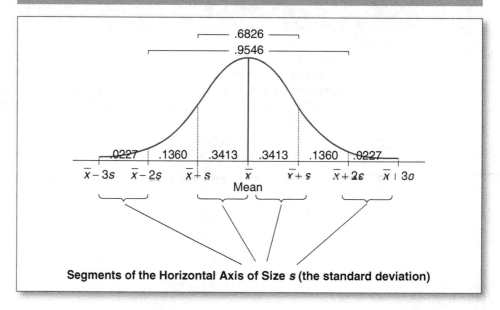

Figure 5.7 A Normal Curve Subdivided by Units of Standard Deviation With Corresponding Proportions of Area Under the Curve

Segments of the Horizontal Axis of Size *s* (the standard deviation)

in most cases here, as the normal curve. To distinguish the theoretical normal curve from an at least roughly bell-shaped distribution of actual data, we will call the latter a normal distribution. Just remember that statisticians often use normal curves as approximations of normal distributions.

The normal curve has characteristics especially useful for statistical analysis, many of which were first described by the statistician R. A. Fisher, building on the earlier work of Abraham De Moivre, the Marquis de la Place, and Karl Fredrich Gauss. In honor of the latter's work, the normal curve is sometimes referred to as the **Gaussian curve or distribution.** Many of the features and procedures we will be discussing here, and in subsequent chapters on descriptive and inferential statistics as well, are among Fisher's extraordinary contributions to modern statistical analysis (Fisher, 1995; Stigler, 1999). To comprehend and make use of these special properties, we must understand the relationship we have discussed above between particular segments of the area under the normal curve and the frequency or percent of times particular variable values (such as particular test scores) have been observed.

Means, Standard Deviations, and Areas Under the Normal Curve

Suppose we have an approximately normal frequency distribution of a continuous variable measured at the interval or ratio level. By using the procedures discussed in Chapter 4, we can calculate the frequency distribution's mean ($\bar{x}$) and standard deviation (s). Once we know the values of these two statistics for our frequency distribution, we can use them to divide the possible variable values arrayed along the horizontal axis of the distribution's line graph into segments of size s, the value of our distribution's standard deviation. By erecting lines perpendicular to the horizontal axis at the division points between the segments, we divide the total area in the graph into several parts. The areas of those parts represent the frequencies or percents with which corresponding possible variable values along the horizontal axis occur in the distribution. Now suppose we approximate this distribution using a normal curve. Consider the horizontal axis of the normal curve in Figure 5.7. We can calculate and use the values of a distribution's mean and standard deviation. Using the value of the mean as a reference point on the horizontal axis of this normal curve, we can locate other points (possible variable values) on the horizontal axis by adding or subtracting multiples of the standard deviation. Thus, we could locate points corresponding to $\bar{x} + s$, $\bar{x} + 2s$, $\bar{x} + 3s$, $\bar{x} - s$, $\bar{x} - 2s$, and $\bar{x} - 3s$, for example. Remember, we are not counting the frequency of variable values in the distribution (or under the curve) at this point. We are only using the mean and standard deviation to divide up the possible variable values arrayed along the horizontal axis of our graph into equal-sized segments of size s—we might say into s-sized units. Now suppose we draw a line perpendicular to the horizontal axis at the division points we have located. When we do, we will divide the total area under the normal curve into parts, as illustrated in Figure 5.7.

The statistically most useful special characteristic of the normal curve is the fixed relationship between the s-sized units of possible variable values on the horizontal axis and corresponding **areas under the normal curve** defined by the perpendicular lines. As with areas in a normal distribution, these areas under the normal curve represent the frequencies with which the different s-sized ranges of possible variable values on the horizontal axis occur in the distribution. In general, statisticians do not typically refer to the frequency or percent with which a particular variable value occurs under a normal curve. Rather, they refer to areas under the curve corresponding to the frequency or percent of times that the observed variable values are above or below a specified variable value, or to the frequency or percent of times the observed variable values fall between two specified variable values. As you can see in Figure 5.7, of the total area under the normal curve, the proportion of the area and the proportion of scores in the distribution included between $\bar{x}$ and $\bar{x} + s$ is always .3413; the proportion between $\bar{x} + s$ and $\bar{x} + 2s$ is always .1360; and the proportion beyond $\bar{x} + 2s$ is always .0227.

Note that, as we might expect, if the proportions of areas under the curve on one or the other side of the mean are summed, the result is .5000 or 50%, and if we sum the proportions on both sides of the mean, we get 1.000 or 100%. Because the normal curve is symmetrical about the mean, the proportions of the area under the curve corresponding to the s-sized units on the horizontal axis below (less than) the value of the mean are the same as those corresponding to the segments above (greater than) the mean. That is, the proportion of the observed variable values under the curve between $\bar{x}$ and $\bar{x} - s$ is the same as the proportion between $\bar{x}$ and $\bar{x} + s$ and the proportion between $\bar{x} - s$ and $\bar{x} - 2s$ is the same as the proportion between $\bar{x} + s$ and $\bar{x} + 2s$, and so on. Similarly, we can say that 68.26% of the area under the curve (.3413 + .3413 = .6826 or 68.26%) falls within one standard deviation (one s-sized unit) of the mean, or between $\bar{x} - s$ and $\bar{x} + s$.

We now have the final piece of information we need to complete our definition of the **normal curve**. It is a bell-shaped curve (unimodal and symmetric about its mean), whose mean, median, and mode have the same value. In addition, there are fixed proportions of area under the curve corresponding to units of standard deviation (s-sized units) above and below its mean, as indicated in Figure 5.7.

Let's apply what we have just learned about areas under the normal curve and standard deviation units above and below the mean to a real-world example. Suppose we have a distribution of the blood alcohol levels of 200 drivers stopped randomly at a checkpoint on a busy highway. Suppose, further, that when we analyze the data we have gathered, the distribution of these readings is approximately normal, with a mean reading of .055 and a standard deviation of .010. We can use the normal curve to approximate the normal distribution of blood alcohol levels. To divide the horizontal axis of the normal curve into segments, we would begin with the mean ($\bar{x}$ = .055). To locate the first division point above (greater than) the mean, we would add one standard deviation (s = .010) to the mean. Thus, we would have .010 + .055 = .065. To locate the first division point below (less than) the mean, we would subtract one standard deviation from the mean. The result would be .055 − .010 = .045. To locate the second division point above the mean, we would add two standard deviations (2 × .010 = .020) to the mean. We would then have .055 + .020 = .075. We have illustrated these and the remainder of the calculations for the division points in Figure 5.8.

Applying the relationships between units of standard deviation on the horizontal axis and corresponding areas under the normal curve, we can say that .3413 or 34.13%

Figure 5.8 Frequency Distribution Line Graph of Breathalizer Readings

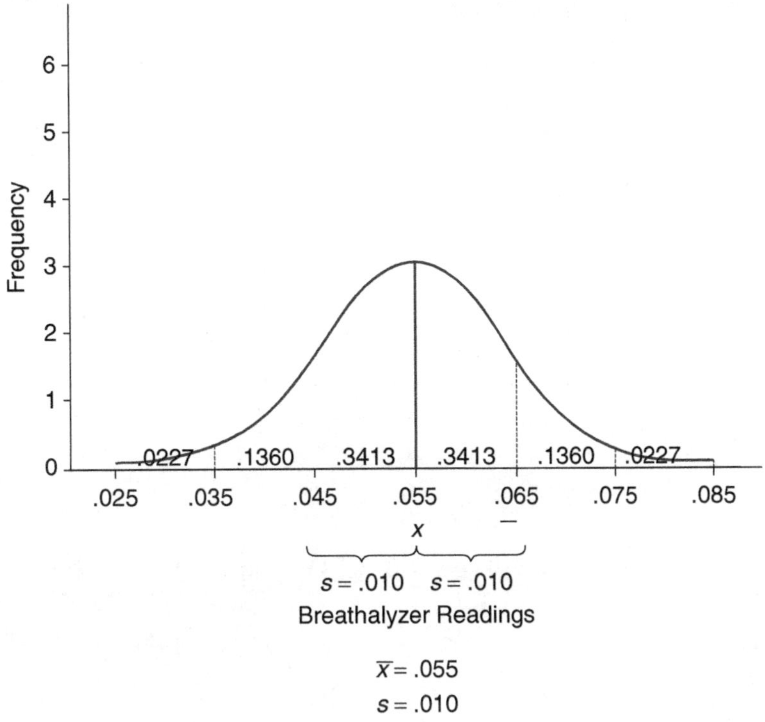

of the breathalyzer readings fell between $\bar{x}$ and $\bar{x} + s$, which, in our example, is between .055 and .065. That would be .3413 × 200 scores = about 68 of the scores. We can also say that .1360 or 13.60% of the readings fell between $\bar{x} + s$ and $\bar{x} + 2s$, which is about 27 readings (scores) between .065 and .075 in our example. About five scores or .0227 or 2.27% of the 200 readings are lower than .035, which is $\bar{x} - 2s$ or .055 − (2 × .010) = .055 − .020 = .035. We can also say that .8186 or 81.86% of the readings (about 164 readings) fell between .045 and .075, which is between $\bar{x} - s$ and $\bar{x} + 2s$.

Note that this particular relationship between units of standard deviation and corresponding proportions of areas under the curve holds only for normal curves and their at least approximately normal distribution counterparts. We can calculate a mean and standard deviation for any distribution, including skewed ones, of course. We can also use those statistics to mark off the horizontal axis in units of standard deviation from the mean and divide areas under the curve accordingly. But the relationship between these *s*-sized units and areas under the curve we find in normal curves no longer holds. You can see why this is so by comparing the areas under the curve between units of standard deviation (*s*-sized units) in the skewed curves in Figure 5.9 with the areas under the normal curve in Figure 5.7.

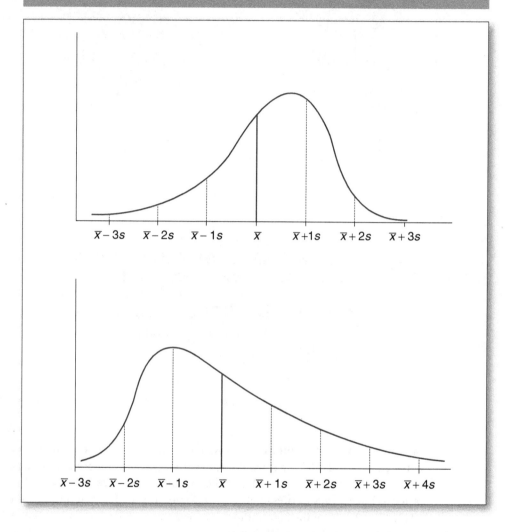

Figure 5.9 Skewed Distributions, Means, and Standard Deviations

The Theoretical Standard Normal Curve and z Scores

For basically the same reasons that it is often useful to convert frequencies into the standardized quantities of percents, statisticians standardize approximately normal distributions by converting them into standard normal distributions. Like percents, standard normal distributions facilitate describing and interpreting the data in the distribution and comparing normal distributions with different ranges of scores or numbers of observations. Once the raw-score distributions are converted into standard normal distributions, the standard normal curve can be used to approximate them.

The conversion requires finding **standard normal score** or **z-score** equivalents for each of the original raw scores. How do we find the z-score equivalents of our raw scores? The procedure for doing so is given by Formula 5.1:

$$z = \frac{x - \bar{x}}{s} \tag{5.1}$$

Pause, Think, and Explore z

Obviously, z is equivalent to a fraction or ratio that can be converted to a decimal or proportion. Is z a continuous or discrete variable? What will the value of z be if $x = \bar{x}$? What will the value of z be if $x - \bar{x} = s$? If $x - \bar{x} = 2s$? What will happen to the value of z if s stays the same and the difference between x and $\bar{x}$ goes up? If it goes down? What will happen to z if the numerator stays the same and s goes up? If it goes down? Can you tell anything about the shape of a raw-score distribution from knowing all of the raw score's z-score equivalents?

Note that the order of the score (x) and the mean score ($\bar{x}$) in the numerator of Formula 5.1 is different from the order in the formulas for the variance and standard deviation we gave in Chapter 4. There, the order was unimportant because we were using squared deviations. Here, the order is important because we want to preserve the correct sign on z. That is, if the original raw score (x) is less than the mean (usually referred to as below the mean) and we subtract the mean from it, we get a negative z, which tells us that both the original raw score and its z-score equivalent are below the mean. Similarly, if an original raw score is greater than the mean (usually referred to as above the mean), when we subtract the mean from it, its z equivalent will be a positive z. Hence, the order in the terms of the numerator in Formula 5.1 must be followed when converting raw scores to their z-score equivalents.

The denominator of the fraction on the right side of the equal sign in Formula 5.1 is the distribution's standard deviation, which, as you will recall, is a measure of how much, on average, all the scores in the distribution vary from its mean. The numerator is a measure of a particular score's deviation from the mean. So, z is a ratio of the deviation from the mean of a particular score to the standard deviation of all the scores. When the particular score is equal to the mean score, the difference between that score and the mean equals 0 ($x - \bar{x} = 0$). When the numerator of a fraction is zero, the fraction equals 0 and, therefore, $z = 0$.

Again, we'll use the set of police recruit test scores for purposes of illustration. The first column of Table 5.1 contains all 36 of the recruits' test scores. We need to convert each of these raw scores into its z-score equivalent. The first individual score listed is 8. To find the z-score equivalent, we need to know the distribution's mean score (which

Table 5.1 Police Recruit Test Raw Scores and z-Score Equivalents

Raw Test Scores	z-Score Equivalents
8	−2.08
9	−1.67
9	−1.67
10	−1.25
10	−1.25
10	−1.25
11	−.83
11	−.83
11	−.83
11	−.83
12	−.42
12	−.42
12	−.42
12	−.42
12	−.42
13	0.00
13	0.00
13	0.00
13	0.00
13	0.00
13	0.00
14	+.42
14	+.42
14	+.42
14	+.42
14	+.42
15	+.83
15	+.83
15	+.83
15	+.83
16	+1.25
16	+1.25
16	+1.25
17	+1.67
17	+1.67
18	+2.08

Note: $n = 36$, $\bar{x} = 13$, $s = 2.4$.

we found to be $\bar{x} = 13$) and standard deviation (which we found to be $s = 2.4$ scores). The z score corresponding to the score of 8, then, is given by the following:

$$z = \frac{x - \bar{x}}{s}$$
$$= \frac{8 - 13}{2.4}$$
$$= \frac{-5}{2.4}$$
$$= -2.08$$

So, for this 8 in the original raw-score distribution, we substitute a z of -2.08. Let's do one more calculation. To convert an original raw score of 17 on the test, we would have

$$z = \frac{x - \bar{x}}{s}$$
$$= \frac{17 - 13}{2.4}$$
$$= \frac{4}{2.4}$$
$$= +1.67$$

So, for each of the two scores of 17, we have $z = +1.67$. Repeating these calculations for each of the original scores will yield 36 z scores. The second column of Table 5.1 shows the z-score equivalents of all 36 scores in our original test score distribution.

Now let's make a frequency distribution line graph of the z scores we have calculated. Using the z-score equivalents of all the scores in the distribution from Table 5.1, the resulting distribution is displayed in Figure 5.10.

Note that the possible z scores are arrayed along the horizontal axis in ascending order. Note also that if we calculated the mean and standard deviation of this distribution, we would find the mean of this z-score distribution = 0 and the standard deviation = 1 (within the limits of rounding error). We will leave it to you to verify that this is the case in an exercise at the end of the chapter.

Consider what we have learned about z scores so far in a different way. If you think about the values of z we have just illustrated, you will recognize that they tell us how many standard deviations their raw-score equivalents are from the raw-score mean. That is, if a raw score converts to a z of +1, it means that that raw score is one standard deviation above the raw-score mean. And if a raw score converts to a z of -1.25, the raw score is one-and-one-fourth standard deviations below the raw-score mean.

Remember our police recruit test score example? We found that our one raw test score of 8 converted to a z-score equivalent of $z = -2.08$ (see Table 5.1). Hence, a score of 8 is more than two standard deviations below the mean, which indicates it is on the far left side of the distribution, which is, in fact, where the score of 8 falls in the distribution in Figure 5.5. Because the z-score distribution is derived from the original

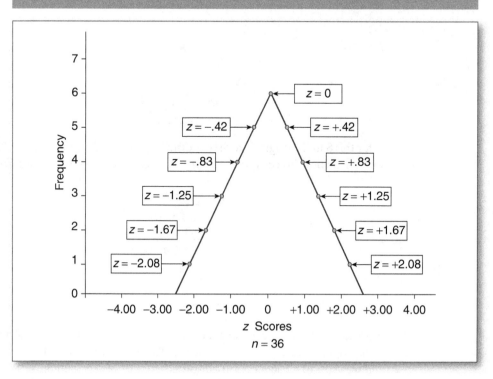

Figure 5.10 Frequency Distribution Line Graph of z-Score Equivalents of Recruit Test Scores

frequency distribution of police recruit test scores, we can work back and forth between them. We found that the mean test score for this group was 13 and the standard deviation was 2.4 scores. Hence, if we have an original test score of 15.4, that score would have a z-score equivalent of +1. It is positive because 15.4 is above the mean of 13, and it is 1 because it is 1 standard deviation above the mean of 13 (13 + 2.4 = 15.4). And, if we know an original score is 2 standard deviations below a mean of 13, it would be 13 − 2(2.4) = 13 − 4.8 = 8.2. The original test score in this case, then, is 8.2. Finally, if we know the mean of a frequency distribution and the z-score equivalent of an original score, we can determine the original score. For our distribution, if an original score had a z-score equivalent of +1.4, we would know the original score was 13 + 1.4(2.4) = 16.36.

Now suppose that we had a test with a large number of possible scores (say, a range from 100 to 800) taken by a large number of recruits (say, 12,000) and that the distribution of these raw scores was approximately normal. Suppose also that we used the procedure described above to convert the 12,000 scores to their standard normal z-score equivalents. Finally, suppose we constructed a frequency distribution of these z scores. The result would be a smoother distribution (that is, there would be many more data points in the graph and the lines connecting them would be shorter) looking a lot more like a bell than the one we drew in Figure 5.10, based on 36 scores having a range of 8 through 18.

As we noted earlier, z scores are called standard normal scores. As with approximately normal raw-score frequency distributions, z-score frequency distributions based on normally distributed raw-score data don't conform precisely to the smooth profile of a normal curve. But a normal curve can be used to approximate the distribution of z scores. The curve of z scores is called the theoretical standard normal curve, or as we call it here the **standard normal curve**. If we drew a curve to approximate this distribution, it would look like the one in Figure 5.11.

Note that this curve is like the one in Figure 5.7, except that it has a mean of zero and a standard deviation of one. Nevertheless, as in the curve in Figure 5.7, .3413 of the area under the curve lies between the mean and one standard deviation above the mean ($z = 1$), .0227 of the area lies beyond $z = +2.00$, and so on.

In this curve, the z score is assumed to be a continuous ratio variable and can, in principle, assume an infinite number of values between 0.00 and 1.00, between 1.00 and 2.00, beyond 3.00 and so on. In practice, z seldom exceeds a value of ±3.00.

Remember that in the normal curve, there is a fixed association between units of standard deviation from the mean and proportions of areas under the curve. When we convert normally distributed variable values to their z-score equivalents and create a standard normal (z-score) curve approximation of them, this relationship still obtains. This, in turn, makes it possible to construct a z-score table specifying the areas under the standard normal curve corresponding to scores above or below any given z score or between two specified z scores.

Figure 5.11 The Standard Normal Curve Subdivided by Units of Standard Deviation With Corresponding Proportion of Area Under the Curve

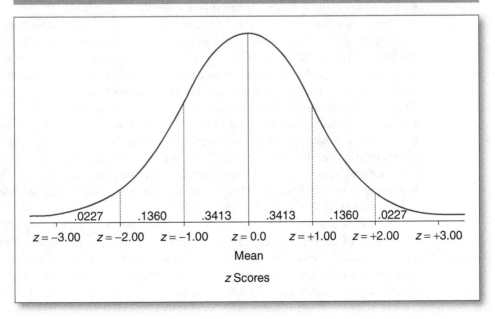

The z-Score Table

A **z-score table** is based on a cumulative proportion or percent normal curve similar to those we discussed in Chapter 3. (You might want to review the discussion on pp. 67–71 of Chapter 3 now to refresh your memory about cumulative percent distribution tables and line graphs.) As we saw in our discussion there, a cumulative frequency distribution permits us to say what proportion of the scores in a distribution falls above or below any particular score. It also allows us to specify what proportion falls between two scores in the distribution. If we were to make a cumulative proportion line graph of z scores, it would have the general shape illustrated in Figure 5.12, which is the general shape of any cumulative distribution based on a normal raw-score frequency or percent distribution. Compare Figure 5.12 to Figures 3.6 and 3.7 on pages 70 and 72 in Chapter 3. We can use the z-score table in the same ways we used the cumulative proportion or percent distributions we discussed in Chapter 3 and earlier in this chapter. The only difference is that, in this case, we have a cumulative percent or proportion curve of the z-score equivalents of raw scores. A z-score table is provided in Appendix D on the study site (www.sagepub.com/fitzgerald).

Using the z-Score Table

Have a look at the z-score table in Appendix D and read "How to Use the z-Score Table" now. Note that the table contents apply to the area under only half of the standard normal curve. This is so because this curve, like all bell-shaped normal curves, is symmetric about its mean—that is, its shape on one side of the mean is the mirror image of its shape on the other side of the mean. The information in the table about the z scores and corresponding areas under the standard normal (z-score) curve for one side of the distribution applies to the other side as well. Look again at Figure 5.11. If the z-score table includes areas under the curve for z scores below the mean, they would simply replicate those above the mean—an unnecessary duplication.

Remember that the mean of a z-score distribution and of the z-score curve approximating the distribution equals zero and the standard deviation is one. Note also that the z scores in the table are not signed but the z scores we calculate *are* signed. The plus or minus sign of the z we calculate indicates whether it (and, of course, its raw-score equivalent) lies above (is greater than) or below (is less than) the mean, respectively. That is, it tells us in which half of the z-score curve our calculated z lies. To interpret properly the information provided in the table, you have to keep track of the sign on the z score you have calculated and remember what the sign signifies regarding the score's location relative to the mean in the z-score distribution and curve.

Look at column A of the z-score table, where the possible values of z are listed, beginning at the top with $z = 0.00$. If you read down column A, you will see that the values of z gradually rise until reaching 4.00.

Now look at columns B and C in the z-score table. Note that column B gives the proportion of the area under half the z-score curve between the mean of zero and a given z. Column C gives the proportion of the area under half the z-score curve beyond (greater than) a given z. Note that if the z we calculate is positive, the values beyond z would be greater than our calculated value. If the z we calculate is negative, the values

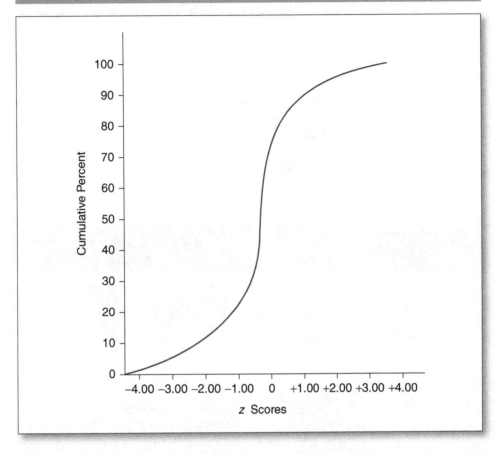

Figure 5.12 Cumulative Percent Line Graph of z Scores for a Normal Distribution

beyond z would be less than our calculated value. For any given z in column A, the sum of columns B and C equals .500 (allowing for rounding error). So, the sum of the proportions in columns B and C always includes the entire half of the distribution.

Starting at the top, read down column B and you will see that the proportions begin at .0000 and rise, reflecting the growing area under the curve between the mean and z as the values of z rise. Starting at the top, read down column C and you will see the quantities begin at .5000 and gradually decline as the values of z and the quantities in column B rise.

Thus, different values of z in the table divide half of the standard normal curve in different proportions depending on how far the particular value of z is from the mean of z. Note that the rate at which the cumulative proportions in columns B and C change varies as the values of z go up, as we would expect from looking at the areas under the curve corresponding to the zs. For example, the change in column B from

$z = .05$ through $z = .09$ is from .0199 to .0359, which is a change of .0160. The change in column B from $z = 3.40$ through $z = 3.70$ is from .4997 to .4999, a difference of only .0002. Note also that if we wish to know the area under the whole curve above or below a particular z, we would need to add .500 to the proportions in some cases. Let's use some examples to see how all of this works.

Areas and Proportions Under Half of the z-Score Curve Between the Mean and z and Beyond z

Suppose we have done the appropriate calculations and found $z = +1.31$ for a particular raw score in an approximately normal distribution. To find the proportion of the area under the standard normal curve between the mean and $z = +1.31$, we locate $z = 1.31$ in column A of the z-score table. The corresponding entry in column B is .4049 or 40.49%, as illustrated in Figure 5.13.

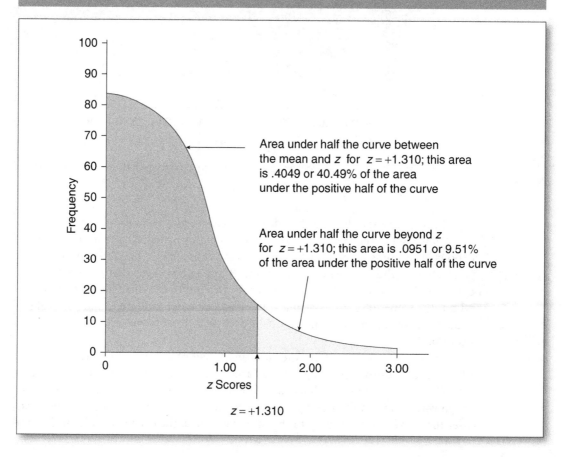

Figure 5.13 Illustrations of Areas Under Half the z-Score Curve Between the Mean and z and Beyond z

The proportion of the area under the curve beyond z is found in the corresponding column C. The entry there is .0951, indicating that 9.51% of the area under the curve lies beyond $z = +1.31$. Note that $.4049 + .0951 = .5000$.

Note, again, that, taking the whole z-score curve into consideration, there is an important distinction between positive and negative z scores when referring to values of z "beyond" (that is, greater or less than) a specified value of z. Remember, the values of z scores beyond (to the right of) a positive z are larger than the specified z, and the values of z scores beyond (to the left of) a negative z are less than the specified z. We will need to bear this distinction in mind when we consider areas beyond (greater or less than) a specified z.

Areas and Proportions Under Half of the z-Score Curve Between Two zs With the Same Sign

Suppose we want to know the proportion of the area under the curve between $z = -0.95$ and $z = -1.83$. In this case, we find the area between the mean and $z = -0.95$ and between the mean and $z = -1.83$. From the z-score table, we find the entry in column B for $z = 0.95$ to be .3289 and the entry in column B for $z = 1.83$ to be .4664. To find the area under the curve between $z = -0.95$ and $z = -1.83$, we subtract the smaller from the larger area. We then have $.4664 - .3289 = .1375$, as illustrated in Figure 5.14.

Figure 5.14 Illustrations of the Area Under Half the z-Score Curve Between Two zs With the Same Sign

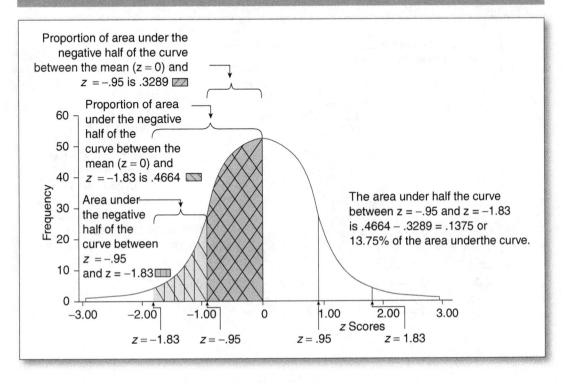

Areas and Proportions Under the Whole z-Score Curve Between Two zs With Different Signs

Suppose we wish to find the area under the curve between $z = -1.26$ and $z = +1.78$. In this case, we would sum the area between the mean and $z = -1.26$ and the area between the mean and $z = +1.78$. Remember that the area between the mean and $z = -1.26$ is the same as the area between the mean and $z = +1.26$, which, again, is why the table presents proportions of area under the curve for only half the z-score curve. Consulting the table for $z = 1.26$ in column A, we find the corresponding entry in column B to be .3962. The entry in column B of the table for $z = 1.78$ is .4625. Summing these two areas, we have $.3962 + .4625 = .8587$, as illustrated in Figure 5.15.

Let's do one more of these. Suppose we wanted to know the area under the curve between $z = -1.96$ and $z = +1.96$. Locating $z = 1.96$, we find the corresponding column B entry to be .4750. So, we sum the two areas, which is $.4750 + .4750 = .9500$. Note that this means .0250 of the area under the curve lies under each of the curve's two tails of the distribution, for a total of .05 or 5%, as indicated in Figure 5.16.

Areas Under the Whole z-Score Curve Below (Less Than) z or Above (Greater Than) z

Suppose we want to know the area under the curve below (less than) $z = +1.64$. Locating $z = 1.64$ in column A of the table, we find the area between the mean of zero

Figure 5.15 Illustration of the Area Under the Whole z-Score Curve Between Two zs With Different Signs

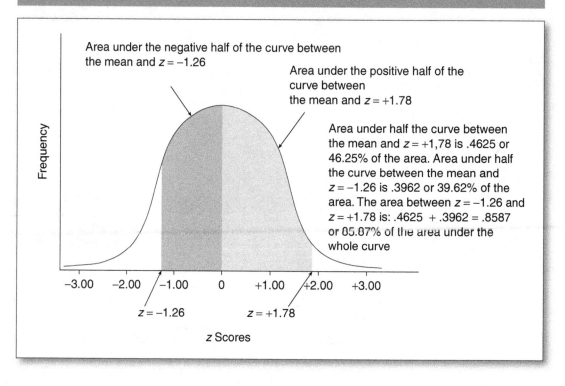

Figure 5.16 Illustration of the Area Under the Whole z-Score Curve Between $z = -1.96$ and $z = +1.96$

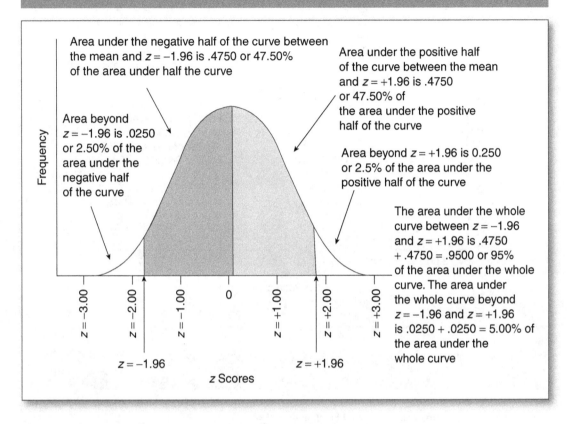

and $z = 1.64$ to be .4495. Note that in this case, because we have asked for the area under the curve for values of z less than $z = +1.64$, we need to add the area under the left side of the curve, which is .5000, as well. Why? Because all of the z scores in that half of the z-score curve are also below $z = +1.64$. So, we have .4495 + .5000 = .9495, as illustrated in Figure 5.17a. Note that this is equivalent to saying a z score of +1.64 (and its corresponding original score) lies at the 94.95th percentile of the curve.

On the other hand, if we had asked for the area under the curve below $z = -1.64$, the correct answer would be given in column C of the table corresponding to $z = 1.64$, as illustrated in Figure 5.17b. Why? Because all of the values of z in the other half of the curve are above, not below, $z = -1.64$. In percentile terms, a z of -1.64 (and its corresponding original score) lies at the 5.05th percentile.

The same basic arguments apply for areas under the curve for values above a particular value of z. For example, the area (and proportion of z scores) above $z = +1.64$ is found in column C. The entry there is .0505. Why? Because all of the z scores in the other half of the curve are below, not above, $z = +1.64$, as illustrated in Figure 5.17c.

Figure 5.17a Illustration of the Area Under the Whole z-Score Curve Below (Less Than) a Positive z

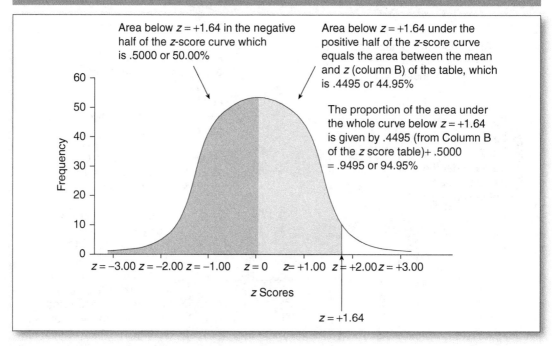

Figure 5.17b Illustration of the Area Under the Whole z-Score Curve Below (Less Than) a Negative z

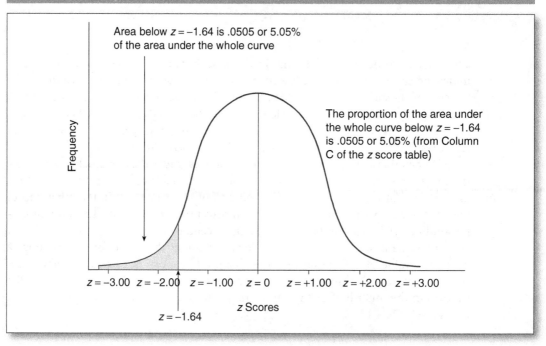

Distributions: Normal and Otherwise ❖ **157**

Figure 5.17c Illustration of the Area Under the Whole z-Score Curve Above a Positive z

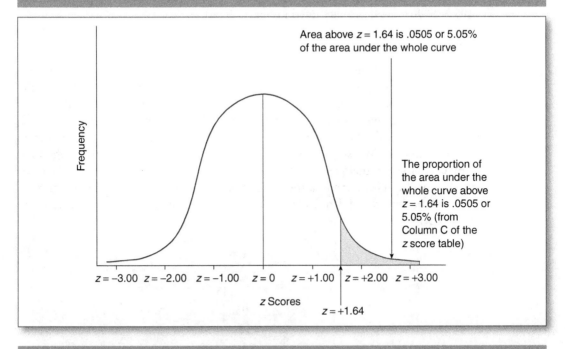

Figure 5.17d Illustration of the Area Under the Whole z-Score Curve Above (Greater Than) a Negative z

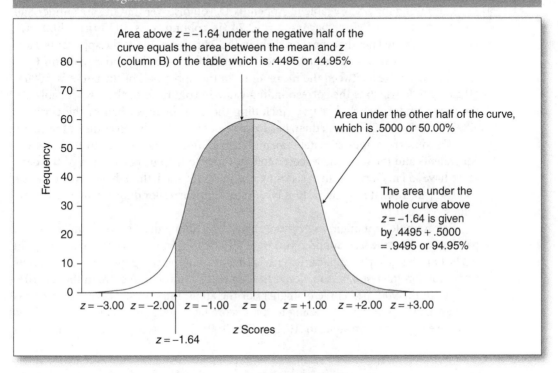

On the other hand, finding the area above $z = -1.64$ requires adding the area under the other half of the curve to the entry in column B, which is .4495. So, we would have .4495 + .5000 = .9495, as illustrated in Figure 5.17d.

A Few More Examples Using z Scores

Suppose that the FBI has given a written entrance test to 3,410 applicants for entry-level positions with the agency. You are charged with the responsibility of analyzing the scores. In doing so, you discover that the scores the applicants received on their tests range from 125 to 765 and are approximately normally distributed around a mean score of 445, with a standard deviation of 95. If one of the applicants writes you inquiring about her score on the test and how her performance compared to the others who took it, you could look up that person's test paper and determine that she received a score of 658. What will you tell her about the place of her score in the distribution of scores?

It will be very convenient to transform the raw score of 658 into a z-score using Formula 5.1.

$$z = \frac{x - \bar{x}}{s}$$
$$= \frac{658 - 445}{95}$$
$$= +\frac{213}{95}$$
$$= +2.24$$

Consulting the z-score table in Appendix D, you discover that the area under half the standard normal curve beyond $z = +2.24$ (in column A) is .0125 (in column C). Hence, you can tell her that she scored above the 98th percentile of the applicants. How did we arrive at this conclusion? Remember that if the area beyond z (column C) is .0125, then the area between the mean and z in the upper half of the curve is .5000 − .0125 = .4875, which is the corresponding value in column B of the z-score table. All the scores under the whole curve (including those in the lower half of the curve) is .4875 + .5000 = .9875. In fact, then, her score was at the 98.75th percentile of the curve.

We convert an approximately normal distribution of raw scores to their z-score equivalents and then use the z-score table in order to help us make sense of the data, as we have so far. Once the analysis using z scores is finished, though, in many cases we will want to translate z-score values back into their corresponding original raw-score values.

For example, you might use z-score analysis, including the z-score formula, to set a passing score for the test. Suppose you were told that there were 341 actual openings in the FBI for this group of applicants. This is 10% of the applicant pool. You want to know what score on the test a person would have to receive in order to score in the top 10% (that is, in the 90th percentile or higher) of the applicants. What z score corresponds with an area beyond $z = .10$? Going to the z-score table, we look in column C until we find the entry nearest in value to .10. Locating .1003 (which is the closest we can come) in column C, we read the corresponding z score, $z = 1.28$, in column A. We now know that this z score marks the point in the distribution and on the standard normal curve such that approximately the top 10% of scores lie above it. Hence, we need to substitute the information we have into Formula 5.1 and solve for the unknown, x.

Recall from your high school algebra course that $z = z/1$ and that to solve such equations, we can cross-multiply. That is, we multiply the numerator on one side of the equation by the denominator on the other side.

$$z = \frac{x - \bar{x}}{s}$$

$$\frac{1.28}{1} = \frac{x - 445}{95}$$

$$95(1.28) = x - 445$$

$$121.6 = x - 445$$

$$445 + 121.6 = x$$

$$x = 566.6$$

About 10% of the applicants received scores of 566 or above, so you might set the passing grade as a score of 567. Or, if we were to think about this in percentile terms, we could say that a score of 566 is equal to or higher than 90% of the scores, which means a score of 566 is equivalent to the 90th percentile of the curve and the distribution. Like quantiles, z scores are of considerable utility when questions about the location of particular scores relative to others in the distribution are the analyst's concern.

As indicated at the outset of our discussion of z scores, we can also think of them as having uses analogous to those of percents. Percents permit us to compare proportions with different base numbers (denominators) by converting them to equivalent expressions, all with a common base of 100. Similarly, converting approximately normal raw-score frequency distributions into their standard normal z-score equivalent curves allows meaningful comparisons when measurement ranges or scales in the raw-score distributions are different. For example, one police recruit test may be marked in such a way that scores range from 20 to 150, whereas another may produce scores ranging from 400 to 800. If the raw scores received by test takers are normally distributed in both cases, converting the distributions to their standard normal equivalents (z scores) makes comparing performances on the two tests as easy as comparing percents, despite the differences in raw-score ranges.

Finally, just as we can calculate a mean and standard deviation for distributions of any shape, any raw-score distribution can be converted to a z-score distribution regardless of its shape. The resulting z-score distribution will retain the shape of the original raw-score distribution. That is, a skewed raw-score distribution will yield a skewed z-score distribution. Applying the z-score procedures we have described in this chapter to non-normal distributions is likely to produce misleading results. Hence, the z-score applications we have described earlier should be used only for those z-score distributions derived from raw-score distributions that are approximately normal.

A Note About Tests for Normality

In the earlier sections of this chapter, we discussed the normal curve as a theoretical distribution. As we noted then, when data about the real world are gathered, variable value distributions almost never conform exactly to the smooth contour of a normal curve. However, many distributions, though slightly skewed and/or otherwise somewhat non-normal in shape, can be approximated by the normal curve for the purposes of statistical analysis. But this raises an important question: How close to a normal curve does a distribution of real data have to be to justify using the normal curve as an analytical tool?

Statisticians have developed a number of different quantitative measures to help researchers determine the degree to which a data distribution may depart from normal and still qualify as a normal distribution for purposes of analysis. Some measure how well observed distributions match or "fit" the normal curve. They are often referred to as "goodness-of-fit" tests. Some measure a distribution's degree of skewness, whereas others focus on other characteristics. New measures are proposed from time to time. The prerequisite conditions under which the various measures of departure from normality may be applied are subjects of considerable debate among statisticians. (See http://spcforexcel.com/are-skewness-and-kurtosis-useful-statistics for a discussion of some of the issues involved.) Furthermore, statisticians differ on how much departure from normality is acceptable when analyzing data distributions as if they were normal. Most do agree, however, that the acceptable degree of departure varies depending on the statistical analysis tools being applied. The formulas for these measures, the difficulties surrounding the establishment of appropriate standards to help decide whether a distribution is "normal enough," and the questions surrounding their use are beyond the scope of this text.

Whether or not statistical measures of departure from normality or descriptive statistics are used to assess the normality of a distribution, we recommend that you construct (or have a computer construct) a frequency distribution line graph of the values for each of the variables of interest. Then "eyeball" them and compare them with the normal curve as a first step in data analysis. It is the easiest and perhaps even the best way to test for normality. The graph should readily reveal whether the distribution is unimodal and symmetric about its mean. If the graph reveals the distribution to be skewed or bi- or multimodal, this should be reported and appropriate cautions should be used when interpreting measures of central tendency, dispersion, and location as well as z scores for the distribution. Of course, we are still left with the question of exactly how much departure from normal is acceptable, but at least a graph provides useful visual information about the nature and degree of a distribution's departure from normality.

In any event, we can use what we know now about means, standard deviations, and corresponding areas under the normal distribution curve to determine if a distribution is approximately normal or not. If the distribution's mode and median values differ considerably from that of the mean, we know the distribution is not a normal one. Similarly, if a reported mean is not near the center of the range of possible variable values, the distribution is likely to be skewed. The farther the mean is from the center of the range, the greater is the likelihood of substantial skewness.

Furthermore, when a mean and standard deviation for a distribution are reported, we can tell something about the shape of the distribution from those statistics. If dividing the horizontal axis using the reported values of the mean and standard deviation results in division points that quickly (within one or two units of standard deviation) exceed the upper or lower boundaries of the range of possible variable values, we know the distribution is not normal. For example, if a distribution with a range of possible variable values from 5 to 55 is reported to have a mean of 35 and a standard deviation of 15, we know that the distribution is not normal. Why? Because the upper boundary of the range of scores (55) is just a little more than one standard deviation above the mean, whereas the lower boundary (5) is slightly more than two standard deviations below the mean. In a normal distribution, the upper and lower boundaries should be about the same number of standard deviations from the mean.

Still, we must remember that a distribution that is symmetric about its mean and whose mean, median, and mode are equal is not necessarily normal. Nor is a mean in about the middle of the range of possible variable values necessarily a sign of a normal distribution.

Summary

In this chapter, we revisited and expanded our discussion of proportional area graphs, focusing on the relationship between percents (proportional frequencies) and total areas encompassed by the graph. We used this relationship to understand some of the special characteristics of normal distributions, as well as normal curves and areas under them. In the process of describing these characteristics, we completed our definition of a normal distribution. In addition to being bell shaped, unimodal, and symmetric about its mean, a normal distribution and a normal curve have fixed proportions of the areas under the curve corresponding to the number of standard deviation units from its mean. The fixed relationships between the units of standard deviation from the mean and areas under the curve are displayed in Figure 5.7.

The procedure for converting any normal raw-score distribution to a standard normal distribution was described. To accomplish the conversion, we used a formula for converting each variable value in the original distribution to its standard or z-score equivalent. We then constructed a frequency distribution of the z scores that was also normal. A standard normal distribution and its standard normal curve approximation are unimodal and symmetric about the mean, with a mean, a median, and a mode equal to zero and a standard deviation equal to one.

Ways of using z scores, the distribution of z scores, the standard normal curve, and the z-score table for analyzing and interpreting data were described and explored. Understanding these procedures and concepts is essential for many kinds of statistical analysis. We will make considerable use of the normal curve, the standard normal curve, and z scores in subsequent chapters.

Finally, we used what we learned about normal distributions together with our knowledge of measures of central tendency and dispersion to identify distributions that depart from normality. Whatever those measures suggest about the distribution's shape, we recommend that a frequency or percent distribution line graph be constructed for each of the variables of interest. This will provide some useful visual information about the shape of the distribution and indicate whether it can reasonably be approximated by the standard normal curve. If it can't, of course, the standard normal curve approximating procedures we have described in this chapter should not be used for the analysis.

Concepts to Master

Areas under the normal curve
Gaussian curve or distribution
Normal curve
Proportional area bar graph
Standard normal curve (theoretical)
Standard scores
Theoretical normal curve
z scores
z-score table

Review Questions

1. What are proportional area frequency and percent bar graphs?

2. In a proportional area bar graph, what is the relationship between the area of a particular bar and the frequency or percent with which the corresponding variable value occurs in the distribution?

3. How are bar graphs converted into line graphs?

4. In a proportional area line graph, what is the relationship between the area under the line (curve) associated with a particular variable value and the frequency or percent with which that variable value occurs in the distribution?

5. What is the complete definition of the normal curve?

6. What is a theoretical normal distribution? How do normal curves differ from approximately normal distributions based on gathered data?

7. What are the special characteristics of the normal curve?

8. What are the relationships between areas under the normal curve and the frequency or percent with which variables' values occur?

9. How might the special characteristics of the normal curve be useful in statistical analysis? Give examples.

10. What is a standard normal curve, and how might it be useful in statistical analysis? Give examples.

11. How does a normal distribution for data on a particular variable differ from a standard normal curve?

12. What is the value of the mean and the standard deviation of any standard normal curve?

13. What are z scores, and how are they calculated?
14. Describe the process of converting a raw-score distribution into its z-score equivalent.
15. Are all z-score conversions of raw-score distributions normal? Why or why not?
16. What are the relationships between areas under the theoretical standard normal curve and the frequency or percent with which variables' values occur?
17. How can z scores be used in statistical analysis? Give examples.
18. What is a z-score table? Why is it called a cumulative distribution?
19. How is a z-score table used? What do the entries in a z-score table tell the user? Give examples.
20. Why does a z-score table include entries for only half of the z-score distribution?
21. Under what circumstances would it be necessary to add the other half of the z-score distribution to answer a question about areas under the curve?
22. What is a simple and basic test for how close a distribution of variable values approximates the theoretical normal curve?
23. What are some other ways of assessing how closely a distribution of variable values approximates the theoretical normal curve?
24. Define each of the terms in the "Concepts to Master" list and use each in three different sentences.

Exercises and Discussion Questions

1. If you haven't already done so, answer the questions in the "Pause, Think, and Explore" box in this chapter.
2. Identify and discuss the special characteristics of the normal curve.
3. Draw a theoretical normal curve with a mean of 48 and a standard deviation of 13, labeling the horizontal axis in units of standard deviation, dividing the area under the curve into parts, and indicating the corresponding proportions of area under the curve.
4. Draw a theoretical normal curve with a mean of −10 and a standard deviation of 3. Label the horizontal axis in units of standard deviation, dividing the area under the curve into parts and indicating the corresponding proportions of area under the curve.
5. Draw a theoretical normal curve with a mean of .59 and a standard deviation of .15. Label the horizontal axis in units of standard deviation, dividing the area under the curve into parts and indicating the corresponding proportions of area under the curve.

6. Draw a standard normal curve for each of the theoretical normal curves you drew in Exercises 3, 4, and 5. Compare them with each other and with the graphs you drew in Exercises 3, 4, and 5.

7. Verify that the z scores in Table 5.1 have a mean of zero and a standard deviation of one (allowing for rounding error).

8. Suppose you have a distribution with a mean score of 98 and a standard deviation of 25. Convert the following scores from the distribution to their z-score equivalents. Round your answers to the nearest thousandth.

   10

   108

   180

   25

   98

   64

   143

9. Using the z-score table in Appendix D, find the areas under the curve (and proportions of variable values) for the values of z as indicated. (Draw graphs of the z-score distribution illustrating the result if that helps you.)

   The area between the mean and $z = +0.51$

   The area between the mean and $z = -3.01$

   The area between the mean and $z = +3.01$

   The area between the mean and $z = +1.96$

   The area between the mean and $z = -1.07$

   The area beyond z when $z = -0.79$

   The area beyond z when $z = -2.54$

   The area beyond z when $z = +1.43$

   The area beyond z when $z = +0.66$

   The area beyond z when $z = -0.66$

   The area between $z = +0.67$ and $z = +1.35$

   The area between $z = +1.35$ and $z = +2.59$

   The area between $z = -0.84$ and $z = -1.89$

   The area between $z = -2.25$ and $z = -2.75$

   The area between $z = -0.67$ and $z = +3.01$

   The area between $z = -2.15$ and $z = +1.35$

   The area between $z = -1.47$ and $z = +0.64$

   The area for z scores above (greater than) $z = +2.26$

The area for z scores below (less than) $z = +2.26$

The area for z scores above (greater than) $z = -2.26$

The area for z scores below (less than) $z = -2.26$

The area for z scores above (greater than) $z = +.79$

The area for z scores below (less than) $z = +2.98$

10. Suppose you have gathered breathalyzer readings for 350 adults recently arrested for assault. In the initial stages of your data analysis, you determine that the readings are approximately normally distributed with a mean reading of .075 and a standard deviation of .021. The prosecutor asks you where one of the defendants whose reading was .083 stands among those arrested. Use these data, what you have learned about z scores, and the z-score table to answer the following questions:

   a. What proportion and how many of the readings were above .083?
   b. What proportion and how many of the readings were above .035?
   c. What proportion and how many of the readings were below .054?
   d. What proportion and how many of the readings were below .075?
   e. What proportion and how many of the readings were between .054 and .119?
   f. What proportion and how many of the readings were between .038 and .185?

11. Suppose you teach a course in statistics and you grade on the curve (the *normal* curve, that is). You have given a final exam to your statistics class of 65 students. The scores, which are approximately normally distributed, range from 5 to 145 with a mean of 73 and a standard deviation of 22. If you wish to give As to the top 10% of your class, how many As would you give and what score on the exam would be the division point between As and Bs? If 40% of the class were to get Cs, what would be the highest and lowest score to earn a C?

12. Suppose you read reports of measures of central tendency and dispersion for distributions as follows. Using this information alone, which distributions are not normal? Which ones are normal? Draw graphs to help you decide. Explain each of your answers.

Range of Possible Scores	Mean	Standard Deviation
0–100	50	35
45–75	65	4
10–206	139	33
80–200	100	45
5–35	20	5.5

13. Go to www.google.com and search for "normal curve" and "standard normal curve." Click on "images of normal curve" and "images of standard normal curve" and explore.

Student Study Site

Visit the open-access student study site at **www.sagepub.com/fitzgerald** for access to several study tools including eFlashcards, web quizzes, and additional appendices as well as links to SAGE journal articles and audio, video and web resources.

An Introduction to Probability Theory and Probability Distributions

Learning Objectives

What you are expected not only to learn but to master in this chapter:

- The nature of probability and probability theory
- Seven rules of probability theory
- The nature of probability distributions
- The characteristics of binomial distributions
- The binomial distribution's use as a probability distribution
- Normal curve approximations of the binomial distribution
- The relationships among probability, probability distributions, and random sampling

Introduction

In Chapters 3, 4, and 5 of this book, we discussed univariate descriptive statistics. In this chapter, we provide the basis for moving beyond description to univariate, bivariate, and multivariate inferential statistics, which will occupy us for most of the remainder of the book. That basis is probability theory and probability distributions.

As we noted in Chapter 3, inferential statistical analysis builds on, but differs from, statistical description in important ways. We use descriptive statistics (e.g., frequency counts, proportions, means, and standard deviations) to describe data and data distributions, whether the data are from a sample or a whole population. If the data are from a random sample of a population, however, the sample statistics, together with probability theory, can be used to estimate the corresponding statistics of the population from which the sample was drawn. The procedures for doing so are called **inferential statistics**.

In the context of inferential statistical analysis, the statistics we calculate to describe sample data (e.g., a sample mean) are called **sample statistics** and the corresponding statistics for the population from which the sample was drawn (e.g., mean for the population) are called **population parameters**.

We begin with a discussion of probability theory, including some basic rules for assigning and calculating probabilities. Binomial distributions and binomial probability distributions, as well as normal curve approximations of binomials, are described. Finally, we explore the relationships among probability theory, probability distributions, and random sampling.

Probability Theory

The origins of probability theory can be traced to the work of Blaise Pascal and Christiaan Huygens in the 17th and 18th centuries. Inferential statistics, which we discussed briefly in Chapter 3, rely heavily on probability theory. To take the next steps in developing our understanding of inferential statistics and their uses in making sense of the data we have assembled, we need to consider the nature of probability, as well as how statisticians assign and calculate probabilities, in more detail.

For our purposes, a **probability** (symbolized here as p) may be defined as the relative frequency (percent) or proportion of times a particular outcome occurs or is expected to occur. An **outcome** (sometimes called an **event** by statisticians) is the result of a theoretical random experiment. We say theoretical random experiment because, as we will see, activities that meet the assumptions of a random experiment are seldom found in the real world. (In this sense, theoretical random experiments are like theoretical normal curves.) A theoretical **random experiment**, often referred to as a **trial**, is an imaginary activity whose outcome (result) is due to chance. (Note that this use of the term *experiment* is different from its use in reference to an experimental research design that we discussed in Chapter 2, pp. 35–38.) **Probability theory** is a branch of mathematics that provides rules for determining the probabilities of outcomes from theoretical random experiments, given certain specified assumptions.

However, we can use these theoretical experiments to approximate and help analyze events in the real world.

To illustrate theoretical random experiments and the rules of probability theory, statisticians often use simple imaginary examples from everyday life, such as flipping a coin, rolling a six-sided die, blindly selecting a card from a deck of 52 playing cards, or drawing at random an element from a population for inclusion in a sample for study. Corresponding examples from real life of the outcomes of theoretical random experiments include getting a head in a coin flip, rolling a 2 on a die, drawing the ace of spades from a deck of cards, and you being drawn for a sample. We use these examples, too, because they are easy to describe and relatively simple to grasp. As we do so, though, just bear in mind that real coins and coin flips, or real dice and die rolls, or actual decks of cards and draws from them do not always conform to the theoretical assumptions in probability theory. Real coins, for example, are rarely completely fair (that is, the probability of heads is not exactly .5000).

In probability theory, probabilities are also often said to apply to outcomes from an infinite number of trials. Of course, by definition, we can't actually perform an infinite number of trials. This is another reason probability theory must be considered an abstract mathematical exercise.

It's also important to remember throughout our discussion that probability theory doesn't tell us what specific outcome will, in fact, occur in any particular trial or series of trials. It tells us only what proportion of times the outcome(s) are expected to occur over an infinite number of trials, given the assumptions governing the theoretical random experiment and its outcomes.

Nevertheless, as we will see, the basic principles of probability theory illustrated by coin flips, die rolls, and so on (trials) and their outcomes can be applied to help shed light on complex issues or test hypotheses criminal justice professionals might encounter in their own practice or research or in the research of others. Examples might include adjudication by jury (which can be regarded as a trial, in the random experiment sense) and being sentenced to jail time for a minor violation (an outcome); taking a test (a trial) and getting a particular score or higher on the test (an outcome); being issued a warning instead of a citation (an outcome) after a stop for speeding (a trial); being placed on probation (a trial) and then failing probation and being sent back to jail (an outcome); or a citizen completing a survey question about local traffic court performance (a trial) and the citizen's rating of traffic court performance as excellent (an outcome). Of course, each of these trials might have other outcomes as well. Often, as we noted earlier, data like these are analyzed by comparing them with the mathematical model of trials and outcomes produced by applying probability theory. When you finish this book, you should understand how this is accomplished and have some appreciation for the many uses of probability theory in criminal justice practice and research.

Some Rules of Probability Theory

Probability theory requires that probabilities be assigned to and/or calculated for specific outcomes or combinations of outcomes according to some basic rules. To understand the basics of how statisticians use probability theory as a tool for making statistical inferences about population parameters from sample statistics, we need to learn about these rules and how they are applied.

Our consideration of probability theory rules is divided into two parts. In the first part, we consider rules that pertain to assigning and calculating probabilities associated with single trials and their outcomes. In the second part, we consider probability rules pertaining to combinations of outcomes from more than one trial.

Rules for Outcomes of a Single Trial

We begin our discussion of the rules for assigning and/or calculating probabilities by considering a single trial and its outcomes. To illustrate the applications of these rules, we'll use examples such as a coin toss or a die roll.

The first rule of probability theory is as follows: *An exhaustive list of the possible outcomes of a trial must be specified.* An **exhaustive list of possible outcomes** is a list that specifies every possible outcome of a trial—it "exhausts" all the possibilities.

Specifying an exhaustive list of the possible outcomes of a trial is usually pretty straightforward, at least theoretically. For example, we might specify that there are only two possible outcomes of a coin flip: head up (H) or tail up (T). We can also identify a complete list of six possible outcomes of a die roll: 1, 2, 3, 4, 5, and 6, corresponding with the six faces of the die that may face up after a roll. Similarly, we can specify all possible answers to a survey question or all possible criminal court rulings or all possible ratings of a rookie's performance.

Note that the theoretical nature of these specifications is revealed when we acknowledge that our exhaustive list of possible outcomes ignores some that may occur in a "real" trial. Our coin might land on edge, for example, or disappear through the street gutter grate. Still, for reasons that will become clear later when we consider the sum of probabilities of outcomes, the list of possible outcomes must be regarded as exhaustive for the purposes of theoretical probability analysis.

The second rule of probability theory is as follows: *The possible outcomes of a single trial must be mutually exclusive.* **Mutually exclusive possible outcomes** are outcomes such that one and only one can occur in any single trial.

Do the criteria of exhaustive and mutually exclusive outcomes sound familiar? They should, because they are the same two criteria we used in Chapter 2 to specify the requirements for the different values of a variable if we are going to subject them to statistical analysis. (For a review of the concepts of mutually exclusive and exhaustive as applied to variable values, see Chapter 2, p. 23.) When a variable's specified values are exhaustive and mutually exclusive, they conform to the first two rules of probability theory.

In a coin flip, the two possible outcomes we have specified (H or T) are exhaustive and mutually exclusive because only the two specified outcomes are possible, and we can get either H or T, but not both, in a single trial (flip). In the case of a die roll, the six possible outcomes are exhaustive and mutually exclusive because we know there are only six possible outcomes and we can get only one of the six outcomes in a single trial.

We can't get both a 2 and a 6, for example, with one roll of a die. Similarly, guilty, not guilty, mistrial, and hung jury are the exhaustive and mutually exclusive possible outcomes of a jury trial.

Once we have specified the exhaustive and mutually exclusive outcomes of a trial (in the random experiment, not judicial, sense), we can assign a probability to each of the outcomes. Theoretically, these assignments are arbitrary. That is, we can assign any probabilities we wish, so long as they satisfy the third and fourth rules of probability theory.

The third rule of probability theory is as follows: *None of the possible outcomes in a trial can be assigned a probability larger than 1.00 or less than 0.00.* A probability of 1.00 is equivalent to certainty that the outcome to which this probability is assigned *will* occur. A probability of 0.00 assigned to an outcome means that the outcome is impossible, that it will never occur. Probabilities greater than certainty or less than impossible make no sense in probability theory (or in real life, for that matter).

The fourth rule of probability theory is as follows: *The probabilities assigned to the mutually exclusive, exhaustive possible outcomes in a single trial must sum to 1.00.* In the case of a coin toss, we might assign to heads a probability of ½ or .50 and to tails a probability of ½ or .50, which when summed equals 1.00. This would be assuming a fair coin, one for which each of the two possible outcomes is equally likely. In the die roll, each face of the die might be assigned the probability of 1/6 or .1667 (rounded to the nearest ten thousandth). Summing the probabilities associated with the six faces, we get 1.0002, rounded to the nearest ten thousandth. This would be a fair die, one for which each of the six possible outcomes is equally likely.

As long as the probability assignments conform to the first three rules, this fourth rule holds no matter what probabilities we assign to the possible outcomes. For example, if we assign to one of two possible outcomes a probability of .60, the other outcome must then be assigned a probability of .40, so that the two probabilities sum to 1.00.

It follows from the fourth rule that the probability of getting any outcome other than any one particular outcome is one minus that outcome. For example, the probability of getting an outcome other than, say, a 2 in the roll of a die is p(other than a 2) = $1 - p(2)$ or $1 - .1667$ (rounded), which equals .8333 (rounded).

The fifth rule of probability theory (often referred to by statisticians as a special form of the addition rule) is as follows: *The probability of getting one* or *another mutually exclusive, exhaustive, independent outcomes is the* sum *of the probabilities of each of the outcomes.* We will discuss what independent means in this context in a bit. For now, we'll note that in our coin toss example, where we have specified that $p(H) = p(T) = .5000$, if we want to know the probability of getting a head *or* a tail in one flip, we sum the two probabilities (.5000 + .5000), which equals 1.00. In this case, the result tells us that either one or the other of the outcomes must occur, because we have specified that these are the only two possible outcomes.

In a fair die roll, if we want to know the probability of getting a 1 *or* a 2 in one roll, we sum the probabilities associated with getting each of the two outcomes. In this case, because the probability of getting any one of the six outcomes is .1667 (rounded), we add .1667 + .1667 and get a .3334 probability (rounded) of getting a 1 *or* a 2 in one roll of a die. It follows from the fourth general rule of probability theory that the probability of getting a 3 *or* a 4 *or* a 5 *or* a 6 (the only other possible outcomes) must then be 1 − .3334 = .6666 (rounded), and according to the fifth rule, .1667 + .1667 + .1667 + .1667 = .6668 (rounded). (The discrepancy between .6666 and .6668 is due to rounding error.) If we want to know the probability of getting a 3 *or* a 5 *or* a 6, we would sum .1667 + .1667 + .1667 = .5001 (rounded). This means the probability of getting a 1 *or* a 2 *or* a 4 (the only remaining possible outcomes) must be .5001 (rounded), because the sum of the probabilities for all of the possible outcomes must equal 1.0000 (ignoring rounding error).

You might well ask yourself why you should be concerned with all these rules about the outcomes of a single trial when criminal justice data typically involve the outcomes of many trials, such as drawing random samples of 10 or 50 or 200 or several thousand. Good question! The answer will become apparent when we discuss two probability rules for multiple outcomes, the relationship between these multiple outcome rules and the single outcome rules we have just presented, and the patterns of possible results that emerge when both sets of probability rules are applied to multiple trials. (Hint: each draw for a random sample can be seen as a trial.)

Before proceeding with a discussion of what probability theory tells us about the results from more than one trial, however, we need to introduce an additional concept in probability theory. In particular, we need to consider whether the events under analysis are independent or dependent.

Independent and Dependent Events

Recall from our discussion above that, statistically speaking, an event is an outcome (e.g., getting a head) of a random experiment or trial (e.g., flipping a coin). The term *event* is also applied to sets (combinations) of outcomes from multiple trials (e.g., getting four heads in six coin flips). Events (outcomes), whether of a single trial or multiple trials, are **independent** if the probabilities of the possible outcomes do not change from trial to trial. For example, if events are independent and the probability of getting a head on the first flip is .5000, it is still .5000 on the second flip. Similarly, if events are independent and the probability of getting any one of the six possible outcomes in a die roll is 1/6 = .1667, then the probability of getting any one of the six possible outcomes on the second roll remains 1/6 or .1667 (rounded). Random sampling with replacement (which, you remember, requires that each unit of analysis in the population has the same probability of being included in the sample) ensures that the probabilities of possible outcomes remain the same from one selection for the sample to the next.

Dependent events are events for which the probabilities of outcomes *do* change from trial to trial. Sampling without replacement is an example because the probability of being included in the sample, and hence the probabilities of outcomes, change from one sample selection to the next.

Probability theory includes rules for both independent and dependent events. Here we will be concerned only with rules for independent events.

Rules for Outcomes of Multiple Trials

With the definition of independent outcomes in mind, we are now ready to consider two probability theory rules pertaining to the outcomes from two or more trials. We begin our discussion with the assumptions that the possible outcomes of a single trial, as well as the possible combination of outcomes from a series of trials, are mutually exclusive, exhaustive, and independent unless otherwise indicated. The number of trials can be thought of as sample size. We'll use more than one coin flip and more than one die roll to illustrate the application of these probability theory rules. As we will see, interesting patterns of outcomes begin to reveal themselves when we consider the results from many trials.

Assume again that in a coin toss the probability of an H, which we will symbolize as $p(H)$, and the probability of a T, symbolized as $p(T)$, are each equal to .5000; that is, $p(H) = p(T) = .5000$ in a single coin flip trial. If we flipped our coin six times (a multiple trial), our single trial probability rules suggest that we might get exactly 3/6 Hs (i.e., .5000 Hs) and 3/6 Ts (i.e., .5000 Ts). Because the outcomes are independent and chance determines each flip's outcome, however, we can expect some variation from .5000 in the proportion of Hs we observe, especially over such a small number of trials. But if we flipped a fair coin 5,000 times, the number of heads should be very near 2,500 and the *proportion* of Hs we observe should be very near .5000, the same probability we assigned to the heads outcome in a single trial. In fact, the more times we flip a fair coin, the closer the observed proportion of heads should get to .5000. If we imagine flipping a theoretically perfectly fair coin an infinite number of times, according to probability theory, the proportion of Hs would be exactly .5000.

Likewise, even if we assume that the six outcomes in a die roll are equally likely, several sets of a few die rolls each may yield by chance a variety of results in terms of proportions of, say, 2s. The larger the number of rolls, however, the closer the proportion of each of the six outcomes to .1667 (rounded) if the die is fair. According to probability theory, they would be exactly the same (.1667, rounded) if we rolled a fair die an infinite number of times.

Now suppose we are interested not in the probability of getting one outcome *or* another in multiple trials, but in the probability of getting one outcome *and* another in multiple trials. We'll symbolize such a probability as $p(A \text{ and } B)$ for one outcome of A and one outcome of B, those with three outcomes as $p(A \text{ and } B \text{ and } C)$, and so on. An example would be the probability of getting snake eyes in the roll of a pair of die, or $p(1 \text{ and } 1)$. Because it is less complex, we'll use the coin toss example for the first illustration.

Suppose we toss the coin twice. Remember, we have assigned equal probability to getting a head (H) and a tail (T) in each toss. In two tosses of the coin, we have four independent, mutually exclusive, and exhaustive possible outcomes if we pay attention to the order in which the outcomes occur: HH, HT, TH, and TT.

Note that in this example, we are interested in the probability associated not with getting a head *or* a tail in a single trial, but with getting a head *and* a tail, for example, in two trials. It's important to pay attention to whether there is an *or* or an *and* in the probability question being addressed!

Probabilities that include an "and" are calculated according to the sixth rule of probability theory (often referred to by statisticians as a special form of the multiplication rule): *The probability of getting any specified combination of outcomes in a series of trials whose outcomes are independent is the product of the probabilities of getting each of the outcomes in a single trial.* In the case of our coin toss example, the probability of a head is .5000 in a single trial. So, according to the sixth rule, the probability of getting two heads in two trial flips is .5000 × .5000 = .2500. Note that the probability of each of the other three outcomes is also .2500. If we consider the four possible combinations of outcomes as four independent outcomes of a single trial, the sum of the four probabilities is 1.0000, which is as it should be according to the fourth rule.

Now, suppose we don't care in what particular order the heads occur in a set of single trial outcomes; we just care whether we get no heads or one head or two heads in two coin tosses. In this case, HT and TH are considered equivalent outcomes because each contains one head. So, if we assign equal probabilities to each of the four possible *pairs* of outcomes, we would have a .2500 probability of getting two Hs, a .2500 probability of getting no heads (i.e., two Ts) and a .5000 probability of getting one H (and one T). The latter .5000 probability is derived from the probability of getting TH, which is .2500, plus the probability of getting HT, which is also .2500, and .2500 + .2500 = .5000. So, the probability of getting one head in two tosses is .5000, two heads is .2500, and no heads is .2500, which, when summed, equals 1.0000. Note also that the probability of getting at least one head in two tosses would be .2500 + .5000 = .7500.

Let's take this one step further. Suppose we flip the coin three times. We can treat each of the three possible combinations of outcomes as a set. In probability theory, a **set of outcomes** is a combination of independent outcomes from two or more trials considered as a single outcome. For example, we have the following eight mutually exclusive and exhaustive possible sets of outcomes when we flip a coin three times, taking into account the order of occurrence of heads and tails: TTT, TTH, THH, THT, HTT, HHT, HTH, and HHH.

This brings us to the seventh rule of probability theory: *When probabilities are assigned to sets of outcomes and the sets are independent, mutually exclusive, and exhaustive, the sum of the probabilities assigned to the sets must be 1.0000.* Note that the seventh rule is similar to the fourth rule. The only difference is that the fourth rule applies to the outcomes of a single trial, whereas the seventh applies to sets of outcomes with each set treated as if it was a single outcome.

If we consider each of the eight sets of possible outcomes from three flips as equally probable, then the probability of any one of the sets is 1/8 or .1250. The sum of all eight sets of probabilities is 1.0000, which conforms to our seventh rule. Suppose we wanted to know the probability of getting exactly one H in a set of three coin flips. Following our fifth rule, but now applying it to the sets of possible outcomes, each set considered as a single outcome, we would identify the sets containing exactly one head (H), which are TTH, THT, and HTT. We would then sum the probabilities for these three sets: .1250 + .1250 + .1250 = .3750.

We'll use die rolls as a further illustration of multiple trial probability rules. In any one roll of the die, we may get a 1, 2, 3, 4, 5, or 6. If we assign the same probability to each of these mutually exclusive outcomes, each outcome would have a probability of 1/6 or .1667 (rounded). Summing the six probabilities gives us 1.0002 (rounded). The probability of getting an even die number (that is, a 2 *or* a 4 *or* a 6) would be .1667 + .1667 + .1667 = .5001 (rounded), following the fifth rule.

The probability of getting a 2 *and* a 4 *and* a 6 in three rolls of the die is given by .1667 × .1667 × .1667 = .0046 (rounded), following the sixth rule. The probability of getting a 4 *or* higher would be the sum of the probabilities of getting a 4 *or* a 5 *or* a 6, which would be .1667 + .1667 + .1667 = .5001 (rounded).

Now let's consider all of the possible outcomes when we roll two dice. If we roll two dice and take order of occurrence into account, we would have the 36 possible mutually exclusive and exhaustive outcomes listed in Table 6.1. Note that in Table 6.1 and the text below, $p(1, 1)$ is to be read $p(1$ and $1)$, $p(2, 5)$ is to be read as $p(2$ and $5)$, and so on.

Using the sixth rule, and assuming the dice are fair, the probability of getting each of these sets or combinations of outcomes would be $1/6 \times 1/6 = 1/36 = .0278$ (rounded) or .1667 × .1667 = .0278 (rounded). The probability of rolling snake eyes would be $p(1, 1) = .0278$ (rounded). Using the sixth rule, the probability of rolling seven would be $p(1, 6) + p(6, 1) + p(2, 5) + p(5, 2) + p(3, 4) + p(4, 3) = 6 \times .0278 = .1668$ (rounded). The probability of rolling anything other than a seven is $1 - p(7) = 1 - .1668 = .8332$ (rounded).

Let's pause for a moment and change our perspective on some of what we have said so far about probabilities. Suppose we are known to occasionally indulge in wagers, the settling of which involves the results of real coin flips or die rolls. Suppose also that after gambling for a while, we become suspicious that the real coin flips or die rolls upon which we were wagering were not fair. We could use the observed proportions of outcomes over several trials as a test of whether or not our suspicions are justified. We could do this because we now know what patterns of outcomes to expect if, in fact, the coin or die is approximately fair. (Again, we say approximately here because real coins or dice are rarely, if ever, perfectly fair, as demanded by probability theory.) Thus, in a large number of coin flips, if we did not observe approximately

Table 6.1 The 36 Sets of Possible Outcomes of Two Die Rolls, Taking Order of Occurrence Into Account

1, 1	2, 1	3, 1	4, 1	5, 1	6, 1
1, 2	2, 2	3, 2	4, 2	5, 2	6, 2
1, 3	2, 3	3, 3	4, 3	5, 3	6, 3
1, 4	2, 4	3, 4	4, 4	5, 4	6, 4
1, 5	2, 5	3, 5	4, 5	5, 5	6, 5
1, 6	2, 6	3, 6	4, 6	5, 6	6, 6

.5000 heads, we might well suspect that the coin was not fair. That is, we might well conclude that the probability of heads in a single flip was *not* .5000. Similarly, after a die is rolled many times and the proportion of, say, 2s was quite a bit larger than .1667, we might suspect strongly that the die is "loaded"—that is, weighted in such a way that in a single roll one of the six possible outcomes is more likely than the others.

Note that these are examples of probability theory-based models being compared to real-world observations to help answer questions we might have about what we observe in the real world. We still have a problem, though. To make a judgment about whether the coin or die is fair, we need to decide how much of a difference between the observed proportion of outcomes and the proportions expected based on probability theory would be proof of unfair coins or loaded dice in the real world?

Unfortunately, we're not quite ready to answer this question yet. We will say now, however, that you will have to be content with an answer in terms of probabilities, not certainties. We will also say that many inferential statistical analyses are based on building models using probability theory and comparing them with real-world observations. There, too, though, we will have to be content with probabilities, not certainties.

Probability Distributions

For our purposes, a **probability distribution** is a distribution of the proportions of times the possible combinations of outcomes occur or can be expected to occur in a trial or a series of trials. In probability theory, an infinite number of trials is assumed. The probability distribution in table form for two coin tosses, ignoring outcome order (that is, in this case, treating HT and TH as the same outcome), would look like the one in Table 6.2.

If we did the same for our three coin toss example, again ignoring order of occurrence, we would have Table 6.3.

Alternatively, we could present these probabilities in terms of the number of heads in three coin tosses, as in Table 6.4.

Later in this chapter, we work out the probability distribution for five flips of a coin. When we do so, you will no doubt notice that, as the number of flips (trials) increases, the resemblance between these probability distributions and a normal distribution grows.

Table 6.2   Probability Distribution for Number of Heads and Tails in Two Coin Flips, Ignoring Order of Occurrence

Possible Outcomes	Probability of Outcomes
Two heads	.2500
One head and one tail	.5000
Two tails	.2500

Table 6.3 Probability Distribution for Number of Heads (and Tails) in Three Coin Flips, Ignoring Order of Occurrence

Possible Outcomes	Probability of Outcomes
Three heads	.1250
Two heads and one tail	.3750
One head and two tails	.3750
Three tails	.1250

Table 6.4 Probability Distribution for Number of Heads in Three Coin Flips, Ignoring Order of Occurrence

Possible Outcomes	Probability of Outcomes
Three heads	.1250
Two heads	.3750
One head	.3750
No heads	.1250

We'll spare you the corresponding tasks for die rolls (doesn't that just make your day!) and consider next binomial frequency and probability distributions.

Binomial Distributions and Binomial Probability Distributions

In probability theory, a **binomial** (think bi = 2; nomial—think number or mathematical term) **distribution** is produced whenever there is a series of trials and there are only two possible mutually exclusive, exhaustive, independent outcomes in each trial. The distribution of outcomes when we flip a coin many times (i.e., perform multiple trials) qualifies as a binomial distribution.

Suppose we consider flipping a coin five times. What would the possible outcomes be, ignoring the order of occurrence of heads and tails? We'll spare you all the calculations and give you the results. In Table 6.5, we have listed the frequency distribution of the possible outcomes in terms of number of heads, ignoring order of occurrence. Figure 6.1 is a frequency distribution bar graph for the binomial distribution in Table 6.5.

Table 6.5 Possible Number of Heads in Five Coin Flips and Corresponding Number of Sets of Possible Outcomes for Each Number of Heads, Ignoring Order of Occurrence

Possible Number of Heads	Number of Possible Outcomes With Specified Number of Heads
5	1
4	5
3	10
2	10
1	5
0	1

Figure 6.1 Bar Graph Distribution of Number of Possible Outcomes for Specified Number of Heads in Five Coin Flips

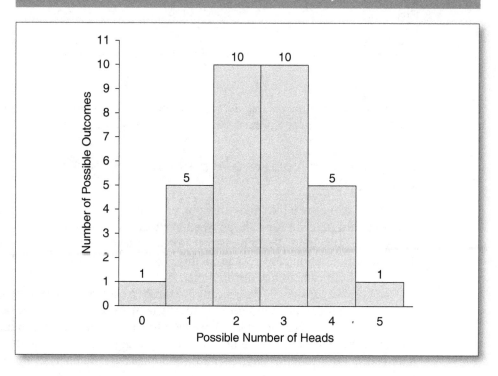

Note that different binomial distributions would be produced for different numbers of trials (e.g., flips), again assuming only two outcomes are possible in a single trial. That is, there is a different binomial distribution for the number of heads in 6 flips, 10 flips, 12 flips, and so on.

Once we determine the number of possible combinations of outcomes of particular types (for example, number of heads), we can assign a probability to each combination and create a binomial probability distribution. A **binomial probability distribution** is a distribution of probabilities associated with each of the possible combinations of outcomes in a series of trials of the same size when there are two possible independent, mutually exclusive, exhaustive outcomes in a single trial, again ignoring the order of occurrence (for example, the order of heads and tails). We can convert the distribution of number of possible outcomes in Table 6.5 to a probability distribution for the various combinations of outcomes.

The first step in the conversion of the binomial distribution to a binomial probability distribution is to sum the numbers of possible outcomes (1 + 5 + 10 + 10 + 5 + 1) in five flips, which results in a total of 32 (see Table 6.5). Using this total, we could then say the probability of getting five heads is 1/32 or .0312 (rounded), the probability of getting an outcome with two heads is 10/32 = .3125, and so on. If we calculated all of the probabilities for each of the numbers of possible outcomes in the above list in this way, we would have Table 6.6, the binomial probability distribution for number of heads in five flips.

Figure 6.2 shows the conversion of this binomial probability distribution table into a bar graph.

Table 6.6 Binomial Probability Distribution for Number of Heads in Five Coin Flips, Ignoring Order of Occurrence

Possible Number of Heads	Probability of Outcomes With Specified Number of Heads
5	.0312
4	.1562
3	.3125
2	.3125
1	.1562
0	.0312

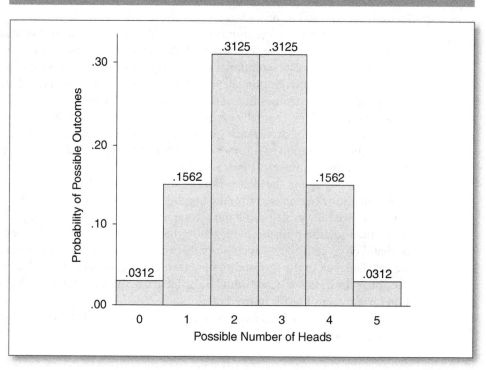

Figure 6.2 Bar Graph Binomial Probability Distribution for Number of Heads in Five Coin Flips

Normal Curve Approximations of Binomial Probability Distributions

Note that the distributions in Table 6.6 and Figure 6.2 resemble in a very general way a bell-shaped, symmetric about the mean, normal distribution. The resemblance is more apparent when the number of trials is 10 or larger, and it is quite clear when the number of trials is 100 or larger. The larger the number of trials, the closer the resemblance. Probability theory tells us, in fact, that when the number of trials is 10 or larger, the normal curve can be used as a pretty good approximation of a binomial probability distribution.

As with any normal curve, these normal probability curve approximations can be transformed into standard normal curve probability approximations. This, in turn, makes it possible to use z scores and their relationships to areas under the normal curve as a way of estimating binomial probabilities. Let's see how that works.

The general formula for transforming a particular outcome into its z-score equivalent is provided in Formula 6.1.

$$z = \frac{x - np}{\sqrt{npq}} \tag{6.1}$$

In Formula 6.1, x is the outcome of interest (the variable value we wish to convert to z), p is the probability assigned to the outcome of interest in a single binomial trial, q is the probability assigned to the other outcome in a single binomial trial, and n is the number of trials (or sample size). Suppose we are interested in the probability of getting five heads in eight flips of a fair coin. In this example, $p = p(H) = .5000$ and $q = p(T) = .5000$ in a single trial, $x = 5$ (the outcome of five heads), and $n = 8$ (the number of flips).

Without offering proof, we will simply note that the mean of any binomial probability distribution equals np and the standard deviation equals $\sqrt{npq}$. Given this information, compare Formula 6.1 with the general z-score Formula 5.1, p. 145.

Now, note that we said the normal curve can be used as a pretty good *approximation* of a binomial distribution and that the approximation is better for large samples (e.g., a large number of flips). The theoretical standard normal probability curve, as represented in the z-score table, is an approximation because the possible combinations of outcomes of a set of binomial trials is always a discrete variable. That is, only some particular outcomes are possible for any given number of trials. The probabilities in a theoretical standard normal probability curve are a continuous variable. (See pp. 23–24 for a discussion of discrete and continuous variables.) Hence, using the z-score table to determine the probability of outcomes for a binomial is likely to be somewhat in error. To adjust for the difference between a discrete and a continuous distribution, statisticians use a correction for continuity when calculating z-score equivalents of particular binomial outcomes.

Correction for Continuity

When samples are less than 100, Formula 6.1 is modified to include a **correction for continuity**. This correction provides a better match between a discrete binomial distribution and the continuous theoretical z-score distribution. The correction for continuity consists of adding and subtracting .5 from the x term in the numerator of Formula 6.1, as indicated in Formula 6.2.

$$z = \frac{(x \pm .5) - np}{\sqrt{npq}} \qquad (6.2)$$

Now suppose we want to know the probability of getting five heads *or more* in eight flips (a cumulative probability). Let's see how using the correction for continuity improves the standard normal (z score) curve approximation of the binomial probability distribution.

We begin by noting that, as a general rule, continuous distribution curves like the z-score distribution use points rather than spaces on the horizontal axis to represent possible variable values. So, look at the horizontal axis in Figure 6.3. If we use the center of the five heads bar as our horizontal axis point representing the outcome of five heads and we want to know the probability of getting five heads or more, we will have to subtract .5 from 5 in order to include the area under the curve consisting of the left half of the five-heads bar, as illustrated in Figure 6.3. If we want to know the

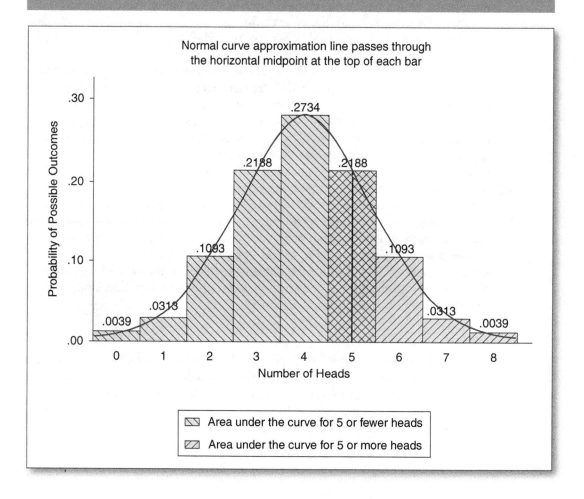

Figure 6.3 Bar Graph Probability Distribution for Number of Heads in Eight Flips of a Fair Coin With Normal Curve Approximation Superimposed

probability of getting five heads or fewer in eight flips, we will need to add .5 to 5 to include the area under the curve consisting of the right half of the five-heads bar, as illustrated in Figure 6.3. This is the meaning and effect of the correction for continuity adjustment of ±.5 in the numerator of Formula 6.2.

Now let's calculate the normal curve approximation of the binomial probability distribution for getting five heads or more in eight flips, using the correction for continuity. Recall that, using the information in the binomial probability bar graph (see Figure 6.3), we previously found the cumulative binomial probability of five or more heads in eight flips to be .2188 + .1093 + .0313 + .0039 = .3633. Because we want to know the probability of getting five heads or more and we are applying the correction for continuity, we subtract .5 from five heads in the numerator of Formula 6.2. To calculate the appropriate z score, we insert the appropriate numbers in Formula 6.2 as follows:

$$z = \frac{(x \pm .5) - np}{\sqrt{npq}}$$

$$= \frac{(5 - .5) - (8)(.50)}{\sqrt{(8)(.50)(.50)}}$$

$$= \frac{4.5 - 4.00}{\sqrt{2}}$$

$$= \frac{.5}{1.4142}$$

$$z = .3536$$

We look up the calculated value of $z = .3536$ in the z-score table in Appendix D to determine the probability of getting 5 heads or more. Because this is a positive z, the applicable area under the curve is found in column C headed "area beyond z." Unfortunately, the table does not give results to the nearest ten thousandth, so our probability approximation for five heads or more is between $z = .35$ ($p = .3632$) and $z = .36$ ($p = .3594$). Because our result is closer to $z = .35$, we will use the corresponding probability of .3632. Our result of .3632 is not equivalent to the .3633 we arrived at from the exact probabilities in the bar graph, but it is pretty close, and that, after all, is what we mean by approximation.

Finally, let's try the approximation without the correction for continuity. In this case, we would use Formula 6.1.

$$z = \frac{x - np}{\sqrt{npq}}$$

$$= \frac{5 - (8)(.50)}{\sqrt{(8)(.50)(.50)}}$$

$$= \frac{5 - 4}{\sqrt{2}}$$

$$= \frac{1}{1.4142}$$

$$= .7071$$

Looking up the area beyond z in the z-score table for $z = .7071$, we find a probability of .2420. As you can see, using the correction for continuity produces a much better approximation. As noted earlier, the correction for continuity should be used whenever sample sizes are less than 100.

Some Concluding Comments About Binomial Distributions

First, a couple of reminders. All of the procedures for calculating areas under the normal curve discussed in Chapter 5, including those using z scores, are applicable when the normal curve is used as an approximation for binomial probability distributions. Also, for statistical analyses involving samples (or number of trials) of less than 100, Formula 6.2, which includes the correction for continuity, should be used to calculate z. For samples larger than 100, Formula 6.1 should be used.

Finally, without going into the details, we will simply observe that the total number of possible outcomes in five coin flips (or any binomial), which we have just learned is 32 (see Table 6.5), is equal to 2^5, which is $2 \times 2 \times 2 \times 2 \times 2 = 32$. This relationship between the sum of the possible outcomes involving a binomial and powers of 2 corresponding to the number of trials holds for all numbers of trials where the number of possible outcomes in a single trial is two and order of occurrence is ignored. Thus, for example, for the number of all possible outcomes in six coin flips, we would have $2^6 = 64$. This relationship is used often in binomial inferential statistics.

Probabilities and Random Sampling

As we noted in Chapter 2, probability sampling is required if we wish to apply some of the most powerful tools in our statistical analysis toolbox. The simple random sample is the most basic type of probability sample. A more complete definition of a simple random sample is one in which each element in the population and each combination of elements must have an equal chance (probability) of being selected for the sample. Furthermore, each draw for the sample must be independent of any other draw, which means that the random selection of one element does not change the probability of the selection of another element. Note that satisfying these criteria requires *sampling with replacement*.

One way to view random sampling is as a series of trials. We randomly choose an element from a population (the trial) and then observe the element's values for those variables we are studying (the outcome[s]). In this context, the number of trials is equivalent to the size of the sample. Each time we randomly select an element of the population for a sample, we are, in effect, randomly selecting the characteristics (that is, the values of the variables that describe the selected element of the population). For example, if we took a simple random sample of the students in your statistics class, we would also be randomly sampling their ages, sexes, majors, grade point averages, career plans, and attitudes toward "stand your ground" laws. We could then record the variable values (outcomes or sets of outcomes) of interest to us for each member of the class and subject these data to inferential statistical analysis, using what we have learned about probabilities.

If each selection of an element (unit of analysis) for a random sample was considered an independent random experiment (trial) and only two possible independent variable value outcomes were possible—such as male or female student, or criminal justice major or other major (or that an inmate did or did not participate in inmate-on-inmate violence, or a juvenile recidivated or did not)—a binomial probability sampling distribution would apply. If more than two outcomes in a trial were possible, or if measures of central tendency such as two means were being compared, other probability theory-based distributions could be constructed.

When used in inferential statistical analyses, binomial probability distributions are referred to as sampling distributions. They provide the probability associated with each of the possible combinations of outcomes when many random samples are taken from the same population and when a variable has two possible values (outcomes) in a trial.

Summary

In this chapter, we have built the foundation for our discussion of probability-based inferential statistics, which will continue in the next chapter. Here we discussed the nature of probability and introduced some basic rules of probability theory. We converted distributions of the number of possible outcomes to probability distributions for possible outcomes. Normal curve approximations of binomial distributions were described and formulas for converting these distributions to standard normal z-score distributions were presented. Finally, the relationship between random sampling and probability distributions was explored. In the next chapter, we will discuss the concept of sampling distributions in some detail.

Concepts to Master

Binomial distribution	Events	Probability
Binomial probability distribution	Independent events (outcomes)	Probability distribution
		Probability theory
Correction for continuity	Inferential statistics	Random experiment
Dependent events (outcomes)	Mutually exclusive possible outcomes	Sample statistics
Exhaustive list of possible outcomes	Outcome(s)	Set (combination) of outcomes
	Population parameters	Trial

Review Questions

1. Distinguish between descriptive and inferential statistics.

2. Distinguish between sample statistics and population parameters. Give two examples of each.

3. What is a probability?

4. What is probability theory?

5. What is a trial (random experiment)?

6. What is an event (outcome)?

7. Distinguish between independent and dependent events (outcomes). Give an example of each.

8. What is an exhaustive list of possible outcomes?

9. What are mutually exclusive outcomes?

10. What does a probability of 1.00 mean?

11. What does a probability of 0.00 mean?

12. What does a probability of .2500 mean?

13. What must be the sum of the probabilities of a list of independent, mutually exclusive, and exhaustive outcomes?

14. Distinguish between single trials and multiple trials. Give an example of each.

15. What is a set of outcomes? Under what circumstances can a set of outcomes be treated as a single outcome?

16. What must be the sum of the probabilities of independent, mutually exclusive, and exhaustive sets of outcomes?

17. What is a binomial distribution?

18. What is a probability distribution?

19. What is a binomial probability distribution?

20. What is a normal curve approximation of a binomial distribution?

21. What is the correction for continuity, and why is it necessary?

22. How is probability involved in random sampling?

23. If you haven't already done so, define each of the terms on the "Concepts to Master" list and use each in three sentences.

Exercises and Discussion Questions

1. Give examples and discuss the uses of probability in everyday life.

2. Discuss how the examples you gave in Exercise 1 above relate to probability theory.

3. Compare and contrast flipping the quarter in your pocket and a statistician's imaginary flipping of a quarter to illustrate aspects of probability theory.

4. Why is it important to select a sample randomly when using inferential statistics?

5. Discuss each of the seven rules of probability theory and give two examples each of how they would be applied.

6. Assume I have an imaginary, fair, eight-sided die, with faces numbered 1-8, and assume that rolls and outcomes are independent. What would the probability be of getting

   a. an 8 in one roll of a die?
   b. a 1 or an 8 in one roll?
   c. a 1 and an 8 in two rolls?
   d. a 2 and a 3 and a 4 in three die rolls?
   e. a 1 or an 8 in two rolls?

7. What are your chances of drawing a five-card flush from a standard deck of 52 cards? Give two answers, first assuming sampling with replacement and then assuming sampling without replacement.

8. Formulate two questions for measuring the variables "current major" and "age at most recent birthday" that you might include on a survey of members of your statistics class. At what level are these variables measured? Are they continuous or discrete variables? Provide a list of the mutually exclusive and exhaustive possible answers (outcomes) to these questions. How might you assign probabilities to these possible responses, and what probabilities would you assign? What rules would you need to follow in doing so? How would you ensure the probabilities you assigned met the rules of probability theory?

9. Construct a binomial distribution for outcomes from four flips of a coin, similar to the one we constructed in the text for three flips. First, identify all of the logically possible permutations of heads and tails in four coin flips—that is, taking order into account. Then, identify and list the possible combinations of outcomes in terms of the number of heads (i.e., from four heads to zero heads). Then, count the number for each possible combination of number of heads—that is, ignoring the order in which heads and tails occur. Show your lists and counts. Create a bar graph binomial distribution for number of heads in four flips. Next, create a binomial probability distribution for number of heads using your results. Finally, assign probabilities to the combinations of outcomes on your list and create a probability distribution bar graph of your results. Show your calculations. Does the resulting probability distribution resemble a normal distribution?

10. What are the possible outcomes in three flips of a coin, taking order of occurrence into account? Ignoring order of occurrence? Check your results by applying the formula in the "Some Concluding Comments" section of this chapter.

11. Identify and discuss how models based on probability theory can be constructed and compared with real-world observations. Give examples of the kinds of questions that might be addressed using such comparisons.

12. Why are there different binomial distributions for different numbers of trials?

13. Discuss what, why, and how a correction for continuity "corrects."

14. How are random sampling and probability related?

15. Calculate z for four heads in six flips with and without the correction for continuity. Use your calculated zs and the z-score table in Appendix D to determine the probability of getting four or more heads in six flips for both calculations. Compare your two results with each other and with your result for four or more heads in Exercise 9. Which of your two results gives the best approximation of your Exercise 9 result?

16. Compare and contrast binomial distributions and binomial probability distributions.

17. Go to www.google.com/imghp, do a search for binomial distribution graph, and explore.

Student Study Site

Visit the open-access student study site at **www.sagepub.com/fitzgerald** for access to several study tools including eFlashcards, web quizzes, and additional appendices as well as links to SAGE journal articles and audio, video and web resources.

Univariate Inferential Statistics

Sampling Distributions and Population Parameter Estimation

Learning Objectives

What you are expected not only to learn but to master in this chapter:

- The role of sampling distributions in inferential statistics, especially their use in estimating population parameters from sample statistics
- How to construct a sampling distribution empirically and mathematically, using the binomial distribution as an example
- How to use sampling distributions as probability of outcomes distributions and as distributions of sampling error
- How to describe a sampling distribution using its mean and standard deviation (standard error)
- The difference between biased and unbiased estimates of population parameters

- Three provisions of the central limit theorem
- The role of the central limit theorem in establishing the means and standard errors of sampling distributions
- How to make point and interval estimates of population means from sample means and standard deviations
- What confidence limits and confidence intervals are
- How to set a confidence level and establish confidence limits for an interval estimate of a population mean
- How to estimate population proportions
- Differences between parametric and nonparametric inferential statistics
- Cautions to be observed when using parametric inferential estimation procedures

Introduction

In this chapter, we build on what we learned about probability, probability distributions, and normal curve approximations in Chapter 6 to understand sampling distributions and their uses in inferential statistics. The most basic application of these concepts and procedures in inferential statistics is in parameter estimation.

As an introduction to sampling distributions and parameter estimation, we review the construction of a binomial probability distribution as a sampling distribution, first empirically and then mathematically. We then consider in a more detailed way sampling distributions for means and proportions that are constructed mathematically. Among the things to be discussed are how such sampling distributions are used, on one hand, to estimate (think infer, hence the name *inferential* statistics) population parameters and, on the other hand, as distributions of sampling error for sample statistics. Sampling distributions and the estimates of sampling error they provide, in turn, make it possible to specify the degree of confidence we have that our population parameter estimates are correct, provided that the statistics come from random samples and, in many cases, that some assumptions about the way variables are distributed in the population are met. The chapter concludes with a discussion of assumptions and cautions necessary for making appropriate and meaningful use of these inferential statistical tools.

Getting your head around the basic idea of sampling distributions is very important for understanding inferential statistics. As a result, we are going to come at sampling distributions from a couple of different directions, repeating ourselves on occasion. Review and be sure you understand the discussion of probability distributions in the previous chapter. Then, read the material in this chapter slowly and carefully. We think your effort will be rewarded.

Sampling Distributions and Their Role in Inferential Statistics

As we begin our discussion of sampling distributions, recall from our discussions in Chapter 6 that descriptive measures calculated from sample data (e.g., the proportions, means, variances, etc., we first discussed in Chapters 3 and 4) are called sample statistics. The corresponding statistics for the population from which the sample was drawn are referred to as population parameters. Recall, too, that probability distributions can be viewed as distributions of the probabilities for getting various outcomes or combinations of outcomes from a series of random trials and that drawing a random sample may be viewed as conducting a number of random trials, the number corresponding with the size of the sample. Each trial can be considered a random sample. In the case of a single coin flip, it is a sample of size one. Five coin flips can be considered as five samples of size one. But it can also be considered one sample of size five, and we can take several such samples of size five (or size eight or 35 or 180 or thousands—whatever size we choose) and examine the distribution of possible outcomes, just as we did when discussing the binomial distribution in Chapter 6.

A **sampling distribution** is a distribution of the probabilities of getting the various possible outcomes or combinations of outcomes when a large (in probability theory, an infinite) number of same-sized random samples are drawn from the same population. Examples of random sample outcomes and combinations of outcomes include getting a head in a coin flip or three heads in five coin flips or finding 30 juvenile offenders out of 50 who recidivated or a particular mean income or standard deviation of the incomes of public defenders.

As we noted in Chapter 2, whenever we sample, we must be willing to accept some uncertainty about the extent to which a sample statistic accurately reflects the corresponding population parameter. We might by chance draw a sample whose statistic is exactly equivalent in value to the corresponding population parameter or one that is close but not exactly equivalent. But we also might get a sample whose statistic is quite different in value from the population parameter. In short, some samples will be more representative of the population than others will be.

Suppose we ask a random sample of county citizens whether they prefer Sheriff Candidate A or Candidate B in an upcoming election. The proportion of our sample supporting Candidate A may or may not be an accurate reflection of the population's proportion supporting Candidate A. Or, suppose we have random sample data on the incomes of public defenders and calculate the sample's mean income. Our calculated mean is not likely to be exactly equivalent to the public defender population's mean income. Statisticians say that any difference between a random sample statistic and the corresponding population parameter is due to **sampling error**—that is, the difference is due to random variation in the sample statistic arising from the process of random sampling. Whenever we take the shortcut of using a sample to study a population, we run the risk of at least some sampling error.

The uncertainty associated with sampling created by the likelihood of at least some sampling error is increased by another troublesome consideration. In most cases, when we are relying on data from a single sample, we do not know and have no way of finding out exactly what the population parameters are. Therefore, at least at first glance, it would appear we have no way of knowing how much, if any, sampling error has occurred—that is, how big a difference, if any, there is between our sample statistic (sample proportion supporting Candidate A, for example) and the corresponding population parameter (proportion in the population supporting Candidate A).

However, appearances, as they say, are often deceiving. It turns out we *can* use sample data to make meaningful statements about a population if we select a random sample and use the tools provided by probability theory-based inferential statistics to estimate population parameters from our sample statistics. Let's see how this can be accomplished.

Recall from our discussion of sampling in Chapter 2 that, in the absence of other information about the population, the best chance we have of obtaining a representative sample—that is, one whose statistic matches the corresponding population parameter—is achieved with random sampling. Of course, random samples don't eliminate sampling error, but, as we will see, they do give us a way of determining *how much* sampling error is *likely* to occur.

"How so?" you may well ask. Recall from Chapter 6 that a predictable pattern in the distribution of outcomes in terms of number or proportion of heads is revealed when many random samples of fair coin flips of a particular size are taken. Over many trials, a discrete but approximately normal binomial distribution emerges that can be considered a probability distribution—a distribution of the probabilities of getting the various possible combinations of outcomes. In a similar way, predictable patterns in the distribution of other sample statistics (outcomes), such as means and standard deviations, emerge when many same-sized random samples are drawn from the same population. Such a distribution also can be considered a probability distribution—a distribution of the probabilities of getting various values of a particular sample statistic (e.g., a mean, a proportion of heads, a proportion supporting Candidate A).

Note also that these probability distributions give us a way of understanding how the amount of sampling error is likely to vary from sample to sample—and, therefore, the likelihood of a specific amount of sampling error for any given sample. The key, then, to understanding and assessing the different likelihoods (probabilities) of different amounts of sampling error is the sampling distribution.

Let's begin our detailed discussion of sampling distributions and their uses with a simple illustration involving a series of trials, each of which has two possible outcomes—in short, a binomial sampling distribution. In the process of working through this example, we will review a few of the basic concepts and procedures discussed in Chapter 6, just to be sure we are all up to speed for the more complex discussions to follow.

A Simple Illustration: Who'll Buy the Coffee?

Suppose you spot a friend standing on the street corner outside a coffee shop. You're broke as usual, but you would like to have a cup of coffee before returning to your study of statistics in criminal justice. You know that your friend likes to gamble. Being a bit of a risk taker yourself, you decide that you might bet her the price of a cup of coffee that in 10 flips of her quarter, she will get no more than four heads (i.e., four or fewer heads). Have you made a good bet? How would you know? Is there a way to determine your chances of winning the bet?

You recognize, of course, that if your friend accepts your bet and flips her quarter 10 times, any number of heads, from 0 to 10, *might* turn up. Furthermore, the outcome of the bet will be determined by the sum of the outcomes of 10 separate flips of the coin. Hence, your chances of winning the bet are tied to the chances or odds of getting a head in any single flip of the coin. You are also aware that once your friend flips the coin 10 times, you will either win or lose the bet. Nevertheless, if you had some way of estimating the probability that your friend would turn up four heads or fewer in a sample of 10 tosses of the coin, you could at least get some idea of your chances of winning the bet. This information could serve as a guide for making this or similar wagers.

Constructing a Sampling Distribution Empirically

One way you might attempt to determine the probability or likelihood that a given proportion of heads will turn up in 10 tosses of the quarter is to do a little empirical exercise. You don't have a quarter to your name, of course, but maybe your friend will let you borrow her quarter. You could flip it 10 times, noting the number of heads that came up. Suppose you found that the coin landed heads eight times. Would you be willing to infer that you would get eight heads in the next set of 10 tosses? Might you not observe three heads in the next set of 10 tosses, six in the next, and so on by chance? In short, if you relied on the sample statistic (in this case, the number or proportion of heads) from any *single* sample of 10 coin tosses to estimate the corresponding parameter (in this case, the number or proportion of heads in an infinite number of samples consisting of 10 coin flips each), you would clearly be in danger of making an incorrect estimate because of sampling error.

Suppose, however, you took a large number of samples, each consisting of 10 tosses of the coin, and recorded the proportion of heads that turned up in each sample. To help you evaluate the data you have assembled, you could construct a frequency distribution bar graph of your sample statistics. Table 7.1 shows our observed results for proportion of heads when we took 100 samples consisting of 10 coin tosses each. Figure 7.1a shows the frequency distribution bar graph for the statistics (number and proportion of heads in 10 flips) from our 100 samples. Figure 7.1b is an empirically derived binomial probability distribution for proportion of heads in 10 flips similar to the ones we derived in different ways in Chapter 6. Figure 7.1b is the binomial probability distribution based on the results reported in Figure 7.1a. To construct Figure 7.1b, we converted the raw frequencies on the vertical axis of Figure 7.1a to relative frequencies (percents), which represent the proportion of times we expect each of the possible outcomes to occur over many trials.

The binomial probability distribution in Figure 7.1b serves as our sampling distribution for proportion of heads in 100 samples of 10 flips each, drawn at random from the infinite population of sets of 10 coin flips.

Table 7.1 Record of Numbers and Proportions of Heads Observed in 100 Samples of 10 Coin Tosses Each

Possible Number of Heads in 10 Coin Flips	Number of Observed Occurrences	Proportion of Observed Occurrences
0	0	0.00
1	0	0.00
2	6	.06
3	11	.11
4	19	.19
5	27	.27
6	22	.22
7	10	.10
8	5	.05
9	0	0.00
10	0	0.00
	Total = 100	Total = 1.00

So far in our illustration, we have discussed a sampling distribution as a distribution of the probabilities of getting the various possible outcomes. The empirically derived sampling distribution in Figure 7.1b can be used to determine the probability that any given proportion of heads will occur in 10 tosses of a coin over the long run, using the procedures we discussed in Chapter 6. It indicates, for example, that the most likely outcome, in proportion of heads, is five (which occurs 27% of the time), followed closely by six (22% of the time), and four (19% of the time). Although the outcomes of 0, 1, 9, and 10 heads are logically possible, they appear highly improbable. In fact, these outcomes did not occur in any of our 100 samples of 10 coin flips.

Following the fifth rule of probability theory (see p. 171), we can use our empirically derived binomial sampling distribution (Figure 7.1b) to estimate the probability of getting more than four heads by observing that in 36 (6 + 11 + 19 = 36) of the samples we took, four or fewer heads turned up, whereas in the remaining 64 samples, more than four heads occurred. Thus, using this empirically derived sampling distribution, we might infer that, over the long run, you will win your bet 36% of the time and lose it 64% of the time.

Remember, as we noted in Chapter 6, that a sampling distribution can't tell you whether you will win or lose your bet on this particular occasion. But it can tell you your odds of winning the bet, which in this case—36 to 64—are not good. Even

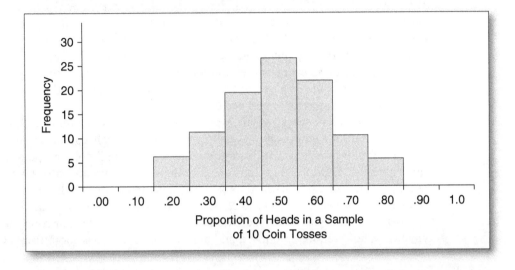

Figure 7.1a Frequency Distribution Bar Graph of Number of Heads in 100 Samples of 10 Tosses of a Real Coin

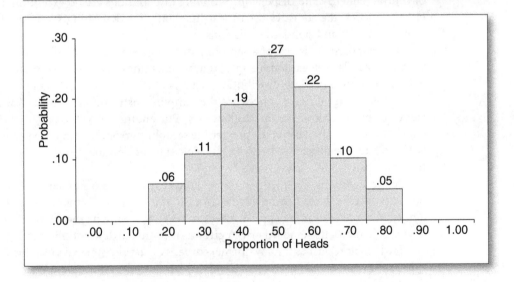

Figure 7.1b Binomial Probability Distribution for Proportion of Heads in 10 Coin Flips, Based on 100 Samples of 10 Flips Each

though you might be lucky and win your bet this particular time, you had probably better offer to make a bet you have a better chance of winning or plan on having that coffee another day. (Don't forget to return your friend's quarter to her whether you win or lose your bet!)

Now suppose we look at the distribution in Figure 7.1b in another way, this time as a distribution of sampling error. We recognize that even if $p(H) = p(T) = .5000$ in each flip, in a series of 10 flips, we will not always get exactly five heads and five tails. When we flip a coin 10 times and do not get exactly five heads and five tails, we might say that an error due to chance (random sampling) has occurred. We can view the distribution in Figure 7.1b, then, as an empirically derived distribution of sampling errors due to random sampling. As we noted, this chance variation in our sample statistic is what statisticians mean by sampling error. So, in effect, when you made your wager that four heads or fewer will occur in 10 flips, you were betting that a certain amount of sampling error would occur.

When no other alternatives are available, statisticians do occasionally derive sampling distributions empirically (usually these days through computer simulation). Fortunately, however, alternative ways of constructing applicable sampling distributions are often available, ways that preserve the convenience and cost advantages of taking a single sample to learn about a population. As we will see, they rely on sample statistics and probability theory to construct sampling distributions mathematically.

Before we consider how to derive a sampling distribution for our coffee bet mathematically, however, we need to expand our inferential statistics vocabulary a bit.

Describing Sampling Distributions: Means and Standard Errors

As we noted in Chapter 4, any distribution can be described by calculating its measures of central tendency and dispersion. Sampling distributions are no exception. In inferential statistics, the statistics used most frequently for describing sampling distributions are means and standard deviations.

The standard deviation of a sampling distribution is called its **standard error**. As with any standard deviation, its quantitative magnitude reflects how spread out the values are in the sampling distribution. That is, the standard error's value reflects the size of the average difference between the sampling distribution's mean value and the values of the outcomes in the distribution. Put another way, the larger a sampling distribution's standard error, the greater the sampling error that can be expected—that is, the greater the difference between a sample statistic and the corresponding population parameter.

As we learned in Chapter 5, once we know the mean and standard deviation of a normal curve, we have a complete description of it. So, if our sampling distribution is a normal curve (or can be approximated by one), knowing its mean and its standard deviation (that is, its standard error) gives us a complete description of it.

Furthermore, just as for any normal curve, we can use a normal sampling distribution's mean and standard error to divide up areas under the curve. (We recommend you review Chapter 5, pp. 141–143, now to refresh your memory about means, standard deviations, and areas under the normal curve before reading further.) When we do so, particular *proportions of the area under the sampling distribution's curve correspond to the probabilities of getting particular possible outcomes (or ranges of outcomes) from a random sample of a population.* That is, given the sample statistic and the probability assumptions used to construct it, we can use the sampling distribution to determine the probability of getting a particular value (or a particular range of values) of the sample statistic in a random sample.

Constructing Sampling Distributions Mathematically

As we noted earlier, having to draw many samples from a population to construct a sampling distribution empirically for the sample statistic of interest (proportion of heads, means, etc.) defeats the purpose of sampling in the first place. If we are to take advantage of the lower costs and greater convenience of studying a single sample instead of the whole population, we need to find another way to construct our sampling distribution.

In many circumstances, our sample statistics and probability theory provide the tools we need. We will apply what we learned about probabilities and probability distributions in Chapter 6, as well as some additional principles of probability theory to construct an applicable sampling distribution based on our sample statistics.

Binomial Distributions as Sampling Distributions

In the case of our coffee wager, we can use a mathematically derived binomial probability distribution exactly like the ones we discussed in Chapter 6. (See the discussion of mathematically derived binomial probability distributions in Chapter 6, pp. 176–179.) This distribution will serve the same purpose as the empirically derived sampling distribution in Table 7.1 (see p. 194). That is, it will tell us what proportion of times we can expect to get various proportions of heads in a series of 10 random flips. (We used the distribution in Table 7.1, you will remember, to tell us what the probability was of getting no more than four heads if we toss a coin 10 times.) The difference, again, is that the binomial sampling distribution we are about to construct will be created not empirically, but mathematically.

To construct the appropriate binomial probability distribution, some of the rules of probability theory with which you are already familiar must be invoked. First, the list of mutually exclusive and exhaustive outcomes of a single trial must be identified and probabilities must be assigned to each of them. That's what we did when we said that the possible outcomes of flipping a coin were a head or a tail, and that a head was as likely as a tail (i.e., $p(H) = p(T) = .5000$). Second, all of the possible mutually exclusive and exhaustive combinations of outcomes from a series of trials must be specified (as we did in the left-hand column in Table 7.1). Third, probabilities must be determined for each of these combinations of outcomes. We arrived at the figures in the right-hand column of Table 7.1 empirically, by calculating the proportion of times each of the possible outcomes occurred in our 100 samples of 10 coin flips. Now we will create the probabilities like those in the right-hand column by mathematical calculation.

To assess our chances of winning the coffee bet, we want to know the probability of getting no more than four heads in 10 tosses of a coin, assuming the equal likelihood of a head and tail in a single flip. Statisticians have provided a formula, based on probability theory, that permits us to calculate the exact probability of any particular outcome in a given number of trials (such as getting exactly four heads in 10 flips) when there are only two possible outcomes in a single random trial.

In working with the binomial probability formula, statisticians typically refer to success (S) or failure (F) in any single trial. You can designate whatever one of the two possible outcomes you like as a success. In our coffee betting example, we might call getting a head in a flip a success. Getting a tail then would be called a failure.

Note that successes and failures can be anything, from going to jail instead of getting probation after a conviction, successfully completing probation or going back to jail, rating police performance as positive or negative, and so on. Just remember that for binomial probabilities to be applied, there must be only two possible outcomes of a single trial, whatever we call them. We just need to keep track of what we are calling a success.

Formula 7.1 yields the exact probability of getting a specified combination of outcomes (e.g., a specific number of heads in 10 coin flips or a specific number of voters supporting Candidate A in a sample of size n).

$$p(K) = \frac{T!}{K!(T-K)!} p(S)^K p(F)^{T-K} \qquad (7.1)$$

This probability calculation involves the following components:

$p(K)$ = the probability (p) of K successes in T trials

T = the number of trials performed

K = the number of successes specified in T trials

T − K = the number of failures in T trials

$p(S)$ = the probability of a success in a single trial

$p(F)$ = the probability of a failure in a single trial

$p(S)^K$ = the probability of a success raised to the Kth power

$p(F)^{T-K}$ = the probability of a failure raised to the (T − K)th power

Remember that $p(S) + p(F)$ must equal 1.000 and, therefore, that $1 - p(S) = p(F)$. This general formula applies no matter what probability we assign to a success.

Now let's translate this general formula (Formula 7.1) in terms of our coffee betting example, where we wanted to know the probability of getting no more than four heads in 10 coin flips. We'll consider getting a head a success and getting a tail a failure in a single coin toss. Assuming the probability of a head is .5000, the calculation for the probability of getting four heads in 10 flips involves the following components:

$p(K)$ = the probability (p) of four (K) heads in 10 (T) flips

T = the number of trials (flips) performed (10)

K = the number of heads in 10 flips (4)

T − K = the number of tails in 10 flips (10 − 4 = 6)

$p(S)$ = the probability of a head in a single flip (.5000)

$p(F)$ = the probability of a tail in a single flip (.5000)

$p(S)^K$ = the probability of a success (.5000) raised to the Kth (4th) power = $.5000^4$

$p(F)^{T-K}$ = the probability of a failure (.5000) raised to the (T − K)th power, so T − K = 10 − 4 = 6 and $p(F)^6 = .5000^6$. In case you have forgotten what "!" means in Formula 7.1, look at the corresponding calculations below. To calculate the probability of getting exactly four heads in 10 flips, we would proceed as follows (we'll round most of our calculations to the nearest ten thousandth):

$$p(4) = \frac{10(10-1)(10-2)(10-3)(10-4)(10-5)(10-6)(10-7)(10-8)(10-9)}{4(4-1)(4-2)(4-3)\,6(6-1)(6-2)(6-3)(6-4)(6-5)} .50^4 50^{10-4}$$

$$p(4) = \frac{10(9)(8)(7)(6)(5)(4)(3)(2)(1)}{4(3)(2)(1)\,6(5)(4)(3)(2)(1)} .50^4 .50^6$$

$$p(4) = 210(.0625)(.0156)$$

$$p(4) = 210(.000975)$$

$$p(4) = .2048$$

Compare this result with that from our empirically derived sampling distribution in Table 7.1. There we found the probability of getting exactly four heads in 10 flips to be .1900, which is pretty close to our mathematically derived result of .2100 using Formula 7.1. How do we explain the difference? Perhaps the difference may be accounted for by the fact that Formula 7.1 assumes a perfectly fair coin ($p(H) = p(T) =$ .5000), whereas our real coin was not perfectly fair or was not flipped fairly. Or, perhaps our coin was fair and was flipped fairly, but we needed to take more than 100 samples of 10 coin flips to get a better match between our empirically derived sampling distribution and our probability theory-based, mathematically derived sampling distribution. It may also be accounted for in part by rounding error. Unless we did an infinite number of 10-flip samples (impossible, right?), there would be at least some difference between an empirically and a mathematically derived sampling distribution.

In any event, Table 7.2 shows the mathematically derived probabilities of obtaining all of the possible number of heads in 10 tosses of an imaginary coin where $p(H) = p(T) = .5000$. Figure 7.2 is a proportional frequency distribution bar graph of the results in Table 7.2. Along the horizontal axis in this graph, we have placed all of the

Table 7.2 Probability Sampling Distribution of Outcomes (in Proportion of Heads) for 10 Trials (Flips of Coin), From Binomial Distribution

Proportion of Heads	Probability (p)
.00	.001
.10	.010
.20	.044
.30	.117
.40	.205
.50	.246
.60	.205
.70	.117
.80	.044
.90	.010
1.00	.001
Total	1.000

possible results (now expressed as proportion of heads) in any single sample of 10 tosses of a coin (0.00 = no Hs; .10 = one H; .20 = 2 Hs, and so on) found in the left-hand column of Table 7.2. The vertical axis of the graph has been converted to proportions as well. That is, instead of representing the raw frequency with which a particular proportion of heads occurs, it indicates the proportion of times in a series of 10 flips a particular proportion of heads is likely to turn up. The height of each bar in the graph corresponds with the probabilities in the right-hand column in Table 7.2.

We now know the exact mathematical probability of getting four heads in 10 flips. To assess the chances of winning our bet, we would have to apply Formula 7.1 to determine the exact probability of getting zero, one, two, and three heads each in 10 flips. These results are found in Table 7.2. Following the fifth probability rule and treating sets of outcomes as if they were single outcomes (see Chapter 6, p. 171), the probability of winning our bet is .001 + .010 + .044 + .117 + .205 = .377. Note how close this mathematically derived estimate is to the empirically derived estimate (.36) we obtained by actually flipping a real coin 10 times on 100 occasions (see Table 7.1).

By this summation method, we can determine the probability of obtaining any specified range of results—say, of getting a proportion of .40 through .60 heads (that is, of getting .40 or .50 or .60 heads). Adding the respective probabilities associated with each of the results (from Table 7.2) would give us .205 + .246 + .205 = .656. Thus,

Figure 7.2 Frequency Distribution Bar Graph of Probabilities of Proportion of Heads in 100 Samples of 10 Tosses of a Hypothetical, Unbiased Coin (from the Binomial Distribution)

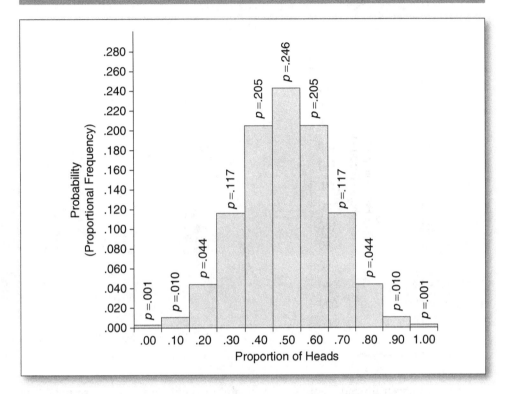

according to the mathematically derived binomial probability distribution, we have a .656 probability of getting four, five, or six heads, if the probability of a head is equal to the probability of a tail in a single flip.

Now, look at the proportional frequency distribution bar graph in Figure 7.2 again. By converting this bar graph to a line graph, we would have the distribution in Figure 7.3. Note the general shape of this distribution and compare it to the shape of the normal curve in Figure 5.7 (see Chapter 5, p. 140). They are remarkably similar, aren't they? It isn't difficult to imagine that, had we chosen to consider the number or proportion of heads in 40 or 100 flips of our imaginary, perfectly fair coin and chosen many samples of those sizes to construct our sampling distribution, we would get distributions whose profiles are increasingly like the smooth normal curve. To put the same point in a different way, the total area of the bars would come closer and closer to matching the area under the normal curve. In general, for practical purposes, we can say that if the number of trials in our sample (in effect, our sample size) is fewer than 10, we should not use the normal curve as an approximation of our sampling distribution

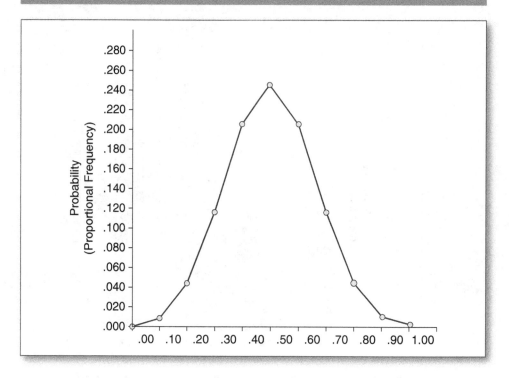

Figure 7.3 Frequency Distribution Line Graph of Probabilities of Proportion of Heads in 100 Samples of 10 Tosses of a Hypothetical, Unbiased Coin (from the Binomial Distribution)

but rely instead on our exact probability calculations using Formula 7.1. If our sample size is between 10 and 99, we can use the normal curve approximation for our sampling distribution, but should also use the correction for continuity to improve the approximation (see Chapter 6, pp. 181–183, for a discussion of the correction for continuity). For samples of 100 or larger, we do not need the correction for continuity.

Note, too, that the number of possible combinations of outcomes gets quite large when working with sample sizes greater than, say, 15, and calculating an exact probability for each using Formula 7.1 in order to construct our sampling distribution would get quite tedious. Imagine calculating 20! or 40! or 100! by hand. Thank goodness for computers and the normal curve approximations!

Point and Interval Estimates of Population Means

Statisticians typically make two kinds of population parameter estimates: point estimates and interval estimates. A **point estimate** of a population parameter is a single variable value used as an estimate of the parameter. For example, we might estimate, on the basis of sample data we have gathered, that the proportion of heads in 10 coin flips will be .5000, or the mean age of first-time offenders in the population we sampled was 14.5 years, or that the proportion of males in a population of first-time offenders was .6810. Each of these is a specific quantity that serves as the single variable value comprising the point estimate of a population parameter. As we will see, the applicable sampling distribution's mean is the corresponding population parameter's point estimate in many cases.

In contrast with a single value point estimate, an **interval estimate** of a population parameter specifies a range of variable values within which the population parameter is estimated to fall. For example, we might estimate that the proportion of heads will be between three and seven heads, or the mean age of first-time offenders in the population fell between 13.5 and 15.5 years, or the proportion of male first-time offenders in the population fell between .6600 and .7020. You may have noted that these intervals were created by adding and subtracting the same quantity from the respective mean estimates above. Thus, for example, the estimate of the mean age of first-time offenders was calculated by first adding 1.0 to and then subtracting 1.0 from the estimated mean of 14.5. If we let the symbol ± (read: plus or minus) represent such additions and subtractions, we could write the interval estimation as $14.5 \pm 1.0 = 13.5$ through 15.5. For the proportion of males estimate, we would have $.6810 \pm .0210 = .6600$ through .7020. We will see why and how interval estimates are built around sample means later in this chapter.

We'll use our coffee bet as a first illustration of constructing point and interval estimates. Look more closely at the mathematically derived binomial sampling distribution we created for our bet (see Figure 7.2). Recall that we began our discussion of the binomial sampling distribution by assuming that the probability of heads was equal to the probability of tails in a single toss of our theoretical coin; that is, $p(H) = p(T) = .5000$. As we noted in Chapter 6, probability theory tells us that, in general, the mean of the sampling distribution for number of successes in n trials is given by np, where n is the number of trials in our sample and p is the probability of success in a single trial. So, our point estimate of the number of heads in 10 flips is $np = 10 \times .5000 = 5$ heads.

For our interval estimate, we will establish a range around the sampling distribution's mean and estimate that the population parameter will fall within that range. How will we do that? First, note that, in the case of fair coin flips, we already know what the mean of the mathematically derived sampling distribution for proportion of heads in 10 flips is. It is 5.0000, and we can build our interval estimate around this mean.

Second, we can use the sampling distribution's standard error to construct the range or interval around the mean. Suppose we want to build an interval estimate consisting of one standard deviation above and one standard deviation below the mean. Again, as we noted in Chapter 6, probability theory also tells us that, in general, the standard error of the sampling distribution for proportion of heads in 10 flips is given by $\sqrt{npq}$. Here, n and p are as before and q is the probability of a failure (i.e., getting a tail in any flip). So, given our assumption that $p(H) = .5000$ in a single trial (flip), its standard error would be $\sqrt{npq} = 10 \times .5000 \times .5000 = \sqrt{2.5} = 1.5811$ heads.

If we perform the calculations, we would have 5 heads (the mean) ± 1.5811(the standard deviation or standard error) heads, yielding an interval around the mean of between 5.0000 − 1.5811 = 3.4189 and 5.0000 + 1.5811 = 6.5811. We know from our discussion in Chapter 5 (see Figure 5.7, p. 140) that about .6826 of the area under a normal curve lies between its mean and ±1 standard error, so we can say about .6826 or 68.26% of the sets of 10 coin flips would result in a number of heads between 3.4189 and 6.5811 heads. Note that this is a case of treating a discrete variable (number of heads in 10 flips) as if it were a continuous one. You can't get 3.4189 heads in 10 flips, only three or four heads, for example. But you get the general idea, we hope. We could say that, roughly speaking, we would get between 3 and 6 heads about 68.26% of the time when we flipped a fair coin 10 times.

We have established that when $p(S) = p(F) = .5000$, the binomial sampling distribution can be approximated by the normal curve if we take many samples, of say 100 or so, even when the number of trials in each sample is as low as 10 (compare Figure 7.3 with a normal curve). Now we can take one further preliminary step in our consideration of parameter estimation. As we noted in Chapters 5 and 6, any normal curve can be converted to a standard normal curve, which has many important properties that can be used in inferential statistics. (You might find it helpful to review the discussion of normal and standard normal curves and z scores in Chapter 5, pp. 140–149 and in Chapter 6, pp. 180–183, before reading further.)

As discussed in Chapter 5, the standard normal curve has a mean of zero and a standard deviation of one. Areas under the standard normal curve can be expressed in ranges of standard units called z scores. So, if we convert a normal sampling distribution to a standard normal (z-score) distribution and use the standard normal curve as an approximation of our distribution, we can use the table for areas under the normal curve (the z-score table) in making our parameter estimates. We discuss and provide examples of how the z score is used in these estimations later in this chapter.

Sampling Distributions for Sample Means

Of course, other sample statistics, such as means and standard deviations, have sampling distributions as well. In fact, the sampling distributions for means and standard deviations are among the most frequently used in inferential statistics. The basic idea of a sampling distribution for means is the same as we have described for proportion of heads. That is, the sampling distribution for means represents the frequency or percent distribution of possible outcomes—in this case, sample means—if we draw a large number (theoretically an infinite number) of same-sized random samples from a population. It turns out that the sampling distribution for means is a normal distribution.

Suppose we want to estimate a population parameter, say, a population mean such as the mean IQ of juvenile offenders in the United States. Just as a mathematically derived binomial distribution can be used as a sampling distribution for proportions of heads in 10 coin flips, a mathematically derived distribution of sample means can be calculated and used as a sampling distribution of juvenile offender sample mean

IQs. Two additional principles of probability theory will help us construct a sampling distribution for sample means.

Two Provisions of the Central Limit Theorem

Recall that a complete description of a normal curve, including a normal curve sampling distribution, requires knowing the value of both its mean and standard deviation. So, we need to determine as best we can the mean and standard deviation of a sampling distribution for means. Three provisions of a probability theorem called the **central limit theorem** will help us construct a sampling distribution for sample means—one that we can use to estimate the mean IQ for the population of juvenile offenders. For now, we consider just two of these provisions.

The first of these three provisions of the central limit theorem pertains to sampling distribution means. According to this provision of the central limit theorem, *the sampling distribution for means from large random samples of the same size drawn with replacement from a population will be an approximately normal curve.* For a theoretically infinite number of samples, it will be a theoretical normal curve.

Again assuming large random samples, the second provision of the central limit theorem tells us that *the mean of the sampling distribution of means will have the same value as the population mean.*

One interesting feature of the first two provisions is that they hold regardless of how the variable values are distributed in the population, as long as the samples are large; that is, they hold whether the distribution of the variable in the population is normal, skewed, multimodal, and so on. In any event, thanks to these two provisions of the central limit theorem, we know the shape of the sampling distribution for means—it's a normal curve. Furthermore, although we don't know in any particular case what the specific quantitative value of the sampling distribution's mean is, we do know that its value is equivalent to the population mean, which, in our example, is the juvenile offender population's mean IQ.

Unfortunately, we often do not know and have no way of knowing (short of doing a juvenile offender population census) the population mean IQ. So, even given what the first two provisions of the central limit theorem tell us about the sampling distribution for sample means, it seems we are still stuck. Is there no hope for us?

Point Estimates of Population Means

Yes, there is hope! We can use the first two provisions of the central limit theorem and a third one we will discuss in a bit, as well as make the best use possible of the information from our sample, to estimate the population mean.

It might not seem so at first, but we do, in fact, have *some* important information about the population mean we are trying to estimate (juvenile offenders' mean IQ). First, we know that we have a random sample from the population, and we can calculate the sample's mean IQ. As we learned in our discussion of random sampling in Chapter 2 (see p. 32), in the absence of other information, sample statistics from random samples are most likely to be representative of the population from which they are drawn. In the absence of any other information, random sample statistics give us the best possible estimates of the corresponding population parameters. Hence, in our example, the mean IQ from a random sample gives us the best possible *point estimate* of the population parameter: mean juvenile offender IQ. The specific quantity of the mean calculated from our sample data becomes our point estimate of the mean IQ population parameter.

Point estimates of population means based on sample means have an attractive simplicity and specificity. Nevertheless, because we know at least some sampling error is almost certain to have occurred when we draw a random sample, an estimate of the population mean IQ based on the sample mean IQ is quite likely to be wrong at least to some degree. It makes sense, therefore, to take sampling error into account when making our parameter estimate.

Interval Estimates of Population Means

As we saw with number of heads, one way of doing so is to construct an interval or range of values around (that is, above and below) our sample's mean value and estimate that the population parameter falls within that interval. This interval, then, would be the interval estimate of our population parameter. As we will see, we can use what we know about the relationship among a normal curve's mean, standard deviation, and areas under the normal curve to create an interval estimate. In particular, if we have the value of our sampling distribution's standard error—or at least our estimate of it—we can determine an appropriate interval estimate. Such an estimate has less specificity than a point estimate, but it offers a greater probability of being correct.

Returning to our example of mean IQ scores, suppose we observe that the sample of juvenile offenders has a mean IQ of 120. Instead of saying that we estimate the mean IQ in the population of juvenile offenders is 120 (a point estimate), we could add to and subtract from the sample mean a fixed quantity (for example, 5 IQ points) and say that the population mean lies somewhere between 115 and 125, which is an interval estimate because it specifies a range (interval) of IQ scores within which we estimate the population mean to fall. Obviously, the wider the range (interval) we specify, the greater the likelihood that the specified interval will include the population mean. The increased confidence we gain by specifying a wide range, however, must be balanced against the decreased precision of our estimate.

As we saw with number of heads, in order to construct our interval, we need to know something about the standard deviation (standard error) of the sampling distributions for means. And here is where the central limit theorem's third provision comes into play.

Estimating the Standard Error of Sampling Distributions for Means

As we begin our discussion of this estimation procedure, recall that the standard deviation of a sampling distribution is referred to as its standard error. So, to complete the creation of our sampling distribution and establish an interval estimate for the population parameter, we need to know, in addition to its mean, its standard error. In keeping with its use in parameter estimation, a sampling distribution's standard error is often referred to as the **standard error of estimate.**

Unfortunately, just as in most cases where we have to estimate the population's mean (and, therefore, the mean of the applicable sampling distribution), we don't know the sampling distribution's standard error of estimate either and will have to estimate it as well. The estimate of a sampling distribution's standard error of estimate, like that for its mean, is based on sample statistics as well as what we know about how random sample statistics vary in normal sampling distributions.

A Third Provision of the Central Limit Theorem

So, how shall we estimate the standard error of the mean for our sampling distribution of means? Once again, the central limit theorem—this time, a third provision of it—comes to our rescue. We have already learned that the central limit theorem tells us that the sampling distribution for means is a normal curve and that its mean is equal to the population mean. A third provision of the central limit theorem tells us that *there is a constant relationship between the standard error of the sampling distribution for a mean ($\sigma_{\bar{x}}$) and the standard deviation of the individual scores in the population (σ) from which the sample was drawn*, so long as we assume random sampling and large samples. Without going into the details of its derivation, the constant relationship between these two quantities is given by Formula 7.2.

$$\sigma_{\bar{x}} = \frac{\sigma}{\sqrt{n}} \qquad (7.2)$$

Here, $\sigma_{\bar{x}}$ is the standard error of the sampling distribution for means, σ is the standard deviation of the individuals' IQ scores in the population, and n is the size of the sample.

> **PAUSE, THINK, AND EXPLORE** $\sigma_{\bar{x}}$
>
> The quantity $\sigma_{\bar{x}}$, the standard error of the sampling distribution for a mean, is derived from a ratio. What happens to its value if σ goes up? If σ goes down? If n goes up? If n goes down? What if the denominator were n instead of $\sqrt{n}$? What does all this say about how $\sigma_{\bar{x}}$ varies with σ and n?

You may have noticed that, even with Formula 7.2, we still have not arrived at our goal of estimating the standard error of the mean. We do not know the value of σ in the formula because we only have our sample statistics, not the population parameter (σ).

We can, however, use our sample standard deviation (s) as an *estimate* of the population's standard deviation. We will symbolize the population standard deviation as σ and our estimate of it as $\hat{\sigma}$. Hence, we are saying $s = \hat{\sigma}$.

For our estimate of the standard error of the sampling distribution for a mean ($\sigma_{\bar{x}}$), we can use Formula 7.3.

$$\hat{\sigma}_{\bar{x}} = \frac{s}{\sqrt{n}} \tag{7.3}$$

In Formula 7.3, $\hat{\sigma}_{\bar{x}}$ is our estimate of the standard error of the mean, s is the standard deviation of the individual scores in our sample, which we are using as our estimate of the population's standard deviation (σ), and n is the size of our sample.

> **PAUSE, THINK, AND EXPLORE** $\hat{\sigma}_{\bar{x}}$
>
> The quantity $\hat{\sigma}_{\bar{x}}$ is also a ratio. How does its value vary as n goes up? Goes down? How do its values vary as s goes up or down?

At this point, we are confronted by another problem. Statisticians tell us that Formula 7.3 produces a biased estimate of the standard error of the mean. What does that mean, and what can we do about it?

Biased and Unbiased Estimates

As we have already learned in our discussion of the central limit theorem, the mean of the theoretical sampling distribution of means is exactly equal to the population mean. In general, when a sampling distribution statistic has the same value as the corresponding population parameter, the sample statistic is referred to as an **unbiased estimate** of the corresponding population parameter. Hence, a sample's mean is considered an unbiased estimate of the population mean. (Remember, however, that even though the sample mean is considered an unbiased estimator of the population mean, any particular sample mean is very likely to differ from the actual population mean to some extent because of sampling error.)

Now consider a sampling distribution for standard deviations—that is, the distribution of standard deviations of some ratio or interval variable from many random samples of the same size drawn from the same population. This sampling distribution of sample standard deviations has a mean as well. For reasons we won't pursue here, the mean of the sampling distribution for standard deviations is not exactly equal to the population standard deviation. A sample standard deviation is, therefore, referred to as a **biased estimate** of the population standard deviation. Furthermore, because the sample standard deviation is used in calculating the estimate of the sampling distribution's standard error, as in Formula 7.3, this estimate is also biased.

When sample statistics are recognized as biased estimators, statisticians make adjustments in calculation formulas to correct for the bias and improve the estimates of the corresponding population parameters. The adjustment typically consists of substituting $n-1$ for n in the denominator of the standard error estimate formula.

Thus, to calculate our *unbiased estimate* of the standard error of the mean, we use Formula 7.4.

$$\hat{\sigma}_{\bar{x}} = \frac{s}{\sqrt{n-1}} \qquad (7.4)$$

> ### PAUSE, THINK, AND EXPLORE $\hat{\sigma}_{\bar{x}}$
>
> Compared to Formula 7.3, does the change in the denominator influence the value of $\hat{\sigma}_{\bar{x}}$ much? What is its effect on the value of $\hat{\sigma}_{\bar{x}}$?

Whew! It's been a long journey, but now that we have a formula for estimating the standard error of a sampling distribution for means, we are in a position to calculate an interval estimate of a population mean—in our example, an interval estimate of the juvenile offender population's mean IQ.

Confidence Intervals, Confidence Limits, and Confidence Levels

Inferential statistics permit us to go beyond calculating an interval estimate of the juvenile offender population's mean IQ. We can calculate the *probability* that our population parameter falls within the interval estimate we establish. In fact, we can use our knowledge of sampling distributions for means to create an interval estimate at whatever confidence level we choose. The range (interval) of values we establish is called a **confidence interval**. The values of the upper and lower boundaries of a confidence interval are called **confidence limits**. And the probability that the population parameter falls within the confidence interval (between the confidence limits) is called a **confidence level**.

How do we determine what interval to establish around our sample mean? Well, it depends on how confident we want or need to be that our estimate is correct. We use the standard error of our sampling distribution, which we will have to estimate from our sample statistics. Then, because we know from probability theory that the sampling distribution of means is a normal probability distribution, we can use the special properties of the standard normal curve and z scores to create intervals of particular sizes depending on how confident we want to be that our estimate is correct. By choosing particular values of z, we can specify the probability that the interval we create includes the population mean.

To help avoid confusion while discussing the process by which these intervals are created, we must introduce some additional mathematical symbols. We will be using sample statistics to estimate measures of the relevant sampling distributions and population parameters, so we will need a set of symbols to represent and distinguish among these various statistics. Statisticians often use Roman letters to represent sample statistics, whose actual value we can calculate from our sample data, and Greek letters to represent the corresponding population parameters, whose values we don't know but want to estimate. To distinguish between the mean IQ score for our sample and the mean IQ score for the population, we use the symbols $\bar{x}$ and μ (the lower-case Greek letter mu), respectively. Likewise, s represents the standard deviation of the IQ scores in our sample and σ (the lower-case Greek letter sigma) represents the standard deviation of IQ scores for the population. The estimated mean of the sampling distribution for means is symbolized as $\hat{\mu}_{\bar{x}}$. The standard error of the mean (that is, the standard deviation of the sampling distribution of means) is symbolized by $\sigma_{\bar{x}}$. As before, n is the number of juvenile offenders in our sample.

Expressed in these mathematical terms, then, we want to make an interval estimate of μ, the mean IQ score of the juvenile offender population we have sampled. To do so, we will make use of the sample statistics $\bar{x}$, s, and n (which, of course, we can calculate from our sample data), as well as the knowledge we have gained about sampling distributions for means, to make estimates of μ, σ, and $\sigma_{\bar{x}}$. These estimates will be used in conjunction with the standard normal curve z scores to create an interval estimate of μ.

Things are going to get a bit complicated and potentially confusing over the next few pages, so take a couple of deep breaths and proceed slowly, doing your best to understand each paragraph before you move to the next one. Table 7.3 provides a handy reference for the various measures and their symbols that we will be using to help you keep track of our discussion. It may help to refer back to Table 7.3 from time to time, just to be sure you understand the procedures we are using to construct our interval estimate of the mean. Pay close attention to whether we are referring to sample statistics or population parameters during the discussion.

Table 7.3 Symbols for Sample Statistics, Population Parameters, and Sampling Distributions

Variables	Sample Statistics	Actual Population Parameters[a]	Estimated Population Parameters	Estimated Sampling Distribution Parameters[b,c]
Mean	$\bar{x}$	μ	$\hat{\mu}$	$\hat{\mu}_{\bar{x}}$
Standard Deviation	s	σ	$\hat{\sigma}$	$\hat{\sigma}_{\bar{x}}$

a. We don't know the values of these parameters, but we want to estimate them.

b. The value of the mean of a sampling distribution of means is equal to the value of the population mean.

c. The standard deviation of the sampling distribution for means is called the standard error of the mean.

The sample mean IQ score ($\bar{x}$) (the point estimate of the population mean) is used to establish the center point for the interval for estimating the population mean IQ score (μ). Next, we need to estimate the standard error of the mean (we symbolize our estimate of $\sigma_{\bar{x}}$ as $\hat{\sigma}_{\bar{x}}$). At first it might seem that the standard deviation of our sample statistic (s) could be used for this estimate. But consider for a moment the dispersion of scores in the two relevant distributions—the distribution of IQ scores in our sample of juvenile offenders and the distribution of the mean IQ scores from a large number of samples of a particular size n (say, 200) drawn from the same population. Suppose that the distribution of individual IQ scores looks like Figure 7.4a, with a mean of 120 and a standard deviation of 10.

The sampling distribution for means from a large number of samples of size $n = 200$ drawn from the same population might look something like Figure 7.4b. Compare Figures 7.4a and 7.4b, which are drawn to the same scale. The mean scores in Figure 7.4b

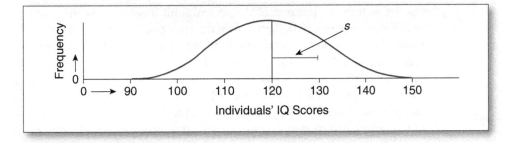

Figure 7.4a Frequency Distribution Curve of Individuals' IQ Scores for a Sample of Size $n = 200$, Showing the Standard Deviation (s) of the Individual Recruits' IQ Scores

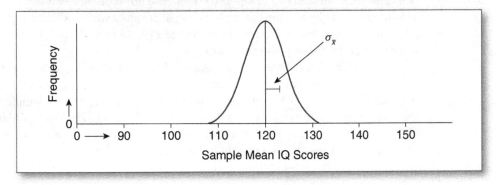

Figure 7.4b Frequency Distribution Curve of Mean IQ Scores for a Large Number of Samples of Size $n = 200$ (that is, a sampling distribution for means from random samples of size 200), Showing the Mean and Standard Error ($\sigma_{\bar{x}}$) of the Mean

are much more closely bunched around the distribution's mean than are the individual recruit IQ scores around their mean in Figure 7.4a. If you think a bit about what quantities are included in the two distributions (raw scores of a single sample in Figure 7.4a and mean scores from many samples of the raw scores in Figure 7.4b), you will understand why. We should expect *much less* variation in the sample mean scores than in the sample raw scores. Put another way, the standard error of the mean ($\sigma_{\bar{x}}$) shown in Figure 7.4b would be many times less than the standard deviation (*s*) of individual raw scores in our sample shown in Figure 7.4a. If we used the sample standard deviation to estimate the standard error of the mean, our estimate would be way too large.

You may have noted that, in constructing the distribution in Figure 7.4b, we assumed that the mean of the sampling distribution has the same value as our sample mean of 120 (see Figure 7.4a)—an assumption that may, of course, be incorrect. We will discuss this issue later. For now, just remember that sampling distribution standard errors are, on average, much smaller than the corresponding sample standard deviations, as illustrated when you compare Figures 7.4a and 7.4b.

Perhaps a review of our progress in parameter estimation is in order. We are constructing an interval estimate of a population mean. We will use sample statistics (in this case, the mean [$\bar{x}$] and standard deviation [*s*] of the IQ scores) to make an estimate of the population mean. We know that some sampling error is likely whenever we sample, and that as a result, $\bar{x}$ probably will not have exactly the same value as μ. We also know from a provision of the central limit theorem how the means of random samples of a fixed size (n), drawn from the same population, are distributed; that is, we know that the sampling distribution for means is a normal curve. We know, too, that there is a constant relationship between the standard error of the sampling distribution for means ($\sigma_{\bar{x}}$) and the standard deviation of the distribution of individual scores in the population (σ), expressed in Formula 7.2. We know that the sampling distributions can be viewed as probability distributions. We don't know the value of μ, but we can put together the statistics we calculate from our sample data with what we know about sampling distributions of means to make an interval estimate of μ, the population mean. To do so, we have to make a number of other estimates. We use $\bar{x}$ as a point estimate of μ and we use *s* and $\sqrt{n-1}$ to calculate $\hat{\sigma}_{\bar{x}}$, an unbiased estimate of the standard error of the sampling distribution for means as indicated in Formula 7.4.

Recall that the range of values in the interval we are going to construct is called a confidence interval. The boundaries or end points of the interval are called the confidence limits. Confidence intervals and confidence limits are just two ways of referring to what is essentially the same thing—the range of values within which we estimate the population parameter to fall. The confidence level is the *probability* that the confidence interval includes the population parameter.

Now, having determined our estimate of the mean and standard error of the applicable sampling distribution, we can turn to a discussion of the use of *z* scores in creating confidence intervals for estimating population parameters from sample statistics. We choose particular *z*-score values that correspond with the desired confidence level. (We recommend that you review our discussion of *z* scores and areas under the normal curve in Chapter 5, pp. 144–149 before reading further.)

Recall from Chapter 5 that the area under any normal curve, including normal sampling distribution curves, can be divided into segments using the value of its mean and its standard deviation. We learned, for example, that approximately .6826 of the area under the curve lies between one standard deviation above and one standard deviation below the mean (see Figure 5.7, p. 140). We showed how any normal distribution can be converted to a standard normal distribution with a mean of zero and a standard deviation of one. Recall, too, that areas under a standard normal curve can be divided up into segments using the curve's mean ($z = 0$) and standard deviation ($z = 1$). In Chapter 5, we also learned how we can specify the proportion of area under the curve falling between two specified z scores or beyond specified z scores using the z-score table in Appendix D. Using that table, we can tell that about .6826 of the area under the standard normal curve lies between $z = -1$ and $z = +1$. Also, about .9546 of the area lies between $z = -1.96$ and $z = +1.96$.

Consider again the sampling distribution of means for juvenile offender mean IQ scores, the mean and standard deviation (standard error) of which we have just finished discussing. What does this distribution represent? We have already noted that sampling distributions are probability distributions. So, our sampling distribution represents the probability of getting various particular outcomes (in this case, mean IQs) when we take a simple random sample. We will divide up the area under this sampling distribution (i.e., divide up the probabilities) using our estimates. To do so, we will use z scores together with our estimates to create confidence intervals at any confidence level we choose. Remember a confidence level is the probability that our interval estimate of the population parameter is correct. Let's see how all this would work in our juvenile offender IQ example.

The general formula for constructing a confidence interval around our sample mean with a specified confidence level that the population mean falls within the interval is provided by Formula 7.5.

$$cl = \bar{x} \pm z(\hat{\sigma}_{\bar{x}}) \qquad (7.5)$$

In Formula 7.5, cl stands for confidence limits, $\bar{x}$ is the sample mean, and $\hat{\sigma}_{\bar{x}}$ is the estimate of the standard error of the mean for samples of size n from Formula 7.4.

PAUSE, THINK, AND EXPLORE CONFIDENCE INTERVALS AND LIMITS

How does the size of the confidence interval (i.e., the distance between the confidence limits) vary as z goes up? As z goes down? How are the areas under the curve in the normal probability distribution changing as z goes up or down? How does the size of the confidence interval vary as $\hat{\sigma}_{\bar{x}}$ goes up and down?

The confidence interval is the range between $\bar{x} - z(\hat{\sigma}_{\bar{x}})$ and $\bar{x} + z(\hat{\sigma}_{\bar{x}})$. We calculate the value of the sample mean ($\bar{x}$) and our estimate of the standard error of the mean ($\hat{\sigma}_{\bar{x}}$) from our sample data. Then, by entering different values of z in this formula, we can construct confidence intervals of different sizes, with corresponding differences in our level of confidence that the range we have determined includes the population mean.

What does having z in this formula accomplish for us? By multiplying our estimate of the sampling distribution's standard error by a chosen z, we are dividing up the area under the sampling distribution curve into segments whose boundaries are multiples of its estimated standard error. So, for example, $\pm 1.96 \times \hat{\sigma}_{\bar{x}}$ (the standard error of estimate) creates boundaries that divide the area under the probability sampling distribution curve into three portions. One portion lies between these boundaries and represents .95 (or 95%) of the total area under the curve, which represents .95 (or 95%) of the outcomes (means) that occur when we random sample. The other two portions lie equally in the tails of the distribution (.025 or 2.5% in each tail), which, taken together, represent the remaining .05 (or 5%) of the sample means we can expect to get if we draw a random sample from the population and calculate the sample's mean IQ. Figure 7.5 illustrates this division of the probability sampling distribution.

So, if we wanted to be 95% confident that the specified range will include the population mean (that is, if we want to construct a 95% confidence interval), we would enter a z value of 1.96 in Formula 7.5. If we wanted a 99% confidence interval,

Figure 7.5 Using the Standard Normal Curve as a Probability Curve for Establishing Confidence Intervals

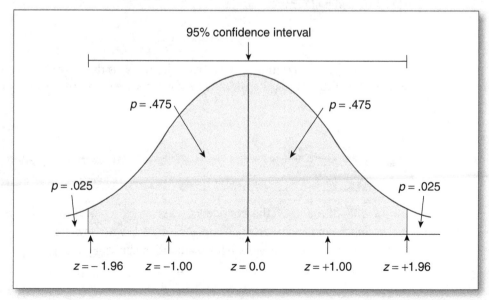

Note: 95% of the area under the probability curve is included in the interval $z = -1.96$ to $z = +1.96$.

we would substitute 2.575 from the corresponding entry in the z-score table for z in Formula 7.5. Note that the z value of 2.575 splits the difference between $z = 2.57$ and $z = 2.58$. For a confidence level of 99%, we are looking for a z corresponding to .0050 of the area under half the curve beyond z. See column C in the z-score table corresponding to $z = 2.57$ and $z = 2.58$.

Returning to our example of juvenile offenders, recall that our sample mean IQ ($\bar{x}$) is 120. We also specified that our sample size (n) is 100 and the standard deviation of IQ scores in our sample (s) is 10, and we decide to establish a 95% confidence interval. Substituting these values from our example in Formula 7.4, our estimate of the standard error of the mean is given by

$$\hat{\sigma}_{\bar{x}} = \frac{s}{\sqrt{(n-1)}}$$

$$= \frac{10}{\sqrt{(200-1)}}$$

$$= \frac{10}{14.1067}$$

$$= .7089$$

Following Formula 7.5 (see p. 213), substituting 1.96 for z and rounding to the nearest one hundredth, our 95% probability confidence limit formula would then be

$$cl = \bar{x} \pm z(\hat{\sigma}_{\bar{x}})$$

$$cl = 120 \pm 1.96(.7089)$$

$$cl = 120 \pm 1.39 \text{ (rounded)}$$

The confidence limits would then be

$$120 + 1.96(.71) = 120 + 1.39 = 121.39$$

and

$$120 - 1.96(.71) = 120 - 1.39 = 118.61.$$

Hence, given our juvenile offender sample data, we can say that there is a .95 probability that the juvenile offender population from which our sample was drawn will have a population mean IQ that falls in the interval between 118.61 and 121.39, inclusive. Does the narrowness of the estimated range surprise you? Our estimate remains an estimate, of course, but we can be 95% confident the actual population parameter falls within this range. It has been a long way getting here, but remember we said we would see that pretty good estimates of population parameters can be made using inferential statistics.

By using the general formula and the table of z scores in Appendix D, we can determine the confidence limits for any confidence level we wish, simply by substituting different values of z in Formula 7.5. The confidence interval that we establish constitutes our interval estimate of the population parameter (in this case, the juvenile offender population's mean IQ) in which we are interested.

Note that in specifying an interval within which we estimate our mean to fall, we are, in effect, making an allowance for sampling error. The larger the interval we specify, the larger the sampling error for which we allow and the safer our estimate.

Note also that the formula we used to obtain our estimate of the standard error of the mean ($\hat{\sigma}_{\bar{x}}$) included the term $\sqrt{n-1}$. Sample size plays a very important role in establishing confidence limits, but the size of the population is irrelevant in these calculations. An examination of Formulas 7.4 and 7.5 shows that as sample size (n) increases, the confidence interval associated with a particular confidence level (for example, 95% or 99%) gets smaller. This, in turn, means that as the sample size increases, the ranges of our interval estimates of population parameters become smaller. That makes sense because larger samples give us more information about the populations from which they were drawn.

Calculating confidence limits for small samples (say, 50 or less) requires the use of additional correctional procedures in the formulas we have discussed. Formulas adjusted for use with small samples are available in more advanced texts.

All that remains in our discussion of estimates of population means is to elaborate on the issue we raised when we constructed Figures 7.4a and 7.4b. As we noted in that discussion, we assumed that our sample mean IQ (120) was equal to the sampling distribution's mean. We pointed out that that assumption may not be correct. In fact, it almost certainly won't be correct. So, we need a way of thinking about what we are doing when we construct confidence intervals and confidence limits around a sample mean without the assumption that the sample's distribution mean is equal to the population's mean.

Remember that to make our interval estimate, we begin by taking the sample mean as our estimate of the population mean and then, using this estimate as a starting point, we construct a range of scores around it to establish as our confidence interval. We now follow this same procedure, except that we assume there likely will be a difference between the mean of the sampling distribution and our estimate of the population mean using the sample mean and particular confidence intervals. Figure 7.6 illustrates more accurately the relationships between the population mean and confidence interval estimates of it.

In Figure 7.6a, we have provided a schematic illustration (not drawn to scale) of one sample mean with a 95% confidence interval ($z = 1.96$) around it. The figure shows the relationship of the interval estimate to the corresponding population mean. In this case, the confidence interval includes the population mean. In Figure 7.6b, we have included two illustrations. One shows a 99% confidence interval ($z = 2.575$), with the population mean included in the interval. The other shows a 50% confidence interval ($z = .67$), with the population mean not included in the interval. As in Figure 7.6a, each illustration begins with the sample mean and then establishes a range around that mean. Remember that a 95% confidence interval indicates that, over the long run, 95% of our interval estimates will include the actual population parameter and 5% will not include it.

Estimating Population Proportions Revisited

Now let's return to a discussion of estimating proportions. In our coin toss example, we knew what the population parameter was (i.e., we knew the number or proportion of heads in 10 flips over an infinite number of trials of 10 flips each) if our coin was fair: five heads in 10 flips or .5000 heads. We were able to build our sampling distribution on the basis of this assumption by calculating exact probabilities for each of the possible outcomes. But suppose you don't know in advance what the population parameter is? Let's consider this more complex situation involving population proportions.

Suppose you are a candidate for sheriff in High Crime County. You are locked in what appears to be a close race with the chief of police in the largest city in the county. A random sample poll by a reputable polling firm has been published showing that, among the 700 likely voters they interviewed, you are currently ahead 52% to 48%. The pollsters report that the margin of error in the poll is ±2%. Does this report have a ring of familiarity to it? It should, because the pollsters have used the sample statistics

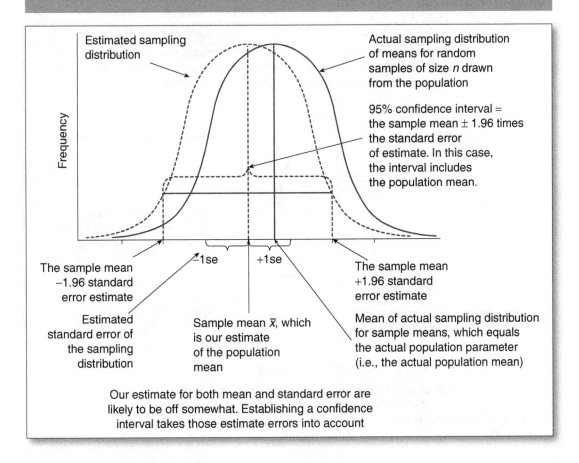

Figure 7.6a Illustration of the Relationship Between "Actual" and Estimated Sampling Distributions for a Population Mean and a 95% Confidence Interval

Figure 7.6b Illustration of "Actual" and Estimated Sampling Distributions for Sample Means, One Showing a 99% Confidence Interval and One Showing a 50% Confidence Interval

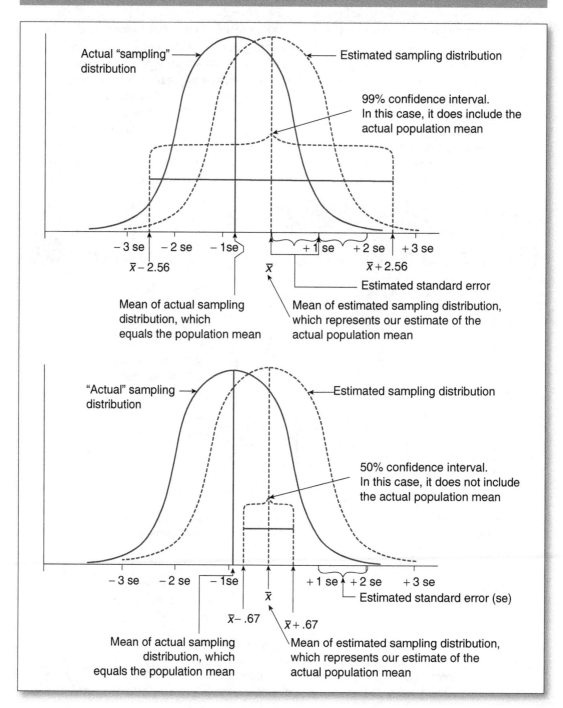

from their poll (the proportions) to make point and then interval estimates of the corresponding population parameter—in this case, proportion of likely voters in the population who say they will vote for you. Given the poll result of 52% who say they will vote for you, the ±2% **margin of error** is a confidence interval.

Here, in contrast with our coin toss example, we don't know and have no way of knowing the real proportion of the voting population that supports you. So, as we did when building our sampling distribution for means, we will have to use our sample statistics and probability theory to construct an applicable sampling distribution for proportions.

Fortunately, a proportion can be treated in many respects as if it were a mean. To see how, think of scoring a vote for you as a 1 and a vote for someone else as a 0. The different poll respondents' answers might then be scored as 1, 0, 1, 1, 1, 0 and so on. If we find the mean of these scores by adding the ones and dividing by the total number of votes, we would get a decimal that could be converted to a proportion. If our sample included only the six scores above, we have four ones in six scores, so 4/6 = .67 (rounded) = 67% (rounded). The proportion .67 is, in effect, the mean of the scores. Assuming the poll is a random sample of likely voters, we can use the central limit theorem pertaining to means to help us construct our sampling distribution.

Following the example of our estimation of a population mean, we will use the proportion of the sample who said they will vote for you (52%) as our point estimate of the proportion of the population who say they will vote for you. We will also need an estimate of the standard error for the sampling distribution of proportions for samples of size 700. We can calculate this standard error estimate from our sample statistics. The calculations for doing so are presented in Formula 7.6.

$$\hat{\sigma}_p = \sqrt{\frac{p(1-p)}{n}} \quad (7.6)$$

In this formula, $\hat{\sigma}_p$ is our estimate of the sampling distribution's standard error, p is the sample proportion saying they will vote for you (p = 52%), and (1 − p) is the proportion saying they will not vote for you (1 − p = 48%), and n is the sample size (700).

PAUSE, THINK, AND EXPLORE $\hat{\sigma}_p$

Our estimate of the standard error ($\hat{\sigma}_p$), of our sampling distribution is a fraction or ratio. What happens to its value as n increases? As n decreases? What happens to its value as p increases? As p decreases? Would the value of $\hat{\sigma}_p$ change faster or slower if it varied by p(1−p)/n instead of the square root of this quantity?

Entering our sample statistics in Formula 7.6, we have

$$\hat{\sigma}_p = \sqrt{\frac{p(1-p)}{n}}$$

$$= \sqrt{\frac{52(48)}{700}}$$

$$= \sqrt{\frac{2496}{700}}$$

$$= \sqrt{3.57}$$

$$= 1.89$$

Now, we need the formula for confidence limits for proportions, which is provided by Formula 7.7.

$$cl = p \pm z(\hat{\sigma}_p) \tag{7.7}$$

We can now select the z score from the z-score table in Appendix D corresponding to whatever confidence level we choose. Suppose we select a 99% confidence level. The z score corresponding to a 99% confidence is $z = 2.575$. (Again, this value of z splits the difference described previously.) Entering our sample proportion and our standard error estimate in Formula 7.7, we have

$$cl = 52 \pm 2.575(1.89) = 52 \pm 4.87$$
$$cl = 56.87 \text{ to } 47.13$$

This result means that you can be 99% confident that the true proportion of likely voters in the population who say they will vote for you is between 47.13% and 56.87%. Or, put in a different way, given a random sample of size 700 and a sample proportion of 52%, 99 times out of 100, the actual proportion saying they will vote for you in the population is between 56.87% and 47.13%. Although it is seldom reported, the margin of error typically used by pollsters is for the 95% confidence level. We'll leave it to you to calculate the confidence interval and limits for the 95% confidence interval in an exercise at the end of the chapter.

One final note is in order here. You may have recognized that the procedure for estimating population proportions can be treated as a binomial problem for which a binomial probability distribution can serve as an approximation of the sampling distribution. One way of exploring this similarity would be as follows. If each voter is as likely to vote for you as not (the equivalent of assuming a head and tail are likely in the toss of a coin), how likely is it that the pollsters would observe that 52% say they would vote for you (the equivalent of observing 52 heads in 100 tosses of the coin or 364 votes out of 700)?

Parametric and Nonparametric Inferential Statistics

Statisticians distinguish between two general kinds of inferential statistics: parametric and nonparametric. They cite two main differences between the two types. The first is that the appropriate levels of measurement for the variables being analyzed differ between the types of analysis. The second is that different shapes of the variable value distributions *in the population* are assumed. In general, **parametric inferential statistics** are used with variables that are measured at the interval or ratio level and are distributed normally in the population. **Nonparametric inferential statistics** are typically used only with nominal- or ordinal-level data and do not require that variable values be distributed normally in the population. The analyses discussed in this chapter are parametric inferential statistics. Numbers and proportions of outcomes are ratio-level variables and are assumed to be distributed normally in the population.

Although parametric and nonparametric statistics may be distinguished in the ways we have discussed, they have one very important similarity. Both types of statistical procedure assume that data from a random sample are being analyzed.

When a variable is measured at the nominal or ordinal level, and when it seems inappropriate to assume that the variable is normally distributed in the population, nonparametric inferential statistics are the best choice. We present and discuss three of the more frequently used nonparametric statistics in Chapter 13. In most of the chapters that follow, we discuss parametric inferential statistics.

Assumptions and Cautions

A few words of caution about inferring population parameters from sample statistics are in order. First, when you encounter a statistic, such as a crime rate, that purports to refer to the characteristics of a large population, you should ask yourself whether the data reported are actual population data or whether they are sample statistics used as point estimates of population parameters. Of course, it is permissible to make point estimates of population parameters, but it is important to indicate that this is what has been done and to understand that such estimates are very likely to be in error to at least some degree.

Second, inferential statistics are based on probability theory principles that assume random sampling with replacement. Sampling with replacement is important when populations are small. When samples are relatively small and the populations from which they are drawn are large, however, most statisticians believe that random sampling without replacement is acceptable. In any event, in practice, most random sampling in the sciences is sampling without replacement.

Third, confidence limits and intervals should be interpreted with care. A confidence level of 95%, for example, tells us that if we took a large number of random samples and used the sample means and standard deviations to construct confidence intervals, approximately 95% of those confidence intervals would include the mean and approximately 5% would not. It does not tell us whether, in the particular case of our juvenile offender sample, our calculated interval estimate actually includes the population mean IQ.

Fourth, sampling distributions enable us to estimate sampling error. However, they do not enable us to assess the influence of other types of biases that may have entered our research procedures, such as poor research design, careless operationalization of the variables, and all of the other examples of "garbage in" we discussed earlier.

Finally, although many estimated sampling distributions, such as those for proportions and means, are normal, some are not. Those for small samples are often skewed. An example is the sampling distribution of the chi-square (χ^2) statistic for small samples, a statistic we will consider in the next chapter.

Summary

In this chapter, we continued the discussion we began in Chapter 6 of probability distributions, applying them here as sampling distributions. We constructed a binomial sampling distribution for assessing our chances of winning a coffee bet empirically. We then derived a sampling distribution for the same bet mathematically, using some principles of probability theory and mathematics. We also derived sampling distributions for means and proportions mathematically. To construct these sampling distributions, we built upon much of what we have learned in previous chapters. Univariate descriptive measures from Chapter 4, the standard normal curve from Chapter 5, as well as probability theory and probability distributions from Chapter 6 were all applied. In addition, some new principles of probability theory, including those of the central limit theorem, were brought to bear. We described ways in which the means and standard errors of sampling distributions are estimated and the differences between biased and unbiased estimates. Then, we discussed how these estimated sampling distributions can be used to calculate point and interval estimates of population means and proportions. Table 7.4 recaps the sample statistics, population parameters, and associated formulas we used in these calculations.

Table 7.4 Summary of Symbols and Formulas for Parameter Estimation

	Sample Statistics	Actual Population Parameters[a]	Estimated Population Parameters	Formula for Estimate	Sampling Distribution Parameters to be Estimated[b]	Formula for Unbiased Estimate of Sampling Distribution Parameter[c]
Mean	$\bar{x}$	μ	$\hat{\mu}$	$\bar{x} = \hat{\mu}$	$\mu_{\bar{x}}$	$\bar{x} = \hat{\mu} = \hat{\mu}_{\bar{x}}$
Standard Deviation	s	σ	$\hat{\sigma}$	$s = \hat{\sigma}$	$\sigma_{\bar{x}}$	$\dfrac{s}{\sqrt{n-1}} = \hat{\sigma}_{\bar{x}}$

a. We don't know the values of these parameters, but we want to estimate them.
b. The value of the mean of a sampling distribution of means is equal to the value of the population mean.
c. The standard deviation of the sampling distribution for means is called the standard error of the mean.

Finally, we distinguished between parametric and nonparametric statistics. The former generally assumes interval level or ratio levels of measurement and, in most cases, variable values normally distributed in the population. The latter can be used with variables measured at the nominal or ordinal levels and regardless of how the variable values are distributed in the population. Both parametric and nonparametric statistics assume random sampling.

The chapter closed with a review of some basic assumptions upon which these estimation procedures are based and some words of caution about their use.

Concepts to Master

Biased estimate
Central limit theorem
Confidence interval
Confidence level
Confidence limits
Interval estimate

Margin of error
Nonparametric inferential statistics
Parametric inferential statistics
Point estimate

Sampling distribution
Sampling error
Standard error
Standard error of estimate
Unbiased estimate

Review Questions

1. Distinguish between a sample statistic and a population parameter.
2. What is a parameter estimate?
3. What is a sampling distribution?
4. What is sampling error?
5. What are the two basic uncertainties associated with sampling when the objective is to estimate a population parameter?
6. Compare and contrast standard deviations and standard errors.
7. What are the two ways sampling distributions may be constructed?
8. What is the binomial probability distribution, and how might it be used as a sampling distribution?
9. Describe the sampling distribution for means.
10. What are the two basic principles of the central limit theorem as they apply to the sampling distribution for means?
11. What is a point estimate of a population parameter?
12. What is an interval estimate of a population parameter?
13. Compare and contrast point and interval estimates of population parameters.

14. What is a standard error of estimate?
15. What is a confidence interval?
16. What are confidence limits?
17. What is a confidence level?
18. What is the third provision of the central limit theorem mentioned in the text, and how does it apply to the construction of interval estimates?
19. How should a 95% confidence interval be interpreted?
20. Compare and contrast a biased and unbiased parameter estimate.
21. How should 95% confidence limits be interpreted?
22. What role do z scores play in constructing interval estimates of means and proportions?
23. Describe the steps to be taken to make a point estimate of a population mean using sample data.
24. Describe the steps to be taken to make an interval estimate of a population mean from sample data.
25. What sample statistics are used to create an interval estimate of a population mean and why does it require all three? What additional information is used?
26. What sample statistics are used to estimate the standard error of a sampling distribution of means, and how are they used to construct the estimate?
27. Describe sampling distributions for proportions.
28. What are the basic assumptions on which parametric statistics are based?
29. What are the main cautions to be observed when using inferential statistics?
30. Distinguish between parametric and nonparametric statistics.
31. What is the basic assumption that underlies both parametric and nonparametric inferential statistics?
32. What are the main cautions to be observed when estimating population parameters?
33. Define all of the terms in the "Concepts to Master" list and use each of them in three different sentences.

Exercises and Discussion Questions

1. Why would a variable's level of measurement be important in the choice between parametric and nonparametric statistics?
2. Why is it essential to select a sample randomly when using inferential statistics?

3. Discuss the origins and nature of sampling error.
4. Why are sampling distributions so important in inferential statistics?
5. How do sampling distributions give researchers a way of measuring sampling error?
6. How do inferential statistics give researchers a way of taking sampling error into account?
7. What is the relationship among population parameters, sampling distributions, and sampling error?
8. Discuss the central limit theorem and its role in estimating population means.
9. Why is it important in many cases that a variable be distributed normally in a population when applying inferential statistics? Can you identify an exception to this general rule?
10. What advantages do large samples have in inferential statistics?
11. Construct a sampling distribution empirically for number of heads in six flips of a coin. Take at least 30 samples of six flips each, recording the results for number of heads in each sample. Be sure the coin turns over at least three times in the air on each flip. Put your results at each stage in table and bar graph form. Convert your number of heads distribution into a proportion of heads distribution and then into a probability distribution. Use this distribution as an empirically derived approximation of the sampling distribution for proportion of heads in six flips. What does your probability distribution tell you about your chances of getting exactly four heads in six flips? What does it tell you about the probability of getting four or more heads in six flips? Show your calculations and discuss why you calculated as you did. Does your probability distribution resemble a normal curve? Compare the probability distributions for three and five flips (from Chapter 6) with the probability distribution for six flips you just created. Do you see a trend? Now, use Formula 7.1 to calculate the exact probabilities for each of the possible number of heads outcomes in six flips, assuming $p(H) = .5000$ in each flip. Show your calculations. Construct a bar graph probability distribution for your results. Compare this distribution with the one you derived empirically above. Discuss the similarities and differences.
12. Suppose you have selected a random sample of 60 persons from a population of 1,000 and measured their ages. Suppose further that the ages in your sample have a range of 15 to 37, are approximately normally distributed, and have a mean of 26 years and a standard deviation of 2.5 years. Sketch a distribution curve for these raw data, showing the mean and the standard deviation of the raw score distribution. Sketch the sampling distribution for the mean on the same scale as your raw score distribution. Show estimates of its mean and standard error. Calculate 50%, 95%, and 99% confidence limits and confidence intervals for estimates of the population means. Interpret and discuss your results. Was the size of the population included in any of your calculations? Why or why not?
13. Using the same sample statistics in Exercise 12, calculate the 95% confidence limits and interval for a sample size of 100. Do the same for a sample size of 200. Show your calculations. Write a paragraph discussing what the results show about the relationship of parameter estimates to sample size.

14. Suppose you are interested in the mean number of drug offenses for a population consisting of 10,000 drug offenders. Suppose you know that the distribution of the number of drug offenses is approximately normal in the population and that the standard deviation for the number of offenses in the population is 2.4. How large a sample would you need to draw to estimate the population mean within a 95% confidence interval? Do you have sufficient information to answer the question? What else, if anything, would you need to know? Is there any information given that is irrelevant?

15. Calculate the 95% confidence limits and interval for the sheriff's race poll example in the text. What would be the margin of error for this confidence level?

16. Suppose you are the chief of police in Middle-Sized City, which has been experiencing a rapid increase in crime. A referendum has been put on the ballot to increase the number of police officers by 25% over the next 2 years. You want to gauge the degree of support in the community for the referendum so you can determine how much effort your department should put into educating the public. You commission a random sample poll of 250 likely voters, and the pollster tells you that 56% of respondents said they were in favor of the proposal to increase the number of police officers. What would be your point estimate of the true proportion in the population of Middle-Sized City in support of the referendum? How and why did you choose that estimate? Now suppose you want to construct an interval estimate of the true proportion in support of the referendum. How confident do you want to be that your interval estimate is correct? Why have you chosen that confidence level? Once you decide how confident you want to be, describe the process you would use to construct your interval estimate. Include the value of z you would need to use in your confidence interval calculations. Calculate an interval estimate of the true proportion in the population who support the referendum such that you can be 99% confident that the true population proportion is included in the interval estimate. Calculate the margin of error for your estimate for the 95% confidence level. Discuss your results. How much effort does your department need to put into public education about the referendum?

17. If you haven't already done so, answer all the questions in the "Pause, Think, and Explore" boxes.

18. Go to www.fbi.gov/about-us/cjis/ucr/frequently-asked-questions/ucr_faqs and click on methodology to learn how population parameters are estimated in the Uniform Crime Reports.

Student Study Site

Visit the open-access student study site at **www.sagepub.com/fitzgerald** for access to several study tools including eFlashcards, web quizzes, and additional appendices as well as links to SAGE journal articles and audio, video and web resources.

Bivariate Hypothesis Testing With Nominal and Ordinal Variables

Learning Objectives

What you are expected not only to learn but to master in this chapter:

- What hypothesis testing means
- The difference between Type I and Type II errors
- How to compare frequency distributions to test nominal- and ordinal-level variable hypotheses
- How to construct a cross-tabulation (contingency table)
- How to title and label a cross-tabulation
- How to use percents in cross-tabulations
- How to read diagonals in cross-tabulations
- How to conduct an elaboration analysis
- How to distinguish among replication, explanation, interpretation, and specification in the results of elaboration analysis

- The basic ideas underlying chi-square analysis
- How to calculate chi square, including the calculation of expected cell frequencies
- How to test chi square for statistical significance
- How to present the results of a chi-square analysis
- Assumptions and cautions when using chi-square analysis

Introduction

Is there a relationship between ethnicity of judge and type of court on which the judge serves? Is there a relationship between sex of judge and type of court on which the judge serves? Is there a relationship between sex of offender and type of offense? Is there a relationship between region of the country and type of offense? Is there a relationship between rank on the force and marital status? Are marital status and type of offense related? Is sex of defendant related to trial outcome? Is sex of defendant related to whether or not there is a successful plea bargain? Is there a relationship between type of offense and psychiatric diagnosis? Are birth order of siblings and type of offense related? Is there a relationship between type of police or court response to domestic violence and subsequent repeat of domestic violence? The statistical analyses we will consider in this chapter can often help answer questions like these.

As we saw in Chapters 3, 4, and 5, frequency distributions, as well as measures of their central tendencies and dispersions, are useful when a researcher wishes to describe or analyze data for a single variable. As we saw in Chapters 6 and 7, these descriptive statistics can be incorporated into inferential statistical procedures for making population parameter estimates from random sample data. These procedures included constructing sampling distributions and determining the probability of specified outcomes due to sampling error alone. In this chapter, we apply much of what we have already learned in Chapters 3 through 7 to another basic research activity, testing hypotheses. Although we will introduce some new statistics related to hypothesis testing, statistical analysis always begins with descriptive statistics and often involves inferential statistics as well. Hypothesis testing is no exception.

We first review some general aspects of hypothesis testing, including the relationship between research and null hypotheses. Next, we consider three approaches to hypothesis testing when only nominal or ordinal variables are involved: comparing frequency distributions, cross-tabulation, and elaboration analysis. Finally, we describe and discuss the uses of chi square, an inferential statistic for determining the statistical significance of the results of such analyses.

Some Basics of Hypothesis Testing

The most common form of **hypothesis testing** involves assessing whether the empirical evidence (data) supports or does not support the existence of a causal relationship between or among variables. In this chapter, we will be concerned primarily with bivariate hypothesis testing. As we will see later in the chapter, there is another kind of hypothesis testing that applies to the distribution of the values of a single variable called univariate hypothesis testing. We take up the most common type of hypothesis testing first.

As we discussed in Chapter 2 (see p. 29), a **research hypothesis**, sometimes called the **alternative hypothesis**, typically asserts a causal relationship between two or more variables. At least one of the variables is considered the independent or causal variable and at least one is considered a dependent or effect variable. Examples would include length of sentence is related to recidivism, marital status of citizens is related to support for police, or changes in a particular law are related to changes in the behavior addressed by the law. As we also noted, when inferential statistics are used to learn about a population from random sample data, the analyses do not typically test a research hypothesis directly. Rather, what is actually tested is a **null hypothesis**, which states that there is no relationship between the variables in the population. The researcher hopes that the sample evidence gathered indicates the null hypothesis should be rejected, thereby lending indirect support for the research hypothesis.

Some researchers and statisticians insist on restricting the use of the term "hypothesis testing" to only those analyses involving inferential statistics. We understand this preference, but think this restriction elevates one kind of statistical analysis to an exclusive position in scientific research it does not deserve and, in the process, confuses what almost all scientific research is most fundamentally about. Scientists work to construct theories that explain phenomena. Theories are, in turn, composed of related hypotheses. Hypotheses typically assert relationships between or among variables. Research is undertaken to test these hypotheses—that is, to determine whether there is empirical evidence to support the hypothesized relationships and, in turn, the theories from which they are derived. None of this requires using random samples, probability theory, or inferential statistics. After all, when we look at data, not just from a sample but from an entire population, we are also typically testing hypotheses that there are or are not relationships among the variables we are studying. Furthermore, even with population data, it is a good strategy to begin by assuming the null hypothesis is true and demand strong evidence against it before concluding that the data support our research hypothesis. We recommend you think about hypothesis testing as encompassing the full range of statistical analysis tools available. In short, hypothesis testing is at the core of the scientific enterprise, and it can be accomplished using inferential or descriptive statistical analyses. Also, designing the research and beginning the data analysis with the assumption that the null hypothesis rather than the research hypothesis is correct is a relatively unique and powerful aspect of the scientific perspective. It helps avoid one of the most common mistakes humans make in assessing their hunches—namely, assuming that their hunch is true and then looking for evidence to support it, all the while easily ignoring or giving short shrift to contradictory evidence.

Requiring that the null hypothesis be tested and rejected in order to provide support for the research hypothesis also emphasizes that, in scientific research, hypotheses must be **empirically falsifiable**. There are two aspects of falsifiability. First, hypotheses must be formulated and studies must be designed so that *observational evidence* bearing on

Table 8.1 Hypothesis Testing and Types of Error

Null Hypothesis Is	Decision on Null Hypothesis	
	Accept (Fail to Reject)	Reject
True	Correct decision Probability of a correct decision = $1 - \alpha$	Incorrect decision is a Type I error Probability of a Type I error = α (α = significance level)
False	Incorrect decision is a Type II error Probability of a Type II error = β	Correct decision Probability of a correct decision = $1 - \beta$ ($1 - \beta$ = power)

their truth or falsity can be gathered. Second, during the analysis, the possibility that the evidence will indicate support for the null hypothesis must be preserved.

As in many life situations, assessing the available evidence as it bears on our hypotheses is seldom clear cut, necessitating that the researcher exercise *judgment* about the *weight* of the evidence. Consider the researcher's two choices regarding the null hypothesis: She can accept (some would prefer to say "fail to reject") or reject it. Consider also the two possible realities with respect to the null hypothesis: It can be true or false. In some cases, the researcher's decision will correspond with the null hypothesis in reality. In other cases, the researcher will make an incorrect decision and commit one of two types of error. The four possible combinations involving these two sets of choices and symbols for the probabilities associated with each are presented in Table 8.1.

Type I and Type II Errors

We first introduced the concepts of Type I and Type II errors in hypothesis testing in Chapter 2 (see pp. 29–30). Here we will explore these concepts in more detail. Note that, as we discussed in Chapter 2 and as indicated in Table 8.1, there are two types of incorrect decisions or errors, labeled as Type I and Type II errors in the table. In a **Type I error**, the researcher rejects a null hypothesis that is, in fact, true. The probability of committing a Type I error is symbolized as α (the Greek letter **alpha**) and, as we will see, is often referred to as the alpha level or significance level in inferential statistics. When data from random samples are used to infer something about the relationship between variables in populations from which they were drawn, they permit us to assign a precise probability—an α—to making a Type I error. The probability of correctly not rejecting the null hypothesis when it is true is $1 - \alpha$.

In a **Type II error**, the researcher decides to accept a null hypothesis that is, in fact, false. The probability of committing a Type II error is symbolized as β (the Greek letter beta). The probability of correctly rejecting the null hypothesis when it is false is $1 - \beta$ and is referred to as the **power** of an inferential statistic.

The details of calculating the power of inferential statistics are often complex and beyond the scope of this text. We will simply note that, as a general rule, statistics based on larger sample sizes, higher levels of measurement, and parametric (as contrasted with nonparametric) statistics have greater statistical power. In this book, we focus primarily on assessing the likelihood of Type I error, though obviously the power of an inferential statistic is very important as well.

Whatever variables the hypothesis may be about, it can usually be translated into an assertion about a population parameter or a relationship between population parameters. When we gather data on an entire population, we can determine the value of whatever parameter is of interest and decide whether to accept or reject the null hypothesis simply by examining the data we have.

Frequently, however, we must rely on sample data to test hypotheses about population parameters. Fortunately, we can use what we learned in Chapters 6 and 7 about samples, probability, and sampling distributions to help us perform these tests. In such tests, the null hypothesis is that there is no causal relationship between the variables because there were no changes in the dependent variable, *except for those that may have resulted from random (sampling) error.*

We can construct a sampling distribution of a relevant sample statistic based on the assumption that any changes we observe in the dependent variable are due to sampling error. This sampling distribution permits us to determine the probability that the sample statistic(s) we observe will occur *if the null hypothesis is correct.* If the changes we observe in the dependent variable have a very low probability of occurring when the null hypothesis is true, we can reject the null hypothesis and argue that the evidence supports our alternative hypothesis—our research hypothesis. We must remember, though, that even in deciding to reject the null hypothesis when our observed results have a very low probability of occurring if the null hypothesis is true, we are still risking an error in judgment. That is, even though the results we obtain are unlikely to have occurred by chance under the null hypothesis, they still may have, in fact, occurred by chance in this particular instance and we have committed a Type I error.

Before discussing the details of hypothesis testing with nominal and/or ordinal variables using inferential statistics, we will discuss comparing frequency distributions, a more basic analytic procedure that does not necessarily involve inferential statistics.

Comparing Frequency Distributions

In this section of the chapter, we discuss comparing frequency distributions in two different circumstances. The first is when the independent and dependent variables are both measured at the nominal level. The second is when at least one of the variables is measured at the ordinal level. Before reading further here, it might be useful for you to review the discussion of levels of measurement in Chapter 2.

Both Variables at the Nominal Level

Suppose we are interested in whether there is a relationship between type of offense and sex of offender in a particular population of adult offenders, say, the 26 adults (13 men and 13 women) convicted of petty theft, assault, or drug possession in the fictitious Horsetail Switch County Court in the past 6 months. With sex as the independent variable, our research hypothesis is that there is a relationship between sex and type of offense. The null hypothesis is that sex of offender is unrelated to type of offense. We hope the evidence we gather will permit us to reject the null hypothesis, leaving us with our alternative, the research hypothesis.

How shall we assemble the evidence? Clearly, a frequency distribution of the sex of these offenders alone would not give us sufficient information to answer this question, nor would a frequency distribution of the type of offense. To find out if there is a connection between these two variables, we must find a way of considering both of the variables at once.

One strategy that could be employed is to construct two frequency distribution bar graphs of the type of offense, including only males in one and only females in the other, and compare them. How would the distributions compare if the null hypothesis is correct? If you think about it a bit, you will conclude that the distributions would be approximately the same shape. That is, the number of males would be the same as the number of females in each category of the dependent variable. On the other hand, if there is a relationship between the variables, the distributions would be different. That is, the numbers for males and females would differ in one or more of the dependent variable (type of offense) categories.

Note that because the total number of males is the same as the total number of females in our example, we can directly compare numbers (frequency counts). If the totals for males and females were different (and somewhat larger), we probably would want to convert them to percents of males and females in each category to make comparisons of the distributions easier. We discuss this procedure in more detail a bit later in this chapter.

Suppose the two graphs look like those in Figure 8.1, drawn to the same scale. Major differences in the two distributions are immediately apparent. The heights of the bars in the graph are quite different, and the modal category for males is assault whereas the modal category for females is petty theft.

Is there a relationship between the two variables? If the apparent relationship were perfect, all males would be in the assault category and all females would be in the petty theft category. Although the relationship is not perfect, it appears the differences are large enough to permit us to reject the null hypothesis and conclude that it supports our research hypothesis. How large the difference must be is a matter of the researcher's judgment and of considerable debate within the scientific community. Even if the consensus is that the null hypothesis should be rejected, however, we may not be justified in concluding that the relationship is causal, for reasons we will discuss later in this chapter.

Why do differences in distributions suggest a relationship between the variables? Consider what we have done in constructing the distributions. In each distribution, we have held the sex variable constant (that is, we used only one value of the sex variable)

Figure 8.1 Frequency Distributions of Type of Offense by Sex of Offender

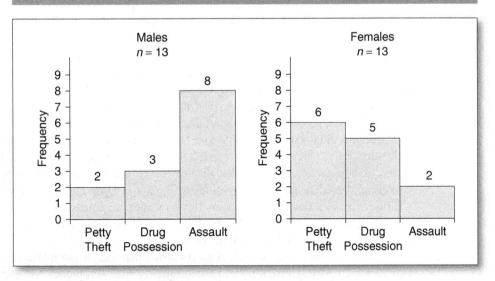

and examined the distribution of the type-of-offense variable *within* that particular value of the sex variable. We proceeded in this way (rather than holding the type-of-offense variable constant and examining the distribution of the sex variable within each of these values) because we assumed that sex was the independent (causal) variable and type of offense was the dependent (effect) variable. Another way of saying this is that we constructed the distributions to answer the question: If we know what an offender's sex is, does that tell us anything about the type of offense he or she has committed? When we compare the two distributions, the data indicate that the type of offense distribution is different for the two sexes and we have some reason to believe that sex is related to type of offense. In our example, if we know the offender is male, we would be right 8 out of 13 times if we said that the person committed assault. If we know the offender is female, we would be right only 2 out of 13 times if we said the person committed assault. If we know that the offender is female, we would be right 6 out of 13 times if we said that the offense committed was petty theft. If we know the offender is male, we would be right only 2 out of 13 times. These differences suggest that there is a relationship (though, as we noted earlier, clearly not a perfect one) between sex and type of offense.

Note that, because the dependent variable is measured at the nominal level, we focused our attention on differences in the modal type of offense category for each sex. Also, the order in which the categories of the dependent variable are listed is irrelevant for the purposes of comparison, so long as they are listed in the same order in the two distributions.

The basic idea of looking for differences between or among distributions as an indicator of a relationship between variables can be extended to include variables measured at other levels, as well as to any of the measures of central tendency, dispersion, and location where appropriate.

One Variable at the Nominal Level and One Variable at the Ordinal Level

There are two possibilities here. The independent variable may be ordinal and the dependent variable nominal, or the dependent variable may be ordinal and the independent variable nominal. Remember that when comparing distributions where ordinal variables are included, the order in which the ordinal variable's values are presented matters. They should be presented in the same (either ascending or descending) order.

When the independent variable is ordinal and the dependent variable is nominal, a frequency distribution of the dependent variable would be constructed for each value of the ordinal variable. Suppose we have fictitious data on all of the high school juniors in a particular city. Our research hypothesis is that success in school is causally related to delinquency. We operationalize (measure) the success in school as the ordinal variable "median grade" with values A, B, C, and D or lower. We operationalize "delinquency" as a nominal variable with two values: no court record of delinquency and delinquent record. The null hypothesis would be that there is no relationship between success in school and delinquency.

To develop the frequency distributions for purposes of comparison, we would construct a frequency distribution of delinquency/no delinquency for each median grade, one for those students with a median grade of A, one for those with a median grade of B, and so on. To facilitate comparisons, we would probably want to convert the delinquency/no delinquency data to percents because the numbers of students in the grade categories are likely to be unequal. There probably would be many fewer students with a median grade of A than of C, for example. We could then compare the percent with no delinquency record in each of the median grade categories.

Suppose the distributions looked like the hypothetical ones in Figure 8.2. Is there a relationship between success in school and delinquency? The mode (no delinquent record) is the same for each median grade. However, the percent with a delinquency record increases with each decline in median grade. Hence, we have evidence that the null hypothesis should be rejected, lending support for the research hypothesis that there is a relationship between the two variables.

When the independent variable is nominal and the dependent variable is ordinal, we would create a frequency distribution of the values of the ordinal dependent variable for each category of the nominal independent variable. We might then look for general differences in the shape of the ordinal dependent variable distributions. In addition, we could compare the modal categories and the median rank orders of the ordinal dependent variable's distributions.

Figure 8.3 presents fictitious data pertaining to the independent variable sex and the dependent variable seriousness of offense. The null hypothesis would be that there is no relationship between these variables; the research hypothesis asserts that there is a relationship. What does the evidence indicate?

Because the ns are different, it might be advisable to convert to percents in order to facilitate comparisons of the distributions. Comparing the distributions clearly indicates there is a relationship. There is a higher percent of females than males in the minor offense category and a higher percentage of males than females in both the

Figure 8.2 Percent With and Without a Delinquency Court Record By Median Grade

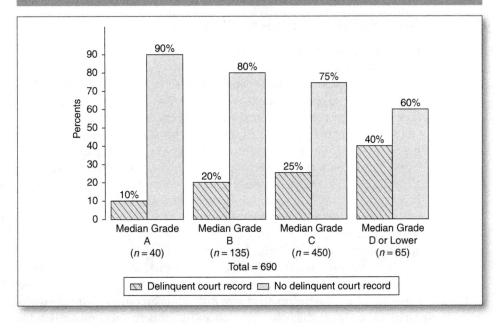

Figure 8.3 Percent of Types of Offense Seriousness By Sex of Juvenile Offender

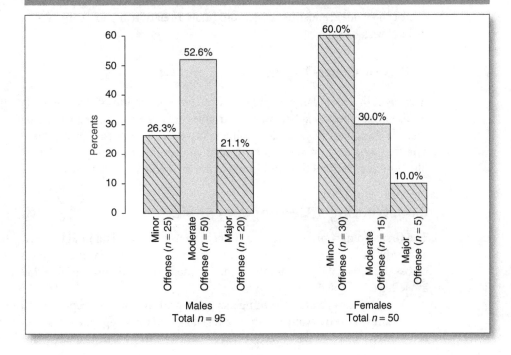

moderate and major offense categories. We might also note that the modal and median categories are different for males and females.

Both Variables at the Ordinal Level

Our research hypothesis might assert a causal relationship between two variables, both measured at the ordinal level. For example, do persons of different social classes (the independent variable) rank differently in their degree of support for the local police? To test this hypothesis, we could, of course, construct frequency (or relative frequency) distributions, just as we have in the previous examples.

Comparing frequency distributions can be an effective strategy for analyzing data no matter what level of measurement is used—even, as we shall see in the next chapter, where the dependent variable is measured at the interval or ratio level. The primary advantage of this analytic strategy is that the distribution graphs provide *visual* cues pointing to possibly important numerical similarities or differences. We strongly recommend constructing and comparing frequency distributions at least as an initial step in data analysis. If you are using any one of the most popular statistical analysis packages, as most analysts do these days, constructing them is very easy.

Nevertheless, frequency distribution comparisons do have limitations. The more frequency distributions you have to eyeball in order to make a judgment about the existence of a relationship, the more difficult it becomes. If you are dealing with two variables, each of which has 8 or 10 values, this method might become somewhat impractical. For this and other reasons, statisticians also rely on cross-tabulation as a form of basic data analysis, especially when variables are measured at the nominal or ordinal level. In fact, cross-tabulation is often a better procedure for assessing whether or not the evidence justifies concluding that a relationship exists between nominal or ordinal variables.

Fundamentals of Cross-Tabulation

A **cross-tabulation** can be thought of as the intersection of two frequency distributions. Cross-tabulating data on two variables creates a **contingency table** that, in many cases at least, permits us to determine relatively easily whether or not they are related. The fictitious data on sex and type of offense presented in Figure 8.1 will be used to illustrate the construction and interpretation of contingency tables.

Constructing a Contingency Table

The first step in constructing a contingency table for the data in Figure 8.1 is to create a two-dimensional data grid. We might begin by placing the values of the sex variable across the top of the grid and the values of the type-of-offense variable down the side, as we have in Table 8.2.

We have now created a contingency table grid that has two separate **columns** (corresponding to the two values of the sex variable) and three separate **rows** (corresponding to the three values of the type-of-offense variable). In statistical analysis, such a table is

Table 8.2 Type of Offense by Sex of Offender

Type of Offense	Sex of Offender	
	Male	Female
Petty theft	cell 1	cell 2
Drug possession	cell 3	cell 4
Assault	cell 5	cell 6

often referred to as a 2 × 3 table. A table with three columns and four rows would be called a 3 × 4 table.

The spaces in the table defined by the intersections of the columns and rows are called **cells**. We can think of the cells as representing all of the possible combinations of the two variables' values. Note that we could have placed the type-of-offense variable across the top and the sex variable down the side, thereby creating a table with three columns and two rows. In this case, too, the order in which the males and females are listed could have been reversed, and the order of the types of offense could have been changed. The choice among these options is essentially arbitrary because the variables are measured at the nominal level. For variables measured at the ordinal, interval, or ratio level, the values should be placed either in ascending or descending order on the grid. Note that a 3 × 4 table has 12 cells and a 2 × 3 table has six cells.

The next step is to make entries in the cells by searching the data set for the different possible combinations of the values of the two variables among the Horsetail Switch convicts (the units of analysis). If Individual A is a male convicted of petty theft, he would be counted in the cell of the table corresponding to the intersection of the male column and the petty theft row. For this table, that means the individual is counted in the upper left-hand cell—Cell 1. If the next person is a female convicted of assault, we place her where the female column and the assault row intersect, or Cell 6. If each person in the population of offenders was included, the table would look like Table 8.3. The numbers that appear in each of the cells are called **cell frequencies**. In

Table 8.3 Type of Offense by Sex of Offender

Type of Offense	Sex of Offender	
	Male	Female
Petty theft	2	6
Drug possession	3	5
Assault	8	2

short, the cell frequencies indicate the number of persons in our data set who possess the various possible *combinations* of values of the two variables.

We can now add the cell frequencies that appear in each of the rows and in each of the columns to get the results shown in Table 8.4. The row sums—8, 8, and 10—are called **row marginal frequencies**. The column sums—13 and 13—are called **column marginal frequencies**.

The number 26 in the lower right-hand corner of the table is the total number of cases included. This table total (often referred to as n or N, as in $n = 26$) can be computed for any table by summing either the row or the column marginal frequencies. Because these two sums must be equal, comparing them provides a simple (though not fail-safe) check on the accuracy of our table construction procedures and cell entry calculations. If the marginal row and column sums are different, a mistake has been made in one or more of the cell entries or in the additions of those figures. Furthermore, if the table total is not equal to the total number of cases in the study, some cases were either left out or counted more than once in the process of generating the contingency table. Of course, any mistakes must be corrected before proceeding with the analysis.

We are now in a position to observe other connections between frequency distributions and contingency tables. The row marginal frequencies constitute a frequency distribution of the types-of-offense variable, whereas the column marginal frequencies are a frequency distribution of the sex variable. Hence, a by-product, as it were, of constructing a contingency table of the sex and type-of-offense variables is the frequency distribution of each of the two variables. Again, this fact can be used to check the table, because the frequency distribution of each of the two variables must be the same as its respective marginal frequencies. If either is not, the process of cross-tabulation must be reexamined in order to correct the mistakes that have been made. Finally, the alert reader will have noted that the male and female columns of the table are the frequency distributions we constructed in Figure 8.1, this time expressed in numerical frequencies rather than as bars in a bar graph.

It should not be inferred from our discussion of the connections between frequency distributions and contingency tables, however, that marginal frequencies

Table 8.4 Type of Offense by Sex of Offender

Type of Offense	Sex of Offender		Total
	Male	Female	
Petty theft	2	6	8
Drug possession	3	5	8
Assault	8	2	10
Total	13	13	$N = 26$

Table 8.5 Type of Offense by Sex of Offender

Type of Offense	Sex of Offender		Total
	Male	Female	
Petty theft			8
Drug possession			8
Assault			10
Total	13	13	$N = 26$

determine cell frequencies. Consider Table 8.5, where the marginal frequencies are specified, but the cells are empty. Note that the marginal frequencies corresponding to a particular cell do impose some *limits* on that cell frequency. For example, the lowest of the two marginal frequencies corresponding to a given cell is the highest frequency that could appear in that cell. Still, many combinations of different frequencies could be entered in the cells of the table without changing the marginal frequencies associated with a particular cell. Therefore, knowing the frequency distribution of each of the two variables (the marginal frequencies) does not tell us anything about whether there is a relationship between them.

The final step in the construction of a contingency table is creating a title for the table and labeling its components.

Titling and Labeling the Contingency Table

Table titles should be clear and concise, indicating the basic contents of the table and perhaps other pertinent information about the population or sample from which the data come. Labels of the table's columns and rows should also be clear and concise, specifying the variables and their values that define the table's rows and columns. Practices differ regarding the placement of the independent variable values in a contingency table. Some prefer they form the rows and others the columns. We will vary the presentation in this chapter. Whatever the particular presentation, though, it is very important to know which variable is considered the independent variable when interpreting the data.

A contingency table is typically titled by naming the dependent variable first, the independent variable second, and linking the two with the word "by." For example, Table 8.2 is titled "Type of Offense by Sex of Offender." To be somewhat more descriptive, a phrase such as "Horsetail Switch County Court, May 1–31, 2010" might have been added to the title. A good title indicates concisely the data being presented in the table. In addition, if the data come from a source other than the research being reported, that source should be indicated. This permits the reader to go to the original source to verify the data and place it in its original context.

All cross-tabulations are constructed and labeled according to the basic principles we have just illustrated. However, a few complications that may be encountered need to be considered.

Collapsing Categories

You are already familiar in a general way with idea of collapsing variable values (categories) and grouped scores from our discussion in Chapter 4, pp. 103–105. It is a strategy employed often when constructing contingency tables. Suppose we have a variable that we call "citizens' evaluation of police services." We have operationalized (measured) it on an ordinal scale with seven possible categories (values), beginning with (1) "police have provided excellent service" and ending with (7) "police have provided very poor service." We wish to examine the relationship of this variable to another variable (for instance, age) that we have operationalized with many possible values. In analyzing and presenting these fictitious data, we could construct a table having seven rows (for the seven values of the evaluation-of-police-services variable) and as many columns as we had ages in our study group, for example. If the age variable ranges from 21 through 70 (having, therefore, 50 values) and there are seven values for the evaluation of services variable, a 50 × 7 table would be produced. It would have 50 × 7 = 350 cells. Making sense of the data might be very difficult, either because there are so many cells or because there might be numerous empty cells or cells containing very low frequencies, especially if we have relatively few subjects in our study.

Given these circumstances, the presentation of the data could be simplified by collapsing variable values and creating grouped scores. (To review our earlier discussion of these topics, see Chapter 4, pp. 103–108.) By combining (collapsing) two or more of the original values of a given variable into a single new category, we can reduce the total number of cells in a table. For example, our evaluations variable could reasonably be treated as a three-category variable rather than a seven-category variable. The first two values of our original measurement could be collapsed and include every person who scores either 1 or 2, and this new category could form a "positive evaluation" score on our scale. The next three values of the original measurement might be collapsed to form a "neutral evaluation" value, and the remaining two values could form a "negative evaluation" category. Now, the evaluation variable has three values rather than the original seven. Note that this is only one of several possible ways of collapsing categories for this variable.

The variable from which we can gain the most by collapsing categories, however, is age. Again, the investigator must decide whether to collapse categories and, if so, into how many new values. The 50 values of the age variable could be reduced to no fewer than two values; reducing it to one value—that is, putting everybody in the same age category—would, of course, be useless. We might create one new category of ages 21 through 45, and another of ages 46 through 70, or we could create 3 new categories, or 4, or 5, or 10. If we decided on a three-category division of the evaluation variable and a five-category scheme for the age variable, we would then produce a 5 × 3 table that has 5 × 3 = 15 cells—a much more comprehensible table than one containing 350 cells.

What is at stake in deciding whether or not to collapse categories? Obviously, some possibly important detail is sacrificed if our variable is originally measured with a larger number of possible values and the data are then analyzed and presented with fewer values. If, for example, there is a large difference between the evaluations of 35-year-olds and 38-year-olds, and we have combined these two age groups into one new category, the difference will not show up in our analysis. One might also contend that some time and effort was wasted by measuring our variables in such detail if only a few general categories were to be used anyway. Although there is no point in measuring a variable with greater detail and precision than are justified by the purposes at hand, it is also true that, short of doing another study, the researcher will never have a greater level of detail available for analysis than that recorded originally. In analyzing the data, the researcher can always reduce the number of categories, but it is difficult to increase the number of categories beyond those with which the data for a particular variable were recorded in the first place. Within reason, then, the original raw data might deliberately be collected in more detail than the researcher expects to use for the analysis. If, in analyzing the data, the researcher encounters unexpected or otherwise intriguing results, the more detailed data may come in handy as she pursues these leads.

How can you decide which categories to collapse? You can, of course, simply try several different ways of collapsing the data on a trial-and-error basis. However, this procedure is only acceptable as an exploratory strategy. It is especially important, when choosing to collapse categories, not to select for presentation only those collapsing strategies whose results make the strongest case for the author's point of view without informing the reader that this was done as part of an exploratory analysis. As a general rule, the researcher should decide on a collapsing plan *before analyzing* the data and apply as much reason, common sense, and ethical judgment as possible throughout the process.

A number of factors might be considered in deciding which categories to collapse. First, you could locate seemingly natural divisions of a variable; for example, an age variable might be broken down into categories corresponding to infancy, childhood, adolescence, adulthood, and old age if those divisions make sense with respect to the problem being investigated. Second, divisions could be based on the categories included in a theoretical proposition or hypothesis, such as "middle-class people are more likely to support the police than are upper-class or working-class people." If the social class variable were operationalized in terms of annual income, it would be reasonable to break these data into three categories corresponding to the three social classes mentioned in the hypothesis. Third, by examining the frequency distribution of the variable, the original categories could be combined so that a sufficiently large number of cases are represented in each category to permit meaningful analysis. Caution is in order here. Categories should not be collapsed in a way that violates the theoretical substance underlying the study, even though it may be expedient to do so. Finally, in the absence of a better rationale, arbitrary collapsing decisions can be made. Many investigators, for example, divide the age range into 5- or 10-year intervals (such as 0–5, 6–10, 11–15 . . . or 0–10, 11–20, 21–30 . . .) and proceed using those categories in their cross-tabulations. Keep in mind that just as the possible values of the original variable measurement must be mutually exclusive and exhaustive, so must be the grouped values created from them.

Some or all of these considerations may be weighed in any decision to collapse categories in a particular way. You should remember, however, that the way data are collapsed may well influence the results that are produced. Consequently, the procedure/criteria used in collapsing categories should always be reported and in a way that is consistent with the variable categories implicitly or explicitly indicated by the research hypothesis.

Using Percents in Contingency Tables

The cross-tabulations discussed so far have contained raw numbers (frequency counts) in the cells. In many cases, for reasons we noted earlier, it is easier to compare and interpret the data if cell frequencies are converted to percents; however, special complications may arise when converting cell frequencies to percents. The basic complication in using percents in cross-tabulations becomes apparent if we attempt to answer the question: What base numbers shall we use in calculating the percents? Consider the cross-tabulation in Table 8.6 of data concerning the variables "position on police force" and "job stress." Suppose we wanted to convert the cell frequencies in the table to percents. The difficulty is that we could do so using three different base numbers, resulting in three different percent figures for any given cell of the table.

First, we could express each of the cell frequencies as a percent of the total number of cases included in the table and produce Table 8.7. Percents based on the total sample are useful to describe the proportion of cases falling into each of the cells. Thus, Table 8.7 indicates that 43% *of all of the subjects studied* are patrol officers with low stress, 30% are sergeants with high stress, and so on. The sum of all of the cell percents calculated in this way always equals 100%.

The two remaining possibilities for converting cell frequencies to percents are to express them as percents of the row or the column marginal frequencies. The choice between these alternatives is based on which of the two variables we have defined as the independent, or causal, variable in the research hypothesis.

You will recall that an independent (causal) variable (x) must precede a dependent variable (y) in time. Our analysis, then, should address the question: Given each of the

Table 8.6 Job Stress by Position on Police Force

Position on Police Force	Job Stress		Total
	Low	High	
Sergeant	30	60	90
Patrol officer	86	24	110
Total	116	84	$N = 200$

Table 8.7 Job Stress by Position on Police Force (in percents)

Position on Police Force	Job Stress		Total
	Low	High	
Sergeant	15	30	45
Patrol officer	43	12	55
Total	58	42	100% $N = 200$

values of the independent variable, what happens to the dependent variable? To answer this question, the cell frequencies should be converted to percentages with each value of the independent variable treated separately. The percentage distribution, then, of the dependent variable within any one category of the independent variable can be compared to the percentage distribution of the dependent variable within any other category of the independent variable. If the independent variable forms the columns of the table, the column marginal frequencies are used to convert cell frequencies to percentages. If the independent variable forms the rows of the table, the row marginal frequencies are used. This practice is referred to as **percentaging in the direction of the independent variable**.

Consider again Table 8.6. It seems reasonable to consider "position on the police force" the independent variable (x), because job stress (y) probably does not "cause" position. The appropriate strategy, therefore, is to use the row marginal frequencies (90 and 110) as the base numbers to convert the cell frequencies in each row to percents, as in Table 8.8. Note that the sum of the percents in each row (but not each column) equals 100%. This table permits us to compare positions on the police force in terms of the percent of patrol officers whose stress levels are in a particular range with the percentage of sergeants with stress in the same range.

Thus, whereas 30/90 or 33% of the sergeants have low stress, 86/110 or 78% of the patrol officers have low stress, and so on. Note that, in reading the table, we compare categories in the direction opposite from the one we used in calculating the percents. If the row marginal frequencies are used as the base for calculating percents (as they were in our example), we compare figures in the same column. If the column marginal frequencies are used to calculate percents, we compare figures in the same row. The table as a whole shows that sergeants tend to experience more stress than patrol officers.

Reading the Diagonals in Contingency Tables

When reading and interpreting the evidence you have assembled in a contingency table, it is useful to look for patterns in the way the data fall in the table's cells. For example, you might examine the table's diagonals. If you draw a straight line from the

Table 8.8 Job Stress by Position on Police Force (in percents)

Position on Police Force	Job Stress		Total
	Low	High	
Sergeant	33	67	100% ($n = 90$)
Patrol officer	78	22	100% ($n = 110$)

lower left cell in a table to its upper right cell, the cells your line passes through or near constitute one of the **diagonals** in the table. The other, of course, would be defined by a line from the upper left to the lower right. In general, if the numbers or percents are higher in the cells through which one or the other of these lines passes than in the other cells of the table, a relationship between the variables is indicated. Be aware, however, that cell numbers (frequencies) can be misleading when reading diagonals unless the marginal frequencies are about equal. It's best to convert cell frequencies to percents before examining the data for cell patterns, including diagonal ones. Figure 8.4 identifies the two diagonals, labeled A and B, in a 4 × 4 table.

When the variables are measured at the ordinal level or above, the values of each variable are arranged in either ascending or descending order on the corresponding axis of the table. Note that, in Figure 8.4, the variables are arranged from lowest to highest beginning in the lower left corner of the cell grid. Compared with other numbers or percents in a table, larger numbers (but remember the numbers caution noted in the previous paragraph) or percents in the cells through which the diagonal line passes indicate a linear relationship between the variables. A **linear** (think straight line) **relationship** can occur in two ways. First, the values of one variable may go up as the values of the other variable also go up. This is called a **positive linear relationship** and is represented by Diagonal A in Figure 8.4. Second, the values of one variable may go down as the values of the other variable go up. This is called a **negative linear relationship** and is represented by Diagonal B in Figure 8.4. Of course, these lines represent a positive or negative relationship as long as the variables are arranged in ascending order along the table's axes as indicated in Figure 8.4. Using these definitions of positive and negative relationships, can you figure out which diagonals would represent positive and negative linear relationships in a table if the order of the variable values on one or both of the axes was reversed?

Linear relationships may be contrasted with curvilinear relationships. A **curvilinear relationship** is one best characterized or approximated by a line or curve other than a straight line. These relationships, too, can be spotted in a cross-tabulation including variables with three or more values on at least one of the table's axes. For example, there may be a change in the direction of the relationship as the values of the variables change. That is, as the values of one variable steadily go up, the values of the other variable go up for a time and then reverse course, going down as the values of

Figure 8.4 Diagram Showing Where to Look for Diagonal (Linear) Relationships and Curvilinear Relationships in a Contingency Table

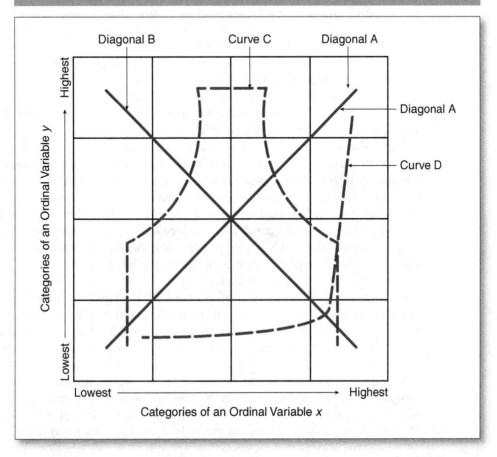

the other variable continue to go up. Or, as the values of the independent variable increase, the values of the dependent variable may increase slowly at first and then rise sharply. If the higher numbers or percents occurred in the cells lying on or near Lines C or D in Figure 8.4, for example, a curvilinear relationship is indicated. Can you identify other patterns of results in a contingency table that would indicate a curvilinear relationship?

Elaboration Analysis

As you will recall from our discussion in Chapter 2, there are three necessary conditions for a causal argument: the correct time sequence, concomitant variation (relationship between or among the variables), and the elimination of other possible causal variables. Hence, even if we have good evidence of the right time sequence and of a relationship between variables, whether from comparing frequency distributions or reading tables, it does not necessarily follow that the relationship is a causal one. As we noted earlier and as we will see in our discussion of elaboration analysis, any observed relationship may turn out to be spurious rather than causal. The search for and elimination of other possible causal variables is a crucial part of the argument in support of a causal research hypothesis. Elaboration analysis, first developed by Paul Lazarsfeld and his associates, especially Patricia Kendall, is one strategy for identifying other possible causal variables (Kendall & Lazarsfeld, 1950). As we will see in subsequent chapters, the logic of elaboration analysis can be applied with variables measured at any level. Here we discuss its logic and application in analyzing cross-tabulated variables measured at the nominal or ordinal level.

In **elaboration analysis**, the investigator examines the effect of a third variable, referred to as a **control variable** or **test factor** (*tf*), on the relationship between the two variables that were the original focus of the analysis. This additional analysis of the data may, depending on the outcome, assist the researcher in eliminating alternative causal variables and strengthening his argument that the relationship between the variables is causal. When a contingency table indicates a relationship between the variables, an elaboration analysis can produce four readily interpretable possible outcomes: replication, explanation, interpretation, and specification.

Consider once again the relationship we have observed between position on police force (x) and stress (y). Note that we can say the table depicts a *concomitant variation* between these two variables; that is, that stress level varies with position on the police force. By observing that position on police force precedes stress in time and that the two variables do vary concomitantly, we have satisfied two of the three conditions for making a causal argument (see Chapter 2, pp. 30–31). The third condition, eliminating other causal factors, remains to be met. If the researcher has used an experimental design to generate the data, considerable control has already been exercised over possible alternative causal variables by the structure of the research design. In other cases, the analyst may simply assume, on the basis of common sense and in the absence of other data or controls, that the relationship revealed by cross-tabulation may be genuine and not spurious. This is, as we have seen, a risky assumption at best, because probably there are many other potential causal variables that have not been considered.

Suppose we are confronted by a skeptic who has examined Table 8.6 but contends that, because females tend to occupy positions of lower status in an organization or to experience less stress than males even when they hold identical positions, sex is the real cause of the stress differentials observed. How could we test the contribution of the sex variable to the apparent relationship between position on the police force and stress?

By constructing two separate contingency tables, one for each value of the sex variable (male, female), we can consider all three variables at once. Using a third variable in this way is referred to as performing a **partial** (think dividing into parts) **analysis**. In effect, we will break the original relationship in Table 8.6 between position on the force and stress level—which, in partial analysis, is called the **zero-order relationship**—into two separate parts (two separate relationships), one for males and one for females. The tables in which the data are entered are called **zero-order tables** and

Table 8.9 Job Stress by Position on Police Force, Males

Position on Police Force	Job Stress		Total
	Low	High	
Sergeant	14	46	60
Patrol officer	58	12	70
Total	72	58	$n = 130$

Table 8.10 Job Stress by Position on Police Force, Females

Position on Police Force	Job Stress		Total
	Low	High	
Sergeant	16	14	30
Patrol officer	28	12	40
Total	44	26	$n = 70$

first-order partial tables, respectively. The relationships, if any, revealed in the partial tables are called **first-order partial relationships** because each, in a way, represents a first division of the original relationship into its "parts." A zero-order relationship or table is so called simply because it is the relationship or table from which the analyst chooses to begin the elaboration analysis. The analyst may choose any bivariate relationship or table to initiate an elaboration analysis.

In any first-order partial analysis, there will be as many first-order partial tables as there are values of the third variable being included in the partial analysis. Because our third variable, sex, has two values (male and female) we will break the original zero-order relationship between positions on the police force and stress level (see Table 8.6) into two first-order partial relationships. Suppose that Tables 8.9 and 8.10 were the result.

First-order partial tables always bear the following relationships to the zero-order table (which, in this case, is Table 8.6):

1. The sum of the total number of cases in the two partial tables equals the total number of cases in the zero-order table. (In this case, 130 + 70 = 200.)

2. Each of the cell frequencies in the zero-order table can be recovered by adding the two corresponding cell frequencies in the partial tables (in our example, 28 + 58 = 86, and 46 + 14 = 60).

3. Similarly, the zero-order marginal frequencies can be obtained by adding the two corresponding marginal frequencies in the partial tables (in our example, 60 + 30 = 90; 58 + 26 = 84).

These relationships occur whenever first-order partial tables are constructed from a zero-order table. If the zero-order table cannot be reconstructed by combining the partial tables in this way, a mistake has occurred; the reasons for any discrepancies must be sought and the tables corrected before proceeding with the analysis.

Again, we can convert the cell frequencies to percents to facilitate interpreting the data, using the row marginal frequencies as in Tables 8.11 and 8.12.

Replication

In both tables, the proportion of patrol officers in the "low stress" category is greater than the proportion of sergeants in the same stress category, and the proportion of sergeants in the "high stress" category is greater than the proportion of patrol officers in the same category. Hence, the same general pattern or relationship between position on police force (x) and stress level (y) found in the zero-order table holds for each of the partial tables as well. In elaboration analysis, this result is called **replication**.

Table 8.11 Job Stress by Position on Police Force, Males (in percents)

Position on Police Force	Job Stress		Total
	Low	High	
Sergeant	23	77	100% ($n = 60$)
Patrol officer	83	17	100% ($n = 70$)

Table 8.12 Job Stress by Position on Police Force, Females (in percents)

Position on Police Force	Job Stress		Total
	Low	High	
Sergeant	53	47	100% ($n = 30$)
Patrol officer	70	30	100% ($n = 40$)

Our skeptic can take some consolation in the data, however, because the relationship between these two variables seems to be considerably stronger among males than among females. That is, when the differences in percents for sergeants and patrol officers within a given stress category are compared in the two tables, these differences are larger for males than for females. For example, in the "low stress" category for males, the difference is 83 − 23 = 60%, whereas for females in the same category, the difference is 70 − 53 = 17%. It appears that both position on the force and sex are related to stress.

The procedure we have just used to test the effect of the sex variable on the relationship between position on police force and stress can be repeated with all of the potentially causal variables for which the researcher has data. The objective is to eliminate as many alternative, possibly causal variables as possible, thereby strengthening the argument that the original zero-order relationship is indeed causal. If the general relationship observed in the original zero-order contingency table is observed in all the partial tables that are constructed, we can infer more confidently that the independent variable is at least one of the causal factors involved. Not all partial analyses result in the confirmation of the relationships observed in the zero-order table, however. In some cases, the relationship between the two zero-order variables will be substantially reduced, or even disappear, in *all* of the partial tables. When the elaboration analysis yields this result, the first step is to construct bivariate contingency tables to determine if the *tf* is related to *x* and to *y*. If it is, what happened to the zero-order relationship in the partial tables can be accounted for in two ways: explanation and interpretation. The crucial factor that distinguishes between these two accounts is the time sequence of the variables.

Explanation

First, if the test factor (*tf*) coincides with or precedes the independent variable, the zero-order relationship is **spurious**. That is, what appears to be a causal relationship between the two original variables is a result of the causal relationship between a third variable (*tf*) and each of the two original variables. This account might be diagrammed as in Figure 8.5, where *x* is the independent variable, *y* is the dependent variable, and *tf* is the test factor third variable. In such cases, the result is called an **explanation**. That is, the test factor is said to explain the apparent, but spurious, relationship between *x* and *y* in the zero-order table. (Note that this is a specialized use of the concept of explanation—not exactly equivalent to the way the term is typically used in science.)

Interpretation

The second account for the partial table results described above is that the test factor intervenes in (comes between) the *x* variable and the *y* variable in time. In this case, the three variables form a causal chain, which can be diagrammed as in Figure 8.6. When the test factor (*tf*) intervenes in time between *x* and *y*, the result is called an **interpretation** and *tf* is called an **intervening variable**.

Again, the determination of whether the analysis has resulted in an explanation or an interpretation is entirely dependent on the time sequence of the variables—the

Figure 8.5 *tf* Explains the Spurious Relationship Between *x* and *y*

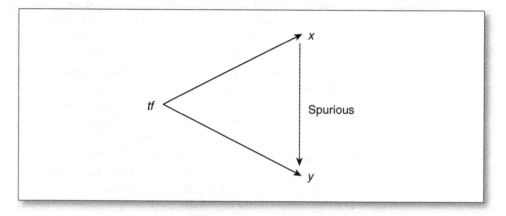

Figure 8.6 *tf* Intervenes Between x and y

$$x \rightarrow tf \rightarrow y$$

numbers or percents in the corresponding cells of the tables could be identical. Note further that in both explanation and interpretation, the test factor must be related to both of the original variables. To be sure that this latter condition has been met, we would have to construct two additional contingency tables to determine that there is a relationship between *tf* and *x* and *tf* and *y*.

Specification

It is also possible that when a test factor is introduced, the original relationship between the two variables may be substantially reduced or disappear in *some* but not all of the partial tables. When our analysis produces these results, the next step is, again, to determine if *tf* is related to *x* and/or *y*. If *tf* is related to one but not both, the result is called specification. That is, we can specify those categories or values of the test factor within which the original relationship still holds and those in which it does not. This is called **specification**, for obvious reasons. When the original relationship holds only for some values of the test factor (control variable), or when its strength or even direction changes with different values of the control variable, the control variable is said to interact with the (original) independent variable. Such **variable interactions** are commonly found in criminal justice research, not only in elaboration analysis but in many types of statistical analysis, such as partial correlation to be discussed in Chapter 11.

Remember, we are justified in calling these results "specification" only if the test factor is *not* related to at least one of the original variables. If the test factor was related to both of the original variables, we would have an instance of either explanation or interpretation.

No Apparent Relationship in the Zero-Order Table

As a general rule, if there is no relationship in the zero-order table, elaboration analysis is not pursued to test the absence of a relationship for other possible causes, for obvious reasons. Instead, another zero-order table with at least one new variable is constructed. If that table indicates a relationship, elaboration analysis proceeds from that zero-order table base.

Nevertheless, we should note that finding no relationship between the variables in the zero-order table does not necessarily mean they are unrelated in any way. If we were to proceed with a partial analysis, we might find the relationship between the two original variables within some categories of the test factor are the opposite of the relationship between the two original variables within other categories of the test factor. These opposing relationships cancel each other when combined in the zero-order table, resulting in the apparent absence of a relationship.

We have summarized our discussion of elaboration analysis and its outcomes in Table 8.13, where x is an independent variable; y is a dependent variable; and *tf* is a third, test variable.

Some Examples of Elaboration Analysis

All of the data reported in the following examples are fictitious. Suppose that we had conducted a questionnaire survey of the relationship between ethnicity and support for the police in a Midwestern city. We have measured the nominal ethnicity variable by asking our respondents to indicate in which of the following ethnic groups they belong: Black, White, Hispanic, Asian, Native American, and Other. Moreover, the ordinal support-for-the-police variable has been operationalized as a 5-point scale: (1) very supportive, (2) supportive, (3) neutral, (4) unsupportive, and (5) very unsupportive.

We hypothesize that ethnicity is the cause of support for the police; that is, ethnicity is our independent variable and support for the police is our dependent variable. As a first step to discovering whether a relationship exists between these two variables, we construct a cross-tabulation. Because there are so few respondents in some categories of both variables, we decide to collapse categories. We make our original six-category ethnicity variable into a new three-category variable, taking Black and White as two of the categories and using "Other" to combine the four categories of Hispanic, Asian, Native American, and Other to create the third category. For the support variable, the original Categories 1 and 2 are collapsed into one new category, 4 and 5 are collapsed into a second new category, leaving the original category 3 the same in our new category system. Suppose that when we placed our data into the cross-tabulation, it looked like Table 8.14.

Table 8.13 Outcomes in Elaboration Analysis

If in the zero-order table	and	in the partial tables	and	the time sequence of the variables	then	the tentative conclusion (inference) is
$x \to y$*		$x \to y$ (in all partials)		x with/before y		**Replication:** x causes y
$x \to y$		$x \mid y$** (in all partials)		tf with/before x and before y		**Explanation:** x is not a cause of y; if $tf \to x$ and $tf \to y$, tf explains relationship between x and y
$x \to y$		$x \mid y$ (in all partials)		x with/before tf and before y		**Interpretation:** If $tf \to x$ and $tf \to y$, x, tf, and y form a causal chain; x causes tf, tf causes y; tf interprets relationship between x and y
$x \to y$		$x \to y$ (in some but not all partials)		x with/before y; tf before y		**Specification:** If $tf \mid x$ or $tf \mid y$, tf specifies causal relationship between x and y; x causes y only in some categories of tf; tf interacts with x

*for $\to$ read "is related to."

**for $\mid$ read "is not related to."

Table 8.14 Support for the Police by Ethnicity

	Ethnicity			
Support for Police	Black	White	Other	Total
Supportive	100	400	250	750
Neutral	150	100	150	400
Unsupportive	400	200	250	850
Total	650	700	650	$N = 2,000$

Table 8.15 Support for the Police by Ethnicity (in percents)

Support for Police	Ethnicity		
	Black ($n = 650$)	White ($n = 700$)	Other ($n = 650$)
Supportive	15	57	38
Neutral	23	14	23
Unsupportive	62	29	38
Total*	100%	100%	99%

*Totals not equal to 100% are due to rounding error.

Next, we can convert the cell frequencies in the table to percentages. Because ethnicity is our presumed independent variable, we use the column marginal frequencies for the conversion. Our table would look like Table 8.15 (with percents rounded to the nearest whole percent).

These data suggest that Blacks are predominantly unsupportive of the police whereas Whites are predominantly supportive. The others are about evenly divided in their level of support for the police. Hence, there appears to be a relationship, perhaps a causal one, between ethnicity and police support:

$$\text{Ethnicity} \rightarrow \text{Support for Police}$$

Now suppose that we have also gathered data about whether our respondents have ever reported a crime to the police. We think that this might have a great deal to do with support for the police. Hence, we decide to perform an elaboration analysis. We divide our respondents into two categories (those who have and those who have not reported a crime to the police) and construct a cross-tabulation of our original two variables for each of these categories. Suppose the data looked like those in Table 8.16.

In this case, the relationship we observed in the original zero-order table (Table 8.15) holds in both of the partial tables (a replication). Hence, reporting a crime to the police does not appear to affect the relationship between ethnicity and police support. We are then still left with

$$\text{Ethnicity} \rightarrow \text{Support for Police.}$$

But suppose the data appeared as in Table 8.17. In this case, the relationship between ethnicity and support for the police observed in the zero-order table (Table 8.15) disappears in the "reported crime" partial table. In the "never reported crime" partial, however, the zero-order relationship remains; in fact, it is even stronger (that is, there are larger differences in percentages between ethnicities on police support) in this partial than in the zero-order table.

Table 8.16 Support for the Police by Report of Crime and Ethnicity (in percents)

Support for Police	Reported Crime			Never Reported Crime		
	Black ($n = 325$)	White ($n = 350$)	Other ($n = 325$)	Black ($n = 325$)	White ($n = 350$)	Other ($n = 325$)
Supportive	16	59	38	15	56	38
Neutral	22	14	23	24	14	23
Unsupportive	62	27	38	61	30	39
Total*	100%	100%	99%	100%	100%	100%

*Totals not equal to 100% are due to rounding error.

Table 8.17 Support for the Police by Report of Crime and Ethnicity (in percents)

Support for Police	Reported Crime			Never Reported Crime		
	Black ($n = 290$)	White ($n = 270$)	Other ($n = 290$)	Black ($n = 360$)	White ($n = 430$)	Other ($n = 360$)
Supportive	31	33	34	3	72	42
Neutral	34	33	31	14	2	17
Unsupportive	34	33	34	83	26	42
Total*	99%	99%	99%	100%	100%	101%

*Totals not equal to 100% are due to rounding error.

Assuming that the report-of-crime variable is related to one (but not both) of the zero-order table variables (although we haven't done so here, we would have to construct the two tables—report of crime by ethnicity and report of crime by support for police—to determine whether this condition holds), this example of elaboration analysis has resulted in a specification. That is, we can now specify in which category of the test variable the zero-order relationship is maintained (in this case, the "never reported crime" category).

Ethnicity → Support for Police (among those who have never reported a crime)

Let's look at another example of elaboration analysis. Suppose we have studied 500 16- to 18-year-old juveniles and examined the relationship between their social class (the independent variable) and the number of self-admitted delinquent acts committed in the past year. We measured the social class variable in three categories (upper, middle, and lower) and the number of delinquent acts in three categories (two or less, three to five, and six or more). Suppose further that we have already constructed the zero-order table and discovered that there is indeed a relationship between these variables: the higher the social class, the lower the number of self-admitted delinquent acts. We then introduce the test factor of ethnicity, measured in two categories (White and non-White) and obtain the results in Table 8.18. (We've left out other ethnicities here for purposes of simplifying the illustration.)

In this case, the zero-order relationship disappears in both partial tables. Recall that when we get this result in an elaboration analysis, we have an instance of either explanation or interpretation. Which of these has occurred depends on the time sequence of the variables. If the test variable (in this case, ethnicity) occurs at the same time as or before the independent variable (social class) and before the dependent variable (number of delinquent acts), we have a spurious relationship in the zero-order table. It seems reasonable in our example to regard ethnicity as occurring simultaneously with the independent variable and prior to the dependent variable. That is, a person's ethnicity and social class are established at birth because a child's ethnicity and social class are determined by the ethnicity and social class of his or her parents, and both of these variables affect the individual well before the delinquent acts being studied. Hence, assuming that our test factor (ethnicity) is also related both to the original independent variable (social class) and to the original dependent variable (number of delinquent acts), we may say that ethnicity is an explanation of the zero-order relationship. That is, the zero-order relationship is spurious, as illustrated in Figure 8.7.

Now suppose that instead of ethnicity, we introduced junior high school attended (measured in two categories for the two junior high schools our subjects attended) as our test factor and obtained the same cell percentages as those in Table 8.18. In this

Table 8.18 Self-Admitted Delinquent Acts by Ethnicity and Social Class (in percents)

Number of Delinquent Acts	White			Non-White		
	Upper Class ($n = 42$)	Middle Class ($n = 108$)	Lower Class ($n = 100$)	Upper Class ($n = 25$)	Middle Class ($n = 95$)	Lower Class ($n = 130$)
2 or less	35	33	34	36	34	34
3 to 5	33	35	33	32	33	32
6 or more	31	31	33	32	33	34
Total*	99%	99%	100%	100%	100%	100%

*Totals not equal to 100% are due to rounding error.

Figure 8.7 Ethnicity Explains the Relationship Between Social Class and Number of Delinquent Acts

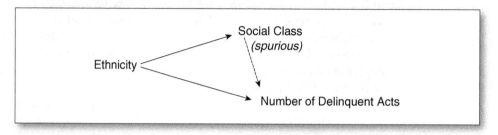

case, we could reasonably argue that the school-attended variable occurs in time after the social class variable (our original independent variable), but before the number-of-delinquent-acts variable (our original dependent variable). The social class of juveniles is usually established at the time they are born; the delinquent acts in question are those committed by 16- to 18-year-olds in the year prior to the study, which means that, in most cases at least, they would have finished junior high school before they committed the delinquent acts in question. Hence, this result of our elaboration analysis is an instance of interpretation. The school-attended variable intervenes and interprets the relationship between social class and number of delinquent acts. The relationships among the three variables as suggested by our analyses might be diagrammed as follows:

Social Class → School Attended → Number of Delinquent Acts.

As a last example of the possible results of elaboration analysis, suppose that our research produced the zero-order Table 8.19. In this case, there is no apparent relationship between the type of defense attorney and trial outcome. As we noted earlier in our discussion of outcomes, we would not ordinarily pursue elaboration analysis with such a finding. To help us make a point, however, suppose we do so in this case.

Table 8.19 Trial Outcome by Type of Defense Attorney (in percents)

	Type of Attorney	
Trial Outcome	**Public Defender ($n = 50$)**	**Private Attorney ($n = 50$)**
Guilty	54	56
Innocent	46	44
Total	100%	100%

Suppose that we introduced sex of offender as a test factor and obtained the results shown in Table 8.20. This result is interesting because, although there was no relationship between the variables in our zero-order table (Table 8.19), there is a strong relationship in each of the partials. Note, however, that the relationships in the partials run in opposite directions. That is, males are more often found guilty when defended by a private attorney and innocent when defended by a public defender, whereas females are found guilty more often when defended by a public defender and innocent when defended by a private attorney. These two partial relationships cancel each other out, resulting in the absence of a relationship in the zero-order table.

Some additional observations about elaboration analysis are in order. The variables with which we begin our zero-order table are essentially arbitrary. That is, we could have begun our analysis with a zero-order relationship between ethnicity and reported crime and used our support for police variable as a test factor, or we could have begun with a zero-order table looking at the relationship between support for police and reported crime with ethnicity as our test factor. The point is that the researcher conducts the analysis as he sees fit, guided by the theoretical propositions that interest him and limited in his inferences about the results only by the time sequence of the variables and whether the contingency tables actually show relationships among the variables.

Note that second-order partial analysis is also possible. It would entail dividing each of the first-order partial relationships (tables) into parts on the basis of the values of a fourth variable. As you can imagine, interpreting the results can get complicated very quickly, and usually, rather than going to a second-order partial analysis, a series of first-order partial analyses is performed, each with a different third variable.

Contingency tables and elaboration analyses may be used on variables at any measurement level (by collapsing categories in the case of interval- or ratio-level data, for example), but they are most appropriate when all the variables are measured at the nominal level. They are also often used when one of the variables is measured at the nominal and one at the ordinal level. However, more powerful statistical tools are available when variables are measured at the ordinal, interval, or ratio level. We will discuss some of these measures in the remaining chapters of this book.

Table 8.20 Trial Outcome by Sex of Offender and Type of Defense Attorney (in percents)

Trial Outcome	Sex of Offender			
	Male		Female	
	Public Defender ($n = 24$)	Private Attorney ($n = 26$)	Public Defender ($n = 26$)	Private Attorney ($n = 24$)
Guilty	25	81	81	33
Innocent	75	19	19	67
Total	100%	100%	100%	100%

Chi-Square Analysis

So far, we have been "eyeballing" distributions and cross-tabulations to judge if the evidence is strong enough to reject the null hypothesis and assert that our research hypothesis is supported. If we have selected a random sample from a population and wish to infer something about the population from our sample data, however, we can use the inferential statistic chi square to test null hypotheses. That is, the chi-square statistic has sampling distributions that can be used to assess the probability of a particular calculated value of chi square if there is no relationship between two variables. Chi square is sometimes referred to as chi squared, symbolized by χ^2 and pronounced "ky" as in "sky." The inferential statistical test using the chi-square statistic and its sampling distributions was developed by Karl Pearson (Plackett, 1983).

Chi square is among the most frequently used inferential statistics in the social sciences, including criminal justice. Its sampling distribution plays an important role in many other statistical tests as well. It is used with frequency counts or proportions from random samples to test the "goodness-of-fit" of an observed distribution of the values of a single nominal or ordinal variable with an expected distribution of the values of the same variable. We discuss the use of chi square as a goodness-of-fit test in a later section of this chapter. It is also used with random samples to test for a relationship in a population between two variables measured at the nominal or ordinal level in a contingency table. In this case, it should be used with raw frequencies only. Percents, means, rates, and so on, are not appropriate for bivariate or multivariate chi-square analysis. In the next few sections, we discuss the use of chi square as a test for a relationship between two variables in a contingency table.

Assumptions

Chi-square analyses are appropriate in research situations that meet the following criteria:

For all applications:
- Data from a random sample
- No expected cell frequency less than 5

    Note that use with very small or very large samples can produce misleading results.

For testing univariate hypotheses (i.e., testing for "goodness-of-fit" of a single variable value distribution):
- Raw frequencies or proportions

For testing bivariate hypotheses (i.e., testing for a relationship between two variables):
- Raw frequencies only
- Independent and dependent variables measured at the nominal or ordinal level

Chi-square analysis can assess the likelihood of a bivariate relationship, but not how strong the relationship is.

You are already familiar with many of the concepts in these assumptions. Don't be concerned if you are unfamiliar with some of the other terms, such as expected cell frequencies. Their meanings will become clear as our discussion proceeds.

The Basic Ideas Underlying Chi-Square Analysis for Contingency Tables

Recall that, in inferential statistics, the null hypothesis as it pertains to bivariate hypotheses is that there is no relationship between the two variables in the population, and the research hypothesis is that there is a relationship between the two variables in the population. As with most inferential statistics, chi-square analysis tests the null hypothesis, in this case by comparing **observed frequencies**—those we assemble from our sample data—with corresponding **expected frequencies**—those we would expect to find if the null hypothesis, in this case was true and there was no relationship between the variables in the population. The χ^2 statistic and its applicable sampling distribution allow us to determine the probability that any differences between the frequencies we expect to find in a contingency table's cells under the null hypothesis and the cell frequencies we actually observe in our sample data are due to random sampling error alone. When the chi-square analysis, indicates that the differences between the observed and expected frequencies are so large that they are very unlikely to have occurred by chance alone (e.g., $p < .05$), we can reject the null hypothesis and argue that the evidence supports our research hypothesis that there is a relationship between the variables in the population. When used in this way, the chi-square test is often referred to as a **test of independence**. This label refers to the fact that the test helps us determine if two variables are independent of each other or not—that is, if they are unrelated or related to each other.

Note that chi-square analysis helps us decide if there is a relationship between two variables, but it does not tell us anything about the strength of the relationship. We discuss the concept of the strength of a relationship between variables in more detail in Chapters 11 and 12. For now, we will only say that strength of a relationship between two variables refers to how closely changes in one variable track with changes in another variable.

The procedure for calculating the expected cell frequencies will be discussed shortly. Once we determine the expected cell frequencies, we can calculate chi square using Formula 8.1.

$$\chi^2 = \Sigma \frac{(O-E)^2}{E} \tag{8.1}$$

In Formula 8.1, χ^2 is chi square, O is the observed frequency in a given cell of the observed contingency table, E is the expected frequency in the corresponding cell of the expected contingency table, and Σ tells us to sum the ratios calculated for the cells.

> ## PAUSE, THINK, AND EXPLORE χ^2
>
> χ^2 is a ratio. Note that the formula involves the sum of squared deviations, this time of an observed from an expected frequency. Does that remind you of any formula we have considered in a previous chapter? Which one? How about the one for variance? If, for all cells, O = E, what is the value of χ^2? What does that result mean in terms of the null hypothesis? What happens to the value of χ^2 if O stays the same and E goes up in any cell? If E stays the same and O goes up? Can the value of χ^2 be negative? Why or why not? Are there any ns in the formula? What would the sum of observed cell frequencies be? What would the sum of expected cell frequencies be?

Note that if we did not square the numerator in Formula 8.1, the results of the calculations for each cell would be the proportion of the expected frequency by which the observed frequency differed from the expected frequency and could be positive or negative. As we saw with the sum of unsquared differences between individual scores and their distribution's mean, the sum of these unsquared differences between expected and observed frequencies would always be zero. Squaring the numerator makes the result for each cell positive (because, as you will recall, a minus times a minus is a plus and a plus times a plus is a plus) and, hence, the sum of the results for all cells is positive.

Note, too, that regardless of the contingency table's size, if the observed cell frequencies and the expected cell frequencies are identical, the value of the numerator in Formula 8.1 would be zero and chi square would have a value of zero. The greater the differences between the observed and expected frequencies in the cells of the table, the larger the value of chi square. Using the chi-square table in Appendix E on the study site (**www.sagepub.com/fitzgerald**), we can determine the likelihood of finding a chi square of the size we have if the null hypothesis is, in fact, true. Put in another way, we can determine the likelihood of getting a chi square of the size we have if the differences between observed and expected cell frequencies were due to random variation (sampling error) alone.

There is a family of sampling distributions for chi square because the sampling distributions are different depending on the number of cells in the contingency table. Fortunately, the characteristics of the family of chi-square sampling distributions can be derived using probability theory and are known. For small tables (say, for those with less than a total of 12 cells), the sampling distributions are highly skewed to the right. For cross-tabulations with more cells, the sampling distributions are less skewed. The number of cells in the table is used to calculate the degrees of freedom for that table, and the shape of the chi-square sampling distribution varies according to the number of degrees of freedom. Figure 8.8 illustrates the general shapes of the chi-square sampling distributions for different degrees of freedom. Note that as *df* reaches 10 and beyond, the chi-square sampling distributions more closely resembles the normal curve.

Figure 8.8 Approximate χ^2 Distributions for df = 1, 3, 5, and 10

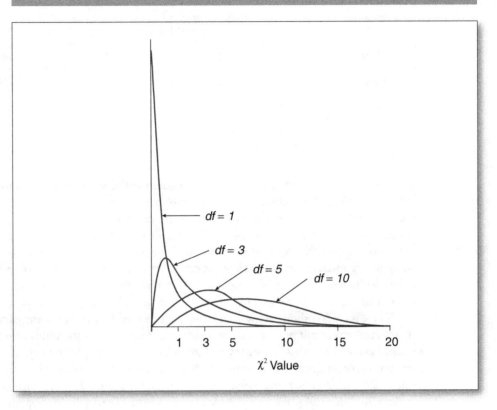

We can say the normal curve approximates the chi-square sampling distribution at this number of degrees of freedom. We discuss degrees of freedom in just a bit.

As with the sampling distributions we discussed in Chapters 6 and 7, the chi-square sampling distributions may be regarded as probability distributions, with the total area under each curve equal to 1.00 and proportions of area under the curve corresponding to specified values of the chi-square statistic. The details of creating these sampling distributions are beyond the scope of this text, but we suggest one way of thinking about them in probability terms later in the chapter.

A fictitious illustration will help us better understand chi-square analysis. Suppose we are interested in the effects of the sex of juvenile delinquents on court dispositions. Our null hypothesis states that there is no relationship between the sex of delinquents and court dispositions. We collect the random sample data shown in Table 8.21.

Calculating Expected Cell Frequencies

Assuming, under the null hypothesis, that sex (the independent variable) and disposition (the dependent variable) were unrelated, we would expect that the proportional

Table 8.21 Court Disposition by Sex of Juvenile (Observed Cell Frequencies)

Court Disposition	Sex of Juvenile		Total
	Male	Female	
Jail Time	84	30	114
Released to Parents	16	20	36
Total	100	50	$N = 150$

distribution of the study group on the dependent variable would be the same in each category of the independent variable. Because males comprise two-thirds of our sample (100/150 = 2/3), two thirds of the jailed delinquents and two-thirds of those released to parents should be males. Two thirds of 114 (the number of delinquents jailed) is 76. Two-thirds of 36 is 24. Because we have a 2 × 2 table and we know the marginal frequencies do not change, we can subtract these figures from their respective column totals in our table of sample data to arrive at the expected frequencies (E) for each of the cells in the table. The results are shown in Table 8.22.

There is an easy shortcut for calculating the expected frequency for any particular cell in any size table. Multiply the cell's row marginal frequency by its column marginal frequency and divide by n. Give it a try in Table 8.22. In this example, our expected frequencies are whole numbers. Often, however, they will not be, and neither will be the results of our other calculations. It is generally recommended that such results be rounded to the nearest third decimal place, as are the values in the chi-square table in Appendix E.

Caution is in order here. Chi-square analysis is not recommended if any of the expected cell frequencies is less than 5. Should your calculations yield any expected frequency less than 5, perhaps you can collapse one or more of the categories (variable values) into a new variable category in order to raise the associated cell frequencies above this minimum limit. See the discussion earlier in this chapter and in Chapter 4, pp. 103–105, for a review of collapsing variable values (categories).

Table 8.22 Court Disposition by Sex of Juvenile (Expected Cell Frequencies)

Court Disposition	Sex of Juvenile		Total
	Male	Female	
Jail Time	76	38	114
Released to Parents	24	12	36
Total	100	50	$N = 150$

Here's another way of thinking about and calculating expected frequencies, assuming the null hypothesis is true, this time in terms of probabilities and the sampling distributions for chi square. Suppose we begin by converting the raw marginal frequencies in Table 8.21 into relative frequencies—that is, into percents. The result would be as indicated in Table 8.23.

The marginal relative frequencies of the values for each variable can be seen as a probability distribution for the values of that variable. For example, the probability of being a male in this sample is .667, and the probability of being released to parents is .240. Note that these probability distributions are arrived at independent of each other. That is, the probability distribution for one of the variables is determined without taking the other variable's probability distribution into account.

Next, we can ask what the probability is of each possible *combination* of the two variables' values. There are four possible combinations represented by the four cells of the table. Answering this question requires applying the multiplication rule for calculating probabilities. As you will recall from Chapter 6 (see p. 174), the probability of a combination of independent events is the product of each of the independent events. So the probability of "male" and "jail time" under the null hypothesis is $.667 \times .760 = .507$. The probability of "female" and "release to parents" is $.333 \times .240 = .080$. You can calculate the remaining two probabilities. The results will be as indicated in Table 8.24.

Table 8.23 Marginal Frequencies of Table 8.21 Converted to Relative Frequencies and Considered as Probability Distributions

Court Disposition	Sex of Juvenile		Total
	Male	Female	
Jail Time			.760
Released to Parents			.240
Total	.667	.333	1.000 $N = 150$

Table 8.24 Probabilities Calculated from the Marginal Probabilities in Table 8.22

Court Disposition	Sex of Juvenile		Total
	Male	Female	
Jail Time	.507	.253	.760
Released to Parents	.160	.080	.240
Total	.667	.333	1.000 $N = 150$

To determine the expected frequencies associated with these probabilities, we just multiply each cell probability by the total frequency, which, in our case, is $N = 150$. We'll leave it to you to verify that when you do so, you end up with the expected cell frequencies in Table 8.22.

Calculating Chi Square

We can now compute chi square for our table using Formula 8.1. Doing the calculation, we find that

$$\chi^2 = \frac{(8)^2}{76} + \frac{(8)^2}{24} + \frac{(8)^2}{38} + \frac{(8)^2}{12} = 10.526.$$

Determining the Degrees of Freedom

One way of thinking about **degrees of freedom** is as a measure of a variable's "freedom to vary." As we will see in subsequent chapters, degrees of freedom play a crucial role in the application of many different kinds of inferential statistics. Here, we will illustrate its role in chi-square analysis.

Suppose, for example, we have a 3×3 contingency table, which has nine cells. Suppose further that we assume that the row and column marginal frequencies (which, as you will recall, are the frequency distributions of each of the two variables included in the table) cannot change. Nevertheless, within the limits imposed by their respective row and column marginal frequencies, the cell frequencies may vary.

Consider Table 8.25, where we have a 3×3 table with specified row and marginal frequencies. As we noted earlier in this chapter, if you think about it a bit and try a few different combinations, you will find that the cells of the table can be filled in with many different combinations of cell frequencies, while leaving the marginal frequencies unchanged.

Table 8.25 A 3×3 Table With Marginal Frequencies Determined

				Row Marginal Frequencies
				36
				14
				10
Column Marginal Frequencies	24	20	16	60

Now, beginning with Table 8.25 again, put any frequency you choose in any one cell, so long as it is no higher than the lowest marginal frequency associated with that cell. You will find you can still fill the remaining cells in several different ways. Fill in two cells. You can still fill in the remaining cells in several different ways. Fill in three cells. The remaining cells can be filled in different ways, though you will note that your options are narrowing quite a bit. Once you fill in four cells, however, the frequencies for the remaining cells are determined; the freedom of the frequencies in the cells to change is gone. Degrees of freedom reflect how many cell frequencies can vary before the remaining cell frequencies are determined. For a 3 × 3 table, then, the degrees of freedom would be four. The more cells there are in a table, the greater are the degrees of freedom associated with it. As we saw in Figure 8.8, the sampling distribution of chi square is different for different degrees of freedom, though as the degrees of freedom reach 10 or more, the normal curve is a reasonable approximation of the chi-square sampling distribution.

Let's return now to our example of the 2 × 2 contingency table in Table 8.21. Having obtained a χ^2 of 10.526, we must now calculate the degrees of freedom (df) associated with this particular contingency table because the sampling distribution of chi square is different for each different table size. For any particular table, we can calculate the degrees of freedom according to Formula 8.2:

$$df = (r-1)(c-1) \qquad (8.2)$$

In Formula 8.2, r is the number of rows and c is the number of columns. In our example (Table 8.21), the table has two rows and two columns, so degrees of freedom equal one. Using one degree of freedom, then, we can look in a chi-square table to determine the probability that a χ^2 of 10.526 or greater would be observed if the null hypothesis is true.

Using the Chi-Square Table

The chi-square table in Appendix E presents the critical values for chi square for a variety of combinations of degrees of freedom and levels of significance (probabilities). The **critical value** for a chi square hypothesis test is the minimum value of chi square that must be attained in order to reach the specified level of significance (probability) for the specified degree of freedom. The **significance level** for a hypothesis test is the probability of rejecting a true null hypothesis. Thus, for example, if we select a .05 level of significance, we are saying that we are willing to reject a true null hypothesis 5 out of 100 times. For a given degree of freedom and a given level of significance (probability), the chi-square value you calculate from your data must be at least as large as the chi-square value in the table in order for you to reject the null hypothesis and argue instead that the evidence supports your research hypothesis.

To use the chi-square table in Appendix E, we need two pieces of information: the degrees of freedom and the calculated numerical value of chi square. Locate the degrees of freedom in the far left column of the table. Using the df to mark the row, read across the row until you come to a value approximately equal to your calculated chi square. Using that value to mark the column, read up the column to the top of the table. The probability at the top of the table is the likelihood that the chi square you observed is due only to random variation. In our example, our χ^2 of 10.526 falls between $p = .01$ (critical value of $\chi^2 = 6.635$) and $p = .001$ (critical value of $\chi^2 = 10.827$) of arising purely by chance if the null hypothesis is true.

Note that the probabilities associated with the chi square values in Appendix E are cumulative. That is, for a particular *df* and a specified chi-square value, the corresponding probability at the top of the table is the probability of getting a chi-square value as large *or larger* than the specified chi-square value.

Statistical Significance and Rejection Regions

We must now decide whether to accept or reject the null hypothesis. Given our data, if the probability of the null hypothesis being true is less than .01, is that "good enough" to reject the null hypothesis and say the evidence supports our research hypothesis? Your decision depends on how conservative you want to be—that is, how much risk you want to take of rejecting a true null hypothesis. You might ask, What is the maximum probability of committing a Type I error that I am willing to accept?

Generally accepted standards regarding rejecting null hypotheses in many fields of research, including criminal justice, help us decide. Although the standards may vary depending on the implications of the results if they were to be applied in a real-life situation, the maximum probability of rejecting a true null hypothesis is usually set at .05. Thus, in general, we need to know the critical value of our test statistic at $p \leq .05$ and the chi square we calculate must be at least as large as that critical value. If we had set our significance level as .05, we can reject the null hypothesis. The cross-tabulation of sample data and the chi-square analysis of it provide evidence that there is, indeed, some relationship, possibly causal, between sex of delinquent and court disposition in the population. If we wanted to be more conservative, we would set our standard at .01 or .001. A less conservative standard would be .10 or .15.

Whatever the standard chosen ($p = .05$, $p = .01$, etc.), it is, as we noted earlier, referred to as the significance level, α (the Greek letter alpha), or the alpha level. Researchers often refer to their results as being **statistically significant** when their results have a probability less than or equal to whatever they have established as the significance level under the null hypothesis. In our example, we would report that our results were significant at $p \leq .05$.

Recall our discussion of areas under a sampling distribution curve in Chapter 5, pp. 148–153 and Chapter 7, pp. 197–202. (It may be helpful for you to reread the relevant portions of those chapters before proceeding with this discussion.) We noted that a sampling distribution can be considered a probability distribution. The chi-square sampling distributions are no exception (see Figure 8.8), even though it is not a good approximation of the normal curve until $df = 10$ or larger.

Suppose that we select a critical value for chi square corresponding to $p \leq .05$. In doing so, we have chosen a chi-square value on the horizontal axis of the sampling distribution such that 95% of the area under the curve lies below that value and 5% of the area lies at that critical value or above.

To illustrate this general point, suppose that we have a 4 × 5 contingency table ($df = 12$) and set our significance level at .05. Looking in the chi-square table, we find the critical value for this significance level to be 21.026. Therefore, the chi-square value we calculate for our data must be 21.026 or higher to meet the .05 significance level criterion. Figure 8.9 represents an approximation of the chi-square sampling distribution for $df = 12$.

The area under the chi-square sampling distribution curve equal to and beyond whatever critical value of χ^2 we have chosen (in our example, equal to or beyond $\chi^2 = 21.026$) is called the **rejection region** or the **critical region**. These areas under the curve are called rejection or critical regions because if our calculated chi-square value falls anywhere in this area, we reject the null hypothesis and argue instead that the evidence supports our research hypothesis. Setting .05 as our significance level means that, given our calculated chi-square value, there is .05 probability or less (i.e., a probability of 5 times in 100 or less) that we will reject a true null hypothesis (i.e., commit

Figure 8.9 An Approximation of the χ^2 Sampling Distribution for $df = 12$ Showing the Critical Value and Rejection Region for the $p \leq .05$ Significance Level

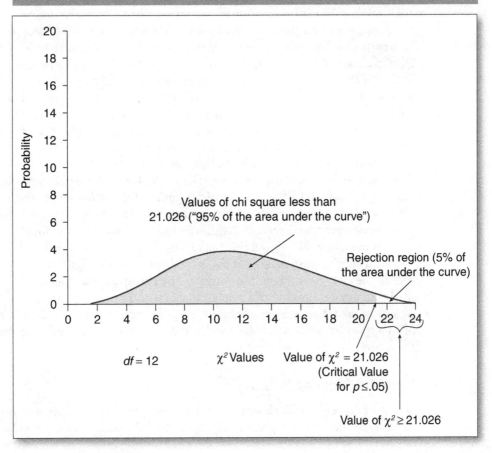

a Type I error—see pp. 230–231 of this chapter and Chapter 2, pp. 29–30) and a .95 or more probability that we will correctly reject a false null hypothesis. We say .05 or less and .95 or more because the chi-square table in Appendix E is a cumulative distribution (see Chapter 3, pp. 67–73, for a discussion of cumulative distributions). We will discuss rejection or critical regions in greater detail in the next chapter.

Chi Square as a Univariate Goodness-of-Fit Test

As we have just discussed, the chi-square statistic may be used as a test of association between two variables. When applied in this way, it is sometimes referred to as a **two-way statistic** because the relationship between two variables is being assessed. Chi square can also be used as a **one-way statistic**. In this application, it may be used to assess whether an observed frequency distribution for a single nominal or ordinal variable is different in a statistically significant way from any distribution we specify as our expected frequency distribution. When used in this way, chi-square analysis is called a **goodness-of-fit** test. In general, the researcher proposes a "theoretical model" consisting of a predicted (expected) frequency for each of the variable's categories. The observed frequencies are then compared with the model's expected frequencies using the chi-square statistic and its sampling distribution. As in the two-way test, it is assumed that the data come from a random sample.

Suppose we have random sample data on the ethnicity of drivers stopped by police in a particular city and that we have five categories of ethnicity: African American, Hispanic, Asian American, Euro-American, and Other. We might wish to examine how likely it is that any observed differences in frequencies of stops among the categories are due to random sampling variation. If we know the proportions with which these ethnic groups are found in the population, we can calculate the expected frequencies for each group by multiplying its proportion by the total sample size. Thus, for example, if the most recent census of the city's population showed that Hispanic Americans made up 20% of the population and there were a total of 540 stops in our sample, the expected frequency for Hispanics would be $540 \times .20 = 108$. Degrees of freedom in this case would be given by the number of categories of the ethnicity variable minus one. In our example, because we have five categories of ethnicity, $df = 5 - 1 = 4$. We can now plug our observed and expected frequencies into Formula 8.1, solve for chi square, and look up the probability in the chi-square table in the row for $df = 4$. If the chi square we calculate is at least as large as the critical value for the significance level we have chosen, we can reject the null hypothesis. The chi-square goodness-of-fit test can be used with any distribution of a single variable we care to specify, including one where we expect the frequencies in all categories of the variable to be equal. The goodness-of-fit test would, nevertheless, tell us what the likelihood is that the differences between the expected and observed frequencies arose by chance.

How to Present Results

To report the results of a chi-square analysis, the following three types of information must be included: the degrees of freedom, the calculated chi-square value, and the probability of finding a chi-square value with the specified degrees of freedom at least as large as the one reported. Just below a contingency table that is the subject of chi-square analysis, this information might be reported as follows:

$$\chi^2 = 17.48$$
$$df = 9$$
$$p \leq .05$$

The results of a one-way chi-square (goodness-of-fit) test would contain the same information and be reported in the same way as two-way results. The From the Literature Box 8.1 includes excerpts from a research report using chi-square analysis.

From the Literature Box 8.1

Larry K. Gaines analyzed data from all of the traffic stops reported in 2003 by the Riverside, California Police Department to determine if there was evidence of racial profiling in the stops. As a part of his analysis, he constructed a contingency table cross-tabulating ethnicity of driver and type of disposition (warning, ticket, etc.). Reprinted below is an excerpt from his research report, including the contingency table and his discussion of the chi-square analysis of the data in the table.

The disposition of traffic stops by the traffic officers was another consideration. When officers stop a motorist, there are several possible dispositions as a result of the stop, including arrest, citation, field interrogation, release, crime report, and supplemental report to a previously opened case. Table 4 provides a breakdown of the disposition of the traffic stops by race and ethnicity.

There are a number of blank cells in Table 4. This indicates that there were no citizens who received those dispositions. With only a few exceptions, the traffic officers cite or release those citizens they stop. A review of the cite percentages contained in the table shows that the citation rate for African Americans was 84.7%, 88.5% for Hispanics, and 88.9% for Whites. There is little difference in the rate of citations across race and ethnicity by the traffic officers. The arrest rate for African Americans was 1.6%, 4.4% for Hispanics, and

(Continued)

(Continued)

Table 4 Traffic Stops by Traffic Officers by Ethnicity and Disposition

Disposition	African American		Hispanic		White	
	Count	%	Count	%	Count	%
Arrest	19	1.6	200	4.4	62	1.2
Cite	981	84.7	4,022	88.5	4,764	88.9
Field interrogation	3	0.3	1	0.0	9	0.2
Release	155	13.4	324	7.1	522	9.7
Report Supplemental report					1	0.0

1.2% for Whites, indicating little disparity. A chi-square analysis of the dispositions for traffic stops made by traffic unit officers found no significant differences ($\chi^2 = 4.74$, $p = .5776$).

Source: From Gaines, L. K. (2006). An analysis of traffic stop data in Riverside, California. Police Quarterly, 9, 210–233. Retrieved June 5, 2012, from http://pqx.sagepub.com/content/9/210. Reprinted with permission.

Assumptions and Cautions

When comparing frequency distributions, regardless of measurement level, the variable values must be arranged in the same order in all the distributions being compared. If both variables are measured at the ordinal level, variable values should be arranged in ascending or descending order.

Converting raw cell frequencies to percents is advisable only when the marginal frequencies are relatively large. When marginal frequencies are small, converting them to percents artificially magnifies any numerical differences. It should also be remembered, though, that when marginal frequencies are very large, percent differences may be quite small.

Although converting cell frequencies to percents often helps us understand the results in a contingency table, bivariate chi-square analysis should be performed only on random sample data presented as raw cell frequencies (that is, not with percents, means, rates, etc.) and only if all of the *expected* cell frequencies are 5 or larger. If any expected frequency is less than 5, perhaps categories can be collapsed to raise expected cell frequencies above 5 before proceeding with the analysis. Furthermore, each placement of an observation in the table's cells must be independent of the placement of any other observation in the cells. That is, the placement of a person in a category of one of the variables must not depend on the placement of another person in the same or any other category. The categories (values) for each of the variables must also be mutually exclusive and exhaustive.

Although chi square helps us determine whether or not a relationship exists between variables, it does not indicate how strong the relationship is. When applied to contingency tables involving ordinal variables, it does not take the order of the variable values into account, thereby losing available information in the analysis. Inferential statistics that do take the order of ordinal variables into account are more powerful statistically and permit us not only to determine if there is a relationship, but to assess its strength. Some of these are discussed in Chapters 11, 12, and 13.

Chi square may be used with almost any size table, including 2×3, 3×4, 4×6, and so on. It assumes data collected from a random sample, but it is "distribution free"—that is, it may be used even if any ordinal variables included in the cross-tabulations are not normally distributed in the population.

The numerical size of chi square, and hence its probability of occurring by chance, is strongly related to sample size. Data from large samples yield larger observed and expected cell frequencies. With them comes greater potential for numerically large differences between those observed and expected frequencies and, therefore, for numerically large chi-square values. The chi-square test, then, is less useful for very large samples because they are more likely to yield statistically significant chi-square results even though, if we converted the raw frequencies to percents, there may be very little or no discernible association between the variables. Results from very small sample data, on the other hand, especially if any of the expected cell frequencies are less than 5, are also of dubious value.

Some words of caution about decisions concerning null hypotheses, as well as interpreting levels of significance and confidence intervals, are also in order. First, inferential statistical tests provide a probability standard (usually .05) for rejecting or failing to reject a null hypothesis. Even if we reject the null hypothesis at the .05 significance level, there remains the 5% chance that the rejected null hypothesis is true and we have committed a Type I error. The statistical tests we will be considering do not help us assess the probability of a Type II error. It is also worth noting that failing to reject a null hypothesis is not quite the same as accepting it. Saying you failed to reject the null hypothesis is a more tentative assertion, and in some ways technically more correct, than saying you accepted the null hypothesis. We are, after all, dealing with probabilities and not certainties. Nevertheless, the practical effect of the two assertions is essentially the same. The interpretation of statistically insignificant results typically proceeds as if the null hypothesis were accepted and there is no evidence of a relationship between the variables. As a general rule in this text, we refer to accepting or rejecting the null hypothesis. Also, significance levels and confidence intervals tell us the probability of obtaining a particular result by chance over the long run if the null hypothesis is true. They do *not* tell us whether any *particular* inferential statistic we have calculated is the result of chance or nonchance factors.

Furthermore, it should be remembered that inferential statistical analyses, whether univariate or bivariate, can't compensate for errors arising from sources in the research process other than random sampling. Errors due to defective research designs; faulty sampling procedures; poorly operationalized variables; and sloppy field note taking, data recording, or data entry, for example, are "garbage in" and cannot be compensated for through the application of inferential statistics.

Finally, assessing the statistical significance of some result should not be confused with determining what we might call its practical significance. **Statistical significance** is a term that refers only to applying probability theory to testing null hypotheses. **Practical significance**, on the other hand, refers to the practical implications or ethical importance of applying some research result in real human life. Statistically significant results, even at very low significance levels, may say little, if anything, about the practical significance of the variables being investigated or the potential impact of the results on people's lives if the research results were to be acted upon.

Summary

In this chapter, we began our discussion of inferential statistics as they apply to hypothesis testing. Research hypotheses and null hypotheses were differentiated. We emphasized that all scientific hypotheses must be falsifiable by empirical evidence. We noted the scientific practice of designing research and structuring data analysis assuming the null hypothesis is true. That assumption prevails unless the evidence strongly indicates it should be rejected. Type I and Type II errors regarding decisions concerning the null hypothesis were discussed and the relationship between them explored. Inferential statistics help us assess the likelihood of a Type I error, which is rejecting a true null hypothesis. It was also noted that testing a null hypothesis provides only an indirect test of the research hypothesis. Frequency distribution comparisons and contingency tables were discussed as hypothesis-testing strategies. Introducing a third variable to help eliminate other possible causal variables, a procedure called elaboration analysis, was described. Elaboration analysis results, which consist of replication, explanation, interpretation, and specification, were defined and discussed.

Finally, a new sample statistic, chi square, was introduced. This distribution-free statistic has known sampling distributions and can, therefore, be used in a two-way analysis to help determine whether the null hypothesis should be rejected in favor of the research hypothesis. The chi-square sampling distribution permits the researcher to assess the likelihood that differences between expected and observed cell differences in contingency tables are due solely to sampling error when the data are from a random sample. As a one-way statistic, chi square permits the analysis of differences between observed and expected frequencies in the distribution of a single nominal or ordinal variable. Limitations of chi-square analysis, whether one- or two-way, were described. The chapter concluded with a reminder that research results may achieve a very high level of statistical significance (that is, have a very low probability of having occurred by chance), but may have little or no practical significance in the real world.

Concepts to Master

- α (alpha)
- Alternative hypothesis
- β (beta)
- Cell
- Cell frequencies
- Chi square(d) (χ^2)
- Column marginal frequency
- Columns (in tables)
- Contingency table
- Control variable
- Critical region
- Critical value
- Cross-tabulation
- Curvilinear relationship
- Degrees of freedom
- Diagonals
- Elaboration analysis
- Empirically falsifiable (hypotheses)
- Expected frequencies
- Explanation (in elaboration analysis)
- First-order partial relationships (tables)
- Goodness of fit
- Hypothesis testing
- Interpretation (in elaboration analysis)
- Intervening variable
- Linear relationship
- Negative linear relationship
- Null hypothesis
- Observed frequency
- One-way statistic
- Partial analysis
- Percentaging in the direction of the independent variable
- Positive linear relationship
- Power (of a statistical test)
- Practical significance
- Rejection region
- Replication
- Research hypothesis
- Row marginal frequencies
- Rows (in tables)
- Significance level
- Specification (in elaboration analysis)
- Spurious relationship
- Statistical significance
- Test factor (variable)
- Test of independence
- Two-way statistic
- Type I error
- Type II error
- Variable interactions
- Zero-order relationships (tables)

Review Questions

1. What is a hypothesis? What is hypothesis testing? What is the role of inferential statistics in hypothesis testing?
2. What is the difference between a research hypothesis and the corresponding null hypothesis?

3. What is the difference between Type I and Type II error? What are α, $1 - \alpha$, β, and $1 - \beta$?
4. What is the power of a statistic? In general, what factors increase the power of statistical tests?
5. Which variable, the independent or dependent, would be used to determine how many frequency distributions would be constructed for purposes of comparison? Why?
6. How does comparing frequency distributions help determine if there is a relationship between two variables?
7. What is cross-tabulation?
8. What is a contingency table?
9. What are cells in a contingency table?
10. What is a cell frequency?
11. What are row and column marginal frequencies in a contingency table?
12. What is the relationship between marginal frequencies in a contingency table and frequency distributions of single variables?
13. How can the accuracy of a cross-tabulation be checked?
14. What is collapsing categories for cross-tabulation? Under what circumstances is collapsing categories advisable? What are the advantages and disadvantages of collapsing categories?
15. When converting cell frequencies to percentages, which marginal frequencies should be used? Why?
16. What is elaboration analysis?
17. What is the difference between zero-order tables and first-order partial tables?
18. What is a test factor or control variable? What role do control variables play in elaboration analysis?
19. On what basis might we conclude that an elaboration analysis has produced an explanation? An interpretation? A specification? A replication?
20. What is the difference between an explanation and an interpretation in elaboration analysis?
21. What is a spurious relationship?
22. What is an intervening variable?
23. What is χ^2, and how is it used?
24. What is an expected frequency?
25. What is statistical significance?
26. What is a significance level?
27. What is a critical value?

28. What is a rejection region?
29. What is a critical region?
30. Distinguish between one-way and two-way analyses.
31. What is goodness-of-fit?
32. What are some cautions to be observed in hypothesis testing with nominal or ordinal variables?
33. What are some cautions to be observed in using chi square?
34. Distinguish between statistical and practical significance.
35. If you haven't already done so, define all the terms in the "Concepts to Master" list and use each in three different sentences.

Exercises and Discussion Questions

1. Convert the percents in Figure 8.2 to raw frequencies.
2. Create a contingency table of the raw frequencies for the data in Figure 8.2.
3. Formulate a research hypothesis and a null hypothesis for the random sample data in the following contingency table.

   Number of Days in Jail for First Offense Theft Over $150 by Sex of Offender

Sex of Offender	Number of Days in Jail		Total
	4 Days or Less	5 Days or More	
Male	32	148	180
Female	15	5	20
Total	47	153	$N = 200$

4. What are the expected frequencies for this table? What is the df for this table? Calculate χ^2 for the data in the table.
5. What is the probability of the χ^2 you calculated? What does this result mean? Would you accept or reject the null hypothesis?

   Use the following hypothetical random sample data for the exercises below. Convert the data in zero-order and partial tables to percents where appropriate.

Subject	Ethnic Group	Convicted of a Crime?	Social Class	IQ Score
1	Non-White	No	Middle	101
2	White	No	Lower	98
3	Non-White	Yes	Lower	112
4	White	Yes	Lower	100
5	White	Yes	Middle	115
6	Non-White	No	Lower	130
7	White	Yes	Middle	99
8	Non-White	No	Middle	100
9	Non-White	No	Middle	126
10	Non-White	Yes	Lower	118
11	White	No	Middle	107
12	White	No	Middle	113
13	Non-White	Yes	Middle	121
14	Non-White	No	Lower	99
15	Non-White	No	Middle	92
16	Non-White	No	Middle	119
17	White	Yes	Lower	101
18	Non-White	No	Middle	140
19	White	No	Lower	132
20	Non-White	No	Middle	123

6. Formulate a research hypothesis and a null hypothesis involving the ethnicity and crime variables. Construct a zero-order table relating ethnic group to conviction of a crime. Is there a relationship?

7. Construct first-order partial tables for the two variables in Exercise 6, using social class as the third variable or test factor. Is there a relationship between social class and ethnic group? Between social class and conviction record? How would you interpret the results of this elaboration analysis?

8. Collapse the IQ scores into three ordinal categories and construct a table for examining whether there is any relationship between social class and IQ. Discuss why you collapsed categories as you did. Is there a relationship?

9. Use Ethnic Group as a control variable (test factor) for an elaboration analysis of the zero-order social class/IQ table. Discuss the results of your analysis.

10. Assume that the data are from a random sample and calculate a chi square for the zero-order table in Exercise 6.

11. Discuss the differences in interpretation of the data if we assume the hypothetical data are from a population and if we assume they are from a random sample.

12. Perform a one-way chi-square analysis on the following hypothetical observed random sample data pertaining to a particular type of CIA operative. Test the model that there are no differences in the frequencies among the geographic assignments.

CIA Geographic Assignments	Number of Agents
Western Europe	26
Eastern Europe	48
Southeast Asia	69
Africa	21
Other	35

13. What data from the contingency table in From the Literature Box 8.1 were used in the chi-square analysis? Did the author percentage the table correctly? Why or why not? Compare the frequency and percent distributions. Do the percent distributions help make sense of the data? How would you describe and discuss the data in the table?

14. Go to http://faculty.vassar.edu/lowry/newcs.html and experiment with contingency tables and chi-square analysis.

15. Go to http://faculty.vassar.edu/lowry/csqsamp.html and explore the shapes of the chi-square sampling distributions for different degrees of freedom.

Student Study Site

Visit the open-access student study site at **www.sagepub.com/fitzgerald** for access to several study tools including eFlashcards, web quizzes, and additional appendices as well as links to SAGE journal articles and audio, video and web resources.

Bivariate Hypothesis Testing for the Difference Between Two Means

Learning Objectives

What you are expected not only to learn but to master in this chapter:

- To distinguish between independence and dependence within a random sample and between random samples
- The basic ideas underlying the t test for the difference between two independent random sample means
- The difference between heteroscedasticity and homoscedasticity
- The mean and shape of the sampling distributions for the difference between two independent random sample means

- How to calculate *t* for two independent random samples
- The mean and shape of the sampling distributions for *t*
- The difference between one- and two-tailed hypotheses and one- and two-tailed hypothesis tests
- The difference between the sampling distributions for the difference between means and the sampling distributions for *t*
- The mean and shape of the sampling distribution for the difference between two dependent sample means
- How to calculate *t* for two dependent random samples
- How to present results for *t* tests
- The relationship between *t* and *z*
- How to construct confidence limits and intervals for the difference between means

Introduction

Are male and female correctional officers with the same rank and number of years of service paid the same? Do male and female offenders with the same prior record and convicted of the same offense get the same length of sentence? Are the property offense rates the same in a neighborhood where a new community policing initiative has been implemented as they are in a neighborhood where the new initiative has not been implemented? Do parolees who participate in a new program stay out of trouble longer than parolees who don't participate? Do juries in southern states assign higher monetary civil penalties than those in northern states for similar civil liabilities? Do male or female traffic officers give more warnings? Is there a relationship between sex of judge and length of sentence for felony domestic assault? The inferential statistical analyses we discuss in this chapter can often help answer questions like these.

In the previous chapter, we considered univariate, bivariate, and multivariate inferential statistics and hypothesis testing when all of the variables being studied were measured at the nominal or ordinal level. We discussed the chi-square statistic in some detail, noting it was a nonparametric statistic. In this chapter, we turn our attention to some parametric statistical tools for use when the independent variables are nominal or ordinal but the dependent variables are measured at the interval or ratio level.

So far in our discussion of inferential statistics, too, we have been concerned with analysis of data drawn from a single random sample. In this chapter, we consider statistical inferences involving the comparison of data from two random samples. In particular, we describe procedures for testing bivariate hypotheses when the nominal or ordinal independent variable is dichotomous—that is, it has only two values. The tests compare the difference between two observed random sample means (one each from two random samples corresponding to the two values of the independent variable) with a sampling distribution for the difference between two random sample means.

The test statistic, which we calculate using random sample data and probability theory, is called Student's t statistic, which we will shorten to the **t statistic,** and the inferential statistical tool used in these research situations is called the Student's t test (which we shorten to **t test**). The sampling distributions for testing t are called Student's t distributions (which we shorten to **t sampling distributions**). We say distributions because the shape of the sampling distribution for t varies with sample sizes, at least for sample sizes less than or equal to 50.

The t statistic and associated t sampling distributions were developed primarily by W. S. Gosset, one of Karl Pearson's students. He published his work under the pen name "Student." As a result, the statistic came to be known as Student's t. He developed the t statistic and t test as he studied variables related to the length of beer's shelf life (his dependent variable). The necessity of taste tests (his way of measuring the shelf life dependent variable) probably limited him to relatively small samples of bottles, do you think?

The formula for calculating the test statistic t varies depending, among other things, on the type of random sample from which the data come. So, before beginning our discussion of t and its use in hypothesis testing, we will distinguish between independent and dependent random samples. Be alert for possible confusion between the use of the terms *independent* and *dependent* referring to different sample types and the use of the same terms referring to different variable types. In the discussion that follows, we will be referring frequently to these different sample and variable types. It's important to keep straight what the terms are referencing as you encounter them in the text.

When discussing statistical significance tests for t, we introduce an additional hypothesis testing option available in some research situations. In particular, t tests and many other inferential statistics provide analysts with a choice between one- and two-tailed hypothesis tests. We explore the similarities and differences between these two tests and how they are applied.

We also discuss and illustrate another analytic strategy based on inferential statistics that helps us make sense of our results. In addition to statistical significance, we will consider confidence intervals and confidence limits for sample statistics used to estimate population parameters. As we discussed in Chapter 7, establishing a confidence interval and confidence limits entails constructing a range around a parameter estimate, which helps us understand how precise our parameter estimate is.

For each of the statistics to be discussed in this chapter, we consider the general ideas underlying the test statistic, the procedures for calculating the test statistic, the characteristics of its sampling distributions, and the performance of tests for statistical significance. The chapter concludes with a summary of the assumptions underlying each of these tests and some cautions in their uses and interpretations. First, though, we need to discuss some important matters related to the selection of an appropriate formula for t.

Independent and Dependent Random Samples

To select the appropriate version of the *t* test for a difference between two means, it is necessary to know whether the data come from independent or dependent random samples. To make this distinction as clear as possible, we review our earlier discussion of independence and dependence within random samples and then define independence and dependence between random samples.

Independence and Dependence Within a Random Sample

In Chapter 2, we defined a simple random sample as one in which each element or unit of analysis (e.g., person, object, or event) and each possible combination of elements in the population being sampled has the same probability of being drawn for the sample. Element selection is independent when drawing one element does not alter the probability of drawing any other element for the sample. These criteria define **independence (of element selection) within a random sample**. Randomly drawing a sample with replacement is an example. When the selection of one element for a sample does alter the probability of another element's selection for the same sample, as in sampling without replacement (see Chapter 2, p. 33), we have **dependence (of element selection) within a random sample**. All of the statistical procedures we will be discussing in this chapter assume the data have come from simple random samples characterized by the independence of element selection within the samples. As we noted in Chapter 7, however, many statisticians consider sampling without replacement acceptable when relatively small samples are selected from large populations.

Independence and Dependence Between Random Samples

In order to apply properly the statistical tools we discuss in this chapter, we must be concerned not just with independence within a sample, but also with independence and dependence between (or among) samples. **Independence between random samples** is established when randomly drawing an element for one sample does not alter the probability of drawing an element for another sample, whether the other sample is from the same or a different population. It can be achieved, for example, by selecting two simple random samples from one population or from two different populations using a random numbers table for each element selection. It can also be accomplished by randomly assigning elements of a larger group to different subgroups (samples), such as an experimental group and a control group in an experimental research design. In any event, when the criteria listed above are satisfied, the samples are called **independent random samples**.

Dependence between random samples occurs when the random selection of an element for one sample changes the probability of the selection of an element for *another* sample, whether the other sample is being selected from the same or different populations. Such samples are referred to as **dependent random samples**. Two general types of dependent random sampling are used frequently in research. They are often referred to as repeated measurement matching and pair matching.

In **repeated measurement matching**, the same group of subjects is measured at least twice, as would be found in research designs involving before-after comparisons of dependent variable measurements for an experimental group, for example. (It may be appropriate to review the discussion of research designs in Chapter 2, pp. 34–38, now.) In such cases, the same study group is treated as if it were two samples. One sample is the study group at the time of the first measurement and the other is the same study group at the time of the second measurement. Obviously, these two samples are not independent, because being included in one of the samples makes the chances of being included in the other 1.00.

In **pair matching**, two elements having the same characteristics—that is, having the same value on one or more variables—are paired. Typically, one of the matched pair is randomly assigned to one of two study groups, for example, to either the experimental or the control group in an experimental research design. The other member of the pair, of course, is assigned to the other study group. Obviously, these samples are not independent either, because the selection of one of the pair for a sample makes the probability that the other will be selected for the other sample 1.00. Examples of matched pairs might include monozygotic twins, husband and wife, and two siblings. Subjects might also be matched on age, sex, number or type of offenses, and so on.

As we noted, the formulas for calculating t and performing t tests differ for independent and dependent random samples. Several other theoretical and research circumstances also require adjustments in the formulas for t tests. Whether the samples are large or small and whether they are about equal size or not, as well as what is known or assumed about population variances, are among the most important. We will not attempt to discuss all of the different research situations and corresponding versions of the formula for t here. Information about many of these variations is available in more advanced texts. Rather, we consider just two that are perhaps most frequently encountered in research, one of the versions of the t test for independent random samples and one of the versions for dependent random samples.

A "heads-up" is in order before we continue. We will be introducing some new concepts that apply not just to t tests but to many other inferential statistical tests as well. The discussion is complex and, without a very careful reading, likely to be confusing. We've done our best to make it as clear as possible, but to master these materials will require your full attention. In our discussion, we will be referring to independent and dependent variables; independent and dependent random samples; sample statistics and population parameters; sum(s) of squares, standard deviations, standard errors, and variances; samples and sampling distributions; theoretical formulas and quantities; and calculated estimates of those quantities. You have already learned something about all of these concepts in this and previous chapters, but you will need to be clear about the definitions of these terms in order to make sense of our discussion in this and subsequent chapters. We will refer you to relevant earlier discussions from time to time, but you should satisfy yourself that you know these terms and how they are used in statistical analysis before you proceed. You will almost certainly need to read the text slowly—and even then, more than once—trying hard to keep straight what exactly is being referred to at each point along the way.

Exposure to a Violent TV Cartoon and Violence in Children's Play

To make our discussion of the t test more concrete, suppose we have designed a research project to examine the effect, if any, on the frequency of violence in children's play after watching a violent TV cartoon. We'll refer to this as our TV cartoon study in the remainder of the chapter. To assemble the relevant data, we draw two independent random samples of 10 students each from first-grade students in a large urban school. Assume we have operationalized "violent acts" in an appropriate way. Assume also that we have obtained informed voluntary consent from the children's parents to participate in the study. The data we will present are fictitious.

Our independent variable (x) has two values: watches violent TV cartoon and watches nonviolent TV cartoon. Our dependent variable (y) is the number of violent acts each of the children displays. Note that, technically speaking, our dependent variable should be continuous rather than discrete when samples are small and the sampling distribution to be applied is a normal curve, for reasons we discussed in Chapter 7. But to make our calculations easier to follow, we will stick with whole numbers for our dependent variable values.

We set up our study as a classic experimental research design. (See our discussion of experimental research designs in Chapter 2, p. 36.) One of the samples will serve as the experimental group and the other will serve as the control group. There will be pre- and postmeasurements of the dependent variable in both groups. The research design can be diagrammed as in Table 9.1.

The two groups are placed in separate but identically arranged play rooms equipped with the same toys and allowed to play for one half-hour. Observers record the number of violent acts each child performs during the play period. These data constitute the **premeasurements** of the dependent variable for each group—that is, dependent variable measurements that occur in each group before the change in the value of the independent variable is introduced in the experimental group. The experimental group is shown a half-hour violent television cartoon with lots of crashes, smashes, bams, and booms with physical objects. The control group watches a half-hour nonviolent cartoon with the same characters but only gentle, nonviolent play with the same physical objects. The experimental group's exposure to the violent TV cartoon is the change in the independent variable. Each group is then taken to its own play room again for a half-hour play period. The violent acts of each child in each group are again counted by observers. These data are our **postmeasurements** of the dependent variable—that is, dependent variable measurements that occur after the independent variable value change in the experimental group. We can then calculate the mean number of violent acts per child in the experimental and control groups during both the pre- and postmeasurement phase of the experiment, as well as other relevant sample statistics, for the two groups.

Table 9.1 Experimental Research Design for TV Cartoon Study

	Premeasurement of the Dependent Variable ↓	Independent Variable Change ↓	Postmeasurement of the Dependent Variable ↓
Experimental group	Number of violent acts in play before	Violent TV cartoon	Number of violent acts in play after
Control group	Number of violent acts in play before	Nonviolent TV cartoon	Number of violent acts in play after

We can frame the question we are trying to answer with our experiment as whether the evidence indicates the two samples (that is, the experimental group and the control group) came from one population or two different populations. If the evidence suggests the two samples came from one population, we will say there is no relationship between the kind of cartoon watched and frequency of violent acts. If the evidence indicates the two samples come from two different populations, we'll say there is a relationship between the two variables.

Our TV cartoon study data will be used to illustrate the application of and calculations for the t test in two general research situations. In the first, we compare the postmeasurement means for the experimental and control groups under the null hypothesis for two independent random samples. In the second, we focus on the difference between the pre- and postmeasurement means for the experimental group only, which can be analyzed statistically as the difference between the means of two dependent random samples. In the exercises at the end of the chapter, we will invite you to think about and analyze some other differences that might be used to test for the effects of our independent variable.

A t Test for the Difference Between Two Independent Random Sample Means

As a point of departure for our discussion of one version of the t test for independent random samples, we suggest you review the list of symbols and terms in Table 7.3, p. 210, in Chapter 7. To help you keep track of the old and new terms and symbols used in t tests, we have listed some of them and their meanings in Table 9.2. Most are just modifications of those with which you are already familiar from Chapter 7. Pay close attention to the subscripts on the symbols in Table 9.2 as well as in the formulas and discussions in the text.

This version of the t test entails the following assumptions and offers the following possible hypotheses.

Table 9.2 Symbols and Their Meanings in *t* Tests

Symbol	Meaning
μ	Population mean
$\bar{y}$	Sample or group mean
σ^2	Population variance
$\sigma^2_{\bar{y}-\bar{y}}$	Variance of the sampling distribution for difference between sample means of *y*
$\hat{\sigma}^2_{\bar{y}-\bar{y}}$	Estimate of the variance of the sampling distribution for difference between sample means of *y*
$\sigma_{\bar{y}-\bar{y}}$	Standard error of the sampling distribution for difference between sample means of *y*
$\hat{\sigma}_{\bar{y}-\bar{y}}$	Estimate of the standard error of the sampling distribution for difference between sample means of *y*
D	A difference score for the *t* test for two dependent samples
$\bar{D}$	Mean of difference scores for dependent samples
$\sigma_{se\bar{D}}$	Standard error of the sampling distribution for $\bar{D}$
$\hat{\sigma}_{se\bar{D}}$	Estimate of the standard error of the sampling distribution for $\bar{D}$
σ_D	Standard deviation of *D* in the population
$\hat{\sigma}_D$	Estimate of the standard deviation of *D* in the population

Assumptions and Hypotheses

Assumptions:

- Two independent random samples
- Population variances of the dependent variable *y* are unknown and assumed to be heteroscedastic (unequal)
- Dependent variable measured at the interval or ratio level
- Independent variable measured at the nominal or ordinal level, with two values
- Dependent variable normally distributed in the population(s)

Possible hypotheses:

- Null hypothesis: $\mu_1 = \mu_2$

   That is, the two dependent variable sample means ($\bar{y}_1$ and $\bar{y}_2$) come from two populations whose means (μ_1 and μ_2) are equal—which is equivalent to saying the samples come from the *same* population and there is no relationship between the independent and dependent variables.

- Possible research hypothesis: $\mu_1 \neq \mu_2$ or $\mu_2 > \mu_1$ or $\mu_1 > \mu_2$

    That is, the two dependent variable sample means come from two populations whose means are not equal—which is equivalent to saying the samples come from *two different* populations and there is a relationship between the independent and dependent variables.

An important distinction between this and other versions of the t test for independent random samples are the assumptions about the dependent variable population variances. Other versions of the test assume these population variances are known and/or that they are equal. Remember that the version of the t test we are discussing now assumes that the dependent variable population variances are unknown and unequal, assumptions that are safest for most actual research situations.

Directional and Nondirectional Hypotheses

Before we discuss the basic ideas underlying this version of the t test and calculating t under these assumptions, note a basic difference between the first research hypothesis ($\mu_1 \neq \mu_2$) and the other two. In the first research hypothesis we assert only that the population means differ, without specifying which will be larger. Hypotheses like these, whether in the context of a t test or some other descriptive or inferential statistical analysis, are referred to as **nondirectional hypotheses**. In the second and third possible research hypotheses, we specify that one mean will be larger than the other. These are called **directional hypotheses** because they specify which of the two populations' dependent variable means will be larger.

Heteroscedasticity and Homoscedasticity

The term **heteroscedastic** also needs definition and brief comment. The term has Greek roots, with *hetero* meaning "different" and *scedastic* meaning "dispersion" or "scatter." The opposite of heteroscedastic is **homoscedastic**, composed of *homo* meaning "same" and *scedastic* meaning "dispersion." We already know a term for the scatter of scores in a distribution, namely, variance. Assuming we are dealing with two or more populations, heteroscedasticity means that the *distributions of y have different variances in the different populations*. It is also possible, of course, to assume that the dependent variable (y) distributions in the populations are homoscedastic—that is, that they have approximately equal variances for each value of the independent variable. Of the two, heteroscedasticity is almost always the safer assumption. Dependent variable distributions in different populations are much more likely to be different than to be the same. It is also true, however, that many inferential statistical analyses assume homoscedasticity, especially for small samples (say, less than 20 or so).

A full consideration of the role of homoscedasticity and heteroscedasticity in hypothesis testing is beyond the scope of this text, but we will have occasion to refer to scedasticity assumptions at several points in this chapter and several subsequent ones as well. We can get some idea of its potential importance, however, by remembering that when we construct estimates of a sampling distribution's standard error, estimates of population variances are necessary. If those population variances are assumed *not* to be at least approximately equal, this additional kind of variation in the dependent variable must be taken into account when devising the formula for the *t* statistic and interpreting the *t*-test results. In some cases, especially for small samples, statistical test results are rendered invalid if the assumption of homoscedasticity is violated. For larger samples (say, $n > 50$), the assumption of homoscedasticity can often be relaxed. In any event, it is important to know the sample size and assumptions about population variances for the particular inferential statistical test, including a *t* test, being used.

Figure 9.1 illustrates the difference between homoscedasticity and heteroscedasticity for a dependent variable in two different populations.

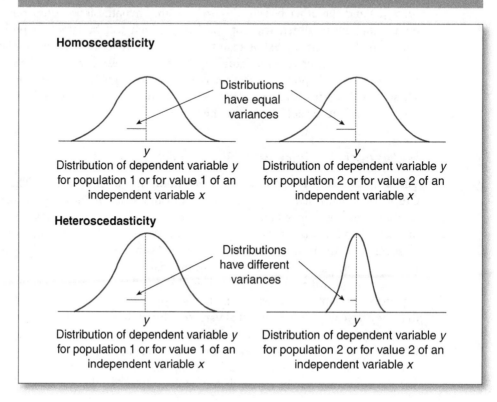

Figure 9.1 Illustration of Homoscedasticity and Heteroscedasticity

The Basic Ideas Underlying the Independent Random Samples Version of the t Test

As we noted in the introduction, the t statistic and t distributions are used for testing bivariate hypotheses when the dependent variable (y) is interval or ratio and the nominal or ordinal independent variable (x) has only two values. As usual in inferential statistics, we will use sample statistics to make inferences about population parameters. Also as usual, the null hypothesis is that x is not related to y in the population(s) and the research hypothesis is that x is related to y in the population(s). We will test the null hypothesis directly, hoping to be able to reject it in favor of our research hypothesis. As we will see, for the purposes of conducting the t test, these hypotheses about the relationship (or lack thereof) between x and y are translated into hypotheses asserting a difference or no difference between two population means.

Consider, again, our TV cartoon study. Suppose our study yielded the data in columns 1, 3, 7, and 9 of Table 9.3. (Ignore the rest of the columns in Table 9.3 for now.) Our research hypothesis is that exposure to a violent TV cartoon (x) increases the frequency of a child's violent acts (y). To assess that hypothesis, we will examine the difference between the mean number of violent acts per child in the experimental and control groups. In particular, we will examine the differences between the postmeasurements of y in the experimental group (column 3) and the postmeasurements of y in the control group (column 9). For the purposes of our present discussion, we will call the experimental group postmeasurements y_2 (and the mean of these scores $\bar{y}_2$); we will call the control group postmeasurements y_1 (and the mean of these scores $\bar{y}_1$). Note that we calculated the means of the ys and found $\bar{y}_2 = 2.9$ and $\bar{y}_1 = 2.0$ (see the means for the ys in columns 3 and 9 below those columns in Table 9.3).

We learned in Chapter 7 (p. 205) that the mean of a sampling distribution of means was equal to the population mean, μ. Now, bearing this in mind, think about what the difference between the two means ($\bar{y}_1$ and $\bar{y}_2$) would be if the two samples were drawn from the same population (that is, if the null hypothesis was true) and *if there were no sampling error*. In this case, both sample means would be exactly equal to the corresponding population parameter (that is, the population mean, μ). In short, under these conditions, the difference between the two sample means would be zero. That is, $\bar{y}_1 = \bar{y}_2 = \mu$ and $\bar{y}_2 - \bar{y}_1 = 0$. If, on the other hand, the research hypothesis is true (that is, the two samples are from different populations with means μ_1 and μ_2) and there was no sampling error, $\bar{y}_1 \neq \bar{y}_2$, $\mu_1 \neq \mu_2$, and $\bar{y}_2 - \bar{y}_1 \neq 0$. (The symbol "$\neq$" means "does not equal.")

Of course, when we sample randomly, we have to expect some sampling error, so we can expect the two means to differ at least somewhat due to sampling error alone, even if they were drawn from the same population. (Review our discussion of sampling distributions and sampling error in Chapter 7 before proceeding.) How is an observed difference between two sample means to be interpreted, then, in relation to whether the data support our null or research hypotheses? How can we judge whether an observed difference between two means is due to sampling error alone or reflects some influence of our independent variable?

Table 9.3 Fictitious Data from TV Cartoon Study

Cols.	1	2	3	4	5	6		7	8	9	10	11	12
	Experimental Group							Control Group					
First Graders	Pre-measurement	$(y-\bar{y})^2$	Post-measurement	$(y-\bar{y})^2$	D score	$(D-\bar{D})^2$	First Graders	Pre-measurement	$(y-\bar{y})^2$	Post-measurement	$(y-\bar{y})^2$	D score	$(D-\bar{D})^2$
A	1	1	2	.81	1	.01	K	3	1.44	3	1	0	.04
B	2	0	3	.01	1	.01	L	1	.64	2	0	1	.64
C	3	1	4	1.21	1	.01	M	1	.64	1	1	0	.04
D	2	0	4	1.21	2	1.21	N	2	.04	1	1	−1	.64
E	1	1	2	.81	1	.01	O	1	.64	2	0	1	.64
F	3	1	4	1.21	1	.01	P	0	3.24	0	4	0	.04
G	1	1	1	3.61	0	.81	Q	3	1.44	4	4	1	.64
H	3	1	4	1.21	1	.01	R	3	1.44	3	1	0	.04
I	1	1	2	.81	1	.01	S	2	.04	2	0	0	.04
J	3	1	3	.01	0	.81	T	2	.04	2	0	0	.04
$n=10$							$n=10$						
Σy	20	8	29	10.9	9	2.9		18	9.6	20	12	2	2.8
$\bar{y}$	2.0		2.9		.9			1.8		2.0		.2	
$\Sigma(y-\bar{y})^2$													
$s = \sqrt{\Sigma(y-\bar{y})^2/n}$		.894		1.044		.538			.980		1.095		.529
$s^2 = \Sigma(y-\bar{y})^2/n$		.8		1.09		.29			.96		1.2		.28
$\hat{\sigma}^2 = \Sigma(y-\bar{y})^2/n-1$		.889		1.211		.322			1.067		1.333		.311
ΣD					9							2	
$\bar{D}$					.9							.2	
$\Sigma(D-\bar{D})^2$						2.9							2.8
$s_D = \sqrt{\Sigma(D-\bar{D})^2/n}$						.538							.529
$s_D^2 = \Sigma(D-\bar{D})^2/n$						.29							.28
$\hat{\sigma}_D^2 = \Sigma(D-\bar{D})^2/n-1$						.322							.311
$\hat{\sigma} = \sqrt{\dfrac{\Sigma(D-\bar{D})^2}{n-1}}$						.567							.558

Note. Dependent variable = Number of violent acts during one-half hour play period.

As you can imagine, whether we decide the sample comes from two populations or one depends in part on how large the difference between the sample means is. As we have noted many times, we can expect some difference due to sampling error alone. If the observed difference between the means is small, we might conclude that they came from the same population and the observed difference is due to sampling error alone. If the difference is large, however, we might conclude that it is unlikely to be due to sampling error alone and, therefore, that the two means came from two different populations. That is, if the difference between the means is large enough that it is very unlikely to have occurred by sampling error alone, we might say that the two samples are so different, at least with respect to the mean of y, that they should be regarded as coming not from the same (one) population, but from two different populations. The t statistic, together with an applicable sampling distribution for t, give us a way of assessing whether an observed change in y, reflected in an observed difference between two means of y, is large enough to make an argument that the two samples come from two different populations and, therefore, support our research hypothesis.

Because inferential statistics are always about probabilities, we know that the question of whether the two samples come from one or two populations can't be answered with complete certainty. However, the t test can be used to determine the probability that an observed difference between two random sample means of y is due to sampling error if they were drawn from one population. If we construct our t test assuming the null hypothesis is true and then find that the probability of the t we calculate based on that assumption is low (say, $p \leq .05$, which is read as "a probability of less than or equal to 5 times in 100"), we will reject the null hypothesis and argue, instead, that the means come from two different populations. That conclusion, in turn, lends support for the research hypothesis that x is related to y.

The Theoretical Formulas for the Independent Random Samples Version of the t Test

With these basic ideas in mind, let's turn to the mathematics of the t statistic. Remember that, as usual in inferential statistics, we use t to test the null hypothesis directly, hoping the results of the test will permit us to reject the null hypothesis and argue instead that it provides indirect support for our research hypothesis. Recall, too, that the null hypothesis is that there is no difference between the *population* means (i.e., $\mu_1 = \mu_2$) and that any observed difference between the sample means ($\bar{y}_1$ and $\bar{y}_2$) is due to sampling error alone, which is the same thing as saying that the two sample means come from the same population.

The general "theoretical" formula for the t statistic *under the null hypothesis* is given in Formula 9.1.

$$t = \frac{\bar{y}_2 - \bar{y}_1}{\sigma_{\bar{y}-\bar{y}}} \tag{9.1}$$

We have already identified the factors in the numerator of Formula 9.1. The numerator ($\bar{y}_2 - \bar{y}_1$) consists of the observed difference between the two sample means. As we discussed earlier in this chapter, if there were no sampling error and the null hypothesis is true, $\bar{y}_2 - \bar{y}_1 = 0$. Because the numerator in Formula 9.1 would be zero under the null hypothesis, $t = 0$ regardless of the particular value of the denominator.

The denominator in Formula 9.1 ($\sigma_{\bar{y}-\bar{y}}$) is the standard error of the sampling distribution for the difference between two independent random sample means drawn from two populations. So, the t statistic is a ratio of the observed difference between the two sample means and the standard error of the sampling distribution for the difference between independent random sample means drawn from two populations.

Unfortunately, we almost never know the value of the denominator (the standard error of the applicable sampling distribution for t) in Formula 9.1. So, we will need to estimate it using data from our samples. That gives us Formula 9.2 for t under the null hypothesis.

$$t = \frac{\bar{y}_2 - \bar{y}_1}{\hat{\sigma}_{\bar{y}-\bar{y}}} \qquad (9.2)$$

Recall that the caret (^) over a mathematical symbol signifies an estimate of that quantity.

> **PAUSE, THINK AND EXPLORE t**
>
> Note that t is a ratio. What is a standard error (see Chapter 7, p. 196)? What is the difference between Formulas 9.1 and 9.2? Describe in words what the standard error for the difference between means is. What is the relationship between the standard deviation of a variable in the population and the standard error of the variable's sampling distribution? Is the latter larger or smaller? Why? Why do we have to estimate $\sigma_{\bar{y}-\bar{y}}$ in almost all situations? What changes on the right side of the equation would yield a larger t? Describe what the t ratio is reflecting. Does the ratio make sense as a test for difference between means? Why?

Let's note two more things about the t test for two independent random samples. First, which mean is subtracted from the other will be dictated by your research hypothesis. For example, your research hypothesis may be that there will be a difference between the means, without specifying which will be larger. As we noted earlier, such hypotheses are called nondirectional hypotheses. Which mean is subtracted from which in such circumstances is essentially arbitrary so long as you keep your research hypothesis in mind, are consistent throughout your calculations in which mean you subtract from which, and keep track of which mean came from which sample. On the other hand, your research hypothesis may specify which of the two means will be larger. Such hypotheses are called directional hypotheses, and we discuss an example later in this chapter.

Second, note that, because the standard error is always positive and one sample mean is likely to be larger than the other due to sampling error alone even if the null hypothesis is true, t can be positive or negative in value. Which sign it has in any given analysis will depend, of course, on which sample mean you subtract from the other. When testing a directional hypothesis, it is important to make the subtraction consistent with the hypothesis, note the corresponding sign of the t you calculate, and know why it has the sign it has when it comes time to interpret your results. We turn now to a discussion of the sampling distributions for t.

The Sampling Distributions for the Difference Between Two Independent Random Sample Means

As indicated in the denominators of Formulas 9.1 and 9.2, calculating t requires the standard error of the sampling distribution for the difference between random sample means. To define this sampling distribution, we need to know its shape, mean, and standard error. From our discussion in Chapter 7, you are already familiar with the idea that probability theory's central limit theorem can help determine the defining characteristics of many sampling distributions. As will be evident, if the null hypothesis is true, the sampling distribution will have the same defining characteristics whether we draw two independent random samples from one population or an independent random sample from each of two separate populations.

The Mean and Shapes of the Sampling Distributions for the Difference Between Two Means

You can get a pretty good idea about what the sampling distribution for the difference between means would look like without doing any calculations. Recall from our discussion of estimating a population mean from a sample mean in Chapter 7 that, according to a provision of the central limit theorem, the mean of the sampling distribution of means equals the population mean. Now suppose we draw two random samples from one population, calculate the mean for each of the two samples, and then calculate the difference between the two means. Suppose we repeat this process an infinite number of times and construct a sampling distribution from the differences between the two means. If you think about this a bit, you will conclude that, whatever the value is of the population mean (μ), if the two samples were drawn from that *same* population, the mean of the sampling distribution for the difference between sample means must be zero. That is, a*ssuming the null hypothesis is true* (i.e., that the samples are drawn from the same population), any difference between two observed sample means $\bar{y}_1$ and $\bar{y}_2$ would be due to sampling error alone.

A little thought about how the differences between sample means due to sampling error alone would be distributed will persuade you that they will be distributed on either side of the mean of zero symmetrically. Most will be small (near the sampling distribution's mean of zero), and a few will be large. You are already familiar, in fact, with how sampling error is distributed in many cases, and this one seems likely to be a normal curve. Provisions of the central limit theorem confirm that the mean of this sampling distribution will be zero; its shape will be unimodal; it will be symmetric about its mean; and, for large samples, it will be a normal curve. For small samples, it will be unimodal and symmetric about its mean, but platykurtic.

Now suppose we draw two simple random samples from two *separate* populations and compare their means. How would we make sense of any difference we observe between these two sample means? This, too, requires a sampling distribution. In this case, a related provision of the central limit theorem tells us that the sampling distribution for the difference between the means will be a normal curve with a mean equal to the difference between the two corresponding population means (we've labeled them μ_1 and μ_2). Note that here, too, however, *under the null hypothesis* the two populations are assumed to be the same population and there is no difference between the population means—that is, the population means would be equal. Hence, the mean of this sampling distribution would also be zero. That is, assuming the null hypothesis is true, for the population means $\mu_1 = \mu_2$, $\mu_1 - \mu_2 = 0$, and any observed difference between sample means $\bar{y}_1$ and $\bar{y}_2$ is due to sampling error alone. So, if the null hypothesis is true, the mean of the sampling distribution for the difference between sample means drawn from two separate populations will also be zero. This means that the mean of the sampling distribution under the null hypothesis will be the same (i.e., zero) whether we draw two independent random samples from one population or an independent random sample from each of two separate populations.

Furthermore, the arguments we made regarding the shape of the distribution for two samples from the same population, then, hold in this case as well. Again, provisions of the central limit theorem confirm that, assuming the null hypothesis is true, the mean of the sampling distribution for differences between independent random sample means drawn from two separate populations is zero, it will be unimodal; symmetric; and, for large samples, a normal curve.

The Standard Error of the Sampling Distributions for the Difference Between Two Means

To complete our description of a sampling distribution for the difference between two random sample means, we need to know its standard error. Another provision of the central limit theorem tells us that the standard error of the sampling distribution for the difference between the sample means of two independent random samples of sizes n_1 and n_2 drawn from two populations is given by Formula 9.3a. We might call this the "theoretical" formula for the applicable sampling distribution's standard error. (Formulas 9.3b, 9.3c, and 9.3d are mathematical equivalents of Formula 9.3a.)

$$\sigma_{\bar{y}-\bar{y}} = \sqrt{\frac{\sigma_1^2}{n_1} + \frac{\sigma_2^2}{n_2}} \qquad (9.3a)$$

$$\sigma_{\bar{y}-\bar{y}} = \sqrt{\frac{\sigma_1^2}{n_1}} + \sqrt{\frac{\sigma_2^2}{n_2}} \qquad (9.3b)$$

$$\sigma_{\bar{y}-\bar{y}} = \frac{\sqrt{\sigma_1^2}}{\sqrt{n_1}} + \frac{\sqrt{\sigma_2^2}}{\sqrt{n_2}} \qquad (9.3c)$$

$$\sigma_{\bar{y}-\bar{y}} = \frac{\sigma_1}{\sqrt{n_1}} + \frac{\sigma_2}{\sqrt{n_2}} \qquad (9.3d)$$

In these formulas, $\sigma_{\bar{y}-\bar{y}}$ is the standard error of the sampling distribution for the difference between the means of two independent random samples drawn from two populations, with subscripts indicating it is for the difference between means of y; σ_1^2 and σ_2^2 are the two populations' variances of y; and n_1 and n_2 are sample sizes.

PAUSE, THINK, AND EXPLORE $\sigma_{\bar{y}-\bar{y}}$

Describe the two factors under the square root sign in Formula 9.3a. Are they variances? Why or why not? What is the square root of a variance? What is the relative size of the variance of the sampling distribution in these formulas compared with the two population variances?

We now know, at least theoretically based on probability theory, what the standard error of the required sampling distribution for our TV cartoon study is. For the purposes of the present discussion, we refer just to Formula 9.3a. If we knew what the population variances were, we'd just plug them into Formula 9.3a; divide them by n_1 and n_2, respectively; and calculate $\sigma_{\bar{y}-\bar{y}}$.

Estimating the Standard Error of the Sampling Distributions for the Difference Between Two Means

Unfortunately, we almost never know and have no way of finding out what the population variances are. As we will see, however, we can use our sample data to estimate the population variances and use these to estimate the sampling distribution's standard error. Again, you are already familiar with such a procedure from our discussion in Chapter 7 (see pp. 207–208).

Let's return to our fictitious TV cartoon experiment to illustrate the t-test calculations for this case. Refer back to the data in Table 9.3, pp. 290–291.

As we did in Chapter 7 for a single sample, we will use our two sample variances to estimate the two population variances. Of course, we want the best estimates possible, so we want unbiased estimates. As you will recall, to obtain an *unbiased* estimate of a population variance from a sample variance, we need to divide the sample's sum of squares not by n but by $n-1$. Recall that we are assuming the population variances for y are heteroscedastic (i.e., not equal), so we have two population variances to estimate. The two populations may, in fact, be the same population, but we don't know (and have no way of knowing) that. We will use each sample's variance to calculate an estimate of the corresponding population's variance. We will use our fictitious TV cartoon study data from Table 9.3 in these calculations, again assuming the population variances of y are not equal.

Because we are testing the observed difference between the postmeasurement violent act means of our experimental and control group samples, only the data and associated calculations from columns 3 and 4, as well as 9 and 10, of Table 9.3 will be used in this analysis. First, we calculate these unbiased estimates of σ_1^2 and σ_2^2 by dividing each of the sample's sum of squares (i.e., $\Sigma(y_1-\bar{y}_1)^2$ and $\Sigma(y_2-\bar{y}_2)^2$) by $n-1$. The results of these calculations are provided at the bottom of Table 9.3. For $\Sigma(y_1-\bar{y}_1)^2/(n-1)$ we have 1.211, and for $\Sigma(y_2-\bar{y}_2)^2/(n-1)$ we have 1.333.

With these population variance estimates determined, we are ready to calculate our estimate of the sampling distribution's standard error. Formula 9.4a or 9.4b will give us the standard error estimate we need.

$$\hat{\sigma}_{\bar{y}-\bar{y}} = \sqrt{\frac{\hat{\sigma}_1^2}{n_1} + \frac{\hat{\sigma}_2^2}{n_2}} \qquad (9.4a)$$

$$\hat{\sigma}_{\bar{y}-\bar{y}} = \sqrt{\frac{\frac{\Sigma(y_1-\bar{y}_1)^2}{n_1-1}}{n_1} + \frac{\frac{\Sigma(y_2-\bar{y}_2)^2}{n_2-1}}{n_2}} \qquad (9.4b)$$

Formula 9.4a is similar to Formula 9.3a. The difference is that Formula 9.4a indicates we are using estimates of the two population variances. In Formula 9.4b, we have substituted the calculation formulas we just used for these two unbiased population variance estimates.

> ### PAUSE, THINK, AND EXPLORE $\hat{\sigma}_{\bar{y}-\bar{y}}$
>
> Describe the two fractions in the numerators under the square root sign in Formulas 9.4b. How would you calculate them? Why are they called unbiased estimates? What makes them unbiased estimates? If everything else stayed the same, what effect on $\hat{\sigma}_{\bar{y}-\bar{y}}$ would larger differences between means have? If everything else stayed the same, what effect would larger ns have?

Once we have our unbiased estimates of the population variances, we then divide each by their respective ns, as indicated in Formulas 9.4a and 9.4b; sum these two quantities; and find the square root of this sum to complete the calculations for our estimate of the sampling distribution's standard error. We'll use Formula 9.4b and show all the calculations, including those for the two population variance estimates we reported earlier, to calculate our standard error estimate.

$$\hat{\sigma}_{\bar{y}-\bar{y}} = \sqrt{\frac{\frac{\Sigma(y_1-\bar{y}_1)^2}{n_1-1}}{n_1} + \frac{\frac{\Sigma(y_2-\bar{y}_2)^2}{n_2-1}}{n_2}}$$

$$= \sqrt{\frac{\frac{10.9}{9}}{10} + \frac{\frac{12}{9}}{10}}$$

$$= \sqrt{\frac{1.211}{10} + \frac{1.333}{10}}$$

$$= \sqrt{.121 + .133}$$

$$= \sqrt{.254}$$

$$\hat{\sigma}_{\bar{y}-\bar{y}} = .504$$

Thus, our estimate of the applicable sampling distribution's standard error is .504.

We are now almost at the point when we can calculate t using Formula 9.2. We know the estimated value of the standard error of the applicable sampling distribution for the difference between means, which we found to be .504 using Formula 9.4b. This result gives us the denominator in Formula 9.2 for t.

One detail remains before we can calculate the t for this analysis, and it pertains to the numerator of t. As we noted at the beginning of the discussion, our research hypothesis can take one of two basic forms. We can hypothesize simply that there is a difference between the means in the populations without specifying which mean will be higher—a nondirectional hypothesis. Or, we can hypothesize that one mean will be higher than the other—a directional hypothesis. As we will see, a nondirectional hypothesis calls for a two-tailed test, whereas a directional hypothesis calls for a one-tailed test. But more about this distinction between types of t tests a bit later when we discuss testing the t we calculate.

For now, let's hypothesize that the postmeasurement mean number of violent acts for the population from which our experimental group was drawn will be larger than the postmeasurement mean for the population from which our control group sample was drawn. That would be consistent with our theory that exposure to violent TV cartoons increases the number of violent acts expressed by the cartoon viewers. So, in this case, we will subtract the control group sample mean from our experimental group mean.

Calculating t for the Independent Random Samples Version of the t Test

We recommend that, as a general rule and unless otherwise directed, you round all calculations for t tests to three decimal places. Most sampling distribution tables for t like those in Appendix F on the study site (**www.sagepub.com/fitzgerald**) are constructed in that way. Also, it helps avoid rounding error problems, which, in some circumstances, can be quite substantial—substantial enough, in fact, to tip results from statistically significant to not statistically significant or vice versa.

The formula for t under our set of assumptions and the null hypothesis is Formula 9.2. Plugging into Formula 9.2 the appropriate quantities from our Formula 9.4b calculations and remembering that the numerator is $\bar{y}_2 - \bar{y}_1$, we have the following:

$$t = \frac{\bar{y}_2 - \bar{y}_1}{\hat{\sigma}_{\bar{y}-\bar{y}}}$$

$$= \frac{2.9 - 2.0}{.504}$$

$$= \frac{.9}{.504}$$

$$t = 1.786$$

The value of the t statistic for our study, then, is 1.786.

Testing t for Statistical Significance

Testing t for statistical significance requires identifying the sampling distribution for t applicable in our particular research situation.

The Sampling Distributions for t

Just as the difference between independent random sample means has a sampling distribution, so, too, does t. The sampling distribution for t mimics that for the difference between means. It has a mean of zero; is unimodal; is symmetric about its mean; and, for large samples, is a normal curve. For smaller samples, it is platykurtic. As we will see, however, there is one major difference between the sampling distribution for the difference between two sample means and the sampling distribution for t. For large samples, the sampling distribution for t is a *standard normal* curve, which, as you will recall, has a standard deviation—in this case, because we are talking about a sampling distribution, a standard error—of one.

Once t is calculated using the appropriate formula, it must be compared with an applicable t **sampling distribution**. For small samples (say, ≤ 50), the sampling distributions for t vary with the degrees of freedom. For larger samples, t is equal to z, and the standard normal (z-score) curve can be used as the sampling distribution for t.

Figure 9.2 illustrates the general differences between the t distributions for smaller and larger samples (and the corresponding lower and higher degrees of freedom).

Figure 9.2 *t* Distributions

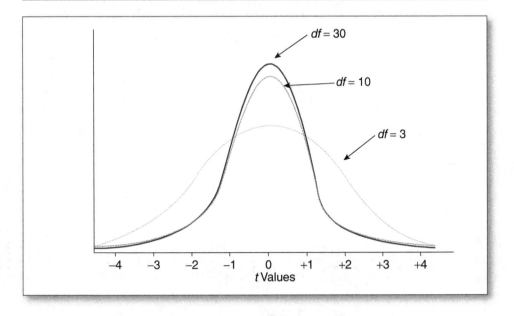

Calculating Degrees of Freedom

Unfortunately, for reasons beyond the scope of this text, when we assume as we have that the population variances are not equal, calculating degrees of freedom is a bit complicated (Blalock, 1972, pp. 226–228). Statisticians recommend that Formula 9.5 be used to estimate degrees of freedom in such cases.

$$df = \frac{\left[\dfrac{\frac{\sum(y_1-\bar{y}_1)^2}{n_1-1}}{n_1} + \dfrac{\frac{\sum(y_2-\bar{y}_2)^2}{n_2-1}}{n_2}\right]^2}{\left[\dfrac{\frac{\sum(y_1-\bar{y}_1)^2}{n_1-1}}{n_1}\right]^2 \left(\dfrac{1}{n_1}\right) + \left[\dfrac{\frac{\sum(y_2-\bar{y}_2)^2}{n_2-1}}{n_2}\right]^2 \left(\dfrac{1}{n_2}\right)} - 2 \qquad (9.5)$$

We have already calculated several of the quantities to be entered into Formula 9.5 (see calculations below Table 9.3, p. 290). The others are squares of some of these quantities. Doing the calculations, we have

$$df = \frac{\left[\dfrac{\Sigma(y_1-\bar{y}_1)^2}{n_1-1} + \dfrac{\Sigma(y_2-\bar{y}_2)^2}{n_2-1}\right]^2}{\left[\dfrac{\Sigma(y_1-\bar{y}_1)^2}{n_1-1}\right]^2\left(\dfrac{1}{n_1}\right) + \left[\dfrac{\Sigma(y_2-\bar{y}_2)^2}{n_2-1}\right]^2\left(\dfrac{1}{n_2}\right)} - 2$$

$$= \frac{\left(\dfrac{1.211}{10} + \dfrac{1.333}{10}\right)^2}{\left(\dfrac{1.211}{10}\right)^2\left(\dfrac{1}{10}\right) + \left(\dfrac{1.333}{10}\right)^2\left(\dfrac{1}{10}\right)} - 2$$

$$= \frac{(.1211 + .1333)^2}{(.1211)^2\left(\dfrac{1}{10}\right) + (.1333)^2\left(\dfrac{1}{10}\right)} - 2$$

$$= \frac{(.2544)^2}{.0015 + .0018} - 2$$

$$= \frac{.0647}{.0033} - 2$$

$$= 19.606 - 2$$

$$= 20 - 2$$

$$df = 18$$

The practice in applying Formula 9.5 is to round the resulting degrees of freedom estimate (in this case, 17.606) to the nearest whole number. When we do so in our example, we get $df = 18$.

If we were to assume the population variances were equal (rather than unequal, as we have for this illustration), calculating the degrees of freedom is much simpler. The formula for the degrees of freedom assuming equal population variances is $df = (n_1 - 1) + (n_2 - 1)$. If the samples were the same as in our illustration, the result would be $(10 - 1) + (10 - 1) = 18$, the same as we achieved above in our illustration using Formula 9.5. This will not always be the case, however, and you should use Formula 9.5 when the safest assumption about population variances is that they are unequal.

You may wonder why statisticians advise using Formula 9.5. A detailed answer is beyond the scope of this text. But we can say that Formula 9.5 yields fewer degrees of freedom than the simpler formula, as it did in our calculations. It was rounding that brought us back up to the same degrees of freedom as the simpler formula for use when we assume population variances are equal. In general, using Formula 9.5 for degrees of freedom gives a more conservative result than does the simpler formula. That is, fewer degrees of freedom mean that a higher calculated value of t would be required to achieve any particular level of statistical significance. You can confirm this by looking at the t table and comparing the entries in any particular column for more and fewer degrees of freedom. You will find that the critical values for t are higher for fewer degrees of freedom.

Although we now have our calculated t and degrees of freedom, we are not quite ready to use a t table to perform the statistical significance test. Why? Because how we use the t table to set the critical value(s) and rejection region(s) depends on a decision we have mentioned but not yet discussed in detail regarding hypothesis testing, namely, whether our test will be one-tailed or two-tailed.

One- and Two-Tailed Tests of Significance

Recall that in our discussion of significance levels, critical values, and rejection regions for chi square, the values in our chi-square sampling distribution ranged from zero upward; that is, there are no negative chi-square values in the table. As we noted previously, an examination of Formula 9.2 reveals that t can be positive *or* negative (depending on which of the two means being compared is larger and which is put first in the t formula numerator). Furthermore, an examination of Figure 9.2 illustrates that the sampling distributions for t have two tails, just like the z-score distribution. This presents us with some new options for hypothesis testing, namely, a choice between one- and two-tailed tests of significance.

As we noted briefly in Chapter 4 (see Figure 4.1 and accompanying discussion in Chapter 4, p. 95), many frequency distributions may be said to have two tails. The same can be said for many sampling distributions (which, remember, are probability distributions) used in hypothesis testing. The tails of a distribution are the areas under the curve farthest toward the left and toward the right in the frequency or probability distribution graph. The tails correspond, respectively, to the lowest and highest values of the statistic (variable) whose possible values are arrayed along the horizontal axis of the graph. When the tails are closer to the graph's horizontal axis (compared with the rest of the curve), they represent the possible values of the variable that have the lower frequencies (or probabilities), as illustrated in Figure 9.3.

The easiest way to illustrate the difference between one- and two-tailed tests of significance for t is to begin by assuming we have two large independent random samples drawn from the same population. In such a case, as we noted above, the sampling distribution for both the differences between the two sample means and for t are approximately normal. Recall also that the central limit theorem tells us that the mean of the sampling distribution for differences between independent random sample means for samples drawn from the same population is zero. So, assuming large samples, the sampling distribution for t is a normal curve with a mean of zero. You might find it helpful to review Figure 5.11 and reread the section on significance levels, critical values, rejection regions, and areas under the curve for chi-square tests in Chapter 8, pp. 266–268, before proceeding further.

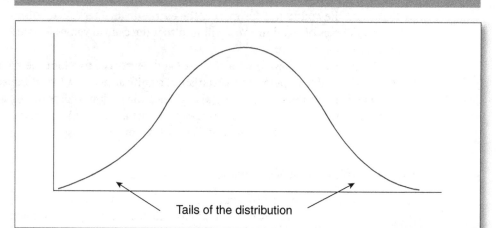

Figure 9.3 A Generic Normal Curve Sampling Distribution Showing the Tails of the Distribution

Let's return to our TV cartoon study for a minute. Recall that our research hypothesis was not just that there will be a difference between the mean number of violent acts, but that the mean number of violent acts for the experimental group will be larger than that for the control group—that is, we hypothesize that $\bar{y}_2 > \bar{y}_1$. This is a directional hypothesis. Directional hypotheses are tested using a one-tailed, rather than a two-tailed, test. Why? Because directional research hypotheses state which of the two means will be the larger. That, in turn, means we are identifying the tail of the sampling distribution (the positive t tail or the negative t tail) where our observed difference between means should fall and where we will look for the critical value of t and associated rejection region for our test. The advantage of a directional hypothesis, as compared with a nondirectional one, is that the entire rejection region for our test statistic is concentrated in one tail of its sampling distribution, rather than being divided evenly between the two tails. This means that for any given significance level, a lower critical value of our test statistic will permit us to reject the null hypothesis.

Our directional research hypothesis for our TV cartoon study calls for a one-tailed test. We expect the mean number of violent acts for the experimental group will be larger than the mean for the control group. When we subtract the control group mean from the experimental group mean, we expect t to be positive so the applicable critical value and associated rejection region is on the right (positive) side of the sampling distribution for t.

The t table, showing the critical values of t and their associated cumulative probabilities, is found in Appendix F. Remember that cumulative probabilities means here that the probabilities (levels of significance) are for ts as large *or larger* than those listed in the table. Note that the values of t in the table can be read for different degrees of freedom and different levels of significance, as well as for one- or two-tailed tests.

To use the table, first we locate the degrees of freedom we have calculated in the left column of the table. That identifies the row for the critical values for t at various levels of significance and for one- or two-tailed tests.

In our TV cartoon study example, we found the degrees of freedom from Formula 9.5 to be 18.

A One-Tailed t Test

As we noted earlier, **one-tailed significance tests** place the entire rejection region into one of the tails of the sampling distribution. Consider the sampling distribution for t in Figure 9.4, assuming a 5% significance level (which is equivalent to a 95% confidence level).

Note that the entire 5% of the area under the curve constituting the rejection region lies in the tail to the right (i.e., the positive t area) of the probability distribution. We would use this distribution and its rejection region in our TV cartoon study example for a one-tailed test of significance for t.

Checking the left column (the *df* column) in the t table in Appendix F, we locate our *df* of 18. For a one-tailed test at the .05 level of significance, we find, in the second column of t values from the left, the critical value for t is 1.734. Thus, for a one-tailed hypothesis test, our calculated value of $t = 1.786$ exceeds the critical value of t at

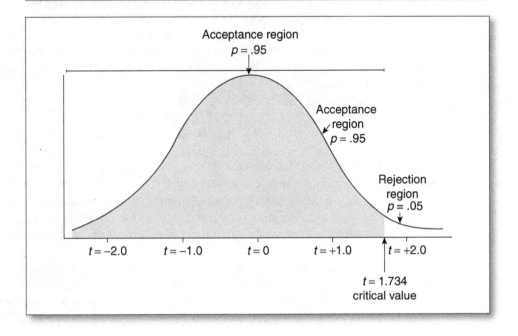

Figure 9.4 Sampling Distribution for *t* Showing Critical Values, Rejection Region and Corresponding Areas Under the Curve for the .05 Level of Significance and a One-Tailed Test for a Directional Hypothesis

the .05 level of significance. Therefore, we can reject the null hypothesis that the two samples came from the same population and argue instead that the samples came from two different populations. Hence, our findings lend support for our research hypothesis that there is a relationship between the kinds of TV cartoon first graders watch and play violence afterwards. More particularly, there is support for our directional research hypothesis that viewing violent acts in a TV cartoon increases the mean number of first graders' violent acts in a subsequent play period.

A Two-Tailed t Test

Two-tailed significance tests divide the rejection region evenly between the two tails of the sampling distribution. Suppose that an investigator is torn between two theories about the effects on children of watching a violent TV cartoon. One of the theories holds that children will mimic the violence they see and the number of violent acts will go up. The other theory holds that children tend to have a certain inborn drive level for aggression/violence. As they watch TV cartoon violence, they will participate in it vicariously and their natural drive for aggression will be reduced, at least temporarily, resulting in fewer violent acts.

If the researcher is uncertain about which theory is the better one, she will simply test the research hypothesis that the two means will differ without asserting which one will be larger—that is, she will assert only that $\bar{y}_2 \neq \bar{y}_1$. Such nondirectional hypotheses call for a two-tailed test. With a two-tailed test, there are two critical values (one positive and one negative) of our test statistic (t) and two corresponding rejection regions for our decision about the null hypothesis for each degree of freedom. The significance level we choose determines the two critical values and the two corresponding rejection regions (areas under the sampling distribution curve), one under the left tail and one under the right tail.

If we selected the .05 level of significance, for example, the 5% of the area under the curve corresponding to the 5% rejection region is divided evenly between the two tails, each containing 2.5% of the area. Figure 9.5 illustrates the .05 two-tailed test of the significance for t.

If we chose the .01 level of significance, the rejection region would be divided into two equal portions, with each tail including .005% of the area under the curve.

Using the data from our TV cartoon study and the same value of t, but this time performing a two-tailed test at the .05 significance level, we look in the third column of t values from the left. The critical value for $df = 18$ is 2.101. For this two-tailed test at the .05 level of significance, our positive $t = 1.786$ does not reach the critical value for t. Therefore, we would not reject the null hypothesis and conclude instead that the two samples came from the same population. In this case, our evidence indicates there is no relationship between the kind of TV cartoon (violent or not) first graders watch and the frequency of violence in their subsequent play activities.

Finally, we should note that in order to apply the t test for small independent samples, as we have in our TV cartoon study with samples of size 10, the sample ns need to be approximately equal. However, if both samples are relatively large (say, ≥ 50), they need not be approximately equal in size, as long as the difference in sample size is not extreme.

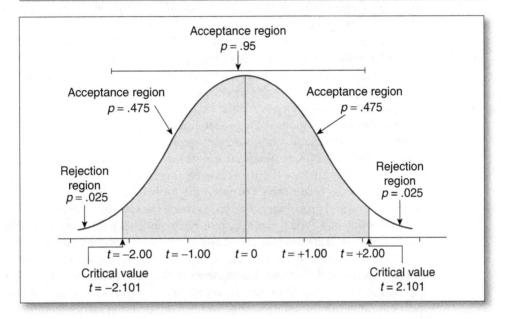

Figure 9.5 Sampling Distribution for t Showing Critical Values, Rejection Regions, and Corresponding Areas Under the Curve for the .05 Level of Significance and a Two-Tailed Test for a Nondirectional Hypothesis

Some Reflections on Statistical Significance Tests

Perhaps this is a good place to step back a bit and reflect again on statistical significance and what we called earlier practical significance. We have just encountered an instance where a one-tailed test is statistically significant and a two-tailed one is not. That is, in one case we rejected the null hypothesis, and in the other we accepted it. Neither the t value nor the data used to calculate t changed. Rather, what changed was the kind of research hypothesis we tested (indirectly, of course). Obviously, statistical tests of significance only help us make decisions about our findings; they do not, by themselves, determine our decisions.

Furthermore, if you look at the t table for $df = 18$, you will see that the two-tailed probability of a t of 1.786 or larger is less than 10%. Why? Because the critical value for t at the 10% level of significance for a two-tailed test is 1.734, and our t exceeds that value. You might well say I'm willing to run a less than 10% risk of a Type I error (which, remember, is the probability of rejecting a null hypothesis that's true); reject the null hypothesis; and argue that my findings support my research hypothesis. Should anyone say you are being entirely unreasonable? It certainly doesn't seem to us you are. Although widely accepted by researchers, the .05 significance level standard for rejecting a null hypothesis is basically arbitrary. Its appropriateness depends on what is at stake in accepting or rejecting the null hypothesis. If people's lives were directly implicated in applying the research results, you might well decide a higher standard (that is, a lower significance level, such as .01) should be required. The .05 standard is only a guideline, however widely accepted in many research situations it may be. You as researcher or consumer of research must make a judgment about what a reasonable standard for avoiding a Type I error is, and it may vary from one research project to another. Statistical analysis must always be combined with good understanding and judgment.

Remember, too, not to confuse the probability of a Type I error with the strength of a relationship. A test result may indicate a very low probability under the null hypothesis, but that does not necessarily mean there is a strong relationship between the variables. A t statistic helps us decide whether or not a relationship between the independent and dependent variables exists, but not how strong it is.

We should also note that the probabilities of Type I and Type II errors are linked. If we decrease the chances of making a Type I error (rejecting a null hypothesis that's true) by choosing a lower significance level (i.e., a .01 instead of .05), we increase the chances of making a Type II error (i.e., accepting a null hypothesis that is false). Figure 9.6 illustrates the relationships between the probability distributions for α (i.e., significance level and probability of a Type I error if the null hypothesis is true) and β (i.e., the probability of a Type II error if a research hypothesis with a specified value is true). Recall that statistical power is defined as $1 - \beta$ (review the discussion of Type I and Type II error in Chapter 8, pp. 230–231). Hence, there is a relationship between α and statistical power as well. In general, as α increases, β decreases and power $(1 - \beta)$ increases.

The From the Literature Box 9.1 on pp. 308–309 provides an example of an independent random samples t-test analysis from the criminal justice literature.

A t Test for the Difference Between Two Dependent Random Sample Means

In our discussion of t for independent random samples, we compared fictitious postmeasurements of an experimental and a control group that were drawn as independent random samples from an urban school's first graders. But this is only one of the comparisons that might be made in order to assess the potential effects of our independent variable (exposure to the violent TV cartoon). For example, we might compare the pre- and postmeasurements of our dependent variable (ys or numbers of violent acts) for the experimental group by itself. That is, we might compare the ys in column 1 and column 3 of Table 9.3 (see p. 290). In this case, we will call the experimental group's premeasurements of y, y_1, and we will call the experimental group's postmeasurements of y, y_2. In this comparison, we are treating the pre- and postmeasurement groups *as if* they may be random samples from two different populations. More specifically, we will be examining whether the changes (differences) in the values of the ys from the pre- to the postmeasurements are large enough to conclude that they did not arise from sampling error alone—that is, the differences are large enough that it is *as if* the two sets of ys came not from one population but from two different populations, and there is a relationship between exposure to the violent TV cartoon and number of violent acts. The two samples clearly would *not* qualify as *independent*

Figure 9.6 Illustration of the Relationships Among, β and Power in Statistical Tests of Significance

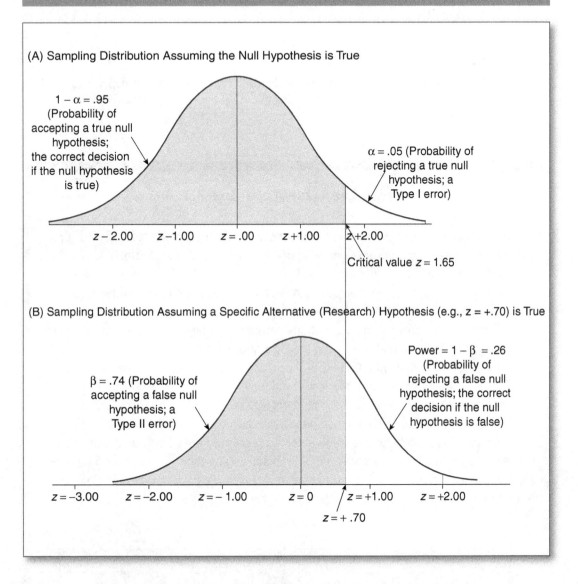

random samples, however. Why? Because when a person is randomly selected for the experimental group (sample) for premeasurement, that person is automatically included in the experimental group (sample) for postmeasurement. In short, the two samples consist of exactly the same individuals.

As we noted in our earlier discussion, examples of dependent samples include research situations when two samples have been matched (called paired or matched samples) or the same group is measured before and after a "treatment" in an experimental design (called repeat measurement samples). Although the *t* distribution serves as the sampling distribution for the *t* statistic we calculate, the formula for calculating a dependent random sample *t* is different from the one we used for independent random samples.

Assumptions and Hypotheses

The *t* test we will be performing for the difference between two dependent random sample means is based on the following assumptions and offers the following possible hypotheses:

From the Literature Box 9.1

Bonnie Carlson and colleagues studied traumatic and stressful experiences as well as drug use before incarceration and postrelease service needs of mothers and fathers in selected Arizona prisons. The data come from inmate surveys. The sample of fathers was a separate (independent) sample from that of mothers. Among the different analyses of their data, they used *t* tests to examine differences between independent random sample means. They combined inmates' responses to survey questions pertaining to physical and sexual abuse in childhood and adulthood (did they or did they not experience such abuse) into a scale with scores ranging from 0 to 4 (with 0 indicating neither physical nor sexual abuse in childhood or adulthood). They treated these scores as ratio-level measurements. They calculated and compared the means of these scores for mothers who reported drug abuse/addiction prior to incarceration with those for mothers who reported no drug abuse/addiction prior to incarceration. They also compared these mean scores for fathers, as well as the means for mothers and for fathers who reported no alcohol abuse/addiction and those who reported alcohol abuse/addiction prior to incarceration. The following is an excerpt from their research report, including *t* tests for independent random samples.

Hypothesis 2 examined the associations between victimization history and having a substance abuse problem. We performed these *t* tests separately by gender and separately for drug and alcohol problems. As shown in Table 2, for mothers, having a self-reported alcohol problem was significantly associated with having experienced more lifetime physical and sexual abuse. The same was true for drug problems. Similarly, for fathers, both self-reported alcohol and drug abuse or addiction were associated with having experienced more forms of lifetime victimization by a family member. Thus, Hypothesis 2 was supported.

Table 2 Self-Reported Drug and Alcohol Problems in Relation to Lifetime Abuse, by Gender

	Mothers[a]				Fathers[b]			
	M	SD	t	P	M	SD	t	P
Lifetime abuse (0-4)								
No drug problem	1.19	1.03	9.01	.000	.62	.77	4.46	.000
Drug abuse/addiction	1.72	1.12			.89	.88		
No alcohol problem	1.34	1.05	8.25	.000	.70	.81	3.26	.001
Alcohol abuse/addiction	1.83	1.56			.89	.88		

a. *n*s vary between 1,410 and 1,418.

b. *n*s vary between 813 and 821.

Source: From Carlson, B. E., Shafer, M. S., & Duffee, D. E. (2010). Traumatic and stressful life events of incarcerated parents II: Gender and ethnic differences in substance abuse and service needs. *The Prison Journal, 90,* 494-515. Retrieved June 2, 2012, from http://tpj.sagepub.com/content/90/4/494. Reprinted with permission.

Assumptions

- Two dependent random samples
- Population variances of the dependent variable *y* unknown and assumed to be equal (i.e., homoscedastic)
- Dependent variable measured at the interval or ratio level
- Independent variable with two values measured at the nominal or ordinal level
- Dependent variable normally distributed in the population

Possible hypotheses:

- Null hypothesis: $\mu_1 = \mu_2$
- Research hypothesis: $\mu_1 \neq \mu_2$ or $\mu_2 > \mu_1$ or $\mu_1 > \mu_2$

The Basic Ideas Underlying the Dependent Random Samples Version of the t Test

For the purposes of illustrating the basic ideas on which the dependent samples difference between means test is based, let's return to our TV cartoon research data. Consider each of the individuals in our experimental group of first-grade violent TV program watchers, such as Maria. The number of violent acts in which Maria engaged would be measured twice, once during the premeasurement phase (y_1) and once during the postmeasurement phase (y_2) of the experiment. If we subtract the latter from the former number of violent acts ($y_2 - y_1$), we can call the result a **difference score** for Maria, which we will symbolize as D. If we repeated this process with each individual in the experimental group, the result would be a single array of D scores that we can analyze as if they were raw scores. (See column 5 of Table 9.3.) We could then calculate a mean for these D scores (i.e., $\bar{D}$). If we found the mean to be zero, there would be no evidence of any violent cartoon effect on children's play. If it was larger than zero, it would suggest exposure to the violent cartoon may have had some effect. In general, the larger the mean of D ($\bar{D}$), the greater the impact of watching the violent TV cartoon on children's violence in play. Note that each subject serves as his or her own control for the second measurements, ensuring that many variables other than exposure to the violent TV cartoon do not change during the experiment. This eliminates the possible impact of changes in the values of those other variables on play violence, thereby helping to isolate the effects of the TV cartoon.

The Theoretical Formula for the Dependent Random Samples Version of the t Test

Formulas 9.6a and 9.6b give us the theoretical formulas for the dependent sample t under the null hypothesis.

$$t = \frac{\bar{D}}{\sigma_{\bar{D}}} \tag{9.6a}$$

$$t = \frac{\bar{D}}{\frac{\sigma_D}{\sqrt{n}}} \tag{9.6b}$$

In Formula 9.6a, $\bar{D}$ is the mean of the sample difference scores and $\sigma_{\bar{D}}$ is the standard error of the sampling distribution for $\bar{D}$. A provision of the central limit theorem tells us that the standard error of the sampling distribution for $\bar{D}$ (i.e., $\sigma_{\bar{D}}$) is equal to $\sigma_D / \sqrt{n}$. So we can rewrite Formula 9.6a as Formula 9.6b. In Formula 9.6b, σ_D is the standard deviation of the difference scores (Ds) in the population and n is the sample size. Note that if we calculated the mean number of violent acts for each of the two samples separately, the difference between those two means would be $\bar{D}$. That is, $\bar{y}_2 - \bar{y}_1 = \bar{D}$. So, the t test for dependent samples is, like the independent samples t test, a test of the difference between two observed sample means, assuming the null hypothesis is true (i.e., in the populations, $\mu_1 = \mu_2$ and $\mu_1 - \mu_2 = 0$, and in the samples, any difference [D] between $\bar{y}_1$ and $\bar{y}_2$ is due to sampling error).

We know that sampling error is likely to produce a mean of D ($\bar{D}$) greater or less than zero. So, similar to the question we raised with respect to independent random sample means, the issue here is, how much different from zero must our sample $\bar{D}$ be to permit us to conclude that something more than sampling error has occurred? The something more is the effect of our independent variable (TV cartoon violence) on our dependent variable (play violence).

The Sampling Distributions for $\bar{D}$

As usual, using inferential statistics to assess an observed difference between two dependent sample means requires a sampling distribution (or distributions) of such differences. We need to know its shape, mean, and standard error.

The Mean and Shape of the Sampling Distributions for $\bar{D}$

Suppose we took a very large number of such repeated measurement samples from a population, calculated the Ds, and then calculated the mean of the Ds (i.e., $\bar{D}$) for each of the repeated measurement samples. What would the mean of the $\bar{D}$ scores be if the null hypothesis is true—that is, if viewing the violent TV program (x) had no effect on the frequency of violence in our first graders' play (y)? A little thought should persuade you that the mean of this sampling distribution of means must be zero, because a $\bar{D}$ of zero is what we would expect if there were no sampling error and no change in y after x was introduced (which is to say that y and x are not related). Note that if $\bar{D} = 0$, then according to Formula 9.6a, $t = 0$. Recall our discussion of the shape and mean of sampling distributions for differences between independent samples means. The same arguments apply here as well. That is, if you think about it a bit, you can see why the $\bar{D}$ sampling distributions' shape would be unimodal; symmetric about their means; and, for large samples, a normal curve. Provisions of probability theory's central limit theorem confirm that the sampling distribution for D score means (i.e., $\bar{D}$) and for t calculated using them has a mean of zero and is a unimodal, symmetric curve. For large samples, it is a standard normal curve with a standard error of one.

Estimating the Standard Error of the Sampling Distributions for $\bar{D}$

As usual, estimating the sampling distribution's standard error depends on knowing the standard deviation of the relevant variable values in the population. Also, because we don't know the population standard deviation of D (σ_D) in Formula 9.6b, we will have to estimate it using our sample data. So we rewrite the formula for t in Formula 9.6b as the formula for t in Formula 9.7, indicating we are estimating the standard deviation of the difference scores (Ds) in the population.

$$t = \frac{\bar{D}}{\frac{\hat{\sigma}_D}{\sqrt{n}}} \tag{9.7}$$

> **PAUSE, THINK, AND EXPLORE THEORETICAL t FOR DEPENDENT SAMPLES**
>
> Compare Formula 9.7 with Formula 9.2 and the denominator in Formula 9.7 with Formula 9.6. How are they similar? How are they different?

Of course, we want an unbiased estimate of σ_D, which is given by Formula 9.8.

$$\hat{\sigma}_D = \sqrt{\frac{\Sigma(D-\bar{D})^2}{n-1}} \qquad (9.8)$$

For the estimate of the population standard deviation for our cartoon study, then, we have

$$\hat{\sigma}_D = \sqrt{\frac{\Sigma(D-\bar{D})^2}{n-1}}$$
$$= \sqrt{\frac{2.9}{9}}$$
$$= \sqrt{.322}$$
$$= .567$$

So, our unbiased estimate of the population standard deviation for D (σ_D) is .567.

We are now ready to calculate an estimate of the applicable sampling distribution's standard error, which is the denominator in Formula 9.7. This estimate is given by Formula 9.9.

$$\frac{\hat{\sigma}_D}{\sqrt{n}} = \frac{\sqrt{\frac{\Sigma(D-\bar{D})^2}{n-1}}}{\sqrt{n}} = \hat{\sigma}_{\bar{D}} \qquad (9.9)$$

Plugging the results from our Formula 9.8 calculations and the number of D scores ($n = 10$) into Formula 9.9 and doing the calculations indicated by Formula 9.9 gives us our estimate of the D score sampling distribution's standard error.

$$\hat{\sigma}_{\bar{D}} = \frac{\hat{\sigma}_D}{\sqrt{n}}$$
$$= \frac{.567}{\sqrt{10}}$$
$$= \frac{.567}{3.162}$$
$$= .179$$

Thus, our estimate of the standard error of the sampling distribution is .179.

Once again, we will note that the sampling distribution for t mimics the sampling distribution for $\bar{D}$. Just as $\bar{D}$s have sampling distributions that have a mean of zero and that are unimodal, symmetric curves, so also does t. In fact, we use the same t distributions with which you are already familiar.

Calculating t for the Dependent Random Samples Version of the t Test

Plugging the result from our Formula 9.9 calculations and our value for $\bar{D}$ (.9) into Formula 9.7 for t, we have

$$t = \frac{\bar{D}}{\frac{\hat{\sigma}_D}{\sqrt{n}}} = \frac{\bar{D}}{\frac{\sqrt{\frac{\sum(D-\bar{D})^2}{n-1}}}{\sqrt{n}}}$$

$$= \frac{.9}{\frac{.567}{\sqrt{10}}}$$

$$= \frac{.9}{\frac{.567}{3.162}}$$

$$= \frac{.9}{.179}$$

$$= 5.028$$

Thus, we get $t = 5.028$ for our repeated measurement (dependent) experimental group (samples) difference scores (Ds).

As we noted before for independent samples, t for dependent samples can be positive or negative because our sample $\bar{D}$ can be positive or negative. In our case, it is positive because the postmeasurements are, on average, larger than the premeasurements, as we expected them to be, and we subtracted the latter from the former to determine our D scores.

Calculating Degrees of Freedom

As we noted in our discussion of the independent random sample version of the t test, the sampling distributions for t vary depending on sample sizes, reflected in degrees of freedom. So, we need one final piece of information, degrees of freedom, before we can determine whether our t is statistically significant at $p \leq .05$. Degrees of freedom for the dependent samples t test is calculated on the basis of the number of D scores (n_D), which is 10. To find df for our dependent sample D scores, we have Formula 9.10.

$$df = n_D - 1$$
$$= 10 - 1$$
$$= 9 \qquad (9.10)$$

Following the example for independent samples, we'll test a directional hypothesis with a one-tailed test. Our research hypothesis is that the postmeasurements are larger than the premeasurements in the population and there is a relationship between our independent and dependent variables. The null hypothesis is that there is no difference between these two measurements in the population.

Interpreting the Results

Checking the t table for $df = 9$, we find the critical value for $p \leq .05$ for a one-tailed test is 1.833. Because our calculated value of 5.028 exceeds the critical value, we can reject the null hypothesis and argue that our data lend support for our research hypothesis that the number of violent acts increases after exposure to a violent TV cartoon.

Note that our result is even statistically significant at the .0005 level for a one-tailed test (because it exceeds the critical value of 4.781 for that test) and at the .001 level for a two-tailed test. Remember, though, that such low probabilities of no relationship between the variables (the null hypothesis) do not indicate the *strength* of the relationship between the variables.

None of the calculations we have made so far, though, takes full advantage of our experimental research design. Remember that the power of this design lies in its use of a control group to measure the pre- and postmeasurement difference when the independent variable hasn't changed. The pre- and postmeasurement of the control group provides a measure of whatever else may be changing that might affect the dependent variable *besides the change in the independent variable.* To get the best measurement of the *net effect* of our independent variable on our dependent variable, we could subtract any difference between the pre- and postmeasurements of the control group from any difference in those measures for the experimental group. We'll leave it for you to figure out what data from Table 9.3 you might assemble and what kind of t test you would perform for these differences to assess the effect of violent cartoon watching on children's play. (Hint: Think about what the D scores are measuring and what a difference between the experimental and control group D scores would measure.)

Presenting Results for t Tests

Reports of t-test results include the version of the t test that has been performed, the calculated value of t, degrees of freedom, and the probability of the calculated t under the null hypothesis, as well as whether the test and associated probability being reported is for a one- or two-tailed test and whether the samples are independent or dependent.

The two independent random samples t-test result we discussed first in this chapter might be presented as follows:

$$n = 20$$
$$df = 18$$
$$t = 1.786$$
$$p \leq .05 \text{ (independent samples, one-tailed)}$$

From the Literature Box 9.2

Jacqueline Sandifer studied the effectiveness of a parenting program for incarcerated mothers in a southern correctional institution for women. The data came from a questionnaire designed to measure various kinds of parenting skills. The research design was quasi-experimental with an experimental group exposed to the parenting program and a control group that did not take part in the program. The questionnaire was administered to both groups twice, once before the experimental group was exposed to the program (the premeasurement) and once after (the postmeasurement). As a part of her analysis, she analyzed the differences between the premeasurement and the postmeasurement scores of the experimental group on a test of parenting skills. The following is an excerpt from her research report discussing her findings.

Hypothesis 3. It was hypothesized that participants in the parenting program would show an increase in knowledge about child discipline techniques after completing parent education training.

The results of the paired sample t test on before and after instruction mean scores on the AAPI-2 Belief in Use of Corporal Punishment scale produced a t-value of -3.48, which was found to be significant at the .001 level. An examination of mean scores (Time 1 M = 4.55, Time 2 M = 5.23) indicates increased knowledge and changed attitudes about how and when to discipline children, and a reduced preference for physical force as the chosen method of teaching children appropriate behavior changed for mothers who completed parenting classes. Hypothesis 3 is supported.

Hypothesis 4. It was hypothesized that participants in the parenting program would show a change in attitudes consistent with dealing with crises in a mature manner through increased knowledge about healthy parent-child relationships after completing parent education training.

The parent-child relationship targeted in this study was parent-child role reversal. The paired sample t test for difference in test scores from Time 1 (preinstruction) to Time 2 (postinstruction) on the AAPI-2 Parent-Child Role Reversal scale produced a t-value of -3.48, which was statistically significant at the .000 level. An examination of the direction of mean score differences (Time 1 M = 4.17, Time 2 M = 5.00) indicates that, after parenting class instruction, this group of incarcerated mothers was more likely to accept an adult role by taking ownership for their own behavior and acting like responsible parents and, conversely, less likely to expect their child to "parent" them or be responsible for them. Hypothesis 4 is supported.

Source: From Sandifer, J. L. (2008). Evaluating the efficacy of a parenting program for incarcerated mothers. *The Prison Journal, 88,* 423–445. Retrieved May 4, 2012, from http://tjp.sagepub.com/content/88/3/423. Reprinted with permission.

The two dependent random samples *t*-test result we just discussed might be presented as follows:

$$n = 10$$
$$df = 9$$
$$t = 5.028$$
$$p \leq .0005 \text{ (dependent samples, one-tailed)}$$

From the Literature Box 9.2 provides an example of the application of *t* tests for dependent random sample means from the contemporary research literature.

The Relationship Between t and z

For larger samples (say, ≥ 50), the sampling distribution for the inferential statistic *t* is approximately normal and $t = z$, so the standard normal distribution can be used as the sampling distribution. You can confirm this by comparing the values for $df =$ infinity (corresponding to samples with a combined total of more than 120) in the *t* table (Appendix F) with the values of *z* in the *z*-score table (Appendix D). For example, find the row in the *t* table corresponding to $df =$ infinity (that is, the last row in the *t* table). Find the column in this table corresponding to a .025 level of significance for a one-tailed test and observe that the critical *t* value is 1.96. Now turn to the *z*-score table. Remember the *z*-score table gives us areas under one half of the curve and we are looking for the area under the curve beyond $z = 1.96$. So, find the entry in column C of the table corresponding to a *z* value of 1.96 in column A. You will find the area beyond *z* to be .0250. Figure 9.7 illustrates this relationship.

Recall that the *z*-score distribution has a mean of zero and a standard deviation (when used as a sampling distribution, a standard error) of one. For large samples, then, because $t = z$, the calculated value of *t* is equivalent to the number of standard errors our observed result is from the mean of the sampling distribution (zero)—that is, from the assumption under the null hypothesis that the two population means are equal and that the difference between them is zero.

Confidence Limits and Intervals for the Difference Between Means

In a way paralleling what we did in our discussion of the estimation of a population mean in Chapter 7, we can calculate confidence limits and intervals for the difference between means using the *z*-score table and our estimate of the sampling distribution's standard error. (Reviewing the discussion of *z* scores in Chapter 5, p 144–149, and confidence limits for means in Chapter 7, p 209–217, now is highly recommended.) Consider again our *t* test for two independent random samples.

The formula for constructing confidence limits and a confidence interval for differences between means in this case is given in Formula 9.11.

$$cl = \bar{y}_2 - \bar{y}_1 \pm z(\sigma_{\bar{y}-\bar{y}}) \tag{9.11}$$

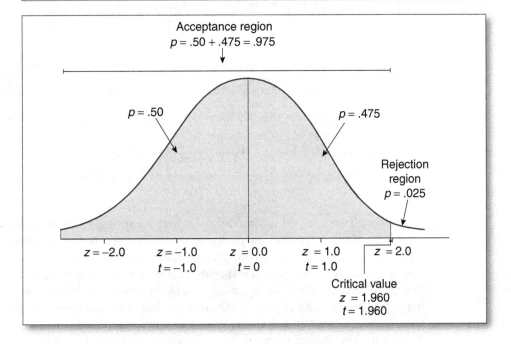

Figure 9.7 Sampling Distribution for Difference Between Means From Two Large Random Samples Drawn From the Same Populations, Treating t as a z Score, .025 Level of Significance-One-Tailed Test

In this formula, $\hat{\sigma}_{\bar{y}-\bar{y}}$ is our estimate of the standard error of the sampling distribution for the difference between means for whatever data we are analyzing, and z is a standard normal score.

To construct confidence limits for a 5% significance level and a 95% confidence interval, for example, we would substitute 1.96 for z. Or, we can choose a .01 significance level and a 99% confidence interval by inserting 2.575 for z in Formula 9.11.

Suppose we chose to calculate a 95% confidence interval and confidence limits for our results from our independent samples TV cartoon data. Recall that our estimate of the standard error was .504, and it came from applying Formula 9.4b. In our TV cartoon study, we found $\bar{y}_2 - \bar{y}_1 = 2.9 - 2.0 = .9$. So, plugging the appropriate numbers into Formula 9.11, we have

$$cl = \bar{y}_2 - \bar{y}_1 \pm z(\hat{\sigma}_{\bar{y}-\bar{y}})$$
$$cl = .9 \pm 1.96(.504)$$
$$= .9 \pm .988$$
$$.9 + .988 = 1.888$$
$$.9 - .988 = -.088$$

So, $cl = -.088$ and 1.888, and the confidence interval is $-.088$ through 1.888.

Remember that we are establishing confidence limits and an interval for our observed difference between means. Thus, given our sample data, we can be 95% confident that the difference between the means in the number of violent acts *for the population(s)* from which our experimental and control groups (samples) were selected lies between −.088 and 1.888, a range of about 2. This is a pretty large interval, considering that the most the raw scores could differ, given our data set, would be −4 to +4, a range of 8.

> ### PAUSE, THINK, AND EXPLORE CONFIDENCE LIMITS
>
> Would it be useful to use the lower confidence limit (−.088) as a difference between means to compute a *t* score and see if that *t* is still statistically significant? If it weren't, what would you conclude from that?

Although we won't do so after this point here, we strongly recommend calculating confidence intervals for all of your inferential statistical results. Finding results that are statistically significant is important, but it should be regarded as just the first indication that you have data worth additional analysis. It is especially important not to be dazzled by findings of statistical significance with very low probabilities under the null hypothesis (say, $p \leq .0001$) because they may produce confidence intervals that are way too large to be of any practical use. You won't know that if you don't calculate confidence intervals. Those intervals indicate the size of the range surrounding your results for a given confidence level and, therefore, add substantially to your understanding of your findings. They are especially important if you or others are contemplating applying your research results. Confidence intervals that are wide relative to the possible range of raw scores should be taken as a sign that applying the results may not provide much benefit and that more research is needed to narrow the intervals with better explanations (i.e., identifying independent variables with greater effect).

Assumptions and Cautions

The general assumptions for the most appropriate use of the *t* test include a bivariate hypothesis, two random samples, and a dichotomous (two-value) independent variable measured at the nominal or ordinal level. Because the test involves a difference between means, the dependent variable must be measured at the interval or ratio level and, for small samples, it must be normally distributed. Different formulas are used for estimating the standard error of the applicable sampling distribution depending on sample size, whether or not homoscedasticity is assumed, and whether the random samples are independent or dependent. For large samples of about equal size, the assumptions of homoscedasticity and normal distributions of the dependent variable in the population can be relaxed.

Use of t tests is not limited to comparing means in an experimental research design. They may be applied whenever any two random sample means of the same dependent variable are being compared and the assumptions on which the particular t inferential statistic is based are satisfied. Any random sample study with an interval- or ratio-dependent variable and a dichotomous nominal or ordinal independent variable may be analyzed using the t test. General examples of such dichotomous independent variables include program participant/not a program participant and exposed to the treatment/not exposed to the treatment. You can imagine that the t test is a widely used inferential statistic in criminal justice and other fields as well.

Some words of caution about interpreting levels of significance and confidence intervals are in order. First, significance levels and confidence intervals can tell us only the *probability* of obtaining a particular result or range of results (for example, differences between means) by chance when we draw random samples from a population or populations. They *cannot* tell us whether any *particular* sample statistic we calculate is the result of chance or nonchance factors.

Furthermore, significance levels should not be confused with the strength of relationships between or among variables. Even very low probabilities under the null hypothesis may be associated with very weak variable relationships. Statistical tests that do assess the strength of relationships are available and should be used whenever possible. Also, calculating confidence intervals provides important additional information for assessing the application of research results in the real world.

The differences between the random assignment of a group of subjects to two research conditions and random sampling from a larger population must be clearly understood. Random assignment is essentially a method of randomizing any differences that might exist between two or more subgroups of the total study group. When we randomly assign the members of some group of subjects to different subgroups for a study, we are actually taking two random samples (usually without replacement) of the group. This group may or may not itself be a random sample of some other larger population.

Let's also take this opportunity to reflect on generalizing our results—that is, arguing that the results of our data analysis are true for or can be applied to some larger group of units of analysis. We have said repeatedly that inferential statistics help us infer something about populations on the basis of sample statistics. But it is important always to keep in mind which populations have been randomly sampled. In our TV cartoon study, for example, we found statistically significant results. What is/are the population(s) to which these results apply? The answer always is the population(s) that have been sampled—no more and no less. In our pretend study, we randomly drew two independent random samples of first graders from a particular school for the experimental and control groups. Our results may be generalized legitimately to the population of first graders in that school. That's it. Statistically speaking, they should not be generalized to all first graders in other schools in the world, the nation, the state, or even the city. A researcher can hope, believe, even argue that research results apply to other populations, but additional evidence from those populations is required to confirm these aspirations and assertions. Always keep in mind what population has been sampled when interpreting and generalizing your results or those of others.

Similarly, if we simply identified a particular small first-grade class and randomly assigned its members to the experimental and control groups, what we have randomly sampled is that particular class. Generalizations beyond that class are not warranted, even if our results are statistically significant beyond the $p \leq .000001$ level.

The same cautions we cited at the end of Chapter 8 regarding statistical tests and garbage in-garbage out, as well as the difference between practical and statistical significance, apply to the *t* test as well.

Summary

In this chapter, we discussed Student's *t* test for the difference between two random sample means, a widely used parametric inferential statistic. To use *t* tests, dependent variables must be measured at the interval or ratio level, and independent variables are usually measured at the nominal or ordinal level. If the independent variable is also measured at the interval or ratio level, more powerful techniques for assessing relationships between or among variables, such as correlation analysis, should be used. We describe some of these procedures in Chapters 11 and 12.

We distinguished between independent and dependent samples. We noted that the formula for calculating *t* varies depending on whether the two random samples are independent or dependent and whether the population variances are assumed to be equal (homoscedasticity) or not (heteroscedasticity). We also noted that the sampling distributions for *t* differ depending on degrees of freedom. Remember that normal distributions may have different variances.

To use any of the *t*-test formulas presented earlier, we must assume that we have drawn random samples, even when they are dependent (e.g., repeated measurement or pair-matched) samples. In general, especially when samples are small or very uneven in size, approximately normal distribution(s) of the dependent variable in the population(s) must be assumed. When samples are large and of about equal size, the distributions' normality assumptions may be relaxed.

Caution must be exercised in making generalizations from statistically significant findings using sample data. Strictly speaking, generalizing results from any sample-based inferential statistical analysis is appropriate only for the population(s) sampled.

Significance levels must be distinguished from the strength of variable relationships. Strength of relationships should be assessed through the application of statistical tests designed for this purpose. Statistical and practical significance are not the same thing. Confidence intervals provide important information regarding the desirability and feasibility of applying research results in real-life situations.

Whenever possible, calculating confidence intervals and limits is highly recommended. Among other things, doing so can help us decide whether it makes sense to apply the results now or to wait for a better theory and/or more research to provide more narrow confidence intervals. Narrower confidence intervals mean more precise parameter estimates and provide more assurance that implementing the result will achieve the desired effects.

Concepts to Master

Dependence between random samples

Dependence (of element selection) within a random sample

Dependent random samples

Difference *(D)* score

Directional hypotheses

Heteroscedastic

Homoscedastic

Independence between random samples

Independence (of element selection) within a random sample

Independent random samples

Nondirectional hypotheses

One-tailed significance tests

Pair matching

Postmeasurements

Premeasurements

Repeated measurement matching

t sampling distributions

t statistic

t test

Two-tailed significance tests

Review Questions

1. Compare and contrast independence and dependence within random samples. In what research situations might they be used?

2. Compare and contrast independence and dependence between random samples. In what research situations might they be used?

3. Compare and contrast repeated measurement and pair matching. In what research situations might they be used?

4. Compare and contrast homoscedasticity and heteroscedasticity.

5. What is the general objective of t tests?

6. How is the standard error for the applicable sampling distribution estimated?

7. How do you calculate t for independent random samples when the population variance is assumed not to be equal?

8. How do you calculate t for dependent random samples, assuming homoscedasticity?

9. Is an unbiased estimate a correct estimate? Why or why not?

10. Why is it necessary to use different formulas for t for independent and dependent samples?

11. What are the general assumptions underlying the different versions of the t test? Under what circumstances is it possible to relax some of those assumptions? Which assumptions may be relaxed?

12. What are the degrees of freedom in a *t* test?

13. What is a directional hypothesis? Give two examples. What is the opposite of a directional hypothesis? Give two examples. In what research situations would the two kinds of hypotheses be used?

14. What are the similarities and differences between one- and two-tailed tests of significance?

15. Describe the relationship between area(s) under the sampling distribution probability curve and a one-tailed test at the .01 and .05 levels of significance. Do the same for a two-tailed test at the same levels of significance.

16. Describe how to use the *t* table and find a critical value in it.

17. What is a *D* (difference) score, and under what research circumstances should it be used?

18. What basic information should be included in a report of the results of a *t* test?

19. What is the relationship between the sampling distribution for *t* and the standard normal curve (z)? How is the value of *t* related to the value of z?

20. Describe how confidence intervals and limits for a difference between two means are calculated.

21. What does a confidence interval tell you about your results that finding them statistically significant does not?

22. What can a confidence interval tell you about applying your research findings in the real world?

23. Define all the terms in the "Concepts to Master" list, and use each in three sentences.

Exercises and Discussion Questions

1. Formulate three research hypotheses and corresponding null hypotheses for which a *t* test would be appropriate. Discuss why the *t* test would be appropriate and how it would be applied in each case.

2. Discuss the differences among a biased estimate, an unbiased estimate, and a correct estimate of a population parameter.

3. For each of the three research/null hypotheses sets you constructed in Exercise 1, write them in a way appropriate for a one-tailed test and then for a two-tailed test.

4. Suppose the significance levels you select for the three hypotheses you formulated in Exercise 1 were .001, .01, .05, and .25. Assume that the appropriate sampling distribution for the test of your hypotheses is a normal curve. Draw the sampling distribution for each null hypothesis, identifying the rejection region for a one-tailed test of your hypothesis for each significance level. Do the same for a two-tailed test.

5. Below are calculated values for t and their corresponding dfs. At what level of significance would these data permit you to reject the null hypothesis for a one-tailed test? For a two-tailed test?

$$t = 2.481, df = 26$$
$$t = 2.481, df = 3$$
$$t = 1.265, df = 456$$
$$t = 64.001, df = 1$$
$$t = 3.321, df = 121$$
$$t = 3.321, df = 2$$

6. Discuss what you have learned about the different sampling distributions for t from completing Exercise 5. (Hint: Discuss the relationships among significance level, t, and df by comparing and contrasting results when t is the same, but df differs, and so on.)

7. What would be the critical value of t for each of the following?

Sig. Level	df	Test Type
.05	3	one tail
.01	3	one tail
.05	12	two tails
.05	12	one tail
.10	100	one tail
.025	25	two tails
.025	25	one tail

8. Using the t table and the z table, show that for large samples, $t = z$. Does this hold for both one- and two-tailed tests? Why or why not?

9. Does a finding with a very low probability of occurring under the null hypothesis mean that the relationship between the variables is very strong? Why or why not?

10. How can calculating confidence intervals add to the understanding of research results?

11. Consider the data for the TV study in Table 9.3. Can you think of other comparisons of means that might shed light on whether there is a relationship between the kind of cartoon first graders watch and their play? What does the control group add to the causal analysis? How might you build the control group's results into your analysis? (Hint: think D scores.) Do the t test and interpret your results.

12. Which do you think is the preferable strategy for managing possible alternative causal variables: independent random sampling or dependent random sampling? Can they be combined in the same research? How might this be accomplished? Would it be desirable to do so? Why or why not?

13. Which do you think is the better strategy for controlling alternative causal variables: random assignment or pair matching? Can they be combined in the same research? How might this be accomplished? Would it be desirable to do so? Why or why not?

14. Are the scores used in the research report excerpt in From the Literature Box 9.1 really ratio-level data? If you decide they aren't, what might be the advantages and risks of treating them as if they are?

15. Can you think of other ways of using t tests to analyze the data in From the Literature Box 9.2? What version of the t test would you use for each alternative analysis you identify? Explain why you chose a particular version of the t test for each alternative analysis.

16. If you haven't already done so, answer all the questions in the "Pause, Think, and Explore" boxes.

Student Study Site

Visit the open-access student study site at **www.sagepub.com/fitzgerald** for access to several study tools including eFlashcards, web quizzes, and additional appendices as well as links to SAGE journal articles and audio, video and web resources.

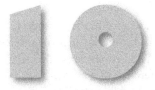

Bivariate Hypothesis Testing With One-Way Analysis of Variance

> **Learning Objectives**
>
> What you are expected not only to learn but to master in this chapter:
>
> - The basic ideas underlying analysis of variance (ANOVA)
> - The nature of the ANOVA test statistic F
> - How to calculate F
> - How to use the F distribution tables
> - How to present ANOVA results
> - How to follow up a significant F with Tukey's HSD test
> - The relationship between F and t

Introduction

Are Anglo American, African American, Asian American, and Hispanic American correctional officers with the same rank and number of years of service paid the same? Do Anglo Americans, African Americans, Asian Americans, and Hispanic Americans differ in age at first offense? Is there a difference in number of property offenses among similar neighborhoods with auto patrol, bicycle patrol, foot patrol, and no patrol? Do judges in the Northeast, the Midwest, and the Southwest give the same length of sentence for the same offense? Do those with recent undergraduate degrees in criminal justice get more job offers than those with recent degrees in sociology and political science? Is there a relationship between ethnicity of judge and length of sentence for felony drug possession? Is there a relationship between current marital status (never married, married, divorced) of offender and length of sentence? Are the floor plans of correctional institutions and number of inmate incidents related? The inferential statistical analyses we consider in this chapter can often help answer questions such as these.

In the previous chapter, we discussed the inferential statistical comparison of two sample means using the t test. In this chapter, we consider analysis of variance, a procedure for comparing three or more means. This inferential statistical procedure, called analysis of variance, is often referred to as ANOVA, which we will do here, and its basic procedures were formalized by R. A. Fisher.

Like the t test, ANOVA is applied most appropriately when the independent variable is measured at the nominal or ordinal level and the dependent variable is interval or ratio. Also like the t test, it assesses the null hypothesis that the means are equal in the populations (that is, there are no differences among them in the populations and thus there is no relationship between the independent and dependent variables). Unlike the t test, however, ANOVA uses the F distribution for statistical inferences and making decisions about hypotheses.

As with parameter estimation, chi-square analysis, and t tests, ANOVA assumes the data being analyzed have come from random samples. In contrast with chi-square analysis, but like the t test, the appropriate use of ANOVA depends on the dependent variable being normally distributed in the population with approximately equal variances (homoscedasticity), at least for small ($n < 50$) samples. For larger samples of about equal size, the assumptions of normal distribution of the dependent variable and homoscedasticity can be relaxed somewhat. Finally, although ANOVA procedures for analyzing data from dependent random samples are available, they are beyond the scope of this text. The ANOVA procedures discussed in this chapter apply only to data from three or more independent random samples.

We consider the general ideas underlying ANOVA, the procedures for arriving at the test statistic, the characteristics of its sampling distribution, and tests for statistical significance. The chapter concludes with a summary of the basic assumptions underlying ANOVA and some cautions about its use and interpretation of its results.

Analysis of Variance (One-Way)

Assumptions and Hypotheses

The **analysis of variance** (ANOVA) test for differences among three or more means entails the following assumptions and hypotheses:

Assumptions:

- Three or more independent random samples
- Population variances unknown, but for small samples assumed to be normal and homoscedastic
- Dependent variable measured at the interval or ratio level
- Independent variable measured at the nominal or ordinal level

Hypotheses:

- Null hypothesis: $\mu = \mu_1 = \mu_2 = \mu_3 = \mu_4 = \mu_5 = \ldots$
- Research hypothesis: $\mu \neq \mu_1 \neq \mu_2 \neq \mu_3 \neq \mu_4 \neq \mu_5 \neq \ldots$

The t test is applicable when we have an interval or ratio dependent variable, a nominal independent variable with two values, and random samples for each of the two variable values. But what if your nominal independent variable has three or more values and you have three or more sample means to compare?

You might be tempted to say we could just run t tests for all the possible combinations of two variable means to sort out which, if any, differences between the means are statistically significant. There are two important downsides to this procedure, however.

One is relatively easy to understand. The laws of probability dictate that the more significance tests of any kind you run, the greater the likelihood you will commit a Type I error—that is, mistakenly reject a null hypothesis that is true. Remember, for example, that if the significance level we have chosen is .05, 5 times out of 100 we will reject a null hypothesis that is, in fact, true. So, the more t tests we run, the more likely it is that we will commit a Type I error. If we were to conduct five t tests, for example, the probability that at least one of them would lead to a Type I error would be .05 + .05 + .05 + .05 + .05 = .25. As you can see, it doesn't take very many groups (samples) to result in a large number of two mean comparisons and a high probability that at least one difference between means will be found statistically significant even when the null hypothesis is true, and that, of course, would be a misleading result.

The second downside is not as readily apparent as the first, and a full explanation is beyond the scope of this text. We will simply note that ANOVA may yield a statistically significant result even when none of the possible two-means comparisons using t tests does.

OK, you might say, but suppose we find a statistically significant ANOVA result. Could we then run t tests to refine our results, identifying which of the possible two-mean comparisons, if any, are significant? Statisticians tell us that the answer is no. The first argument against using *t* tests we made above applies here as well. As we will see, there are more appropriate procedures for comparing the possible pairs of means as a followup to a significant ANOVA. For these reasons, statisticians strongly recommend against using multiple *t* tests when comparing more than two means.

As with the *t* test, the null hypothesis in ANOVA is that the population means are equal (that is, that the real differences among the means in the populations equal zero, and any observed differences in the sample means are due to sampling error). As we pointed out in our discussion of the two means being compared in the *t* test in Chapter 9, this is equivalent to saying that the three or more population means are equal, which is, in turn, equivalent to saying that the samples come from the same (one) population. The sample statistic of concern in ANOVA is called the *F* statistic, and the applicable sampling distribution is the *F* distribution.

As we begin our discussion, let's review the basic procedures we used for conducting an inferential statistical test for the difference between two independent random sample means using *t*. We suspected that children who watched a violent cartoon would display violence more frequently in a subsequent play period than would children who watched a nonviolent cartoon. Our research hypothesis, then, was that there is a relationship between an independent variable (the kind of TV cartoon children watched [violent or nonviolent]) and a dependent variable (the number of violent acts in a subsequent play period) in the population(s).

Our strategy for testing this hypothesis was to select two independent random samples of first graders from a large, urban elementary school's population. We observed both groups at play, counting the number of violent acts for each child, before the experimental group was exposed to a violent cartoon and the control group was exposed to a nonviolent cartoon. Then we observed the children in each sample at play after viewing the cartoon, again counting the number of violent acts they displayed. We calculated the mean number of violent acts per person for each play period. This gave us two sample mean numbers of violent acts to compare, one for the sample who watched a violent cartoon and one for the sample who watched a nonviolent cartoon. The question we addressed was, How likely is a difference of the size we observed between these two independent random sample means if the two samples were actually drawn from the same population and the observed difference is due to sampling error alone?

The null hypothesis we formulated asserted that the difference between the population means is zero—that is, for the purposes of our difference between two means test, the two samples came not from two populations but from one population (or we could say the samples come from two populations with the same mean). The observed difference between the sample means is attributable to random sampling error alone, and therefore, there is no relationship between the independent and dependent variables in the population. We used the observed sample statistics and probability theory to estimate the corresponding population parameters (means and standard deviations), as well as the mean and standard error of the applicable sampling distribution. We used the sample statistic of interest (difference between means) and the standard error of its estimated sampling distribution to test the null hypothesis. We decided that, if the observed difference between means was large enough, it was very unlikely (a probability of .05 or less, for example) to have occurred by chance alone (i.e., through sampling error alone) and we would not accept the null hypothesis. Instead, we would argue that our observed difference between means result favors our research hypothesis that the two samples came from different populations and there is a relationship between the two variables in the population(s).

This basic logic of the t test for the difference between two random sample means can be extended to research situations involving the comparison of more than two random sample means. For ANOVA, however, we will need to approach the analysis in a somewhat different way and make a few adjustments in the parameter estimation procedures we used in performing a t test. ANOVA is, as we will see, about variances as well as means.

To facilitate our discussion, it will be useful to have a handy reference for some symbols/abbreviations and their meanings in ANOVA. Such a reference is provided in Table 10.1.

It will also be easier to understand what we are doing if we have a particular, if fictitious, example to illustrate the analysis. Suppose that four large cities use the same written examination as a part of their selection process for new police officers. Each city has a program for attracting police applicants, and the programs differ among the four cities. It seems reasonable to wonder whether their different recruitment approaches may attract recruits with different characteristics and abilities. It would be useful to know, for example, which approach tends to produce a police officer applicant pool with the most desirable characteristics.

One way of measuring desirable recruit characteristics is the written exam all of the recruits take as a part of the application process. To determine if there are differences among the applicant pools, we take a random sample of the exam scores from each of the four cities. Comparing the written exam scores of the recruits from the four cities may shed some light on the differences, if any, among the applicants that may be due to differences in the cities' recruiting programs. (Of course, to make a strong causal argument, we must be willing to assume that all other things that might influence the exam scores are equal among the four cities. This is admittedly a very risky assumption at best, but for now, we are just exploring whether the four recruit groups are different as measured by their exam scores. If we find significant differences, we can follow up with a more elaborate research design and analysis.) To determine if the recruit groups (i.e., the populations) from the four cities do differ, we decide to compare their samples' mean exam scores. Thus, we have data from four independent random samples with which to work, and we want to compare the mean exam scores of the four city groups to determine if the four recruit populations differ.

Just as we did in Chapter 9 when we compared two means with the t test, we want to know whether the recruits' exam performances differ more than would be expected by chance if the four samples were drawn randomly from one population. In this case, we have not two but four samples to compare. As we noted earlier, performing all of the logically possible pairs of means with a series of t tests is not recommended. The more appropriate test for comparing three or more means is ANOVA.

Table 10.1	Symbols and Their Meanings in Analysis of Variance
Symbol	Meaning
μ	Population mean
$\bar{y}$	Sample mean
y_i	An individual variable value (score) without regard to the particular sample of which it is a part
y_{ik}	An individual variable value (score) in a particular sample
$\bar{y}_k$	Mean of the scores for a particular sample or group
$\bar{Y}$	Grand mean
σ^2	Population variance
Σ	Sum the following
$\Sigma\Sigma$	Sum the following sums of
k	The number of groups (samples or categories [values] of the independent variable)
TSS	Total sum of squares
BSS	Between-group sum of squares
WSS	Within-group sum of squares
MSB	Mean (sum of) squares between
MSW	Mean (sum of) squares within
Q	Tukey's Honestly Significant Difference test statistic

Suppose the individual applicants' scores in our four samples were those in the four columns headed y_1 through y_4 in Table 10.2.

In the interests of brevity, we'll label our nominal-level independent variable "city," although what we mean by that is "approaches to recruiting police applicants." Our independent variable has four values, and we have an independent random sample for each of those values. Our dependent variable is "exam score," and we have four mean exam scores to compare. Our null hypothesis is that the four samples come from populations with the same mean exam score (which is equivalent to saying they come from the same population), and any observed differences among the four samples' mean exam scores are due to sampling error. In other words, our null hypothesis is that city and exam scores are unrelated. Our research hypothesis is that the exam score

Table 10.2 Exam Scores (y) for Police Recruits in Four Cities

	City A (y_1)	City B (y_2)	City C (y_3)	City D (y_4)
	y_{i1}	y_{i2}	y_{i3}	y_{i4}
	18	18	31	15
	16	25	39	26
	30	22	17	19
	38	37	19	19
	22	40	23	21
	35	31	20	11
	19	40	26	13
	25	34	29	10
	33	28	22	26
		40	31	32
		36	21	28
		32	26	
N_k	9	12	12	11

Note: $N = 44$; $k = 1$ through 4.

means for the populations do differ, which is the same thing as saying the samples were drawn from different populations. That is, the recruit samples' mean scores do differ more than can be attributed reasonably to sampling error, and there is a relationship between city and exam scores.

The Basic Ideas Underlying ANOVA

There are two basic ideas underlying ANOVA. One is that the total variation of the dependent variable (y) can be divided into two additive components. The other is similar to the basic idea underlying the t test for the difference between two means.

Dividing the Total Variation in y Into Two Additive Components

One of the basic ideas in ANOVA is that the total variation in the values of the dependent variable (in our example, variation in recruits' test scores) can be divided into two separate, independent, and additive components. Join us in a thought experiment. Suppose we begin by considering one individual's exam score, which we will symbolize as y_i. Next, we combine the scores from all four of our samples into a single group and calculate the mean for this combined group. We'll call this the **grand mean** and symbolize it as $\bar{Y}$. Next, we subtract the individual score from the grand mean ($\bar{Y} - y_i$). As we have in earlier chapters, we will consider a difference between an individual score and a mean score a *deviation*—in this case, a deviation of the score from the grand mean. If we summed these deviations for all of the subjects included in a study, we would have the total variation in y.

The deviation of one individual score from the grand mean can be partitioned into two components, and the total variation in y can also be divided into two components. We will spare you all of the gory details regarding how each of these deviations is divided into two components statistically and what the relationship between them is, but we will try to give you a pretty good idea of what is involved.

First, as we suggested above, let's combine the four city samples into one group, calculate the mean for all groups combined and the deviations of each of the individual scores from the grand mean and then sum these deviations. This sum of deviations is the *total variation in exam scores*—that is, the total variation in *our* dependent variable y.

Second, let's consider each of the our city samples separately. We calculate the mean of each sample and then the deviation of each individual score in that sample from its mean. In the case of our example, we calculate the mean of each of the four samples, which we will symbolize as $\bar{y}_k$, where $k = 1$ through 4 (for the four city samples). Then we subtract each score in a sample from that sample's mean (using absolute values), which we can symbolize as $\bar{y}_k - y_{ik}$ (where $\bar{y}_k$ is a sample mean and y_{ik} is an individual's score in sample k). We can think of these differences as the *within-sample deviations*. We'll call the sum of these deviations for each sample *the sum of the within-sample deviations*. Finally, we sum the sums of the four within-sample deviations to determine the total of the within-sample deviations for all four of our city groups, which we can symbolize as $\Sigma\Sigma(\bar{y}_k - y_{ik})$, where again $k = 1$ through 4.

As a final preliminary calculation, we find the deviation of each of the sample means from the grand mean (that is, we find $\bar{Y} - \bar{y}_k$). Let's call these four deviations *the between-sample deviations*. We can then sum these four deviations again using absolute values, and call the result *the sum of the between-sample deviations*. With the results of these preliminary calculations in hand, we can return to our consideration of the partition of the deviation of one score from the grand mean, as well as the partition of the total variation of y, into two components.

So, what are the two components, and how are they derived? Let's consider the deviation of an individual's score from the grand mean first. The deviation of a single score from the grand mean can be expressed as the two additive components in the general Formula 10.1, again using absolute values.

$$\bar{Y} - y_i = (\bar{Y} - \bar{y}_k) + (\bar{y}_k - y_{ik}) \qquad (10.1)$$

One of the components is the deviation of the recruit's sample mean score from the grand mean score ($\bar{Y} - \bar{y}_k$). The other is the deviation of the recruit's exam score from her sample's mean exam score ($\bar{y}_k - y_{ik}$). The subscript k indicates we are referencing a particular sample of which the individual is a part.

Now imagine substituting each of the individual exam scores (y_i) from all four samples; the y_is in each particular sample (i.e., y_{i1} for the y_is in Sample 1, y_{i2} for the y_is in Sample 2, and so on); and the appropriate corresponding sample means ($\bar{y}_1, \bar{y}_2, \bar{y}_3,$ and $\bar{y}_4$) as well as the grand mean in this equation. This would give us a total of 44 equations (one for each of the 44 y_is in our data set in Table 10.2). Now imagine summing these 44 equations by summing the terms on each side of the equal sign to obtain the total deviations. (Again, remember that in the calculations, we'll have to use the absolute value of the deviations, for reasons we discussed in Chapter 4 [pp. 112–113]). Then, we could express the sum of these deviations as in Formula 10.2.

$$\Sigma(\bar{Y} - y_i) = \Sigma n_k(\bar{Y} - \bar{y}_k) + \Sigma\Sigma(\bar{y}_k - y_{ik}) \qquad (10.2)$$

Recall that Σ stands for "sum the following" and $\Sigma\Sigma$ stands for "sum the sums of the following." Here, as we did before, we let k stand for each of the samples (i.e., $k = 1$ through 4). Whenever there is a k subscript, the mathematical operations indicated are performed for each sample separately before the summation. We will discuss the first term on the right side of the Formula 10.2 equation, which contains an n factor, in just a bit. You are already familiar with part of the second term on the right side of the equation ($\bar{y}_k - y_{ik}$). The $\Sigma\Sigma$ in front of that term tells us to sum the deviations of the individuals' scores in a particular sample from that sample's mean for each of the four samples and then sum the four deviations. The result is the contribution of the second term on the right side of the equation to the total deviation of y from the grand mean ($\Sigma(\bar{Y} - y_i)$).

Now, what about the first term on the right side of the equal sign in Formula 10.2? It looks roughly the same as the corresponding term in Formula 10.1, except for the n_k factor. Where did that n come from? Return for a moment to the corresponding component in Formula 10.1 ($\bar{Y} - \bar{y}_k$). *Within* each sample, this component of the deviation of the individual score from the grand mean will not change from one y_i to another. In this component, each sample's mean score represents (can be substituted for) each of the individual scores in that sample. So, for the purposes of calculating this component of the total deviation of individual scores from the grand mean, we multiply the deviation between the grand mean and each sample mean by the size of each respective sample (that is, n_k, the number of scores for which we have substituted the mean in each sample) and then sum these four products. In our example, we would multiply the deviation between the grand mean and the mean of the sample for City A by the size of the City A sample. We would perform this same calculation for each of the other three samples and sum these four deviations to determine the magnitude of this component's contribution to the total variation.

Perhaps we have gone far enough now with our thought experiment to give you a good general idea of the deviation partitions that underlie ANOVA. We won't actually do the calculations we have described because, as we have learned in previous chapters, statisticians prefer to work with *squared* deviations and the *sum(s) of squared deviations*, which they refer to as the *sum(s) of squares*.

Accordingly, we will square the deviations on both sides of Formula 10.2. Among other things, this frees us from having to use absolute values in our calculations. Recall from your algebra class that when we square a binomial such as $(a + b)$ we get $a^2 + 2ab + b^2$. We'll spare you the algebra of squaring the deviations on both sides of the equal sign in Formula 10.2 and ask you to trust us that when we do so and then sum them, the middle terms (similar to $2ab$) cancel out and we are left with the general formula for sums of squares provided in Formula 10.3.

$$\Sigma(\bar{Y} - y_i)^2 = \Sigma[n_k(\bar{Y} - \bar{y}_k)^2] + \Sigma\Sigma(\bar{y}_k - y_{ik})^2 \tag{10.3}$$

Applying Formula 10.3 to our exam score example, $\Sigma(\bar{Y} - y_i)^2$ tells us to find the deviation of each individual's exam score in all of the samples from the grand mean, square it, and sum these squared deviations. $\Sigma[n_k(\bar{Y} - \bar{y}_k)^2]$ tells us to find the deviation from the grand mean of each of the k sample means, square it, multiply the result by the number of scores in the corresponding sample, and sum these results. In our example, there would be four samples, so as we noted above, $k = 1$ through 4. The four ns corresponding to the four samples are 9, 12, 12, and 11 (see Table 10.2). So, for the first term on the right side of the equation, we have

$$\Sigma[n_k(\bar{Y} - \bar{y}_k)^2] = n_1(\bar{Y} - \bar{y}_4)^2 + n_2(\bar{Y} - \bar{y}_2)^2 + n_3(\bar{Y} - \bar{y}_3)^2 + n_4(\bar{Y} - \bar{y}_4)^2$$

or, in the case of our example,

$$\Sigma[n_k(\bar{Y} - \bar{y}_k)^2] = 9(\bar{Y} - \bar{y}_4)^2 + 12(\bar{Y} - \bar{y}_2)^2 + 12(\bar{Y} - \bar{y}_3)^2 + 11(\bar{Y} - \bar{y}_4)^2$$

$\Sigma\Sigma(\bar{y}_k - y_{ik})^2$ tells us to find the deviation of each of the individual scores in a sample from its corresponding sample mean, square it, sum these squared deviations for each sample, and sum these four sums. In our exam score example, we would have

$$\Sigma\Sigma(\bar{y}_k - y_{ik})^2 = \Sigma(\bar{y}_1 - y_{i1})^2 + \Sigma(\bar{y}_2 - y_{i2})^2 + \Sigma(\bar{y}_3 - y_{i3})^2 + \Sigma(\bar{y}_4 - y_{i4})^2$$

So, Formula 10.3 divides the **total sum of squares** ($\Sigma(\bar{Y} - y_i)^2$) into two additive sums of squares. One, $\Sigma n_k(\bar{Y} - \bar{y}_k)^2$, is referred to as the between-group or sample sum of squares. (Note that in ANOVA vocabulary, the term *group* or *category* [as in nominal independent variable category] is often used instead of *sample*. We will use *group* in the following discussion.) It is called the **between-group sum of squares** because it represents the variation between (maybe we should actually say *among*, because in ANOVA, we are comparing three or more means) the different group means and the grand mean. Note that it also reflects the differences among the means, because the larger the differences among the means, the larger the sum of the squared deviations between the sample means and the grand mean. The other component ($\Sigma\Sigma(\bar{y}_k - y_{ik})^2$) is referred to as the **within-group sum of squares.** Formula 10.3, then, can be expressed as

$$\text{Total Sum of Squares} = \text{Between-Group Sum of Squares} + \text{Within-Group Sum of Squares}$$

Let's examine the two terms on the right side of this equation in more detail, using our recruit exam score example. First, consider the within-group sum of squares. This sum of squares is derived from the sum of squared deviations within each sample. We calculate the sum of squares for each city group separately and then sum these four sums of squares. Within each city sample, recruits' scores vary around that particular city group's mean score. Because we have taken an independent random sample from each city, differences between the mean of each sample and the individuals' scores within that sample reflect sampling error *alone*. For this reason, it is sometimes referred to as the *error* component of the total variation in *y*.

Now, note that neither the magnitude of these within-group sums of squares taken separately nor the magnitude of their sum is related to whether or not the null hypothesis is true (that is, whether or not there are differences among the four groups' means). Why? These sums of squares are calculated separately for each sample using that sample's mean; therefore, they cannot, either alone or together, reflect any differences *between or among* the samples. So, we can consider these two components as independent of each other; that is, the within- and between-group components can vary independent of each other. Furthermore, for the purposes of our analysis, the within-group sum of squares is referred to as the **unexplained sum of squares** or **error** component of the total sum of squares (i.e., the total variation in *y*) because it is attributable to sampling error alone.

Next, consider the between-group sum of squares. This variation includes sampling error, too, of course, and it *varies with the sizes of the differences among the means*. The larger the differences among the means, the larger this sum of squared deviations from the grand mean. This second component, the remainder of the total of the squared deviations of individual scores from the grand mean, is, as we noted earlier, called the between-group sum of squares. The effects of our independent variable, if any, will be reflected in differences among these means and, therefore, in the squared deviations of the sample means from the grand mean. This between-group variation is referred to as the **explained sum of squares**; that is, that portion of the total sum of squares that is "explained" by the effects of our independent variable. It is sometimes referred to as the **effect** component of the total variation in *y*.

So, the general equation for total sum of squares might be written as follows:

Total Sum of Squares = Explained (Between-Group) Sum of Squares + Unexplained (Within-Group) Sum of Squares

or

Total Sum of Squares = Between-Group Sum of Squares (Effect) + Within-Group Sum of Squares (Error)

Now let's think about a ratio of the two component sums of squares as follows:

$$\frac{\text{Between - Group Sum of Squares (Effect)}}{\text{Within - Group Sum of Squares (Error)}}$$

Recall that the between-group sum of squares component includes both sampling error and the effects, if any, of our independent variable, whereas the within-group sum of squares includes sampling error alone. So, if our independent variable has no effect, any differences among the sample means in the population(s), as reflected in the between-group sum of squares, would be due to sampling error alone. That means that, under the null hypothesis that there are no differences among the means, the ratio above would be one of sampling error to sampling error, which is likely to approximately equal one. Ratios larger than one to one would indicate at least the possibility of some independent variable effect.

Testing the Null Hypothesis in ANOVA

Now that we have considered the first of the two basic ideas underlying ANOVA, we can turn our attention to the second. It is similar to the one we described in our discussion of the basic idea underlying the *t* test for the difference between two sample means and its relationship to the null hypothesis. In particular, in ANOVA, we test the null hypothesis that there are no differences among three or more sample means.

Let's back up a bit and consider the research and null hypotheses in our exam score example in a little more detail. Assuming the null hypothesis is true, the four samples come from four populations with equal means, which is the same as saying the samples come from the same (one) population. Thus, our null hypothesis is

$$\mu = \mu_1 = \mu_2 = \mu_3 = \mu_4$$

and our research hypothesis is

$$\mu_1 \neq \mu_2 \neq \mu_3 \neq \mu_4$$

or that at least two of the population means differ from each other.

Again assuming the null hypothesis is true, *if there were no sampling error*, the four sample means would be equal among themselves and equal to the one population mean (μ) as well (i.e., $\bar{y}_1 = \bar{y}_2 = \bar{y}_3 = \bar{y}_4 = \mu$). But, of course, because we have selected random samples, we do have to contend with sampling error. As we noted earlier, just as individual recruit scores in each sample vary around their respective sample means, the group (sample) means will vary around the grand mean at least to some extent due to sampling error. So, the between-group sum of squares contains both the effect, if any, of our independent variable and a random factor as well. The question we need to answer, then, is, How large must the aggregate difference among the sample means be in order for us to conclude that it did not occur by chance alone when four independent random samples are drawn from the same population (that is, when the null hypothesis is true)? Any effects of the independent variable (city, in our example) on the dependent variable (recruit exam score) would increase the differences among the group mean scores and, in turn, increase the between-group variance beyond what would be expected from sampling error alone.

The Theoretical ANOVA Test Statistic F

In ANOVA, the statistic comparable to the theoretical t statistic is the theoretical F statistic. Recall that the formula for calculating the theoretical test statistic t was a ratio of the observed difference between two sample means and the standard error of the corresponding sampling distribution assuming the null hypothesis is true (see Formula 9.2, p. 292). The **F statistic** in ANOVA, on the other hand, is a ratio of two population variances. The theoretical formula for F is given in Formula 10.4.

$$F = \frac{\text{Population Variance Between}}{\text{Population Variance Within}} \qquad (10.4)$$

Just as we did above with the total sum of squares, we can think of the **total variance** of y in the population as divided into two additive components: the **between-group variance** (or **explained variance**) and the **within-group variance** (or **unexplained variance**). So, we can write the general formula for total variance of y in the population as

Total Variance = Between-Group (Explained) Variance + Within-Group (Unexplained) Variance

As we encountered when discussing the t test for the difference between two means, we almost never know the population variances, so we have to estimate them using the sample data that are available to us.

In ANOVA, the two variance estimates specified in Formula 10.4 are called the between-group (explained or effect) variance estimate and the within-group (unexplained or error) variance estimate. (We suspect you can see where this is going!) The theoretical formula for F (Formula 10.4) can be rewritten and framed in terms of population variance estimates as in Formula 10.5.

$$F = \frac{\text{Population Variance Estimate Based on the Between-Group Sample Variance (Explained or Effect)}}{\text{Population Variance Estimate Based on the Within-Group Sample Variance (Unexplained or Error)}} \qquad (10.5)$$

Estimating Population Variances

The estimates are calculated using the sample data, and, as we noted with respect to the two components of the total sum of squares, each of the variance estimates varies independently from the other. As we saw in Chapters 7 and 9, sample variances can be used as a basis for estimating the corresponding populations' variances. We will see exactly how when we consider some illustrative calculations for our four-city exam score study later.

Calculating the Population Variance Estimates

How are the two estimates of the population variance in Formula 10.5 calculated? Let's begin by recalling from Chapter 4 that a variance is arrived at by dividing the sum of squared deviations by sample size (n) (see Formula 4.2, p. 113). Recall also from Chapter 9 that we divided a sample sum of squares by ($n-1$) to obtain an unbiased estimate of the corresponding population's variance. Recall, too, from Chapter 9 that the ($n-1$) in these equations represents the degrees of freedom associated with those sums of squares. In ANOVA, the unbiased population variance estimates in the formula for F are also calculated by dividing the sums of squares by the degrees of freedom associated with those sums of squares.

So, we can rewrite Formula 10.5 as Formula 10.6.

$$F = \frac{\dfrac{\text{Between - Group Sum of Squares}}{k-1}}{\dfrac{\text{Within - Group Sum of Squares}}{N-k}} = \frac{\text{Mean Squares Between}}{\text{Mean Squares Within}} \qquad (10.6)$$

Now let's interpret Formula 10.6, which consists of a ratio of two ratios using our exam score example. The top ratio represents one estimate of the population parameter of interest (i.e., the population variance). In the top ratio, the numerator is the square of the difference between the grand mean and each of the sample means, multiplied by their respective sample size and then summed. The bottom ratio is another estimate of the population variance, independent of the first estimate. In the bottom ratio, the numerator is the sum of the squared deviations of the individual scores from their respective sample means for each of the four samples, the results of which are then summed. The denominators of the top and bottom ratios are the degrees of freedom associated with the particular corresponding sum of squares. In those denominators, k is the number of samples or categories of the independent variable (in our study, $k = 4$, so $k - 1 = 3$). N is the total number of observations or people included in the study (in our study, $N = 44$, so $N - k = 40$). When we divide the between-group sum of squares by $k - 1$ to get the ratio in the numerator for Formula 10.5, the result is the population variance estimate based on the between-group sum of squares and is referred to as the **mean squares between**. Dividing the within-group sum of squares by $N - k$ gives us the population variance estimate based on the ratio that is the denominator in Formula 10.6. It is referred to as the **mean squares within**. These two mean squares now become our estimates of the population variance, one based on the between-group sum of squares (effect) and one based on the within-group sum of squares (error).

> ### PAUSE, THINK, AND EXPLORE F
>
> F is a ratio of two ratios. Can F ever be negative? What would an $F = 1$ indicate? What values of F would indicate support for our null hypothesis? For our research hypothesis? If everything else stayed the same in the formula and the number of samples increased, what would happen to the value of F? If the between-group sum of squares goes up, what, if anything, happens to the within-group sum of squares? To the F statistic?

Let's now calculate these two population variance estimates using our four cities' police recruit exam scores. We begin by finding the total, between-group, and within-group sums of squares. Although we are interested primarily in the between-group and within-group comparison, we will also calculate the total sums of squares as a way of checking the accuracy of our other calculations. Then we divide by the degrees of freedom associated with each of the sums of squares in order to complete our two population variance estimates.

In Table 10.3, we have recorded the fictitious scores from our four city samples in the four columns headed y and most (though not all!) of the calculations needed to complete the ANOVA for our study.

For the total, between-group, and within-group sums of squares (Formulas 10.7, 10.8, and 10.9, which follow), we report two mathematically equivalent formulas for each. Remember, Formulas 10.8 and 10.9 will be formulas only for the sums of squares numerators in the two ratios of Formula 10.6. We will complete our calculations of the population variance estimates we need for our F statistic by identifying the appropriate denominators once we determine the numerators' sums of squares.

We will label the first of the two equivalent formulas as "a" and call it the easier-to-understand formula. It expresses the desired quantities in terms of sum of squares. (As you will see, we shouldn't confuse "easier to understand" with "easy" here; easier is obviously a relative term! Be thankful for computers!) The second formula, which we will label "b," is mathematically equivalent (within rounding error) to the first, but easier to use when calculating by hand. Another significant advantage of the easier-to-calculate formulas are that they involve less rounding and thus less distortion due to rounding error.

We express the step-by-step calculation instructions for each of the formulas in words, but we show the actual calculations only for the easier-to-calculate versions of the formulas. You can verify the mathematical equivalence (within rounding errors)

Table 10.3 Exam Scores (y) for Police Recruits in Four Cities and ANOVA-Related Calculations[a]

	City A (y_1)		City B (y_2)		City C (y_2)		City D (y_4)	
	1	2	3	4	5	6	7	8
	y_{i1}	y_{i1}^2	y_{i2}	y_{i2}^2	y_{i3}	y_{i3}^2	y_{i4}	y_{i4}^2
	18	324	18	324	31	961	15	225
	16	256	25	625	39	1,521	26	676
	30	900	22	484	17	289	19	361
	38	1,444	37	1,369	19	361	19	361
	22	484	40	1,600	23	529	21	441
	35	1,225	31	961	20	400	11	121
	19	361	40	1,600	26	676	13	169
	25	625	34	1,156	29	841	10	100
	33	1,089	28	784	22	484	26	676
			40	1,600	31	961	32	1,024
			36	1,296	21	441	28	784
			32	1,024	26	676		
Σy_{ik}	236		383		304		220	$\Sigma y_i = 1{,}143$
n_k	9		12		12		11	$N = 44$
$\bar{y}_{ik}$	26.2		31.9		25.3		20.0	
Σy_{ik}^2		6,708		12,823		8,140		4,938
								$\Sigma y_i^2 = 32{,}609$
$(\Sigma y_{ik})^2$	55,696		146,689		92,416		48,400	
$\dfrac{(\Sigma y_{ik})^2}{n_k}$	6,188.4		12,224.1		7,701.3		4,400.0	
Grand Mean	$\dfrac{\Sigma y_i}{N} = \dfrac{1{,}143}{44} = 25.98$						$\dfrac{(\Sigma y_i)^2}{N} = 29{,}692$	

a. The subscript i denotes an individual recruit's score, and k denotes a particular group ($k = 1$ through 4). So, y_{i1} stands for the individual's scores (i) in Group 1 (City A), for example.

of the formulas if you wish by doing the calculations both ways for any of the quantities that follow. To simplify matters a bit for illustrative purposes, we will also set aside our own previously stated general rule of rounding to the nearest three decimal places. Instead, we will round to just one decimal place. As we noted earlier, the double summation sign, as in $\Sigma\Sigma$, should be read "sum the sums of the following"; y_i is an individual's score regardless of the sample of which it is a part; y_{ik} is the score of an individual who is part of a particular sample (k); $\bar{y}_k$ is the mean of a particular sample; $\bar{Y}$ is the grand mean; n_k ($k = 1$ through 4) is the size of a particular sample; and N is the total number of observations in all four groups.

We begin our calculations of the sums of squares by recalling that

Total Sum of Squares (TSS) = Between-Group Sum of Squares (BSS) + Within-Group Sum of Squares (WSS)

To calculate the total sum of squares (TSS), we can use either of two mathematically equivalent formulas, Formulas 10.7a and 10.7b. Formula 10.7a makes clearer what we are doing theoretically; that is, we are calculating a sum of squared deviations of all of the individual's scores from all four groups from the grand mean. Formula 10.7b yields the same mathematical (again, within rounding error) result, but is easier to calculate.

$$\text{TSS} = \Sigma(\bar{Y} - y_i)^2 \qquad (10.7a) - \text{easier to understand}$$

Formula 10.7a in words:

To find the total sums of squares (TSS):

First, find the grand mean ($\bar{Y}$), which is given by $\Sigma y_i / N$ (i.e., add all the 44 individual scores [y_is] and divide by the total number of scores in all four groups [N; in our study, $N = 44$]).

Next, subtract each of the 44 individual scores (y_is) in all four groups from the grand mean ($\bar{Y}$).

Square each of these 44 differences.

Sum the 44 squared differences.

$$\text{TSS} = \Sigma y_i^2 - \frac{(\Sigma y_i)^2}{N} \qquad (10.7b) - \text{easier to calculate}$$

$$= 32,609 - \frac{(1,143)^2}{44}$$

$$= 32,609 - \frac{1,306,449}{44}$$

$$= 32,609 - 29,692$$

$$\text{TSS} = 2,917$$

Formula 10.7b in words:

To find the total sum of squares (TSS):

First, square each of the 44 individuals' scores in columns 2, 4, 6, and 8 in Table 10.3.

Sum those 44 squared scores.

That gives us Σy_i^2 in Formula 10.7b.

Next, sum the 44 individuals' scores in columns 1, 3, 5, and 7 in Table 10.3.

Square the result.

Divide that result by N, the total number of individuals in all four groups (44).

That gives us $(\Sigma y_i)^2/N$ in Formula 10.7b.

Subtract the latter from the former.

That gives us TSS (2,917) in Formula 10.7b.

For the between-group sum of squares (BSS), we have Formulas 10.8a and 10.8b. Formula 10.8a reflects more clearly what we are doing theoretically—calculating a sum of squared deviations, this time involving the four group means and the grand mean. In these calculations, we treat each individual's score in a particular group as if it were equivalent to that group's mean score. Accordingly, we find the deviation of each group mean from the grand mean, square this deviation, and multiply this deviation by the corresponding group size (n_k; k = 1 through 4). We then sum these four results.

$$BSS = n_1(\bar{Y} - \bar{y}_{i1})^2 + n_2(\bar{Y} - \bar{y}_{i2})^2 + n_3(\bar{Y} - \bar{y}_{i3})^2 + n_4(\bar{Y} - \bar{y}_{i4})^2$$

(10.8a) – easier to understand

Formula 10.8a in words:

To find the between-group sum of squares (BSS):

Find the grand mean ($\bar{Y}$).

Find the mean score for each of the four groups ($\bar{y}_{i1}$, $\bar{y}_{i2}$, etc.).

Subtract each of the four group means from the grand mean.

Square each of those four differences.

Multiply each of the four squared differences by its respective group size (n_1, n_2, etc.).

Sum these four results.

$$\text{BSS} = \Sigma \left[\frac{(\Sigma y_{ik})^2}{n_k} \right] - \frac{(\Sigma y_i)^2}{N} \qquad (10.8\text{b}) - \text{easier to calculate}$$

$$= \left[\frac{(236)^2}{9} + \frac{(383)^2}{12} + \frac{(304)^2}{12} + \frac{(220)^2}{11} \right] - \frac{(1{,}143)^2}{44}$$

$$= \left[\frac{55{,}696}{9} + \frac{146{,}689}{12} + \frac{92{,}416}{12} + \frac{48{,}400}{11} \right] - \frac{1{,}306{,}449}{44}$$

$$= (6{,}188.4 + 12{,}224.1 + 7{,}701.3 + 4{,}400) - 29{,}692$$

$$= 30{,}513.8 - 29{,}692$$

$$\text{BSS} = 821.8$$

Formula 10.8b in words:

To find the between-group sum of squares:

> First, sum the individuals' scores for each group separately in columns 1, 3, 5, and 7 in Table 10.3 (Σy_{i1}, Σy_{i2}, etc.).
>
> Square each of these four sums.
>
> Divide each of these four squared sums by its respective group size (n_1, n_2, etc.).
>
> Sum the four results.
>
> That gives us $\Sigma[(\Sigma y_{ik})^2/n_k]$ in Formula 10.8b.
>
> Next, sum the 44 individual scores in all four groups in columns 1, 3, 5, and 7.
>
> Square this sum.
>
> Divide the result by $N = 44$, the total number of scores in all four groups.
>
> That gives us $(\Sigma y_i)^2/N$ in Formula 10.8b.
>
> Subtract the latter from the former.
>
> That gives us BSS (821.8) in Formula 10.8b.

Because TSS = BSS + WSS, we can write WSS = TSS − BSS and calculate WSS from our results for TSS and BSS. Nevertheless, we will go through the steps of calculating WSS because it provides a good check on the accuracy of our other two calculations.

For the within-group sum of squares (WSS), we have Formulas 10.9a and 10.9b. The within-group sum of squares consists of a sum of the sums of squared deviations from means, this time the sum of the sum of squared deviations of the individual scores in each group from that group's mean.

$$\text{WSS} = \Sigma(\bar{y}_{i1} - y_{i1})^2 + \Sigma(\bar{y}_{i2} - y_{i2})^2 + \Sigma(\bar{y}_{i3} - y_{i3})^2 + \Sigma(\bar{y}_{i4} - y_{i4})^2 \quad (10.9a) - \text{easier to understand}$$

Formula 10.9a in words:

To find the within-group sum of squares:

> For each of the four groups separately, find the mean of the scores for that group.
>
> Subtract the individual scores in each group from its mean.
>
> Square these differences.
>
> Sum these squared differences for each of the four groups separately.
>
> Sum the four sums.

$$\text{WSS} = \Sigma y_i^2 - \Sigma \left[\frac{(\Sigma y_{ik})^2}{n_k} \right] \quad (10.9b) - \text{easier to calculate}$$

$$= 32{,}609 - (6{,}188.4 + 12{,}224.1 + 7{,}701.3 + 4{,}400.0)$$
$$= 32{,}609 - 30{,}513.8$$
$$= 2{,}095.2$$

Formula 10.9b in words:

To find the within-group sum of squares:

> First, square each of the 44 individual scores in columns 1, 3, 5, and 7 in Table 10.3 (as we have done in columns 2, 4, 6, and 8).
>
> Sum these 44 results.
>
> That gives us Σy_i^2 in Formula 10.9b.
>
> Next (see columns 1, 3, 5 and 7), sum the individual scores in each group separately.
>
> Square each of these four sums.
>
> Divide each of those sums by their respective group size (n_1, n_2, etc.).
>
> Sum the four results.
>
> That gives us $\Sigma[(\Sigma y_{ik})^2/n_k]$.
>
> (Note that this quantity is the same as the one calculated for BSS.)
>
> Subtract the latter from the former.
>
> That gives us WSS (2,095.2) in Formula 10.9b.

As a check on our calculations, note that the sum of the between-group sum of squares (821.8) and the within-group sum of squares (2,095.2) must equal the total sum of squares (2,917).

You might well say at this point: I thought we were testing for differences between means. What is all this stuff about sums of squares? It is a perfectly reasonable question. Our calculations do involve sums of squares. Remember, though, that under our null hypothesis, the between-group sum of squares in the numerator of our formula for F may be interpreted as a measure of the amount of variation among the means of our four groups. So, it is analogous to the difference between two means in the numerator of our formula for t. The within-group sum of squares, which is an estimate of the sampling distribution's sampling error, is analogous to the t formula denominator (see Formula 9.2, p. 292).

As we noted earlier, the variation of the group means around the grand mean includes, in addition to some random sampling error, the effects, if any, of our independent variable. For any given data set, the greater the difference between each of the sample group means and the grand mean, the larger the BSS. Because WSS = TSS − BSS, the larger the BSS, the smaller the WSS. This, in turn, makes BSS larger relative to WSS and yields a larger F. Hence, when we calculated the sums of squares, we were actually taking into account differences among means.

Now let's complete our calculations of the two estimates of the population variance assuming the null hypothesis is true by dividing each of the sums of squares (BSS and WSS) by the applicable degrees of freedom. In ANOVA, as we noted earlier, it is conventional to refer to the results of these divisions as mean squares. For the mean squares between, we have BSS/$(k-1)$ = 821.8/3 = 273.93. For the mean squares within, we have WSS/$(N-k)$ = 2,095.2/40 = 52.38. Thus, our two estimates of the population variance are 273.93 and 52.38.

Calculating F

Calculating F and comparing it with an applicable sampling distribution permits us to determine the probability that any *aggregate* or combined differences among the observed sample means is due to sampling error alone if the null hypothesis is true—that is, the probability that the samples were all drawn from the same population. The great advantage of this approach to testing for differences among means is that it is applicable with any number of samples (categories of the independent variable) and the corresponding sample means.

Now that we have values for the mean squares between and mean squares within for our city data, we can rewrite Formula 10.6 as Formula 10.10:

$$F = \frac{\text{Mean Squares Between}}{\text{Mean Squares Within}} = \frac{\frac{BSS}{k-1}}{\frac{WSS}{N-k}} \qquad (10.10)$$

So, using the results of our mean squares calculations and applying Formula 10.10, we have

$$F = 273.93/52.38 = 5.23$$

The Sampling Distributions for F

The ratio of the two population variance estimates derived from independent random samples (F) has known sampling distributions called **F distributions**. As with t distributions, there are many different sampling distributions of F. In the case of ANOVA, however, two different degrees of freedom must be considered simultaneously, which greatly multiplies the number of possible applicable F distributions. Tables of critical values for F at the .05 and .01 significance levels and for different combinations of degrees of freedom (dfs) are found in Appendix G on the study site (www.sagepub.com/fitzgerald). All F sampling distributions assume that y is normally distributed in the population(s) from which the samples are drawn and that the variances of y in the populations are equal (homoscedastic). F, in contrast with t, is always positive, and, for all practical purposes, F tests are one-tailed.

Figure 10.1 contains a few schematic examples of continuous F distributions. Note that as the two dfs increase, the distribution curve appears more like a normal curve. Note also that the distributions tend to peak at or near $F = 1.00$. In general, we are interested only in findings where the mean squares between is larger than the mean squares within, which would yield an $F \geq 1.00$. As in the Appendix G tables, most F distribution tables begin with $F = 1.00$.

Figure 10.1 Representations of Sampling Distributions for the F Statistic for Larger and Smaller Degrees of Freedom (Larger and Smaller Samples)

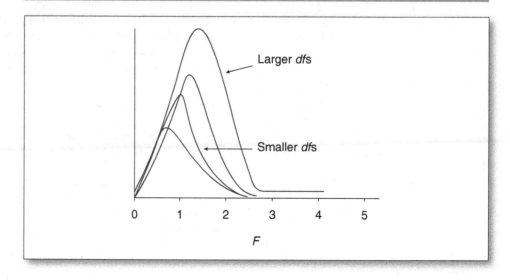

Using the F Tables

Our first task is to determine the significance level for our hypothesis test. Recall that the significance level is the probability of making a Type I error (i.e., rejecting a true null hypothesis). Usually, .05 or .01 is selected. Appendix G includes two F distribution tables, one for the .05 level of significance and one for the .01 level of significance.

To find the critical value of F for the significance level we have chosen, we first find the F table corresponding to the significance level we have selected. Then we locate the critical value of F in that table corresponding to the two dfs. The formula for $df\,1$ is $k - 1$, where k is the number of samples (groups) whose means are being compared. We find the table column corresponding to that df. The formula for $df\,2$ is $N - k$, where N is the total number of observations in all samples (groups). We find the table row corresponding to that df. The value of F where the column and row intersect is the critical value of F for our hypothesis test.

Recall that in Formula 10.6, the numerator is the between-group unbiased estimate of the population variance and the denominator is the within-group unbiased estimate of the population variance. Hence, only when that portion of the total variance around the grand mean ($\overline{Y}$) that can be attributed to (explained by) the independent variable (that is, the between-group variance) is larger than the portion that can be attributed to the within-group (unexplained) variance will we have reason to argue that the means differ significantly. That's why F tables typically include only values of F equal to or greater than 1. So we can restate the question before us as, How much larger than 1 should the F ratio be before we conclude that the observed differences among the means for the dependent variable are unlikely to have occurred by chance?

In general, if the F we calculate is smaller than the critical value in the table, we accept the null hypothesis that there are no significant differences among the means. If the F we calculate is as large or larger than the critical value from the table, we may reject the null hypothesis that the population means are equal, leaving us with our alternative or research hypothesis that the populations' means do differ, and that the independent variable (city) does have some effect on the dependent variable (exam scores).

Suppose we chose a significance level of .01. To find the critical value of F, we would locate the .01 F table, go to the column $k - 1 = 3$, and proceed down this column to the row corresponding to $N - k = 40$. The entry in the cell ($F = 4.31$) is the critical value of F for our study. Because the F in our study (5.23) exceeds the critical value, we can reject the null hypothesis at the .01 level of significance.

Presenting ANOVA Results

The results of an analysis of variance are presented in research reports in a variety of forms. A common one is illustrated in Table 10.4, using data from our study for illustrative purposes.

Table 10.4 ANOVA Summary

Source of Variation	Sums of Squares	Degrees of Freedom	Mean Squares	F
Between SS (treatment)	821.8	$k - 1 = 3$	273.9	5.23
Within SS (error)	2,095.2	$N - k = 40$	52.4	$p < .01$
Total SS	2,917.0	$N - 1 = 43$		

The analysis we have just completed is called a **one-way analysis of variance**. "One-way" refers to the fact that only one nominal-level independent variable (in our example, city) has been used to analyze the values of an interval or ratio dependent variable y. ANOVA for independent random samples can be extended to research situations where two or more nominal independent variables are used simultaneously. For example, we might have included data on recruits' genders, as well as city, as possible independent variables and conducted a **two-way analysis of variance**. Although beyond our scope here, discussions of these procedures may be found in advanced statistics texts. Versions of ANOVA for dependent random samples and procedures for calculating confidence limits are also available, but beyond the scope of this text.

Follow-Up Analysis After a Significant F

It is important to remember that ANOVA is a test of the *aggregate* (total combined) effect of the independent variable on the dependent variable. It tells us whether or not there is a statistically significant difference among the means, considering all the means at once. As we noted at the beginning of our discussion, ANOVA is preferable to a series of *t* tests at the initial stage of analysis because it does in one test of statistical significance what would require several *t* tests to accomplish, thereby reducing the likelihood of a Type I error, rejecting a null hypothesis that is true.

A statistically significant *F* often means that the difference between at least one pair of the means included in the analysis is statistically significant. However, it is possible to have a significant aggregate difference without having a significant difference between any two of the means. In any event, to complete and properly interpret the results of the analysis, the difference between each of the logically possible pairs of means must be examined to determine if it is statistically significant.

Recall that statisticians tell us several procedures are superior to the multiple *t* test strategy as followups to a significant *F*. These procedures generally result in fewer significance tests being run, and they take into account the fact that the comparison of any two means is taking place in a larger context involving other means as well. Most are quite complex, however, and beyond the scope of this text. We consider the basics of only one approach here, often referred to as Tukey's HSD (honestly significant difference) test.

Tukey's HSD Test

Tukey's HSD test can be viewed as a modification of one version of the *t* test. Like the *t* test for independent random samples, it can be used to compare two of the three or more means included in the analysis at a time. It does this by identifying the *minimal* difference between any two of the means that must be observed for a specified significance level. It assumes homoscedasticity (that is, equal variances of the dependent variable *y* in the population[s]) and normal distributions of *y* in the populations, at least for small samples. The formula for the HSD test varies depending on a number of factors, including whether the sample sizes are equal or unequal. We will confine ourselves here to a discussion of research situations in which the samples are all the same size.

We will spare you the details and just illustrate one way of using the basic ideas underlying the HSD test. The goal is to determine how large the difference between two means must be to be statistically significant. This is the difference referred to as an honestly significant difference (HSD).

The HSD test is based on a quantity, often symbolized as **Q**, whose distribution is related to the *t* distribution. The general formula for HSD *assuming sample sizes are equal* is given in Formula 10.11. (Note that in our four-city exam scores example, the samples are not of equal size so Formula 10.11 would have to be modified. Such modifications are available, but beyond the scope of this text.)

$$\text{HSD} = Q \sqrt{\frac{\text{WSS}}{n_{ps}}} \qquad (10.11)$$

HSD is calculated using Q, which is derived from a Q table (see Appendix H on the study site: **www.sagepub.com/fitzgerald**), and data from the ANOVA, including the within-group sum of squares (WSS), as well as sample size. The n_{ps} in this formula is the size of *one* of the equal-sized samples ($n_{\text{per sample}}$). Note that the WSS term in the formula refers to the within-group sums of squares from all of the samples included in the ANOVA analysis. The WSS in the formula ensures that some of the data from all of the samples included in the ANOVA are included in the HSD analysis, making HSD analysis preferable to a series of *t* tests.

The sampling distributions of Q vary depending on the number of samples included in the ANOVA analysis (symbolized as *k*) and the degrees of freedom for the WSS in the ANOVA analysis. To use the Q tables in Appendix H, we need to decide on a level of statistical significance. The Q tables in Appendix H are for a .01 or a .05 level of significance. We also need to know *k*, the total number of samples (and sample means) compared in the ANOVA analysis, and the degrees of freedom associated with WSS in the ANOVA analysis.

Suppose there are six equal-sized samples (*k* = 6) in an original ANOVA study, the WSS was 215, degrees of freedom for WSS was 15, and we have decided on a .05 level of significance. Consulting the Q distribution table for the .05 level of significance in

Appendix H, we locate the k value of six across the top and the degrees of freedom value of 15 down the left column. Looking at the values in each table where the corresponding row and column intersect, we find the critical value of Q = 4.59. Substituting these values in Formula 10.11, we have

$$HSD = Q\sqrt{\frac{WSS}{n_{ps}}}$$

$$= 4.59\sqrt{\frac{215}{6}}$$

$$= 4.59\sqrt{35.8333}$$

$$= (4.59)(5.986)$$

$$= 27.476$$

So, in this case, the minimum difference between the means necessary for statistical significance at the .05 level is about 27.5. The observed differences between the possible pairs of means included in the ANOVA analysis can be compared with this minimum difference to determine which of them, if any, are significantly different at the .05 level.

The From the Literature Box 10.1 includes excerpts from a report on a research project that used analysis of variance (ANOVA) and Tukey's HSD Test in the data analysis.

From the Literature Box 10.1

Brad Smith and colleagues were interested in how different types of criminal justice officials (police, prosecutors, defense attorneys, and judges) viewed who was responsible and what went awry when people were wrongfully convicted of criminal offenses. The researchers created scales that measured the officials' perceptions of the extent to which certain kinds of errors were made by different criminal justice officials. The scales ranged from 1 (never make this error) to 9 (always make this error). They calculated mean scores for each type of criminal justice official for each error and used ANOVA to test for differences among the mean scores for the four types of criminal justice officials. When they found a statistically significant F, they used Tukey's HSD Test to compare differences between pairs of means and determine which differences were statistically significant. The following reprinted table displays some of the analyses and results.

Perceptions of Defense Attorney and Judicial Error (Mean Responses)

Type of Error	Police	Prosecutors	Defense Attorneys	Judges	Statistics
Defense attorney error					
Not adequately challenging witnesses	3.37[a]	3.05[b]	5.13[ab]	4.18[ab]	$F(3,459) = 48.39$, $p = .000$
Unwarranted plea bargaining concessions	3.74[a]	3.00[b]	5.01[ab]	3.93[b]	$F(3,459) = 24.76$, $p = .000$
Failing to file proper motions	3.67[a]	3.55[b]	5.35[ab]	4.40[ab]	$F(3,459) = 43.78$, $p = .000$
Not adequately challenging forensic evidence	3.46[a]	3.05[b]	5.77[ab]	4.42[ab]	$F(3,459) = 71.40$, $p = .000$
Inadequate investigation	4.19[a]	3.86[b]	5.79[ab]	4.89[ab]	$F(3,457) = 37.68$, $p = .000$
Judicial error					
Admissibility of eyewitness testimony	2.70[a]	2.35[b]	4.68[abc]	2.71[c]	$F(3,459) = 88.32$, $p = .000$
Judicial bias	2.69[a]	2.74[b]	4.97[abc]	2.65[c]	$F(3,459) = 81.29$, $p = .000$
Admissibility of physical evidence	2.72[a]	2.87[b]	4.67[abc]	2.99[c]	$F(3,459) = 88.12$, $p = .000$
Admissibility of expert testimony	2.61[a]	2.78[b]	4.83[abc]	3.09[c]	$F(3.459) = 87.62$, $p = .000$

Note: Mean values that share common row superscripts are significantly different ($p < .05$) in pairwise comparisons using Tukey's procedures.

Source: From Smith, B., Zalman, M., & Kiger, A. (2011). How justice system officials view wrongful convictions. *Crime and Delinquency, 57,* 663-685. Retrieved May 23, 2012, from http://cad.sagepub.com/content/57/5/663. Reprinted with permission.

The Relationship Between *F* and *t*

As you might imagine, there is a relationship between t and F for two sample cases, the only circumstances in which they are directly comparable. In a two-sample case, if you calculate both statistics, you will find that $F = t^2$. Note that F cannot be negative, and squaring t takes care of the possibility that t may be negative.

Assumptions and Cautions

The version of ANOVA we have described in this chapter assumes independent random samples for each value of the independent variable and is most appropriately used when the independent variable is measured at the nominal or ordinal level. The dependent variable must be measured at the interval or ratio level. In general, especially when samples are small or very uneven in size, an approximately normal distribution of the dependent variable in the population(s) as well as homoscedasticity must be assumed. For larger samples of about equal size, the assumptions of homoscedasticity and a normally distributed dependent variable in the population may be relaxed.

Some words of caution about interpreting levels of significance are again in order. As we noted in Chapter 8, significance levels tell us the probability of obtaining a particular result or range of results (for example, differences between or among means) by chance when we draw random samples from a population. They do *not* tell us whether any *particular* sample statistic is the result of chance or nonchance factors.

Furthermore, statistical significance levels should not be confused either with the strength of relationships between or among variables or with practical significance. The other cautions regarding statistical tests and garbage in-garbage out, as well as the difference between statistical and practical significance, apply to ANOVA, too.

Summary

ANOVA is applied when more than two means from random samples are being compared. The sampling distributions for F differ depending on degrees of freedom and two different degrees of freedom must be taken into account simultaneously. The formula for ANOVA we presented here applies when the random samples are independent and, for small samples, when the dependent variable is normally distributed in the population and the assumption of homoscedasticity is justified. Modifications of the formulas are available in more advanced texts for use in studies involving dependent random samples, as well as for assumptions other than those we used. ANOVA is applied when dependent variables are measured at the interval or ratio level and independent variables are usually measured at the nominal level. If the independent variable is measured at the ordinal, interval, or ratio level, more powerful statistical tests for assessing relationships between or among variables, such as correlation analysis, should be used. We describe some of these procedures in the next chapter.

A statistically significant F should be followed up by a search for which, if any, pairs of means included in the ANOVA differ significantly. Several procedures for identifying the pairs of means are available, and one of the more commonly applied is Tukey's HSD test. Statisticians strongly recommend Tukey's HSD test or other similar procedures for following up on a significant F instead of a series of t-test comparisons for the logically possible pairs of means.

Concepts to Master

Analysis of variance (ANOVA)

Between-group sum of squares (BSS)

Between-group variance

Effect (in ANOVA)

Error (in ANOVA)

Explained sum of squares

Explained variance

F distributions

F statistic (in ANOVA)

Grand mean

Mean squares between

Mean squares within

One-way analysis of variance (ANOVA)

Q

Total sum of squares (TSS)

Total variance

Tukey's HSD test

Two-way analysis of variance

Unexplained sum of squares

Unexplained variance

Within-group sum of squares (WSS)

Within-group variance

Review Questions

1. Compare and contrast the t test and ANOVA.
2. What is the basic objective of one-way analysis of variance (ANOVA)?
3. What is the basic formula for ANOVA?
4. On what general assumptions is ANOVA based, and for what research situations is it appropriate?
5. Define, compare, and contrast total variance, between-group variance, and within-group variance.
6. Define, compare, and contrast total sum of squares, between-group sum of squares, and within-group sum of squares in ANOVA.
7. What are explained and unexplained variances? In what sense are they explained or unexplained?
8. Compare and contrast mean squares between and mean squares within.

9. What is the numerator in the ANOVA F ratio? What is the denominator?
10. How are the differences among group (sample) means reflected in the F ratio?
11. Describe the sampling distributions for F.
12. What basic information should be included in a report on the results of an analysis of variance?
13. What is Tukey's HSD test? What is its purpose? When is it used? What can it tell you?
14. Why is Tukey's HSD test preferable to a series of t tests?
15. What is the relationship between t and F in two-sample cases?
16. Define all the terms in the "Concepts to Master" list and use each in three sentences.
17. If you haven't already done so, answer all the questions in the "Pause, Think, and Explore" boxes.

Exercises and Discussion Questions

1. Can you think of other ways of comparing the exam scores from the four city recruit groups? (Hint: think measures of central tendency and dispersion.)
2. Formulate three research hypotheses and their corresponding null hypotheses for which ANOVA would be appropriate. Discuss why ANOVA would be an appropriate test for these hypotheses.
3. Discuss why in ANOVA the between-group variance is said to be explained and the within-group variance is said to be unexplained.
4. Below are six calculated values of F and the corresponding dfs for ANOVA tests of significance. Would any of them be statistically significant? If they are, at what level(s) would each be significant?

F Value	$df1$	$df2$
2.55	5	29
2.55	40	10
1.00	∞	∞
99.00	1	2
12.00	60	4
12.00	4	60

5. Discuss what you have learned about the sampling distributions for F from completing Exercise 4.

6. Suppose you have developed two new marksmanship training programs for law enforcement or correctional officers and you wish to know which, if either, achieves better results compared with the current training program. You select a group of new officers and randomly assign each person to one of three conditions: current training program, new Training Program A, and new Training Program B. You score each person for marksmanship before the training, provide each group its training program, and score their marksmanship after the training. You record the following marksmanship scores (higher is better):

Group 1 ($n = 6$) Current Training Marksmanship Scores		Group 2 ($n = 6$) Training Program A Marksmanship Scores		Group 3 ($n = 6$) Training Program B Marksmanship Scores	
Before	After	Before	After	Before	After
5	6	3	5	1	3
3	5	2	4	6	5
7	6	5	6	3	4
4	5	1	3	3	5
2	4	6	4	2	5
1	2	5	7	4	7

Describe the ANOVA that you think best captures whether there are any differences in the effectiveness of the different training programs. Describe what data you have chosen to include in your analysis and discuss why you have chosen those data. Perform an ANOVA using the data you have selected to determine if there are any differences in the effects of the different training programs on marksmanship. Describe what level of significance you would choose and why. What are the degrees of freedom? What is the critical value? Describe and interpret the results of your analysis. Is your test statistically significant? Discuss what your results mean and what they don't mean. Are there other ANOVA tests that you could run? What would be the next best ANOVA to detect any differences in the effectiveness of the training programs? Could you conduct an ANOVA on D scores? What D scores would you use?

7. Perform a Tukey's HSD test on the data in Exercise 6. Describe your procedures and interpret your results.

8. Discuss the data in the table in the From the Literature Box 10.1. Why was ANOVA chosen for this analysis? Are the differences among the mean scores what you expect? What means were

compared in each ANOVA? Are the data ratio level? Why or why not? Do the very low probabilities for the F statistics indicate a strong relationship between type of official and perception of error on the part of defense attorneys and judges? Why or why not? Why do you suppose defense attorneys are more critical of defense attorneys and judges than are the other types of criminal justice officials? Should they be? Why was Tukey's HSD test used instead of t tests as a follow-up when ANOVA was statistically significant?

Student Study Site

Visit the open-access student study site at **www.sagepub.com/fitzgerald** for access to several study tools including eFlashcards, web quizzes, and additional appendices as well as links to SAGE journal articles and audio, video and web resources.

Bivariate Linear Regression and Correlation and Linear Partial Regression and Correlation

Learning Objectives

What you are expected not only to learn but to master in this chapter:

- The basic ideas underlying linear correlation and regression analysis
- What a scattergram is and how to construct one
- What a best fitting regression line and a best fitting linear equation are
- What the constants a and b in a linear regression equation represent and how to calculate them
- What positive, negative, and no relationships between two variables mean in regression and correlation analysis
- The difference between linear and nonlinear relationships

- What standardized betas (βs) are and why they are useful in statistical analysis
- What can go wrong when using linear regression equations for predictions
- The similarities and differences between linear regression and correlation analyses
- What a correlation matrix is and how to read one
- Why outliers are a problem in linear correlation and regression analysis
- How Pearson's correlation coefficient r and coefficient of determination r^2 are calculated and what they mean
- The relationship between r and b
- The relationship between correlation and cross-tabulation
- Tests of statistical significance for r and b
- What linear partial regression and partial correlation analysis are and their relationship to elaboration analysis
- The relationships among Pearson's correlation coefficient r, regression analysis, and analysis of variance
- Assumptions and cautions to be observed when using linear regression and correlation analysis

Introduction

Is there a relationship between traffic officers' salaries and number of traffic citations issued? Is there a relationship between the number of property offenses in neighborhoods and the frequency of police officer patrols? Is there a relationship between number of years on the bench and length of sentence for felony assault? Is there a relationship between population density of urban blocks and number of drug offenses? Is inmate density related to number of inmate incidents? Is the length of time between arraignment and trial start related to length of sentence for those convicted? How strong are these relationships? How much do crime rates change for every $10,000 added to the police department's budget? How much will the speed of cases coming to trial change for every $10,000 added to the court budget? The statistical analyses we consider in this chapter can often help answer questions like these.

In this chapter, we discuss some forms of bivariate and multivariate analysis when all independent and dependent variables are measured at the interval or ratio level. When variables are measured at these levels, variable relationships are usually examined through statistical procedures called correlation and regression analysis.

To better understand what these analyses entail, we first consider some new ways of graphing data and introduce the general idea of correlation between two variables. Because we think the details are a little easier to understand, we discuss bivariate regression analysis first and then turn to a consideration of bivariate correlation. Included in the discussion are tests of significance for the relevant sample statistics.

The introduction of a third variable into the analysis leads to a description of partial regression and partial correlation analyses. As their names suggest, these analyses have parallels with the partial tables in elaboration analysis as discussed in Chapter 8.

As usual, we need a number of new symbols to facilitate our discussion of these procedures. Table 11.1 lists them and provides brief definitions for your reference as you read through this chapter.

The Basic Ideas Underlying Linear Correlation and (Regression) Analyses

Both correlation and regression analyses are based on what should now be the familiar idea of sums of squares, this time focusing on minimizing these measures of difference or deviation. They differ in the particular kinds of research question for which they are appropriate. Correlation analysis measures the strength of the relationship between two or more variables. Regression analysis focuses on predicting the values of a dependent variable from the values of one or more independent variables.

The general idea of correlation is relatively simple. Variables are correlated if their values tend to change together. If the number of police officers in a large city (our independent variable x) goes up each year for 10 years, for example, and the burglary

Table 11.1 Symbols and Their Definitions in Regression, Correlation, Partial Regression, and Partial Correlation

a	The y intercept in a linear least squares regression equation
b	Beta—the slope of a linear least squares regression line; the amount of change in y for every unit change in x in a linear equation
b^*	Standardized beta (beta weight)
r	The coefficient of correlation (or the correlation coefficient)
r^2	The coefficient of determination
x,y	The coordinates of a data point in a scattergram
$y.x$	The regression of y on x
$x.y$	The regression of x on y
$b_{y.x}$	The regression coefficient (beta or slope of the regression line) for $y.x$
$b_{x.y}$	The regression coefficient (beta or slope of the regression line) for $x.y$
$r_{xy.T}$	The correlation between x and y, controlling for T; the partial correlation of x and y, taking T into account

rate (our dependent variable *y*) goes down each year for the same time period, we say the two variables are correlated; that is, their values change together. In this case, they change in opposite directions. If we had the relevant data, we could do a correlation analysis to see how strong the relationship is. If this analysis indicates a relatively strong linear relationship (more about these terms later) between the variables, the researcher might then proceed to a regression analysis.

The objectives of regression analysis are also pretty straightforward. They are to predict the values of *y* from the values of *x* and also specify how much *y* (in our example, burglary rate) typically changes for every unit of change in *x* (in our example, the addition of one police officer).

First, however, to facilitate the understanding of both procedures, we introduce a new kind of graph and discuss both data points and straight lines within the graph.

Scattergrams

Suppose we have two continuous ratio-level variables for each of a group of 35 cities, such as expenditure on police services and the crime rate for a particular year. One could argue that either of these variables could serve as the independent variable, but suppose our research hypothesis is that larger expenditures on police services (our independent variable *x*) will be associated with higher crime rates (our dependent variable *y*). We are interested in examining the data from our 35 cities to see if there is a relationship between these two variables.

We create a graph with perpendicular axes, much as we did for constructing a line graph frequency distribution. As before, we array the possible values of the independent variable *x* along the horizontal axis. This time, however, instead of putting possible frequencies for our *x* variable along the vertical axis, we put the possible values of the dependent variable *y* along it. The point in the graph at which the two perpendicular axes cross is designated as zero for both variables. We will make one other important change in constructing our graphic space. The axes cross each other, extending beyond the point of intersection both horizontally and vertically, allowing for positive and negative values of each of the two variables. We'll call the horizontal axis along which the possible *x* values are arrayed the **x axis** and the vertical axis along which the possible *y* values are arrayed the **y axis**. We could then locate each city in our study group on this graph by placing a dot where its scores on variables *x* and *y* intersect. To simplify our illustrations, we will reduce our variables (police expenditures and crime rates) to ratio-level scores ranging from 0 to 11.

The precise location of each dot in the graphic space is determined as follows. Suppose City A scored 4 on variable *x* (police expenditures) and 6 on variable *y* (crime rate). We would draw an imaginary line perpendicular to the *x* axis at the point corresponding to a score of 4 on variable *x* and a line perpendicular to the *y* axis corresponding to a score of 6 on variable *y*. At the point where these two perpendicular lines intersect, we place a dot (see Figure 11.1). This dot, called a **data point,** is said to have **coordinates** with the independent variable listed first and written as (x,y)—in this case (4,6). If we plotted the paired scores for each of the 35 cities on our graph, the result would be a graph space with 35 data points representing the intersection of the paired scores for each city on our two variables. This kind of graph is called a **scattergram**, and sometimes a scatterplot or a bivariate distribution. Here, we will use the term *scattergram*.

Straight Lines in Scattergrams

Now suppose that we add another data point with coordinates (5,7.5) representing City B, to the graph in Figure 11.1. With two data points in the graph, we can draw a straight line that passes through the two data points, as illustrated in Figure 11.2.

Let's consider the line in Figure 11.2 for a few moments. Any straight line in this kind of graph can be described by an equation of the general form indicated in Formula 11.1:

$$y = a + bx \tag{11.1}$$

This equation says that the values of variable y are determined by the values of two constants (a and b) and another variable, x. Note that any of these values may be positive or negative.

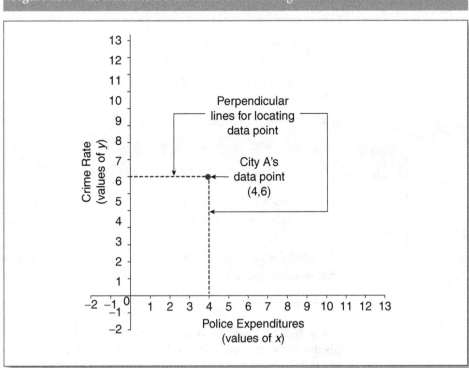

Figure 11.1 Location of a Data Point in a Scattergram

Figure 11.2 A Scattergram Showing the Location of Two Data Points and a Straight Line Passing Through Them

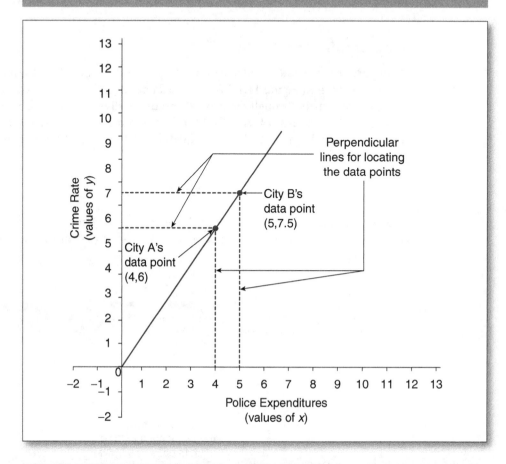

PAUSE, THINK, AND EXPLORE $y = a + bx$

Can you think of uses for this equation? If we know the value of x at a point on the line, could we determine the value of y at the same point on the line? What else would we need to know to do so? Try solving the equation for x. If $a = 0$, what would y equal? If $b = 0$, what would y equal? If $x = 0$, what would y equal? If $y = 0$, what would x equal?

What does it mean to say the formula describes a line? We might approach answers to this question in a number of different ways. For one thing, it means that once we specify the values of a and b in the equation, we can draw a *unique* line in the graph corresponding to those values. We discuss how this is done a little later. It also means that, once we have specified the values of *a* and *b* and drawn our line, we can determine the value of *y* associated with any particular value of *x* (or vice versa) *if the data point lies on the straight line.*

What are the values of the constants for our particular line? Determining the value of **a** for our straight line (and any other straight line) is relatively easy, at least in mathematical terms. All we need to do is play with Formula 11.1 a bit. If $x = 0$, the point on the *x* axis at which the axes in our graph intersect, then $bx = 0$ and $y = a$. So, for any straight line, the value of *a* is the point where the line crosses the *y* axis. For this reason, *a* is referred to as the **y intercept**. We'll find an exact quantitative value of *a* for our particular line shortly.

The constant *b* is referred to as the slope of the line. Consider Figure 11.3. The **slope** of a line is defined as the number of units of change in one (usually the dependent) variable for each one unit of change in the other (usually the independent) variable.

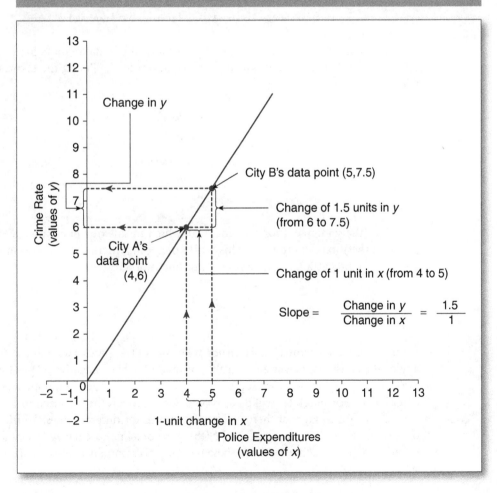

Figure 11.3 A Scattergram Showing the Interpretation of the Slope of a Graph Line

Suppose we move one unit on the x axis (say, from $x = 4$ to $x = 5$), draw two imaginary lines perpendicular to the x axis at these two points, and mark the points where these perpendicular lines and our graph line intersect. Next, we draw two imaginary lines perpendicular to the y axis so that they intersect our graph line at the same two points where our lines from the x axis intersect our graph line. Then, we measure the distance between the two points where these lines intersect the y axis. That would give us the value of b, the number of units of change on the vertical y axis for every one unit of change on the x axis. In our example, as the value of x moved one unit—say, from 4 to 5—y moved 1.5 units (from 6 to 7.5). If we repeated this exercise for x moving from 2 to 3 or from 6 to 7, for example, we would find the same 1.5-unit change in y in each case. This relationship of 1.5 units of change in y for every unit of change in x would hold for *any* one-unit change in the value of x we would care to specify, so long as the data points lie on the line.

In the most general terms, we can express the slope of any straight line in the graph as a ratio of the change in y over the change in x, as in Formula 11.2.

$$\text{slope} = b = \text{change in } y/\text{change in } x$$
$$\text{In the case of our particular line, } b = 1.5/1 = 1.5. \tag{11.2}$$

We can now substitute the coordinates of any of our data points for x and y and 1.5 for b into Formula 11.1 and solve the equation for a. Taking the coordinates for City A (4, 6), we would have

$$y = a + bx$$
$$a = y - bx$$
$$a = 6 - 1.5(4)$$
$$a = 6 - 6$$
$$a = 0$$

So a (the y intercept for our line) = 0, which means our line passes through the point on the y axis where $y = 0$. This is also the point where the two axes intersect, as Figure 11.3 indicates. The equation for our line is now:

$$y = a + bx$$
$$y = 0 + 1.5x$$

Let's note a few more characteristics of Formula 11.1. First, as we pointed out before, any of the constants or variables in the formula may have negative or positive values. We'll discuss what a negative slope (i.e., $-b$) is a little later. Second, not all graph lines described by Formula 11.1 will pass, as ours does, through the intersection of the x and y axes, which is to say that there will be different *a*s for different lines. Third, note that once we know a (the y intercept) and b (the slope of a line), we have all the information we need to draw the line. In short, these two factors essentially determine the line.

We can now use the equation to find any *y* corresponding to any *x* (or vice versa) in our data set if the data point lies on the straight line described by our formula. All we need to do, for example, is plug a specific value of *x* into Formula 11.1 and solve it for *y*.

With our knowledge of data points, scattergrams, and straight lines and their slopes in mind, we turn now to a discussion of regression analysis.

Linear Bivariate Regression Analysis

As you can readily imagine, we rarely come across a data set where every data point lies exactly on a straight line in the graphic space. The data points for our cities data set would be very unlikely to do so. Instead, we would probably find that the data points were at least somewhat scattered about in the graph.

Suppose that when we constructed the scattergram for our fictitious cities data set, it looked like the one in Figure 11.4. Although the data points certainly don't all lie on a straight line, there is a discernable pattern in the way they are distributed in the graph. In general, we can say that the pattern flows from the lower left-hand corner to the upper right-hand corner of the graph. The data points in the lower left area of the graph represent cities with lower levels of expenditures on police and lower crime rates. Those in the upper right area reflect cities with higher police expenditures and higher crime rates. In general, then, we could say that as the values of *x* (police expenditures) increase, so also do the values of *y* (crime rates). At first glance, this is not a result either the police or citizens would likely find pleasing. Even so, can you think of why the data might indicate such a relationship? And if it did, would you say the apparent relationship might be spurious? In any event, just keep in mind that these are fictitious data we're using for illustrative purposes. We'll use some other equally fictitious examples a little later.

Remember that one of the general objectives of **regression analysis** is predicting the values of a dependent variable (*y*) from the values of an independent variable (*x*). In order to make these predictions, we will use a straight line like the one we just discussed. When used in regression analysis, the line is called a **regression line,** and the equation for the line is called the **regression equation.** The regression line is used to approximate the pattern of data points in the scattergram and the regression equation is used to calculate estimates of the values of *y* from those of *x*.

Once we have a regression line and equation for our data, we can use it to make predictions of *y* from *x* in the following way. We begin with a value of *x* (the *x* coordinate of one of our data points). We erect a line perpendicular to the *x* axis at that value of *x*, extending upward to the regression line. We then find the *y* value (coordinate) that corresponds to that point on the regression line by erecting a line perpendicular to the *y* axis that passes through this point. The point at which this line intersects with the *y* axis is our predicted value of *y* for the value of *x* with which we began. (Is this beginning to sound familiar?) When the data points don't lie exactly on the line, which will be the case almost all of the time, our prediction will be in error to some extent. Nevertheless, we want a regression line that best approximates the data points and we want a regression equation that does the best job of predicting the values of *y* from the values of *x*.

Figure 11.4 Scattergram Showing Data Points for 35 Cities

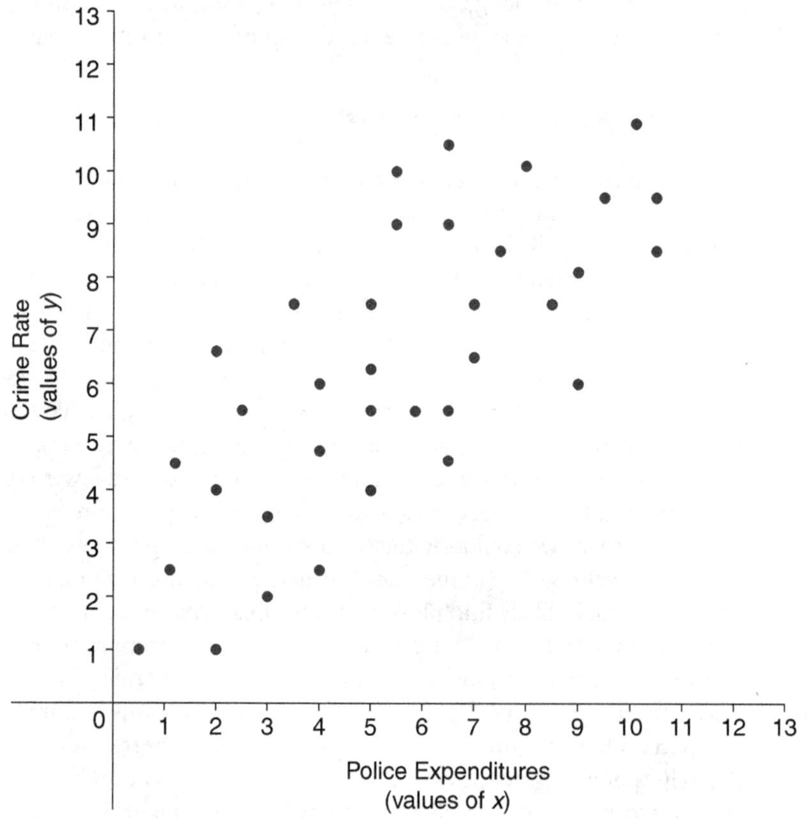

A regression line in a scattergram (bivariate distribution) is analogous to the mean in a univariate frequency distribution. Each is, in a statistically important way, the best representative of the data in the distribution. The mean best represents a univariate distribution because, as we have noted before, its value minimizes the difference between it and the scores in the distribution. Similarly, we can establish a precise criterion that the straight regression line must satisfy. *The straight line that best represents the data points, referred to as* **the best fitting line**, *is the one that minimizes the sum of the distances between it and those data points.* The equation for this line is the one that minimizes the error when we predict y from x. To know whether the regression line and equation meet the minimization of error criterion, of course, we need to measure the distance between each data point and the line.

Before we can measure, though, we have to resolve a dilemma. The alert reader may recognize that there are at least three ways of measuring this distance. It may be measured perpendicular to the x axis (and parallel to the y axis), perpendicular to the y axis (and parallel to the x axis), or perpendicular to the regression line itself. Each of these ways of measuring has its uses in data analysis. For now, we will focus on the way of measuring most appropriate for our regression analysis purposes, which you will recall is predicting the values of y on the basis of the values of x.

For regression purposes, it makes the most sense to measure the distance perpendicular to the x axis and parallel to the y axis. After all, it is the distance along the y axis that represents the difference between two values of y: the value of y we predict from a particular value of x using the best fitting line and the value of y corresponding with that x we observe in our data set. The difference between the observed and predicted values of y is referred to as the **residual** or **error of estimate**, as indicated in Figure 11.5. For the purpose of regression analysis, then, the best fitting regression line minimizes the errors of estimate. To reflect the fact that using the regression line and equation to predict the values of y from the values of x is likely to be in error, we can revise Formula 11.1 and write Formula 11.3.

$$y = a + bx + \text{error of estimate} \qquad (11.3)$$

Figure 11.5 Scattergram Showing a Data Point, a Regression Line, and a Residual or Error of Estimate

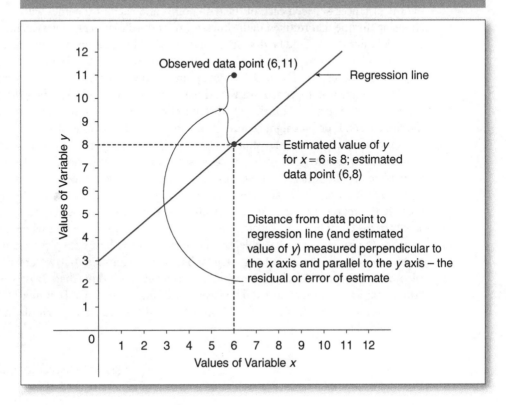

As in Formula 11.1, the formula for any particular linear (straight) regression line will include a and b as constants and x and y as variables. Here also, a, b, x, and y can have either positive or negative values. As we discovered earlier, the constant a is the y intercept of our regression line. Also as before, b is the slope of a straight line, but this time it is the slope of a straight regression line. In the context of regression analysis, b is referred to as **beta** or as the **regression coefficient.**

The slope of a regression line (b or beta) indicates the amount of change in y for every unit change in x. The quantitative size of the beta indicates the steepness of the slope—that is, the speed or pace at which y is changing with respect to x. Like the line itself, beta is an approximation (estimate) of the amount of change in y for a unit change in x because not all the data points lie on the regression line.

Calculating the Best Fitting (Regression) Line Constants *a* and *b*

How do we determine the numerical value of the constants a and b in the equation for the best fitting regression line? We could do it just by eyeballing the pattern of data points and making our best guess about the line that would minimize these differences, noting its y intercept and calculating its slope. As you will no doubt recognize, this would be an imprecise procedure at best. We could also take a more empirical, trial-and-error approach. We might draw a number of straight lines in the field of data points, measuring the distances between each of the data points and each of the lines with a ruler and choosing the line that resulted in the lowest sum of the differences. However, the number of straight lines that could be drawn and tested using this procedure would be large, and we would likely become cross-eyed in our attempts to measure the distances. Imagine the difficulties if there were 200 or 2,000 data points in the scattergram. Even if we pursued this more empirical approach, we would never know if we had identified *the* line that meets the criterion of minimizing the distances between it and the data points. Adjusting the slope just a little bit might reduce the errors in our predictions of y.

Once again, however, statisticians come to the rescue, employing what is called the **least (sum of) squares** or **ordinary least squares** (OLS) criterion. The least squares referred to are the squared differences between the observed y coordinates of the data points and the predicted values of y using the regression equation. The objective is to identify the regression equation that minimizes the sum of these squared deviations. The proof is complicated. For our purposes, we will simply note that when x is designated as the independent variable, the slope ($b_{y.x}$) of the best fitting regression line is given by Formula 11.4a or 11.4b. The subscript y.x signifies that we are predicting y from x, or, alternatively, we are regressing y on x. As we did in Chapter 10, we present both an easier-to-understand and an easier-to-calculate formula. Formula 11.4a is the easier-to-understand formula and 11.4b is the easier-to-calculate formula, if you are working by hand.

$$b_{y.x} = \frac{\Sigma(x-\bar{x})(y-\bar{y})}{\Sigma(x-\bar{x})^2} \qquad (11.4a) - \text{easier to understand}$$

$$b_{y \cdot x} = \frac{\Sigma xy - \frac{(\Sigma x)(\Sigma y)}{n}}{\Sigma x^2 - \frac{(\Sigma x)^2}{n}} \qquad (11.4b) \text{ – easier to calculate}$$

Remember that each data point has an x and a y coordinate. To calculate the numerator in Formula 11.4a, for each data point we first subtract the mean of x ($\bar{x}$) from the x coordinate for a given data point. Then we subtract the mean of y ($\bar{y}$) from the y coordinate for the same data point. The results of these two subtractions are multiplied, giving us what is called the **cross-product of x and y**. Then these cross-products are summed for all the data points. For the denominator, we subtract the mean of x ($\bar{x}$) from each x in our data set (which is the x coordinate for each data point), square those differences, and sum the squared differences. This gives us the sum of squares for x. In Formula 11.4b, Σxy is the sum of the products of the x and y coordinates for all data points. The other terms should be familiar to you by now. Although it is not readily apparent, the two formulas will produce the same result within rounding errors.

PAUSE, THINK, AND EXPLORE b (BETA) FOR A REGRESSION LINE

Formula 11.4a for b is a ratio. What is it a ratio of? Do any of the factors in this equation look familiar? Which one(s)? Why? Are any of them new? Which ones? What's new about them? What will happen to the value of b if the sum of squares of x is larger?

Statisticians tell us that the y intercept (a) of our least squares regression line is provided by Formula 11.5.

$$a = \bar{y} - b\bar{x} \qquad (11.5)$$

PAUSE, THINK, AND EXPLORE a FOR A REGRESSION LINE

Solve Formula 11.5 for $\bar{y}$ and compare it with Formula 11.1. What are the similarities and differences? Do you have any ideas about why the means of x and y are used in this formula?

Having determined the values of constants a and b, we can enter them in Formula 11.1, which then becomes the least squares regression equation for the best fitting regression line—the one that minimizes the squared differences between the predicted and observed values of y (i.e., minimizes the errors of estimate or residuals). For brevity's sake, we'll usually just refer to residuals. For every value of x in our data, we can predict the corresponding y value by entering the values of x, a, and b and solving Formula 11.1 for y.

Suppose that when we calculate the constants a and b of the regression equation for a best fitting regression line for our data set, we find that $a = 1.5$ and $b = 2.1$. This result indicates that the y intercept for our regression line would be $y = 1.5$ when $x = 0$. The interpretation of b changes somewhat when all the points do not lie exactly on a straight line. As you can imagine in such cases, changes in y are irregular, sometimes changing more and sometimes less with a one-unit change in x. Look at the scattergram in Figure 11.4 again. When data points are scattered around the line instead of lying exactly on it, the b calculated by Formula 11.4 is interpreted as measuring how much, *on average*, y changes with one-unit change in x. Because the slope of our regression line is 2.1, the quantity 2.1 indicates that for every one unit of change in the x axis, there will be, on average, 2.1 units of change on the y axis for the data set as a whole. The formula for our regression line, following Formula 11.1, would be

$$y = a + bx$$
$$y = 1.5 + 2.1x$$

Substituting values of x (in our example, police expenditure amounts) in this formula, we can solve the equation for ys (crime rates). This would give us the best predictions or estimates of the crime rates associated with those expenditures. So far in our discussion of regression analysis, we have assumed that the residuals have been measured parallel to the y axis and perpendicular to the x axis of the graph, reflecting the error in the prediction of the y coordinate produced by our regression equation. This way of measuring the residuals is dictated by our designation of x as the independent variable. Formulas 11.4a, 11.4b, and 11.5 (for the values of b and a for a least squares regression line) are based on this designation. The regression line formula that results is referred to as the equation for the **regression of y on x**, often symbolized as y.x.

Best Fitting Lines and the Means of x and y

As Formulas 11.4a and 11.4b indicate, there is a relationship between the best fitting regression line and the means of x and y. Recall that, in the absence of any other information, the best estimate we can make of the value of y is the mean of y ($\bar{y}$), and the best estimate we can make of x is the mean of x ($\bar{x}$). Suppose we calculate the means of x and y and locate their values on their respective axes. Then, the intersection of the perpendicular lines drawn from the values of x and y on the corresponding axes would locate the data point ($\bar{x}, \bar{y}$). That point will lie on the best fitting regression line. In particular, the best fitting regression line for any particular data set will always pass through the data point whose coordinates correspond to the means of x and y. In fact, we can think of regression lines as pivoting on this data point. This fact presents us with a way of visualizing what improving our predictions of y by taking x into account means. Consider the scattergram in Figure 11.6. We have drawn a dashed line perpendicular to the y axis at the point $y = \bar{y}$. This line would represent our best estimate of y if we had no other information except the distribution of y. Note that the y intercept (the value of y when x is zero) for this line's equation would be $a = \bar{y}$. For the beta (slope), we would have $b = 0$, because on this line, the value of y does not change no matter what change in x occurs. Note that, even though $\bar{y}$ minimizes the difference between it and the other scores in the distribution of y, using the line representing the mean of y ($\bar{y}$) to predict y would entail large errors. Note also that in Figure 11.6, we have located the point on this line corresponding to the mean of $\bar{x}$. This point would have the coordinates $(\bar{x}, \bar{y})$.

Figure 11.6 Scattergram Illustrating Improvement in Prediction of y by taking x into Account

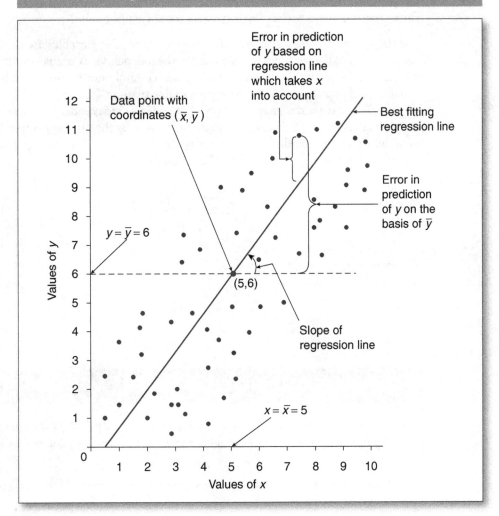

The solid slanting line in Figure 11.6 represents the best fitting regression line. It pivots on the point with coordinates $(\bar{x}, \bar{y})$. Note that if we used this line, rather than the dashed line representing the mean of y, the error in predicting the values of y would be, on average, much smaller. The angle of the regression line relative to the horizontal dotted line representing the mean of y is the slope of the line. The value of a for the best fitting regression line would, of course, be different from $a = \bar{y}$. We locate the points on the regression line (and, hence, our predictions of y) by multiplying the value of x by this slope and adding the value of a. Note that the accuracy of our prediction of y using the regression equation would not improve much for all ys, particularly those closest to the pivot point. It would, however, improve greatly for other ys. The difference in the accuracy of the predictions of y based on these two lines is the improvement we attribute to taking not just the mean of y but also the values of x into account.

Designating y as the Independent Variable

The data points in the scattergram for any two particular variables are the same no matter which of the variables is designated as the independent variable. But the regression line and equation for the data will almost certainly not be the same. So, which variable we designate as the independent variable matters.

Suppose that we designated y, instead of x, as the independent variable in a particular scattergram. In this case, we would be measuring the residuals (errors) parallel to the x axis and perpendicular to the y axis. The formula for b in the regression equation assuming this way of measuring the residuals would become

$$b_{x.y} = \frac{\Sigma(x-\bar{x})(y-\bar{y})}{\Sigma(y-\bar{y})^2} \quad (11.6)$$

The formula for a would be

$$a = \bar{x} - b\bar{y} \quad (11.7)$$

> **PAUSE, THINK, AND EXPLORE FORMULAS 11.6 AND 11.7**
>
> Compare Formula 11.4a with 11.6 and Formula 11.5 with 11.7. What similarities and differences do you find? Would a and b likely have the same values in the comparable formulas? Why or why not?

It should be clear that, in most cases, when we designate y as the independent variable for the same data set and calculate the values of b and a by Formulas 11.6 and 11.7, they would almost certainly be different from those arrived at by Formulas 11.4a and 11.5 based on x as the independent variable. Obviously, substituting the two different values for b and a into Formula 11.3 will result in different regression lines and equations, and hence, different predictions of the dependent variable and different sums of least squares. The lines will almost certainly have different slopes (b), and in the regression line for $x.y$, a will be the x intercept.

To visualize the difference, consider the two scattergrams in Figures 11.7a and 11.7b, which represent the same data set. Assume that the line in Figure 11.7a is the best fitting regression line for the scattergram when x is the independent variable. Assume that the line in Figure 11.7b is the best fitting regression line for the same scattergram, assuming y is the independent variable. Note that the lines would almost certainly have at least somewhat different slopes, which means that the least sum of squares would be different. To illustrate, in each of the figures, we selected the same three data points. Then, in Figure 11.7a, again assuming x is the independent variable, from each of these data points we drew a line perpendicular to the x axis from the data point to our estimate of the best fitting line. In Figure 11.7b, again assuming y is the independent variable, we drew a line from each of the same data points perpendicular to the y axis. The lengths of the lines represent the errors of estimate for these data points under the two different assumptions about which is the independent variable. It's pretty clear that the sum of squares (the sum of squared deviations) for these lines would differ at least somewhat.

Finally, let's put together what we said in the immediately preceding section about means and our observations about differences in regression lines in this section. Although the best fitting lines for the regression of y on x and for x on y are likely to have at least somewhat different slopes, they would nevertheless intersect and pivot on the data point in the graph where the mean of x and the mean of y intersect. In effect, they rotate on this center point.

Positive, Negative, and No Relationship

In our fictitious example of research on police expenditures and crime rate, we found that the pattern of data points in the scattergram flowed from lower left to upper right in the graph (see Figure 11.4). So also would our regression line. When the values of one variable increase as the values of the other variable increase, the relationship between the variables is called a **positive relationship**. Although we didn't mention it at the time, the implicit + sign on b, the slope of our regression line, indicates this positive relationship between the two variables.

What if our scattergram looked like the one in Figure 11.8? In this case, the pattern of data points flows from the upper left to the lower right in the graph. This scattergram presents a case where the values of y decrease as the values of x increase.

Our regression line would conform to this pattern, slanting from the upper left to the lower right. In this case, the variables are said to have a **negative relationship**. If we were to calculate a least squares regression equation for these data, the sign on b would

Figure 11.7a Scattergram Showing Distances to the Best Fitting Line for *x* as the Independent Variable

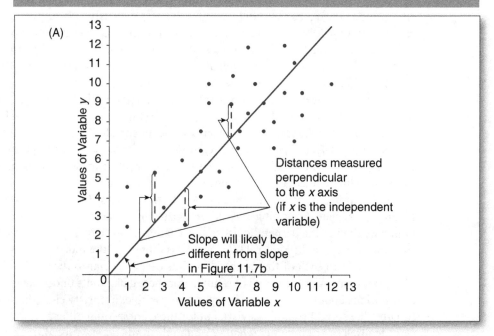

Figure 11.7b Scattergram Showing Distances to the Best Fitting Line for *y* as the Independent Variable

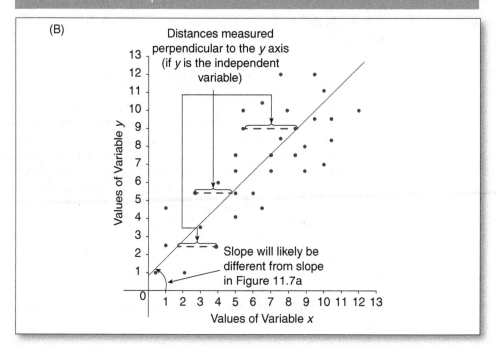

Figure 11.8 Scattergram Showing a Negative Relationship Between Variables x and y

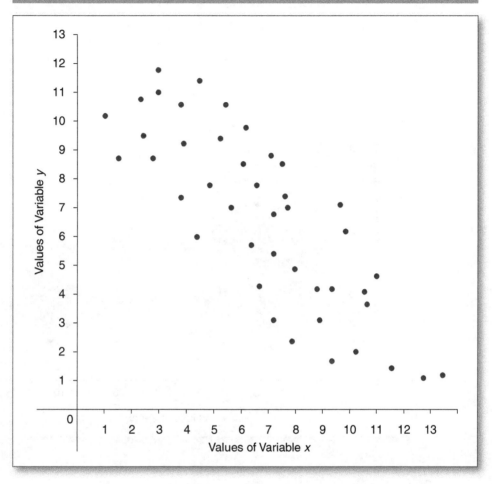

be negative, indicating a negative relationship between the variables. For example, perhaps if we used per capita instead of gross police expenditures for our independent variable in our fictitious data set, the scattergram data points and the regression line would indicate a negative relationship between expenditures and crime rate.

Now suppose that when we constructed our scattergram, it looked like the one in Figure 11.9. Note that the data points are scattered fairly evenly over the graph. The scattergram in Figure 11.9 would not permit us to say anything useful about the value of variable y given a particular value of variable x. Choose any value of x and examine the corresponding values of y arrayed directly above it. They are as likely to correspond to low as they are to medium or high values of y. Hence, the scattergram represents a situation in which the two variables are unrelated. If we calculated a regression equation for these data, b, the slope of the regression line would be near zero.

Figure 11.9 A Scattergram Showing No Relationship Between Two Variables

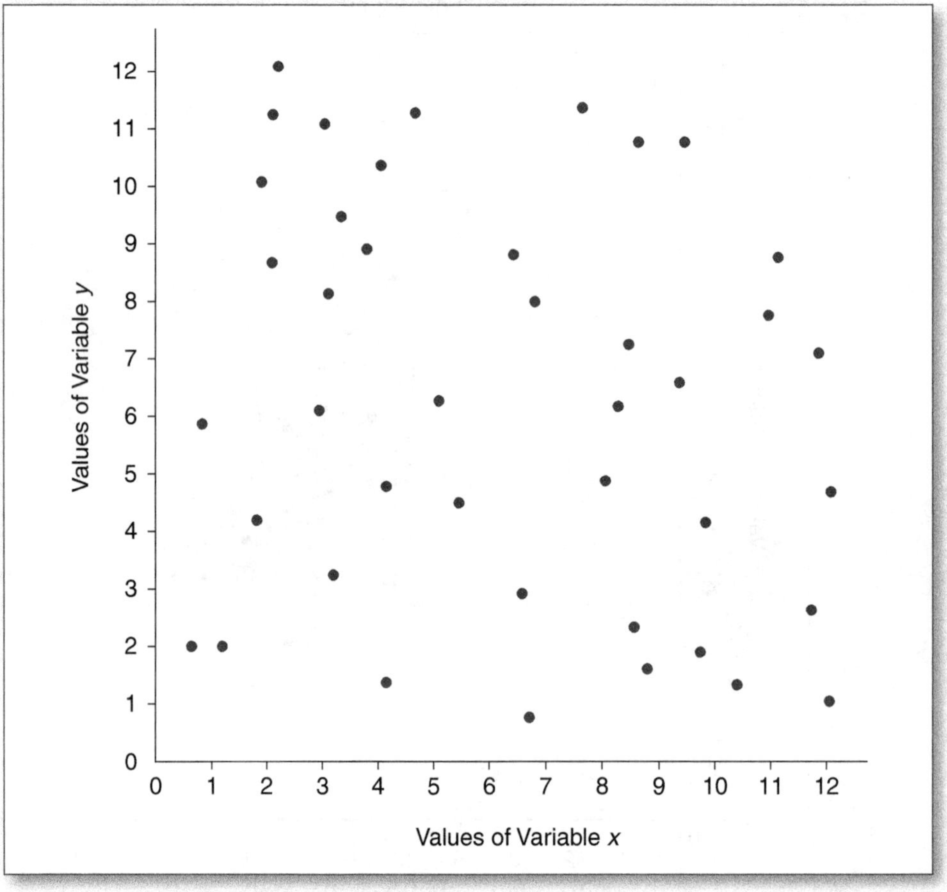

Linear and Nonlinear Relationships

The positive and negative relationships of the kind we have described above are **linear relationships**, because the pattern of the data points can be represented reasonably well by a straight line that runs diagonally across the graph.

Of course, a scattergram can reveal a nonlinear relationship as well. Suppose our scattergram looked like one of those in Figures 11.10a, 11.10b, or 11.10c. In these, the data points clearly fall into a pattern, but not one well approximated by a straight line. A curved line does much better, reflecting what is called a **curvilinear relationship**. Although there are formulas for describing curvilinear data patterns, they are beyond the scope of this text. Many other patterns may, of course, be revealed by scattergrams as well. Figures 11.10d through 11.10h are just a few. Some can be described relatively well by mathematical equations, but they are beyond the scope of this text.

Figure 11.10 Scattergrams Showing Curvilinear and Other Nonlinear Relationships Between Two Variables

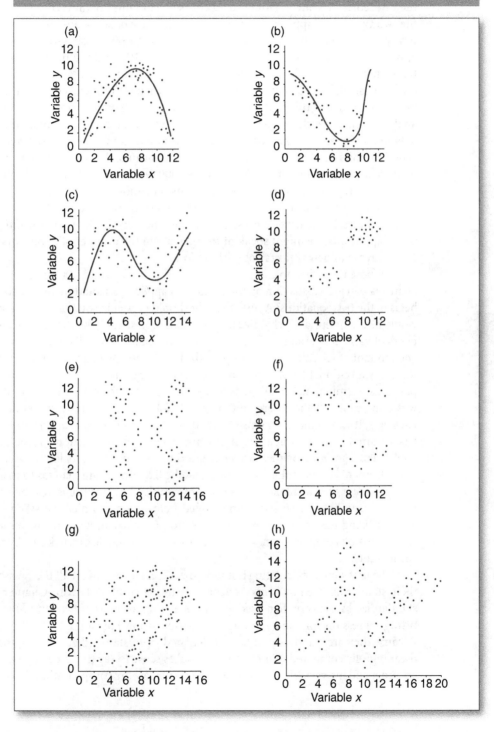

Standardized Betas

So far in our discussion of betas (regression line slopes), we have calculated them from the raw scores of x and y. Doing so, of course, maintains the units of measurement for the two variables. Suppose, for example, that we have data on annual compensation of newly appointed officers (measured in units of $1,000), job satisfaction of newly appointed officers (measured on a scale from 1 to 10), and the number of applicants for each position on the police force. Furthermore, suppose that we are interested in the relationship between each of the first two variables (that we regard as independent variables) and the third (dependent) variable. We have performed two regression analyses (one for each of the two independent variables) and determined the values of beta in the regression equations. In one regression analysis where x is annual compensation in units of $1,000 and y is number of applicants, the beta would be interpreted in those terms, number of applicants per $1,000 of compensation. That is, the value of beta in this regression equation would tell us the amount of increase (or decrease) in the number of applicants for every $1,000 increase in compensation for first-year police officers. In the other regression analysis where x is job satisfaction and y is number of applicants, we might speak of the increase in the number of applicants for every unit increase in new officers' job satisfaction.

Suppose we wished to compare the effect of an increase in $1,000 compensation and an increase in job satisfaction on the number of applicants. Could we simply compare the betas in the two equations? A little thought should persuade you that such a comparison would be inappropriate. Why? Because the betas representing the change in the two independent variables pertain to different units of measurement—amount of compensation and amount of job satisfaction. Suppose the beta for the first equation was 20, indicating for every additional $1,000 in annual compensation, the number of applicants for a particular criminal justice job goes up by 20. Suppose the beta for the second equation was 2, indicating that for every unit increase in job satisfaction, the number of applicants rises by 2. It would make no sense to say that a $1,000 increase in annual compensation has 10 times as much impact as a unit increase in job satisfaction on the number of applicants. The units of measurement are different (dollars and job satisfaction scale scores), and to compare them directly would be like comparing mangos to marmosets.

Is there a way to make the betas comparable? The answer is yes, by calculating **standardized betas**, also sometimes called **beta weights**, which we symbolize as b^*. Standardizing the betas removes their ties to particular units of measurement (such as amount of compensation and amount of job satisfaction), making them directly comparable.

The first step in calculating a standardized beta is to convert all the raw scores into their standardized equivalents (z scores) using Formula 5.1 from Chapter 5. These standardized scores are then used when calculating the constants (a and b) for the best fitting regression line and regression equation using Formulas 11.4, 11.5, and 11.3. Because they are standardized betas calculated from standardized scores, they can be meaningfully compared. For example, it makes sense to say that a particular change in an independent variable (such as a $1,000 increase in compensation) has twice the effect on one dependent variable (such as number of applicants) compared to another (such as job satsifaction) if the standardized beta for the former is 4 and the latter is 2.

Cautions With Predictions From Linear Regression Equations

When using regression equations for prediction, two important cautions must be observed. First, remember that the residuals or errors of estimate can be quite large, even when the relationship is generally linear, which means, of course, that our predictions of y are not very good, as in Figure 11.10g, for example. Knowing the value of x helps in predicting y in such a data set, but not much. Many points lie a long distance from the best fitting regression line, and the residual sum of squares (errors of estimate) would be quite large. Second, it is dangerous to use a regression formula to predict much beyond the range of the values in the data used to calculate the regression formula in the first place. Doing so essentially assumes the variable relationship remains linear over an extended range of variable values, and that, of course, may not be true.

Consider scattergrams (a) and (b) in Figure 11.10. Suppose our data on both x and y are limited to a range of 0 to 7. Place a piece of paper over the scattergrams so that only the data points falling in those ranges are visible. Then suppose we calculated a regression equation using values of x from 0 to 7 and values of y from 0 to 7. Now we use the regression equation to predict the value of y for $x = 12$. How accurate would our predictions of y be if the actual relationship were as depicted in Figures 11.10a and 11.10b for values of x greater than 7?

Finally, a few scores that are exceptionally large or small compared to other scores in the data set can have a significant impact on the calculated slope of a regression line. They are called **outliers** and contribute disproportionately to the residual sum of squares and, therefore, to the statistics we calculate to describe and analyze the data. We have more to say about outliers in our discussion of correlation analysis.

Linear Bivariate Correlation Analysis

Our understanding of OLS regression analysis will help us make sense of correlation analysis. As we noted earlier, **correlation analysis** is primarily concerned with measuring the strength of a linear relationship between two variables. One way of measuring the strength of a linear bivariate relationship, called the correlation between the two variables, is by calculating the average distances between the data points and the corresponding best fitting line. In general, the smaller these distances, on average, the stronger the relationship and the higher the correlation between the two variables.

But as we have previously noted, the distances can be measured in different ways. In regression analysis, we wanted to find the best fitting line and corresponding regression equation, where best fitting was defined as the line that minimized the distance between the line and the observed values of y, measured parallel to the y axis (and perpendicular to the x axis). For correlation analysis, the best fitting line is the one that minimizes the distance between it and the data points as *measured perpendicular to the line itself*. One of the most commonly used measures of correlation was developed by Karl Pearson. It is called the correlation coefficient, or sometimes the Pearson product moment correlation coefficient, and it is symbolized by r. A **correlation coefficient** ranges from +1.0 to −1.0 and indicates both the direction (positive or negative) and the strength of the *linear* relationship between two variables. Assume that the possible variable values are arrayed from lowest to highest on the scattergram axes, beginning at the point where the axes intersect. In this case, a perfect correlation of $r = +1.0$ would be produced if all of the data points in the scattergram fall precisely on a straight diagonal line slanting up and to the right. A perfect negative correlation of $r = -1.0$ would be produced if all the data points fall precisely on a straight diagonal line slanting down and to the right. The closer the data points to such diagonals, the closer to +1.0 or −1.0 the correlation coefficients calculated from the data. There are a number of other ways of thinking about r, and we discuss a few of them now.

Let's begin with what is perhaps the most general description. We can think of the tendency of x and y to vary together as the **correlation** or **covariance** of the two variables. This tendency, if it exists, is reflected in the pattern of the paired coordinates of data points (x,y). In general, the statistic r may be described as a ratio of the covariance we observe in our data set to the maximum possible covariance of the two variables. Such a ratio would necessarily vary between 0 and ±1. We've already learned what the maximum covariance would look like in a scattergram. It is the circumstance in which all the data points fall exactly on a slanting line, which, by definition, would be the best fitting line.

Although the proof is beyond the scope of this text, we can also think about the maximum covariance of x and y as the square root of the product of the sum of squares of x and the sum of squares of y. That is, we find the sum of squares of x and the sum of squares of y and multiply these two quantities. Consider that if all the values of y are the same, the sum of squares of y would be 0 and there could be no covariance with x. Similarly, if all the values of x were the same, its sum of squares would be 0 and there could be no covariance with y. Only if both variables vary can there be covariance. The calculated values of the sum of squares of x and y represent the extent of the variance for each of these variables taken separately. When these two sums of squares are multiplied and the square root of this product is taken, the result is the maximum possible covariance of the two variables. This quantity becomes the denominator (the maximum covariance) of the ratio that defines r as indicated in Formula 11.8a.

The numerator for the r ratio is the amount of covariance actually observed in the data set. This covariance is reflected in the x and y coordinates for each data point. To determine this observed covariance, we begin with a data point. We subtract the value of its x coordinate from the mean of x and the value of its y coordinate from the mean of y. We then multiply the results of these two subtractions. The result of this multiplication is, as we have already learned from our calculations for the best fitting regression line's slope, the cross-product of x and y (see Formula 11.4a and accompanying discussion, pp. 368–369). This procedure is repeated for each data point in the data set, and then the products are summed. This sum of the cross-products provides us a measure of the observed covariance of x and y.

Conceived of in this way, the easier-to-understand formula for r is Formula 11.8a. The easier-to-calculate formula for r is provided in Formula 11.8b.

$$r = \frac{\Sigma(x-\bar{x})(y-\bar{y})}{\sqrt{[\Sigma(x-\bar{x})^2][\Sigma(y-\bar{y})^2]}} \quad \text{(11.8a) – easier to understand}$$

$$r = \frac{\Sigma xy - \frac{(\Sigma x)(\Sigma y)}{n}}{\sqrt{\left[\Sigma x^2 - \frac{(\Sigma x)^2}{n}\right]\left[\Sigma y^2 - \frac{(\Sigma y)^2}{n}\right]}} \quad \text{(11.8b) – easier to calculate}$$

PAUSE, THINK, AND EXPLORE r AS LEAST SQUARES

Note that r is a ratio. How would you describe the factors in the numerator and the denominator? What, if anything, about Formula 11.8a suggests to you that the value of r is *not* influenced by whichever variable is considered the independent variable?

Let's consider the numerator of Formula 11.8a a bit more. If the value of x for any data point is greater than the mean of x, the subtraction $(x - \bar{x})$ would yield a positive number. If the value of y for the same data point is greater than the mean of y, the subtraction $(y - \bar{y})$ would also result in a positive number. Multiplying the two results would yield a positive number. Similarly, if the x and y coordinates were both smaller than their respective means, subtractions would produce negative numbers. Their multiplication (cross-product), however, would also yield a positive number. When both of a data point's coordinates are either above or below their respective means, it is evidence of a positive relationship between the two variables. When the data point coordinates vary in opposite directions from their respective means, the result of the subtractions will be a negative number in one case and a positive number in the other case. Their cross-product will result in a negative number. This is evidence of a negative relationship between the variables. For any data set, some of these cross-products are likely to be positive and some negative. When they are summed, the result will be positive or negative, depending on whether the sum of the positive cross-products is larger or smaller than the sum of the negative cross-products. If the sum of these cross-products is 0, $r = 0$, indicating no relationship between the variables. Statisticians say that such a result would indicate that the two variables are independent of each other. Because the denominator of Formula 11.8a consists of squared deviations, it will always be a positive number. So, the sign of the numerator will be the sign of the calculated r, indicating whether there is a positive or negative relationship between the variables.

We can also think of r as an average of the two slopes (bs) of the regression lines $x.y$ and $y.x$. That is, r has the same value whether we consider x or y as the independent variable. It is in this sense that we might think of r as based on minimizing the residuals measured perpendicularly to the best fitting line. In this sense, too, we can think of r as a **goodness-of-fit** test. That is, it tells how well a straight line equation "fits" the data in the scattergram. A good fit would be one that left small errors or residuals; a bad fit would leave large errors or residuals. It's sort of like the way your pants may or may not fit (tight or loose).

A formula for calculating r that reflects its dependence on a combination of the two slopes (bs) of $x.y$ and $y.x$ is

$$r = \sqrt{(b_{x.y})(b_{y.x})} \qquad (11.9)$$

> **Pause, Think, and Explore r as a Function of b**
>
> Try substituting Formulas 11.4a and 11.6 for the slopes (bs) in Formula 11.9 and compare it with Formula 11.8a. What similarities and differences do you see?

In this formula, we calculate the regression coefficient $b_{x.y}$ using Formula 11.6, which assumes y is the independent variable, and using Formula 11.4a to calculate the regression coefficient $b_{y.x}$, which assumes x is the independent variable. Then, we multiply the two bs and take the square root of the result to find the value of r.

Let's examine one more formula for r expressed in terms of z scores.

$$r = \frac{\sum (z_x)(z_y)}{n} \qquad (11.10)$$

To use this formula, we would first convert the values of x and y into their standard score equivalents using Formula 5.1 in Chapter 5. Now recall that each data point in our scattergram can be designated by its coordinates (x,y). In this formula, z_x is the standard or z-score equivalent of the x coordinate for a data point, and z_y is the z-score equivalent of the same data point's y coordinate. The numerator in this equation says that we should multiply the z-score coordinate values for x and y for each data point in our scattergram, sum these cross-products, and then divide by n, the number of units of analysis in our study group.

> **PAUSE, THINK, AND EXPLORE r AS A FUNCTION OF z**
>
> Formula 11.10 is an average. What makes it an average? What is it an average of? Try substituting the formula for z scores (Formula 5.1 from Chapter 5) for the zs in Formula 11.10 and compare with Formula 11.8a. What similarities and differences do you see?

Correlation Matrixes

Often, when many variables are included in an analysis, bivariate correlations are reported in a **correlation matrix**. A correlation matrix is a table containing all of the possible bivariate correlation coefficients (rs) of the variables. The variables included in the matrix are typically listed beginning in the upper left-hand corner and going down the side, as well as across the top, in the same order. Each cell in the table contains the correlation coefficient for two variables, one defining the row and the other the column corresponding to that cell. The diagonal of a correlation matrix is always filled with ones because every variable correlates perfectly with itself. Usually, just half of the matrix is presented because the halves are mirror images of each other. This arises from the fact that the value of r is the same no matter which variable is designated the independent variable.

The From the Literature Box 11.1 provides an example of a correlation matrix from the professional literature.

Note that there is a formula for how many bivariate correlations there will be in any given correlation matrix. The formula for the number of combinations of n things taken two at a time is $n(n-1)/2$, where n is the number of variables being correlated. The correlation matrix in From the Literature Box 11.1 has 12, so applying the combination formula, we have $12(11)/2 = 66$ bivariate correlations.

The Problem of Outliers

Note that, like the mean and variance of a frequency distribution, as well as many of the other statistics we have discussed in this text, the magnitude of r can be influenced substantially and disproportionately by a few coordinate values that are very large and/or very small relative to the other values in the distribution. Such values are often referred to (for obvious reasons) as **outliers** in a scattergram. If a scattergram includes outliers, as does the one in Figure 11.11, for example, great caution must be exercised in interpreting quantitative results. As we have seen, statistical calculations include not just deviations from the mean, but squared deviations, greatly amplifying the impact of outliers.

Because of their disproportionate influence on sum of squares calculations, statisticians often recommend eliminating outliers from the data set before performing final data analysis. Eliminating data before final analysis, however, is always a risky business. First,

From the Literature Box 11.1

Gregory B. Morrison studied differences among deadly force training programs in several larger police departments in the United States. The data came from a police firearms training survey. One part of the data analysis included constructing a Pearson's r bivariate correlation matrix of several ratio-level variables in his data set. The following matrix is one he includes in his research report.

Box 11.1

	1	2	3	4	5	6	7	8	9	10	11	12
Average cost per in-service officer	1.000	0.747**	-0.424*	0.030	0.336	-0.265	-0.144	0.163	-0.286	-0.244	-0.131	0.360*
Ratio of full-time to part-time instruction		1.000	-0.154	0.015	0.726**	0.185	0.117	-0.077	0.259	0.075	0.065	0.031
Ratio of trainees-to-instructors			1.000	0.139	-0.056	0.025	-0.177	0.053	-0.218	-0.015	0.181	0.148
OISs for 1998–2000				1.000	0.426*	-0.165	-0.173	-0.225	-0.188	-0.056	0.342*	0.102
Hours of instruction update training					1.000	0.006	-0.004	-0.062	-0.125	0.219	-0.031	0.225
% department support for extradepartmental instructor development courses						1.000	0.346*	-0.019	0.237	0.102	0.050	0.107

Hours of handgun activities	1.000	0.370**	0.049	−0.374**	−0.166	0.147
Number of training sessions		1.000	0.048	−0.243	−0.120	0.077
Minimum requalifying percentage score			1.000	−0.007	−0.026	−0.238
% hours for requalification				1.000	−0.128	−0.224
Number of officers in field assignments					1.000	−0.102
Average cost per recruit officer						1.000

Note: OIS = officer-involved shooting.
*p > .05; **p > .01.

Source: From Morrison, G. B. (2006). Deadly force programs among larger U.S. police departments. *Police Quarterly, 9,* 331–360. Retrieved May 2, 2012, from http://pqx.sagepub.com/content/9/3/331. Reprinted with permission.

Note: the greater than (>) signs following *p* at the bottom of the table are as printed in the article from which the table was excerpted, but they are almost certainly a misprint and were intended to be less than (<) signs indicating statistical significance of the correlation coefficients at the .05 and .01 levels.

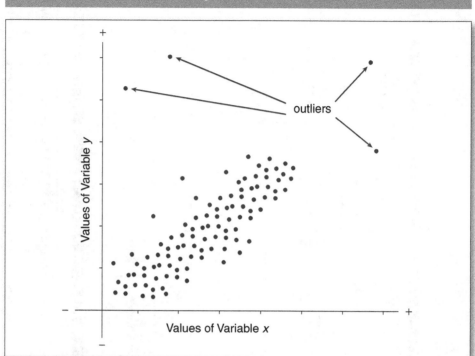

Figure 11.11 Outliers in a Scattergram

the researcher must decide which data points depart from the general pattern enough to be considered outliers. Some data points are pretty obviously outliers, but it is likely that others are borderline cases. Whether the outliers are obvious or borderline, leaving them in or taking them out will often substantially impact the outcome of the analysis, determining whether it is statistically significant or not, for example. Whenever such choices are involved, there is a temptation to fudge the data so that the outcome preferred by the researcher is produced. Furthermore, because various assumptions, such as random sampling, on which statistical tests of significance for r are based may be undermined by throwing out data, the validity of the results may be threatened. In any event, removing outliers must always be noted and thoroughly explained in research reports.

Comparing r and b

A comparison of r (the correlation coefficient) and b (the regression coefficient which is the slope of the regression line) is instructive. Like regression coefficients, correlation coefficients indicate the direction of the relationship between two variables and may have predictive value. As with b, r can be positive or negative, indicating a positive or negative bivariate relationship. If r or b is close or equal to zero, knowing the value of one variable does not help us predict the value of the other. Furthermore, both r and b are indicators of the amount of change in y associated with changes in x.

There are some important differences, however. First, in discussing regression analysis, we noted that different regression lines and, therefore, different sums of squares would be obtained depending on whether x or y was designated the independent variable. In contrast, r does not depend on the designation of an independent and a dependent variable. It has the same value whichever variable we designate as independent. Note also that r is a standardized statistic with values restricted from -1.00 to $+1.00$. Because r is a standardized statistic, comparisons of rs (i.e., comparisons of the relative sizes of the changes in y that can be attributed to different xs) are legitimate and meaningful. The values of b, however, are neither restricted in range nor standardized when they are calculated from raw scores. It is not appropriate, therefore, to compare bs to assess the relative sizes of the changes in y that can be attributed to different xs. Nevertheless, there is a connection between r and b as indicated in the mathematically equivalent Formulas 11.11a and 11.11b.

$$r = b_{y.x}(s_x/s_y) \qquad (11.11a)$$

$$b_{y.x} = r(s_y/s_x) \qquad (11.11b)$$

In both formulas, $b_{y.x}$ means the slope (beta) of the line regressing y on x, r is the correlation coefficient, and s_x and s_y are the standard deviations of x and y, respectively. Note that in Formula 11.11a, multiplying $b_{y.x}$ by s_x/s_y results in a standardized quantity, in this case equal to r.

Finally, as we noted earlier in this chapter, the values of any variable can be converted to standard scores, using Formula 5.1 from Chapter 5 to facilitate relative magnitude comparisons. After we do so, we can calculate b for the linear equation using these standardized scores. As we noted earlier, the result is a standardized beta or beta weight, which we symbolized as b^*. We use the same asterisk (*) marker to denote the standardized scores of x (x^*) and y (y^*). Without offering proof, we will note that, when we are analyzing standardized rather than raw scores, we are concerned only with the slope (b) of the line and not its y intercept. Therefore, a drops out of the raw score regression equation (see Formula 11.1) and we are left with Formula 11.12.

$$y^* = b^* x^* \qquad (11.12)$$

Also without going into the proof, we will report that in any standardized bivariate linear equation, $b^* = r$. We have more to say about r (and r^2) in just a bit. For now, we simply note the close relationship between regression and correlation manifested in these equations.

> ### PAUSE, THINK, AND EXPLORE $y^* = b^* x^*$ AND $b^* = r$
>
> Compare and contrast the formulas for standardizing raw scores (Formula 5.1), $b_{y.x}$ (Formula 11.4a), and r (Formula 11.8a). What similarities and differences do you see? Can you see why b^* would equal r?

The Coefficient of Determination r^2

The quantity r^2, called the **coefficient of determination**, is somewhat easier to interpret than r. We can think of r^2 as a measure of the proportion of the variance in the dependent variable accounted for or, statistically speaking, "explained" by the independent variable in much the same way we did when discussing analysis of variance. Consider the three scattergrams in Figure 11.12 representing data from three different studies involving the same independent and dependent variables. As usual, the independent variables are on the horizontal axes and the dependent variables are on the vertical axes. We have raised a vertical dotted line above a given value of the independent variable in each scattergram and marked the range of values of the dependent variable that are associated with this independent variable value. This range is an indication of the amount of variance in the dependent variable associated with the specified independent variable value. Note that in the scattergram in Figure 11.12a, the range of scores on the dependent variable associated with the independent variable value $x = 6$ is larger (from about 4 to 13) than the corresponding range (from about 7 to 10) in Figure 11.12b. One way of describing this difference is to say that the correlation between x and y is stronger in Figure 11.12b than in Figure 11.12a. Note also that in both scattergrams, knowing the value of the independent variable does not permit one to predict perfectly what the value of the dependent variable will be. (Perfect prediction would result only if all of the data points fell on a straight line.) This means that in both cases some of the variation in the dependent variable remains unexplained by the independent variable.

Consider the scattergram in Figure 11.12c. The values of y associated with $x = 6$, for example, encompass nearly the full range of the y variable. Here, the independent variable accounts for none of the variation in y.

Now imagine drawing an approximation of the best fitting line in each of the three scattergrams. Drawing the approximate lines for Figures 11.12a and 11.12b would be pretty easy. They would have the same general direction, up and to the right, indicating a positive relationship between the variables, but they would likely have different slopes (bs), as calculated by Formula 11.4a. We will leave it to you to explain why this is the case.

Note that the residuals (and, therefore, the sum of the squared residuals) would be much larger in Figure 11.12a than in Figure 11.12b. Conceived of in terms of the best fitting line, then, there is much greater unexplained variation in the former than the latter.

You may have some trouble figuring out how to draw the best fitting line in Figure 11.12c. In this case, knowing the value of x doesn't help at all in predicting the value of y. The best prediction would be the mean of y. The line would be nearly horizontal and parallel to the x axis, beginning at the point on the y axis equal to the mean of y. The slope of the line would be $b = 0$, indicating no change in y for a unit change in x. The residual sum of squares would be equal to the sum of squares for y, and the coefficients of regression (b) and correlation (r) as well as the coefficient of determination (r^2) would equal approximately zero.

Finally, when interpreting the coefficient of determination r^2, it's important to remember that it refers only to statistical explanation. Suppose the correlation coefficient (r) between crime rates and the proportion of the population that owns handguns is

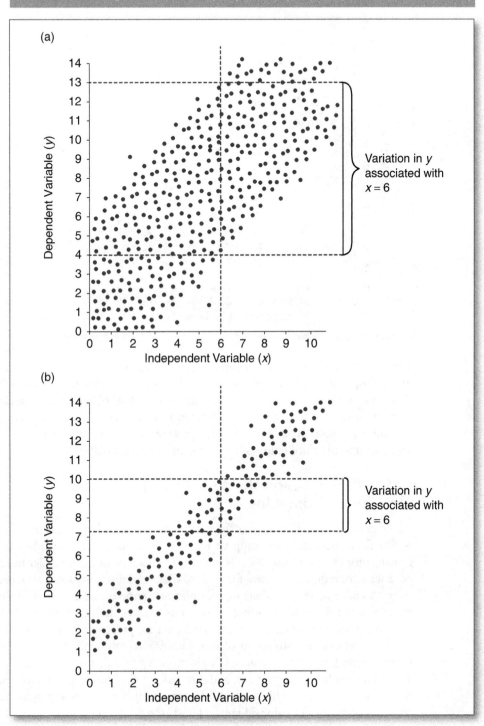

Figure 11.12 Three Scattergrams Showing Different Amounts of Variation in the Dependent Variable y Explained by the Independent Variable x

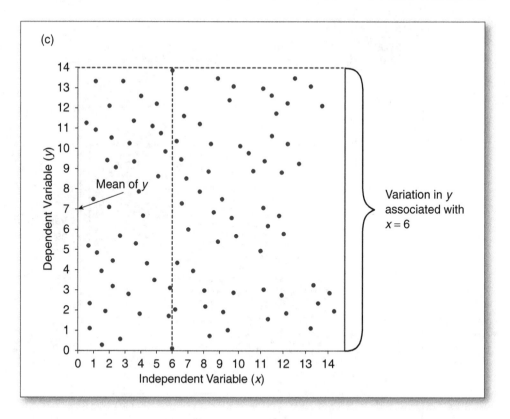

+0.6 and the coefficient of determination $(r^2) = (0.6)(0.6) = 0.36$. In this case, variations in the proportion of handgun owners can be said to account for (explain) 36% of the variations in the crime rate. Of course, that means that 64% of the variation in crime rates remains unaccounted for. Remember, though, that statistical explanation is not the same as causal explanation. Causal explanation also requires an appropriate time sequence and the elimination of other potential causal variables.

Calculating r, r^2, and the Constants (a and b) for a Best Fitting Line

Let's calculate r and r^2, as well as the constants for a best fitting line, and interpret the results for a small data set. Suppose we have fictitious police expenditure and crime rate data for five fictitious cities. To make our calculations a little easier to follow, suppose we have reduced our data for each of these variables to ratio-level scores ranging from 1 to 6. To further facilitate our calculations, suppose we also set aside our recommended general rule of rounding calculations to three decimal places and round them here to two decimal places. The converted data are presented in Table 11.2.

First, let's do a scattergram of our data. We recommend this step in all of your regression and correlation analyses. It gives you a good picture of your data, indicating at a glance the linearity, strength, and direction of the correlation, if any, and whether there are any outliers. This general information also serves as a rough check on the accuracy of your calculations. Figure 11.13 is the scattergram for our five-city data.

Table 11.2 Police Expenditure and Crime Rate Scores for Five Cities

	Police Expenditures (x)			Crime Rates (y)			Covariance
	x	$(x-\bar{x})$	$(x-\bar{x})^2$	y	$(y-\bar{y})$	$(y-\bar{y})^2$	$(x-\bar{x})(y-\bar{y})$
City A	5.50	1.56	2.43	4.20	.76	.58	1.19
City B	2.00	−1.94	3.76	1.50	−1.94	3.76	3.76
City C	3.20	−.74	.55	3.00	−.44	.19	.33
City D	4.00	.06	.00	3.50	.06	.00	.00
City E	5.00	1.06	1.12	5.00	1.56	2.43	1.65
	$\bar{x} = 3.94$			$\bar{y} = 3.44$			
			$\sum(x-\bar{x})^2 = 7.86$			$\sum(y-\bar{y})^2 = 6.96$	$\sum(x-\bar{x})(y-\bar{y}) = 6.93$

Figure 11.13 Scattergram for Data in Table 12.1

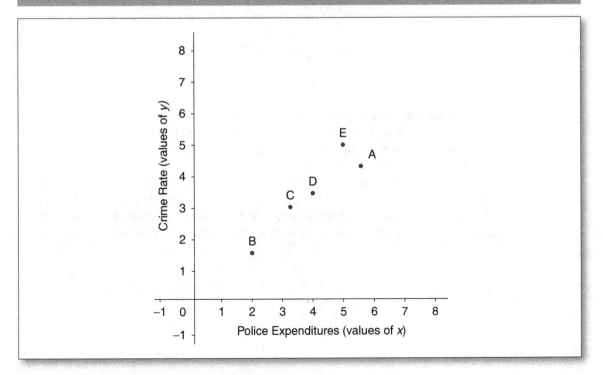

The scattergram indicates there are no outliers. The data points can be very closely approximated by a straight line slanting from the lower left to the upper right of the graph. This suggests a strong positive correlation between our variables. It also suggests the b for $y \cdot x$ should be about 1, because a one-unit change in x seems to be associated, on average, with about one unit of change in y.

Now let's do the calculations for r using Formula 11.8a. You may calculate r following the easier-to-calculate Formula 11.8b to confirm their equivalency. The denominator in Formulas 11.8a and 11.8b will always be positive because it is a squared quantity. Be sure to keep track of the signs on numbers as you do the calculations for the numerator. (Remember that a plus times a plus equals a plus, a plus times a minus equals a minus, and a minus times a minus equals a plus.) Again, the sign on the r you calculate will indicate whether the relationship between the variables is positive or negative.

$$r = \frac{\Sigma(x-\bar{x})(y-\bar{y})}{\sqrt{[\Sigma(x-\bar{x})^2][\Sigma(y-\bar{y})^2]}}$$

$$r = \frac{1.19 + 3.76 + .33 + .00 + 1.65}{\sqrt{(7.86)(6.96)}}$$

$$= \frac{6.93}{\sqrt{54.71}}$$

$$= \frac{6.93}{7.40}$$

$$r = .94$$

$$r^2 = (.94)^2$$
$$r^2 = .88$$

As we guessed from eyeballing the scattergram, the correlation coefficient of $r = .94$ is quite high, as is the coefficient of determination ($r^2 = .88$). This indicates that 88% of the variance in y is statistically explained by the variance in x and that 12% (the residual) is the statistically unexplained variance in y.

Now let's calculate the constants b and a for the least squares regression line and regression equation for our data set, assuming x is the independent variable. For calculating the regression coefficient b for the $y \cdot x$ regression line, we use Formula 11.4a. Again, remember to keep track of the signs on the numbers in your calculations.

$$b_{y \cdot x} = \frac{\Sigma(x-\bar{x})(y-\bar{y})}{\Sigma(x-\bar{x})^2}$$

$$= \frac{6.93}{7.86}$$

$$b_{y \cdot x} = .88$$

A slope (the regression coefficient) b of .88 is about what we would expect from looking at the scattergram for our data (see Figure 11.13). Note that although $b = r^2$ in this case, the two quantities are not usually equal. We'll leave it to you to explain why. (Hint: compare Formulas 11.4a and 11.8a and think about the range of r.)

Now that we know the value of the constant b in our best fitting line equation, we can use Formula 11.7 to calculate the value of the other constant, a.

$$a = \bar{y} - b\bar{x}$$
$$a = 3.44 - .88(3.94)$$
$$a = 3.44 - 3.47$$
$$a = -.03$$

As should be clear from the scattergram of our data (Figure 11.13), the best fitting regression line will cross the y axis near the point where $y = 0$. The calculated value of $-.03$ for a (the y intercept) indicates just that.

We can now enter the values of a and b in Formula 11.1 to complete the equation for our data's best fitting regression line, which then becomes $y = -.03 + .88x$.

Other Statistical Measures of Strength of Relationship

Correlation analyses assume interval or ratio measurements of at least two of the variables being correlated. There are other measures of strength of association, some of which may be used with tables for variables measured at the nominal level, such as lambda. Others can be used on variables measured at the ordinal level, such as Kendall's tau, phi, and Spearman's rank order correlation coefficient. Like Pearson's r, they all rest upon certain assumptions about sampling, levels of measurement, size of the study group, and so forth. We discuss one, Spearman's rank order correlation coefficient, in Chapter 13.

Correlation and Cross-Tabulation

Our earlier discussion of cross-tabulation focused on the importance of specific rows and columns and their comparison. However, as we noted in Chapter 8, when a cross-tabulation involves two variables measured at the ordinal level or above, it is often useful to examine the diagonals of a table to determine whether or not the two variables are correlated. Similarly, a regression line provides a way of interpreting a scattergram. Figure 11.14a is a scattergram with a data grid like the ones we used in constructing cross-tabulations superimposed over it. Suppose we counted the data points included in each of the cells in the data grid and entered the number in the corresponding cells. We would then have a cross-tabulation of the two variables corresponding to the scattergram with which we began, as illustrated in Figure 11.14b.

To create Figure 11.14b, we counted the number of data points in each cell of the table and entered the totals in the corresponding cells. In converting the scattergram in Figure 11.14a into the cross-tabulation in Figure 11.14b, we have collapsed the

Figure 11.14 A Scattergram and Corresponding Cross-Tabulation

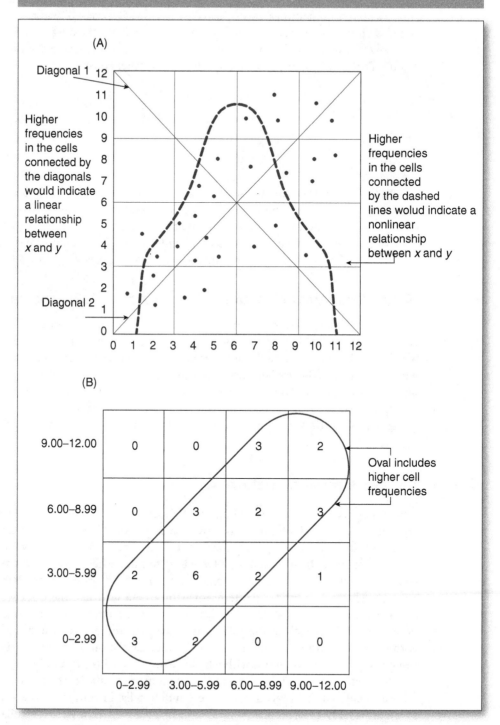

original scattergram range of the values (0 through 12) on both the vertical and horizontal axes into four values: 0.00–2.99, 3.00–5.99, 6.00–8.99, and 9.00–12.00.

As we have just discussed, we can also approximate the pattern of the data points in some scattergrams by drawing a straight, solid line to represent the general pattern of the data. Consistent with the data points in Figure 11.14a, such a line would pass from the lower left-hand cell of the table to the upper right-hand cell, corresponding to the diagonal marked 1. If the data points indicated a negative relationship, it would pass from the upper left to the lower right, corresponding to the diagonal marked 2.

If the cell frequencies tend to be larger in the cells that lie on or near either one of the two diagonals than in those remote from it, this constitutes some evidence that an approximately linear relationship exists between the two variables. (We'll leave it to you to figure out which of the diagonals would correspond to a positive relationship and which to a negative relationship, as well as which best fits the data points in Figure 11.4a.) As in the case of correlation, the absence of a linear relationship (concentration of higher frequencies or percentages in or near the diagonals) does not necessarily mean that the variables are unrelated. If the cells we have connected with a dotted line in Figure 11.14 contained the higher frequencies, the possibility of a curvilinear relationship between the variables would be indicated.

Although we have done so here for comparative purposes, we hasten to point out that turning a scattergram into a contingency table is not recommended as a data analysis strategy. A great deal of information about both variables available in the scattergram is lost in the conversion because many different data points are treated as if they are equal in the table's cells. When data are originally measured at the interval or ratio level, potentially valuable information contained in the variations and covariations of the two variables is ignored when variable values are collapsed for presentation in a table.

Test of Statistical Significance for r and b

If the data we are subjecting to correlation analysis come from a random sample, the results may be tested for statistical significance. The sample statistic of interest is r. The corresponding population parameter is symbolized as ρ (the Greek letter rho, pronounced row, as in row your boat). We use the sample statistic, r, to estimate ρ. As usual, the null hypothesis is that there is no relationship between the variables in the population ($\rho = 0$), and the research hypothesis is that a relationship does exist ($\rho \neq 0$). The question to be addressed in a statistical significance test is how much larger than zero must our observed sample r be before we conclude that it is unlikely to have occurred by random error (chance) alone if $\rho = 0$. As usual, to perform significance tests, in addition to the sample statistics we need to know the mean and standard error of the sampling distribution(s).

The proof is beyond the scope of this text, but a little thought will persuade you that the mean of the sampling distribution for r is 0 if the null hypothesis is true. It also turns out that we can use the t distribution, the same distribution we used in Chapter 9 for testing the difference between two means, as our sampling distribution for r, again assuming the null hypothesis is true. The assumptions required for the population are normal distributions of both x and y, a linear relationship between x and y, homoscedasticity, and a normal distribution of y about x.

You should recognize all of the assumptions except the last one. We can think about a normal distribution of y about x as equal variances of y for different values of x. This would be indicated in a scattergram in which the data points are evenly spread out above and below the best fitting line throughout the length of the line, as in Figure 11.6.

The formula for calculating t for the purposes of a significance test for r is given by Formula 11.13.

$$t = \sqrt{\frac{r^2}{1-r^2}(n-2)} \tag{11.13}$$

In the formula, r^2 is the coefficient of determination; n is the sample size. The formula for the degrees of freedom is $n-2$, which is used to determine the critical value of t in the t table.

Pause, Think, and Explore the Test of Significance for r

Ignoring the $n - 2$ factor, what is the ratio under the square root sign expressed in terms of explained and unexplained variance in y? How would the value of t change if the amount of unexplained variance in y went up? If it went down?

Let's calculate the test of significance for r for our five-city data in Table 11.3. Recall that we found $r = .94$ and $r^2 = .88$.

$$t = \sqrt{\frac{r^2}{1-r^2}(n-2)}$$

$$= \sqrt{\frac{0.88}{0.12}(5-2)}$$

$$= \sqrt{7.33(3)}$$

$$= \sqrt{21.99}$$

$$t = 4.69$$

$$df = n - 2$$

$$= 5 - 2$$

$$df = 3$$

Now that we have our value for t, we can use the t table in Appendix F in the usual way, as described in Chapter 9. Suppose our research hypothesis is that the r for these two variables (police expenditure and crime rate) will be positive. This permits us to use a one-tailed test of significance. If we hypothesized only that there would be a relationship between the variables, without specifying whether it would be positive or negative, we would use a two-tailed test. Suppose, also that we choose the .05 level of significance. For three degrees of freedom, a one-tailed test, and a .05 level of significance, the table tells us the critical value of t is 2.353. Our obtained t value of 4.69 exceeds that value, so we can reject the null hypothesis and conclude there is a relationship between the two variables.

Because we have learned that $b^* = r$, testing for the statistical significance of b^* is the same as testing the significance of r under the null hypothesis. Procedures for calculating confidence intervals for r, b, and b^* are described in more advanced texts.

Linear Partial Regression and Correlation Analysis

Recall that bivariate regression and correlation analyses have two different but closely related objectives. Bivariate regression analysis aims to predict a value of a dependent variable from the values of an independent variable. Bivariate correlation analysis seeks to determine the strength of a relationship between two variables in terms of the proportion of variation in y accounted for by an independent variable x. We can think of **partial regression analysis** as predicting the values of y from the values of x, taking one or more other possibly causal (independent) variables into account. **Partial correlation analysis** may be thought of as a way of determining the amount of variation in y accounted for by a particular independent variable x, taking one or more other independent variables into account. In the discussion that follows, we will consider including only one additional independent variable in the analysis, but the basic procedure is extendable to any number of additional independent variables. As we noted in our discussion of causality in Chapter 2, the argument that an observed relationship between two variables is causal is strengthened if we can include other possibly causal variables in our analysis. The objective of doing so would be to either eliminate them from consideration as causal by demonstrating they have little or no effect on the original relationship, or describe how the original relationship is modified by them. We have already encountered this general idea in our discussion of elaboration analysis with contingency tables in Chapter 8. There we examined what happened to the relationship between two variables in a zero-order table when partial tables, defined by the categories of a third nominal or ordinal variable, were created. For the purposes of this discussion, we call the third variable the test variable and abbreviate it here as T. (Don't confuse this abbreviation with the t test for statistical significance we discussed in Chapter 9 and earlier in this chapter.)

If the third variable was measured at the nominal or ordinal level, we could proceed in much the same way we did in elaboration analysis. We would calculate regression or correlation coefficients for each value (category) of T and examine any changes in the bs or rs. Interpreting the results of such an analysis follows essentially the same lines of argument we used in elaboration analysis. For example, assuming the time sequence of the variables was appropriate, if all of the partial rs stayed essentially the same and T preceded y in time, we would have a replication. If they were all approximately zero, we would say the apparent zero-order r was spurious; if the r for one of the partials was higher than the zero-order r, whereas the rs for the other partials were near zero, we would have a specification; and so on. These interpretations would, of course, depend on the time sequences and the relationships between T and the other two variables as described in our discussion of elaboration analysis. This is an effective strategy for multivariate analysis, especially when only one or at most two additional nominal or ordinal independent variables (or categories of variables) are to be included in the analysis. If more than two such variables are involved, the strategy quickly becomes unwieldy and interpretation of the results is very difficult.

When all three variables under consideration are measured at the interval or ratio level and the general assumptions underlying the procedure can be met, partial regression and partial correlation analyses are good options. In partial correlation, the same general strategy we used in contingency table partial analysis is employed. We want to hold the value of a second independent variable "constant" and examine the relationship between the remaining independent variable and the dependent variable. We put the word *constant* in quotation marks because, as we shall see, holding a variable constant in partial correlation means something a bit different than it means when constructing partial tables.

Suppose we are interested in the relationship between "rate of gun ownership" as the independent variable and "homicide rate" as the dependent variable, and that we find a negative correlation between these two variables. That is, as the rate of gun ownership goes up, the homicide rate goes down. Then suppose someone suggests that the size of the population in cities may be an important factor in determining the homicide rate. Partial correlation analysis, examining the relationship between the rate of gun ownership and the homicide rate, holding population size constant, would be an appropriate way of approaching this question.

Holding population constant here is really more like taking population size into account or controlling for population size *statistically*. It does not involve dividing up the population size variable into discrete categories and doing the correlation analysis for each category, as in contingency table partial analysis. Rather, we might think of it as a process of measuring the relationship between the test variable (T) and each of the original two variables and then removing those effects statistically, leaving whatever remains of the original relationship. In our example, the partial correlation question might be, What happens to the relationship between the rates of gun ownership and homicide rates when city population is taken into account?

Calculating $r_{xy \cdot T}$

For purposes of illustration, we calculate a partial correlation coefficient. Calculating the partial correlation coefficient involves determining the bivariate correlations between all the possible combinations of the three variables under consideration. The general formula for a partial correlation coefficient is

$$r_{xy \cdot T} = \frac{r_{xy} - (r_{xT})(r_{yT})}{\sqrt{(1 - r_{xT}^2)(1 - r_{yT}^2)}} \quad (11.14)$$

The statistic $r_{xy \cdot T}$ can be read as the correlation between x and y, controlling for the test variable. The zero-order correlation coefficient between x and y is r_{xy}, the correlation coefficient between y and T is r_{yT}, and the correlation coefficient between x and T is r_{xT}. For illustrative purposes, we calculate one partial correlation coefficient using Formula 11.14, for fictitious bivariate correlation data. Suppose we have the following bivariate correlations: $r_{xy} = .62$, $r_{xT} = .45$, and $r_{yT} = .32$. Let's now calculate $r_{xy \cdot T}$.

$$r_{xy \cdot T} = \frac{r_{xy} - (r_{xT})(r_{yT})}{\sqrt{(1 - r_{xT}^2)(1 - r_{yT}^2)}}$$

$$= \frac{.62 - (.45)(.32)}{\sqrt{(1 - .45^2)(1 - .32^2)}}$$

$$= \frac{.62 - .14}{\sqrt{(1 - .20)(1 - .10)}}$$

$$= \frac{.48}{\sqrt{(.80)(.90)}}$$

$$= \frac{.48}{\sqrt{.72}}$$

$$= \frac{.48}{.85}$$

$$r_{xy \cdot T} = .56$$

Interpreting $r_{xy \cdot T}$ is essentially similar to the process discussed above. That is, assuming the time sequence for the variables is correct, if $r_{xy \cdot T}$ is approximately equal to r_{xy}, we would say T has no influence on the relationship between x and y (similar to a replication in elaboration analysis terms). If $r_{xy \cdot T}$ is zero (or nearly so), we would say that r_{xy} is spurious and that T accounts for (statistically explains) the relationship between x and y. In our fictitious sample, the $r_{xy \cdot T}$ of .56 is not too far from our r_{xy} of .62, so we would probably conclude that T has little, if any, effect on r_{xy}—a replication. Here, too, as we noted in our discussion of partial analysis with contingency tables, interpreting partial correlation analysis results is not just a matter of the statistics themselves but also of analysts' judgments. The consumers of such statistics must also place these results in the context of their own experiences to assess their importance.

Partial regressions and correlations may also be tested for statistical significance if the data are from a random sample. Those procedures are beyond the scope of this text.

Assumptions and Cautions

As descriptive data analysis procedures, least squares bivariate correlation and regression, as well as partial regression and correlation, assume normally distributed variables measured at the interval or ratio level. They assess the strength of only *linear* relationships between variables. Other types of relationship, including curvilinear relationships, may exist, but would not be revealed by these analyses. To detect the nature of the relationship between variables, constructing a scattergram of the data is highly recommended as an initial step in data analysis. If the scattergram does not reveal at least an approximately linear relationship, alternative strategies for analyzing the data should be selected.

It is also especially important to ensure that the measurements of the variables are independent of each other. If they are not, the analysis will produce a misleadingly high regression or correlation coefficient, one that reflects nothing more than that the same variable has been measured in two different ways. This would be a prime example of garbage in-garbage out.

Correlation should not be confused with causation. Such confusion may be fostered by terms like *explained* and *unexplained variance*, which are used in discussing correlation and regression analysis. As we pointed out in Chapter 2, correlation (or concomitant variation) is a necessary but not sufficient condition for causation. In the context of correlation and regression analysis, variance in the dependent variable is explained only in statistical terms (sum of squares). Although a finding that a correlation exists, even a very high one, between or among variables satisfies one of the three criteria for a causal inference (concomitant variation), the appropriate time sequence of changes in variable values and the elimination of other possible causal variables remain to be fulfilled. In fields of study where multiple causes are common, such as in criminal justice and other social sciences, high correlation or regression coefficients arouse the suspicion that they are spurious for one reason or another. The reader should keep this point in mind whenever correlation coefficients are presented as part of a data analysis.

It is very risky to project correlations or regressions beyond the range of the variable values used to calculate them. Even if a relationship is linear over a certain range of variable covariance, it does not necessarily follow that it will remain so over the entire range of possible variable values.

Finally, bivariate correlation and regression, as well as partial correlation and regression analyses, can be performed only on units of analysis for which data are available on all of the variables included in the analysis. As we noted in Chapter 4, missing data can pose difficult issues in statistical analysis. Missing data may be dealt with in a variety of ways, but the typical solution is to remove from the analysis the units of analysis for which data on one of the variables is missing, at least for the analysis involving that variable. It should be noted, however, that deleting units of analysis from a sample jeopardizes the assumption of randomness required for inferential statistics, including significance tests. As a consequence, the results of the analysis may be misleading. The amount and nature of the missing data should be reported and discussed.

Regression analysis is similar to correlation analysis, except that in the former, one of the variables is designated as the independent variable. In correlation analysis, the results are the same no matter which variable we designate as the independent variable.

Partial correlation analysis has parallels with partialing contingency tables. It can result in evidence indicating a spurious correlation between the original variables, as well as a replication or specification.

The tests of statistical significance for r and b assume random sampling, normally distributed variables measured at the interval or ratio level, homoscedasticity, and approximately equal variances of y for all values of x.

Summary

In this chapter, we considered bivariate regression and correlation analysis as well as partial regression and correlation for variables measured at the interval or ratio level. Regression analysis is aimed at predicting the value of a dependent variable from the value of an independent variable. Correlation analysis assesses the strength of the relationship between the variables. Partial regression analysis assesses the effect of a third variable on the zero-order regression coefficients. Partial correlation analysis assess the impact of a third variable on the zero-order correlation. These descriptive analytic procedures are obviously closely related.

Correlation analyses provide measures of the amount of variation in a dependent variable that is statistically explained by the variation in an independent variable. It is important to distinguish between this use of explanation and its meaning in the context of causal inference. Correlation establishes only one of the three prerequisite conditions, concomitant variation, for a persuasive causal argument.

Regression analysis permits the researcher to determine how many units of change in y are, on average, associated with a single unit of change in x. This leads to statements summarizing research results such as when the police force was increased by one foot patrol officer for a month in a neighborhood, there is a reduction of 10 personal assault reports from that neighborhood for the month. Assuming we have good evidence that the relationship is causal and not spurious, the regression coefficient may provide some guidance in estimating the magnitude of the impact of interventions (changes in policy or practice) designed to increase desirable outcomes in applied settings. Thus, we might propose to increase the number of foot patrol officers in neighborhoods next year and say we can expect a reduction of 10 personal assault reports from the neighborhood for each officer added. Of course, such predictions may or may not turn out to be true and should be subjected to ongoing study.

Caution must be exercised in such applications of correlation and regression analysis, however. First, as we have already noted, other unrecognized and/or unmeasured variables may account for some or all of the changes in assault reports. Correlation, by itself, is not causation. Second, predictions of the impact of independent variable values beyond the range of those values included in a particular study should be regarded as highly speculative.

Concepts to Master

- a (in a linear equation)
- b (or beta, in a linear equation)
- b^* (standardized beta or beta weights)
- Best fitting line
- Coefficient of determination
- Coordinates
- Correlation
- Correlation analysis
- Correlation coefficient
- Correlation matrix
- Covariance
- Cross-product of x and y
- Curvilinear relationship
- Data point
- Error of estimate
- Goodness of fit
- Least (sum of) squares
- Linear relationship
- Negative relationship (correlation or regression)
- OLS (ordinary least squares)
- Outliers
- Partial correlation analysis
- Partial regression analysis
- Positive relationship (correlation or regression)
- r
- r^2
- $r_{xy.T}$
- Regression analysis
- Regression coefficient
- Regression equation
- Regression line
- Regression of y on x
- Residual
- Scattergram
- Slope
- Standardized beta (b^*)
- x axis
- x,y
- x,y
- y axis
- y intercept

Review Questions

1. What are the basic ideas underlying correlation and regression analysis? How are they different? How are they similar?

2. What is a scattergram?

3. What is a data point? How is one located in a scattergram graph?

4. What is the general formula for any straight line in a scattergram graph?

5. What is the basic definition of the slope (b) of any straight line in a scattergram graph? What would a slope of +2 mean? A slope of –2?

6. What is the general formula for the slope of any straight line in a scattergram graph?

7. What is the definition of the y intercept (a) for any straight line in a scattergram graph?

8. What is the general formula for the y intercept of any straight line in a scattergram graph?

9. What is the objective of regression analysis? What does the regression of y on x mean?

10. What is a regression line? How does it differ from just any straight line in a scattergram graph?
11. What is the general equation for a regression line? Distinguish between constants and variables in the equation.
12. What is the y intercept of a regression line?
13. What is the general formula for the y intercept for a regression line?
14. What is the general formula for the slope (b) of a best fitting line?
15. What is a standardized beta (b^* or beta weight)? What are the similarities and differences between b and b^*? What is the advantage of b^*?
16. What is a sum of squares? What is a least sum of squares?
17. Why would the regression line for the regression of y on x ($y.x$) likely have a different slope than the regression line for the regression of x on y ($x.y$)?
18. What is the regression coefficient?
19. What is a residual or error of estimate?
20. Define outliers and discuss why they are problematic in statistical analyses.
21. What is correlation analysis, and what is its objective?
22. What is a linear relationship? How do linear and curvilinear relationships differ?
23. What is a positive relationship between two variables?
24. What is a negative relationship between two variables?
25. What is the correlation coefficient? What is its range of values?
26. What are explained and unexplained variances in correlation analysis?
27. What is a correlation matrix?
28. What is the coefficient of determination? How is the coefficient of determination interpreted in terms of explained and unexplained variance?
29. Is there a relationship between the slope of a regression line (b) and the correlation coefficient (r)?
30. What does $r = +1.0$ mean? $r = -1.0$? $r = 0.0$? $r = +0.5$? $r = +0.2$?
31. What is partial correlation analysis, and what is its objective?
32. What does holding a variable constant mean in partial correlation analysis? How does it differ from holding a variable constant in elaboration analysis?
33. What distribution is used for testing the statistical significance of r?
34. What are the assumptions underlying the test of significance of r?
35. What does y evenly distributed about x mean?
36. Define all the terms in the Concepts to Master list and use each of them in three sentences.

Exercises and Discussion Questions

1. What is the difference between the slope of just any straight line and the slope of a least squares regression line in a scattergram graph?

2. What is the difference between just any straight line and a least squares regression line in a scattergram?

3. Compare and contrast the y intercept for just any straight line and a least squares regression line in a scattergram graph.

4. Compare and contrast regression and correlation analysis.

5. Compare and contrast correlation and causation.

6. What do contingency table diagonals and best fitting least squares lines have in common? How do they differ?

7. Draw an approximate regression line in a scattergram you create. Estimate the slope of the regression line and identify the y intercept. Write the general formula for the regression line you have drawn.

8. In a scattergram space you create, draw least squares regression lines with $a = 4$ and slopes of $0, +1, -1, +3, -6, +4$. Discuss the results. What does each of these regression lines tell you about the relationship between the variables?

9. Suppose you have matched two low-income neighborhoods on other relevant variables and gathered the following data for assessing the effects of after school until 10:00 p.m. bicycle patrols and automobile patrols on preteens' perceptions of the police and their safety in their neighborhoods.

	Bicycle Patrol Neighborhood				Automobile Patrol Neighborhood		
Citizens	View of police	Safety of neighborhood	Age	Citizens	View of police	Safety of neighborhood	Age
A	3	4	10	H	4	4	9
B	1	2	12	I	3	1	11
C	4	3	11	J	1	2	10
D	2	1	9	K	5	2	12
E	5	4	12	L	2	1	11
F	4	3	11	M	3	3	12
G	3	5	10	N	2	3	10

Assume that: the two groups of preteens are random samples of the preteens in their neighborhoods; the "view of police" and "neighborhood safety" ratings are ratio-level measures, each with a possible range of 1 to 5, as is age; and higher numerical ratings indicate more favorable views of the police and feeling more safe.

Use these data for the following exercises. You will need to use statistical analyses you have learned about in previous chapters as well as those covered in this chapter to address the following exercises.

   a. Discuss the nature of the research design underlying this study.
   b. Formulate at least four null and corresponding research hypotheses that could be addressed by these data. Discuss how you would use the data (what kinds of analysis you would perform) to determine whether the data supported your research hypotheses.
   c. Is there a relationship between type of neighborhood patrol and view of the police? Select an appropriate test of statistical significance and discuss why it is appropriate. Do the calculations, report and interpret the results.
   d. Is there a relationship between type of neighborhood patrol and feelings of safety?
   e. Ignoring the difference in type of patrol (that is, combining the two samples and treating them as if they were one sample), is there a relationship between age and views of the police?
   f. Ignoring the difference in type of patrol, is there a relationship between age and feelings of safety?
   g. Ignoring the difference in type of patrol, is there a relationship between views of police and feelings of safety? Construct a scattergram for these data and discuss what it indicates. Draw your best guess of a regression line in the scattergram. Discuss what a regression line is for this data. What is a y intercept, and what would be your best guess of the y intercept for this scattergram? How did you arrive at your guess? What is the slope of a regression line, and what would be your guess about its value for this scattergram? How did you arrive at your guess? What would you guess the coefficient of correlation might be? How did you arrive at your guess?
   h. Construct a scattergram for the views of police and feelings of safety variables for the bicycle patrol sample and the automobile patrol sample separately. Discuss what the two indicate compared to each other and to the combined scattergram you constructed in Exercise 9g.
   i. Using only the views of police and feelings of safety data from the bicycle patrol neighborhood, calculate the constants for the best fitting (regression) line, interpret those constants, and state the corresponding formula for the line. Discuss what it means to call the regression line the best fitting line. What are the residuals for the regression line? Why are they called residuals? What would the opposite of the residuals be?
   j. Using only the views of police and feelings of safety data from the bicycle patrol neighborhood, calculate the correlation coefficient and the coefficient of determination.

Discuss and interpret your results. Test your obtained r for statistical significance. Interpret and discuss the results.

k. Using only the views of police and feelings of safety data from the bicycle patrol neighborhood, calculate a partial correlation coefficient using age as the test factor. Interpret and discuss your results.

10. Discuss the correlation matrix in the From the Literature Box 11.1. Which of the variables in the matrix are ratio-level variables? Why are they ratio-level variables? Which variables correlate highest with each other? Which correlate lowest with each other? What would you need to do to calculate the coefficient of determination for the rs in the matrix?

11. If you haven't already done so, answer all the questions in the "Pause, Think, and Explore" boxes.

Student Study Site

Visit the open-access student study site at **www.sagepub.com/fitzgerald** for access to several study tools including eFlashcards, web quizzes, and additional appendices as well as links to SAGE journal articles and audio, video and web resources.

12

Multivariate Linear Regression and Correlation Analysis and Logistic Regression

An Introduction

Learning Objectives

What you are expected not only to learn but to master in this chapter:

- The similarities and differences between correlation and regression analysis
- Some ways of dealing with missing data

- The assumptions of linear multiple regression and correlation analysis
- The basic ideas underlying multiple regression analysis
- How to graph a trivariate best fitting plane
- The components of a general multiple regression equation
- The nature and uses of standardized betas
- Some versions of stepwise regression
- The basic ideas underlying linear multiple correlation
- What dummy variables are and how they are used in multiple regression and correlation analyses
- What statistical models are and how they are used in multiple regression and correlation analyses
- What main effects and interaction effects are in multiple regression and correlation analyses
- What the problem of multicollinearity is in multiple regression and correlation analyses
- Tests of statistical significance for linear regression and correlation statistics
- How to report the results of multiple regression and correlation analyses
- The basic ideas underlying logistic regression analyses
- The use of natural logs in logistic analyses
- The components of the logistic regression equation
- How logits are derived
- How the constants α and β are estimated in logistic equations
- How the results of logistic analyses are reported

Introduction

Is there a relationship among years of education completed, years of residence in a particular city, sex, and jail time served for a serious misdemeanor? Is there a relationship among judges' ages, judicial circuits' population sizes, and lengths of sentence for felony assault? Is there a relationship among officers' ages, weights, years in service, and accuracy in the use of firearms? Is there a relationship among years of education completed, number of drug-using friends, parents' marital status, and amount of marijuana consumed per week? What two or more variables best predict whether a probationer or parolee will succeed or fail? What two or more variables best predict whether a domestic assault perpetrator will repeat the offense within 1 year? The statistical analyses we consider in this chapter can often help answer questions such as these.

Let's begin by recalling from our discussion in Chapter 11 that bivariate least squares correlation and regression analyses are closely related, but have somewhat different objectives. Correlation analysis tells us the strength and direction (positive or negative) of the relationship between two variables. More specifically, it is aimed at determining how much of the variation in a dependent variable can be accounted for (explained) by variation in an independent variable. The purpose of regression analysis, on the other hand, is prediction. In particular, the aim is to predict the values of a dependent variable from the values of an independent variable. We said that both bivariate correlation and bivariate regression were linear analyses. That is, they both relied on a straight line to approximate the data. Multivariate correlation and regression analyses are also closely related linear analyses and have the same corresponding differences in objective. What's new is the inclusion of more than two variables in the analyses. Multivariate correlation and regression are usually referred to as multiple correlation and regression. We follow that convention on most occasions here.

In the social sciences, including criminology and criminal justice, those who wish to develop knowledge based on quantitative research methods must routinely confront complexity both in theoretical issues and in the practical problems they wish to resolve. Much of the complexity arises from the fact that *many* variables influence the phenomena they are interested in explaining and/or predicting. The analytic and statistical procedures we have discussed in previous chapters are limited in their usefulness by the relatively few variables that can be included in a particular analysis.

As we noted in Chapter 2, one of the great advantages of experimental research designs, especially those that can be implemented in laboratory settings, is that they provide a powerful way of managing at least some of this complexity. In laboratory experiments, the researcher exercises what we call **physical control** over numerous potentially causal variables. Typically, physical control of variables occurs before or during the data-gathering process. For example, the researcher controls the physical setting in which the study will take place, the selection of study participants, and the deliberate introduction (or exclusion) of changes in particular variables. As a result, the effects, if any, of a single independent variable often can be at least partially isolated. In some instances, such as studying the effects of different perpetrator identification procedures on the accuracy of eyewitnesses, criminal justice theories, policies, and practices can be examined in laboratory settings. Unfortunately, opportunities for such highly controlled studies are, for a variety of reasons (including ethical considerations), relatively rare in criminal justice.

Something approaching experimental design can sometimes be achieved by criminal justice researchers in the field, that is, in the natural settings where people live their day-to-day lives. Studies comparing the impact of two different patrolling practices in two neighborhoods that have been matched on what are believed to be significant variables are examples. So also are studies of different responses to domestic violence. Still, strategies such as randomization and matching are often both difficult and imprecise in field research settings. Furthermore, implementing changes in policies or procedures based on research results often poses difficulties in natural settings because unanticipated circumstances and events (that is, changes in unanticipated variables) often intervene in real-life settings. The difficulties and imprecision in these aspects of the field research process can undermine the validity and applicability of research results.

So, the criminal justice researcher or practitioner must, in many instances, resort to other ways of contending with complex research questions, including controlling many possibly influential variables and sorting out their individual effects. Again, statisticians have come to our rescue and developed procedures for the analysis of more complex theoretical and applied questions involving multiple independent variables.

The most commonly applied strategy is to impose **statistical controls** over variables. In contrast with physical controls, statistical controls are imposed *after* the data have been gathered and during the data analysis phase of the research process. Statistical controls take two basic forms. First, they may be imposed by dividing the data set into subsets on the basis of the values of potentially important independent variables and examining relationships between a dependent variable and other independent variables within those categories. You are already familiar with this basic approach when dealing with two or three nominal or ordinal independent variables. It is the strategy we used when performing elaboration analysis with contingency tables in Chapter 8 and partial regression and correlation analysis in Chapter 11.

Second, as we learned in Chapter 11, sophisticated statistical controls can be applied mathematically when analyzing interval- or ratio-level independent variables. In Chapter 11 we learned about how the effects of one independent variable are determined while controlling statistically for the effects of another independent variable included in the analysis. This statistical control strategy can be extended to analyses involving more than two independent variables.

When a researcher has data on three or more variables of interest that are measured at the interval or ratio level, multiple correlation and regression analyses offer many advantages. Among the most important is the capacity of these analyses to measure both the total combined effects of all independent variables included in the analysis and the contribution each of the independent variables makes to the prediction or explanation of changes in the values of a dependent variable. To accomplish the latter, it is necessary to impose statistical controls over many independent variables simultaneously.

In this chapter, we introduce and discuss in general terms some procedures for analyzing data sets involving many independent variables. These procedures are called multiple correlation and multiple regression analyses. In some cases, as we shall see, even nominal- or ordinal-level independent variables can be included in these analyses through the creation of dummy variables. Also, in recent years, statisticians have developed logistic procedures that permit multiple regression and correlation analysis with nominal or ordinal dependent variables.

A detailed treatment of multiple correlation and regression is beyond the scope of this introductory text, as are most of the calculations associated with them. We do hope, however, to provide a basic introduction to these procedures. Our objectives in this chapter are to (a) convey a basic understanding of these procedures, (b) provide a foundation for further study in statistical analysis, (c) assist researchers in selecting an appropriate analytic strategy for their own data, and (d) help you interpret and make basic critiques of such analyses when they are encountered in criminal justice research reports in the professional literature or elsewhere. As we did in the previous chapter, because we think it is easier to understand, we will begin with a discussion of multiple regression analysis.

There are a few new symbols introduced to facilitate the discussion, and they are summarized in Table 12.1.

Table 12.1 Symbols and Their Meaning in Multiple Regression and Correlation and Logistic Regression

Symbol	Meaning
a	The y intercept in a multiple regression equation
A	The y intercept in a logistic regression equation
b	Beta (beta weight, slope coefficient, regression coefficient)
b^*	Standardized beta
β	Beta in a logistic regression equation
β^*	Standardized beta in a logistic regression equation
b_{yx}	The coefficient of regression of the dependent variable y on independent variable x
$b_{yx_1 \cdot x_2}$	The coefficient of regression of the dependent variable y on independent variable 1 (x_1), controlling for or taking into account independent variable 2 (x_2); parallel interpretations for other combinations of subscripts
$\log_e$	The natural log (base of 2.7182)
R	Coefficient of multiple correlation
R^2	Coefficient of multiple determination
$\text{Exp}(\beta)$	The odds ratio of the effect of a one-unit change in an independent variable, which is $\log_e$ raised to the power of β, on the dependent variable
r_{xy}	The correlation between x and y
$r_{x_1 y \cdot x_2}$	The correlation of independent variable 1 (x_1) and the dependent variable (y), controlling for or taking independent variable 2 (x_2) into account; parallel interpretations for other combinations of subscripts

Dealing With Missing Data

Before we turn to the details of multiple regression analysis, we need to consider again a problem we first discussed in Chapter 4: missing data. It is a potentially serious problem in all statistical analyses, even univariate ones. But it is very likely to become more serious as the number of variables included in an analysis increases. The basic issue can be stated simply: Analysis can be performed only on variables for which data are available. In the real world of research, it is quite common that some data are missing on some variables for some units of analysis. Some subjects may refuse to answer or inadvertently skip one or more survey questions, for example. The almost universal reality of missing data is easy enough to understand, but dealing with the problems missing data pose when conducting analyses is anything but simple.

Statisticians have developed a number of strategies for dealing with missing independent variable data. The details of some of them are beyond the scope of this text, but we briefly identify and discuss three of the most basic approaches: listwise (sometimes called casewise) deletion, pairwise deletion, and variable deletion. The first two approaches remove units of analysis from the data set, whereas the third leaves all units of analysis in the data set, but excludes variables for which data are missing from the analysis.

In **listwise deletion** (sometimes called casewise deletion), if data are missing on one or more independent variables for a unit of analysis (i.e., case), that unit of analysis is dropped entirely from the data set (the list of cases) for all analyses.

Unlike listwise deletion, where missing data on any one variable removes the unit of analysis entirely from the data set (and, of course, all subsequent calculations), **pairwise deletion** excludes those units of analysis for which there are missing data only from those calculations involving those independent variables for which information is missing. Those units of analysis are included in other calculations on the data set not involving those variables. This means, of course, that there are different *n*s for different analyses of the "same" data set. In the case of bivariate correlation analyses (which, as we will see, play a large role in multivariate regression and correlation analyses), the correlation analyses include only those units of analysis for which data were available for both variables being correlated.

In **variable deletion**, when data on an independent variable are missing for any unit of analysis, that variable is removed from the list of variables included in the analysis. Unlike listwise deletion, where units of analysis for which any data are missing are excluded from the data set to be analyzed, variable deletion excludes *variables* from analyses of the data set.

Finally, of course, there is the problem of missing data on dependent variables. If data on the dependent variable for any unit of analysis are missing, that unit must be dropped from the analysis.

Listwise and pairwise deletions (as well as unit-of-analysis deletions due to missing dependent variable data) threaten the validity of many multivariate analyses, especially those involving inferential statistics. Why? Because when you remove units of analysis from a sample, the sample becomes less random, thereby undermining the assumption of randomness required for inferential statistics, including tests of significance. The greater the number of units of analysis dropped from an analysis due to missing dependent or independent variable data, the greater the likelihood that randomness has been severely compromised. Analyses compromised by listwise deletions usually include fewer of the original units of analysis than those compromised by pairwise deletions, but the former analyses at least have the virtue of being based on the same list of remaining cases and, therefore, the same *n*s. Analyses involving pairwise deletions usually include more of the units of analysis in the original data set, at least for some analyses, but they have the disadvantage of being based on at least somewhat different numbers of units of analysis (that is, different *n*s). Variable deletions have the great advantage of not threatening the randomness of the sample required for inferential statistical analysis, but they can result in the loss of a very large number of variables, some of which may be very interesting or important variables. The truth is, there are no really good solutions to the problems posed by missing data, especially when the amount of missing data is large. Vigorous efforts to minimize missing data in the first place are strongly recommended. In any event, researchers should always report the kinds and amounts of missing data, how they have dealt with these problems, and the implications for interpreting the results of their analysis.

Assumptions of Linear Multiple Regression and Correlation Analyses

The general assumptions for the appropriate application of linear multiple regression and correlation analyses include many of the same ones we noted for bivariate regression and correlation, and a couple of new ones as well. They are as follows:

Variables are measured at the interval or ratio level (except for a limited number of dummy variables; see the discussion later in the chapter).

The relationships among the variables are linear.

Variables are normally distributed and homoscedastic.

The independent variables must be statistically independent of each other (i.e., all of the possible bivariate correlations between them must be relatively small; this is referred to as an absence of multicollinearity. (See the discussion of multicollinearity later in the chapter).

The effects of the independent variables must be additive.

Like their bivariate counterparts, multiple regression and correlation are descriptive statistics. If the data are from a random sample, multiple regression and correlation statistics can be tested for statistical significance using inferential statistics.

Linear Multiple Regression Analysis

In Chapter 4, we discussed univariate analysis and noted that the mean was the score that minimized the distance between it and the rest of the scores in a distribution. As such, if we wanted a single score that best represented the distribution, it would be the mean. In Chapter 11, we discussed bivariate regression analysis involving an independent variable (x) and a dependent variable (y). In that chapter, we described the process of searching for the best fitting regression line. That was the straight line, you will recall, that minimizes the distance between it and the data points in the bivariate scattergram, as measured perpendicular to the x (independent variable) axis. Put in a different way, the regression line minimizes the residual (error) sum of squares when regressing y on x. Recall that the formula for the straight best fitting regression line had the form $y = a + bx$. The formula includes two constants (a and b) and two variables (x and y). We defined a as the y intercept, and b as the slope of the best fitting line. As we learned in Chapter 11, statisticians provide formulas for calculating these constants for any particular straight line. Once their values are determined, we can use the linear regression equation to make the best (i.e., error-minimizing) predictions of y from particular values of x. Multiple regression analysis is an extension of the same basic ideas, though they are very difficult to represent graphically when more than three variables (and, hence, more than three dimensions) are involved.

When two, rather than one, independent variables are used to predict the dependent variable, the analog of the best fitting straight line in bivariate regression is the best fitting flat plane. As with bivariate linear regression analysis, the absence of a strong linear relationship among the variables in a multivariate analysis does not necessarily mean there is no relationship between the variables. Rather, there may be a relationship best represented by a curved plane.

The Basic Ideas Underlying Linear Multiple Regression Analysis

The basic aim of **multiple regression analysis** is to make the best possible prediction of the value of a dependent variable, this time from the values of two or more independent variables.

A Trivariate Best Fitting Plane

Let's begin with a multiple regression analysis we can visualize. Consider the case of predicting the value of y from two independent variables, all three variables measured at the interval or ratio level. For example, we might want to predict the annual number of disciplinary incidents for juveniles in a long-term detention facility from the juveniles' ages (which we call variable x_1) and number of previous adjudicated offenses (which we call variable x_2). The juveniles are our units of analysis. Annual number of disciplinary incidents, age, and previous adjudicated offenses are the variables pertaining to the units of analysis. Annual number of disciplinary incidents is the dependent variable and the other two variables are the independent variables. We can represent this situation with a three-dimensional scattergram. To create the scattergram space, on a two-dimensional table top we draw two axes (one for each of the independent variables, age and number of previous offenses) that cross at right angles. (They will look like an x viewed from the side.) The third axis, representing the dependent variable y (annual number of disciplinary incidents), would extend vertically from and perpendicular to the first two x axes, as would a long pencil sticking straight up from the table top, passing through the point where the two x axes cross.

Each data point in the three-dimensional scattergram (representing one of the juveniles in our data set) has three coordinates (x_1, x_2, y). To locate a data point in this three-dimensional scattergram, we find the point where the two x values intersect on the table top. Through this point of intersection, we draw a straight line perpendicular to the two x axes (i.e., perpendicular to the table top). Next, we locate the point on the y axis corresponding to the value of the data point's y coordinate. From this point on the y axis, we draw a straight line perpendicular to the y axis. Where this line intersects with the perpendicular line drawn from the point of intersection of the two x values on the table top, we place a dot. This dot is a data point in the three-dimensional scattergram, as illustrated in Figure 12.1. We would repeat this process for each set of three observed variable values in our data set.

Then, instead of identifying a best fitting straight line as we did in the bivariate case, here we search for the best fitting flat plane we'll call the **regression plane**, as

Figure 12.1 Location of a Data Point in a Trivariate Scattergram

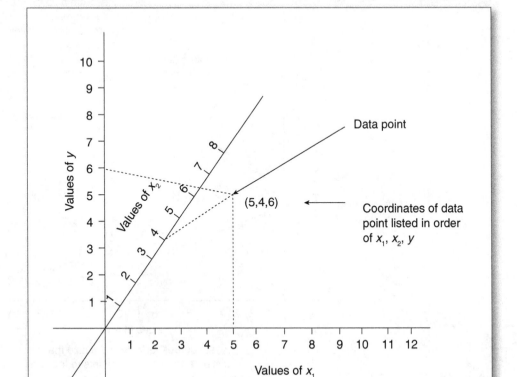

indicated in Figure 12.2. The basic criterion is the same, however. We want the plane that minimizes the average distance between the data points and the plane (that is, the plane that minimizes the errors when we use x_1 and x_2 to predict y, and the residual sum of squares for y). Here, too, as in bivariate regression analysis, we measure the distance we are trying to minimize parallel to the y axis.

The general formula for any plane in three-dimensional space is

$$y = a + b_1 x_1 + b_2 x_2 \qquad (12.1)$$

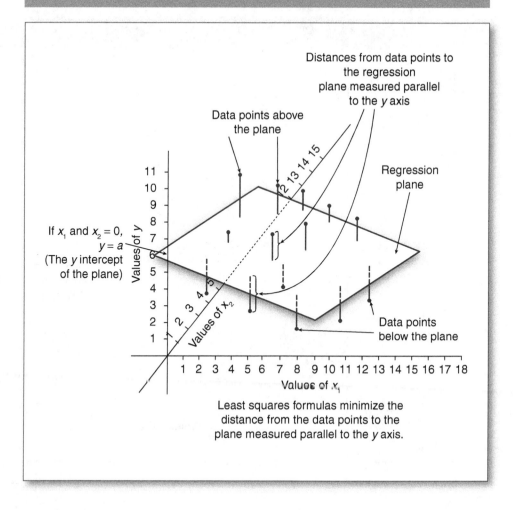

Figure 12.2 A Regression Plane and Data Points in a Trivariate Scattergram

> **PAUSE, THINK, AND EXPLORE A REGRESSION PLANE**
>
> Compare Formula 12.1 with Formula 11.1. What similarities and differences do you see?

As in the general formula for a straight line in a bivariate scattergram (Formula 11.1), in Formula 12.1 for a flat plane in a trivariate scattergram, a and b are constants for any particular multiple regression equation and x_1, x_2, and y are variables. When x_1 and x_2 are equal to zero, $y = a$. So, the constant a is the y intercept of the regression plane—that is, the point where the regression plane crosses the y axis. As in the bivariate regression equation, the bs in a multiple regression equation are called betas, slopes, or regression coefficients, in this case, **partial betas, partial slopes,** or **partial regression coefficients**. The constant b_1 is called the partial beta, slope, or regression coefficient of the linear partial regression of the first independent variable x_1 (which, in our example, is age) on y. The constant b_2 is the partial beta, slope, or regression coefficient of the second independent variable x_2 (the number of previous offenses) on y.

From our discussion in Chapter 11, you are already familiar with the general idea of partial regression. Recall that in the absence of any other information, the best prediction we can make about a value of y is the mean of y ($\bar{y}$). When we multiply the value of an independent variable x by its corresponding b, we are improving our prediction of y based on $\bar{y}$ by taking the average change in y for each unit change in x into account. Recall also that a partial regression predicts a dependent variable y from a particular independent variable (say, x_1) after the effects of another independent variable (say, x_2) have been "controlled" or taken into account. In the term $b_1 x_1$, the factor b_1 represents the average change in y for every unit change in x_1 *after the effects of x_2 have been taken into account*. Similarly, in the term $b_2 x_2$, the factor b_2 represents the average change in y for every unit change in x_2 *after the effects of x_1 have been taken into account*. It makes sense, then, to add these two quantities to determine their combined effects on y. So, Formula 12.1 says that the best prediction of y (based on the best fitting plane) is obtained by adding the product of each of the two partial regressions and their respective x coordinates to the constant a—the point where the regression plane crosses the y axis, which, as you will recall, is called the y intercept.

As we did when discussing bivariate correlation (see Formula 11.3, p. 367), we might add an error of estimate term to Formula 12.1 to remind us that our predictions of y will almost never be perfect. As in bivariate regression analysis, the error term represents the amount of variance in y unexplained by the combined effects of the independent variables.

The betas (bs) are roughly analogous to the partial tables in elaboration analysis (see Chapter 8). That is, they indicate the effects on the dependent variable of an independent variable while controlling for the effects of other independent variables included in the analysis. Figure 12.3 provides a geometric interpretation of the partial regression of y and x_1, holding x_2 constant.

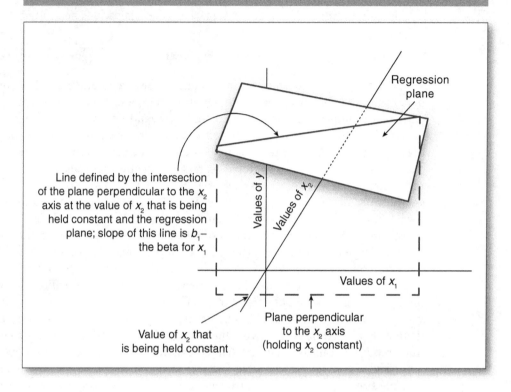

Figure 12.3 A Trivariate Scattergram Showing the Partial Regression of y on x_1, holding x_2 constant

The General Linear Multiple Regression Equation

You can imagine that it would be possible to extend Formula 12.1 to include as many independent variables as available or desirable. The general formula would then be

$$y = a + b_1x_1 + b_2x_2 + b_3x_3 + \cdots + b_jx_j + \text{error of estimate} \quad (12.2)$$

Statisticians have provided formulas for the constants a and b in multiple regression equations. The formulas for b_1 and b_2 in our trivariate multiple regression equation example (see Formula 12.1) are given by Formulas 12.3a and 12.3b, respectively.

$$b_1 = b_{yx_1.x_2} = \left[\frac{r_{yx_1} - (r_{yx_2})(r_{x_1x_2})}{1 - r_{x_1x_2}^2}\right]\left[\frac{s_y}{s_{x_1}}\right] \quad (12.3a)$$

$$b_2 = b_{yx_2 \cdot x_1} = \left[\frac{r_{yx_2} - (r_{yx_1})(r_{x_1 x_2})}{1 - r_{x_1 x_2}^2}\right]\left[\frac{s_y}{s_{x_2}}\right] \quad (12.3b)$$

The formula for *a* is given in Formula 12.4.

$$a = \bar{y} - (b_{yx_1 \cdot x_2})(\bar{x}_1) - (b_{yx_2 \cdot x_1})(\bar{x}_2) \quad (12.4)$$

In Formulas 12.3 and 12.4,

$b_{yx_1 \cdot x_2}$ is the partial slope (partial regression coefficient) of *y* on x_1, controlling for the effects on *y* of x_2;

$b_{yx_2 \cdot x_1}$ is the partial slope (partial regression coefficient) of *y* on x_2, controlling for the effects on *y* of x_1;

s_y is the standard deviation of *y* (the dependent variable, number of disciplinary incidents);

s_{x_1} is the standard deviation of x_1 (the first independent variable, age);

s_{x_2} is the standard deviation of x_2 (the second independent variable, number of previously adjudicated offenses);

r_{yx_1} is the bivariate correlation of *y* and x_1;

r_{yx_2} is the bivariate correlation of *y* and x_2;

$r_{x_1 x_2}$ is the bivariate correlation of x_1 and x_2;

$r_{x_1 x_2}^2$ is the square of the bivariate correlation between x_1 and x_2;

$\bar{y}$ is the mean of *y*;

$\bar{x}_1$ is the mean of x_1; and

$\bar{x}_2$ is the mean of x_2.

PAUSE, THINK, AND EXPLORE MULTIPLE REGRESSION ALPHAS AND BETAS

Compare Formulas 12.3a and 12.3b with Formula 11.14 (p. 399). Compare Formula 12.4 with Formula 11.5 (p. 369). What similarities and differences do you see?

As with the bivariate best fitting regression line, once the constant quantities a and b have been determined for our particular data set, we can insert them in Formula 12.1, the general formula for the best fitting regression plane (two independent variables), and use it to make our best predictions of y for any given x_1 and x_2.

Standardized Betas

We introduced the concept of the standardized beta in Chapter 11. Remember that the basic definition of a slope (b) is the ratio of the change in y to the change in x. When the variables included in an analysis are measured in different kinds of units, such as ages and proportion of time during a week watching television and miles from school, the unstandardized regression coefficients (bs) necessarily reflect those units. Because they are expressed in different units, their relative sizes are not directly comparable. As we have seen, it is often useful, therefore, to standardize the raw scores before calculating the statistics required for a particular analysis. As you will recall, the usual way of standardizing scores is to convert them into z scores, as we discussed in Chapter 5 (see Formula 5.1). As we noted in Chapter 11, when these conversions are completed and the calculations for b are carried out on these standardized scores, the results are called **standardized betas,** sometimes also called **beta weights,** often symbolized as b^*.

The formulas for calculating standardized betas for our two independent variable example are given in Formulas 12.5a and 12.5b.

$$b_1^* = b_1 \left(\frac{s_{x_1}}{s_y} \right) = b_{yx_1.x_2}^* = \frac{r_{yx_1} - (r_{yx_2})(r_{x_1.x_2})}{1 - r_{x_1.x_2}^2} \tag{12.5a}$$

$$b_2^* = b_2 \left(\frac{s_{x_2}}{s_y} \right) = b_{yx_2.x_1}^* = \frac{r_{yx_2} - (r_{yx_1})(r_{x_1.x_2})}{1 - r_{x_1.x_2}^2} \tag{12.5b}$$

To get a general idea of the relationship between raw score slopes (bs) and the corresponding standardized betas (b^*s), consider Formulas 12.6a and 12.6b for the two independent variables in our trivariate multiple regression example.

$$b_{x_1}^* = b_{x_1} \left(\frac{s_{x_1}}{s_y} \right) \tag{12.6a}$$

$$b_{x_2}^* = b_{x_2} \left(\frac{s_{x_2}}{s_y} \right) \tag{12.6b}$$

In Formula 12.6a, the standardized beta for the juveniles' ages equals the raw score b for age multiplied by the ratio of the standard deviation of the juveniles' ages (s_{x_1}) divided by the standard deviation of the number of disciplinary incidents (s_y).

In Formula 12.6b, the standardized beta (beta weight) for the number of previous offenses is the raw score b for number of previous offenses multiplied by the ratio of the standard deviation of the number of previous offenses (s_{x_2}) divided by the standard deviation of the number of disciplinary incidents (s_y). These formulas could be adapted to calculate b's for any number of (independent variables) that may be included in the analysis.

> **PAUSE, THINK, AND EXPLORE STANDARDIZED BETAS**
>
> Compare Formulas 12.5a and 12.5b as well as Formulas 12.6a and 12.6b. What similarities and differences do you see? How would you interpret the similarities and differences? Substitute the formula for the standard deviation (Formula 4.2) in Formulas 12.6a and 12.6b. Then compare Formulas 12.6a and 12.6b with Formula 11.4a. What similarities and differences do you see?

Again, the great advantage of standardized betas is that their relative sizes, and hence their proportionate contributions to changes in y, are immediately apparent in the values of the regression coefficients themselves. This is not the case with raw score slope coefficients (bs) because they are expressed in terms of the units of the variables to which they correspond. Of course, using Formula 12.1 to make predictions of the raw score values of y requires converting the standardized betas back into raw bs and the original units of the raw variables (ages, miles, etc.).

Stepwise Regression

Multiple regression analyses are often used to compare the effects of different combinations of two or more independent variables on y. One procedure for doing so is called stepwise regression. Several varieties of stepwise multiple regression are used in criminal justice research. We will consider only two common ones here, forward and backward **stepwise regression.**

Recall that the aim of a multiple regression equation is to predict the value of some dependent variable from two or more independent variables (see Formula 12.1). Basically, the equation entails adding the "effects" of each individual variable to produce a total combined effect. (We put effects in quotation marks because it is important to remember we are not necessarily referring to cause-and-effect relationships. Correlation is not causation.)

One way of using stepwise multiple regression analysis is to begin with just 2 or 3 independent variables, perhaps those with the highest bivariate correlations with the dependent variable, and then add other independent variables to the regression equation one at time or in conceptually or theoretically related blocks (groups of independent variables), examining the impact of the added variable(s) to the prediction of the dependent variable. This procedure is called **forward stepwise regression**. **Backward stepwise regression** essentially reverses this process. It begins with a multiple regression analysis that includes a large number of independent variables. Individual variables or blocks of variables are then removed one at a time and the regression analysis is rerun. The multiple regression analyses are then compared to determine the amount of reduction, if any, in the combined total effects on y.

Multiple correlation and regression statistics are calculated before and after each variable or block is added to or deleted from the equation. If the data are from a random sample, any difference between the before and after statistics may be tested for statistical significance. If adding a variable produces a statistically significant difference between the regression or correlation coefficients, the added variable is kept in the equation. If it does not, it is discarded. The process is repeated until all of the available variables that make a significant impact on the summary statistic are identified. The final regression equation then includes only those variables making a statistically significant difference when added to or subtracted from the equation.

Linear Multiple Correlation

Multiple correlation analysis is basically an extension of bivariate correlation. The aim is to determine how strong the linear relationship is between two or more independent variables (xs) and a dependent variable (y)—that is, how much of the variance in y is explained by changes in the xs.

The Basic Ideas Underlying Linear Multiple Correlation Analysis

You will recall that in bivariate correlation, the coefficient of determination (r^2) is interpreted to mean the proportion of the variance in a dependent variable accounted for or explained by the independent variable. The **coefficient of multiple determination** (sometimes called the **multiple correlation coefficient**), symbolized as R^2, is interpreted in the same way as r^2, except that it pertains to the proportion of the variance in y explained by the combined effects of two or more independent variables. Remember again, as we noted in our discussion of bivariate correlation, "explained" here means only statistical and not necessarily causal explanation.

For purposes of illustration, let's take the trivariate example we used earlier. **Multiple correlation analysis** permits us to determine how much of the variance in y, our dependent variable (number of disciplinary incidents) can be statistically explained by the two independent variables x_1 (age) and x_2 (number of previous adjudicated offenses) *combined*. In the process, we will also determine how much change in y can be attributed uniquely to each of the xs—that is, each x's contribution to changes in y after controlling for the effects of all of the other xs included in the analysis. You should recognize this language from our discussion of partial correlation and regression analyses in Chapter 11.

The formula for R^2 for our trivariate example is given in Formula 12.7.

$$R^2 = r_{yx_1}^2 + r_{yx_2 \cdot x_1}^2 (1 - r_{yx_1}^2) \tag{12.7}$$

In Formula 12.7, $r_{yx_1}^2$ is the zero-order coefficient of determination for x_1 and y and $r_{yx_2 \cdot x_1}^2$ is the **partial correlation coefficient** (also sometimes called the partial coefficient of determination) for y and x_2 controlling for x_1. So, to determine the coefficient of multiple determination (R^2), we begin with the zero-order coefficient of determination for y and the first independent variable (x_1), which gives us a measure of how much variance in y that first independent variable explains without considering the effect of x_2. We add to this explained variance another amount comprised of two factors that are multiplied. The first factor ($r_{yx_2 \cdot x_1}^2$) is the amount of variance in y explained by the second independent variable (x_2) after the variance in y explained by x_1 has been statistically controlled (i.e., the first factor is the partial correlation of y and x_2 controlling for x_1). The second factor ($1 - r_{yx_1}^2$) is an unexplained residual. Specifically, it is the remaining, unexplained residual (sum of squares) after the variance in y explained by x_1 has been determined. These two factors are multiplied and added to the zero-order coefficient of determination for y and x_1 to give us the coefficient of multiple determination. This coefficient tells us how much of the variance in y is statistically explained by the two independent variables (x_1 and x_2) combined.

Formula 12.7 can be expanded to include any number of independent variables, though the subscripts for keeping everything straight can get quite complex and confusing when more than four variables are involved. Fortunately, computers do a good job of keeping things sorted out in such situations.

You should also be aware that, when R^2 calculated from a *small* random sample is to be tested for statistical significance, the value is often corrected downward by a formula we will not present here. The correction is made necessary by the fact that R^2 tends to be inflated when ns are small.

Dummy Variables in Multiple Regression and Correlation Analyses

Many of the variables of interest to criminal justice researchers are measured at the nominal or ordinal level. Examples include sex, type of offense, type of correctional institution, and ethnicity. As a general rule, multiple correlation and regression analyses require continuous variables measured at the interval or ratio level. However, procedures have been developed to transform nominal- and ordinal-level independent variables in a way that permits them to be incorporated into regression and correlation analyses. This is accomplished by coding each value of the nominal or ordinal variable as a new variable. The values of these new variables, called **dummy variables**, are substituted for the original nominal or ordinal variable values in the analysis. We illustrate the use of dummy variables with multiple regression, but the same principles apply in multiple correlation as well.

Some nominal variables, such as sex (divided into male and female) or the answer to an interview question (divided into yes and no or true and false), may be coded as binary (that is, two-value) variables. One of the two answers would be entered into the database as a 1 and the other as a 0. Female may be scored as 1 and male as 0, for example. In effect, the code becomes an indicator of the presence or absence of a particular characteristic. Means and standard deviations can be calculated for these binary scores. The mean of such scores is equivalent to the proportion of those who were scored 1 on that particular variable value. Of course, 1 minus this proportion equals the proportion coded 0 for that variable value. In a multiple regression equation with female scored as 1, the beta associated with the sex variable is interpreted as the effect of being female (and not male) on the dependent variable, controlling for the effects of other independent variables in the equation. If male is coded as 1, the beta is interpreted as the effect of being male (and not female).

Although things get a bit more complicated, nominal or ordinal variables with more than two categories (values) can be converted to dummy variables as well. To do so, it is necessary to specify a "reference category" (variable value) and then treat each of the other categories (values) of the variable as a dichotomous variable with the value of the reference category coded 0. Suppose our research hypothesis is that the type of offense committed by a person is related to the person's success on probation (measured, say, by a length of time before revocation or release). Suppose also that the categories (values) of our "type of offense" variable are "property offense," "offense against persons," and "other offense." To transform the nominal-level values of this variable to dummy variables for the purposes of a multiple regression analysis, we might choose "other offenses" as our reference category. The remaining two variable values would each be scored separately as a binary variable. The "property offense" variable value might be coded 1 for "property offense" and 0 for "not a property offense." "Offense against persons" might be coded 1 for "offense against persons" and 0 for "not an offense against persons." Again, the mean for each of these binary category codes would be the proportion coded as 1. Table 12.2 indicates the basic coding scheme for the analysis of our example data.

As you can see in Table 12.2, two of three dummy variables are represented by unique combinations of 1s and 0s. The third dummy variable, for "other offense," is

Table 12.2 Coding Scheme for Dummy Variables for a Three Value Nominal Variable With "Other Offense" as the Reference Category

Dummy Variables	Coding for Dummy Variables	
Property offense	1	0
Offense against persons	0	1
Other offense	0	0

our reference category and is represented by all 0s. It is included in the analysis too, however, because the effect of each of the other two variable values on parole success is measured against the reference category, "other offense." When we perform a multiple regression analysis, the beta associated with the "property offense" dummy variable is interpreted as the difference between the effect on parole success of "property offense" and the effects of the reference category, "other offense after taking the effects of all other independent variables into account." If we subject the beta to a significance test and find a statistically significant beta for "property offense," for example, it would mean that the effect of "property offense" on parole success is significantly different from the effects on parole success of "other offense." If we find a statistically significant beta for "offense against persons," it would mean that the effect of "offense against persons" on parole success is significantly different from the effects on parole success of "other offenses." In these two comparisons, all three of the original nominal variable categories are included in the analysis. The basic rule is that, for any nominal or ordinal variable with k categories, we need $k - 1$ dummy variables and a reference category to replace the original variable with k values for a multiple regression analysis.

Which of the variable value categories is chosen as the reference category is largely a matter of the researcher's preference. Often, the category with the largest frequency is chosen as the omitted variable value. This facilitates a comparison of its impact on the dependent variable (in our example, parole success) with the variable values that are explicitly included (i.e., coded as 1 or 0). For example, if "property offense" had the highest frequency in our data set, we might choose to dummy code the other two values of the offense variable. We would then look for significant betas for each of the other two dummy variables. A significant beta would indicate that the difference in effect on the dependent variable between the particular included variable value whose beta was tested (offense against persons or other offense) and the excluded variable value "property offense" was significant. Obviously, it's important to keep track of which category of the variable is being used as the reference category and which of the binary options for each of the variable categories was scored 1 so that the results of a multiple correlation or regression analysis using dummy variables can be properly interpreted.

For reasons beyond the scope of this text, the number of dummy variables included in any particular multiple correlation or regression analysis must be relatively small. We'll simply note that dummy variables tend to inflate the value of R and, in extreme cases, render the results of either multivariate analysis meaningless.

Models

The term *model* is used in two related but slightly different ways in multivariate analysis. On one hand, researchers may refer to different blocks or combinations of independent variables for predicting or explaining a dependent variable as different models. On the other hand, analysts often refer to how well their data fit a particular model. We consider each of these uses of the term *model* in turn.

Multiple regression and correlation analyses are often described, discussed, and interpreted in terms of comparing models. Both types of analysis address the relationship between one particular dependent variable and two or more independent variables. Multiple regression, as we have noted, is intended to predict the values of a dependent variable from the values of two or more independent variables. Multiple correlation determines how much of the variance in a dependent variable can be statistically explained by the independent variables. In this context, a **model** can be defined as a particular set of two or more independent variables being used to predict the value or explain the variance of a particular dependent variable. In this meaning of the term, if we put a new variable in or take a variable out of an analysis, we are using a different model. Similarly, each of the different steps in a stepwise regression represents a different statistical model because adding or removing a variable or variables changes the combination of variables included in the analysis.

As a general rule, different models are constructed in order to compare their predictive or explanatory capacities. The analyst chooses which variables to include in particular models in order to facilitate the comparisons of particular interest. Her choices may be guided by a desire to compare the explanatory power of two theories about recidivism she is testing, for example. Suppose we are attempting to account for variances in the dependent variable, severity of sentence for first-time armed robbery. We have data on the independent variables age, ethnicity, previous convictions, and marital status of offenders, as well as the age and length of time on the criminal court bench of the presiding judges. If one were interested in whether offenders' characteristics or judges' characteristics played a larger role in determining the sentence, we might construct two models. Model 1 would be composed of all of the independent variables pertaining to the offenders, and Model 2 would include only those pertaining to the judges who issued the sentence. Multiple regression and/or correlation equations would be formulated, analysis for each model would be performed, and the results for the different models compared.

There are, of course, other possible models that could be constructed with this data set and compared in terms of their capacity to predict the values of or explain the variance in sentencing. Model 3 might be composed of the independent variables offenders' age and previous convictions as well as the ages of the presiding judges. Model 4 might consist of the offenders' marital status and previous convictions. Model 5 might include judges' length of time on the criminal bench, offenders' age and offenders' marital status, and so on. Alternatively, all of the offender and judge variables might be combined in a single model.

The severity of sentence data set we have been discussing might be analyzed with stepwise regression. For starters, we might run a multiple regression analysis that included all the variables. That might be considered one statistical model, and its goodness of fit could be judged by how much of the variance in incarceration rate their combined effects produced. Each subsequent step, in which we removed one or more of the independent variables, would be another model.

At least two other models for analyzing these data suggest themselves, based on the two different types of variables involved. One would consist of what we might call biological variables (median age and percent male) and their effects on incarceration rates. The other would consist of what we might call the socioeconomic variables (median family income, percent minority, and percent represented by public defenders) and their effects on incarceration rates. We could run separate multiple regression equations for the all-variables model and each of the two other models.

The second version of the term *model* arises when analysts speak of fitting their data to a model. Basically, that means they are searching for a regression equation (a mathematical model) that approximates their data with as little error as possible. Such models are constructed from sets of assumptions like the ones we have cited for the various statistical procedures and tests we have discussed in previous chapters (linear relationships, normal distributions, homoscedasticity, etc.). The extent to which the data fit the mathematical model is called **goodness-of-fit**. We discussed this concept earlier in Chapters 8 and 9. For example, bivariate regression analysis offers the model of a straight line represented by an equation that best fits the data (i.e., that minimizes the errors when predicting y from x) for a particular data set. However, how well a particular data set fits a model (i.e., its goodness of fit) varies. Data sets that leave large error terms or residuals after the model has been applied are not good fits. In such cases, another model might be tried, perhaps a curvilinear one, to see if it is a better fit. In this sense, many of the types of statistical analyses we have discussed in this book are models to which we try to fit our data. For example, the regression and correlation analyses we have discussed are linear least squares models. The two variations on the use of the term *model* are closely related. Recall that the results of a multiple regression analysis can be represented by a mathematical equation. Each set of independent variables would produce its own unique equation. So, to speak of a model as consisting of a particular set of independent variables for predicting y from xs is not really very different from speaking of it as a mathematical equation for predicting y from xs.

Main Effects and Interaction Effects

In analyzing the results of multiple regression, statisticians distinguish between main effects and interaction effects. The definitions of these terms vary somewhat depending on the analytic context, but we will consider only the most basic ones here. We also take this opportunity to review and illustrate several of the concepts we have discussed so far in this chapter.

Suppose we have data on five independent variables and a dependent variable. Perhaps we are interested in exploring the variables that might help account for differences in the federal incarceration rates among several federal court jurisdictions. In addition to the data for this dependent variable, we have data on the percent of the jurisdiction's population consisting of ethnic minorities and the median family income in the jurisdiction, age and sex of defendants, and whether or not the defendant was represented by a public defender or a private lawyer.

Suppose the general multiple regression equation reads as follows:

$$y = a + b_1 x_1 + b_2 x_2 + b_3 x_3 + b_4 x_4 + b_5 x_5 + \text{error of estimate}$$

where y is the federal incarceration rate and

a is the y intercept (i.e., the value of y when all xs equal zero),

x_1 is the percent minority in the jurisdiction,

x_2 is median family income in the jurisdiction,

x_3 is age of defendant,

x_4 is sex of defendant, and

x_5 is type of legal representation (public defender or private lawyer).

In general, **main effects** may be defined as bivariate effects, controlling for the effects of the other variables in the analysis. So, in our example, we would have the following main effects:

- Effect of percent minority on incarceration rates
- Effect of median family income on incarceration rates
- Effect of median age on incarceration rates
- Effect of percent of males on incarceration rates
- Effect of percent of defendants represented by public defenders on incarceration rates

Each of these main effects is measured, controlling for or taking into account all of the other independent variables included in the analysis.

As you will recall, the betas in a multiple regression equation are measures of the change in y for every unit change in x, controlling for the effects of other variables in the equation. If we converted our data to standard scores and ran our multiple regression analysis on them, standardized betas would indicate the relative size of each variable's contribution to changes in incarceration rates.

We introduced the concept of interaction in Chapter 8 when we discussed specification as an outcome when partialing contingency tables in elaboration analysis. In that context, zero-order relationships held only for a particular value of a second independent variable. The basic idea is the same here. **Interaction effects** can be defined in this context as the effects on a dependent variable of two or more independent variables that, when combined, are not additive.

What are additive and nonadditive effects? We begin with bivariate relationships and note how much effect the independent variable has on the dependent variable in each. In our example, suppose median family income changes the incarceration rate such that an increase of 10% in median family income reduces the incarceration rate by 5%. Suppose also that for every 5% increase in the minority population, the incarceration rate increases by 8%. If the effects of two or more variables are additive, their total combined effect on the dependent variable is equal to the sum of their separate effects. If the effects of median family income and percent minority are additive, their combined effects would increase the incarceration rate by 3 percentage points (the difference between the 8% increase and the 5% decrease). Note that percents are standardized statistics and can be directly compared.

We might find, however, that when we combined the two variables in our multiple regression analysis, the result was a 15% increase in the incarceration rate. Such a result would indicate that the two independent variables interact with each other and/or with the dependent variable to produce a larger change than would be expected from their separate bivariate results. In our example, note that if our analysis indicated an interaction between the two independent variables, we would expect there to be a correlation between percent minority and median family income, which could be confirmed (or not) by examining the appropriate cell in a bivariate correlation matrix. Interaction effects greatly complicate the interpretation of regression equations because they tend to inflate betas and make predicting the effects on the dependent variable of changes in the interacting independent variables very uncertain.

Dealing with evidence of interaction effects usually takes one of two paths. First, one or more of the variables that interact may be removed from the regression analysis and equation, which prevents their interaction effects from distorting the analysis but also removes those possibly important variables from the analysis. This strategy may be preferable if the interacting variables are not central to the questions of interest to the analyst. Second, as long as they are not just different measures of the same thing, interaction terms may be built into the regression equation. This strategy seeks to assess the interaction effects directly and is perhaps most appropriate when two or more of the independent variables of primary interest to the analyst interact. Such an equation might look like this:

$$y = a + b_1 x_1 + b_2 x_2 + b_3(x_1 x_2)$$

The term $x_1 x_2$ is the interaction term in this equation. It would be a new variable whose values would be the product of the two original variable values for each individual or other unit of analysis. Its beta (b) would be interpreted in the usual way, except that it would reference the newly created interaction variable, indicating how much variation in y is explained by the interaction term.

The Problem of Multicollinearity

Any high bivariate correlation indicates collinearity. In bivariate analyses, we usually like to see collinearity. In this case, collinearity is another name for a correlation between two variables, one independent and one dependent. In multiple regression and correlation analysis, however, collinearity refers to a correlation between *two of the independent variables* included in the analysis. When two or more pairs of independent variables in a multivariate analysis are correlated, the condition is referred to as **multicollinearity**. Multicollinearity poses serious problems for those doing or interpreting multivariate analyses. First, correlation suggests that two variables may be measuring the same thing. Second, the standard errors of the betas are inflated and tests of statistical significance on them are unreliable. Third, multivariate analysis aims to assess the unique contribution of changes in each independent variable to changes in the dependent variable. When independent variables are correlated, the unique effects of each variable cannot be determined. Finally, when several pairs of the independent variables included in an analysis are correlated, the multiple correlation coefficient R (and, of course, R^2) can be inflated, thereby yielding a misleading result.

The basic test for multicollinearity is to examine a bivariate correlation matrix involving all of the possible combinations of two independent variables to be included in the analysis. The matrix is examined to determine if there are high bivariate correlations and, if so, to identify the independent variables that are highly correlated. One often-cited standard is that bivariate correlations (rs) above .60 (or coefficients of determination [r^2s] above .35) should be regarded as evidence of multicollinearity requiring some adjustment in order not to be misled by the results of the multivariate analysis.

Solutions to the problem of multicollinearity include dropping at least one of the highly correlated variables from the analysis or statistically adjusting the formula for calculating R. Details for the latter are available in more advanced texts.

Multiple regression and correlation analysis reports should include information about any collinearity that has been detected and the steps that have been taken to manage its effects. If a report does not include multicollinearity information, be very skeptical about the results.

Tests of Statistical Significance for Linear Multiple Regression and Correlation Analyses

Tests of statistical significance are available for coefficients of multiple determination (R^2s) and partial correlation coefficients, both raw and standardized, as well as regression betas both raw and standardized (i.e., bs and b^*s) and for differences between them. These significance tests assume random sampling as well as a number of other conditions. The t or F distributions are used as sampling distributions, and the null hypothesis is typically that the statistic in question is zero. Their derivations and applications are beyond the scope of this text, but we have already discussed some of their uses. Recall our discussion of stepwise regression, for example, where variables are added to (or removed from) the regression equation when their addition (or subtraction) produces a statistically significant change in R^2.

Reporting the Results of Multiple Regression and Correlation Analyses

Multiple regression and multiple correlation results are often reported together because the researchers are interested in both the contributions that changes in each independent variable make to changes in the dependent variable (the bs or b^*s, i.e., the raw or standardized partial regression coefficients) and the total amount of dependent variable variance that is statistically explained by the combined effects of all of the independent variables (R^2).

Reports on multiple regression analysis results sometimes include the multiple regression prediction equation with a format like that of Formula 12.2. More often, however, the report consists of a table (or tables) containing a list of the independent variables included in a particular analysis and the betas and/or standardized betas (beta weights) associated with each of the independent variables. The coefficient of multiple determination (R^2) is also often reported. A bivariate correlation matrix is sometimes included in order to make clear the degree of multicollinearity among the independent variables. Finally, standard errors for the sampling distributions of all of the statistics, including the betas and the multiple correlation coefficient (R), as well as the significance levels of significance tests on these statistics, are also reported.

As noted earlier, interpretation of the results usually emphasize standardized betas because the reader can tell at a glance the relative contribution to changes in y made by each independent variable or block of variables. Tables 12.3a and 12.3b present fictitious examples of some types of multiple regression and correlation analysis reports similar to those that might be found in the professional research literature. The from the Literature Box 12.1 includes an excerpt from a recent research report published in a national criminal justice journal.

Table 12.3a A Fictitious Multiple Regression Report

Predictor Variables	b (Unstandardized Coefficients)	b^* (Standardized Coefficients)	SE (Standard Error)
Age	−4.63	−.07*	.10
Weight	0.45	.01	.005
Blood Alcohol	8.13	.08**	.278
Speed	6.98	.04*	.191
Male	12.12	.11**	.364
Time of Day	6.76	.05	.312

Note: $n = 215$; $R^2 = .36$.

*$p < .05$; **$p < .01$.

Table 12.3b A Fictitious Trivariate Multiple Correlation Report

$n = 26$
$r^2_{x_1 y} = .291$
$r^2_{x_2 y \cdot x_1} = .151$
$R^2 = .346$
$R^2 \text{ (adjusted)} = .335$

From the Literature Box 12.1

Robert J. Homant explored the question of whether altruism was a predictor of criminal victimization. Data came from a survey distributed to four samples (college students, and residents of low-, medium-, and high-crime neighborhoods). Among other things, items on the survey, combined into scale scores, measured different types of altruism (safe and risky) and how many times they had been victims of various kinds of crime. The author used analysis of variance, t tests, and Pearson's r, as well as multiple correlation analyses.

The following are excerpts from the research report. The correlations reported in the excerpts are for the altruism scale scores and the number of victimizations of all types. (Note: We have reversed the order of the first two excerpts in order to make the research report more understandable for our purposes.)

❖ ❖ ❖

The primary measure for this research, for the most direct test of the hypotheses, was the total victimization score, found by adding together the reported property and personal victimizations. For the total group, this gave a mean victimization score of 3.3. Seventy-nine percent of the sample ($n = 212$) reported at least 1 victimization. Ten percent of the sample ($n = 27$) had 8 or more victimizations, with 2 respondents reporting 20 total victimizations. (The total victimization score was later recoded to reduce the positive skew by compressing the scores of the top 10%; in effect, this reduced the range from 0 to 20 down to 0 to 10. This recoded variable correlated .96 with the raw scores and made no difference in any analysis.)

. . .

A statistical test was done on the victimization variable to determine whether respondents were indeed representative of significantly different crime areas. The overall analysis of variance was significant ($F = 6.42$, $df\ 3/264$, $p < .001$). Post hoc comparisons (Scheffe) showed that the high-crime sample experienced significantly more crime than either the student or low-crime groups ($p < .01$), but other group comparisons were not significant. Because the low- and moderate-crime samples had been specifically selected from the

Table 3: Risky and Safe Altruism Items' Correlations With Victimization

Altruism Scale	r	P
Risky items		
1. I have given directions to a stranger.	.299	.000
2. I have made change for a stranger.	.182	.003
3. I have given money to a stranger who needed it or asked me for it.	.190	.002
6. I have helped carry a stranger's belongings (e.g., books, parcels, etc.).	.188	.002
9. I have given a stranger a lift in my car.	.248	.000
10. I have let a neighbor whom I didn't know too well borrow an item of some value (e.g., tools, a dish, etc.).	.187	.002
Safe items		
4. I have donated goods or clothes to a charity.	.004	.944
5. I have done volunteer work for a charity.	.000	.997
7. I have delayed an elevator and held the door open for a stranger.	.111	.070
8. I have allowed someone to go ahead of me in a line (e.g., supermarket, copying machine, etc.).	.051	.404
11. I have bought "charity" Christmas cards deliberately because I knew it was for a good cause.	.055	.368
12. 1 have helped a classmate who I did not know that well with a homework assignment when my knowledge was greater than his or hers.	.029	.639
13. I have, before being asked, voluntarily looked after a neighbor's pets or children without being paid for it.	.092	.133
14. I have offered to help a handicapped or elderly stranger across a street.	.083	.173

Note. All *p* values are two-tailed.

(Continued)

(Continued)

same city to represent areas that differed in crime rates, these two samples were also compared by t test. The t showed that respondents from the moderate-crime area did indeed report a higher level of victimization than did those from the low crime area: $t = 2.01$; df 142; $p = .05$, two-tailed.

. . .

Table 3 shows the 14 altruism items subdivided into Risky Altruism and Safe Altruism and gives each item's correlation with total victimization. Although all 14 altruism items had at least a slightly positive correlation with total victimization, the correlations were significant only for the 6 risky items.

. . .

Altruism and Victimization

The basic hypothesis for this research is that risky altruism has a positive correlation with crime victimization. Safe altruism is expected to show a much smaller, probably non-significant, correlation with victimization. This relationship is expected to be true for the total group and to be basically the same for the subgroups. Total victimization is the primary measure of victimization.

. . .

Correlations between altruism and victimization are shown in Table 4. For the total sample, risky altruism correlated .310 (df 266, $p < .001$) with total victimization, whereas the correlation with safe altruism was only .088 (ns); the difference between these two correlations is highly significant ($z = 2.68$, df 265, $p < .01$). This pattern held for the breakdown into property and personal victimizations. (The differences in these pairs of correlations are significant at the .05 level.) The analysis according to subgroup is complicated somewhat by the differences in n in each sample. In general, however, risky altruism is a significant predictor of victimization, and safe altruism is not. It should be noted that in the one case where risky altruism failed to significantly predict total victimization (a .182 correlation in the low-crime group), the correlation does reach the .05 p value if a one-tailed test is used.

. . .

Controlling for Demographic Variables

It was expected that various demographic variables, especially age and gender, would correlate with victimization. If these variables also correlated with risky altruism, this would raise the issue of spurious correlation between victimization and risky

(Continued)

Table 4 Correlations Between Risky and Safe Altruism and Crime Victimization

	Total Crime		Property Crime		Personal Crime	
Group	Risky	Safe	Risky	Safe	Risky	Safe
Student	.306**	−.066	.250*	−.106	.305**	.039
Low crime	.182	.133	.215*	.134	.000	.055
Moderate crime	.272*	.144	.188	.123	.301*	.106
High crime	.386*	.337	.374*-	.419*	.228	.039
Total sample	.310***	.088	.276***	.093	.240***	.038

*$p < 05$; **$p < .01$; ***$p < .001$, all two-tailed.

altruism. . . . Age, gender, and race were found to have significant correlations with both altruism and victimization. Therefore, it will be important to look at the correlations of risky and safe altruism with victimization with these variables controlled for. Education did not correlate with victimization or with risky altruism and was dropped from further analysis. The effect of religious affiliation was examined by analysis of variance and was found to have no relation to either victimization or altruism; it, too, is deleted from further analyses.

Table 7 shows the overall predictability of victimization (total, property, and personal) when using both measures of altruism and the main demographic variables. In addition, partial correlations are given for each variable, showing how well that variable predicts victimization with the other variables controlled for. As can be seen from Table 7, risky altruism remains a consistent and significant predictor of victimization, and safe altruism has virtually no relationship. Only gender (male) and sample (based on crime level) make additional independent contributions to the multiple Rs.

To summarize the results thus far, risky altruism has been shown to be a significant predictor of victimization. This has held true for both personal and property victimization, for victimization limited to the previous 12 months, and for altruistic victimization. The relationship between risky altruism and victimization was found for all four subsamples, and with demographic variables controlled for. In contrast, safe altruism, although highly correlated with risky altruism (.49), was generally unrelated to victimization. (The main exception was that safe altruism was the better predictor of property crime victimization for the high-crime subgroup—see Table 4.)

(Continued)

(Continued)

Table 7 Multiple and Partial Correlations With Victimization

Predictor	Victimization					
	Total		Property		Personal	
	r	P	r	P	r	P
Risky altruism	.205	.002	.154	.018	.205	.002
Safe altruism	.008	.904	.045	.494	−.067	.307
Age	.014	.906	.040	.544	−.044	.505
Gender (male)	.204	.002	.224	.001	.066	.313
Race (Black)	.054	.410	.056	.394	0?4	.716
Sample	.151	.021	.153	.019	.073	.264
Multiple R	.422	.000	.411	.000	.289	.002

Note. N = 240 throughout $(df = 6/233)$. Except for the Multiple R row, all correlations are partial correlations, with the effect of the other predictor variables controlled for.

Source: From Homant, R. J. (2010). Risky altruism as a predictor of criminal victimization. *Criminal Justice and Behavior, 37,* 1195–1216. Retrieved June 4, 2012, from http://cjb.sagepub.com/content/37/11/1195

Logarithm-Based Analyses

By using dummy variables, a small number of nominal *independent* variables can be included in the multivariate correlation and regression analyses we have discussed so far in this chapter. But these analyses assume the *dependent* variable is an interval- or ratio-level variable. Yet many of the dependent variables of interest to criminal justice theorists and practitioners alike are measured at the nominal level. Both theorists and practitioners may want to know, for example, what variables might be related to the success or failure of a new policy or program or of a parolee or probationer. Many of these nominal dependent variables are dichotomous; that is, they have only two values. As we discussed in Chapter 8, elaboration analysis using contingency tables and chi square are a viable option in some research situations. But as we noted in Chapter 8, there are some rather severe limitations to such analyses.

In recent years, a variety of logarithm-based procedures have been developed as alternative and, indeed, preferable ways of assessing the effects of independent variables on nominal-level dependent variables. The development of these procedures is attributed to Joseph Berkson, Chester Bliss, and George Barnard. They have become quite widely used throughout the social sciences, including criminal justice. Contemporary journal articles frequently feature log-based analyses.

The general objectives of such analyses remain the same as in multiple correlation and regression analyses. For example, as in multiple regression analysis, one log-based procedure aims to determine the contributions of each of several independent variables (called predictors) to a change in a dependent variable (called an outcome).

Log-based analyses do not rely on the least squares formulas with which you have become familiar in previous chapters for calculating betas. Rather, they invoke a repetitive (iterative) process of approximation and maximization to arrive at the regression equation that achieves the best estimates (predictions) of a nominal dependent variable. Furthermore, they are nonparametric statistics. That is, unlike multiple correlation and regression, they do not require normal distributions of the variables in the population, homoscedasticity, or equal distributions of y about x, for example. The calculations on which they are based, however, are complex and laborious, typically requiring a computer to complete them.

Several varieties of logistic analysis may be applied, depending on the particular research situation, the kinds of variables involved, and the objectives of the researcher. Our purpose in the next few pages is to give you a general idea of these procedures and to help you interpret the research reports involving logistic analyses you will encounter in the criminology and criminal justice literature. We focus here on just one type of log-based analysis, called logistic regression, which is used to predict the value of a dichotomous nominal dependent variable from the values of independent variables. Discussions of this and other varieties of logistic analysis, including ones designed for ordinal dependent variables, have been developed, but are beyond the scope of this book. We turn now to an introductory exploration of logistic regression.

Logistic Regression

In general, **binomial logistic regression** analysis is applicable when the dependent variable is nominal and dichotomous. Recall that in least squares regression analysis, the aim is to predict the values of a ratio or interval level dependent variable for units of analysis. In binomial logistic regression, the aim is to predict whether the units of analysis are in one of two categories (i.e., one of the two possible values of the dependent variable). Perhaps, for example, we want to predict whether a parolee will or will not succeed in staying arrest free for 2 years after release or whether a new recruit will or will not remain on the force. Let's use the former for illustrative purposes. Our dependent variable is parolee outcome, with two nominal values: success, which we code as 1, or failure which we code as 0. We will define and discuss the probabilities involved in these predictions and describe some of the analyses and outputs of commonly used logistic regression programs. Our aim is only to give you a general idea of what is involved in logistic regression analysis. More complete information is available in more advanced texts.

Suppose we have some data on the characteristics (independent variables) of a number of parolees, some of whom succeeded by remaining arrest free for 2 years and some of whom failed and were reincarcerated. We want to use those characteristics to help us explain why some succeeded and some failed. In the case of each particular parolee, whether he or she succeeds is an outcome (like a head or tail in a coin toss). In binomial logistic regression we are predicting the probability of a success. For our group of parolees as a whole, we can determine the proportion who succeeded and think about that proportion as an estimate of a probability that a parolee in the group would succeed without taking the effects of any independent variable into account.

Assumptions of Logistic Regression

In general, binomial logistic regression assumes that the dependent variable is discrete, dichotomous, and that observations (measurements) of the independent variables are independent of each other. Logistic regression is a nonparametric analytic procedure; that is, it is not necessary to assume the variables are normally distributed and homoscedastic. It is also recommended that samples be relatively large—say, $n \geq 100$ or so—and more or less evenly divided between the two values of the dependent variable for the study group as whole.

Odds

We can also think about the outcome of a parolee's success or failure in terms of odds. **Odds**, you will recall, are ratios of wins to losses, or, in this case, of successes to failures on parole. So we can say that a particular parolee has a certain odds of succeeding (or failing), the specific odds depending on the proportion of a parolee group that succeeds. You will probably also recall that odds can be converted easily to proportions and probabilities. For example, suppose 5 of a group of 9 parolees succeeded. The odds of succeeding are 5 to 4, and the probability of succeeding is

$$p_{success} = 5/(5 + 4) = 5/9 = .56$$

The odds of failing in this example are 4 to 5, which can be converted to the probability

$$p_{fail} = 4/(5 + 4) = 4/9 = .44$$

As expected, the probabilities of success and failure sum to 1.0 and the probability of failing is $1 - p_{success}$. The odds of interest in logistic regression are defined as the ratio of the probability that an event (e.g., a parole success) will occur to the probability the event won't occur, which can be written as Formula 12.7 and illustrated by the data from our example.

$$\text{Odd}_{success} = p_{success}/p_{fail} = p_{success}/(1 - p_{success}) = .56/.44 = 1.273 \qquad (12.7)$$

For reasons we won't go into here, to perform a logistic regression, we convert odds of $p/(1-p)$ to **logits**, which are the odds natural log (sometimes labeled $\log_e$ or ln - here we'll use $\log_e$) equivalents.

Natural Log (Log_e)

The **natural log** ($\log_e$) is the logarithm to the base e. As you may recall from your math classes, logarithms transform numbers to some common base number and an exponent. The exponent is called the log of the number. In general, given an original number and a base number, the log is the power to which the base number must be raised in order to recover the original number. In logs with a base of 10, for example, the number 100 would be 10 raised to the second power (10^2), so the $\log_{base10}$ of 100 = 2. In the case of the natural log ($\log_e$), the base number is approximately 2.7182. The power to which this base number is raised to recover any original number is the $\log_e$ equivalent of that original number. It's OK to say "good grief" or something similar at this point! Fortunately, computers make conversions of numbers to their $\log_e$ equivalents easy.

You should be aware of some restrictions when using $\log_e$s. Only variable values (original numbers) above zero have $\log_e$ equivalents. For variable values between 0 and 1, $\log_e$ equivalents are negative. For variable values greater than 1, $\log_e$ equivalents are positive. A variable value with the $\log_e$ of 1 equals the variable value—that is, it is a number raised to the power of 1, which is that number. When a variable value equals 1, the $\log_e$ is 0. Any variable value raised to the power of 0 equals 1. Like standardized statistics, logs transform variable values in a way that permits assessing their relative size. In $\log_{base10}$, for example, the relative sizes of numbers change in multiples of 10. For the number 10, for example, the change from a $\log_{base10}$ of 1 to a $\log_{base10}$ of 2 is a tenfold increase (from 10 to 100), and the change from $\log_{base10}$ 1 to $\log_{base10}$ 3 is a hundred-fold increase (from 10 to 1,000). The same relationships hold for $\log_e$s except that the base is different. So, instead of representing relative increases by multiples of 10, they represent increases by multiples of 2.7182.

Logistic regression uses the $\log_e$ of the odds of $p/(1-p)$ as the new values of the dependent variable, the probabilities we want to predict using our independent variables (xs). These new values, as we noted above, are called logits. A $\log_e$-enabled calculator or an online $\log_e$ conversion program is used to convert odds to their $\log_e$ equivalents. In our example, we would find the $\log_e$ conversion of our odds of 1.273 to be $\log_e(1.273) = 0.2412$. We can summarize the relationships as follows:

$$\log_e(\text{odds}) = \log_e[p/(1-p)] = \text{logit}(Y) \tag{12.8}$$

where p is the probability that a parolee succeeded (coded 1) or failed (coded 0); odds are for the odds of being a success or failure, and $\log_e$ is the natural log. Using our example for the $\log_e$ of the odds of a parolee succeeding, we have:

$$0.2412 = 0.2412 = 0.2412$$

The Logistic Regression Equation

In addition to knowing whether parolees succeeded or failed, we have data on a number of independent variables that, in logistic regression analyses, are called **predictor variables** for the parolees. We want to determine what contribution, if any, they make to the probability of a parolee succeeding. In light of what we discussed in the immediately preceding paragraph, we can restate our objective as wanting to determine how much, if any, change in logit(Y) (our new dependent variable) is associated with changes in the predictor (independent) variables.

We will capitalize the letters to indicate we are dealing with logistic, rather than least squares, regression and express the general predictive logistic regression equation as

$$\text{logit}(Y) = A + \beta_1 X_1 + \beta_2 X_2 + \beta_3 X_3 + \cdots + \beta_j X_j + \text{error}, \qquad (12.9)$$

where the number of independent variables in the equation is 1 through j.

> **PAUSE, THINK, AND EXPLORE LOGIT(Y)**
>
> Compare this formula with Formula 12.2. What similarities and differences do you see?

Even though, as we will see, the procedures for arriving at the constants in Formula 12.9 are very different from those in least squares analysis, the general form of the equation should look familiar to you. It is, of course, similar to the least squares regression equation, which, you will recall, is $y = a + bx$. Once the values of of A and the βs are determined, Formula 12.9 can be used to predict the values of logit(Y), just as the least squares regression line formula can be used to predict y.

In the logistic regression formula, A is a constant and has an interpretation similar to a in a least squares regression equation [that is, it is the Y intercept, the value of logit(Y) when all the Xs equal zero] and the βs are the logistic regression coefficients. Interpretation of the coefficient βs is similar to, though not exactly the same as, that of bs in a least squares regression equation. Whereas b in least squares regression represents the average amount of change in the dependent variable y for a one-unit change in x, β represents the average amount of change in logit(Y) for every unit change in X. Interpreting the sign of β is also similar. When β is larger than zero, the relationship between the variables is positive; when it is less than zero, the relationship is negative. When β = 0, logit(Y) does not change with changes in the corresponding X and there is no relationship between the variables. When testing β for statistical significance, the null hypothesis would typically be β = 0. To make really good sense of the βs in a logistic regression equation, though, it is necessary to convert the logit(Y)s back into their original probabilities (odds).

Deriving Logits

Now let's consider in more detail one way of thinking about the derivation of logits and determining the effects of independent variables on the probability of correct predictions of parolee success for a particular data set. We can think about the process as consisting of a number of steps. First, the study group is divided into subsets on the basis of the values of the predictor variables, each subset defined by a particular combination of the predictor variables' values. There are as many such subsets as there are possible mutually exclusive and exhaustive combinations of the values of the predictor variables. For example, suppose we have two predictor variables. One is the nominal variable "sex," with values male and female. The other is an ordinal variable "parole officer's rating of the parolee's chances of success," with values high, medium, and low. The possible subsets of the study group would be the six possible combinations of these variable values as indicated in Table 12.4. In effect, this procedure divides the study group into six mutually exclusive and exhaustive subsets, each defined by a different **predictor blueprint**.

Second, the parolees who match each blueprint are identified and placed into the subset defined by that blueprint.

Third, the proportion of the parolees in each of these blueprint subsets who succeeded is determined. This, of course, also determines the proportion for that blueprint group who did not succeed, because the outcome (dependent) variable is dichotomous. If a particular predictor blueprint yields no successful parolees, it is ignored for the remainder of the analysis because it contributes nothing to determining the factors that predict who succeeds and who fails.

As we have seen before, with a small change in perspective, proportions can easily be seen as probabilities. The proportion who succeeded in a particular subset can be viewed as an estimate of the probability that a parolee in that subset will succeed. Odds of success can also be converted to probabilities of success by summing the numerator and denominator of the odds and dividing the numerator of the odds by that sum. Thus, for 3 to 2 odds, the probability of success is 3/5, which equals a .60 or 60% probability of success, and the probability of failure is 2/5 = .40 = 40%. Conceived of in this way, an objective of logistic regression is to determine which

Table 12.4 Subsets of a Study Group Defined by Possible Combinations of Two Predictor Variables With Two and Three Variable Values

Subset	Sex	Rating
1	Male	High
2	Male	Medium
3	Male	Low
4	Female	High
5	Female	Medium
6	Female	Low

combination of independent (predictor) variable values best predicts *(maximizes the probability)* that a parolee will succeed.

Fourth, each of the parolees who succeeded in a particular blueprint group is assigned a variable value equivalent to the proportion of parolees in that particular group who succeeded ($p_{success}$). Each parolee in the group who did not succeed is assigned a score equivalent to the proportion of that particular group who did not succeed ($p_{failure}$). This process is repeated for each predictor blueprint, resulting in scores of p and $1 - p$ for each parolee in the entire study group.

Fifth, these p and $1 - p$ scores are turned into odds of $p/(1 - p)$. These odds will differ for those who succeed and those who fail in a particular blueprint subset, unless, of course, the subset has the same proportion of successes as of failures. If the chances of a parolee succeeding are equal to the chances of not succeeding (i.e., if success is a 50%/50% proposition), the odds equal 1. The odds are greater than 1 if the probability of succeeding is greater than .50. The odds are less than 1 if the probability of success is less than .50, but they are never less than zero. Describing data in terms of odds and their equivalent probabilities invites comparisons among the subsets because they reflect relative contributions to success. In our example, we might compare the odds of a parolee succeeding for the predictor blueprint for males rated low with that of the predictor blueprint for females rated low, or we might compare the odds of a parolee succeeding of males rated low with males rated high.

Finally, $p/(1 - p)$ is converted to its $\log_e$ equivalent. This $\log_e$ equivalent is assigned to each parolee in the corresponding predictor blueprint group, and it becomes the new outcome variable score (logit[Y]) for that parolee. This means, of course, that all of the parolees in a particular predictor blueprint group who succeeded will have an equivalent logit(Y) value and all of those who failed in that group also have an equivalent logit(Y). In this sense, the aim of binomial logistic regression is to find the predictor blueprint (the combination of independent variable values) that has the highest logit (Y)—that is, the highest $\log_e p/(1 - p)$ for those parolees who succeed.

For illustrative purposes, let's take just the first predictor blueprint category from Table 12.4, males with high ratings from their parole officers. Suppose that when we looked at our data, we found five parolees conforming to this blueprint. Suppose further that three of the five succeeded by remaining on parole and two had failed and been reincarcerated. We have included the calculations for the steps outlined above in Table 12.5. For each of the five parolees in the subset, remaining arrest free (success) is coded as 1 and rearrest (failure) is coded 0.

The logit(Y)s in the right-hand column are the new values for the dependent variable for these five parolees. The same process would be repeated for each of the parolee blueprint groups. As you can see from Table 12.5, the successful parolees are assigned logits by this process and the unsuccessful parolees are also assigned equivalent logits.

Assuming at least one parolee succeeded in every predictor blueprint group, if we did this analysis for the parolees in each of the six predictor blueprints, we could compare the logit (Y)s of success for the different predictor blueprints and determine which combination produced the largest logit and, therefore, the highest odds of success.

Table 12.5 Calculations for p, $1-p$, Odds, and Logit (Y) for One Subset of Five Parolees

Parolee	Code Success = 1	Proportion or Probability of Success for This Subset p	$1-p$	Odds $p/1-p$	Logit (Y); $\log_e$ (Odds) Ratio Logit
A	1	.600	.400	1.500	.4055
B	1	.600	.400	1.500	.4055
C	1	.600	.400	1.500	.4055
D	0	.400	.600	.667	−0.405
E	0	.400	.600	.667	−0.405

Now consider for a moment adding to our two predictor variables (sex and supervisor's rating) a third predictor variable, ethnicity, with six categories. This would increase greatly the number of possible combinations of these independent variable values. In fact, there would be $2 \times 5 \times 6 = 60$ combinations for just these three variable values. If we were to add more predictor variables, some of which were interval or ratio, creating the predictor blueprints would be, for all practical purposes, impossible. When many independent variables are included in the analysis, especially if some of them are interval or ratio variables, we need a different procedure for determining the combination of those values that best predicts (or maximizes our odds of predicting) parolee success.

Estimating the Constants A and β in Logistic Regression Equations

In least squares regression, to find the regression equation that best "fits" the data is the one that minimizes the residual (error) least squares in predicting the values of the dependent variable. In logistic regression, we want the equation that maximizes the probability of correctly predicting parolee success—i.e., that maximizes the logit(Y)s of success. Similar to least squares analysis, the task is to estimate the constants A and β for the best fitting logistic regression equation. Instead of the least squares procedure, logistic regression uses a different method for estimating the value of A and βs for a logistic regression equation. The alternative is preferred because, although it is a linear model, it does not rely on sample statistics as does ordinary least squares regression analysis, and it is not necessary to make the assumptions of normality, homoscedasticity, and so on associated with least squares regression analysis. Furthermore, formulas are not used to calculate the estimates of A and β. (Aren't you glad about that?)

Instead, a process called **maximum likelihood estimation** is employed. The process can be crudely thought of as a computer beginning with a guess about the value of A and the values of however many βs (one for each predictor variable) are required for the logistic regression equation (see Formula 12.9). The logistic regression analysis program instructs the computer to calculate the logit(Y)s for the parolees who succeed on the basis of the guessed values of A and the βs for each of the possible combinations of predictor variable values. The resulting equation is used to predict the logit(Y)s. Then the computer makes another set of guesses (i.e., constructs another predictor blueprint) and computes the predictions of the logit(Y)s (i.e., $\log_e$ of the probability of parolee success), noting if the predictions using the second equation have improved over the previous equation. If it has, the next set of guesses takes that into account. Each equation and its predictions is called an iteration. The computer continues in this way, tweaking the guessed values of A and β and using the new equation to make new predictions of the logits. When a new equation yields little or no improvement over the previous one in the predictions of the logits, the results are said to converge, the iterations cease, and the constants A and β for the logistic regression equation that best fits the data have been found. The equation thus arrived at becomes the maximum likelihood estimation equation for the logit(Y)s. Perhaps now you can see why a computer is necessary to do logistic regression!

Interpreting the Results of Logistic Regression

In least squares regression analysis, predictions of y based on the best fitting regression equation are compared with the predictions of y using only the mean of y ($\bar{y}$). The question for the analysis is whether using one or more xs to predict the ys improves the predictions over what can be obtained from knowing $\bar{y}$ alone. In logistic regression, the baseline model and predictions against which the accuracy of the predictions of other regression equations are compared is the $\log_e$ of the odds [the logit(Y)] of being a parolee success based on the study group as a whole. For example, if the entire study group has 60% who succeeded and 40% who didn't, the baseline prediction would be the $\log_e$ of these odds. The impact, if any, of independent variables added to the regression equation is reflected in the difference between the baseline $\log_e$ odds of succeeding and the $\log_e$ odds of succeeding calculated for each predictor blueprint. In logistic regression analysis, the null hypothesis usually is that we cannot improve on the logit(Y) predictions of the baseline model. The research hypothesis is that we can improve on the baseline model predictions by taking into account the predictor variables. Comparisons may also be made between the predictions of models with different predictor variables. Testing for the statistical significance of differences between the model predictions is often made using a statistic with a chi-square sampling distribution. Such chi-square tests do not tell us *how much* one model has improved (or is better) in its predictions over another, only that the two models' outcomes are significantly different. Procedures for measuring the amount of improvement (sometimes called pseudo R^2), as well as for calculating confidence intervals, have been developed, but are beyond the scope of this text.

As we noted above, logistic regression coefficients (βs) have a roughly similar interpretation as bs in least squares regression. But to interpret them properly we need to translate the logit(Y)s and the regression coefficients (βs) back into their original odds in order to understand what the regression analysis tells us about the effects of the independent variables on the dependent variable. The key to understanding this translation is knowing the relationship between $\log_e$ of the odds of $Y = 1$ (a parole success) and a quantity called Exp(β)—namely that they are the inverse of each other. That is, $\log_e$ odds of Y (success) is equal to $1/\text{Exp}(\beta)$ and Exp(β) is equal to the $\log_e$ odds of success raised to the power of β. For example, if $\beta = 2$, Exp(β) = Exp(2) = $\log_e$

raised to the power of 2. Recall that $\log_e = 2.72$ (rounded). So, if a logistic regression coefficient $\beta = 2$ the corresponding odds of parolee success are 2.72 squared or 7.40 (rounded). This result is interpreted as the odds of correctly predicting a parolee success and is about seven times greater when the corresponding independent variable is included in the equation.

To conclude our discussion, we will review some of the more common kinds of results produced by a logistic multiple regression analysis. Note that outputs and symbols will vary from one statistical analysis package to another, and some outputs are produced only at the request of the analyst. Our aim here is only briefly to describe some of the typical contents of such reports and some of the most commonly reported statistics. Most statistical analysis packages have help functions that will aid the user in understanding and interpreting the results of a logistic regression analysis.

Reports provided by a logistic regression analysis program typically include the following:

a. Basic descriptive statistics, as appropriate, such as
   - frequencies and cumulative frequencies
   - missing data
   - relative frequencies (percents) and cumulative percents
   - measures of central tendency (means, medians, modes)
   - measures of dispersion (range, standard deviation)
   - bivariate correlation matrix and contingency tables

b. Inferential statistics, such as
   - standard error (*SE* or *S.E.*)—the estimate of the standard error of the parameter estimate for the applicable sampling distribution
   - inferential statistic (χ^2, Z, Wald, Cox and Snell, etc.) and calculated values of the statistics (see discussion of specific statistical tests that follows)
   - degrees of freedom (*df*) associated with tests of significance;
   - probability (*p*) or significance (sig.), which is the probability of the calculated statistic under the null hypothesis (note that sometimes a statistically significant result is desirable, and sometimes it is not—see the discussion of the Homer-Lemeshow Test that follows)

c. Coding for the dependent variable (*Y*)—which value of *Y* is coded 1 and which is coded 0

d. Dummy variable coding for nominal or ordinal independent variables included in the analysis (if the coding for a particular value of a variable shows all zeros, that value is the reference category and is omitted from the analysis—see the discussion of dummy variables earlier in this chapter)

e. Factors in the prediction equation, including
   - *A* (alpha): The *Y* intercept; it is sometimes included in the models (regression equations), but can usually be ignored for purposes of interpreting other statistics.
   - β *coefficient* (β coeff.): The regression coefficients, one for each of the independent variables in the regression equation. As noted above, the coefficients

have a similar interpretation as *b* in bivariate and multivariate least squares regression equations, except that the predicted change is in logit(Y) They reflect the amount of change in logit(Y) with each unit change in X. As with *b*, they should *not* be compared to assess *relative* impact on logit(Y).
- *Standardized* β (β^* coeff.): These are standardized logistic regression coefficients. They may be compared for relative size of impact on logit(Y).
- *Exp(β)*: This is the beta expressed as an **odds ratio** in raw score units of measurement for an independent variable, which is equivalent to $\log_e$ raised to the power of β; an odds ratio is the ratio of the odds of being a success in one group to the odds of being a success in another group—e.g., a ratio of the odds of being a parolee success if you are a male and the odds of being a success if you are female; it is interpreted as the predicted change in Y (*not* in logit[Y]) of a one-unit change in the corresponding independent variable; in effect, it translates the logit(Y) from the prediction equation (see Formula 12.9) back into the original units of Y. Exp(β)s of less than 1 indicate decreases in the odds of Y with an increase in X (a negative relationship); Exp(β)s greater than 1 indicate increases in the odds of Y with an increase in X (a positive relationship). The larger the Exp(β)s, the greater the change in Y; however, because they are not standardized, they cannot be compared for determining their relative contribution to changes in Y. If Exp(β) equals 1, Y does not change with X. An Exp(β) or odds ratio reported as 1.5, for example, would mean a success was 1.5 times as likely in one group than in the other. (Note: Any variable with a negative β ($-\beta$) should have an Exp(β) of less than 1; any variable with a positive β should have an Exp(β) greater than 1. If this is not the case, something is wrong in the analysis.)
- *Log likelihood:* A likelihood is a probability. The log likelihood is $\log_e$ of the likelihood (probability) of a correct prediction of Y with the model being tested.
- *−2 log likelihood* (−2 log L): Sometimes called Deviance, refers to the difference between observed and expected probabilities of Y being a success. Using a chi-square sampling distribution, it compares the predictions of Y from two models (for example, the baseline model with no independent variables with a model including all of the independent variables). If the chi square is statistically significant at a given significance level, it means the improvement in the prediction was statistically significant at that level.
- *Maximum likelihood estimate* (MLE): The equation that maximizes the probability of correctly predicting Y from the independent variables included in the analysis. The higher the maximum likelihood estimate, the better the model predicts the logit Ys.

f. Baseline model calculations (sometimes labeled Block 0 or Beginning Block)—these calculations predict logit(Y)s (the dependent variable) with the coefficients of all predictor (independent) variables set at 0. Because no variables other than the dependent variable are included in the model, the probability of a correct predicton is equal to the proportion coded 1 for the study group as a whole.

g. Calculations for a model (or models) with independent (predictor) variable(s) included; sometimes called Block 1. The computer tries different combinations of variable values (predictor blueprints) and calculates statistics indicating improvement in the prediction of logit(Y) compared with the previous model until the improvement is very small. Each of these tries is called an iteration, or sometimes a step. The analysis report usually indicates the number of iterations before the best fitting model is determined.

h. Specific tests of statistical significance: A number of tests of statistical significance have been developed for logistic regression statistics. Many use the chi-square distribution as the sampling distribution. When a test of significance is reported for the β of a particular independent variable, typically the model including that variable only is being tested against the model that includes none of the predictor variables (the Block 0 model). Hence, it is testing whether the difference between the two predicted odds ratios are significantly different under the null hypothesis that they are not different. In these cases, we want to be able to reject the null hypothesis and argue that the independent variable(s) does (do) improve our prediction of logit(Y). Again, note that statistical significance is not always the desired result. (See the discussion of the Hosmer-Lemeshow Test below.)

- *Wald Test:* A Wald test is a statistical significance test for logistic regression using the chi square distribution to test the null hypothesis. The null hypothesis tested is that β = 0. The test may be performed for each variable coefficient in the analysis. The test computes a statistic Z, which is equal to β/s, where s is the standard error of the applicable sampling distribution. Z^2 is then tested using the chi-square distribution. (Don't confuse this Z with standard z scores.)
- *Likelihood Ratio Test:* The likelihood ratio test compares the $\log_e$ maximum likelihood for the model with some or all of the predictor variables included to the $\log_e$ maximum likelihood for a model with fewer or no predictor variables included.
- *Hosmer-Lemeshow Goodness-of-Fit Test:* This test assesses goodness-of-fit of the logistic regression equation by comparing observed probabilities of success with the predicted probabilities of success for each of 10 groups (deciles) into which the subjects are divided. The 10 groups are selected so that they are ordered in terms of the observed probabilities (those with probabilities less than .1, those with probabilities .1 to .19, from .2 to .29, and so on to .9 to 1.0.). The differences between expected and observed probabilities are then tested using the chi-square distribution. In this case, a *non*significant chi square is the desirable result because it means the model fits the data pretty well. Reports may show the expected and observed table for this test.
- *Cox & Snell R square:* This test assesses the strength of association among the variables; it is somewhat similar to the least squares coefficient of multiple determination (R^2), but its maximum can be less than 1.
- *Nagelkerke R square:* This test adapts Cox & Snell R square so that it varies between 0 and 1, making its interpretation more comparable to the least squares multiple regression statistic, the coefficient of multiple determination (R^2).

- *Confidence intervals:* You are already familiar with these kinds of statistics. They provide a range of estimated values for population statistics and add greatly to the information available when there has been a finding of statistical significance. The breadth of the confidence interval range has implications for successfully applying the results of the research in real-life settings.

Again, the main goal of logistic regression analysis is to identify the significant independent variable predictors (estimates) of logit(Y) and, ultimately of Y. The confidence intervals for these estimates are also of interest, especially if applied uses of the results are contemplated. Remember that logits and the regression coefficients (βs) must be reconverted to their original units or categories to interpret the results of logistic regression analysis. Exp(β) gives the results in those units.

Reporting the Results of Logistic Regression

Logistic regression reports vary depending on which of the statistics and tests just described are included. The From the Literature Box 12.2 contains excerpts from a recently published study using logistic regression analysis, including several of these statistics and tests.

From the Literature Box 12.2

Mathew J. Giblin studied the effectiveness of a program that included police officers in the supervision of juvenile probationers. Data came from the Anchorage (AK) Coordinated Agency Network (CAN) project. The experimental research design included two independent random samples of juvenile probationers, one of which was part of the program and the other not. Among other analyses, Giblin used logistic regression analysis to examine the contributions of several independent variables to each of two dichotomous dependent variables. The dependent variable for what he labeled Model 1 was whether or not the probationer committed any new probation violations. The dependent variable for what he termed Model 2 was whether or not the probationer was charged with new criminal violations. The following are excerpts from the research report.

The final sample used in the analysis consisted of 155 juveniles (91 experimental, 64 control). Table 1 presents descriptive statistics for juveniles in both groups. A chi-square test statistic was computed to examine the differences between control and experimental group members. The chi-square statistic assesses differences in observed and expected frequencies where the expected frequency distribution for both groups is hypothesized to be equal. For example, if the expected frequency distribution for the two groups is expected to be equal, the proportion of females in each group and the proportion of juveniles with substantiated

(Continued)

Table 1 Characteristics of Control and experimental Groups

Variable	Control		Experimental		x^2
	n	%	n	%	
Age at program start					8.421
11	0	0.0	1	1.1	
12	0	0.0	0	0.0	
13	3	4.7	3	3.3	
14	2	3.1	3	3.3	
15	5	7.8	18	19.8	
16	19	29.7	15	16.5	
17	13	20.3	21	23.1	
18	18	28.1	24	26.4	
19	4	6.3	5	5.5	
20	0	0.0	1	1.1	
Race/ethnicity					9.307
White	25	39.1	48	52.7	
African American	7	10.9	16	17.6	
Alaska Native/Native American	10	15.6	12	13.2	
Other[a]	22	34.4	14	15.4	
Missing	0	0.0	1	1.1	
Gender					0.117
Male	57	89.1	79	86.8	
Female	7	10.9	12	13.2	
Prior history of substantiated abuse/neglect					0.493
Yes	29	45.3	39	42.9	
No	34	53.1	49	53.8	
Missing	1	1.6	3	3.3	
Working during the pilot phase					
0% to 50% of lime	47	73.4	72	79.1	2.113
51% to 100% of lime	14	21.9	18	19.8	
Missing	3	4.7	1	1.1	
Attending school during the pilot phase					
0% to 50% of time	27	42,2	40	44.0	.278
5i% to100% of time	33	51.6	47	51.6	
Missing	4	6.3	4	4.4	

Note: Percentages may not total 100 due to rounding, a. Includes juveniles who are multiethnic.

(Continued)

(Continued)

histories of child abuse should be similar for each group. The larger the difference between the observed and the expected frequencies, the more likely that the differences will be significant. Chi-square tests reveal that the two groups have similar frequency distributions for each of the variables analyzed. That is, there do not appear to be any significant differences between the control and CAN groups on the variables included in the study. Such a finding is expected given the random assignment of juveniles to control and experimental groups. As stated earlier, the benefit of random assignment is based on the presumption that the assignment produces groups that are equal in all respects. This analysis reveals that the disproportionate attrition of juveniles from the control group did not create differences between the two groups on any of the variables examined.

A t test was conducting on both prior record variables. The t test, unlike the chi-square test, compares the means of a continuous variable for two groups. Like the results presented in Table 1, the t test results indicated that the differences between the mean number of prior misdemeanor adjudications for CAN participants ($M = 2.60$) and control group participants ($M = 2.48$) are not significant. Similarly, the mean number of prior felony adjudications for CAN participants ($M = .34$) did not significantly differ from control group juveniles ($M = .40$).

An important caveat is worth noting. The discussion above revealed that the control and experimental group both experienced preprogram participant attrition. Although the reasons for the attrition were noted and the initial random assignment would lead to the expectation that attrition would occur equally in each group, the results show that control group participants were much more likely to be excluded from the program than treatment group members. The chi-square test indicated that the groups appear to be similar on the measures used in this analysis, but this does not preclude the possibility that the two groups are dissimilar on other characteristics not measured here (see Grossman & Tierney, 1993). The results presented below are based on the assumption that the control and treatment groups, after preprogram attrition, are similar due to the initial random assignment.

Dependent Variables

To examine the impact of the CAN program, several different analyses are conducted using two different outcome (dependent) variables. The first dependent variable is new probation violations (ANY_PROB). This variable identified whether a particular juvenile was referred with any new probation violation during the pilot period (June 1, 1999 to December 31, 1999). The variable is dichotomous and coded yes (new violations) or no (no new violations).
. . .
The second dependent variable is new charges (ANY_OFF). Again, the variable is dichotomous—coded yes or no. This variable measures whether the juvenile committed any new

(Continued)

criminal offenses that resulted in new charges being filed; this did not include probation violations. Like the ANY_PROB variable, this variable covered the offenses that occurred during the CAN pilot phase.

Independent Variables

Because the purpose of the study was to examine the impact of CAN program participation on the outcomes variables discussed above, the most important independent variable included in the analysis is group membership (CON_EXP). That is, the primary interest is determining whether experimental group members (CAN participants) have more favorable outcomes than control group members. The CON_EXP variable is dichotomous and indicates whether the juvenile was a member of the CAN group or the control group. Given the findings in the ISP literature, two hypotheses are tested. First, the expectation is that individuals in the CAN group will be more likely to have new technical violations than their control group counterparts due to increased surveillance and monitoring. Second, CAN participation is expected to decrease the likelihood of new charges. Unlike technical violations, new charges are less likely to be detected by police and/or probation contacts. However, it is hypothesized that the increased contacts will have a deterrent effect and reduce the likelihood of new charges.

RESULTS

Contacts

CAN police officers made a total of 186 contacts with CAN participants between June 1, 1999, and December 31, 1999. The majority of visits occurred in August and September 1999. Ninety-six contacts were made during these 2 months, whereas 90 contacts were made in the other 4 months combined. Most visits were made during September (50), followed by August (46), July (32), October (32), June (15), November (10), and December (1). It is not surprising that the pattern of contacts takes on a bell-shaped curve. In June, the pilot phase was just beginning, and officers were becoming acquainted with their role. As they learned about the expectations of the program, they gradually increased the number of contacts they were making. At the end of the pilot phase, the number of visits tapered off. This reduction can likely be attributed to several factors. Some juveniles were charged with new offenses or violated conditions of their probation and were institutionalized. Other juveniles simply completed their probation and were no longer a part of the program. In either case, there were fewer juveniles to supervise and contact at the latter stages of the pilot phase than at the beginning.

(Continued)

(Continued)

The number of contacts received by each CAN program juvenile varies and likely indicates that the program was only partially implemented for some probationers. . . .

. . .

Logistic regression analysis . . . takes into account the fact that CAN participation is likely not the only factor that influences outcomes. This statistical procedure can include additional variables thought to contribute to the outcome and identify the relative importance of each factor while considering the effects of others. This is where the control variables (e.g., age, race, prior abuse) discussed above become important for this evaluation. The analysis can assess the impact of CAN participation while holding all of these other variables equal. This type of analysis is a stronger test of the influence of CAN on new charges and new probation violations. A separate analysis was conducted for each outcome variable (new charges, new violations). The results are presented in Table 7. Model 1 presents the logistic regression coefficients and odds ratios for the dependent variable ANY_PROB (new probation violations). Model 2 presents the logistic regression coefficients and odds ratios for the dependent variable ANY_OFF (new charges). Each model will be examined separately.

The first analysis assessed the impact of CAN program participation on the dependent variable ANY_PROB (new probation violations). The dependent variable is dichotomous (new violations, no new violations) and does not include any new criminal charges. The model fits the data well; the significance level is less than .001. The results indicate that three variables are significant predictors of new probation violations: participation in the CAN program (CON_EXP), juvenile race/native, and prior history of substantiated abuse/neglect.

To further explain these findings, the odds ratios need to be addressed. The odds ratio represents the "increase (or decrease if the ratio is less than one) in odds of being in one or more outcome category when the value of the predictor increases by one unit" (Tabachnick & Fidell, 1996, p. 607). The results in Table 7 indicate that the odds of a juvenile in the CAN program having new probation violations, all else being equal, are nearly 3.1 times greater than the odds of a juvenile not in the CAN program having new probation violations. Stated differently, CAN program juveniles are nearly 210% more likely to have new probation violations than control group participants. This finding is consistent with the intensive supervision probation literature that suggests that increased supervision leads to an increased likelihood of technical violations. Two additional significant findings deserve mention. First, Alaska Natives/Native Americans were more than 460% more likely to have new technical violations than White juveniles, independent of CAN participation. Second, juveniles with a prior history of substantiated child abuse

(Continued)

Table 7 Logistic Regression Coefficients for Predictors of Outcome Variables

	Model 1 (ANY_PROB)		Model 2 (ANY_OFF)	
Variable	Beta	Odds Ratio	Beta	Odds Ratio
CON_EXP	1.116*	3.054	−.390	.677
Race				
White	Reference		Reference	
African American	.218	1.244	.754	2.126
Alaska Native/Native American	1.537*	4.653	.892	2.441
Others	.533	1.703	−.113	.894
Age in years	−.208	.813	−.413**	.661
Gender				
Female	Reference		Reference	
Male	−.507	603	.724	2.063
Prior misdemeanors	.063	1.065	.056	1.058
Prior felonies	−.021	.979	−.115	.892
Prior abuse	1.370***	3.935	.291	1.338
Work time	−1.476	.229	−1.061	.346
School time	−.798	.450	.090	1.095
Constant	.279	1.322	5.082	161.025
n	141		141	
Model −2 log likelihood	129.550		132.891	
Model chi-square	34.789**		20.550*	

Note: CON_EXP = Coordinated Agency Network group membership. ANY _PROB = new probation violations. ANY_OFF = new charges.

*$p < .05$; **$p < .01$; ***$p < .001$.

(Continued)

(Continued)

and/or neglect were much more likely to have new technical violations than juveniles with no history of abuse. In fact, the odds of a juvenile with a history of abuse having new probation violations were nearly 4 times greater than the odds for juveniles without prior history of abuse or neglect.

Model 2 presents the findings using new charges as the dependent variable (ANY_OFF). The only significant relationship found to exist is between age and new charges. The relationship is negative, indicating that older juveniles were less likely to have new charges filed against them than younger juveniles. In other words, for each unit increase in age (e.g., 1-year increase in age), the odds of new charges being filed are reduced by 35%. In this analysis, participation in the CAN program did not significantly affect the likelihood of new charges being filed. This finding is consistent with some ISP literature in that intensive supervision did not lead to either increases or decreases in new arrests (see Turner & Petersilia, 1992).

Source: From Giblin, M. J. (2002). Using police officers to enhance the supervision of juvenile probationers: An evaluation of the Anchorage CAN program. *Crime and Delinquency, 48,* 116–137. Retrieved June 2, 2012, from http://cad.sagepub.com/content/48/1/116

Assumptions and Cautions

The analytic techniques we have discussed in this chapter are well suited to some of the kinds of theoretical and applied issues confronting criminal justice researchers and practitioners. They permit analysis of complex data sets in which many variables need to be taken into account simultaneously. However, they are not without their limitations.

The most effective use of least squares regression and correlation analyses can be made when all of the variables are measured at the interval or ratio level. Many of the variables of interest in criminal justice are nominal or ordinal, however. The incorporation of nominal or ordinal independent variables in least squares regression analyses using dummy variables increases the range of variables that can be addressed, but their use must be kept to a minimum in order not to distort the correlation and regression statistics.

Least squares correlation and regression analyses assess only the extent to which relationships between or among variables are linear. Interaction effects distort correlation and regression statistics. Even if there is little or no evidence of linear relationships, variables still may be strongly related in curvilinear ways.

The least squares analytic procedures assume the independent variables are statistically independent of each other, which means in this context that they are not correlated with each other. In the purest sense, this means their bivariate correlations are zero but in practice, correlations of .60 or less are considered low enough. When the independent variables are correlated with each other, the condition is called multicollinearity. Bivariate correlation matrices are sometimes included in research reports involving multiple correlation and regression to permit readers to assess the extent to which this criterion has been met. We recommend they always be included.

To the extent that any of the above cautions and assumptions cannot be satisfied, the results of least squares multiple correlation and regression are unreliable. There are procedures for dealing with some of these problems in some research situations, but they, too, have their limitations. Ultimately, if the assumptions can't be met, data analysis must be performed using alternative procedures like those we have discussed in previous chapters.

Logistic regression analysis assumes independent observations and that independent variables are linearly related to the logit of the dependent variable. The other assumptions associated with least squares multiple regression, such as homoscedasticity and that the independent variables be unrelated to each other, may be set aside for logistic regression. Logistic regression coefficients are not standardized statistics, so they cannot be compared directly to assess the relative impact of different independent variables on the dependent variable. Furthermore, as we have noted on several occasions earlier in the book, statistical significance by itself means relatively little. The results of logistic regression analyses are often tested for statistical significance using a chi-square sampling distribution. As we noted earlier, Cox and Snell R square and Nagelkerke R square—statistics similar to the coefficient of multiple determination (R^2) and designed to measure the size of the effects (strength of relationships) in logistic regression analysis—have been developed, but detailed consideration is beyond the scope of this text.

Finally, as we have seen, logistic analysis programs produce a large volume of statistical output, including many different descriptive and inferential statistics. They look impressive and sophisticated, and in some senses, they are. However, we urge you not to confuse this volume of output and complex appearance with the reliability or validity of results.

Summary

In this chapter, we have considered least squares multiple regression analysis, which permits us to predict the values of an interval or ratio level dependent variable from two or more independent variables. We also discussed least squares multiple correlation analysis, which can tell us how much of the total variance in an interval or ratio level dependent variable is statistically explained by two or more independent variables combined. Logistic analytic procedures, which permit the use of nominal- or ordinal-level dependent variables in multiple regression and correlation procedures, were also explored.

These multivariate procedures have the advantage of permitting analysis of complex data sets, taking many variables into account simultaneously. They are especially useful when using any large data set, such as the ones we mentioned in Chapter 1 and others, to test hypotheses. They are statistically sophisticated and can shed light on many important questions in both theory and practice. Still, such analyses are especially susceptible to the charge of garbage in-garbage out. Their validity rests on the quality of the data being analyzed and the degree to which the assumptions that underlie them are satisfied. When data quality is suspect and/or when the underlying assumptions are violated, the results of these analyses must be regarded with great skepticism. Remember—garbage in-garbage out.

Concepts to Master

a	Goodness-of-fit	Odds ratio
A	Interaction effects	Pairwise deletion
α	Listwise deletion	Partial beta
b	Log likelihood	Partial slope
b^*	Logistic regression	Partial correlation coefficient
β	Logits	
β^*	Main effects	Partial regression coefficient
Backward stepwise regression	Maximum likelihood estimation	Physical control (of variables)
Beta weight		Predictor blueprint
Coefficient of multiple correlation (multiple correlation coefficient)	Model	Predictor variables
	Multicollinearity	R^2
	Multiple correlation analysis	Regression plane
Coefficient of multiple determination	Multiple correlation coefficient	Standardized beta
		Statistical control (of variables)
Dummy variables	Multiple regression analysis	
Exp(β)	Natural log ($\log_e$, ln)	Stepwise regression
Forward stepwise regression	Odds	Variable deletion

Review Questions

1. Distinguish between physical and statistical controls over variables.
2. Why is controlling variables important in research?

3. Distinguish among listwise, pairwise, and variable deletions. Discuss why they are necessary and why they pose problems for multivariate inferential statistical analysis.

4. What is linear multiple regression analysis? What is its objective? When is it an appropriate choice for data analysis?

5. What is a best fitting plane? What is a regression plane?

6. What is a standardized beta?

7. What is the relationship between standardized betas and raw score betas?

8. What is a partial slope? What is a partial regression coefficient? What is a partial correlation coefficient?

9. What is stepwise regression? What is forward stepwise regression? What is backward stepwise regression?

10. What is linear multiple correlation? What is its objective? When is it an appropriate choice for data analysis?

11. What is the coefficient of multiple determination? How should it be interpreted?

12. What is a dummy variable?

13. How are dummy variables used in multiple regression and correlation?

14. What are models in multivariate analysis?

15. What are main effects in multivariate analysis?

16. What are interaction effects in multivariate analysis?

17. What is multicollinearity? Why is it a problem? How is the problem managed?

18. How are results of multiple regression and correlation reported?

19. What is logistic regression? When is it an appropriate choice for analyzing data?

20. How does logistic regression differ from least squares regression? Why is it preferable to use least squares regression in particular data analysis situations?

21. What are odds ratios, and what role do they play in logistic regression?

22. Why are logs of raw scores or odds ratios used in logistic regression?

23. What is natural log or log_e? What role does it play in logistic regression?

24. How does the logistic regression equation differ from the least squares regression equation?

25. What is a logit? How are logits derived?

26. What is a predictor blueprint?

27. What is a log likelihood?

28. What is a maximum likelihood?

29. What is a maximum likelihood estimation?

30. What are the assumptions of multiple regression and correlation analysis?

31. What are the assumptions of logistic regression?

32. Define all the terms in the "Concepts to Master" list and use each in three sentences.

Exercises and Discussion Questions

1. Identify three research hypotheses that would be suitable for a multiple regression analysis and three that would be suitable for a multiple correlation analysis.

2. What are some of the major problems associated with studying subject matter that is complex (i.e., involving many variables)? How do laboratory settings help solve those problems? What alternative approaches to solving those problems exist when research is conducted in natural settings?

3. Why is controlling variables important in science?

4. Between physical and statistical controls, which is the superior means of controlling variables? What are the advantages and disadvantages of each?

5. What are missing data? What problems do missing data pose for multivariate analysis? What are some possible strategies for dealing with missing data?

6. Compare and contrast least squares regression lines and least squares regression planes.

7. What are the advantages and disadvantages of raw score and standardized betas?

8. How would stepwise regression inform the analyst about the relative impacts of her independent variables on her dependent variable?

9. Why are least squares regression and correlation analyses considered linear models?

10. What is a dummy variable?

11. Discuss the role of dummy variables in least squares multivariate analysis.

12. How might an analyst use stepwise regression?

13. Discuss the similarities and differences between least squares multiple regression and multiple correlation.

14. What are the two meanings of the term *model* in multivariate analysis? How are they related?

15. Formulate a multivariate research hypothesis and identify at least two models that might be analyzed.

16. Discuss the similarities and differences between least squares multiple regression and logistic regression.

17. Discuss the difference between main effects and interaction effects in multivariate analysis.

18. Why do interaction effects and multicollinearity pose problems for multivariate analysis?

19. What problems do nominal or ordinal dependent variables pose in least squares regression analysis?

20. What is a natural log, and what role does it play in logistic regression?

21. What are logits, and what role do they play in logistic regression?

22. Use each of the two data set statistics below to calculate the specified least squares statistics. (Pay attention to whether the formula calls for r or r^2!) Discuss the general meaning of the results of your calculations.

Exercise 22 Data Set Table

	$r_{x_1 y}$	$r_{x_2 y}$	$r_{x_1 x_2}$	s_y	s_{x_1}	s_{x_2}	$\bar{y}$	$\bar{x}_1$	$\bar{x}_2$	$r_{yx_2 \cdot x_1}$
Data Set 1	.30	.16	.07	4.12	7.83	1.10	18	26	49	.40
Data Set 2	−.19	−.43	−.81	5.25	1.19	3.67	31	35	24	.58

s = standard deviation.

a. Calculate $b_{yx_1 \cdot x_2}$
b. Calculate $b_{yx_2 \cdot x_1}$
c. Calculate a.
d. Calculate $b^*_{yx_1 \cdot x_2}$
e. Calculate $b^*_{yx_2 \cdot x_1}$
f. Calculate R^2

23. In the second paragraph of From the Literature Box 12.1, the authors refer to an analysis of variance (ANOVA). Discuss why ANOVA is appropriate here. Discuss the correlations in Table 4. Is risky or safe altruism more closely associated with crime victimization? Discuss the correlations in Table 7. What do the multiple Rs represent? What would the coefficient of multiple determination be in each case?

24. For the statistics in Table 1 of From the Literature Box 12.2, discuss what data are included in each chi-square analysis reported and what a significant and a nonsignificant chi square would indicate. For the data in their Table 7, what do beta and odds ratio mean? Compare the

results for Model 1 and Model 2. What does the term *reference* in the table refer to? What do the model chi squares represent?

25. If you haven't already done so, answer all the questions in the "Pause, Think, and Explore" boxes.

Student Study Site

Visit the open-access student study site at **www.sagepub.com/fitzgerald** for access to several study tools including eFlashcards, web quizzes, and additional appendices as well as links to SAGE journal articles and audio, video and web resources.

Nonparametric Statistics

Learning Objectives

What you are expected not only to learn but to master in this chapter:

- The difference between parametric and nonparametric inferential statistics
- The basic ideas underlying the Mann-Whitney (U) test for two independent random samples
- How data are prepared for U analysis
- How to calculate U
- How to test U for statistical significance
- How to report U test results
- The basic ideas underlying the Kruskal-Wallace (H) test for three or more independent random samples
- How data are prepared for H analysis
- How to calculate H
- How to test H for statistical significance
- How to report H test results
- The basic ideas underlying Spearman's rank order correlation (ρ) analysis
- How data are prepared for ρ analysis
- How ρ is calculated
- How ρ is tested for statistical significance
- How to report ρ results
- Cautions that should be observed when using nonparametric statistics

Introduction

Do men and women differ in their degree of support for local police? Do those 20 to 25 years old and those 60 to 65 years old differ in their beliefs about the fairness of the criminal courts? Do those under age 35 adjust more easily to first-time incarceration than those over age 55? Do Catholics, Protestants, and Jews differ in their evaluation of police effectiveness in preventing crime? Do central city residents, suburbanites, and rural residents differ in their evaluation of prisons as rehabilitative institutions? Is there a relationship between political philosophy (on a scale from very conservative to very liberal) and evaluation of police services in their neighborhood? The statistical analyses we will consider in this chapter can often help answer questions like these.

In previous chapters, we have explored the underlying ideas, calculations, and significance tests for several parametric statistics. In Chapter 9, we discussed the t test for two independent random samples. In Chapter 10, we considered one-way analysis of variance for three or more independent random samples. We also described a linear correlation statistic, Pearson's product moment correlation coefficient (r), in Chapter 11. All of these statistics assume dependent variable measurements at the interval or ratio level and, in the case of r, the independent variable as well. They also assume normal distributions of the dependent variable in the population.

In Chapter 8, we introduced chi square, a nonparametric statistic used to test for relationships between two variables measured at the nominal or ordinal level. In this chapter, we describe three additional nonparametric statistics for use with variables measured at the ordinal level or higher. The Mann-Whitney U (M-W U) test is used to examine differences between two random samples, and, in this sense, it is like the t test. The Kruskal-Wallace H (K-W H) test is used for examining differences among more than two random samples and is similar to analysis of variance (ANOVA). Like Pearson's product moment correlation statistic r, Spearman's rank order correlation statistic, often symbolized as the Greek letter rho (ρ), measures the strength of the relationship between two variables (x and y) pertaining to each of the units of analysis (e.g., persons, institutions, arrests) included in the study.

The nonparametric statistics we consider in this chapter are arguably the most commonly used. You should be aware, however, that many other nonparametric statistics, some of which are modifications of the statistics we describe here, are available and may be more suitable in particular research situations.

Choosing Between Parametric and Nonparametric Inferential Statistics Revisited

In general, as we noted at the end of Chapter 8, when a good case can be made for applying them, parametric are preferable to nonparametric inferential statistics. The primary reasons are that parametric statistics have greater statistical power (that is, they reduce the chances of a Type II error, as discussed in Chapter 8 [see pp. 230–231]). and permit more complex analyses than do nonparametric statistics. But, as we noted in previous chapters, **parametric statistics** are appropriate only when several assumptions about the data being analyzed are satisfied. Among them are (a) at least the dependent variable is measured at the interval or ratio level, (b) the dependent variable values are approximately normally distributed in the populations from which the samples are selected, (c) the samples are randomly selected, and (d) the population variances are approximately equal (homoscedasticity). It is often difficult to meet some of these assumptions and/or to verify that they have been met for the data we are proposing to analyze.

It is true, as we also noted in previous chapters, that in some circumstances, the parametric statistics we have discussed are quite robust, and strict adherence to one or more of these assumptions is not required. Assumptions b and d can be violated to some degree, for example, when samples are large. It is also true that parametric statistical formulas can sometimes be modified to accommodate unequal population variances, as we discovered in our discussion of the t test.

Furthermore, in the absence of definitive information, there are ways of exploring whether the assumptions of parametric statistics are met. Given today's technology, for example, it is not difficult or expensive, in terms of either time or money, to determine the shapes of sample variable distributions. Computerized statistical analysis programs will print frequency polygons, as well as measures of central tendency and dispersion, for any variable at the push of a key or the entry of a simple instruction. If the samples indicate wide departures from normality or large differences in variances, the strong possibility of non-normal distributions and unequal variances (heteroscedasticity) in the population must be considered. There is also an inferential statistical test to help determine the likelihood that sample variances come from random samples drawn from the same population. These investigations can help the analyst decide whether a parametric or nonparametric statistical analysis is more appropriate. You should also be aware that procedures, some of which are based on logarithms, are available for converting some raw score data that are not normally distributed into scores that are more normally distributed. These procedures, often referred to as data transformations, are beyond the scope of this text.

Still, there are many research situations where the requirements for applying parametric statistics are not satisfied, or the analyst doesn't know whether they are satisfied or not. The variable(s) of interest may not be normally distributed in the population, for example. Perhaps, too, our samples are small and/or we suspect the population variable variances are unequal, violating the assumption of homoscedasticity, and no formula accommodation is available. It is quite common, too, for analysts to treat ordinal measurement scales, such as many evaluations, ratings, or degree of agreement or disagreement, as if they were ratio-level measurements. This practice is understandable. It permits analysts to take advantage of the greater statistical power and sophistication of parametric statistics, but it is also a violation of parametric statistic assumptions.

In many cases, then, applying parametric statistics remains questionable at best and, because the assumptions of parametric statistics are compromised, the results of such analyses may be very misleading. When dependent variables are measured at the nominal or ordinal level, we think nonparametric statistics should be the first choice, even if the analytic sophistication and statistical power of parametric statistics are sacrificed. In our view, in fact, parametric statistics are too often applied inappropriately in social science research because it is not clear whether the assumptions on which they rest have been satisfied. Whether you are a producer or consumer of statistics, you should always ask, "Do the data satisfy the assumptions of the statistics used for the analysis?"

When dependent variables are measured at the interval or ratio level and there is some doubt about which statistical analysis is best, it can be appropriate to use both a parametric and a nonparametric statistical analysis. Again, given available technology, this is not an expensive or burdensome task once the database has been established. Similar outcomes in terms of accepting or rejecting the null hypothesis would add to the confidence in your results. Should one method lead to a rejection of the null hypothesis and the other not, it is tempting to just report the one that supports your research hypothesis. Should you ever be so tempted, sit down, take a deep breath, and listen to your statistics guardian angel. You must report the results of both your parametric and your nonparametric statistics. You must also do everything you can to understand the causes of any differences in results and then make a case for accepting one or the other of the results—and that is not necessarily the one that permits rejection of the null hypothesis.

General Assumptions of Nonparametric Inferential Statisics

A significant advantage of **nonparametric statistics**, compared to their inferential statistics counterparts, is that they are "distribution free." That is, we do not need to assume, as we do with parametric statistics, that variables are normally distributed in the population. Also, nonparametric statistics can be used when both independent and dependent variables are measured at the nominal or ordinal level. As we saw in Chapter 8, chi square can be used when both are nominal. The statistics we describe in this chapter can be used when at least the dependent variable is ordinal.

As with their parametric counterparts, if the nonparametric statistics are to be tested for statistical significance, random sampling is required. In some instances, the samples must be independently randomly selected, as with the M-W U and K-W H tests for independent random samples. Also, as with some of their parametric counterparts, some nonparametric statistics formulas may be modified to analyze data from dependent random samples.

Nonparametric statistics can be used even if our variables are measured at the interval or ratio levels of measurement. When doing so, however, statistical power is lost (i.e., the probability of a Type II error is increased). When our dependent variables are affected by several independent variables, many of which have relatively small effects, as is generally the case in criminal justice research, we must be cognizant of Type II errors. Still, especially if sample sizes are small and the other parametric statistics assumptions are either in doubt or clearly violated, nonparametric statistics should be chosen for the data analysis even when variables are measured at the interval or ratio level.

We turn now to a detailed description and application of three of the more commonly used nonparametric statistics, beginning with the M-W U for two independent random samples.

The Mann-Whitney U Test for Two Independent Random Samples

The Mann-Whitney U test was developed by statisticians H. B. Mann and D. R. Whitney. F. Wilcoxon also contributed to the development of the test and it is sometimes referred to as the Mann-Whitney-Wilcoxon Test. The **Mann-Whitney U test (M-W U)** is most appropriate when the independent variable is nominal, the dependent variable is ordinal, and the null hypothesis asserts that there is no difference between two independent random samples. It is also applicable when interval or ratio dependent variable data are available and a t test might be appropriate, except that there is doubt about whether the assumptions on which the parametric t test are satisfied.

Assumptions of the M-W U Test

The M-W U test can be used as a nonparametric alternative to the t test provided that (a) the two samples are randomly and independently drawn, (b) the dependent variable measure is continuous (that is, its value is capable in theory, at least, of being carried out to many decimal places), (c) the dependent variable is measured at the ordinal level or higher, and (d) the dependent variable has a similar distribution (though not necessarily a normal distribution) in the two populations. It is not necessary to assume normal population distributions or equal sample variances for the dependent variable to use M-W U.

The Basic Ideas Underlying the M-W U Test

As we will see, calculations for M-W U are relatively simple, but the underlying logic is somewhat complex. We won't provide proof of all the underlying principles or calculation formulas, but we try to convey some of the basic ideas on which the test rests.

Just as a t test assesses the difference between two dependent variable means from two independent random samples, we can think of M-W U as assessing the difference between two dependent variable mean *ranks*. To perform a M-W U analysis, the raw dependent variable values must be converted into ranks, whatever their original measurement level (as long as it is not nominal, of course; nominal-level variable values cannot be ranked). M-W U analysis uses these ranks rather than the raw variable values to calculate the test statistic.

The underlying rationales for the M-W U test and the t test are similar, except that in the case of M-W U, we are testing observed differences between the mean ranks rather than the mean raw scores from two samples. The null hypothesis is that the two samples come from the same population and there is no relationship between the independent variable (x) and dependent variable (y). The research hypothesis is that the difference between the two samples is so large that it is not reasonable to conclude that they are due to sampling error alone. Therefore, they do not come from the same population and there is a relationship between *x* and *y*. We construct the sampling distribution for the test statistic *U* assuming the null hypothesis is true and determine the probability of obtaining the *U* we did under that hypothesis. If the probability of our observed *U* is low (say, ≤.05) under that assumption, we reject the null hypothesis and argue that our data support the research hypothesis.

Preparing Data for M-W *U* Analysis

To illustrate the various steps in carrying out a M-W *U* analysis, we'll use some fictitious data. Suppose the administrator of a state correctional system has designed two different in-service training programs for newly hired (rookie) correctional officers. She wants to know whether there is any difference in the performance of rookies who have gone through the two different programs. To find out, she draws an independent random sample of rookie officers in each of the two programs, consisting of seven officers in one case and six in the other. The senior officers directly supervising the rookies have evaluated (rated or "graded") the rookies' performance at the end of the probationary period on a scale of 1 (lowest) through 10 (highest). Suppose the ratings for the two samples (Samples 1 and 2) were as indicated in Table 13.1.

In this table, the rookie officers' performance evaluations for each of the two samples have been arranged from highest to lowest. You can think of the evaluations as grades given to the rookie officers (1 = F, 5 = C, 10 = A, etc.), if you like. Preparing these data for M-W *U* analysis requires three steps.

Step 1: Combining the Two Samples' Ratings. The first step is to combine the two samples into a single group and arrange the supervisors' raw ratings ("grades") for the two samples into a single ordinal rating list (as in column 2 of Table 13.2), again from

Table 13.1   Supervisors' Ratings of Rookie Correctional Officers

Sample 1 Ratings	Sample 2 Ratings
8	10
7	9
6	8
4	5
2	3
1	1
1	

Table 13.2 Samples, Ratings, and Possible Ranks for Supervisors' Evaluations

Sample	Ratings	Possible Ranks
2	10	13
2	9	12
2	8	11
1	8	10
1	7	9
1	6	8
2	5	7
1	4	6
2	3	5
1	2	4
2	1	3
1	1	2
1	1	1
$n = 13$		Sum of Ranks = 91

highest to lowest. When doing so, you must keep track of the sample from which each rating comes, as we have in column 1 of Table 13.2, because later in the analysis we need to separate the combined ratings back into their samples of origin.

Step 2: Converting the Combined Samples' Ratings to Ranks. The next step is **conversion of the raw data to ranks**. That is, we want to replace each of the original raw rating scores with its corresponding rank in the combined array of scores. Note that the number of possible ranks must correspond to the total number of raw ratings in the combined list (see column 3 in Table 13.2). In our case, the total number of raw ratings in both samples is 7 + 6 = 13, so the ratings would be ranked from 1 (lowest) to 13 (highest).

If none of the rookies received the same rating, this task would be easy. We would simply assign the rookie who was rated highest the rank of 13, the rookie who rated next highest the rank of 12, and so on until we reached the rookie who was rated lowest, assigning him the rank of 1, as indicated in Table 13.2, column 3, headed "possible ranks."

Often, however, as in the case of our example, three rookie officers received the same "1" rating and two received the same "8" rating. Such identical ratings are called tied scores, and they require a special procedure for assigning their corresponding ranks. Why? Because it makes no sense to assign different ranks to the three rookies who received the same "1" rating, as we did in column 3 of Table 13.2, for example. They have equal ratings, so they should have equal ranks.

How will we ensure that tied ratings receive appropriately tied ranks? When raw ordinal ratings are tied, we calculate their mean possible rank and assign each of the tied ratings that mean rank. For example, three of the rookie officers in our example received a rating of 1. As indicated in column 3 of Table 13.2, they "occupy" possible rank positions 1, 2, and 3 of the 13 ranks in our combined list. To determine what rank to assign these scores, we would add these three ranks (1 + 2 + 3 = 6) and divide by the number of tied ranks (3) and arrive at the result: 6/3 = 2. Therefore, each of the three tied ordinal ratings of 1 would be assigned a rank of 2. The same procedure is followed for the two officers who received a tied rating of 8. Consulting column 3 of Table 13.2, we see that they occupy ranks 10 and 11 in the combined possible ranks list. Each of them would be assigned a rank of 10.5 because (10 + 11)/2 = 21/2 = 10.5.

Table 13.3 shows the samples from which the rookie officers came (column 1); the original raw ordinal supervisors' ratings for each rookie officer in each sample (column 2); and the rank corresponding with each rating, adjusting the ranks for tied ratings using the procedures discussed above (column 3).

Note that both the number of ranks (in our example, 13) and the sum of ranks *for the combined samples* (in our example, 91) is the same before and after these tied rank adjustments are made. The fact that we are dealing with a fixed number of ranks (and, therefore, a fixed sum of ranks) for all the officers combined is important for our later considerations and calculations. For example, it provides the basis for comparing the two sums of ranks when the officers are separated into their respective samples, as we do in Step 3.

Step 3: Separating the Combined Samples and Their Ranks Into the Original Two Sample Groups. The final step in preparing for the M-W U analysis is to separate the combined samples back into their original two sample groups, retaining each rookie officer's rank, which we just established in Step 2. In Table 13.4, we show the ranks of the individual rookies in each of the two samples, this time displaying them side by side. The calculations for the M-W U tests are performed on these ranks.

Let's review what we have accomplished in these three steps and consider the implications for our hypothesis test. First, we combined the supervisors' ratings for the two samples of rookies into a single group and arranged the ratings in an ordinal variable values array, in this case listing them from highest to lowest. Then, we converted the ratings in this combined ordered list to ranks, employing special procedures for tied ranks. Finally, we separated the combined group into the two original samples again, retaining the newly established ranks from the combined samples. The net result is that we have two distributions of ranks (one for each of the original

Table 13.3 Samples, Ratings, and Ranks for Supervisors' Evaluations, With Assigned Ranks Corrected for Tied Ranks

Sample	Ratings	Possible Ranks Corrected for Tied Ranks
2	10	13
2	9	12
2	8	10.5
1	8	10.5
1	7	9
1	6	8
2	5	7
1	4	6
2	3	5
1	2	4
2	1	2
1	1	2
1	1	2
$n = 13$		Sum of Ranks = 91

Table 13.4 Combined Samples' Ranks of Supervisors' Evaluations Separated Into the Two Original Rookie Samples

Sample 1	Sample 2
10.5	13
9	12
8	10.5
6	7
4	5
2	2
2	

samples), but the ranks in these distributions are those we assigned when the samples were combined.

Let's consider what we might be able to say about these two distributions of ranks. Ignore for a moment that our two samples are not of equal size and assume instead that they are. Now suppose we ask what a comparison of the two distributions of ranks ought to show if the null hypothesis is true and there is no difference in rookies' performance for the two different training programs. A little thought should persuade you that higher ranks would be about equally divided between the samples, medium ranks would likewise be about evenly divided between the two samples, and lower ranks would also be about evenly divided between the two samples. It follows that, so long as the sample sizes are equal, the sums of the ranks for the two samples would be approximately equal (and so would the mean of the ranks). We say "approximately" here because, for reasons beyond the scope of this text, when we are dealing with sums of ranks, the two sums will not be exactly equal in many cases. It turns out, however, that the difference between the two sums to be expected under the null hypothesis and in the absence of sampling error can be calculated precisely, even when the sample sizes are not equal. Once this difference is determined, we can argue that, if the null hypothesis is true and there is no sampling error, the sums would differ from this difference only due to sampling error.

Here's another way of thinking about what the M-W U test does. Suppose we begin by examining the ranks in the two samples (Table 13.4) and select the sample that appears to have a greater number of higher ranks (i.e., ranks of 10, 12, or 13 rather than ranks of 1, 3, or 5), which, in our example, looks like it is Sample 2. (We select our sample in this way to make the task we are about to perform easier.) Then, taking each of the ranks in Sample 2 in turn, beginning with the highest rank in Sample 2, we count and record the number of ranks in Sample 1 that have higher ranks than the specified Sample 2 rank. In our example, beginning with the rank of 13 in Sample 2, we record a 0 because there are 0 ranks in Sample 1 that exceed the rank of 13. Then we consider the next highest rank in Sample 2, which is 12. Again, there are no ranks in Sample 1 that exceed the rank of 12, so we record a 0 here too. The next highest rank in Sample 2 is 10.5. One rank in Sample 1 ties with this rank. When a rank in Sample 1 ties with the specified Sample 2 rank, it is counted as .5. So our count in this case is .5. These procedures are repeated for each of the other ranks in Sample 2. If we did so, the counts would be: 0, 0, .5, 3, 4, and 6 (five higher and two tied). Now suppose we sum these counts. We would have $0 + 0 + .5 + 3 + 4 + 6 = 13.5$. This sum of counts gives us a measure of how often the ranks in Sample 1 exceed those in Sample 2. Note that the larger this sum, the greater the difference between the ranks in the two samples and, hence, the more likely it is that there is a relationship between the training program (our independent variable) and rookie performance (our dependent variable). You can perhaps imagine ways in which these counts could be turned into probabilities that ranks in Sample 2 exceed those in Sample 1. In any event, it turns out that the sum of ranks we just calculated equals the M-W test statistic, U.

Calculating M-W U

We have already illustrated one method of calculating U in the preceding paragraph. Our description of this method was intended to help you understand the general principles on which the M-W U test is based, and it can be used with samples of any size. It's easy to see, however, that calculations like these would get quite tedious if sample sizes are large. And in any event, it isn't the one typically used for calculating U, whether the samples involved are large or small. The procedures usually used for calculating U differ for smaller and larger samples. In this section, we will discuss calculating U when both samples are $n \geq 5$.

As a preliminary step, let's add a few summary statistics to the data in Table 13.4, which we will use in our calculations. The results are presented in Table 13.5. We'll round our calculations in this section to the nearest hundredth.

Next, let's define the symbols for the summary statistics at the bottom of Table 13.5 as well as others we will use in our M-W U calculations. We will give examples of the symbols and their meanings at appropriate points. The symbols, their meanings, and some examples from Table 13.5 are found in Table 13.6.

Table 13.5 Combined Samples' Ranks of Supervisors' Evaluations Separated Into the Two Original Rookie Samples With Added Summary Statistics

Sample 1	Sample 2	
10.5	13	
9	12	
8	10.5	
6	7	
4	5	
2	2	
2		
		Totals
$n_1 = 7$	$n_2 = 6$	$N_T = 13$
$\Sigma R_1 = 41.50$	$\Sigma R_2 = 49.50$	$\Sigma R_T = 91$
$\bar{R}_1 = 5.93$	$\bar{R}_2 = 8.25$	$\bar{R}_T = 7$

Note: See Table 13.6 for symbol meanings.

Table 13.6 Symbols and Their Meanings in M-W U Calculations

Symbols	Meanings
K-W BSS$_{obs}$	The observed between-group sum of squares in K-W H analysis
n_1	The number of ranks in Sample 1 (the size of Sample 1)
n_2	The number of ranks in Sample 2 (the size of Sample 2)
N	The number of ranks in a set of ranks
N_T	The total number of observations (ranks) in both samples ($N_T = n_1 + n_2$)
ΣR_1	The sum of the n_1 (7) ranks in Sample 1 (41.5) after Samples 1 and 2 have been combined, ranked, and then separated again.
ΣR_2	The sum of the n_2 (6) ranks in Sample 2 (49.5) after Samples 1 and 2 have been combined, ranked, and then separated again.
ΣR_T	The sum of the N_T (13) ranks after Samples 1 and 2 have been combined (91)
σ_u	The standard deviation of U in the population
μ_u	The mean of the sampling distribution for U (which is the value of U in the population)
μ_{pop}	The mean of U in the population
$\bar{R}_1$	The mean of the ranks in Sample 1
$\bar{R}_2$	The mean of the ranks in Sample 2
$\bar{R}_T$	The mean of all ranks in all samples
U	The M-W sample-based test statistic
U_1	A M-W statistic calculated from Sample 1 data after Samples 1 and 2 have been combined, ranked, and then separated again.
U_2	A M-W statistic calculated from Sample 2 data after Samples 1 and 2 have been combined, ranked, and then separated again.
U_{obs}	U calculated from sample data
$\bar{X}_{K\text{-}W\ BSS}$	The mean of the sampling distribution of K-W BSS

Perhaps you have already recognized that the language and symbols used in discussing M-W U can be confusing. It is especially important to pay attention to the distinction between the **number of ranks** (n) and the **sum of ranks** (ΣR) in the discussion to follow. The number of ranks refers to the number of observations of the dependent variable—in our example, the number of rookies (really, the number of ratings)—in a sample or in both samples combined. Thus, for example, in our rookie study, there are seven officers in Sample 1 ($n_1 = 7$) and six in Sample 2 ($n_2 = 6$) and a total of 13 rookies ($N_T = 13$) in both samples. The sum of ranks refers to adding up the rank values in a sample or both samples combined. When we add the rank values for each of the samples in our example, the Sample 1 $\Sigma R_1 = 41.5$, the Sample 2 $\Sigma R_2 = 49.5$, and the combined samples $\Sigma R_T = 91$. It is also important to notice whether we are discussing these statistics for a sample or for the combined samples. So, pay attention to what is being referred to (numbers of ranks or sums of ranks and whether these are for a particular sample or for the two samples combined) or you will surely get lost.

To make things potentially even more confusing, we will be referring to U (italicized), the statistic used in M-W significance tests, and the closely related statistics U_1 and U_2, which are calculated from Samples 1 and 2, respectively. There are, as we will see, relationships among U, U_1, and U_2. You need to be alert for the differences in these symbols and their meanings as well.

Rank orders are numerical systems with certain fixed mathematical properties that make the M-W U test (and the other tests to be discussed in this chapter) possible. We will simply note some of them without offering proof. First, note that by converting raw score ratings to ranks, we treat the data as strictly ordinal. That is, we ignore any quantitative differences between the original raw ratings other than that one is higher or lower than (or tied with) another. Second, many mathematical properties of *consecutive* ranks are fixed for any particular set of n ranks. Consecutive ranks are ranks that run in numerical sequence without gaps, such as from 1 to 2 to 3 to 4 to 5 in whole-number increments (except when allowing for tied ranks where fractional numbers are permitted). Ranks that run from 1 to 3 to 6 would not be consecutive. These properties can be expressed in relatively simple mathematical formulas involving two quantities: the number of ranks in the set and the sum of those ranks. It can be demonstrated, for example, that there is a fixed relationship between the sum of ranks and the number of ranks in a data set. In particular, the sum of the ranks in any given set of *consecutive* ranks is given by $\Sigma R_T = N_T(N_T + 1)/2$, where N_T is the total number of ranks (i.e., the total number of observations—in our example, the total number of rookie correctional officers in both samples combined, which is $N_T = 13$). Thus, in our example, the number of ranks is 13 for the combined samples, and we have the following relationship between the number of ranks and the sum of ranks: $\Sigma R_T = (13)(13 + 1)/2 = (13)(14)/2 = 182/2 = 91$. Note that this relationship between the number and sum of ranks does *not* hold for the ranks in the samples *after* the samples have been combined, ranked, and separated into the original two samples again. Why? Because the ranks in each sample are not consecutive.

Note, also, however, that $\Sigma R_T = \Sigma R_1 + \Sigma R_2$ and that $N_T = n_1 + n_2$. So, substituting $n_1 + n_2$ for N_T in the formula for ΣR_T above, we can write

$$\Sigma R_T = \Sigma R_1 + \Sigma R_2 = N_T(N_T + 1)/2 = (n_1 + n_2)(n_1 + n_2 + 1)/2$$

Using the numbers from our example, we would have

$$\Sigma R_T = 41.5 + 49.5 = (7 + 6)(7 + 6 + 1)/2 = 91$$

With these preliminary considerations in hand, let's return to the method for calculating U for samples of $n \geq 5$. For reasons again beyond the scope of this text, this way of calculating U requires that we calculate a U for Sample 1 (U_1) and for Sample 2 (U_2) and then select the smaller of the two for our test statistic U. The calculations required for U_1 are given by Formula 13.1.

$$U_1 = n_1 n_2 + \frac{n_1(n_1+1)}{2} - \Sigma R_1 \quad (13.1)$$

In Formula 13.1, n_1 is the size of Sample 1 and ΣR_1 is the sum of the ranks in Sample 1.

The calculation for U_2 can be accomplished by applying Formula 13.2a or 13.2b.

$$U_2 = n_1 n_2 + \frac{n_2(n_2-1)}{2} - \Sigma R_2 \quad (13.2a)$$

$$U_2 = n_1 n_2 - U_1 \quad (13.2b)$$

In Formulas 13.2a and 13.2b, ΣR_2 is the sum of ranks in Sample 2, n_1 and n_2 are the sizes of Samples 1 and 2 respectively, and U_1 is the result of the calculations following Formula 13.1.

Let's apply these formulas to the rank order data in Table 13.5. For U_1, we have

$$U_1 = n_1 n_2 + \frac{n_1(n_1+1)}{2} - \Sigma R_1$$
$$= (7)(6) + (7)(8)/2 - 41.5$$
$$= 42 + 28 - 41.5$$
$$= 70 - 41.5$$
$$= 28.5$$

For U_2, we have

$$U_2 = n_1 n_2 + \frac{n_2(n_2-1)}{2} - \Sigma R_2$$
$$= (7)(6) + (6)(7)/2 - 49.5$$
$$= 42 + 21 - 49.5$$
$$= 63 - 49.5$$
$$= 13.5$$

We can confirm that Formulas 13.2a and 13.2b give the same result by doing the calculations specified in Formula 13.2b.

$$U_2 = n_1 n_2 - U_1$$
$$= (6)(7) - 28.5$$
$$= 42 - 28.5$$
$$U_2 = 13.5$$

Because U_1 is the smaller of the two quantities, we use it for the value of the test statistic U, which, in this case, is 13.5. (Compare this result with what we obtained summing the number of times a rank in Sample 2 exceeded the ranks in Sample 1 on p. 470.)

Let's explore this test statistic U a bit more. If we combine Formulas 13.1 and 13.2a, we can write Formula 13.3.

$$U_1 + U_2 = \left[n_1 n_2 + \frac{n_1(n_1+1)}{2} - \Sigma R_1 \right] + \left[n_1 n_2 + \frac{n_2(n_2-1)}{2} - \Sigma R_2 \right] \quad (13.3)$$

We won't present the details, but applying some algebra to the right side of this equation, we can demonstrate that Formula 13.4 holds.

$$U_1 + U_2 = n_1 n_2 \quad (13.4)$$

In our example, $U_1 + U_2 = 28.5 + 13.5 = 42$ and $n_1 n_2 = (6)(7) = 42$. Look again at Formula 13.2b. If we solve this equation for $n_1 n_2$, we also have $n_1 n_2 = U_1 + U_2$. So, Formula 13.4 gives us a way of checking our calculations for U_1 and U_2.

For any given samples of sizes n_1 or n_2, the sum of U_1 and U_2 will always be equal to the product of n_1 and n_2. Hence, because $U_1 = n_1 n_2 - U_2$ and $U_2 = n_1 n_2 - U_1$ (see Formula 13.2b), once you know the value of U for any one of the samples, you can easily calculate the U for the other and then determine which is the smaller to use as the Mann-Whitney test statistic U.

The Sampling Distribution for U

The sampling distribution for U consists of the probabilities of all the possible combinations of a set of ranks when ranks are taken two at a time (corresponding to the two samples) assuming the null hypothesis is true. U has known sampling distributions. We say "distributions" here because they vary by sample sizes.

We will present the general formulas for the mean and standard error of a U sampling distribution, again without offering proof. Note that these general formulas are *not for estimates* of an applicable sampling distribution's mean and standard error, as we have discussed for other inferential statistics in previous chapters. Rather, because of the special properties of rank order sets, the values of these sampling distribution statistics are *known*; they are determined by the number and sum of ranks in the set.

The applicable sampling distribution's mean, which is the value of U in the population and which we symbolize as μ_{pop}, is given by Formula 13.5.

$$\mu_{pop} = \frac{n_1 n_2}{2} \tag{13.5}$$

The applicable sampling distribution's standard error, which we symbolize as σ_u, is given by Formula 13.6.

$$\sigma_u = \sqrt{\frac{n_1 n_2 (n_1 + n_2 + 1)}{12}} \tag{13.6}$$

Note that Formula 13.6 applies when there are no tied ranks. When tied ranks are present, the formula is more complicated and available in more advanced texts. If only a few tied ranks are present, they can be ignored for the purposes of hand calculations.

Applying Formula 13.5 to determine the applicable sampling distribution's mean (which you will recall is equal to the population mean, μ_{pop}) for our data in Table 13.5, we have

$$\mu_{pop} = \frac{(7)(6)}{2} = \frac{42}{2} = 21$$

Applying Formula 13.6 to determine the sampling distribution's standard error, we have

$$\sigma_u = \sqrt{\frac{n_1 n_2 (n_1 + n_2 + 1)}{12}}$$

$$= \sqrt{\frac{(7)(6)(7+6+1)}{12}}$$

$$= \sqrt{\frac{(42)(14)}{12}}$$

$$= \sqrt{\frac{588}{12}}$$

$$= \sqrt{49}$$

$$\sigma_u = 7$$

Testing *U* for Statistical Significance

For smaller samples (typically when at least one of the samples is $n \leq 20$, but both are $n \geq 5$), the most precise critical values for U at various levels of significance are provided in tables included with more advanced texts. For samples where $n > 5$, the sampling distribution for U is approximately normal and hence can be approximated by the standard normal (z-score) distribution. We'll use this approximation for our example. The formula for converting an observed U to its z-score approximation is given by Formula 13.7a.

$$z = \frac{U_{obs} - \mu_{pop}}{\sigma_u} \qquad (13.7a)$$

In Formula 13.7a, U_{obs} is the observed sample statistic (the smaller of the results from Formulas 13.1 and 2 calculations), μ_{pop} is the mean of U in the population, and σ_u is the standard error of the sampling distribution of U. Compare Formula 13.7a with Formula 9.1 for t in Chapter 9. Remember that for large samples, $t = z$.

> ### PAUSE, THINK, AND EXPLORE...
>
> Compare Formula 13.7a with Formula 9.1. What similarities and differences do you see?

Although our samples in Table 13.5 are not large enough to qualify for the z-score approximation of the sampling distribution for U and we do have some tied ratings, we'll use these data to do the calculations for the z approximation and discuss its use in significance tests of U anyway, just for purposes of illustration.

Applying Formula 13.7a for the z-score approximation of our observed $U = 13.5$, we have

$$z = \frac{U_{obs} - \mu_{pop}}{\sigma_u}$$
$$= \frac{13.5 - 21}{7}$$
$$= \frac{-7.5}{7}$$
$$= -1.07$$

So, we have arrived at a z approximation of the M-W U test statistic as $z = -1.07$. We can now test for the statistical significance of this z-score approximation of U using the standard normal (z-score) distribution as the sampling distribution.

For the z-score value we determined by applying Formula 13.7a, our results are interpreted in the same way we illustrated in Chapters 5 and 9 for areas under the curve, or in this case, areas under the curve of the sampling distribution for U. In our example, the null hypothesis was that rankings of the two samples of rookie officers would not differ, and our research hypothesis was that they would differ in the population. Because our research hypothesis is nondirectional, we use a two-tailed test to determine the likelihood that our null hypothesis is true in the population given our sample data.

Consulting the *z*-score table in Appendix D for a two-tailed test and the .05 significance level, the critical value for *z* is 1.96 (see column C = .025 opposite *z* = 1.96 in column A—because the table gives us values for areas [probabilities] under half the curve, for a two-tailed test we need to divide the .05 in half, and half of .05 is .025). So, because our calculated *z* is less than the critical value of 1.96, there is not a statistically significant difference between the rank orders of the correctional officer rookies. We accept the null hypothesis that the differences in the training made no difference in the supervisors' rookie performance ratings.

If our research hypothesis was directional (i.e., if we hypothesized that one training program is better than the other), we would perform a one-tailed hypothesis test. The critical value of *z* for a one-tailed test at the .05 significance is 1.64. Our calculated value of $z = -1.07$ fails to meet or surpass this threshold as well.

Technically, rank orders are not continuous variables. Therefore, some statisticians recommend that a correction for continuity be added to Formula 13.7a, as we first discussed in Chapter 6. If we did so, Formula 13.7b would be the result. (See pp. 181–183 for a discussion of correction of continuity.)

$$z = \frac{U_{obs} - \mu_{pop} \pm .5}{\sigma_u} \tag{13.7b}$$

We'll do a Formula 13.7b correction for continuity calculation using the data from our example.

$$z = \frac{U_{obs} - \mu_{pop} \pm .5}{\sigma_u}$$

$$= \frac{(13.5 - 21) \pm .5}{7}$$

$$= \frac{-7.5 \pm .5}{7}$$

$$= \frac{-7.0}{7} \text{ through } \frac{-8.0}{7}$$

$$\frac{-8.0}{7} = -1.14$$

and

$$\frac{-7.0}{7} = -1.00$$

$$z = -1.14 \text{ to } -1.00$$

These results do not justify any change in our decision; we cannot reject the null hypothesis.

Reporting the Results of M-W U Analysis

Reports of a M-W U analysis typically include the sizes of the samples, calculated U or z score, and the probability associated with it under the null hypothesis. The sum of ranks for each of the two samples is also sometimes reported.

Concluding Remarks Regarding M-W U Analysis

Recall that at the beginning of our discussion of the M-W U test, we said it was similar to a t test for the difference between two sample means, except that it focused on a difference between mean ranks rather than mean raw scores. Some of you are saying yes, and we have yet to see another reference to mean ranks since. Well, you are correct. Our calculations for U did not involve mean ranks. Without offering proof, there are methods of calculating U that do focus more explicitly on means, but they are more complex and they come to the same results we achieved. Hence, although it might not be obvious, the methods of calculating U we have described do implicitly involve a comparison of mean ranks. For a description of these more complex calculations, consult a more advanced text.

A review and comparison of all the several nonparametric tests for identifying statistically significant differences between two independent random samples is beyond the scope of this text, but it is important to note that several alternatives do exist. Examples include the Median, Kolmogorov-Smirnov, Wald-Wolfowitz, and Moses tests. In addition, there are nonparametric tests that can be used when your samples are dependent. They include the Sign, Wilcoxon, and Kendall coefficient of concordance tests. Each of these tests has its strengths and weaknesses, which are discussed in other texts, and statisticians, of course, are also always attempting to come up with better tests.

Whether you are presenting your own M-W U test results or you are reading about others, you should expect a table (or at least the summary statistics) similar to Table 13.5, the results expressed as either a z score or U; the probability of this result under the null hypothesis; and enough information about the type of research design, samples (Are they random or not? Are they independent or dependent?), and data details (such as how and at what level the variables were measured) to determine whether or not a M-W U test is appropriate.

The From the Literature Box 13.1 discusses a recent research report that includes a Mann-Whitney U test as a part of the data analysis.

The Kruskal-Wallis H Test for Three or More Independent Random Samples

The statisticians William Kruskal and W. Allen Wallis developed the **Kruskal-Wallis H** (**K-W H**) test. The K-W H test is similar to ANOVA in that both tests are designed to identify statistically significant differences, if any, among three or more dependent variable value means. As we learned in Chapter 10, ANOVA focuses on differences among raw interval or ratio variable value means; the K-W H test examines differences among mean ranks. The typical application of the K-W H test is in research situations where the independent variable is nominal with three or more values and the dependent variable is ordinal.

From the Literature Box 13.1

Paul A. Zanderbergen and colleagues noted the rapid spread of residential restriction laws for sex offenders, and they decided to find out if empirical evidence supported such laws. They studied whether sex offender recidivism was related to, among other variables, the distance offenders resided from public schools and child day care centers. Using data from Florida public records, they compared a sample of recidivist sex offenders with a similar sample of nonrecidivist sex offenders. As a part of their analysis, they used a Mann-Whitney U test. The following is an excerpt from their research report.

PURPOSE OF THE STUDY

The purpose of this study is to investigate the relationship between sex offense recidivism and residential proximity to places where children commonly congregate. Specifically, we sought to determine whether sex offenders who lived closer to schools or daycares were more likely to reoffend sexually than those who lived farther away. The null hypothesis proposes that there will be no significant differences between recidivists and nonrecidivists in their proximity to schools or daycares. In addition, the null hypothesis assumes no statistically significant correlation between proximity and recidivism. This research is important for identifying the role that residential distance from child-oriented venues might play in inhibiting sexual recidivism. Policies informed by scientific data are more likely to successfully accomplish their goals of community protection.

...

The general approach used in this study to examine the effect of residential proximity on recidivism consisted of (a) determining the recidivist population for the period from 2004 to 2006, (b) selecting a comparable set of nonrecidivists, (c) geocoding the residential addresses of the two groups as well as all the schools and licensed daycares, (d) calculating proximity metrics for both populations, and (e) analyzing any differences in the distributions of proximity metrics between the two groups. These steps will be described in more detail in the sections below.

...

Statistical Analyses

The distributions of the number of schools and daycares within distance buffers were summarized in tabular form and compared using a chi-square test. The distances to the nearest daycare and school were graphically summarized as cumulative distribution functions. Differences between the distributions were tested using chi-square and parametric and

(Continued)

nonparametric tests of means. The predictive power of distance, controlling for certain risk factors, was assessed through a linear regression model.

RESULTS

Descriptive statistics of the offender population are displayed in Table 3. It is important to remember that this sample was generated by identifying recidivists and then creating a matched sample of nonrecidivists. The sample is therefore not representative of the sex offender population in Florida, and it consists of a more high-risk group than a randomly selected sample would be. The sample ($n = 330$) had accrued an average of 5.5 prior arrests for any crime (mode = 4) and 3 prior sex crime arrests (mode = 2). They were predominantly White and unmarried, and one quarter were designated as predators. Almost all (96%) had at least one minor victim in their criminal sexual history. The sample lived an average of 5,182 ft from a daycare and 4,962 ft from a school. More than half lived within 2,500 ft of a school or daycare.

Facility Counts within Buffer Distances

Counts of the number of daycares and schools within 1,000-ft and 2,500-ft buffers around offenders are summarized in Table 4. Manual inspection of the distributions suggests very small differences. For example, when considering a buffer of 1,000 ft around offenders, 115 out of 165 recidivists have no daycare within this buffer, and 28 have one daycare, whereas 116 out of 165 nonrecidivists have no daycare and 31 have one daycare. Logically, a larger buffer of 2,500 ft results in more offenders having one or more daycares within this buffer, but the differences between the two populations remain small.

Differences between the distributions were tested using chi-square. A total of four tests were carried out, each comparing recidivists and nonrecidivists for one type of facility for one distance value. Consistent with standard practice in chi-square tests, count categories were combined to ensure no observation counts fell below the minimum of five. Results are shown in Table 5. Three of the four tests indicated no significant differences between the distributions of counts for recidivists and nonrecidivists. The only significant difference was found for the count of schools within a 2,500-ft buffer. Although the chi-square test itself does not reveal any particular direction, visual inspection of the results in Table 4 suggests that nonrecidivists are more likely than recidivists to have at least one school within 2,500 ft. Multiple iterations of the chi-square test using only two categories (count = 0 vs. count > 0, count ≤ 1 vs. count > 1, etc.) indicate that the strongest difference

(Continued)

(Continued)

Table 3 Descriptive Statistics (n = 330)

	%	Mean	Median	Mode	Standard Deviation
White	63				
Minority	37				
Currently married	18				
Divorced/separated/widowed	34				
Never married	48				
Priors (all)		5.45	4.00	4	4.18
Priors (sex)		3.35	2.50	2	2.78
Offender	74				
Predator	23				
Minor victim[a]	96				
Offender age		33.1	30.0	24	12.8
Feet to daycare		5,182	1,780		9,116
Within 1,000 of daycare	23				
Within 1,500 of daycare	42				
Within 2,500 of daycare	61				
Feet to school		4,962	2.442		7,740
Within 1,000 of school	13				
Within 1,500 of school	26				
Within 2,500 of school	51				
Recidivist	50				

a. For recidivists, the victim age category is based on prior victim(s) only not the new arrests.

(Continued)

Table 4 Counts of Daycares and Schools Within Buffers Around Offenders

Count	Number of Daycares Within 1,000 Ft		Number of Daycares Within 2,500 Ft		Number of Schools Within 1,000 Ft		Number of Schools Within 2,500 Ft	
	Non-recidivists	Recidivists	Non-recidivists	Recidivists	Non-recidivists	Recidivists	Non-recidivists	Recidivists
0	116	115	65	57	123	127	68	77
1	31	28	30	35	26	25	35	51
2	12	12	14	19	13	10	35	21
3	5	7	17	21	2	2	12	11
4	1	1	13	15	1	1	7	3
5	0	1	8	8	0	0	7	1
6	0	0	7	6	0	0	1	1
7	0	0	4	1	0	0	0	0
8	0	0	3	1	0	0	0	0
9	0	1	1	1	0	0	0	0
10	0	0	0	1	0	0	0	0
>10	0	0	3	1	0	0	0	0
Sum	165	165	165	165	165	165	165	165

(Continued)

(Continued)

between the two populations occurs when comparing the counts for zero or one school within 2,500 ft (103 vs. 128) and more than one school within 2,500 ft (62 vs. 37). This finding confirms that the only statistically significant difference found is the result of nonrecidivists having more schools in close proximity than recidivists.

Table 5 Results of Chi-Square Tests for Counts of Daycares and Schools Within Buffers When Comparing Recidivists to Nonrecidivists

Test	χ^2	df	Two-Tailed p Value
Daycares within 1,000 ft	1.930	3	.587
Daycares within 2,500 ft	10.581	6	.102
Schools within 1,000 ft	0.858	2	.651
Schools within 2,500 ft	35.496	4	<.001

Proximity and Recidivism

The distances to the nearest daycare and school for both populations are plotted as cumulative distribution functions in Figures 3 and 4, respectively. The results for distance to the nearest daycare indicate that there is very little difference in the two distance curves up until approximately 2,000 ft, indicating that recidivists and nonrecidivists are located at very similar distances when considering these shorter distances. At greater distances, the curve for recidivists is above the curve for nonrecidivists, indicating that a larger proportion of recidivists live between approximately 2,500 and 4,000 ft. At greater distances, the difference gets smaller again.

The results for the distance to nearest school indicate that the curve for recidivists falls below the curve for nonrecidivists up until approximately 3,500 ft, indicating that a smaller proportion of recidivists is located close to schools at these distances. At greater distances, the curve for recidivists exceeds the curve for nonrecidivists, indicating that a larger proportion of recidivists live between approximately 3,500 and 10,000 ft. The curves become very similar at greater distances.

. . .

. . . and 8,000 ft for schools), which fall outside of the values of interest. Therefore, differences were tested using parametric and nonparametric tests of means as well as chi-square tests for specific distance values of interest.

(Continued)

Figure 3 Cumulative Distribution Function of Distance to Nearest Daycare

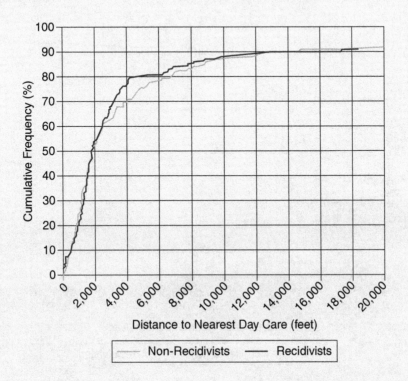

To assess whether sex offenders who lived closer to schools or daycares were more likely to reoffend sexually than those who lived farther away, we utilized two-tailed t tests to compare the mean distance that recidivists and nonrecidivists lived from schools and daycares and found no significant differences between the groups (see Table 6). Nonrecidivists lived slightly closer to daycares, and recidivists lived slightly closer to schools, but neither difference was statistically significant, indicating that these differences were not more than would be expected by chance. In other words, sex offenders who lived in closer proximity to schools and daycares were no more likely to reoffend than those who lived farther away. Because the distributions did not conform to all the assumptions of parametric comparisons of means, we performed a Mann-Whitney U test, a nonparametric

(Continued)

(Continued)

Figure 4 Cumulative Distribution Function of Distance to Nearest School

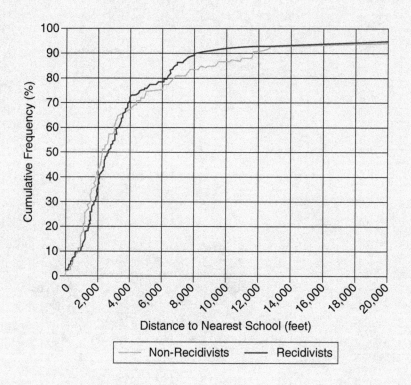

Table 6 Mean Distances From Schools and Daycares

	Recidivist	n	Mean	Standard Deviation	Standard Error Mean	T Test (Difference Between Groups)	Two-Tailed p Value
Feet to daycare	no	165	5144.15	8655.80	673.85	−.075	.940
	yes	165	5219.76	9581.04	745.88		
Feet to school	no	165	5296.75	9029.17	702.92	.785	.433
	yes	165	4627.80	6198.25	482.53		

(Continued)

Table 7 Group Comparisons Between Recidivists and Nonrecidivists Based on Distance

Proximity	Percentage of Recidivists Living		Percentage of Nonrecidivists Living		χ^2	Two-Tailed p value
	Outside the Buffer Zone	Within the Buffer Zone	Outside the Buffer Zone	within the Buffer Zone		
Within 2,500 ft of a school	52	49	47	53	0.776	.378
Within 2,500 ft of a daycare	38	62	39	61	0.115	.734
Within 1,500 ft of a school	78	23	70	30	2.687	.102
Within 1,500 ft of a daycare	59	41	56	44	0.311	.577
Within 1,000 ft of a school	90	10	85	15	1.746	.186
Within 1,000 ft of a daycare	78	21	76	24	0.431	.511

Note: df = 1.

test used for two samples measured on an ordinal scale (Mann & Whitney, 1947; Vogt, 2005). Again, there were no significant differences between recidivists and nonrecidivists in the distances they lived from schools ($p = .485$) and daycares ($p = .934$).

We also compared the proportions of recidivists and nonrecidivists who lived within common buffer zones using chi-square analyses (see Table 7). In these analyses, we tested three distances: the 1,000- and 2,500-ft zones used in previous analyses for the reasons stated above, and a distance zone of 1,500 ft—the distance designated in proposed legislation in 2008 in Florida for expanding the statewide buffer zone. Again, no significant

(Continued)

(Continued)

differences were found, indicating that recidivists were not more likely to live within 1,000, 1,500, or 2,500 ft of schools or daycares than nonrecidivists.

We also examined the bivariate correlations between proximity and recidivism. There was a virtually nonexistent association *between* reoffending and proximity to schools ($r = .004$, $p = .940$) or daycares ($r = -.043$, $p = .433$). Keeping in mind that the sample was matched on relevant risk factors (prior offenses, age, marital status, predator status), when the distances to schools and daycares were entered along with risk factors into a logistic regression model with recidivism as the dependent variable, neither distance variable was statistically significant ($p = .091$ and $p = .141$, respectively). The overall model was not statistically significant ($\chi^2 = 5.767$, $df = 7$, Nagelkerke $R^2 = .024$, $p = .567$), indicating that proximity to schools and daycares, with other risk factors being comparable, explains virtually none of the variation in sexual recidivism.

Source: From Zanderbergen, P. A. (2010). Residential proximity to schools and daycares: An empirical analysis of sex offense recidivism. *Criminal Justice and Behavior, 37,* 482–502. Retrieved June 1, 2012, from http://cjb.sagepub.com/content/37/5/482

The K-W *H* test may be used to analyze data in other research situations as well. You should consider using the K-W *H* test when ANOVA might seem appropriate, but (a) the dependent variable is not approximately normally distributed in the population, (b) the sample variances are not approximately equal, and/or (c) the dependent variable is measured at the ordinal level (neither the ANOVA nor the K-W *H* test is suitable for nominal-level data).

Assumptions of the K-W *H* Test

The K-W *H* test is one of the most commonly used ANOVA alternatives, and it can be used as long as (a) the samples are randomly and independently drawn, (b) the dependent variable is measured at the ordinal level or higher, (c) the dependent variable is continuous, and (d) the dependent variable has the same distribution (though not necessarily a normal distribution) in the populations. Remember, you can always convert variable values at higher levels of measurement to a rank order measure using the procedures for converting raw scores to ranks we discussed earlier and use again in the following.

The Basic Ideas Underlying the K-W *H* Test

Although the K-W *H* test is not based on exactly the same principles and computations as the ANOVA test, the underlying logic is similar. In both tests, the null hypothesis is that there is no relationship between x and y, and in both tests, this null hypothesis is translated into the question of whether the aggregate difference among three or more dependent variable sample means is too large to have occurred by chance alone if the samples were drawn from the same population. The research hypothesis is that the aggregate difference is larger than would be expected by chance alone, which is to say the samples were drawn from different populations and there is a relationship between x and y. In both tests, too, the test statistic is compared with its sampling distribution constructed under the assumption that the null hypothesis is true. Finally, in both ANOVA and K-W H, the test of the null hypothesis focuses on the mean of a between (among) group (sample) sum of squares. For both tests, that measure is referred to as a between-group sum of squares, though in the case of the K-W H test, it uses the sums of squares of ranks rather than raw scores to compute the means.

Two important differences between ANOVA and K-W H analyses should be kept in mind. First, as you will recall, in ANOVA, the between-group sum of squares is calculated using the mean of the *raw scores* of each sample and the grand mean (see Formula 10.8a, p. 342). In K-W H, the between-group sum of squares is calculated using the mean *rank* of the raw scores for each sample and the mean rank for the combined samples. Second, whereas the null hypothesis in ANOVA is that the aggregate difference among the sample raw score means is zero, in K-W H, for reasons beyond the scope of this text, the null hypothesis is that the aggregate difference under the null hypothesis is specifiable and at least somewhat larger than zero. We return to this feature of K-W H analysis later.

For purposes of discussing and illustrating the procedures and calculations in K-W H analyses, suppose we have the fictitious data for three independent random samples 1, 2, and 3 in Table 13.7. You can think of these as supervisors' ratings ("grades") for rookies in three different training programs (instead of the two we used in our discussion of M-W U). There are seven rookies in Sample 1, six in Sample 2, and five in Sample 3.

Preparing Data for K-W *H* Analysis

At the beginning stages, K-W H test procedures are like those for the M-W U test, whereas the logic and calculations emulate to some extent those associated with the ANOVA test.

As we did for the M-W U test, the first step in preparing data for K-W H analysis is to combine the raw dependent variable scores (ratings) from each of the three or more samples under investigation into a single set of raw scores arranged in an ordinal array, keeping track of the sample from which each raw score comes. These scores for the combined samples are then assigned ranks from lowest to highest. As we did before, we'll choose to assign a rank of 1 to the lowest score. (You can assign either the highest or lowest score a rank of 1 in this or any of the other nonparametric statistics we discuss here; you just need to remember what your choice was when interpreting your results.) As in M-W U, the total number of ranks assigned is equivalent to the total number of scores that are ranked. In our example, there are a total of 18 scores,

Table 13.7 Supervisors' Ratings for Three Samples of Rookies, the Ratings for Each Sample Arranged in Order From Lowest to Highest

Sample 1	Sample 2	Sample 3
1	2	8
1	5	9
1	7	9
2	8	10
3	9	10
4	10	
6		
$n_1 = 7$	$n_2 = 6$	$n_3 = 5$

Table 13.8 Ratings and Corresponding Ranks for Three Samples of Rookies

Sample 1		Sample 2		Sample 3	
Ratings	Ranks	Ratings	Ranks	Ratings	Ranks
1	2	2	4.5	8	11.5
1	2	5	8	9	14
1	2	7	10	9	14
2	4.5	8	11.5	10	17
3	6	9	14	10	17
4	7	10	17		
6	9				
$n_1 = 7$		$n_2 = 6$		$n_3 = 5$	

so there are 18 possible ranks. We use the same procedure for dealing with tied ratings (and ranks) as we did for preparing data for M-W U. The results are in Table 13.8.

Next, we focus on the ranks that have been assigned in Table 13.8 and add some summary statistics, as indicated in Table 13.9. We round our calculations in this section to the nearest hundredth.

Table 13.9 Ranks and Summary Statistics for Three Samples of Rookies

Sample 1	Sample 2	Sample 3	k = 3
2	4.5	11.5	
2	8	14	
2	10	14	
4.5	11.5	17	
6	14	17	
7	17		
9			
			Totals
$n_1 = 7$	$n_2 = 6$	$n_3 = 5$	$N_T = 18$
$\Sigma R_1 = 32.5$	$\Sigma R_2 = 65$	$\Sigma R_3 = 73.5$	$\Sigma R_T = 171$
$\bar{R}_1 = 4.64$	$\bar{R}_2 = 10.83$	$\bar{R}_3 = 14.7$	$\bar{R}_T = 9.5$

Below is a key to the symbols in Table 13.9, followed in parentheses by their corresponding data-based equivalents for this example.

ΣR_1 = the sum of the n_1 (7) combined ranks in Sample 1 (32.50)

ΣR_2 = the sum of the n_2 (6) combined ranks in Sample 2 (65)

ΣR_3 = the sum of the n_3 (5) combined ranks in Sample 3 (73.50)

ΣR_T = the sum of the N_T (18) ranks in Samples 1, 2, and 3 combined (171)

$\bar{R}_1$ = the mean of the n_1 (7) combined ranks in Sample 1 (4.64)

$\bar{R}_2$ = the mean of the n_2 (6) combined ranks in Sample 2 (10.83)

$\bar{R}_3$ = the mean of the n_3 (5) combined ranks in Sample 3 (14.70)

$\bar{R}_T$ = the mean of the N_T (18) ranks in Samples 1, 2, and 3 combined (9.50)

k = number of samples (3)

As we noted above, K-W *H* analysis uses the means of the sample ranks to test the null hypothesis that there is no difference among the three or more samples. In particular, it uses the **observed between-group (sample) mean rank sum of squares**, which we will abbreviate as K-W BSS$_{obs}$, as the key to assessing the statistical significance of differences among the sample mean ranks. Similar to the calculations for ANOVA, the between-group sum of squares is derived from the squared differences (deviations) between a "grand mean" (in this case, a mean of all ranks, $\bar{R}_T$) and sample means (in this case, the mean ranks for each sample, $\bar{R}_1$, $\bar{R}_2$, and $\bar{R}_3$). Also similar to ANOVA, a K-W total sum of squares can be calculated using the deviations of the individual ranks from the grand mean, $\bar{R}_T$.

As we saw with ANOVA, there are easier-to-understand and easier-to-calculate formulas for K-W BSS_{obs}. For the sake of brevity, we will provide only the easier-to-calculate general formula, Formula 13.8, for calculating K-W BSS_{obs}.

$$\text{K-W BSS}_{obs} = \left[\frac{(\Sigma R_1)^2}{n_1} + \frac{(\Sigma R_2)^2}{n_2} + \cdots + \frac{(\Sigma R_k)^2}{n_k}\right] - \left[\frac{(\Sigma R_T)^2}{N_T}\right] \qquad (13.8)$$

PAUSE, THINK, AND EXPLORE . . .

Compare Formula 13.8 with Formula 10.8a. What similarities and differences do you see?

Applying this formula to our three-sample example, we would have

$$\text{K-W BSS}_{obs} = \left[\frac{(\Sigma R_1)^2}{n_1} + \frac{(\Sigma R_2)^2}{n_2} + \cdots + \frac{(\Sigma R_k)^2}{n_k}\right] - \left[\frac{(\Sigma R_T)^2}{N_T}\right]$$

$$= \left[\frac{(32.5)^2}{7} + \frac{(65)^2}{6} + \frac{(73.5)^2}{5}\right] - \left[\frac{(171)^2}{18}\right]$$

$$= \left[\frac{1{,}056.25}{7} + \frac{4{,}225}{6} + \frac{5{,}402.25}{5}\right] - \left[\frac{29{,}241}{18}\right]$$

$$= [150.89 + 704.17 + 1{,}080.45] - [1{,}624.5]$$

$$= 1{,}935.51 - 1{,}624.5$$

$$\text{K-W BSS}_{obs} = 311.01$$

Calculating K-W H

The K-W H test statistic is a ratio, and we will describe two ways to calculate it. The first better illustrates the logic and mechanics of the test, and it is the easier-to-understand formula. The second, which is the easier-to-calculate formula, is found more often in statistics textbooks.

As we noted in Chapter 10, easier-to-calculate formulas are preferred because they require less rounding and are, therefore, less subject to rounding error distortion of the results. The results for the two formulas should be approximately the same because you will be using similar values in each formula. You may or may not find it any more convenient to use the formula for H that is often provided in statistics texts.

In the easier-to-understand formula for H, the ratio consists of a numerator, which is the observed value of K-W BSS_{obs} (calculated from our sample data applying Formula 13.8), and a denominator equal to $N(N+1)/12$, as indicated in Formulas 13.9a and 13.9b. Formula 13.9b is mathematically equivalent to Formula 13.9a. We have just substituted the formula for K-W BSS_{obs} from Formula 13.8 for the numerator in Formula 13.9a. The easier to understand formula is given by Formula 13.9a.

$$\text{K-W } H = \frac{\text{K-W BSS}_{obs}}{\frac{N_T(N_T+1)}{12}} \tag{13.9a}$$

$$\text{K-W } H = \frac{\left[\frac{(\Sigma R_1)^2}{n_1} + \frac{(\Sigma R_2)^2}{n_2} + \cdots + \frac{(\Sigma R_k)^2}{n_k}\right] - \left[\frac{(\Sigma R_T)^2}{N_T}\right]}{\frac{N_T(N_T+1)}{12}} \tag{13.9b}$$

If there are three samples, as in our example, Formula 13.9b would be written as Formula 13.10.

$$\text{K-W } H = \frac{\left[\frac{(\Sigma R_1)^2}{n_1} + \frac{(\Sigma R_2)^2}{n_2} + \frac{(\Sigma R_3)^2}{n_3}\right] - \left[\frac{(\Sigma R_T)^2}{N_T}\right]}{\frac{N_T(N_T+1)}{12}} \tag{13.10}$$

The easier-to-calculate formula H is given by Formula 13.11.

$$\text{K-W } H = \left[\frac{12}{N_T(N_T+1)}\right]\left[\frac{(\Sigma R_1)^2}{n_1} + \frac{(\Sigma R_2)^2}{n_2} + \cdots + \frac{(\Sigma R_k)^2}{n_k}\right] - k(N_T+1) \tag{13.11}$$

We'll use Formula 13.11 to calculate K-W H for our three-sample example.

$$\text{K-W } H = \left[\frac{12}{N_T(N_T+1)}\right]\left[\frac{(\Sigma R_1)^2}{n_1} + \frac{(\Sigma R_2)^2}{n_2} + \frac{(\Sigma R_3)^2}{n_3}\right] - k(N_T+1)$$

$$= \left[\frac{12}{18(18+1)}\right]\left[\frac{1{,}056.25}{7} + \frac{4{,}225}{6} + \frac{5{,}402.25}{5}\right] - 3(18+1)$$

$$= \left[\frac{12}{342}\right][150.89 + 704.17 + 1{,}080.45] - 3(19)$$

$$= (.0351)(1{,}935.51) - 57$$

$$= 67.94 - 57$$

$$= 10.94$$

For the data from our example, if we apply Formula 13.9a, instead of 13.11: the value of K-W H would be

$$\text{K-W } H = \frac{\text{K-W BSS}_{obs}}{\frac{N_T(N_T+1)}{12}}$$

$$= \frac{311.01}{\frac{18(18+1)}{12}}$$

$$= \frac{311.01}{\frac{(18)(19)}{12}}$$

$$= \frac{311.01}{\frac{342}{12}}$$

$$= \frac{311.01}{28.5}$$

$$= 10.913$$

Allowing for some minor differences due to rounding error, the results for both methods of calculating K-W H should be approximately the same, as they are in our example (10.91 and 10.94).

Testing K-W *H* for Statistical Significance

To test K-W H for statistical significance, we need to know the applicable sampling distributions for three or more between-groups (samples) mean ranks sums of squares. For reasons beyond the scope of this text, the general formula for the mean of an applicable sampling distribution for H, which we will symbolize as $\bar{X}_{\text{K-W BSS}}$, is given by Formula 13.12.

$$\bar{X}_{\text{K-W BSS}} = (k-1)\left[\frac{N_T(N_T+1)}{12}\right] \quad (13.12)$$

In Formula 13.12, $\bar{X}_{\text{K-W BSS}}$ is the mean of the sampling distribution, k is the number of samples, and N_T is the total number of ranks in all three samples. In our example, $k = 3$ and $N_T = 18$.

Applying Formula 13.12 to our three-sample example, we have

$$\bar{X}_{\text{K-W BSS}} = (3-1)\left[\frac{(18)(19)}{12}\right] = 2(28.5) = 57$$

We now know that our K-W BSS_{obs} (311.01) comes from a K-W BSS sampling distribution with a mean of 57, if our null hypothesis is true and there is no difference among the sample mean sums of squares quite a bit different from our observed value of 311.01.

The K-W H test statistic allows us to assess the statistical probability that the difference between our K-W BSS_{obs} and $\bar{X}_{\text{K-W BSS}}$ (the mean of all possible sample rank orders of the sort in our example) occurred by chance alone.

When each of the samples includes at least five ratings, it turns out that, for reasons we won't pursue here, we can test H for statistical significance directly because the

> **PAUSE, THINK, AND EXPLORE...**
>
> Compare Formula 13.9a with the numerator in Formula 10.10. What similarities and differences do you see?

sampling distribution for H is very closely approximated by the chi-square distribution for degrees of freedom $(df = k - 1)$, where k equals the number of sample means being compared.

Treating $H = 10.913$ as a chi-square value with $df = 3 - 1 = 2$ and consulting the chi-square table in Appendix E, we find that our observed K-W BSS would be expected to occur by chance less than one time in a hundred ($p \leq .01$). Hence, we reject the null hypothesis and argue that the evidence supports our research hypothesis that there is a difference among the sample rank order means and the training program is related to rookie ratings.

Reporting the Results of K-W H Analysis

Whether you are presenting your own K-W H test results or you are reading about others' use of this test, you should expect summary statistics like those in Table 13.9 as well as the total and between-group sum of squares to be reported. The calculated value of H; its probability under the null hypothesis; and enough information about the study design, samples, and data to determine whether or not a K-W H test is appropriate should also be reported.

As with ANOVA, the K-W H test does not tell us which of the possible pairs of mean ranks are significantly different, only that at least one almost certainly is. Often, simply eyeballing the sample mean ranks will indicate which pairs are most likely to be significant, especially when the sample sizes are approximately equal. The M-W U test may be used as a follow-up to determine which specific pairs of mean ranks are significantly different. As we have noted, however, you should be aware that the more significance tests you run, the greater the likelihood that you will commit a Type I error. So far as we know, there is no equivalent of Tukey's test for a K-W H test to avoid this risk.

Concluding Remarks About K-W H Analysis

The K-W H test for three or more independent random samples has no alternatives we would recommend (though a Median test is sometimes noted). Other nonparametric tests can be used when samples are not independently drawn, such as the Friedman two-way ANOVA and Kendall coefficient of concordance tests. Each of these tests has its strengths and weaknesses, and statisticians, of course, are also always attempting to come up with better tests.

From the Literature Box 13.2 includes a recent research report that used the Kruskal-Wallis H test as a part of the data analysis.

From the Literature Box 13.2

Nygel Lenz was interested in public support for the funding of various amenities available for prisoner use in correctional facilities. Data came from three different surveys, one of which was sent to three different random samples of a Florida county's citizens. As a part of their data analysis, they used the Kruskal-Wallis H test. The differences among the surveys and some of their analyses are described in the excerpt from their research report below.

Three different questionnaires were constructed for three groups of respondents (200 participants in each group). The surveys varied their description of how the prison amenities were funded. The first survey asked respondents 10 questions regarding their views about 9 separate amenities (the 10th question was about the Inmate Fund itself) that may be found in prisons. This group (hereinafter "FUND") was informed that all privileges are paid for through an Inmate Fund, which was explained to them as money earned by the inmates themselves, not tax dollars. The survey also made clear that the inmates earned the money to pay for the amenities by working and through commissary sales. For instance, the question about television read "Prison inmates should have access to televisions that are paid for through the Inmate Fund."

The second group of participants (hereinafter "TAX"), received the same questions, with the exception of number 10, but with the additional information that in some states, prisoner privileges are paid for with tax dollars. Each of the questions asked about specific amenities and included reference to the fact that the item was paid for with tax dollars. For example, "Prison inmates should have access to televisions that are paid for with tax dollars."

The third group of participants (hereinafter "CONTROL") received a survey with no special instructions. The questions did not indicate how any of the items were purchased (e.g., "Prison inmates should have access to televisions").

The survey participants in all three groups were asked to circle the choice on a Likert-type scale that most closely represented their opinion. The choices were strongly agree, agree, no opinion, disagree, and strongly disagree. However, in light of the objective of this research (the effect of information about funding sources on support for or in opposition to inmate access to amenities), response categories were combined as agree, disagree, or no opinion.

Besides access to television, the survey asked respondents for their opinions about inmate access to periodicals (newspapers, magazines, and journals), books, cable television, weights, musical instruments, special holiday meals, radios, and air-conditioning. The questionnaires also included demographic questions and provided space for respondents to write comments.

(Continued)

Table 2 Percentage of Respondents Who Agree With Inmate Access to Each Amenity by Survey Version

Description	Inmate Fund Agree	Tax Dollars Agree	Control Group Agree	Mean Level of Agreement
Periodicals***	87.8	46.3	83.1	72.4
Books***	88.4	52.7	90.9	77.3
Televisions*	55.3	23.6	43.3	40.7
Cable television***	30.2	5.5	10.3	15.3
Weights*	29.7	22.6	50.8	34.4
Music instruments***	63.9	29.4	58.8	50.7
Special meals	38.5	16.4	26.0	27.0
Radios***	65.8	36.4	67.1	56.4
Air-conditioning	55.0	44.2	53.8	51.0
Mean level of agreement	57.2	30.8	53.8	47.3

*$p < .01$; ***$p < .001$.

Findings

The survey was designed to determine whether information regarding the source of funding for inmate amenities is related to levels of public support for those privileges. Participants responding to the FUND survey were expected to report greater support for all 9 items than were those responding to TAX and CONTROL surveys. It was further

(Continued)

(Continued)

Table 3   Results of Nonparametric Analysis: Kruskal-Wallis Analysis and Tukey Multiple Comparison Test for Each Amenity

Description	Inmate Fund and Tax Dollars	Inmate Fund and Control Group	Tax Dollars and Control Group
Periodicals	**	NSD	**
Books	**	NSD	**
Televisions	**	NSD	NSD
Cable television	**	**	NSD
Weights	NSD	NSD	**
Musical instruments	**	NSD	**
Special meals	**	NSD	NSD
Radios	**	NSD	**
Air-conditioning	NSD	NSD	NSD

Note: NSD = not significantly different.

**Significantly different at < .05 significance level.

expected that control group respondents would answer similarly to tax dollar respondents because it was presumed that participants who received no information regarding cost would assume—if anything about cost—that the items are purchased with tax dollars.

Source: From Lenz, N. (2002). "Luxuries" in prison: The relationship between amenity funding and public support. *Crime and Delinquency, 48,* 499–525. Retrieved May 29, 2012, from http://cad.sagepub.com/content/48/4/499

Spearman's ρ Analysis

When two variables whose possible relationship is being analyzed are measured at the ordinal level (i.e., they consist of ratings or rankings), you will need to find a suitable nonparametric test of association (correlation). The primary application of **Spearman's rho analysis** is in just this kind of research situation, though it can be applied with variables measured at the interval or ratio level as well, if the variable values are converted to ranks. Often symbolized by the Greek letter rho (ρ) or by r_s, this test was developed by the statistician Charles Spearman. We'll use ρ here.

Should you ever find yourself contemplating an assessment of the direction and strength of association between two variables measured at the ordinal level and you are tempted to use the Pearson product moment correlation (r)—oops! As we pointed out in Chapter 12, Pearson's r is applicable only when variables are measured at the interval level or above (and other assumptions about the variables' distributions can be met).

Assumptions of Spearman's ρ Analysis

In general, Spearman's ρ analysis is the best nonparametric alternative to Pearson's r when (a) the raw data for both variables are ordinal-level measures (ratings or rankings); (b) both variables have a relatively broad range of values (ratings)—say, at least five values; and (c) there are few rating (and, therefore, rank) ties.

Note that ρ is different in one important respect from the other two nonparametric statistics we have discussed previously in this chapter. The M-W U and K-W H tests involve statistics from two or more separate independent random samples, whereas ρ assesses the relationship between two variables pertaining to each unit of analysis in one sample. In this sense, ρ is like the chi-square analysis we discussed in Chapter 8.

Spearman's ρ analysis is like the M-W U and K-W H analyses in other respects, however. It is a nonparametric statistic and is based on the same basic assumptions as the M-W U and K-W H tests. Also, to perform all three of these tests, raw ratings must first be arranged in an ordinal array (i.e., they must be listed from lowest to highest) and converted to ranks. Note that when one of the variables is ordinal and the other is interval or ratio, the interval or ratio variable must first be converted to ranks. Calculations for the test statistics in all three analyses are performed on ranks, not on the raw ratings.

The Basic Ideas Underlying Spearman's ρ Analysis

The basic ideas on which Spearman's ρ analyses are based are the same as those underlying Pearson's correlation coefficient r. The null hypothesis is that there is no relationship between the two variables x and y, and the research hypothesis is that there is a relationship between them. A Spearman's ρ analysis measures how closely changes in an independent variable x are accompanied by changes in a dependent variable y (i.e., ρ measures the strength of the relationship between x and y). To put the same general point slightly differently, it assesses how well we can predict the values of y from the values of x. In this sense, it is like regression analysis. Like its parametric counterpart r, ρ varies between −1.00 and +1.00 (the sign indicating the direction of the relationship, negative or positive, respectively) and measures only the direction and degree to which a *linear* relationship exists between the two ranks. If knowing the value of one variable does not help at all in predicting the other variable's value, ρ will equal 0.00. If our predictions are perfect, ρ will equal −1.00 or +1.00. The better our predictions, the closer ρ will be to −1.00 or +1.00 and the stronger the relationship between x and y. In fact, when there are no tied ranks, Spearman's ρ is equivalent to a Pearson's r calculated using the ranks.

Remember that, just as with Pearson's r, even if ρ is near zero, other important nonlinear relationships may exist between the two variables. Remember, too, that just as with Pearson's r, any relationship indicated by ρ, no matter how strong, may be spurious.

Preparing Data for Spearman's ρ Analysis

It will help if we have some data with which to illustrate the procedures and calculations involved in a Spearman's ρ analysis. Suppose we have data from a survey of criminal court judges. The judges were asked to rate their job satisfaction on an ordinal scale of 1 (very low satisfaction) to 6 (very high satisfaction). They were also asked to rate their political philosophy from 1 (very liberal) to 6 (very conservative). Now suppose we are interested in whether there is a relationship between political philosophy (x) and job satisfaction (y). Our null hypothesis is that there is no relationship between the variables, and our research hypothesis is that there is a relationship between the two variables.

Suppose that each of the judge's ratings on these two variables is as indicated in Table 13.10. For purposes of illustration, in this fictitious data set we have listed the five judges in column 1, their political philosophy ratings (which we are designating variable x) in column 2, and their job satisfaction ratings (variable y) in column 3.

As we have already learned, we don't perform the calculations for ρ on these raw ratings. They must first be converted to ranks from lowest to highest or highest to lowest. It doesn't make any difference which of these two ranking procedures you use as long as you remember which one you used when interpreting your results. Tied ranks are dealt with in exactly the same way as we have described when discussing the M-W U test and the K-W H test.

Table 13.10 Political Philosophy and Job Satisfaction Among Five Circuit Court Judges

Judge	Political Philosophy	Job Satisfaction
A	6	5
B	2	2
C	3	3
D	4	4
E	5	6

For ρ analysis, however, we have only one sample and we convert the raw score ratings for each variable (x and y) *separately* into ranks. In our example, there are five judges. We would assign ranks 1 to 5 to the ratings on variable x, according to the ordinal order of the raw ratings. The number of ranks would be equal to the number of units of analysis (in our example, the number of judges). We have five judges, so we would assign five ranks (1 through 5) for the values of each variable. To assign ranks to the ratings on variable y, we have to eyeball the list of ratings, identifying which is the highest, which the next highest, which the next highest, and so on for all five ratings. If 6 is the highest rating on a variable, we would assign it a rank of 5, and if 5 were the next highest rating, we would assign it a rank of 4 and so on. Table 13.11 shows the raw score ratings and the corresponding ranks we have assigned for the two variables x and y. (Note that the job satisfaction ratings and ranks can easily be seen as ranging from low to high. The political philosophy ratings and ranks, on the other hand, are perhaps best viewed as ranging from less to more, as in less conservative to more conservative.) Ignore the columns on the right side of Table 13.11 headed D_ρ for now.

Just as with Pearson's r, we recommend that before calculating ρ, you draw a scattergram of the paired x and y ranks to get some idea of what kind of relationship, if any, exists between the two variables. We follow the same procedure we discussed in Chapter 11 for constructing a scattergram for two interval- or ratio-level variables. The possible rank values of variable x (political philosophy) are arrayed from more conservative to less conservative along the horizontal axis and the possible rank values of variable y (job satisfaction) from lowest to highest along the vertical axis. The scattergram for our judges' data would look like Figure 13.1.

The scattergram for these fictitious data indicates that judges who rate themselves less conservative rate their job satisfaction higher, that the relationship between the variables is roughly linear, and that it is a fairly strong relationship.

Table 13.11 Political Philosophy and Job Satisfaction Self-Ratings of Five Circuit Judges, With Corresponding Ranks and D Statistics

Judge	Political Philosophy (x)		Job Satisfaction (y)		D_ρ	
	Rating	Rank	Rating	Rank	Rank x – Rank y	D_ρ^2
B	2	1	2	1	1 – 1 = 0	0
C	3	2	3	2	2 – 2 = 0	0
D	4	3	4	3	3 – 3 = 0	0
E	5	4	6	5	4 – 5 = –1	1
A	6	5	5	4	5 – 4 = 1	1
					$\Sigma D_\rho^2 = 2$	

Figure 13.1 Scattergram of Ranks on Political Philosophy and Job Satisfaction for Five Circuit Judges

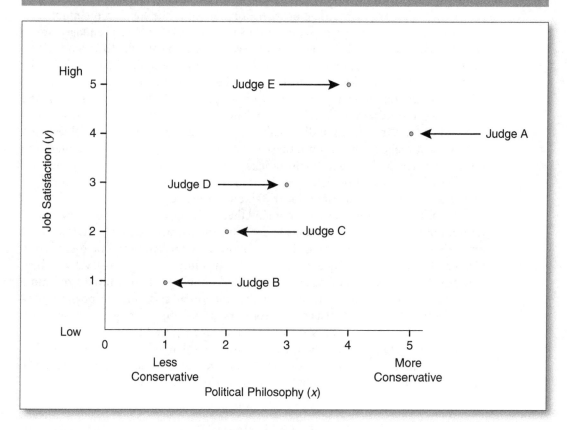

Calculating Spearman's ρ

The first step in calculating ρ is to calculate a difference score, which we will symbolize as D_ρ, and then find the square of D_ρ (i.e., D_ρ^2). The calculations are straightforward. For our example, we simply subtract each judge's rank on variable x from that judge's rank on variable y. This gives us a D_ρ score for each of the five judges. Then, we square each of these scores, yielding a D_ρ^2 score for each of the five judges. Note that squaring the D_ρs gives all the D_ρ^2s a positive sign. Finally, we sum the D_ρ^2 scores for all five judges. The calculations and corresponding results are shown in the columns on the far right side of Table 13.11.

The formula for Spearman's ρ, which is given by Formula 13.13, is pretty straightforward.

$$\rho = 1 - \frac{6 \sum D_\rho^2}{N_T(N_T^2 - 1)} \qquad (13.13)$$

To calculate ρ, we need only know the number of elements in our sample (five judges) and the sum of the D_ρ^2 column for our sample $(0 + 0 + 0 + 1 + 1 = 2)$. For our judges' data, we would have

$$\rho = 1 - \frac{6\sum D_\rho^2}{N_T(N_T^2 - 1)}$$

$$= 1 - \frac{6(2)}{5(25-1)}$$

$$= 1 - \frac{12}{5(24)}$$

$$= 1 - \frac{12}{120}$$

$$= 1 - .10$$

$$\rho = .90$$

Hence, as our scattergram suggested, our calculated ρ = .90 indicates a very strong linear relationship between these two variables; the more conservative in political philosophy, the higher the job satisfaction.

We can also compute a coefficient of determination for Spearman's ρ, which we will symbolize as ρ^2. It is similar to the coefficient of determination for Pearson's r, which is r^2. For our judges' data, the coefficient of determination for ρ would be $(.90)(.90) = .81$. This statistic has an interpretation very similar to that of Pearson's coefficient of determination, r^2. That is, 81% of the variation in the ranks of y is accounted for by the variation in the ranks of x.

In fact, as we noted earlier, if there are no tied ranks and we calculate a Pearson's r using the ranks rather than the raw ratings, the result will be the same as Spearman's ρ. However, in those instances where there are tied ranks in one or both variables, there will be some small differences between r and ρ.

Testing ρ for Statistical Significance

If our data are from a random sample and we want to generalize the results of our Spearman's ρ analysis from our sample to the population sampled, we need to apply an appropriate test of statistical significance. In short, we ask how likely it is that we would find a Spearman's ρ as high as the one we calculated purely by chance.

Given all the other similarities between r and ρ, it probably will not surprise you that the appropriate sampling distribution for ρ is similar to that of r, at least when the sample size is greater than 10. Again, proof is beyond the scope of this text, but it can be shown that the sampling distributions for ρ have a mean equal to 0 and a distribution similar to the t distribution. The general formula for calculating t in order to test ρ for statistical significance is given by Formula 13.14.

$$t = \sqrt{\left(\frac{\rho^2}{1-\rho^2}\right)(n-2)} \tag{13.14}$$

Applying Formula 13.14 to our judges' data, we would have

$$t = \sqrt{\left(\frac{\rho^2}{1-\rho^2}\right)(n-2)}$$

$$= \sqrt{\left(\frac{.90^2}{1-.90^2}\right)(5-2)}$$

$$= \sqrt{\left(\frac{.81}{1-.81}\right)(5-2)}$$

$$= \sqrt{\left(\frac{.81}{.19}\right)(3)}$$

$$= \sqrt{(4.26)(3)}$$

$$= \sqrt{12.78}$$

$$t = 3.57$$

When n is 10 or less (as in our example), we compare the observed value of ρ to a table of ρ critical values that statisticians have developed and we have included in Appendix I on the study site (**www.sagepub.com/fitzgerald**). Consulting that table for a two-tailed test and $n = 5$, we find that the observed ρ of .90 in our example would not be significant at $p < .05$. In short, there is a greater than 5 chances in 100 that a Spearman's ρ of .90 for our sample would occur by sampling error alone if the null hypothesis is true in the population. So, we can't reject the null hypothesis. Note that if we had hypothesized a positive (or negative) relationship between judges' self-ratings of degree of conservatism and job satisfaction our rho of .90 would be significant at the .05 level.

For large samples, the t table in Appendix F identifies the critical values for t for specific degrees of freedom. The degrees of freedom are $n - 2$.

Reporting the Results of ρ Analysis

When reporting the results of a ρ analysis, the calculated ρ, as well as its probability under the null hypothesis, should be included. Enough information about the study design, samples, and data to determine whether or not a Spearman's ρ analysis is the most appropriate test to use should also be reported.

Concluding Remarks Regarding Spearman's ρ Analysis

Several other nonparametric statistical tools are available for assessing the relationship between two variables. They can be divided into two broad categories: (a) those that best fit data that are at least theoretically continuous in nature (i.e., at least theoretically a very large number of ranks could be assigned) and (b) those that best fit data that are restricted to, or can be collapsed into, a small number of rank order categories, say, fewer than five. Examples of the former include gamma, and examples of the latter include Somer's *d* and Kendall's Tau-*b*.

The From the Literature Box 13.3 discusses a recent research report that includes Spearman's ρ as a part of the data analysis.

From the Literature Box 13.3

Mitchell and Mackenzie were interested in testing some hypotheses derived from Gottfredson and Hirschi's general theory of crime. In particular, they studied two aspects of self-control: stability in the amount of self-control over time, and, once an individual's level of self-control has been established, the resilience to change in the amount of self-control over time. Their data came from self-report surveys administered during a randomized experimental evaluation of a Maryland boot camp for adults. The surveys, which contained among other things a scale measuring self-control, were administered monthly to platoons of inmates who were then randomly assigned either to the boot camp or to a regular prison facility. The surveys were administered to the same two groups (experimental and control groups) of convicts in about 6 months. Among the data analyses they performed was Spearman's ρ (which they refer to as Spearman's *r*). The following is an excerpt from their research report.

Many aspects of Gottfredson and Hirschi's theory are controversial; however, two of the theory's propositions appear to be particularly contentious. First, Gottfredson and Hirschi contend that after the age of 8 to 10, one's level of self-control becomes a stable trait in the relative sense. That is, Gottfredson and Hirschi argue that the absolute level of self-control within individuals increases with age, and therefore, the likelihood of involvement in criminal acts declines with age: "Crime declines with age among all groups of offenders and in almost all types of offending" (Hirschi & Gottfredson, 2001, p. 92). However, relative differences between individuals of the same age will endure over time: "Differences between high- and low-rate offenders persist during the life course. Children ranked on the frequency of their delinquent acts will be ranked similarly later in life" (Hirschi & Gottfredson, 2001, p. 91). Thus, Gottfredson and Hirschi propose that within-individuals' self-control increases monotonically with age, but the relative rankings of self-control between individuals remains stable over time.

(Continued)

(Continued)

Second, and perhaps more controversially, Gottfredson and Hirschi follow the stability proposition by predicting that once formed, an individual's level of self-control is resilient to change: "Once tendencies to engage in crime and delinquency have been established, successful treatment is, at a minimum, extraordinarily difficult" (Hirschi & Gottfredson, 2001, pp. 91–92). Continuing in this vein, Gottfredson and Hirschi are unusually bleak in their outlook on the effectiveness of criminal justice interventions in reducing recidivism. In their words, "because low self-control arises in the absence of the powerful inhibiting forces of early childhood, it is highly resistant to the less powerful inhibiting forces of later life, *especially the relatively weak forces of the criminal justice system*" (Gottfredson & Hirschi, 1990, p. 255, italics added). Yet in contrast to their negative predictions regarding the effects of criminal justice intervention, Gottfredson and Hirschi are more positive in regards to the possible effects of early intervention: "Intervention efforts in childhood offer the greatest promise of success in crime reduction"

. . .

In concordance with Gottfredson and Hirschi's (1990) theory, we hypothesize that self-control is stable over time within and between individuals. That is, we expected that an individual's *absolute* level of self-control does not vary during a short period of time, and individuals' *relative* rankings on a measure of self-control do not vary over time. We also hypothesize that self-control is resilient to the specific criminal justice intervention considered in this research. In particular, this research directly assesses the resiliency of self-control to participation in a boot-camp program for adults by taking preintervention and postintervention measurements of self-control using an attitudinal measure that assesses each of the six dimensions of self-control suggested by Gottfredson and Hirschi. Given the findings of prior research indicating boot camps are generally ineffective in reducing recidivism (MacKenzie, Wilson, & Kider, 2001), we expect participation in the boot-camp program of interest to have no influence on self-control.

METHOD

The data used in this study derive from a randomized experimental evaluation of Maryland's only correctional boot camp for adult offenders, the Herman L. Toulson Correctional Boot Camp (TBC). To the authors' knowledge, this research is the only randomized experimental evaluation of an adult boot-camp program. The evaluation was designed to determine whether a correctional boot camp for adults with a treatment orientation (i.e., includes addictions treatment, a life skills component, and intensive adult

(Continued)

basic education classes) reduced recidivism in comparison to a traditional correctional facility that also emphasized treatment but does not have a military component (for a full discussion of this evaluation, see Mitchell, MacKenzie, & Perez, 2005).

. . .

DATA COLLECTION

At the beginning of each month, a new platoon of 8 to 20 inmates was drawn into the research sample. Eligible inmates were contacted by trained survey facilitators, who solicited participation in a 45-min voluntary self-report survey. The self-report survey was administered to each incoming platoon as a group. The first self-report survey (baseline survey) was typically administered 3 to 4 days before each platoon was scheduled to start the boot-camp program. After the research team surveyed consenting inmates, those inmates randomly assigned to the control facility were diverted from the boot camp and transferred to the alternative facility. Inmates were not informed of random assignment decisions until after the administration of the baseline survey. The survey was read aloud to aid inmates with reading deficiencies.

Approximately 6 months later, the same group of trained survey facilitators administered a second voluntary, self-report survey (the exit survey). Typically, 1 week before inmates were released to the community, the survey facilitators traveled to both facilities. The survey facilitators gathered the outgoing group of inmates and asked each inmate to participate in the exit survey, which also took approximately 45 min to complete. Once again, the survey was read aloud as an aid to inmates with reading deficiencies.

Both surveys contained Grasmick et al.'s (1993) self-control scale. Response options were coded on a 5-point Likert-type scale, 0 = *strongly agree* to 4 = *strongly disagree*, with 2 = *neither agree nor disagree*. Thus, higher scores indicate greater levels of self-control. Principal components analysis and examination of scree plots suggested that one dimension underlies the 24-item self-control scale at baseline and exit. Furthermore, this scale was found to be highly reliable (Cronbach's alpha at both time periods = .89).

RESULTS

A correlation matrix of the bivariate Spearman correlations between baseline and exit self-control measures is displayed in Table 3. The correlations on the diagonal of the correlation

(Continued)

(Continued)

matrix indicate the strength and direction of the relationship between the same dimension of self-control at baseline and exit, whereas the off-diagonal values indicate the strength and direction of the relationship between different dimensions at different times. Table 3 also displays the mean scores for each dimension at baseline and exit; the last column of Table 3 presents baseline mean scores, and the last row displays the same information at exit. Comparing the baseline and exit means reveals that in absolute terms, self-control decreases between the two time periods. Specifically, the total score at baseline was 56.21, whereas the total score at exit dropped to 51.65. In fact, the exit scores are lower on each dimension of self-control with the exception of preference for physical tasks. Thus, self-control is not stable in absolute terms, but this finding does not contradict Gottfredson and Hirschi's assertion of the rank-ordered stability of self-control.

Generally, the correlations on the diagonal in Table 3 indicated moderate positive relationships between baseline and exit scores (all diagonal correlations are statistically significant at the .05 level). The strongest correlation was between baseline and exit total self-control score (0.48), whereas the smallest correlation was between baseline and exit scores on the preference for physical activities dimension (0.27). The magnitudes of these correlations, although not trivial, were not nearly as strong as we expected based on Gottfredson and Hirschi's strong assertions about the rank-order stability of self-control. Furthermore, these correlations were substantially smaller than similar correlations reported in Arneklev et al.'s (1998) study of university students. For example, Arneklev and colleagues found that the correlation between Time 1 and Time 2 total self-control scores was 0.82, which is an order of magnitude higher than the correlations revealed in this research. Moreover, these correlations are somewhat smaller than the longitudinal correlations between measures of self-control reported by Turner and Piquero (2002).

To further examine the rank-order stability of self-control over time, offenders in the lowest quartile on self-control (total score) at baseline and exit were distinguished. Of the 55 offenders in lowest quartile (actually 26%) at baseline, 28 (51%) of these offenders were also in lowest quartile at exit. Although such a finding is consistent with the notion of regression to the mean, the stability hypothesis implies that regression to the mean will not occur as self-control is a fixed characteristic after age 10 or so. Thus, both the correlation and quartile analyses indicate that measures of self-control are modestly positively related, but the rank-ordered stability of self-control does not appear to be as robust as Gottfredson and Hirschi suggest.

...

(Continued)

Table 3 Spearman Correlations Between Self-Control Subscales at Baseline and Exit ($n = 209$)[a]

Baseline Measures	Exit Measures							Baseline [Means]
	1	2	3	4	5	6	7	
1. Impulsive	**0.38**	0.17	0.23	0.17	0.12*	0.19	0.29	8.85
2. Simple tasks	0.35	**0.47**	0.21	0.14	0.18	0.20	0.36	10.62
3. Risk taking	0.23	0.11*	**0.45**	0.26	0.17	0.21	0.32	9.23
4. Physical activities	0.30	0.17	0.21	**0.27**	0.10*	0.22	0.29	7.25
5. Self-centered	0.25	0.21	0.26	0.18	**0.41**	0.33	0.38	10.60
6. Temper	0.26	0.14*	0.32	0.23	0.25	**0.44**	0.38	9.66
7. Total Self-control	0.41	0.30	0.40	0.30	0.29	0.38	**0.48**	56.21
Exit means	8.38	9.54	8.89	7.37	8.78	8.70	51.65	

Note: Unless otherwise noted, all correlations are statistically significant at the .05 level (one-tailed). The bolded correlations on the diagonal of the correlation matrix indicate the strength and direction of the relationship between the same dimension of self-control at baseline and exit.

a. Higher scores on all measures of self-control indicate greater levels of self-control

*$p > .05$, one-tailed (not statistically significant).

ANALYSES

To assess the stability of self-control over time, three types of analyses were performed. First, because Gottfredson and Hirschi hypothesize stability in the rank-ordered distribution of self-control between individuals, Spearman's correlation coefficient was computed to examine the relationship between the rank-ordered distribution of scores at baseline and exit. Given Gottfredson and Hirschi's assertions, we expected the correlation between baseline and exit scores for the whole scale and each dimension of the scale to be large

(Continued)

> **(Continued)**
>
> and statistically significant. Second, as an alternative method of examining the between-individual relative stability of self-control, offenders in the lowest quartile on the measure of self-control were distinguished. If self-control was stable, in the relative sense, between baseline and exit, we expected to find that individuals with the lowest levels of self-control at baseline also have the lowest levels of self-control at program exit.
>
> *Source:* From Mitchell, O., & Mackenzie, D. L. (2006). The stability and resiliency of self-control in a sample of incarcerated offenders. *Crime and Delinquency, 52,* 432–449. Retrieved May 23, 2012, from http://cad.sagepub.com/content/52/3/432

Some Final Cautions About Nonparametric Statistics

Perhaps the most important thing to remember, whether you are choosing a test for your own data or reading about the results of other analyses, is to ask whether the data fit the assumptions of the test. Along with your results, you should report how your test fits the data you are analyzing, and you should expect others to report how their data fits the test they are using. If the data do not fit the assumptions of the test or you are not provided with enough information to know, you should be very cautious about accepting the results no matter how they turn out.

Statisticians vary to some extent in terms of how much a data set may violate the assumptions of a particular parametric statistic before it should be analyzed using a nonparametric alternative. We end up having to come to grips with language such as "approximately normally distributed," "variances nearly equal," and so on. As either users or appraisers of others' use of nonparametric statistics, about the best we can expect of ourselves and others is that we devote as much attention to a description of our data and assumptions as to the specific results of our statistical test. We should report, and we should expect others to supply, enough information to specifically identify the nature of our samples, relevant variable distributions, and the populations they represent (when we can) so that others can make their own judgments.

It is also worth noting that because data for the statistics we have discussed are converted to consecutive ranks, the problem of outliers is greatly reduced when applying the statistics we have discussed in this chapter. On the other hand, converting interval or ratio to ordinal data often results in a significant loss of information. That is, any quantitative differences between or among raw scores are collapsed into the usually much smaller differences between ranks.

Finally, many of today's computer-derived statistical procedures will automatically produce the results for several of the available parametric and nonparametric tests simultaneously. Especially when research is aimed at exploring relationships among variables in a preliminary way, it is not a bad idea to examine and report the results of more than one test that fits the nature of the data in question. If similar results in terms of statistical significance or strength of relationships are achieved when different tests are applied to the same data, confidence in the validity of those results is increased. Disparate exploratory research results should also be noted and an explanation for the differences sought. A careful review of the assumptions and calculations inherent in each test might reveal why differences in results occurred. In the later stages of examining hypotheses, however, statisticians recommend you should decide on an appropriate test and level of significance before you gather any data. In doing so, you'll be less tempted to choose only those analyses that produce statistically significant results. Remember, too, that the more significance tests you run, the greater the likelihood that you will commit a Type I error.

Summary

In this chapter, we have described and discussed three nonparametric statistics, the Mann-Whitney U test, the Kruskal-Wallis H test, and Spearman's ρ analysis. Nonparametric statistics such as these are used when the data being analyzed do not meet the assumptions on which parametric statistics are based, such as normal population distributions and homoscedasticity. They do, however, share the assumption of random sampling when tests of statistical significance are to be performed. The nonparametric statistics we have described are typically applied when variables are measured at the ordinal level. They may also be applied when interval or ratio variables are not normally distributed in the population and/or when population variances are not homoscedastic.

To perform each of the three analyses, raw ordinal ratings (or the interval- or ratio-level data to be analyzed) must first be converted to ranks, applying special procedures for dealing with tied ratings. Calculations for the tests are performed on these ranks, rather than on the original raw ordinal ratings.

The Mann-Whitney U and Kruskal-Wallis H tests are used to compare the mean or sum of ranks for independent random samples. The former assesses differences between two samples and the latter assesses aggregate differences among three or more mean ranks (or, in practice, sums of ranks).

Spearman's ρ analysis measures the direction and strength of association (correlation) between two variables, both of which are attributes of units of analysis (e.g., persons, institutions, arrests). When there are no tied ranks and Pearson's correlation coefficient r is performed on the ranks rather than their corresponding raw scores, it produces the same quantitative result as Spearman's ρ analysis.

Concepts to Master

Conversion of the raw data to ranks

D_ρ

H

K-W BSS$_{obs}$

Kruskal-Wallis H test (K-W H)

Mann-Whitney U test (M-W U)

Nonparametric statistics

Number of ranks

Observed between-group (sample) mean rank sum of squares (K-W BSS$_{obs}$)

Parametric statistics

ρ

ρ^2

Spearman's rho analysis

Sum of ranks

U

$\bar{X}_{\text{K-W BSS}}$

Review Questions

1. How are parametric and nonparametric inferential statistics similar, and how are they different?
2. In what research situations might it be appropriate to use both parametric and nonparametric statistics to analyze data?
3. What is the purpose of the Mann-Whitney U test?
4. What are the assumptions of the Mann-Whitney U test?
5. What are the basic ideas underlying the Mann-Whitney U test?
6. How are the raw scores converted to ranks for the Mann-Whitney U test?
7. How is Mann-Whitney U calculated?
8. How is Mann-Whitney U tested for statistical significance?
9. How are Mann-Whitney U results reported?
10. What is the purpose of the Kruskal-Wallis H test?
11. What are the assumptions of the Kruskal-Wallis H test?
12. What are the basic ideas underlying the Kruskal-Wallis H test?
13. How are the raw scores converted to ranks for the Kruskal-Wallis H test?
14. How is Kruskal-Wallis H calculated?

15. How is Kruskal-Wallis H tested for statistical significance?
16. How are Kruskal-Wallis H results reported?
17. What is the purpose of Spearman's ρ analysis?
18. What are the assumptions of Spearman's ρ analysis?
19. What are the basic ideas underlying Spearman's ρ analysis?
20. How are the raw scores converted to ranks for Spearman's ρ analysis?
21. How is Spearman's ρ calculated?
22. How is Spearman's ρ tested for statistical significance?
23. How are Spearman's ρ results reported?
24. Define all the terms in the Concepts to Master list, and use each in three sentences.

Exercises and Discussion Questions

1. Name a nonparametric alternative for the t test, ANOVA, and Pearson's r, and discuss why they are alternatives.
2. State two research hypotheses, corresponding null hypotheses, and appropriate research designs (including data collection methods) for which M-W U would be most appropriate. Do the same for both the K-W H test and Spearman's ρ.
3. Can you use M-W U, K-W H, or Spearman's ρ to analyze nominal-level data? Why or why not?
4. Can you use M-W U, K-W H, or Spearman's ρ to analyze interval- or ratio-level data? Why or why not?
5. Discuss the appropriate circumstances for, as well as the advantages and disadvantages of, using more than one statistical analysis when analyzing the same data.
6. Both the M-W U and K-W H tests use combined samples ranks. How do you create combined samples rank orders? Use the fictitious ordinal rating data below and compute a combined samples rank order and then separate them into their original samples. Then calculate the sum of ranks and mean ranks for the two samples. Discuss whether or not it appears the two samples come from the same population.

Raw Ordinal Score, Sample A	Raw Ordinal Score, Sample B
1	4
5	4
3	5
5	1
2	3
4	2
5	2

7. Compute a M-W U test for the data in Question 6 above.

8. Use the fictitious data for three independent random samples below to compute a K-W H and present your results.

Raw Ordinal Score, Sample A	Raw Ordinal Score, Sample B	Raw Ordinal Score, Sample C
1	7	8
6	1	2
2	5	9
9	10	1
14	3	15
9	14	
3		

9. Consider the raw score data in Table 10.3 to be ordinal ratings of performance. Use the data to compute a K-W H test. Compare and contrast your results with the ANOVA result. Discuss the similarities and differences. Test the K-W H you calculated for statistical significance and discuss your results.

10. Compare and contrast Pearson's r and Spearman's ρ.

11. Suppose we have data from a random sample of 10 criminal justice students on degree of support for the death penalty ranging from 1 (strongly approve) to 6 (strongly disapprove). Suppose we also have data on their grades in the introduction to criminal justice course. The fictitious data are displayed in the following table.

Student	Support for Death Penalty	Grade in Intro Course
1	5	B
2	4	A
3	1	C
4	4	B
5	6	A
6	3	C
7	2	B
8	4	A
9	2	D
10	1	B

Use these data to draw a scattergram, calculate Spearman's ρ, and discuss your results. Test the ρ you calculated for statistical significance and discuss your results.

12. Calculate Pearson's r using the *ranks* for the judges' data in Table 13.11. Compare your results with our calculations of ρ in the text.

13. In the From the Literature Box 13.1, what can you tell, if anything, about the shapes of the variable distributions given the means, medians, modes, and standard deviations reported in their Table 3? Discuss and interpret the results of the chi-square tests referenced in the section headed "Facility Counts with Buffer Distances" and in the section headed "Proximity and Recidivism." What data were included in these chi-square analyses? Discuss and interpret the cumulative distributions in their Figures 3 and 4. How were they constructed? What do they show? Discuss and interpret the results of the Mann-Whitney U test referenced in the paragraph after their Table 7. Why was this test used for this analysis? Was this an appropriate use of this test? Why or why not? How was it calculated? Discuss and interpret the results of the Pearson's r correlation coefficients referenced in the second full paragraph after their Figure 4. Were these appropriate tests? Why or why not? Discuss and interpret the results of the t tests displayed in Table 6. What is a two-tailed test, and why was a two-tailed t test used? Discuss and interpret the results of the logistic regression analysis referenced at the end of the excerpt. What data were included in the analysis? Why was logistic regression used for this analysis? Is it an appropriate test for these data?

14. In the From the Literature Box 13.2, discuss and interpret the results of the data analyses displayed in Table 2. Are means appropriate for these data? Why or why not? Discuss and interpret the results of the Kruskal-Wallis analyses reports in Table 3. What data were included in the analyses? What does the note at the bottom of the table referring to results that are "significantly different at the .05 level (one tailed)" mean?

15. In the From the Literature Box 13.3, discuss and interpret the results of the data analyses in Table 3. What data were included in these analyses? What do the Spearman's ρ (r) correlations in the diagonal (in bold type) represent and indicate? Is Spearman's correlation coefficient an appropriate statistic for these data? Why or why not? Why were one-tailed tests used to test the significance of Spearman's ρ (r) in this case? Compare the baseline (first survey as premeasurement of the dependent variables of self-control) and exit (second survey as postmeasurement of the dependent variables) means. What, if anything, do they tell us about stability and resilience of self-control?

16. If you haven't already done so, answer all the questions in the "Pause, Think, and Explore" boxes.

Student Study Site

Visit the open-access student study site at **www.sagepub.com/fitzgerald** for access to several study tools including eFlashcards, web quizzes, and additional appendices as well as links to SAGE journal articles and audio, video and web resources.

Real-Life Adventures of Statistics Users

Statistics: A Practitioner's View

by John H. Schlaf

Director of Campus Safety, Knox College, and former Chief of Police, Galesburg, Illinois. Used with permission.

Background. I grew up in northwestern Illinois in a town of approximately 35,000 persons. As many young people do, I had vowed to leave the area to seek my fame and fortune in larger and more exciting places, and I was able to talk my parents into giving me permission to join the Air Force at 17. I was fortunate enough to be trained as an intelligence analyst, which consisted of recognizing and gathering data from various sources (I feel I need to remain somewhat vague on this), analyzing the data, and then writing timely reports for "consumption" by other military and governmental "users." It was a great experience for a young person and provided a strong foundation on which to build a law enforcement career.

Upon my return from the Air Force (after traveling around the world during those 4 years) I learned that my hometown was really a pretty nice place to live after all. I worked briefly on the railroad (as my father, grandfather, and great-grandfather had) and then a steel building manufacturing company before I tested for the police department and subsequently was appointed as a police officer. As it turned out, I was able to seek my fame (guess it really wasn't fame) and fortune (wasn't really fortune either) in my hometown as a police officer and became one of those very fortunate persons who then (and now) went to work every day and enjoyed it; not that every day was a joy, but it was a career that could be loved and for that I will remain forever grateful.

I was able to work each patrol shift as an officer and supervisor and then as an investigator. I served in the other divisions (operations and administrative) as well, moving through ranks as a sergeant, lieutenant, and captain before becoming and then retiring as chief of police. After retirement, I was appointed as director of campus safety at a small (approximately 1,400 students) private college in our community. Some of my day-to-day experiences as a municipal police officer and my activities as director of campus safety, as well as the influences "statistics" had on these experiences and activities, are described below.

I'm not sure if this is a good thing or a bad thing, but I should probably report that my "official" exposure to statistics has been primarily as a consumer versus one who has had specific training or education as a statistician. Initially, when first asked to consider writing about my interaction over the years with statistics, I was concerned that the authors had, basically, asked the wrong guy. I noticed, however, while attempting to recall some real-life stories from nearly 45 years as a police officer and law enforcement executive, that statistics, in some form, had been a greater influence on my career than I originally suspected.

Over the years, various persons, generally young persons, tend to ask two questions about law enforcement as they consider a position in the criminal justice system. The first is generally, "What's it like to be a police officer?" As the years go by, the questions seem to change to correlate with the current assignment within the department, so from "What is it like to be a police officer?" the question becomes, "What's it like to be a detective?" and then "What's it like to be a chief of police?" To be honest, I'm not sure I can recall my answers to the first two questions, but in response to "What's it like to be a chief of police" I had to respond, "Being a chief of police is a little like being the guy who mows the grass in the cemetery. You've got a lot of people under you, but nobody listens." I'm not sure that response has anything specifically to do with statistics, but I wanted to share it with the readers in the event that they may have occasion to use it in the future. It can be used for any career field, so maybe someday, with a little tweaking, when someone asks you the question "What is it like to be a senior criminologist (or statistician)?" you can answer in the same way.

The other frequently asked question, though, has a stronger link to the topic of statistics: "What classes should I take if I want to become a police officer?" My response was always a recommendation to follow the course of study suggested by the school the student was considering, with an added personal suggestion of pursuing a philosophy course. That suggestion tended to result in a look from students indicating that they wished they had not asked the question or maybe that it should not have been asked of me.

In response to that look, I tried to explain that, although most books written on law enforcement as a career may not mention philosophy, it was my belief that that course of study tended to broaden a person's ability to consider life's circumstances differently and to think independently. I tried to explain that it was my belief—and still is—that the best police officers, on the street or in the office, are the ones who are not afraid to ask questions and who do not automatically accept the conventional or "approved" answers; they are free thinkers and they see and consider possibilities that others have overlooked or rejected. Those philosophy classes generally aren't easy, and, no doubt, some of those who asked the question quietly elected to ignore my advice.

Making the decision to take a difficult class to become a police officer or to make a better police officer is tough but will not, in any fashion, compare with the difficult decisions that a police officer will make in the future. As a good friend, former partner on the street, and lieutenant in my command staff commented when he had apparently noted that my mood was down a bit, "You know, Chief, if this was easy, anyone could do it." It's the same way with being the best police officer that you can be—it might be tough, but if it was easy, anyone could do it.

As I noted earlier, during the recollection of the real-life stories for this chapter, I recognized that statistics, in some form, had played a significant and positive role in my law enforcement career. It was also interesting to note that, much in the same way that those asking about a recommendation for the best classes to take and in much the same way that philosophy may have been avoided because of the perceived degree of difficulty, statistics may have been considered a tough course by those considering a career in the criminal justice system.

I have not personally experienced the courses, so I can't confirm that suspicion, but I do believe that the same reasons I gave for taking a philosophy course would also apply to a statistics course. It would seem that taking a statistics course should also create a person willing to think openly and not accept a statement or concept "just because" someone else believes it to be so. In the case of statistics, however, I believe that the product of that expanded manner of thinking has been, or should have been, the result of some scientific fact rather than philosophical thought. These comments have reminded me of a lesson learned as a very young patrol officer as it relates to accepting information without sufficient study.

After responding to a report of a traffic crash at a local restaurant (I had been very close to the restaurant when the report came in), a man ran into the parking lot and called out to me that his vehicle had just been struck by a woman in another vehicle who was leaving the scene. He then pointed to a vehicle turning southbound onto a nearby street. He was clearly agitated that pursuit of the female was not immediately initiated, saying, "You're letting her get away!" It was tempting, but something just didn't seem quite right, and my hesitation gave enough time for a female to walk from the restaurant to say, "This guy just hit my car and tried to leave." I'm not sure about the philosophic lesson to be drawn from this incident, but there is clearly a statistical one, which is the very critical need to remain cautious and skeptical about accepting information without adequate analysis and seeking the details required for an accurate resolution. Those memories have caused me regret as it relates to those questions from young persons asking, "What classes should I take?" I realize now I should have said, "Philosophy and statistics—they're both tough, but if they were easy, anyone could do them."

Uniform Crime Reports/Clery Reports. The statistical report probably most familiar to persons both inside and outside of the criminal justice system is the Federal Bureau of Investigation's (FBI's) annual Uniform Crime Reports (UCRs), which have compiled crime data submitted from various law enforcement agencies since 1930. The data are gathered daily by agencies across the country, and each agency is encouraged by the FBI to strive for complete accuracy to "generate a reliable set of crime statistics for use in Law Enforcement administration, operation and management." It is acknowledged that the data are critical to a wide range of users to assist with the understanding of crime, the formulation of policies, operational and strategic decision making, and for criminological research and analysis.

Likewise, senior law enforcement officials expect to have contact from various media sources regarding the annual report. This is normally routine unless there has been a significant increase noted in a certain area. I made an effort personally to avoid the year-to-year comparisons that local reporters attempted to make and instead focused on the trends I noticed and those supported by the UCR data. The data were helpful when developing community programs, promoting departmental activities, and supporting budgetary requests. Likewise, the results of those studies have, over the years, impacted the manner in which the officer on the street performed or was expected to perform his or her duties.

Although there is no doubt that the data should be considered invaluable for those involved in longer term criminal and social studies, it seemed that the degree of interest from the local community, officers, and others in the criminal justice system was limited. The experience of other senior law enforcement officials may have been entirely different, but to me, the level of interest always seemed disappointingly low.

Additionally, the number of UCR inquiries from people interested in becoming a resident of and/or moving a new business to our community also seemed low. It is possible that the wider access of UCR data via the Internet and elsewhere may have contributed to the lack of contact with our police department about the UCR data, or it may have just been a circumstance unique to this area.

The publication of information similar to that available in the UCR, but for campus police and security departments, is the report originally known as the Jeanne Clery Disclosure of Campus Security Policy and Campus Crime Statistics Act, and subsequently the Higher Education Opportunity Act. The Clery Act reports are required by the U.S. Department of Education. The act directs all public and private colleges and universities (postsecondary institutions) that participate in the federal government's Title IV student financial assistance programs to publish annual reports on criminal and fire incidents that have taken place on their respective campuses.

The Clery reporting guidelines utilize basically the same crime classification rules and definitions as those in the UCR and the National Incident Based Reporting System (NIBRS) handbook. The Clery Act requires that institutions disclose three general categories of crime statistics: criminal offenses, hate crimes, and arrest/referrals for disciplinary action. Although the Clery crime categories and classifications are basically the same as those utilized within the UCR system, there are some significant differences, mainly those pertaining to reporting requirements for sexual assaults.

Within Clery, the reporting requirements have been drafted in such a manner as to restrict sexual assault reporting to two categories of "forcible and non-forcible" offenses. Within each category, the offenses have been restricted to four forcible and two non-forcible categories. The four forcible offenses consist of forcible rape, forcible sodomy, sexual assault with an object, and forcible fondling. The two non-forcible sex offenses consist of incest and statutory rape.

Under the Clery Act, a crime should be considered "reported" when it is brought to the attention of campus security authorities—those "authorities" include more than simply the campus security or police department—and may be reported by a victim, witness, other third-party person, or even the actual offender. In the event that they have accurately followed the Clery guidelines, campuses are actually reporting "alleged criminal incidents." Clery reporting actually does not require the report to have been investigated by the police or other campus security authority to be recorded. There is also no requirement that there be a finding of "guilt or responsibility" to disclose the information. As it relates to sexual assaults, the information, which has been restricted as outlined earlier, should be reported regardless of any investigation that may or may not have been done, even if the reporter has elected to share very little information with the campus police or security department. The only requirement for reporting is a reasonable belief that the information is not simply rumor or hearsay and that the report has been made in good faith.

Likewise, the report cannot be unfounded without a determination by sworn or commissioned personnel. Although the reasons for these guidelines are understood, it is also interesting to note the differences between the UCR and Clery reporting realities. I believe that the competition for students among colleges and universities has resulted in unrealistic reporting of major offenses—primarily sexual assaults. It is interesting to note that colleges and universities of similar size, demographic makeup, and location report major differences in the number of sexual assaults. Although I can't prove it, and although other campus security/law enforcement chief executives may disagree, I believe the lower numbers reported by some institutions are the result of the need to ensure that prospective students are not discouraged from attending those institutions rather than an accurate reflection of what is happening at those institutions as reported under the Clery guidelines. It is discouraging to see such decisions being made at the reporting and recording level. It is also discouraging that subtle (or not-so-subtle) pressure to reduce the Clery numbers may come from the executive levels within an institution's administration.

I have no doubt that more potential students and still more parents review the published reports during the college selection process than would others preparing to move to a community. Still, the number of inquiries from parents and prospective students regarding the Clery reports remains disappointingly low.

Prison Study. Our community was one of several under consideration for the construction of a state medium-security prison. The Illinois State Department of Corrections (DOC) conducted a series of hearings within each of the communities under consideration to determine the degree of public support for or opposition to the construction of a prison. At the time of the hearings, the community had the good fortune of a strong economic foundation with several large factories that had been in the community for a long time, a large state mental health center, a major railroad yard, and a well-known and respected private college.

The hearings were painful to watch. The opposition was strong and based in large part on information that had been gathered by a well-organized group that strongly opposed the construction of a prison in the community. The group expressed concerns that the prison would change the general reputation and impression of the community and, more specifically, have a direct impact for the worse on the quality of life for local citizens.

The prediction of a negative local impact was based on data the opposition group had gathered about other communities with prisons throughout the state. The information confirmed that each of the communities had experienced an increase in the local crime rate, as well as specific increases in drug-related crimes; drug sales; increased gang activity. There was also evidence that prisoner families had moved into the community while the family member was in prison and that, once released, the prisoners and their families remained in the community. The information was credible and based on UCR data as well as interviews with various officials from the cities involved.

Based on the emotions stirred up by the opposition group and the statistical information presented, the prison proposal was rejected. The state DOC representatives, who had not received an "open arms" welcome in the first place, were encouraged to leave and not return to subject the community to the negative impact that the prison would cause.

But times and circumstances changed for our community. A major industry that had been a consistent part of our life for many years closed and relocated to Mexico and China. The state mental health center closed, too. The economic foundation of our community crumbled, and along with it, the strong opposition to the DOC prison system, which was still trying to find locations to build within the state. The data that had been used to argue against the prison were still being cited, however, and continued to cause fear and uncertainty regarding the possibility of placing a prison in the area. But the changed circumstances created a desire at least to verify the data that had been gathered. Because much of it was crime based, the Galesburg Police Department was asked to research the information.

Actually, the UCR data were confirmed as accurate. The communities that had agreed to build prisons had, in fact, noted an increase in crime as well as drug and gang activity. It was noted, however, that the interpretation of the data may have contributed to the goals of the opposition at the time. Although those increases had been noted and accurately reported in the various UCR documents, the same increases in drug and gang activity had been noted in communities that had *not* had prisons located there.

Information presented by several sources (unconfirmed but believed to be U.S. Bureau of Justice and ABC News) indicated the movement of several large California-based gangs into the Midwest (especially Chicago) and that increasing drug and drug-related criminal activity could be expected to follow in smaller midwestern communities. As the data were analyzed locally, it appeared that gang and drug activity had indeed increased over time along major transportation lines extending from Chicago and other major midwestern cities. Our community was on one of those major transportation lines.

We also learned that there had, in fact, been an increase in the number of persons from larger communities moving into low-income housing in our own as well as other outlying communities. It was ultimately learned that the increases in criminal activity were correlated with actions being taken within various low-income housing authorities and that the apparent correlation of these increases with the presence of prisons was spurious. The perception that the presence of a prison in a community caused many of the observed changes in drug and criminal activity was strong but frequently unfounded factually.

Our community now has a state prison. The issue remains emotional, and persons still attempt to correlate the negative influences of crime and gangs to the prison, but, in fact, the prison has been a positive asset, and for the most part, the benefits of its presence have been apparent to the local population.

In addition to the very specific manner in which the data were used, by design or simply misunderstanding, the police learned a very valuable lesson: It remains critical that law enforcement, at every level, remain sensitive to the accurate analysis of data to ensure that the proper problem or target has been identified. It was easy to blame the prison for the gang- and drug-related problems that had confronted our department. If the easy explanations had been accepted and measures to correct or suppress the problems had been limited to the prison system, the department would have missed the real reason and potentially failed to protect the safety and well-being of our citizens as we are expected and have personally sworn to do.

Low-Income Housing. During the efforts to analyze data regarding the prison system in the state and the impact that the prison would have on local communities, the department learned that low-income housing was an area that required some additional attention.

Efforts were made to determine who had moved into the area from elsewhere (generally larger cities) and to learn what was needed by the residents of the housing area (especially the younger residents) as well as department officers. Several actions were taken. Some, in cooperation with the local housing authority, were administratively specific, such as tighter controls on visitors and monitoring who was actually living in the units assigned. In an effort to involve the young residents more, officers and community services personnel (nonsworn but uniformed members of the department) were assigned to interact with younger residents on a daily basis, primarily after school.

The program continued for several years, and after initial strong interest and interaction with the department, the younger residents began to withdraw. After the early success of the program, it was disappointing to see the desire for interaction with the department diminish. In an effort to determine where the program had failed, an attempt was made to compare the number of persons participating in the current program with the number who had been involved initially. At the same time, interviews were completed with the younger residents as well as parents and friends of those involved. All the information combined revealed an interesting story.

The program with the youth had not failed. The program had done what it was supposed to do—create the feeling of a real neighborhood where the young residents could come home and simply play. They no longer felt the need for an organized, department-sponsored, after-school program. We learned that in addition to not knowing, for sure, what to do or what was going to work, we were having difficulty recognizing when we had been successful.

We had made a commitment to be willing to try anything new that we felt would be helpful and had pledged to stop a plan or program if it was not successful and then try something new. We were prepared for failure and vowed not to continue just because it was a popular idea. It was felt that we would clearly know when we had failed, but surprisingly, it was not as easy to recognize when we had been successful. The need to have a plan in place, gather information, and then correctly analyze the information was underscored by this effort. In hindsight, those suggestions all seem simple and obvious, but we didn't do it.

Luck Is Often Seat-of-the-Pants Statistics. It seemed that any time I had a conversation with an officer regarding a successful investigation, traffic stop, and subsequent drug arrest or pursuit, the frequent response was something to the effect of, "I was just lucky." That response often provided an opportunity to share my personal belief that the officer needed to take credit for the success and not to praise luck with the comment: "There is no such thing as luck. You make your own luck."

I sincerely believed in the truth of this statement, but honestly, it was without factual support. As the years passed, however, I became convinced that there may be some factual/scientific support for the idea that officers make their own luck. At their core, the best police officers have learned or sensed that the best predictor of future behavior is past behavior, and they have learned to recognize patterns in behavior, much as statistical analysis reveals patterns worth paying attention to.

Although that comment seems simple enough, I believe that scientific research consists of gathering, categorizing, and analyzing data of some activity or behavior. I believe that the best of the best among criminal justice practitioners understand this process, even if unconsciously. The street officer may not check a table, chart, or graph, yet daily, he or she relies on basically the same process, gathering and analyzing information in much the same manner as the criminologist-statistician-researcher.

The operational processes, however, may be dramatically different in several ways. One may be the result of focused conscious thought over an extended period of time, whereas the other may take place without conscious thought over a much shorter, even instantaneous, time frame, but the end result is the same: A decision to act, or not act, made as the result of an analysis of data gathered about some previous actions or behaviors.

One may involve a presentation to a city council, county board, or state appropriations committee and include a comment such as "Based on the statistical analysis of the number of calls for service within that particular area and the average response times by departmental personnel, it is proposed that two additional officers be hired to ensure adequate police service to the citizens who live in the patrol zone in question." The other may consist of the brief comment, frequently made on a police radio channel, "Headquarters ... I'm behind the suspect vehicle ... eastbound on Main Street at Cherry." The actions may be dramatically different, but I believe they involve the same basic process.

In much the same way, officers and sometimes departments use a similar process to design operational stings using the study of past human behavior. We've seen it used successfully on the interstate highway system when signs have been posted to announce that "Vehicle Searches" will be conducted at some location several miles ahead. The signs may be posted in a remote area just before an exit. The searches may not be taking place as announced, but the fact that the driver of a vehicle has elected to exit at that remote location, seemingly to avoid the announced search, has resulted in some significant illegal drug seizures. Likewise, a similar investigative approach has been used at a local train station. Observations of the behavior of persons departing the train have been successful with the same drug enforcement effort. People who often observe the police presence near the train platform may react by attempting to avoid the officers and the police dog. Subsequent conversations or other interactions with officers have resulted in numerous successful arrests for the possession of illegal drugs.

It may explain why some officers always seem to be at the right place at the right time to clear a case, intercept the fleeing suspect, or make that critical arrest. Somewhere inside of those "lucky" officers, they have somehow learned that by using past behaviors and computing the odds, a valid prediction may be made. My comment that "we make our own luck" should more accurately be stated as "Statistically speaking, we make our own luck."

Rapist Story. During conversations with young people interested in pursuing a criminal justice career, I often said that I thought our department was an ideal size for working as a police officer. The department consisted of 54 officers, 30 auxiliary/emergency police officers, and 32 civilian positions. I considered the department's size ideal because it was large enough that, over the course of 20 to 25 years, officers would likely be exposed to just about every criminal and noncriminal event they would care to experience (and some they would not care to experience), but it was small enough not to become lost within the organization. One of the cases investigated by the department was very painful for all involved because of the intimidation and brutality of the perpetrator.

It is generally acknowledged that virtually all sexual assaults are exercises of power and domination, but may be aggravated by the circumstances of the assault, including the age and location of the targeted victim. Every officer will comment that the most painful memories of any criminal case or serious accident are those in which the victim(s) are children or elderly citizens. In this case, the youngest rape victim was in her late 70s, and the oldest was nearly 90 years old.

Initially, the department was unaware of the actual criminal nature of the incidents. We noted that we had experienced a number of late evening calls from persons reporting that a man had come to their residence and had requested to use the telephone to call the police. The man usually stated that he had been involved in a traffic accident nearby and needed police assistance or that he had been the victim of a criminal act and needed to contact the police. In fact, in several cases, residents actually made the call to the police department for the man, and when officers arrived, they found no accident or evidence of a problem in the neighborhood. In several other cases, the man was permitted to enter and make what appeared to be a call to the police department; generally, he was gone shortly thereafter without police contact observed by the resident. The cases received limited follow-up investigation and were believed to be pranks. The descriptions of the suspect were vague due to the darkness and inability of the resident to see the man's face clearly.

The true intentions of the man became clear when the department was contacted by a female in her 80s who wanted to report a "problem" with a man who had come to her door. She actually lived in a second-floor apartment in the city's downtown district. She had answered her doorbell and walked downstairs to find a man who said he was being pursued by some other males and requested to use her telephone to contact the police department for assistance. She agreed to let him and invited him to follow her to the upstairs apartment. Once inside, he moved to the telephone and then, as he lifted the handset, he turned and began to beat her about the face, head, and upper shoulders with the telephone receiver. He continued to beat her and threatened to kill her if she did not submit to his expressed intent to rape her, which he eventually succeeded in doing.

The victim's demeanor during our interviews was that of an embarrassed, subdued, sweet lady. She displayed no anger, she was calm, she was everyone's grandmother, but she was one more thing that we or perhaps her attacker had not counted on; she was as "sharp as a tack." She may have been in her 80s, but she was able to recall specific physical details about the assault, comments made by the perpetrator, smells, what he had touched, and what went on during the moments before he had entered her home. Her recollections proved essential as we intensified our investigations and built our case.

She noted that when she answered the doorbell, she walked to the door and turned on the light to more clearly see the face of the person there. She remembered that the light did not work, but also recalled that she knew that before the attack, it had been working properly. We checked and confirmed that the light did not work but that the reason it did not light was that it had been slightly unscrewed. That observation ultimately resulted in a possible correlation with other, similar cases that had been reported. As noted earlier, those cases had not involved any reported assault or attempted assault but had involved the request to use the telephone to call the police for help. The suspect's method was specifically designed to cause persons to drop their guard and placed him in the position of a victim, causing his potential victims to believe that they could trust him because a person who was asking for police assistance would not be expected to cause harm. They could not have been more wrong.

A detail noted in some of the brief reports written about similar past incidents was that the suspect's face was not identifiable due to the darkness. After follow-ups with those cases, however, it was noted that the homes' porch lightbulbs had been unscrewed or, in some cases, removed. The follow-ups also produced several of the bulbs, which had been dropped in bushes at or near each of the residences. Each of them was processed for fingerprints without success.

The follow-up interviews also produced more details regarding the suspect's conduct. Although always quiet and polite, he seemed to quickly depart when he learned that the person who answered the door was a younger female, a male, or a person who was not alone or appeared not to be alone. It also appeared that he had been targeting a specific age group, the older citizen, who he likely felt would respond in a trusting manner to a person in need who was requesting police assistance. We speculated that, in addition to a personal desire for elderly female victims and his effort to mask his identity by darkness, he also may have felt that the age of his victims would reduce their ability to provide an accurate description. He hadn't considered just how tough, determined, and sharp our grandmother was.

Unfortunately, the follow-up interviews produced more than additional details about the man and his behavior; they also produced more victims. Some had elected not to share all the details when the initial call was made requesting police assistance. Some victims had not called the police, but had shared the information regarding the man coming to their home with neighbors, who then contacted the police. During the follow-ups, officers were referred to the previously unknown victims, who ultimately shared all the details; some of those included either an actual rape or an attempt. As the follow-up investigations continued, so did the attempts. Internally, the department was now deeply aware of the operation of the suspect. Any reports of persons requesting to use a telephone to call the police, late night knocking on doors, or reports of lost/stolen lightbulbs were treated as felony crime in progress calls.

In addition to the crime scene investigations, fingerprinting, photographs, and interviews, an attempt was made to reconstruct every known case that correlated, in any way, to the methods known to have been used by the suspect. The reconstruction efforts were displayed on pin maps to try to identify some unique area in which the contacts and/or attacks were taking place. Likewise, days, dates, and times were displayed on charts in an attempt to identify some pattern in the data that would assist the investigation.

Interestingly, the map was initially disappointing and did not tell us what we had hoped to see. The contacts were not taking place in a specific area but were actually taking place from the north to the south side of the city in no concentrated area. Looking back, I now understand that we were hoping the map would tell us what we expected to see, and when it didn't, we felt that we had failed and the map would not be of help, but we were wrong. The contacts had taken place from the north to south side, but when we stopped looking for a small, concentrated area, the map showed us that contacts with victims had not strayed more than two blocks from a street that ran through the entire city. We tried to imagine why the suspect would limit his activities to persons within that strip. We speculated that because he appeared always to operate on foot (as noted on other charts), this strip was his comfort zone and he was unfamiliar with the city outside this area, which indicated he was not a longtime city resident.

These speculations led to others that were supported by other data we had gathered and charted, and a profile emerged. We developed a list of known businesses in the area that would be expected to transfer persons into our area from elsewhere, that would not include business vehicles as part of the transfer, that may have had a correlation to the north/south street in question, and that would be expected to work the hours, days (and on the dates) of the incidents. Based on the entire effort, we believed that the suspect worked for the railroad. We believed that the suspect worked, in some fashion, on the tracks and/or track bed that paralleled the same north/south street that had seemed to act as his compass as he moved through the city. We felt that the man's job was likely to be a labor rather than a management position. We also felt that he lived on the south side of our city and concentrated our patrol and investigative efforts there. When he was finally apprehended, it was confirmed that he lived within two blocks of where we had predicted he would live.

Ultimately, we confirmed that, not only did he live within the predicted area, but he was a railroad worker who had been transferred (in and out) as part of a track repair crew. He was from Winslow, Arizona; we weren't able to predict *that*, but the maps, graphs, and charts were all a critical part of the investigation effort. Although statistics like these may not make it into television or the movies on a regular basis, they can be a key part of the life of a street officer.

I'd really like to leave it all right there, but unfortunately, I can't. At this point, it may appear that this was a major case solved with the statistics as noted above, but it wasn't. Please don't misunderstand; everything I noted about the case, including the follow-up interviews, other investigative efforts, and statistical analysis, is accurate, as were the assumptions, speculations, and predictions. But the preceding explanation may be misleading. The perpetrator was apprehended, but not as a *direct* result of the investigative efforts or the statistics or the good guesses.

As noted, we became aware of the seriousness of the cases regarding the man knocking on doors asking to use the telephone and the pranks regarding the missing light bulbs only after the report by the woman raped on the second floor of her downtown apartment. There had been months of previous reports filed away before we really moved into the statistical investigative mode. We had elected to keep some of the speculations we had made regarding the incident confidential. Details of the rape as well as the possible number of previous cases were not known to the media. As more information became available through the investigative efforts and more victims became known, the decision was made to release the information to the public and request any additional details regarding the mode of operation of the suspect, and any additional incidents of a similar nature that had been unreported, as well as anything else that might assist the investigation.

We received a call from a woman who stated that she had some information that might be related to the case and requested to speak with an investigator who had spoken with her at her residence months before our first report of this man's activities. The woman did not fit the victim profile that had been developed by the suspect. She was young, and she lived outside the two-block strip that we had identified during our data analysis. His mode was also different. He had not come to her door and asked to use the telephone. He had entered her home as she slept on a couch in her front room. He attempted to attack her, but she fought back, and for whatever reason, thankfully, he departed without causing her any harm.

She had not reported the matter at the time, but when she read about the attacks elsewhere in the city, she felt that she should call and report her experience even though the circumstances were not the same as those reported in the newspaper. She also said, if we thought it would be helpful, that she had the man's wallet, which he had apparently dropped during the attack. The wallet contained his Arizona driver's license and information that took us directly to his home within that two-block area that we had predicted. We again speculated that after his unsuccessful attack of the younger woman, outside his comfort zone, he altered his area of activities, victims of choice, and approach. Sadly, these changes contributed to his success during his subsequent attacks.

The standard investigative efforts coupled with the statistical analysis of the data may not have led to the actual arrest of the suspect, but they made the case basically airtight. I remain confident that, eventually, the data would have led to the apprehension of the suspect, but the reality is, it did not. This story illustrates the case that data gathering, analysis, and interpretation are all critical for criminal investigations, but so is sharing the statistics with others. In this case, sharing the data led to a quicker apprehension of a brutal serial rapist.

Statistics: A Researcher's View

by Jerry Fitzgerald

Former alcohol and drug abuse researcher (for 30 years), most of them in the Department of Psychiatry, University of Iowa, and co-author of this text. Used with permission.

When applied appropriately, statistics are an invaluable tool in almost any endeavor, and statisticians have developed procedures that can help us better understand the increasingly complex world in which we live. Still, every statistic you encounter should be approached with at least some skepticism. I tried to practice this tenet through 30-some years of doing research in the social sciences. When it comes to statistics, I have seen my share of the good (the appropriate application and interpretation of statistics); the bad (the uninformed, unintentional, and inappropriate application or interpretation of statistics); and the ugly (the informed, intentional, and inappropriate application or interpretation of statistics). By sharing some of my more memorable experiences with you sniffing out the bad and ugly, I hope you can gain a better appreciation of the good and a better nose for sniffing out the bad.

First, a bit about myself. I am a born and raised Iowa farm boy (some affectionately call us clod kickers). Upon finishing high school, I went to Cornell College (not University) in Mt. Vernon, Iowa. After graduating from Cornell with a sociology degree, I entered graduate school in the Sociology Department at the University of Iowa. A fellow sociologist (tenured professor in the Psychiatry Department) and clod kicker (PhD Harold A. Mulford) took me under his wing as a graduate research assistant in my first year of graduate school, and except for an all-expenses-paid 2-year stint in the U.S. Army, I worked with my mentor for the next 30 years. Until a colleague from the Psychiatry Department pointed out that Iowa was a terrible place to raise kids (because they grow up trusting everybody, and I did), I thought I could not have asked for a better childhood and educational preparation for the research career that followed, especially because all I really wanted to be was as good a mechanic as my dad and as good a farmer as my grandfather.

The Cornell College Years. Like most first-year college students, when I entered Cornell, I was not sure what I wanted to be when I grew up (and I'm still not entirely sure today that I know what I want to be when I grow up). Social science research, however, was definitely not on my radar. At first, I thought I might pursue a career teaching math in high school, then along came calculus and I decided there might be something I was better at. Biology looked good, but I still was not satisfied. I did have this older brother who was getting a graduate degree in sociology, and he said that was pretty interesting. Though younger brothers generally make it a practice to ignore any older brother's advice, I decided to give it a try. It was interesting, and it turned out I was good at it.

I was not so sure about the elementary statistics to which I was exposed in a combined statistics and methods course at Cornell, but the methods material was very interesting, and the prospect of being a scientist seemed pretty fascinating. Still, though a sociology degree looked appealing, I must admit I did wonder what I was ever going to do with it (maybe a social science literate mechanic would be better than a social science illiterate mechanic). Then, after my junior year at Cornell, I got a summer job with the chairman of the Department of Sociology at the University of Iowa doing some community surveying in Iowa. True to my upbringing, I trusted everyone and was soon completing more surveys than expected (turned out I was out on the streets trying to get interviews at night in areas where I was subsequently told I should not be). Still, I thoroughly enjoyed it, and it felt good to be a part of the scientific enterprise. I was so enthused, I went on in my senior year to take advanced independent studies in social science research methods and analyses (with just enough statistics to not persuade me to abandon this ship).

The Graduate School Statistics Course Years. First, let me begin by assuring you that I approached my first real statistics class with at least as much trepidation as you may have approached your first class. I hope your experience was similar to mine in that I soon found out it really wasn't as bad or difficult as I thought it might be (even though I did not have quite as good a textbook as this one). However, as I progressed through that course and text, I quickly substituted one unhelpful image of statistics—fear and awe—with another unhelpful image—impractical and mostly useless. That is, I found statistics were difficult, but not impossible, to either compute or comprehend. However, given all the caveats and assumptions associated with each statistic, I became convinced that statistics really weren't of very much practical use either, and probably, for the most part, could be safely ignored. Perhaps at least some of you are nodding your heads at this point.

In short, I went from fear and awe (unquestioned faith in the scientific integrity of statistics and their producers) before even cracking open the statistics book to "just about anybody can do this but why bother" at the end of that first class. Please note that, at least in my mind, either set of misconceptions about statistics produced a convenient justification for not having to pursue any further statistics classes. Funny how that worked out or didn't work out, actually. I had to take more courses, and in the ensuing years, I found out I could get over the fear and awe stuff, but perhaps I carried the skepticism a bit too far, at least initially.

I learned to appreciate statistics for what they are—tools that have the potential to produce a high-quality product or a disaster (i.e., useful or misleading results). Like the use of any tool, it was up to me to identify the tool that was most appropriate for the task at hand. Not only that, once I applied the appropriate tool to a specific task, I needed to carefully evaluate the results. Whether I was presenting my own statistical results or interpreting others', I needed to make sure the most appropriate statistic was applied and then determine whether the results were more likely to be useful than misleading. I sincerely hope that is where you are right now, and whether you decide to pursue more statistics classes or not, we think if you share this view of statistics, you are in a good position to both appreciate statistics and carefully assess each application you encounter.

Please note that I still believe skepticism is a good thing to have when you encounter statistics. Just don't let that skepticism blind you to the potential benefits that can be derived from an appropriate statistical application: a complete and accurate description of the data being analyzed; a good description of the analytic strategies (including specific statistical tests used); a comprehensive report of the results of those analyses; and a critique of the research, which lets others know the strengths and weaknesses of the entire research project, including the statistics.

The Graduate Student Research Years. I started my research career as a graduate student research assistant. I was lucky or unlucky enough, depending on your perspective, to be working on a research project at a university that was testing the first versions of the Statistical Package for the Social Sciences (SPSS). The research office in which I was working had just completed a large general population survey that included hundreds of participants and questions—an ideal data set to test this new, fast, and economical means of producing statistics from large data sets.

Because we were getting free computer time, my faculty supervisor was quite excited about giving it a try—a state of mind I did not exactly share. I was one of several research assistants from various departments who were "volunteering" to do SPSS testing, and at the time I often wondered, Why me? It dawned on me later that because I was a relative newcomer to both statistics and computers, I was an ideal guinea pig. If I could master this new software, anyone could.

All our data were stored on paper IBM punch cards (you can probably find some of these in a museum somewhere). Each morning usually meant writing an SPSS program, using those same IBM punch cards, and carrying the program cards and data cards over to the computer center to be read into a card reader so that the analysis could be done. Sometimes, if we were lucky, we might get results late that afternoon, but usually it was not until the next day or later that you received any analysis output, assuming there was any analysis that actually ran. Because this was a trial period for SPSS, glitches of various kinds were common and the process had to be repeated, which often was quite frustrating.

Though computer glitches are more common in the beta versions (testing phases) of new software, they sometimes do not entirely disappear. New software, even after extensive testing, may still contain errors. In addition, there are user errors: entering the wrong variable name, a comma instead of a period, an "and" instead of an "or," and the list goes on.

Exactly how that software and hardware all works eludes me to this day, and I remain in awe of all those 12-year-olds who do seem to know. I also learned early on in my SPSS testing days to have a great deal of respect for computer professionals. I had written an SPSS program that simply would not run, and I could find no reason for it not to. I finally decided I just had to take the risk of making a fool of myself and asked the computer center's SPSS expert what was wrong. He looked over my program, inserted one card in the program that said "stop giving this error message," and told me to resubmit my program. It ran, and I was pretty much convinced that guy could walk on water if the need ever arose.

Computer professionals can, of course, correct many problems that the average user would have no clue as to how to fix. On the other hand, it is often the average software and hardware user that is best at identifying computer-related glitches. Some of us believe there are gremlins inside computers who, ironically, behave randomly. In any event, when users are well acquainted with their data, research design, and analyses, they can often identify a problem that may well be missed by someone who is unfamiliar with the data being analyzed. If something looks funny, check it out. Review carefully what you did, and if that doesn't satisfy you, try looking at some simple frequency distributions or scattergrams. Use a different software package, a different computer, or a statistic that is similar to the one producing results that just do not seem right given what you know about the data being analyzed. In my case, nearly all the problems so identified turned out to be "user error"—a euphemism for "I made some kind of dumb mistake when instructing the computer which data to look at or what to do with the data once it found them." I have reason to believe this still happens to many who use computers for purposes of statistical analysis. And some things did happen in some analyses for which I was never able to identify a satisfying explanation. I was never able to verify that a gremlin was responsible, though. But maybe you will get lucky. I'm still holding out hope their existence will be confirmed.

On one of those days when nothing seemed to be working with SPSS, I was looking for some sympathy from my older faculty supervisor and mentor. Instead of giving me a shoulder to cry on, he shared a story of statistical analyses and computers that he had witnessed in previous years. He remembered that it was not all that long ago that the chi-square statistic (you know the one we discussed in Chapter 8) was first introduced. Prior to the advent of computers, it was, of course, necessary to compute chi square by hand using paper and pencil. As a result, chi-square analyses were completed fairly infrequently and, even then, generally under only the best of circumstances. Once computers and research assistants were created, however, calculating chi squares was easy, and it was not long before the halls of his campus building were ringing excitedly with the words "I got one."

Now those of you who fish would know what an excited "I got one" means, but might be a little puzzled about its application in the halls of academia. My supervisor was similarly puzzled but he soon learned it meant that after many hours or even months of making every comparison faculty members or their research assistants could possibly make from whatever data resource they could lay their hands on, they had found a significant ($p \leq .05$) chi square. Why so excited? Given a significant chi square, there was the potential for an article to be published. Professional journals, then and unfortunately now, are more likely to publish only those manuscripts with statistically significant results. Given that bias, such manuscripts were more likely to be published, and publications are often a prerequisite for promotions and tenure in most large universities.

This statistical strategy—trying all the possible combinations—is sometimes called *data mining*. It can and certainly has been used, and sometimes may be helpful in terms of identifying what subsequent studies might focus on. When statistics are used in this way, however, that should be clearly stated, including the warning that the results are highly susceptible to Type I errors.

Still, is there anything about this that bothers you? I hope so, because if it doesn't, then we have failed to make some important points when it comes to inferential statistics in general. Although the results obtained from the analyses described may well have been very beneficial in terms of faculty advancement, they likely added little to the valid cumulative knowledge about whatever variables were being subjected to a chi-square analysis. In these cases, the cart was put before the horse. Researchers treated the statistic as the end rather than as a means to an end. In short, the statistics proclaimed in those halls were more the consequence of a new statistic's availability and the machines to compute it, than of building a good case for using the statistic with appropriate data to test hypotheses. As a result, they were likely to produce some misleading results.

Why? Well, inferential statistics are all about probability, and the more statistical analyses you perform, the more likely you are to commit a Type I error, rejecting a null hypothesis that is true (see Chapter 8). In short, given enough chi-square analyses, you are bound to find at least one or two significant ones by chance alone (about 5 in 100 chances, actually, when the significance level is $p = .05$). Just because you have a statistical tool, even the one that is currently the most popular and easiest to use, it does not mean that tool is appropriate in every possible application.

Events like that witnessed by my faculty supervisor may be rarer today, or at least not as public, but they have not completely disappeared. As is often the case, individuals who use tools that they do not fully understand are likely to misapply them. Applying the statistic du jour to everything you can get your hands on is, in general, not a wise or helpful thing to do.

Make sure that as a producer of statistics, you provide enough information to judge whether or not a particular statistic was appropriately applied. As a consumer of statistics, you must look for and accept nothing less than a full disclosure of the process that produced any particular statistical result. Perhaps some of those hallway "statisticians" actually described how they got their one significant chi square and appropriately documented the accompanying precautions, but I am sure some did not, and the scientific body of knowledge involved was likely the worse off because of it.

After working with SPSS for a year or so, I began to learn about the existence of several other statistical software packages. At my university, a dichotomy of sorts developed between the various statistical packages and their users: SPSS, for dummies like me in the social sciences, and others, like biomedical statistics packages, for the real scientists. These latter statistical software packages tended to be more complex or sophisticated (usually meaning lots more calculations and a bit harder to understand and use unless you had a mathematics and/or computer degree). The SPSS package was deemed more appropriate for the soft data (and some even thought soft minds) we social scientists were often left to deal with.

Most social scientists were content to leave well enough alone, but some of us dummies, being brutes for punishment, were brave enough (OK, I was forced) to take it upon ourselves to venture into these "sophisticated" software packages to see exactly what was there. As a result, it became clear to me that just because a particular statistical procedure might be more difficult to explain and take more computer time to calculate, that does not necessarily mean any specific application of that statistic and its concomitant results are more valid and useful than any other statistic. More sophisticated statistics often come with more assumptions about the data and/or presume more control of the research design than social scientists can typically aspire to. My point here is not that you can just ignore the more "sophisticated" statistics, but that such statistics may or may not be more appropriately applied than others under all conditions.

The Research Practitioner Years. As I progressed in my career and began to publish research results of my own, it was not uncommon to have to defend the statistics applied and the results reported. This is a good thing and all a part of the process of accumulating a scientifically valid body of knowledge. It has been my experience, however, that these exchanges can be very rewarding and also very frustrating. Critiques are, of course, always a blow to one's ego (especially if they are valid). When they are not valid, they are just plain frustrating. With regard to the latter, I would like to share some of the lessons I learned from such encounters.

First, when someone challenges your statistical results because a better statistic is available, make sure that is the case. To do that, you will need to know how it is better and whether it is applicable to the data and research question at hand. Perhaps the alternative statistic is better, but its assumptions may not be consistent with the data or research design. If it does not fit, no matter how new or sophisticated it is, you should not accept its results over those obtained from an older and perhaps less sophisticated statistic that does fit. The results obtained from a more sophisticated analysis may or may not be better than those obtained from a more simple procedure that you do understand and is applicable to the data and question at hand.

Given that statisticians are constantly developing new and revising old statistical procedures, you may find yourself in the position of feeling unqualified to make such an applicability assessment. If you don't feel comfortable making such an assessment, do not be afraid to ask for help from a statistician. I will warn you, however, that you will find there are statisticians who are good at explaining and willing to take the time to do so, and others who are not. Find a good one. I was fortunate to be able to find a university statistician who was patient and explained things well—an invaluable asset to anyone doing quantitative research who is not a professional statistician. If you are lucky enough to find a good resource, buy him or her a beer once in a while!

Whoever you seek help from, you should expect that person to be able to explain, in a manner that you can understand, what this new super-duper statistic does, how it does it, and why it is better than the older alternatives. This does not mean you have to understand all the mathematical derivatives, but at least you should feel comfortable that you know enough to tell whether this new and unfamiliar statistic was applied appropriately. Keep asking for help until you feel comfortable. The only dumb questions are those that are not asked.

Once you have settled the applicability question to your satisfaction, the next thing you need to turn your attention to is the data. When there are differences in results between statistical procedures that are equally applicable to the data, you need to carefully assess the databases that were used to calculate that statistic. Do not fall prey to that old schoolyard argument that goes something like, my statistic is more sophisticated than yours and therefore my results are more valid. Although this may indeed be the case, it is not necessarily so. It is also possible that a careful reading of the methods will indicate that those differences in results can alternatively be attributed to differences in the data that were used to calculate the different statistics. If you are not using equivalent data, you are not likely to produce similar statistical results. When the databases are different, the question of the validity of the results is less dependent on the sophistication of the statistic than it is on which data set is most applicable to the question (hypothesis) at hand.

Furthermore, no statistical sophistication can compensate for bad data or an ugly research design. Remember, garbage in-garbage out. There are those, however, who will at least implicitly attempt to "wow" the consumers of their statistics into forgetting about the ugly reasoning and/or bad data that were used to generate them. Over the years, I have found one clue that often characterizes the "wow" statistical practitioners: They are long on documenting the sophistication and novelty of a particular statistical procedure, but often short on the documentation of their research design, data collection methods, and description of the data used.

In short, there is nothing inherently wrong with simple when it comes to statistics. In fact, I have often found that when simple is appropriate, it is often a good indication of the quality of the research design and the data collected. Generally, it has been my experience that if you have a good research design and data collection methods, you will often need nothing more than the most basic statistical procedures to assess the results of your research.

It is even often the case that simple visual aids such as graphs and scattergrams, which can be produced before any statistic is calculated, give you some of the most useful insights into your research results. You will note we have encouraged you to produce and examine such visual aids throughout this text, and I want to emphasize them again. Those basic visual aids are often the best means of identifying potential problems with your data (such as outliers), the fit of the assumptions about your data that a particular statistic requires, and the nature (such as linear vs. curvilinear) and strength of any relationship that might exist. The summary statistic is a necessary, but not sufficient, means of adequately describing your data or results.

As we have also emphasized throughout this text, you should never be satisfied as a producer or consumer of statistics with just the report of a particular statistical result. The reporting of statistical results in the absence of a clear and adequate description of the research design and data that were used should raise a red flag—accept these findings at your own risk. Beware of what you do not know or are not told. Good and adequate statistical reports should include a detailed description of the research design and data collected, including the applicability of the statistic used and then, of course, the results of the statistical procedure.

Unfortunately, it has also been my experience that the guidelines of those who often bear the ultimate decision of what to include in a research report (journal editors and administrators) often interfere with good research project reports. Professional journal editors (due ostensibly to space limitations) and administrators (ostensibly because they are so busy) often demand that methods be given short shrift, and the bottom-line results (such as statistical significance or correlation coefficient) are all that can be included in research project reports. The bottom line is all well and good, except that the "real" bottom line (like the devil) is often in the details nobody wants to print or look at.

As a producer of statistics, you should resist any effort on the part of colleagues or publication editors to omit or radically reduce your attempts to adequately describe your research design, data collection methods, missing data and how they were dealt with, and statistical results. In spite of their power, editors, supervisors, and administrators do compromise, at least sometimes. As a consumer of statistics, you should expect a complete description of the research design, data collection, and statistical results. If that is not presented, you should ask for it, and if it is not produced, you should ignore the results presented. As has been observed, it is not so much the things we all agree that we do not know as it is the things we think we know, but do not, that cause the most problems.

If you, as a consumer, are confronted with reports that provide only the results (e.g., even if it is $p \leq .0001$), you need to be especially cautious about accepting those results as valid or useful. You need to demand the details. As a producer of statistics, when you devote the time and space necessary to adequately describe your research design and data collection, you not only help others to better assess your results, but also set the stage for others to replicate your study. And, if we are ever going to build a body of scientifically based knowledge in the social sciences, we will need replication studies.

The replication of a study can take many forms. Others can use the exact same data as yours but use a different statistic. Alternatively, a new sample can be drawn with equivalent data collected and the same statistic applied to see if the statistical result is the same. However the replication is designed, a careful review of all the research design, data collection procedures, and statistics applied must be thoroughly analyzed before an appropriate interpretation of the results can be reached. Replication is the backbone of any science and the only way to help ensure that Type I error is not the cause of the results for any one investigation. Whatever our findings are in any one instance, it is only through replication that we can become more and more confident that our findings are not the result of chance.

However, replication studies and their results must be appropriately interpreted. It is not uncommon, for example, for some to argue that because one particular study finding is inconsistent with the findings of several others, the inconsistent study results must be in error. That interpretation may or may not be true, and the validity of the inconsistent study should be based on the validity of its results, not the observation that it is different. The answer to the question of whether the result of any one study is valid cannot be determined by simply noting that its result is different from similar studies.

One final thought I want to share with you based on my experiences. I was involved in several evaluations of intervention programs (in my particular instance, evaluations of alcoholism treatment centers). Such evaluations can, of course, produce results that indicate the program has been a success or a failure. Obviously, if the evaluation results are positive, everyone will be happy, but if the results are negative, a common by-product is a high level of antagonism between the evaluators and the program staff. Those individuals within the program being assessed have their reputations and their livelihoods put in peril based on a negative outcome for an evaluation study. Politicians may seize on this opportunity to stop funding, not only for the program being assessed but also for all intervention programs in general. The program staff may hold the researchers responsible for everything bad that is happening to them and further accuse the researcher of being insensitive to the plight of those who need interventions. Although these may be the consequences of a negative evaluation result, they are not what good evaluators want and what they should make every effort to avoid.

If the potential that the analysis will indicate the program has failed to achieve its goal is not addressed early on, it can mean not only a nasty fight with respect to the validity of the results for this one study, but also the end of any hope for the program staff and others like them to cooperate in any future study. Just like any other research project, the validity of the results of an evaluation study should be based on the quality of the data, the research design, and the applicability of the statistics employed. With respect to avoiding all the other potential problems that might accompany a valid finding of no program impact, the only thing that seemed to work for us was involving the program staff in the development of the research design and data collection, and making it plain that we viewed the evaluation as part of an ongoing process with the goal of identifying the best interventions possible.

In short, we approached our evaluations from the perspective of a process, with evaluation and intervention activities interacting so that they would, in time, produce the best interventions possible. Program development and research needed to proceed hand in hand if the goal was to have the best intervention possible. Although this approach did not always work, it was the best one we could muster, and we feel it should be a prerequisite for any evaluation study. Progress can be made only when the program provider and evaluator work together to eliminate what does not work, develop new strategies, test them, and then start the process all over again, depending on the results of the evaluation. If everyone involved is on board with this process perspective, negative evaluation results can be seen as a positive contribution to the ongoing process of identifying what may have gone wrong with the program and designing better interventions.

Reflections on a Research Career. Over the years, I feel very fortunate to have been able to lead some interesting and important research projects with my mentor and others, participate in many others, and have the opportunity to make some useful contributions to the growing body of cumulative knowledge in the social sciences. Should you decide to pursue a career, or just participate in a research project, you will find it will not be all fun and games, and you will almost undoubtedly be embroiled in arguments over this or that. My colleagues and I were not always in agreement with each other, let alone all the others in our field of endeavors, but that should be expected. The give and take of conversation and criticism are an essential part of building a useful body of scientific knowledge.

As far as statistics are concerned, what you should expect from yourselves and others is an honest effort to make an informed decision about the appropriateness of whatever statistic is chosen and provide enough of a description of the research methods (design and data collection) to allow others to judge whether or not an appropriate choice of statistics and interpretation of the results was made. And, of course, this information is essential if others wish to replicate the study.

I found research to be a very rewarding experience, definitely not so much in terms of income earned, but more in terms of some satisfaction that I had made a contribution, however small it might have been, to the ongoing accumulation of a scientifically based body of knowledge in the social sciences. Should you find yourself interested in pursuing a research career in the criminal justice field, you are going to have to deal with statistics, as well as with those who use them appropriately and ethically and those who do not. Do your best to keep your own ethical bearings and weigh in when you see something that just isn't right. Scientific advancements—maybe even lives—depend on it. Best wishes for a successful career!

Student Study Site

Visit the open-access student study site at **www.sagepub.com/fitzgerald** for access to several study tools including eFlashcards, web quizzes, and additional appendices as well as links to SAGE journal articles and audio, video and web resources.

15
Summary and Conclusions

Some Concluding Thoughts

Empirical data are essential for understanding what happened in the past, what is going on now, and what might happen in the future. But such data, no matter how large the data sets or how carefully the data have been gathered, are, by themselves, essentially useless. They make no sense unless they are organized and analyzed. Simply put, statistics are the tools—the essential and powerful tools—for making sense of data. When they are applied appropriately to data, they may reveal patterns we can use to improve our understanding of the past, make more informed choices now, and prepare ourselves better for what is to come. Our purpose in this book has been to introduce you to some of those tools and some of the ways in which they can be put to good use.

But just as data require analysis, for all their ubiquity, undeniable importance, and potential uses, for both good and ill, statistics and statistical analyses do not speak for themselves and are not ends in themselves. We humans must invent statistics, choose the particular statistical tools to apply in a particular research situation, and interpret the results of statistical analyses appropriately in light of the data available and the questions for which we are seeking answers. Statistics are best viewed as means to the ends of acquiring knowledge and making better policy and practice decisions.

Statistics of one kind or another have become omnipresent in virtually every aspect of contemporary life. To a large extent, that can be attributed to the advent of computers and statistical analysis packages. Computer and software advances (including rapidly growing memory capacity as well as processing speed and power in smaller and smaller hardware units, improved ease of use, and decreased costs of both hardware and software) are continuing to increase our exposure to statistics. These developments have made it possible for almost anyone to produce statistics and perform statistical analyses at the touch of a button. In fact, modern public and private bureaucracies depend heavily on statistics and statistical analyses in order to function at all. The particular descriptive and inferential statistics we have discussed here are used regularly by policymakers, administrators, researchers, and practitioners in a wide variety of political, social, and scientific arenas. They help shape decisions about what constitutes the current state of scientific knowledge as well as what the best practices are in dealing with real-life problems. They help shape answers to many kinds of important questions, including those that arise in life-or-death situations.

If you are going to make the best of your experiences with statistics, whether as producer or consumer, you obviously need to know something about them, including which statistics are best suited for the data being analyzed and the questions being asked of them, as well as their particular strengths and weaknesses, and the cautions that should be observed when interpreting the results of statistical analyses. You should also be aware that statistics can be misleading both intentionally and unintentionally. We have pointed out how various kinds of errors may distort or invalidate statistics and how statistics and their display, especially in graphs, might be deliberately manipulated to mislead. We have emphasized that maintaining ethical standards in data management, analysis, and reporting is essential. In the preceding chapters, we have attempted to provide you with a basic understanding of statistics in general and of several of the more common specific statistics you might use or otherwise encounter in a criminal justice career. We hope you have gained some appreciation for what statistics can do, as well as some of their limitations. As a way of summarizing some of the factors that go into choosing applicable statistics and statistical analyses, guides for selecting appropriate statistics and statistical analyses may be found in Appendix A. We have considered a number of widely used descriptive and inferential statistics. Descriptive statistics are used to describe and summarize distributions of the values of single variables or relationships between variables. Inferential statistics, using probability theory, including the theory of random sampling, build on descriptive statistics from random samples to estimate population parameters in univariate goodness-of-fit tests, as well as in bivariate and multivariate hypothesis testing.

We use descriptive statistics such as mean, median, and mode to indicate the central tendency of a variable's values in a distribution. Ranges, standard deviations, and variances serve as indicators of the dispersion or variation in a variable's values in a distribution. The information provided by measures of central tendency and dispersion, often supplemented by graphs of the distributions, often help make patterns in data more visible and, hence, more recognizable. When we find patterns in data, we may be on the way to learning something useful.

Goodness-of-fit and hypothesis testing use random sample statistics and probability theory to estimate population parameters. Typically, hypothesis testing involves formulating a research hypothesis asserting a relationship between or among variables and a null hypothesis asserting no such relationship. Using sample statistics and probability theory, sampling distributions for a test statistic are constructed under the assumption that the null hypothesis is true. A sampling distribution is a distribution of the probabilities associated with the various possible values of the test statistic—that is, the possible outcomes of random trials or experiments. If the sampling distribution indicates that the probability of the observed value of the test statistic is low (for example, $p \leq .05$) if the null hypothesis is true, the result is said to be statistically significant. If the result is statistically significant, the researcher rejects the null hypothesis and argues instead that the evidence supports the research hypothesis.

Although many aspects of statistics may seem cut and dried, you should be aware that statisticians don't always agree among themselves about important matters. Furthermore, both the research process and the real world are inevitably messy and require a certain amount of muddling through. The researcher or practitioner is often confronted by circumstances that only partially conform to the assumptions on which statistical analyses are based. How much of a departure from randomness in sampling, normality, or homoscedasticity is permissible when the statistical model being applied is built on these assumptions? Do we assign too much importance to statistical significance in data analyses? What are the relevant variables? How will they be measured? What are the appropriate descriptive and inferential statistical tools for analyzing the data? What is the appropriate significance level? How seriously do the missing data undermine the randomness of the data? Data and other kinds of relevant information are almost always—to some degree, at least—incomplete and/or in error. Addressing these questions and issues requires human judgments and almost always compromises of one sort or another. How these dilemmas are resolved influences the choice of statistical analysis tools to be applied and how the results of those analyses are interpreted. Statistical analysis, then, always requires multiple human judgments and compromises.

Appropriately applying statistics, whether descriptive or inferential, depends on a number of assumptions being satisfied. Each statistic has its own set of assumptions. Of the assumptions that may determine a statistic's applicability, three are especially important: (a) the level of measurement of the variable (some statistics may be used with nominal-level variables, whereas others require interval- or ratio-level measurement); (b) the shape of the distribution of variable values in the sample and/or in the population (for example, parametric inferential statistics assume normal distributions, whereas nonparametric inferential statistics do not); and (c) the nature of the sampling procedure, if any (for example, inferential statistics assume random sampling). Some statistics are robust enough to remain generally valid in spite of minor violations of these assumptions, but it is nevertheless true that, to the extent the assumptions pertaining to any particular statistic are not met, analyses using it may yield misleading results.

Furthermore, it has become routine in the social sciences—and criminology and criminal justice are no exceptions—to treat ordinal data (e.g., data from scales with responses ranging from strongly agree to strongly disagree) as if they were interval or ratio data and to analyze them using statistics (especially inferential statistics) that assume interval- or ratio-level data. It's easy to understand the temptation; parametric statistics permit more sophisticated and complex analyses. But, in our view, the results of such analyses should be regarded with considerable skepticism. It is also quite common to find inferential statistics applied to data from samples whose randomness is, to say the least, suspect. Generalizing to populations from which such samples have been drawn is a very risky business—far more risky than the inherent risk involved in making probability-based decisions about hypotheses when samples are genuinely random. When samples are not random, or the randomness of an original sample has been compromised by the elimination of a variable's units of analysis, it's probably best to learn what one can from the available descriptive statistics and resist the temptation to generalize results to the population from which the sample was drawn.

The formulas for carrying out statistical analyses, no matter how sophisticated and whether they are descriptive or inferential, can't distinguish between good data and bad data. Computers programmed with the formulas will happily draw data as instructed from a database, crunch the numbers as ordered, and spit out the results. It is usually impossible to tell by looking at them on the output screen or the printout whether those results have been obtained using good or bad data. You must do everything you can to ensure the highest quality of the data to be analyzed. That begins with careful attention to the earlier stages of the research process. These include formulating good questions or empirically falsifiable hypotheses, identifying relevant units of analysis and variables pertaining to them, developing valid and reliable operational definitions and measurements of those variables, formulating and executing an appropriate research design, gathering the data carefully, and entering them accurately. You must know the quality of the data being analyzed in order to know how to interpret the results of the statistical analyses. Remember: garbage in-garbage out.

Statistical analyses, including those done by computers, are not foolproof. Make no mistake—computers make far fewer errors than we do working with pen and pencil or a handheld calculator. But electronic bits do occasionally go astray, and other mechanical or electronic glitches do occur. In addition, the database stored in a computer's memory may be corrupted in a variety of ways. Also, we may inadvertently provide faulty instructions to the computer for the analysis we are seeking. In short, computers are incredibly accurate, but they are not perfect, and neither are the humans who tell them what to do. So, trust the computer output—but verify. Simple checks, some of which we have mentioned in previous chapters, will often detect that an analysis has gone awry.

Statisticians are always working on better ways of analyzing data and developing new statistical tests. Before you use or accept any new statistical procedure, it should be carefully reviewed to make sure its assumptions are consistent with the original research design, data collection, and question at hand. Any statistical innovation is likely to have its own strengths and weaknesses. Just because a new, easy-to-use statistic becomes available, it does not necessarily follow that it is either better than older procedures or applicable in a particular research situation.

Furthermore, the usefulness of our research should not be dependent on finding statistically significant results. Although it is certainly exciting to obtain statistical evidence that permits us to reject a null hypothesis and argue that our research hypothesis is supported, it is important to keep in mind that in terms of building a body of scientific knowledge, analyses that produce no statistically significant results are just as important as those that do. You may find it harder to publish statistically nonsignificant results, but such results, if valid, are just as important as statistically significant ones in terms of building our knowledge base.

Remember, too, that correlation is not causation. Just because changes in two or more variables occur together, it does not follow that changes in one or more of those variables cause changes in the others. The possibility of spurious relationships between or among variables always exists. Be on the lookout for the possible effects of variables not included and, therefore, not accounted for in the analysis.

Remember, too, that inferential statistics offer sophisticated and complex analyses, and, when used appropriately, they permit generalizations from samples to populations—truly enormous advantages. But when we avail ourselves of these advantages, we must be content with answers expressed as probabilities of Type I and Type II errors.

Even if you find a statistical analysis persuasive, it's always worth asking, "What else is true?" Properly interpreting the results of a statistical analysis requires not only understanding all aspects of the research process that produced them, but also the larger context within which they should be understood and/or applied. Results that are statistically significant may or may not be practically significant, for example. And although the results of an analysis may be valid, there are probably other valid "facts" that, if known, would reveal the limits of those results and/or change their interpretation in other, sometimes dramatic ways. Statistics never tell the whole story.

As we have noted on many occasions, many statistics other than those we have discussed in this text are available, and one or more of these may be better suited to your particular research situation and data analysis purposes. More advanced texts provide information about the appropriate applications for these additional statistical analysis options. It's also a good idea to ask for help in choosing the best statistical analyses to use, identifying their strengths and weaknesses, and interpreting the results. Many college and university faculties include statisticians who are happy to provide basic assistance free of charge. Your instructor in this course is a good resource. Be aware that asking what seems like a simple statistical question often requires answering several other questions about the research situation, such as how the data were gathered (e.g., the nature of the sampling, if any); the operational definitions of the variables (i.e., how the variables were measured and at what level of measurement); what, if anything, you know about the population, and so on. In fact, if your chosen adviser doesn't ask some follow-up questions, be wary! A dialogue, rather than a one-shot response, will be necessary in almost all cases. Less personal but informative online resources (college and university statistics instructors' sites, forums, etc.) are also available.

Finally, if you have made it this far in our text, congratulations! We knew you could do it. Did you make sense of this chapter? Could you have made sense of it if you had read it before you grappled with the previous chapters? If you have understood this chapter, you have accomplished the crucial task of learning some of the lingo—and, hence, part of the perspective—that statistics provide for making sense of things.

We hope you have gained an appreciation for what statistics and a variety of statistical analyses can (and cannot) do for you as a citizen of a local community, state, nation, and world, as well as in your chosen profession, whether as a practitioner or researcher. In short, we hope that in studying this text, you have acquired some of the knowledge and skills that will help you to become an ethical, informed, and critical producer and/or consumer of basic statistics.

Student Study Site

Visit the open-access student study site at **www.sagepub.com/fitzgerald** for access to several study tools including eFlashcards, web quizzes, and additional appendices as well as links to SAGE journal articles and audio, video and web resources.

Glossary

A

A The Y intercept in a logistic regression equation

a The y intercept in a bivariate or multivariate linear least squares equation; the value of y when all xs are zero.

α (alpha) In statistical significance testing, the significance level; the probability of rejecting a true null hypothesis.

Analysis of variance (ANOVA) A statistical test of differences among three or more means typically used when the independent variable is nominal or ordinal and the dependent variable is interval or ratio.

Appropriate time sequence In a causal argument, the requirement that the causal (independent) variable precedes the effect (dependent) variable in time; one of the three criteria for a causal inference.

Areas under the curve Portions of the space under a smooth frequency or percent distribution line graph; in sampling distributions, portions of the space under a smooth sampling distribution line graph that correspond to the probabilities of obtaining an observed test statistic value, usually assuming the null hypothesis is true.

Average deviation The arithmetic average of the differences between a distribution's mean score and each of the individual scores in the distribution.

B

b (beta) One of the two constants in bivariate or multivariate linear least squares equations, as in $y = a + bx$; a regression coefficient; a measure of how much y changes for each unit of change in x; the slope of a regression line. In multiple regression equations, partial slopes.

b* Standardized beta (b)

β (beta) Beta in a logistic regression equation.

β* Standardized beta in a logistic regression equation.

Backward stepwise regression A series of regression analyses that drops one or more variables or blocks of variables from the list of variables included in each successive regression analysis.

Bar graph A data display in which quantities (e.g., frequencies, percents) are represented by rectangular spaces ("bars") arranged vertically or horizontally in the graph space.

Before-after research design A research plan in which the researcher measures the dependent variable in a study group before the independent variable changes and then measures the dependent variable in the same study group again after the independent variable changes.

Before-after with control group design Often called the classic experimental research design; a research plan involving an experimental and a control group and in which the dependent variable is measured in both groups prior to and then again after the change in the independent variable in the experimental group.

Bell-shaped distribution A distribution that has the appearance of a bell; a unimodal distribution symmetric about its mean.

Best fitting line In linear least squares regression analysis, the line in a scattergram that minimizes the distance between it and the data points as measured parallel to the y axis.

Beta See b and $β$.

Beta weight A standardized beta.

Between-group sum of squares (BSS) In analysis of variance, the sum of the squared deviations of the group means from the grand mean; the explained sum of squares.

Between-group variance In analysis of variance, that portion of the total variance in the dependent variable explained by the independent variable.

Biased estimate An estimate of a population parameter when the mean of the sampling distribution for the corresponding sample statistic is not equivalent to the population parameter.

Bimodal distribution A distribution with two "humps" or modes.

Binomial distribution A distribution of outcomes or combinations of outcomes for two or more trials where each trial has only two possible outcomes.

Binomial logistic regression Logistic regression analysis for a dichotomous dependent variable.

Binomial probability distribution A distribution of probabilities useful as a sampling distribution for determining the probabilities of outcomes of a series of two or more trials, each trial having only two possible (and often equally probable) outcomes.

Bivariate analysis An analysis that includes only two variables.

C

Categorizing Placing units of analysis into groups based on their having at least one shared characteristic (variable value).

Causal chain A sequence of three or more variables, each causally related to the one that follows.

Causal inference Concluding that a causal relationship exists between or among variables; requires concomitant variation, appropriate time sequence, and elimination of other possible causal variables.

Cause/causality/causal relationship A relationship between or among variables satisfying the three criteria for a causal inference.

Cell A location in the grid of a cross-tabulation (contingency table) representing the intersection of one value of one variable and one value of the other variable used to construct the table.

Cell frequency The number appearing in the cell of a contingency table representing the frequency count of the units of analysis in the sample or population who possess the two values of the two variables that intersect in the cell.

Census Data gathered from all the units of analysis in a population.

Central limit theorem A mathematical theorem with several rules and principles used in constructing some sampling distributions.

Chi square (χ^2) An inferential statistic based on the differences between observed and expected cell frequencies; used to determine the probability of these differences if the null hypothesis is true.

Classic experimental design See *Before-after with control group design*.

Coefficient of multiple correlation (R) See *Multiple correlation coefficient*.

Coefficient of correlation See *Correlation coefficient*.

Coefficient of determination (r^2) A measure of the strength of the relationship between two variables; the proportion of the variance in the values of one variable statistically explained by changes in the values of another variable.

Coefficient of multiple determination (R^2) A measure of the strength of the relationship between one dependent variable and two or more independent variables taken together; the proportion of variance in one variable statistically explained by changes in the values of two or more other variables taken together.

Collapsing categories Combining two or more values of a variable, thus creating a smaller number of variable values to facilitate data analysis and presentation.

Column marginal frequencies The sum of the cell frequencies in each column of a contingency table.

Columns The vertical cells in a contingency table.

Concomitant variation Changes in variable values that occur together; a correlation between two or more variables; one of the three prerequisites of a causal inference.

Confidence interval The range of values between the confidence limits for an estimated population parameter calculated from sample statistics using inferential statistics, with a specified probability that the population parameter falls within the range.

Confidence level The probability of committing a Type I error in a statistical test of significance.

Confidence limits The smallest and largest values of the estimate of a population parameter calculated from sample statistics using inferential statistics, with a specified probability that the population parameter falls between these values.

Contingency table A two-dimensional grid in which the values of two variables are cross-tabulated.

Continuous variables Variables that can assume an infinite number of values.

Control group In the classic experimental design, a group of subjects (units of analysis) *not* exposed to a change in the hypothesized independent variable.

Control variable A potential independent variable whose values are held constant during an analysis in order to examine the effects of changes in the values of other independent variables on the dependent variable.

Conversion of raw data to ranks For the purposes of nonparametric statistical analysis of data measured at ordinal or higher levels, listing the raw data (the variable values for each unit of analysis) in ascending or descending order according to their measured values and then substituting corresponding consecutive numerical ranks according to their positions on the list.

Coordinates The variable values that define a data point, as in a scattergram.

Correction for continuity An adjustment in some statistical formulas for use with continuous data when the variables being analyzed are discrete rather than continuous.

Correlation Changes in variable values that occur together; see *Concomitant variation*.

Correlation analysis Data analysis that measures the strength and direction of relationships (covariation) between or among variables in a quantity ranging from –1 to +1 .

Correlation coefficient (*Pearson's r*) A measure of the strength and direction of the relationship between two variables that varies between –1 and +1; see also *Spearman's* ρ.

Correlation matrix A table in which all of the possible bivariate correlation coefficients among several variables are displayed.

Counting Determining the frequency with which some phenomenon (e.g., a variable value) occurs or is observed.

Covariance See *Correlation*.

Cross-product (of *x* and *y*) The multiplication of the paired coordinates of a data point.

Critical region See *Rejection region*.

Critical value The minimum value of a test statistic for a finding of statistical significance at a specified significance level.

Cross-tabulation A procedure for displaying data in a rectangular grid consisting of cells, cell frequencies, and marginal frequencies; often used to examine whether two variables are related.

Cumulative frequency distribution bar graph A bar graph in which each successive bar represents the sum of its frequency and the frequencies preceding it.

Cumulative frequency distribution line graph A line graph in which each successive point represents the sum of its frequency and the frequencies preceding it.

Cumulative frequency distribution table A table in which frequencies are added successively.

Cumulative percent distribution bar graph A bar graph in which each successive bar represents the sum of its percents and the percents preceding it.

Cumulative percent distribution line graph A line graph in which each successive point represents the sum of its percents and the percents preceding it.

Cumulative percent distribution table A table in which percents are added successively.

Curvilinear relationship A relationship between variables such that the values change with respect to each other but not in a linear fashion; for example, as the values of one variable go up, the values of the other variable at first go up and then go down.

D

D (difference score) The difference between the pre- and postmeasurements of a dependent variable for a study group, such as the experimental group in an experimental research design.

D_ρ A difference score used in Spearman's rho analysis for ordinal (rank) data.

Data (pl.); *datum* (sing.) The observation(s) or measurement(s) researchers or others record. Data are compiled, analyzed, and summarized using descriptive and/or inferential statistics, searching for meaningful patterns.

Database An organized collection of quantitative data and/or codes.

Data point A point in a graph representing the intersection of two or more variable values.

Deciles The variable values that lie at the nine division points when a data array is divided into 10 equal-sized groups of variable values.

Decimal A mathematical quantity in which proportions of less than whole numbers are expressed in tenths, hundredths, thousandths, and so on, the specific proportions determined by the number of places to the right of a decimal point.

Degrees of freedom A statistic's freedom to vary; quantities used in identifying an appropriate sampling distribution for an inferential statistical test.

Dependence between random samples When the probability of selecting a unit of analysis for one sample influences the probability of selecting a unit of analysis for another sample.

Dependence within a random sample When the probability of selecting one unit of analysis for a sample influences the probability of selecting another unit of analysis for the same sample.

Dependent events (outcomes) Outcomes of a trial or series of trials when the probability of one outcome or combination of outcomes occurring influences the probability of another outcome or combination of outcomes occurring.

Dependent random samples See *Dependence between random samples.*

Dependent variable A variable hypothesized by the researcher to be an effect of an independent (causal) variable.

Description Identifying the attributes or characteristics of a phenomenon.

Descriptive statistics Statistics that characterize or summarize the distribution of a variable's values, probabilities, or a relationship between or among variables.

Diagonals In a contingency table, the cells that lie on or near a straight line drawn from the upper left to the lower right corners or from the upper right to the lower left corners of a cross-tabulation.

Difference score In the *t* test for dependent random samples, the difference between the pre- and postmeasurements of the dependent variable in the experimental group.

Directional hypothesis A hypothesis that specifies which of two descriptive or inferential statistics of a particular kind (e.g., frequency counts or means) will be larger than the other.

Discrete variables Variables that can assume only a finite number of whole number values.

Due diligence (in handling and analyzing data and reporting the results of statistical analyses) Doing everything one can to create an accurate and complete data set; choose appropriate statistical analyses; report all relevant results; and acknowledge limitations of any kind in the data, analyses, and research reports.

Dummy variable A nominal- or ordinal-level variable whose values are included in a least squares multiple regression or correlation analysis.

E

Effect Changes in a variable caused by changes in another variable; in analysis of variance, the between-group sum of squares.

Elaboration analysis A strategy for testing the influence of a third variable on a relationship observed between two variables by introducing a third, control variable and creating partial contingency tables; helps determine if the original observed (zero-order) relationship is causal or spurious and, if causal, the nature of the relationships among the three variables.

Eliminate (control for) other possible causal variables In a causal argument, the requirement that the relationship between or among variables is not spurious; one of the three criteria for a causal inference.

Empirically falsifiable hypotheses Hypotheses whose falseness can be demonstrated by applying scientific methods and assembling empirical evidence, such as observing, counting, and measuring.

Error The difference between an observed and a predicted measurement; in analysis of variance, the within-group sum of squares; in least squares regression analysis, the distance from the regression line or plane to a data point.

Error of estimate See *Residual error.*

Estimation See *Parameter estimation.*

Event An outcome of a trial.

Evidence-based best practices Procedures that have proven through scientific research to be most likely to achieve desired results.

Exhaustive categories (or variable values) A list of variable values that includes all possible values of a particular variable.

Exhaustive list of possible outcomes A list that includes all of the possible outcomes of a single trial or combinations of outcomes of a series of trials.

Exp(B) A beta expressed as an odds ratio, interpreted as the predicted change in *y* for every unit change in *x* in logistic regression analysis.

Expected frequency In chi-square analysis, the frequency expected in a contingency table cell if the null hypothesis is true.

Experimental design See *Before-after with control group design.*

Experimental group In an experimental research design, the group that is exposed to the change in the independent variable.

Explained sum of squares The amount of the squared deviations of *y* from the mean of *y* ($\bar{y}$) accounted for by the variation in *x*; in analysis of variance, a synonym for between-group sum of squares.

Explained variance The amount of variance in *y* accounted for by variance in *x*; in analysis of variance, a synonym for between-group variance.

Explanation In elaboration analysis, the result when the relationship between the two zero-order table variables disappears in all of the first-order partial tables, the control variable is related to both zero-order variables, and the control variable occurs with/before the independent and dependent variables in time; the zero-order relationship is spurious. (See also *Causal relationship.*)

F

F distributions The sampling distributions of the *F* statistic.

F statistic In analysis of variance, the statistic calculated and tested for statistical significance.

First-order partial relationships The relationships indicated in the contingency tables constructed when a third variable is introduced in elaboration analysis.

First-order partial tables In elaboration analysis, contingency tables created by introducing a third variable (a control variable or test factor) into the analysis of the relationship between two other variables. One partial contingency table displaying the relationship between the two original variables is created for each value of the control or test factor variable.

Forward stepwise regression A regression analysis that adds variables or blocks of variables to successive regression analyses.

Fraction A quantity expressed as one number divided by another; represented as two numbers divided by a line, with the number in front of or above the line called the numerator and the number following or below the line called the denominator, as in ½.

Frequency count The number of observations or units of analysis having a particular variable value.

Frequency distribution bar graph A bar graph with bars representing the frequencies with which each of the values of a particular variable appear in the data set being analyzed.

Frequency distribution line graph A line graph with points representing the frequencies with which each of the values of a particular variable appear in the data set being analyzed.

Frequency distribution table A table showing the number of observations or units of analysis for each variable value.

Frequency polygon A line graph consisting of ordinal or higher level data points connected by straight lines. See *frequency distribution line graph.*

G

Garbage in-garbage out An expression emphasizing that the quality of the results of a statistical analysis depends, in large part, on the quality of the execution of other stages in the research process.

Gaussian curve or distribution See *Normal distribution.*

Goodness-of-fit The degree to which a distribution of observed variable values matches a model distribution, often represented by an equation, sometimes derived from probability theory and usually based on a null hypothesis.

Grand mean In analysis of variance, the mean of all the dependent variable value scores in all study groups combined.

Grouped scores Variable values that have been combined to create a smaller number of variable values for purposes of analysis; see *Collapsing categories.*

H

H The statistic calculated and tested for statistical significance in Kruskal-Wallis analysis.

Heteroscedastic (heteroscedasticity) Inequality among variances, usually of a dependent variable.

Histogram A frequency distribution bar graph for a variable measured at the ordinal level or above.

Homoscedastic (homoscedasticity) Equality among variances, usually of a dependent variable.

Hypothesis An assertion about the distribution of a variable or about the relationships (or lack thereof) between or among variables.

Hypothesis testing Examining empirical evidence to determine if that evidence supports or does not support an assertion about the distribution of a variable or about the relationships (or lack thereof) between or among variables.

I

Independence between random samples When the probability of selecting a unit of analysis for one sample has no influence on the probability of selecting a unit of analysis for another sample.

Independence within a random sample The condition in which the probability of selecting a unit of analysis from a population for a sample does not influence the probability of selecting any other unit of analysis for the sample.

Independent events (outcomes) Events or outcomes of a trial or series of trials when the probability of one outcome or combination of outcomes occurring has no influence on the probability of another outcome or combination of outcomes occurring.

Independent random samples Samples characterized by independence between random samples.

Independent variable A variable whose changes in values are hypothesized by the researcher to cause changes in the variable values of a dependent variable.

Inferential statistics A variety of statistical analyses based on probability theory, random sampling, and a particular set of assumptions for each type. They permit testing results for statistical significance, estimating population parameters, and calculating confidence intervals.

Interaction (effects) Effects on a dependent variable of two or more independent variables that are *not* additive; when a relationship between an independent and a dependent variable is different in strength or direction for the different values of one or more other independent variables.

Interpretation In elaboration analysis, the result when the relationship between the two zero-order variables disappears in all of the first-order partial tables, the control variable is related to both zero-order variables, and the control variable is an intervening variable.

Interval estimate A range of values around a sample statistic (for example, a range around the sample mean value of a particular variable) used to estimate the value of the corresponding population parameter.

Interval-level measurement A measurement scale with an arbitrary zero point but equal distances (intervals) between any two adjacent units on the measurement scale.

Interval (level) variable A variable measured at the interval level.

Intervening variable A causal variable that occurs in time between an independent and a dependent variable, creating a causal chain of variables.

K

Kruskal-Wallis H test (K-W H test) A nonparametric test of statistical significance for differences among three or more mean ranks.

K-W BSS_{obs} In Kruskal-Wallis analysis, the between-group (sample) sum of squares.

Kurtosis The degree to which a distribution is peaked or flat.

L

Least (sum of) squares The minimum sum of squared deviations of observed variable values (scores) from the corresponding predicted variable values, as in the least (sum of squares) regression line.

Leptokurtic distribution A relatively peaked distribution.

Linear relationship A relationship between variables such that the values of the two variables tend to change together at the same rate. When plotted on a scattergram, the data points form an approximately straight line that runs diagonally up or down across the graph space.

Listwise (casewise) deletion In multivariate analysis, the elimination of a unit of analysis from all regression analyses if data are missing for that unit of analysis on one or more variables.

Log likelihood In logistic regression analysis, the natural log ($\log_e$) of the predicted odds of a success.

Logistic regression A type of multiple regression analysis used when the dependent variable is nominal.

Logits In logistic regression analysis, the natural log equivalent of the odds $p/(1-p)$.

M

Main effects In least squares multiple regression, the effects of an x on y, controlling for the effects of other independent variables included in the analysis.

Mann-Whitney U Test A nonparametric test for the statistical significance of a difference between two sets of ranks.

Margin of error The confidence limits for a parameter estimate, expressed as the point estimate plus or minus a quantity.

Marginal frequency The sum of a row or a column in a contingency table.

Matching A procedure for selecting units of analysis for two samples on the basis of shared characteristics, thereby ensuring, for example, that subjects in control and experimental groups are as similar as possible on at least some potential independent variables.

Maximum likelihood estimation In logistic regression analysis, the iterative estimation process that results in identifying the values of the constants A and β of a logistic regression equation that best predicts the values of the logit(Y)s.

Mean The arithmetic average of the variable values (scores) that make up a distribution.

Mean squares A sum of squares divided by n.

Mean squares between In analysis of variance, the mean of the between-group sum of squares.

Mean squares within In analysis of variance, the mean of the within-group sum of squares.

Measures of central tendency Characterizations of variable value distributions focusing on the distributions' "typical" variable values; means, medians, and modes.

Measures of dispersion Characterizations of variable value distributions focusing on the distributions' "spread"; ranges, standard deviations, and variances.

Measures of location (of a score in a distribution) Ways of identifying the location of a score (variable value) in an array of scores that indicate how many scores in the array fall above or below the score; quantiles.

Measuring A procedure for determining specific attribute(s) of units of analysis or for determining to what extent or degree specific attributes characterize units of analysis.

Median The score (variable value) in a distribution of scores above which and below which half of the scores are found; the score occupying the middle position in the array of scores.

Mesokurtic distribution A distribution that is neither flat nor peaked.

Missing data Absence of data on particular variables and/or for particular units of analysis; creates problems of various kinds in data analysis.

Mode The most frequently occurring variable value (score) in a distribution of scores.

Model In regression and correlation analysis, a particular set of independent variables included in an analysis; the equation representing the relationships among the variables included in the analysis.

Multicollinearity High bivariate correlations between independent variables in a multiple regression or correlation analysis; may distort the results of such analyses.

Multimodal distribution A distribution of variable values (scores) with more than one mode.

Multiple causation Several conditions causally related to a single other condition, with each contributing separately or in combination to the determination of that condition.

Multiple correlation analysis A correlation analysis that includes more than two independent variables.

Multiple correlation coefficient (R) A measure of the strength and direction of the relationship between one variable and two or more other variables taken together; varies between +1 and −1.

Multiple regression analysis A regression analysis that includes two or more independent variables.

Multivariate analysis Analyses that include three or more variables.

Mutually exclusive possible categories (variable values) For any particular variable, a set of categories (variable values) in which there is one and only one category or value for each unit of analysis.

N

Natural log (log$_e$, L$_n$) A logarithm with a base of e (2.7182818 . . .).

Negative (linear) relationship A relationship between variables in which as the variable values of one variable go up, the values of the other variable go down at a constant rate.

Negatively Skewed The skew of a distribution toward the lower values of a variable.

Nominal-level measurement A level of measurement in which variables can be placed in mutually exclusive, exhaustive categories, but cannot be ordered further.

Nondirectional hypotheses Hypotheses that do not specify which value of a population parameter will be larger.

Nonparametric (inferential) statistics Inferential statistics that do not assume a normal distribution of variable values in a population (that is, they are distribution free) and are applicable with variables measured at the nominal or ordinal levels.

Normal curve A theoretical, smooth, unimodal, symmetrical curve with special characteristics useful in a variety of statistical calculations.

Normal distribution A unimodal, symmetrical distribution with special characteristics useful in a variety of statistical calculations.

Null hypothesis The hypothesis that there is no relationship between two or more variables; used to generate sampling distributions for testing hypotheses in inferential statistics.

Number of ranks The number of rank order positions, which equals the number of units of analysis included in a set of ranks.

O

Observed between-group (sample) mean rank sum of squares (K-W BSS$_{obs}$) In Kruskal-Wallis H analysis, the explained mean sum of squares calculated from the sample data.

Observed frequency In chi-square analysis, the number of observations in a cell of a contingency table.

Odds The chances (probability) of some event occurring, expressed as the number of times it is expected to occur in relation to the number of times it is not expected to occur.

Odds ratio In logistic regression analysis, the ratio of the probability of success to the probability of failure.

OLS See *Ordinary least squares*.

One-tailed significance test A directional hypothesis test where the rejection region is located in only one of the tails of the sampling distribution.

One-way analysis of variance A test for differences among means involving only one independent variable measured at the nominal or ordinal level.

Operational definition The specification of exactly how the researcher will categorize and/or measure variables.

Ordinal-level measurement A level of measurement in which it is possible not only to categorize but to rank units of analysis according to the degree to which a certain attribute is present.

Ordinary least squares (OLS) A Pearson's linear correlation or regression analysis in which a linear model that minimizes the dependent variable sum of squares is identified.

Outcome(s) The results of a trial or series of trials; also called events.

Outliers Relative to other scores in the distribution, a few very high or very low variable values (scores) in a distribution or scattergram that distort sums of squares calculations.

P

Pair matching Dependent sample selection in which, if one of a pair of units of analysis is chosen for a sample, the other member of the pair is also selected for a sample.

Pairwise deletion In multivariate analysis, the elimination of a unit of analysis from a regression analysis if data are missing for a particular variable included in the analysis.

Parameter See *Population parameter*.

Parametric (inferential) statistics Inferential statistics that assume a normal distribution of variable values in a population and measurement at the interval or ratio levels.

Partial beta A partial regression coefficient.

Partial analysis In elaboration analysis, breaking a bivariate zero order relationship into parts based on the values of a third variable.

Partial correlation analysis Linear least squares analysis of the effect of one independent variable on a dependent variable, holding one or more other independent variables constant.

Partial correlation coefficient The amount of variance in the dependent variable accounted for by one independent variable, holding constant other independent variables included in the analysis.

Partial regression analysis Linear least squares multivariate analysis that predicts the value of dependent variable on the basis of the value of another independent variable, holding constant other independent variables included in the analysis.

Partial regression coefficient A beta or slope in a least squares regression equation.

Partial slope A beta or slope in a least squares multivariate regression equation.

Percent(s) A standardized mathematical quantity in which parts of a whole are expressed as proportions with a base of 100.

Percentaging in the direction of the independent variable Using the marginal frequencies corresponding to the values of the independent variable to convert cell frequencies to corresponding percentages in contingency tables.

Percentiles The variable values that lie at the 99 division points when a data array is divided into 100 equal-sized groups of variable values; often expressed in decimal, as well as whole, numbers, as in the 95.25th percentile.

Physical control of variables Procedures for controlling potential causal variables implemented by the researcher before and during the data-gathering research process, maximized in laboratory research where the researcher controls the setting in which the research takes place, and sample selection strategies such as matching; contrasts with *Statistical control of variables.*

Pictograph A data display using icons in different numbers or different sizes to represent quantities, usually frequency counts or percents, pertaining to the values of a variable.

Pie graph A data display using segments (slices) of a circle (pie) to represent quantities, usually frequency counts or percents, pertaining to the values of a variable.

Plagiarism Claiming others' ideas, work, or words as one's own; failing to give credit to others for their words, work, or ideas used in one's own publications.

Platykurtic distribution A relatively flat distribution.

Point estimate A sample statistic used as a single-value estimate of the corresponding population parameter.

Population The entire group of units of analysis included in an analysis; the entire group of units of analysis from which a particular sample of units of analysis is drawn.

Population parameter The value of a population statistic, such as a measure of central tendency or dispersion.

Positive (linear) relationship A relationship between two variables such that as the values of one variable go up, the values of the other variable go up at the same rate.

Positively Skewed The skew of a distribution toward the higher variable values.

Postmeasurement In experimental design, the measurement of the dependent variable in both the experimental and control groups after the experimental group has been exposed to a change in the value of the independent variable.

Power (of a statistical test) One minus the probability of a Type II error.

Practical significance The implications of applying the results of a statistical analysis in the real world; contrasted with *Statistical significance.*

Prediction Forecasts of variable values based on statistics about their past and/or present values.

Predictive analyses Analyses that calculate predictions of variable values.

Predictor blueprint In logistic regression analysis, a particular combination of independent variable values used to predict a value of the dependent variable.

Predictor variables Independent variables whose values are used in different combinations to predict the values of the dependent variable.

Premeasurement In experimental research design, the measurement of the dependent variable in both the experimental and control groups before the experimental group is exposed to the change in the value of the independent variable.

Probability The likelihood of an outcome or combination of outcomes occurring from a trial or series of trials, usually expressed as a decimal (e.g., .05, .001).

Probability distribution A distribution of the likelihoods of the possible outcomes or combination of outcomes from a trial or series of trials.

Probability theory A branch of mathematics used to construct sampling distributions for use in inferential statistics.

Proportion A mathematical quantity based on the relation of parts to wholes, often expressed as decimals.

Proportional area bar graph A bar graph in which the proportion of the graph's total area occupied by a given bar is the same as the proportion of the total quantity (e.g., total number or 100% of the observations included in the graph) represented by that bar.

Q

Q A statistic whose sampling distribution is used in Tukey's HSD test.

Quantile One of three measures of location (quartiles, deciles, percentiles) of a score (variable value) in an array of scores.

Quartile The variable values that lie at the three division points when a data array is divided into four equal-sized groups of variable values.

Quasi-experimental design Research plans that have the basic elements of an experimental design, but in which the researcher has less than ideal control of, for example, the study environment, selection of units of analysis, and/or changes in the independent variables (e.g., program evaluations).

R

r Pearson's correlation coefficient.

r^2 See *Coefficient of determination*.

R^2 See *Coefficient of multiple determination*.

Random experiment A trial or series of trials in which all of the possible outcomes are equally likely.

Random sample A sample drawn from a population in such a way that each unit of analysis and each combination of units in the population has an equal chance of being selected for the sample.

Range The lowest and the highest scores (variable values) in a distribution.

Rate A mathematical quantity that expresses the frequency of an event in relation to a fixed unit of measurement, often time or population (e.g., "per hour" or "per 1,000").

Ratio A mathematical quantity that expresses the relative frequencies or proportions constituting a whole, as in women in the group outnumbered the men by a ratio of 2 to 1.

Ratio-level measurement A level of measurement with the properties of nominal, ordinal, and interval measurement and, in addition, an absolute zero point.

Raw data The variable values originally recorded and stored in a database; data that have not been processed by applying statistical calculations.

Regression analysis Least squares analysis with the purpose of predicting the values of a dependent variable from the values of one or more independent values.

Regression coefficient See *Beta*.

Regression equation An equation used to predict the values of y from the values of x.

Regression line A straight line that best represents the data points in a scattergram; technically, the line that minimizes the distance between it and the data points in the scattergram, the distances measured parallel to the y axis; see also *Best fitting line*.

Regression of y on x In a regression analysis, the expression indicating that values of the dependent variable (y) are being predicted by the values of the independent variable (x) using a best fitting regression line defined as minimizing the squared deviations of the observed variable values from the line measured parallel to the y axis.

Regression plane Similar to a regression line, except that the values of two independent variables are being used in combination to predict the value of the dependent variable using a best fitting two-dimensional surface (plane).

Rejection region(s) Area(s) under a sampling distribution's curve (and the corresponding range[s] of statistical test values, such as the values of t or F) such that if the calculated test statistic value falls within it (them), the null hypothesis will be rejected.

Relative frequency A percent.

Repeated measurement matching A procedure that involves measuring the same group of units of analysis more than once, as in the pre- and postmeasurement of the experimental group in an experimental research design; when used with random sampling, it creates, in effect, two dependent random samples.

Replication The repetition of a study previously done; in elaboration analysis, the result when the relationship between the two zero-order table variables remains the same in all of the first-order partial tables.

Research design A plan for carrying out research, especially including the number of groups or samples to be included, the times at which the independent and dependent variables will change (or be changed) and the times at which the independent and dependent variables will be measured.

Research hypothesis The hypothesis that two variables are related; in inferential statistics, it is tested indirectly by testing the null hypothesis.

Residual The difference between the predicted value of a variable and the observed value. See *Error of estimate*.

Rho (ρ) Spearman's rank order correlation coefficient.

ρ^2 Spearman's coefficient of determination.

Row marginal frequencies The sum of the cell frequencies in each row of a contingency table.

Rows The horizontal cells in a contingency table.

$r_{xy \cdot T}$ A partial correlation; the correlation of x and y, holding a third variable (T) constant.

S

Sample A group of units of analysis drawn from a population and used to represent the population for statistical purposes.

Sample statistic The value of a statistic, such as a measure of central tendency or dispersion, calculated from the variable values in a sample.

Sampling The process of selecting some units of analysis to represent the population of units of analysis from which they are drawn.

Sampling distribution An empirically or mathematically derived distribution of sample statistics, usually assuming a large (ultimately, an infinite) number of random samples drawn from the same population; used as a probability distribution for tests of statistical significance.

Sampling error In inferential statistics, the difference between the value of a sample statistic and the value of the corresponding population parameter due to randomization, as in random sampling.

Sampling frame A list of the units of analysis in a population from which a sample is to be drawn.

Scale (of a graph) The amount of space on the horizontal and vertical axes allocated to each variable value or unit of measurement.

Scattergram A data display consisting of a two-dimensional space defined by two axes at right angles and data points within the graphic space.

Segmented bar graph A bar graph in which each bar representing the value of one variable is subdivided according to the values of one or more additional variables.

Set (combination) of outcomes A mutually exclusive and exhaustive list of the possible combination of outcomes from 2 or more trials.

Significance level The probability set by the researcher that determines whether the researcher will accept or reject a null hypothesis; the probability of making a Type I error.

Simple random sampling See *Random sampling*.

Size changing icon pictograph A pictograph in which differences in quantities (usually frequencies or percents) are represented by differences in the size of icons rather than in the number of icons.

Skewed distribution A distribution with variable values (scores) bunched toward one tail or the other; a distribution that is not symmetrical.

Skewed to the left See negatively skewed.

Skewed to the right See positively skewed.

Slope In least squares regression analysis, the slant of the regression line, representing the amount of change in the dependent variable for every unit of change in the independent variable.

Spearman's rho (ρ) analysis Spearman's analysis of the correlation between two sets of ranks.

Specification In elaboration analysis, the result when the relationship between the two zero-order variables disappears in *some* but not all of the first-order partial tables and the control variable is *not* related to at least one of the zero-order table variables.

Spurious relationship An observed relationship between two variables that is not a causal relationship between them (e.g., see *Explanation* in elaboration analysis).

Standard deviation The square root of the average of the squared deviations from the mean.

Standard error The standard deviation of a sampling distribution.

Standard error of estimate See standard error.

Standard normal curve A normal curve with a mean of 0 and a standard deviation of 1.0.

Standard score A score computed by subtracting a distribution's mean score from a given score and dividing by the sample standard deviation; a score in a standard normal distribution.

Standardized beta See *Beta weight*; a beta that permits comparisons with other standardized betas in a regression equation.

Standardized size multiple icon pictographs A pictograph in which differences in quantities (usually frequencies or percents) are represented by differences in the number of icons, rather than in the size of the icons.

Statistical control (of variables) The control of variables exercised during the analysis process.

Statistical explanation The amount of variance in the dependent variable accounted for by the variance in the independent variable(s); refers only to correlations, which are not necessarily causal relationships.

Statistical significance Assessment of the results of an inferential statistical analysis on the basis of the probability that a particular test statistic would be observed if the null hypothesis is true; when the results indicate low probabilities (usually .05 or .01 or less) of such an occurrence, the results are assessed to be statistically significant; contrasted with *Practical significance*.

Statistics Any of a number of different kinds of quantities used to describe, predict, analyze, and test for statistical significance.

Stepwise regression Two or more successive least squares regression analyses in which independent variables are added to or dropped from the previous analysis.

Student's t test A statistical test used to determine the probability that mean values of the same variable from two different randomly selected samples came from the same population.

Sum of ranks The sum of a set of ranks.

Sum of squared deviations from the mean The sum of the squared differences between each observed variable value and the mean of the distribution of that variable's values.

Sum of squares See *Sum of squared deviations from the mean*.

Symmetric distribution A distribution with the same shape on either side of its mean.

T

t sampling distributions The sampling distributions for the t statistic.

t statistic The statistic used, among other ways, to test an observed difference between two sample means for statistical significance.

Table A two-dimensional grid consisting of cells into which statistics, such as frequency counts and percents, are entered.

Tails (of a distribution) The portions of the area under a distribution's curve lying to the far left and far right, usually representing the relatively low frequencies (or percents or probabilities) of the lower and higher variable values in the distribution.

Test factor A third variable introduced into an analysis to examine its effect on the relationship between two other variables; used in elaboration analysis and partial correlation and regression analysis.

Test of independence A statistical test to determine the probability that two observed outcomes are independent of (not related to) each other.

Theoretical normal curve A normal curve representing, for example, the distribution of results from an infinite number of random trials or samples.

Total sum of squares (TSS) In analysis of variance, the sum of the squared deviation of each variable value (score) from the grand mean for all units of analysis included in the study.

Total variance In analysis of variance, the sum of the between group and the within group variance.

Trend graph A graph, usually a line graph, showing changes in particular variable values or in measures of central tendency or dispersion for a particular variable over time.

Trial In probability theory, a random experiment whose outcomes or combination of outcomes are assigned probabilities.

t test See *Student's t test*.

Tukey's HSD test After a statistically significant finding from an analysis of variance, a test to determine which pairs of sample means are significantly different.

Two-tailed significance test A nondirectional hypothesis test where rejection regions are evenly divided between the two tails of the sampling distribution.

Two-way analysis of variance An analysis of variance involving two independent variables.

Type I error Rejecting a true null hypothesis.

Type II error Accepting a false null hypothesis.

U

U The test statistic used in the nonparametric Mann-Whitney test for the difference between the means of two sets of ranks.

Unbiased estimate An estimate of a population parameter when the mean of the sampling distribution for the corresponding sample statistic is equivalent to the population parameter; an unbiased estimate may, nevertheless, be incorrect.

Unexplained sum of squares In analysis of variance, the within-group sum of squares; in general, the sum of the squared residuals.

Unexplained variance In analysis of variance, the within-group variance; in general, the variance of the residuals.

Unimodal distribution A distribution with one mode.

Units of analysis The persons, places, things, or events whose characteristics or attributes (variables) are being studied; the elements of a sample or population being studied.

Univariate analysis Analysis involving a single variable, usually the distribution of the values of that variable.

Univariate descriptive statistics Statistics used to describe the distribution of one variable, such as the measures of central tendency and dispersion.

V

Variable An attribute or characteristic whose aspects or dimensions can vary from one unit of analysis to another.

Variable deletion In multiple regression analysis, the elimination of a variable from a regression analysis if data on that variable are missing for any unit of analysis.

Variable interaction See *Interaction*.

Variable values The values (categories, ranks, or measurements) that a particular variable may assume or may be observed.

Variance A measure of the dispersion of scores in a distribution computed by squaring the difference or deviation from the mean of each score in the distribution, summing these squared deviations, and dividing the sum by the total number of scores in the distribution.

W

Within-group sum of squares (WSS) In analysis of variance, the unexplained sum of squares; the sum of the sum of the squared deviations of each score in a sample (group) from the mean of that sample for all the samples included in the analysis.

Within-group variance In analysis of variance, that part of the total variance in the dependent variable unexplained by the variance in the independent variable.

X

x The symbol for an independent variable.

x axis The axis of a graph on which the possible values of the independent variable are arrayed.

x,y The coordinates of a data point.

y.x The regression of y on x.

$\bar{X}_{K\text{-}W\ BSS}$ In Kruskal-Wallis H analysis, the mean of the sampling distribution of K-W BSS.

Y

Y In a logistic regression equation, the dependent variable.

y The symbol for a dependent variable.

y axis The axis of a graph on which the possible values of the dependent variable are arrayed.

Y intercept In logistic regression analysis, the value of Y when all Xs are zero.

y intercept In least squares regression analyses, the point where the regression line crosses the y axis; the value of y when x is zero.

y.x The symbol for the regression of y on x.

Z

z score A standard normal score; a score in a standard normal distribution.

z-score table A table indicating the areas under the standard normal curve that correspond to the frequencies, percents, or probabilities with which particular z scores or ranges of z scores occur.

Zero-order relationship (table) In elaboration analysis, the table showing the original relationship, if any, between two variables; this relationship will be examined further through the introduction of one or more control variables and the creation of partial tables.

Answers to Questions

CHAPTER 2

5.

The establishment of a causal relationship between variables requires that three conditions be met: (1) concomitant variation; (2) appropriate time sequence of changes in the values of the variables, and (3) the elimination of other possible causal variables. Causation is difficult to establish because, while strong evidence that the first two conditions can usually be obtained, satisfying the third condition (the elimination of all other possible causal variables) is essentially impossible to achieve. Why? Because what looks like a causal relationship between two variables may always, in fact, be the result of a relationship between each of these two variables and a third variable. That is, the observed relationship between the original two variables may be spurious.

Concomitant variation (correlation) is not enough to establish a causal relationship between variables, because the other two conditions must be met and because observed concomitant variation may be spurious.

11.

Due diligence must be exercised in all phases of the research process, including determining who or what will be studied; gathering, recording, and analyzing data; and in reporting the results of the analysis. Care must be taken not to introduce biases in the initial selection of subjects and and/or in the removal of subjects from the study group during the analysis. The accuracy of recording raw data and entering the data in a data base must be checked and verified (data cleaning). Appropriate types of statistical analyses must be selected, depending on the variable's measurement level(s), the type of group being studied (population, random sample, or non-random sample). Data analysis must be performed as accurately as possible and results must be verified in whatever ways may be available. When discussing results, missing data and how they were dealt with in the analysis must be reported. Results must be presented completely and honestly, including informing readers of any peculiarities in the data or analysis that might affect the results and/or their interpretation. Also, you should identify the financial underwriters/sponsors of the research in order to consider what untoward influence they might have had on any aspects of the research process.

Remember: garbage in-garbage out!

CHAPTER 3

3.

The contour of the "curve" in a cumulative frequency line graph indicates how the corresponding underlying frequencies are changing. First, note that cumulative frequency curves are either flat or rising; they never fall. Relatively flat sections of a cumulative frequency line graph are generated when the cumulative frequencies are rising little if at all, which means the frequencies corresponding to those sections are zero or near zero; slowly rising sections of the curve indicate the corresponding frequencies are somewhat greater than zero. Steeply rising sections indicate the corresponding frequencies are rising rapidly. Sections curving up indicate gradually rising corresponding frequencies. Sections curving toward flat indicate gradually falling corresponding frequencies. The same general descriptions would hold for the percents in cumulative percent distributions. The contour of the entire cumulative frequency or percent curve, therefore, reflects the general shape of the underlying frequency or percent distribution.

CHAPTER 4

5.

a. The sentence category corresponding to the median is found as follows:

Divide the total number of cases 227/2 = 113.5 this is the point in the array of the data where half the sentences are higher and half are lower. Beginning with the frequency associated with the shortest sentence (sentence of 1–7 days; frequency of 15), the frequencies in the table associated with consecutively higher sentence lengths are added until the cumulative frequency of 113.5 is included in a sentence length frequency category. The length of sentence category associated with this cumulative frequency (31–45 days) is then the median length of sentence category for this distribution.

The sentencing category corresponding to the mode is also the 31–45 sentencing category because this is the length of sentence category that occurs most frequently in this distribution.

The sentencing category corresponding to the 78th percentile of the data is found as follows: First, similar to what we did in locating the median sentence length category, we determine how many sentences constitute 78% of the sentences. There are 227 scores, so 227 × .78 = 177.06, which indicates that, when we consecutively add the frequencies and the cumulative frequency includes 177.06, we will have reached the sentence length category that includes the 78th percentile. The sentence length category that includes the 78th percentile is the 61–90 day category.

The mean length of sentence is found as follows: First, we find the range and midpoint of the range of each sentence length category. For the 1–7 = day sentence length category, these would be: range of 7 − 1 = 6 days; the midpoint of this range would be 6/2 = 3.

The same procedure is followed for each of the other sentence length categories, yielding the following midpoints for all 9 sentence length categories:

3, 3, 3.5, 3.5, 7, 7, 14.5, 14.5, 14.5

Next, we sum each of these midpoints and the lowest value of the corresponding sentence length category. For the 1–7 = day sentence length category, we would sum the lowest sentence length in the category (which is 1 day) and the midpoint for this category we have just calculated (which is 3), giving us 4. Following this procedure for each of the sentence length categories, we have

4, 11, 18.5, 26.5, 38, 53, 75.5, 105.5, 135.5

Next, we multiply each of these values by its corresponding frequency. For example, for the 1–7 = day sentence length category, the sentence length is 4 and the corresponding frequency is 15; 4 × 15 = 60. Following the same procedure for each of the sentence length categories, we have:

60, 198, 407, 927.5, 1,976, 1,643, 1,887.5, 1,688, 1,761.5

We then sum these numbers, which equal 10,545.5, and divide by the total number of sentenced individuals, which in this case is 227.

This yields an estimated mean length of sentence of 46.47 days (rounded) for this group of offenders.

b. The mean of 46.47 days is the estimated arithmetic average length of sentence for the 227 convicts in the study. The accuracy of the estimate depends on a number of assumptions about the distribution of the sentences within the sentence categories, assumptions that are rarely met.

The category of 31–45 days is the modal sentence length category of this distribution. It tells us which sentence length category occurs with the highest frequency in the distribution. It may or may not include the actual mode—that is, the exact sentence length that occurs most frequently in the distribution. In this case, the modal category does not include the estimated mean sentence length.

The median length of sentence category, which is also 31–45 days, is the category that includes the sentence length that lies in the center of the array of the 227 sentence lengths included in the table. It tells us that about half of the sentences exceed 31–45 days and about half are less than 31–45 days.

c. The distribution of length of sentence categories is unimodal, but not quite symmetric. You can tell by comparing the sizes of the frequencies for the lower and higher sentence length categories.

CHAPTER 5

7.

Summing the z scores in the table, paying attention to their signs, yields a sum of 0. Dividing 0 by any number (including the n of 36 in the table) equals 0, so the mean of the z scores equals 0. Following Formula 4.3, squaring the deviations of each of the z scores from the mean and summing those squared deviations yields a sum of 36.5. Dividing the sum of squared deviations by n (36) yields 1.01 (rounded), which is the variance. The standard deviation is the square root of the variance. The square root of 1.01 is 1.00 (rounded), which is the standard deviation of the z scores in Table 5.1.

9.

The area between the mean and $z = +0.51 = .1950$

The area between the mean and $z = -3.01 = .4987$

The area between the mean and $z = +3.01 = .4987$

The area between the mean and $z = +1.96 = .4750$

The area between the mean and $z = -1.07 = .3577$

The area beyond z when $z = -0.79 = .2148$

The area beyond z when $z = -2.54 = .0055$

The area beyond z when $z = +1.43 = .0764$

The area beyond z when $z = +0.66 = .2546$

The area beyond z when $z = -0.66 = .2546$

The area between $z = +0.67$ and $z = +1.35 = .4115 - .2486 = .1629$

The area between $z = +1.35$ and $z = +2.59 = .4952 - .4115 = .0837$

The area between $z = -0.84$ and $z = -1.89 = .4706 - .2995 = .1711$

The area between $z = -2.25$ and $z = -2.75 = .4970 - .4878 = .0092$

The area between $z = -0.67$ and $z = +3.01 = .2486 + .4987 = .7473$

The area between $z = -2.15$ and $z = +1.35 = .4842 + .4115 = .8957$

The area between $z = -1.47$ and $z = +0.64 = .4292 + .2389 = .6681$

The area for z scores above (greater than) $z = +2.26 = .0119$

The area for z scores below (less than) $z = +2.26 = 1 - .0119 = .9881$

The area for z scores above (greater than) $z = -2.26 = .4881 + .5000 = .9881$

The area for z scores below (less than) $z = -2.26 = .0119$

The area for z scores above (greater than) $z = +0.79 = .2148$

The area for z scores below (less than) $z = +2.98 = .4986 + .5000 = .9986$

11.

$.10 \times 65 = 6.5$, so 6 or 7 students would be given As. Let's say the professor is feeling generous and will give 7 As, which is $7/65 = 11\%$ (rounded) of the students. Assuming the distribution of exam scores is approximately normal, to identify the scores that lie in the upper 11% of the curve, we first consult the z-score table to find the value of z when 11% of the area under the whole curve lies beyond (in this case, above) that z. According to the table, that value of z is approximately 1.23, which is 1.23 standard deviations above the standard normal curve mean of 0. The mean of the exam scores is 73 and the standard deviation is 22. If we add 1.23 standard deviations to the mean of the exam scores, we will have the score where approximately 11% of the scores lie above it—i.e., the score that divides the As from the Bs. So, $1.23 \times 22 = 27.06$ and $73 + 27.06 = 100.06$. Thus, a score of 100 is the division point between the As and Bs and scores above 100 get As.

To give 40% of the scores a C, we want to know the value of z where 20% of the area under half the standard normal curve would lie between it and either side of the mean. The z-score table tells us that value is approximately 0.52. With our scores having a standard deviation of 22, we can add and subtract .52 standard deviations from the exam mean score of 73 to determine the range of scores that includes about 40% of the scores. So, $0.52 \times 22 = 11.44$ and $73 + 11.44 = 84.44$ and $73 - 11.44 = 61.56$. Thus, scores between approximately 61 and approximately 84 would be assigned Cs.

CHAPTER 6

3.

When statisticians refer to such real life examples as flipping a coin from your pocket, their purpose is to illustrate and increase understanding of the abstract, theoretical principles of probability theory. The trials and outcomes of probability theory conform strictly to certain specified assumptions; real life examples rarely do so. For example, real coins are rarely perfectly fair and more than two possible outcomes may occur (landing on edge). In real-life coin flipping, the probability distribution might not always conform exactly to the theoretical distribution produced by the statistician's calculations. Also, statisticians often assume an infinite number of trials, which is not possible in real life.

7.

Assuming a standard playing deck with 52 cards and 13 cards of each of four suits, with each card having an equal chance of being drawn on each draw:

Sampling with replacement (putting the card drawn back in the deck before drawing the next card):

The chance (probability) of drawing a card of a particular suit on each draw is 13 out of 52, which reduces to 1 out of 4, or .25. The chance of drawing five cards of the same suit in a row is

$$.25 \times .25 \times .25 \times .25 \times .25 = .00098$$
(rounded) or about 1 in 1,000.

Sampling without replacement (not replacing the card drawn after a draw):

The probabilities change after each draw. Depending on assumptions made, here is one way of calculating the probability of drawing five cards of the same suit in a row (rounding the interim calculations to the nearest hundredth):

$$.25 \times 12/51 \times 11/50 \times 10/49 \times 9/48 =$$
$$.25 \times .24 \times .22 \times .20 \times .19 = .00050$$

13.

A correction for continuity corrects for the situation in which a theoretical curve based on the assumption of continuous data (such as the z-score distribution) is used to approximate a distribution of discrete variable values (such as a binomial distribution) when samples are less than 100. The correction is necessary because the estimations of discrete variable values using the theoretical continuous data curve are more accurate if the correction for continuity is used. The correction is made by subtracting .5 and adding .5 to the appropriate quantity in the numerator of the applicable formula (for example, for calculating a z score).

CHAPTER 7

1.

Typically, parametric statistics are used with variables measured at the interval or ratio levels, while nonparametric statistics are used with variables measured at the ordinal and nominal levels. So, knowing the level at which a variable is measured helps determine which statistical analyses are appropriate for analysis of the data.

3.

We select a sample from a population so that we don't have to study a whole population. Whenever we select a sample to learn something about a population, we run the risk that the sample may not reflect the characteristics of the population. When the sample's characteristics do not match those of the population, we say that sampling error has occurred. So, the origins of sampling error are in the process of selecting a sample. If we sample randomly, we have the best chance of drawing a sample whose characteristics pretty closely match the population. And, if we sample randomly, we can use probability theory to construct sampling distributions and estimate the amount of sampling error that occurs.

5.

Sampling distributions give researchers a way of measuring sampling error by providing a distribution of the possible outcomes of random trials (trials in which each of the possible outcomes [or combinations of outcomes] is equally likely). Using them gives us a way of determining (measuring) how likely a particular outcome (or combination of outcomes) we observe is to occur if the trials are random.

7.

Population parameters are the population statistics we estimate on the basis of the corresponding sample statistics. Sampling error is the difference between the parameter estimate based on sample statistics and the corresponding actual population parameter. Sampling distributions are distributions of sampling error. Sampling distributions give us a way of determining the likelihood of sampling errors of different sizes when we make estimates of population parameters from sample statistics.

9.

The normal distribution of a variable in a population is important in many cases because many of the sampling distributions that are used to estimate sampling error and parameter estimates are constructed assuming that the variable is distributed normally in the population. Exceptions are the sampling distributions for means, which for large samples will equal their population means even if the variable is not distributed normally in the populations. Also, nonparametric statistics do not require a normal distribution of variable values in the population.

13.

To answer this question, we will need the point estimate of the sample mean (26) and unbiased estimates of the sampling distributions' standard errors for samples of size 100 and 200.

For sample size of 100, the unbiased standard error estimate is 2.5 divided by the square root of 99, which is 2.5/9.95 (rounded), which equals 0.25 (rounded).

For sample size 200, the unbiased standard error estimate is 2.5 divided by the square root of 199, which is 2.5/14.11 (rounded), which equals 0.18 (rounded).

The z score corresponding to 95% confidence limits is 1.96. The confidence limits for a sample size of 100 are given by 26 ± 1.96 (.25), which is 26 ± .49. The confidence limits are 25.51 and 26.49 and the interval is 26.49 − 25.51 = .98.

The confidence limits for a sample of size 200 are given by 26 ± 1.96(.18), which is 26 ± 0.35 (rounded). The confidence limits are 25.65 and 26.35 and the interval is 26.35 − 25.65 = .70.

Comparing the confidence limits and intervals for the two different sample sizes indicates that larger sample sizes yield smaller confidence limits for a given confidence level (in this case, the 95% confidence level). This suggests that sample based point estimates of population means are more likely to be closer to the actual population means when samples are larger.

15.

To calculate the confidence interval for a proportion, we need the proportion (in this case, it is 52%), the z score corresponding to a 95% confidence level, which is 1.96, and an estimate of the standard error of the sampling distribution for proportions, given a sample size of 700. The calculation for the latter estimate is the square root of $(52 \times 48)/700$, which is the square root of 2496/700. So, 2496/700 = 3.57 (rounded) and the square root of 3.57 = 1.89 (rounded).

Plugging the numbers into confidence limits for proportions formula (Formula 7.7), we have 52 ± (1.96)(1.89), which is 52 − 3.70 (rounded). The confidence limits are 48.30 and 55.70 and the margin of error for the point proportion estimate of 52% is ± 3.70%.

CHAPTER 8

1 and 2.

Number of Juveniles With and Without a Delinquency Court Record by Median Grade

Median Grade	Juvenile Court Record		
	Yes	No	Total
A	4	36	40
B	27	108	135
C	113*	338*	451
D or lower	26	39	65
Total	170	521	691

* The convention of rounding all decimals of .5 or larger up has been followed; doing so adds 1 to the total N.

3.

Research hypothesis: There is a relationship between sex and number of days in jail for first offense theft over $150.00. (Go to top of column on right)

Null Hypothesis: There is no relationship between sex and number of days in jail for first offense theft over $150.00.

5.

According to the chi squared table, for 1 degree of freedom the probability of a chi squared = 32.78 is less than .001. This means that there is less than 1 chance in 1,000 that the cell frequencies we observed occurred by chance if there is no relationship between sex and days in jail. Reject the null hypothesis and say that the evidence supports the research hypothesis that there is a relationship between sex and days in jail. Males tend to spend more days in jail than do females for this theft offense.

7.

First order partial tables:

Crime Conviction by Ethnicity

Lower Class

	Convicted of a Crime		
Ethnic Group	Yes	No	Total
White	2	2	4
Non-White	2	2	4
Total	4	4	8

Crime Conviction by Ethnicity

Middle Class

	Convicted of a Crime		
Ethnic Group	Yes	No	Total
White	2	2	4
Non-White	1	7	8
Total	3	9	12

Is there a relationship between social class and ethnic group? The contingency table for answering this question is the following:

	Ethnic Group		
Social Class	White	Non-White	Total
Lower	4	4	8
Middle	4	8	12
Total	8	12	20

Is there a relationship between social class and conviction? The contingency table for this questions is the following:

	Convicted		
Social Class	Yes	No	Total
Lower	4	4	8
Middle	3	9	12
Total	7	13	20

There does appear to be a relationship between ethnicity and social class. Non-Whites are more often in the middle class than are whites.

There does appear to be a relationship between ethnicity and conviction. The middle class is less often convicted than is the lower class.

The time sequence of the variables is as follows: ethnicity with/before social class (tf), conviction record. There is a relationship between each of the variables in the zero order table and the test variable. The apparent zero order relationship disappears in one of the two partial tables. So, the result of our elaboration analysis is mixed—a combination of interpretation and specification.

11.

Assume the data are valid and any observed relationships are not spurious. If the data are from a population, any observed relationships between or among variables hold for that population. If the data are from a sample, sampling error must be taken into account when interpreting the data. Inferential statistics help us generalize from the sample statistics to the corresponding population parameters, but we must be satisfied with answers to questions about variable relationships that are expressed in terms of probabilities.

13.

It is not entirely clear which data were included in the reported chi square analysis, in part because we are not provided the df they used for determining the probability of their chi square. A relatively large number of cells with expected frequencies of less than 5 may be problematic for chi-square analysis, even though the sample sizes in this case are large.

The authors did percentage in the direction of the independent variable: the values of the independent variable form the columns and the column totals were used to calculate the percentages.

The total N is large and there are large differences in the total numbers of the different ethnicities. Because they are standardized quantities, the percentages do help make comparisons. There is no apparent relationship between ethnicity and disposition.

CHAPTER 9

5.

For a one tailed test, the significance levels would be (in the order listed in the question):

$$<.01, <.05, >.10, <.005, <.005, <.05$$

For a two-tailed test:

$$<.02, <.10, >.20, <.01, <.001, <.10$$

7.

The critical values for the ts are 2.353, 4.541, 2.179, 1.782, <1.296 (or 1.28 from the z-score table), <2.485, 2.060.

9.

A finding that has a low probability of occurring under the null hypothesis does not indicate anything about the strength of the relationship between variables. A low statistical probability of a finding means only that the chances are small that the observed result occurred by chance alone and that there is a relationship between the variables, but the strength of the relationship is unknown.

15.

A variety of other difference between means t tests could be applied to this data. Some would be for independent samples and some for dependent samples.

CHAPTER 10

1.

We could compare median or modal exam scores; we could also compare the ranges and standard deviations of the exam scores for the four cities.

3.

The between-group variance is called the explained variance because it is based on the deviations of the sample means from the grand mean and these differences include the effect, if any, of the independent variable, as well as sampling error. The within-group variance, based on the deviations of individual scores in each sample and their respective means, includes sampling error alone.

5.

The sampling distributions and associated significance levels for F vary with both sample sizes and the number of samples. When both dfs = infinity, the critical value of F is 1.00. Also, lower critical values are associated with larger sample sizes, relative to the number of samples. (Compare the significance levels for the last two examples.)

CHAPTER 11

1.

The slope of a least squares regression line differs from the slope of just any other straight line in a scattergram in that the slope of the regression line best describes how much change in the dependent variable occurs with each one unit change in the independent variable.

3.

The y intercept of any straight line, including a least squares regression line, in a scattergram is the value of y on the line when the value of x on the line equals 0. The y intercept of a least squares regression line is the y intercept of the line that minimizes the distance between it and the data points in the scattergram.

5.

Correlation is a measure of concomitant variation—of how closely changes in one variable track with changes in another variable. It is only one of three criteria necessary to establish causation. (The other two criteria are appropriate time sequence and the elimination of other possible casual variables.) Even a strong correlation may be spurious.

9.

    a. It is a quasi-experimental research design. The two neighborhoods have been matched to help control for other possible causal variables and the samples are random giving us the best chance of getting a sample that reflects the characteristics of the population from which they were drawn. But there are only "after" and no "before" measurements of the dependent variables and there is no control group. It will provide relatively weak evidence for an argument that one patrol strategy is better than the other.

    b. A few of examples:

Research hypothesis: View of police is related to patrol strategy.

Null hypothesis: View of police is not related to patrol strategy.

Analyze by comparing the two means of the dependent variable "view of police" for the two patrol strategy groups using a t test for the difference between independent random sample means.

Research hypothesis: View of neighborhood safety is related to patrol strategy.

Null hypothesis: View of neighborhood safety is not related to patrol strategy.

Analyze by comparing the two means of the dependent variable "view of neighborhood safety" for the two patrol strategy groups using a t test for the difference between independent random sample means.

Research hypothesis: View of police is related to feelings of safety in the bicycle patrol sample.

Null hypothesis: View of police is not related to feelings of safety in the bicycle patrol sample.

Analyze by constructing a scattergram of "view of police" and "view of feelings of safety" variable in the bicycle patrol sample. Do a bivariate correlation analysis to determine the strength of the relationship, if any, between the two variables in the bicycle patrol sample.

Research hypothesis: View of police is related to age in the auto patrol sample.

Null hypothesis: View of police is not related to age in the auto patrol sample.

Analyze by constructing a scattergram of the "view of police" and "age" variables for the auto patrol sample. Do a bivariate correlation analysis to determine the strength of the relationship, if any, between the two variables in the auto patrol sample.

c. The independent variable (patrol type) is measured at the nominal level with two values. The dependent variable (view of police) is measured at the ratio level. The samples are independent random samples. An appropriate test is the t test for the difference between two independent random sample means. (All calculations rounded.) (See Chapter 9, Formula 9.2b.)

First calculate the means for the two groups:

Bicycle Patrol Mean = 3.14; Automobile group mean = 2.86

Then calculate the sum of the squared deviations from the mean for each sample:

Sum of squared deviations for Bicycle patrol sample = 10.86; sum of squared deviations for Auto patrol sample = 10.86

Divide the sum of squared deviations by $n - 1 = 6$; In both cases, this = 1.81.

Divide each of these results by $n = 7$, which = .26

Sum these two results, which = .26 + .26 = .52.

Find the square root of .52, which = .72.

Then calculate t for the difference between these two independent random sample means.

$t = (3.14 - 2.86)/.72 = .28/.72 = .39$

Assume the population variances are equal and $df = (n_1 - 1) + (n_2 - 1) = 6 + 6 = 12$. The critical value for t at the .05 level (non-directional two-tailed test) = 2.179. The value of $t = .39$ is not statistically significant. The evidence is that there is no difference between the two populations in their views of the police.

d. Follow the same procedures as in c, using the t test for differences between the means for two independent random samples. In this case, the dependent variable is feelings of safety, so the difference between the means for feelings of safety would be analyzed. The means are Bicycle, 3.14 and Auto, 2.29. The sums of the squared deviations are: Bicycle, 10.86 and Auto 7.40. The final calculations for t are $t = 3.14 - 2.29/.66 = .85/.66 = 1.29$. The df and critical value are the same as in c. The $t = 1.29$ is not significant and the evidence indicates there is no relationship in the population between patrol type and feelings of safety.

e. Both age and views of police are assumed to be ratio level variables. Appropriate analyses would be constructing a scattergram of the two variables and calculating a Pearson's r correlation analysis. To calculate r, use Formula 11.8b with x as age and y as view of police. Following are the required sample statistics and the value of r.

$$\Sigma x = 150, \Sigma y = 42, \Sigma x^2 = 1,622, \Sigma y^2 = 148, \Sigma xy = 455, n = 14.$$

$$r = +.28$$

There is a modest positive correlation between age and view of police in the sample;

older preteens tend to have a more positive view of the police. The coefficient of determination is $r^2 = .08$, indicating only about 8% of the variance in views of police is explained by age.

f. Both age and feelings of safety are assumed to be ratio level variables. Appropriate analyses would be constructing a scattergram of the two variables and calculating a Pearson's r correlation analysis. To calculate r, use Formula 11.4b with x as age and y as feelings of safety. Following are the required sample statistics and the value of r.

$$\Sigma x = 150, \Sigma y = 38, \Sigma x^2 = 1{,}622, \Sigma y^2 = 124,$$
$$\Sigma xy = 405, n = 14$$

$$r = -.12$$

There is a small negative correlation between age and feelings of safety in the sample. As age goes up, feelings of safety decline somewhat. The coefficient of determination $r^2 = .02$ indicates only about 2% of the variance in feelings of safety is accounted for by age.

i. To calculate $b_{y \cdot x}$ use Formula 11.4b with x as view of the police and y as feelings of safety. The following statistics are required for the formula:

$$\Sigma x = 22, \Sigma y = 22, \Sigma x^2 = 80, \Sigma y^2 = 80,$$
$$\Sigma xy = 75, n = 7$$

$$b_{y \cdot x} = +0.54$$

To calculate the value of a use Formula 11.5.

$$\bar{y} = 3.14, \bar{x} = 3.14.$$

$$a = \bar{y} - b\bar{x} = 3.14 - (+.54)(3.14) = 3.14 - 1.70$$
$$= 1.44$$

The regression line formula is $y = 1.44 + 0.54x$.

This is the formula for the best fitting least squares regression line. It is called the "best fitting" line because it is the straight line that minimizes the distance between it and the data points, with distance measured parallel to the y axis and perpendicular to the x axis. The residuals are the errors in prediction of the values of y from the values of x using the regression line – that is, the distances between the line and the data points measured as described above. They are called residuals because they represent the variance in y that is left over after the values of x and the regression equation are used to predict the values of y. They are the unexplained variations in y. The opposite would be the explained variance in y, which is the improvement in the prediction of y using the regression equation compared with using the mean of y to predict the values of y.

j. Use Formula 11.4b to calculate r. Use the following sample statistics:

$$\Sigma x = 22, \Sigma y = 22, \Sigma x^2 = 80, \Sigma y^2 = 80,$$
$$\Sigma xy = 75, n = 7$$

$$r = +.54; r^2 = .29$$

The moderately large positive correlation of +.54 and coefficient of determination of .29 indicates that, in the sample, as pre-teens' views of the police become more favorable, they tend to feel safer. The coefficient of determination ($r^2 = .29$) indicates that 29% of the variation in feelings of safety is accounted for by variation in views of the police.

We use Formula 11.13 to calculate t to test r for statistical significance. For $r^2 = .29$ and $n = 7$, we find $t = 1.43$. The critical value for t at the .05 level, $df = 5$, and a two-tailed test is 2.571. We do not reject the null hypothesis. The evidence indicates there is no relationship in the population from which the sample was drawn between views of the police and feelings of safety.

k. Use Formula 11.14 to calculate a partial correlation. For views of the police as x, feelings of safety as y; and age as T, the following statistics are required for the calculations:

$r_{xy} = .54$ (from exercise j), $r_{xT} = .255$, $r_{yT} = .14$ (Calculate r_{xT} and r_{yT} using Formula 11.8b)

$$r_{xy.T} = .53$$

The partial correlation of +.53 is the correlation between view of police and feelings of safety holding age constant. The introduction of T as a test factor did not change the original, zero-order correlation between x and y (which was $r = .54$—see j above), it appears that age has almost no influence on the relationship between view of police and feelings of safety in the sample. In the language of elaboration analysis results, it appears to be a replication.

CHAPTER 12

3.

Controlling variables (holding certain variable values constant) is important in science because, by definition, the values of controlled variables do not change (and, therefore, cannot cause any changes in the dependent variable), thereby allowing the researcher to isolate the effects, if any, of the independent variables that are the primary focus of study, whose values do change. Controlling variables is important in helping meet one of the three criteria for establishing causality, eliminating other possible causal variables.

5.

Missing data occurs when, for one reason or another (e.g., interviewer forgot to ask a question, subject refused to answer a question, data were dropped during data cleaning, etc.) data for one or more variables are not available for one or more units of analysis.

Missing data pose a problem for inferential statistical analysis because it complicates interpretation of the results of statistical analyses. Among other things, it may threaten the randomness of a sample (on which the application of inferential statistics is based) and distort the results of sample statistics calculations, such as means and standard deviations. The larger the amount of missing data, the greater the problems posed. Also, the larger the number of variables included in a study, the more likely there will be missing data.

Some of the ways of dealing with missing data are listwise, pairwise, and variable deletion.

7.

The advantage of raw score betas is that they are calculated using the original units of measurement (e.g., dollars, number of inmates, etc.) being studied. Raw score betas indicate the amount of change in the dependent variable for every 1 unit change in the value of an independent variable expressed in these original units (e.g., For every additional correctional officer, the number of inmate disturbances goes down by 2 disturbances.) The disadvantage of raw score betas is that their relative sizes are not directly comparable, so one cannot assess the relative effects of independent variables measured in different units.

The advantage of standardized betas is that there relative sizes are directly comparable, so one can assess the relative effects of independent variables measured in different units by comparing the size of the standardized betas. The disadvantage of standardized betas is that they are not expressed in the original units of measurements, so they cannot be used to predict the values of y in the original units of y. To do this, standardized betas must be reconverted into their nonstandardized equivalents.

9.

Least squares regression and correlational analysis are considered linear models because they both use a straight line (hence, linear) as the model for fitting the data, for determining the direction and strength of a relationship (in the case of correlation analysis), and for predicting the values of a dependent variable from the values of an independent variable (in the case of regression analysis). Curvilinear models may be used instead of linear models in data analysis.

11.

Dummy variables play the same role as interval or ratio level variables in least squares multiple regression and correlation analyses. Dummy variables convert each value of a nominal or ordinal variable into a two value variable (1 if this value is present and 0 if it is absent). The effect of each dummy variable on the dependent variable can be assessed, their betas can be transformed into standardized betas to assess their relative effects, they can be tested for statistical significance, and they can be included or excluded in stepwise multiple regressions and correlations.

13.

Least squares multiple regression and correlation share the same prerequisite assumptions in terms of level of measurement and random sampling. They both use a linear model for fitting data and involve one dependent variable and two or more independent variables.

They differ in their general purposes. Multiple regression analysis is used to predict the values of a dependent variable from the values of two or more independent variables. Multiple correlation analysis is used to determine the direction and strength of the relationship among variables, as measured by the amount of variation in the dependent variable accounted for (explained by) changes in two or more independent variables.

17.

In general, main effects are bivariate effects, controlling for the effects of any other variables included in the analysis.

When more than one independent variable is included in an analysis, the general assumption of the model is that the effects of the two independent variables will be independent of each other and that their combined effects will be additive. Interaction effects are manifested when the effects of two or more independent variables on a dependent variable are greater than the sum of their effects taken separately—that is, the effects are not additive. (In the analysis of nominal or ordinal independent variables, an example would be "specification" in elaboration analysis, where the effects of an independent variable on a dependent variable are greater for some values than for others of another independent variable.)

19.

Nominal or ordinal dependent variables are problematic in least squares multivariate analyses because most such analyses are parametric statistics, requiring normal distributions, homoscedasticity and measurements at the interval or ratio level. Statisticians have developed alternative analyses, such as logistic regression, that use an iterative process, rather than least squares formulas, for arriving at a best fitting equation for predicting the values of y (through logit (y)).

21.

Logits are the natural logs of odds consisting of the probability of "success" to the probability of "failure" to observe a designated value of the dependent variable. Logistic regression equations predict these $\log_e$ odds called logit (y)s.

23.

ANOVA is appropriate in this analysis because the independent variable is measured at the nominal level with three values (high crime, low crime and student), the samples are independent, and the dependent variable (victimization experienced) is measured at the ratio level. A comparison of the dependent variable means using ANOVA is an appropriate test of the null hypothesis that there is no relationship between the variables.

The correlations between risky altruism and crime victimization are higher than those for safe altruism in almost all groups.

A multiple correlation coefficient (R) is a measure of the direction and strength of the association between a dependent variable and two or more independent variables. Each multiple R in the last row of the table is a measure of the combined effects of the variables listed above it. To determine the coefficient of multiple determination we would square each R. These squared values would represent the amount of variance in the dependent variable y explained by the combined effects of all of the independent variables included in the analysis. The R^2s (from left to right and rounded) are: .178, .169, .084.

CHAPTER 13

1.

A nonparametric alternative for the t test is the Mann-Whitney U test. Both test for differences between two random samples. The Kruskal-Wallace H Test is an alternative to ANOVA. Both test for differences between three or more independent samples. Spearman's rank order correlation statistic is an alternative to Pearson's coefficient. Both measure the direction and strength of the relationship between two variables.

3.

In general, none of these tests can be used with nominal-level data because they are all based on rankings, which are ordinal-level data. Nominal level variable values cannot be ranked.

5.

Different statistical analyses have different strengths and weaknesses. When assumptions of some statistical analyses are questionable, it may be advisable to use different statistical analyses based on different assumptions. If all analyses come to the same results, confidence in the results is increased. Using more than one analysis can reveal different aspects of the data that have been gathered. Given current technology it is fairly inexpensive to perform several types of statistical analyses on the same data. The primary disadvantage of using more than one type of statistical analysis is that results might be different and one might be tempted to report only the more favorable results. Doing so is unethical.

7.

Relevant statistics are $\Sigma R_1 = 58.5$, $\Sigma R_2 = 46.5$, $n_1 = 7$, $n_2 = 7$.

Following Formula 13.1, $U_1 = 30.5$.

Following Formula 13.2a, $U_2 = 18.5$.

(Note that $U_1 + U_2 = 49$ and $n_1 n_2 = 49$).

The smaller of the two Us = 18.5, so this is the observed value (U_{obs}) we will use in our calculations following Formula 13.7a.

Following Formula 13.5, $U_{pop} = 24.5$.

Following Formula 13.6, $\sigma_u = 7.826$.

Following Formula 13.7a, $z = -.767$.

At the .05 level of significance, for a one-tailed test the critical value of $z = 1.64$ and for a two-tailed test $z = 1.96$. Our observed $z = -.767$ does not reach either critical value, so the difference between the ranks for the two samples is not statistically significant.

If we performed our calculations with the correction for continuity, the calculated range of z is from $z = -.703$ to $-.831$; still not statistically significant.

11.

To prepare to calculate Spearman's ρ, convert the raw scores for the two variables into ranks, calculate the difference between the ranks on the two variables for each student, square those differences, and sum the squared differences ($\Sigma D_\rho^2 = 252.00$). Then use Formula 13.13 to calculate ρ.

$$\rho = -.527$$

One test for the statistical significance is to consult the Spearman's rho critical values table in Appendix I. According to that table, the critical values for ρ with $n = 10$ at the .05 level of significance and a one-tailed test is .564 and for a two-tailed test is .648. Our observed ρ is not statistically significant.

For another test of ρ for statistical significance, use Formula 13.14 and the t-distribution table.

At the .05 level significance and with $df = 8$, the critical value of t for a one-tailed test is 1.860 and for a two-tailed test is 2.306. For our data,

$$t = 2.17$$

Our observed ρ is statistically significant for a one-tailed test, but not a two tailed test, at the .05 level.

The two test results are somewhat different. The critical values of rho table should be used with small samples.

13.

In a normal distribution, the mean, median and mode have equal values. While we are not given the ranges for these variables, we can determine the lowest possible value for each variable, which would be 0 for all but age; the minimum value of age is, we presume, in the late teens. Adding a variable's standard deviation to or subtracting its standard deviation from its mean and comparing where that value falls relative to the lowest possible variable value also indicates these are not normal distributions. (Remember the relationship between areas under the normal curve and units of standard deviation above and below the mean.)

The four chi-square tests in their Table 5 examine differences between recidivists and non-recidivists for each of the four conditions in their Table 4. The different dfs reported in their Table 5 for the chi-square tests reflect the different number of cells in the contingency tables after the categories in Table 4 were collapsed to achieve a minimum frequency of 5 (one of the requirements for a chi-square analysis). Two tailed tests were used because the authors were not predicting which frequencies would be larger. Only one of the observed chi-square values achieved statistical significance. The overall model chi square is a test of the difference between the predictions of the logistic regression equation using all of the independent variables and and the equation using none of the independent variables. Its non-significance indicates proximity to schools or daycares accounts for very little of the variation in recidivism.

Their Figures 3 and 4 are cumulative percent distributions. The percents are the percents of each of the two populations living within the specified distances measured in feet from the nearest daycare or school, beginning with the percent living closest to a daycare or school. The cumulative percent graphs are constructed by adding the percents for each successively greater distance from a daycare or school to the cumulative percent from the next closest distance. They show the cumulative percents for distances from day cares and schools track very closely with each other. The steep rise of the cumulative distribution curves for the smaller distances indicate the frequencies and percents rise rapidly over those distance values; the flatness of the curves associated with the longer distances indicates the frequencies and percents are at or near zero for those distances.

The nonparametric Mann-Whitney U test was used because the authors wished to compare two independent random sample means for variables that did not meet the assumptions for the parametric t test. It appears to be an appropriate choice for those reasons. The Mann-Whitney U test compares the sum of ranks of two independent random samples following a formula like the one in this chapter.

The r appears to be appropriate because the two variables being correlated are ratio level. Its value is very low and its non-significance indicates no relationship between proximity and recidivism in the population.

The t tests reported in their Table 6 are apparently for the difference between two independent random sample (recidivists and non-recidivist) mean distances. A two tailed test divides the rejection region equally between the two tails of the sampling distribution curve and is used when the research hypothesis does not specify which mean will be larger.

Logistic regression was used for this analysis because the dependent variable (recidivism) is a nominal variable with two values and two or more independent variables were included in the analysis. The analysis included the dependent variable and the distances, as well as other risk factor independent variables. It appears to be an appropriate test for these data for these reasons.

The results indicate that neither distance to daycare nor distance to school is related to recidivism in the population. Neither the chi-square value for the logistic regression model nor the Nagelkerke R^2 (a measure similar to the least squares coefficient of multiple determination) was statistically significant.

15.

Their Table 3 is a correlation matrix consisting of Spearman's ρs relating the scores on each of the subscales of the measures of self-control at the entrance and exit of an adult offender boot camp program. Note that this is a different kind of correlation matrix than we discussed in Chapter 11. The correlations in the diagonal are for the same subscale at entrance and exit. They all are positive, indicating higher scores at entrance are associated with higher scores at exit from the boot camp.

Spearman's ρ appears to be an appropriate statistic because it is a nonparametric measure of the strength and direction of the relationship between two ordinal level variables. One-tailed significance tests were used because the authors' research hypothesis stated which scores would be larger.

Comparing the baseline (entrance) and exit subscale means for each of the subscales shows that they are pretty close to each other in value, indicating fairly stable self-control scores from entrance to exit, though the measures of self-control, both overall and for each subscale, except physical activities, decreased a bit from entrance to exit.

Bibliography

Bailey, C. (2006). *A guide to qualitative field research* (2nd ed.). Thousand Oaks, CA: Sage.

Bierstedt, R. (1970). *The social order.* New York: McGraw-Hill.

Blalock, H. (1972). *Social statistics* (2nd ed.). New York: McGraw-Hill.

Braga, A., & Weisburd, D. (2010). *Policing problem places: Crime hot spots and preventive policing.* Oxford, UK: Oxford University Press.

Bronowski, J. (1956). *Science and human values.* New York: Harper Torchbook.

Cresswell, J. W. (2007). *Qualitative inquiry and research design* (2nd ed.). Thousand Oaks, CA: Sage.

Crime and Delinquency. (2000a). Special issue 46(2).

Crime and Delinquency. (2000b). Special issue 46(3).

Curtis, Y. (2010). David Weisburd wins the Stockholm Prize in criminology. *NIJ Journal, 266,* 31. Retrieved July 25, 2010, from http://www.ncjrs.gov/pdffiles1/nij/230409.pdf

Denzin, N. K., & Lincoln, Y. S. (1994). *Handbook of qualitative research.* Thousand Oaks, CA: Sage.

Eck, J. E., Chainey, S., Cameron, J., Leitner, M., & Wilson, R. (2005, August). Mapping crime: Understanding hot spots. *NIJ Special Report.* Retrieved August 3, 2010, from http://www.ncjrs.gov/pdffiles1/nij/209393.pdf

Farrington, D. P., Ohlin, L. E., & Wilson, J. Q. (1986). *Understanding and controlling crime: Toward a new research strategy.* New York: Springer-Verlag.

Fisher, R. A. (1995). *Statistical methods, experimental design and scientific inference.* New York: Oxford University Press.

Fitzgerald, J. & Cox, S. M. (2002). *Research methods and statistics in criminal justice: An introduction* (3rd ed.). Belmont, CA: Wadsworth.

Gabor, T. (1986). *Prediction of criminal behavior.* Toronto: University of Toronto Press.

Gill, J. B. (2010, January 17). Calif. police ramping up evidence-based policing. Retrieved August 4, 2010, from http://www.policeone.com/community-policing/articles/1990344-calif-police-ramping-up-evidence-based-policing/. Comment on the article by derb79.

Goffman, E. (1961). *Asylums.* Garden City, NY: Doubleday.

Guba, E. (Ed.). (1990). *The paradigm dialogue.* Newbury Park, CA: Sage.

Harries, K. (1999). *Mapping crime: Principle and practice* (NCJ 178919). Washington, DC: National Institute of Justice. Retrived from http://www.ncjrs.gov/html/nij/mapping/pdf.html

Hatry, H., Blair, L., Fisk, D., & Kimmel, W. (1976). *Program analysis for state and local government.* Washington, DC: The Urban Institute.

Hawkins, N. (2010). Perspectives on civil protective orders in domestic violence cases: The rural and urban divide. *NIJ Journal, 266,* 4-8. Retrieved August 2, 2010, from http://www.ncjrs.gov/pdffiles1/nij/230409.pdf

Jensen, C. J. (2006). Consuming and applying research evidence-based policing. *Police Chief, 73*(2). Retrieved August 7, 2010, from http://PoliceChiefMagazine.org/magazine/index.cfm?fuseaction=display_arch&article_id=815issue_id=22006

Johnson, E. S. (1981). *Research methods in criminology and criminal justice.* Englewood Cliff, NJ: Prentice Hall.

Kelling, G. L., Pate, T., Dieckman, D., & Brown, C. (1974). *The Kansas City preventive patrol experiment: A summary report.* Washington, DC: The Police Foundation.

Kendall, P. L., & Lazarsfeld, P. F. (1950). Problems of survey analysis. In P. F. Lazarsfeld & R. K. Merton (Eds.), *Continuities in social research: Studies in the scope and method of "the American soldier"* (pp. 133–196). New York: Free Press.

Kohout, F. J. (1974). *Statistics for social scientists: A coordinated learning system.* New York: Wiley.

Manning, P., & Van Maanen, J. (Eds.). (1999). *Policing: A view from the streets.* Santa Monica, CA: Goodyear.

Mayo, E. (2011). *The human problems of an industrial civilization.* London: Routledge.

Milgram, S. (1974). *Obedience to authority: An experimental view.* New York: Harper and Row.

Pearsall, B. (2010, June). Predictive policing: The future of law enforcement. *NIJ Journal, 266,* 16–19. Retrieved August 3, 2010, from http://www.ncjrs.gov/pdffiles1/nij/230409.pdf

Plackett, R. L. (1983). Karl Pearson and the chi squared test. *International Statistical Journal, 51,* 59-72.

Reaves, B. A. (2010, December). *Local police departments, 2007* (NCJ231174). Washington, DC: Bureau of Justice Statistics.

Rice, S. K., Dirks, D., & Exline, J. J. (2009). Of guilt, defiance, and repentance: Evidence from the Texas death chamber. *Justice Quarterly, 26*(2), 295–326.

Ritter, N. (Ed.). (2007, June). LAPD Chief Bratton speaks out: What's wrong with criminal justice research—and how to make it right. *NIJ Journal, 257.* Retrieved July 15, 2010, from http://www.ojp.usdoj.gov/nij/journals/257/chief-bratton.html

Schmitt, G. R. (2010). *Overview of federal criminal cases, fiscal year 2009.* Washington, DC: U.S. Sentencing Commission.

Sherman, L. W., Gottfredson, D. C., MacKenzie, D. L., Eck, J., Reuter, P., & Bushway, S. D. (1998, July). *Preventing crime: What works, what doesn't, what's promising* (Research in Brief). Washington, DC: NIJ.

Sherman, L. W., Schmidt, J. D., & Rogan D. P. (1992). *Policing domestic violence: Experiments and dilemmas.* New York: Free Press.

Skolnick, J. H. (1967). *Justice without trial.* New York: Wiley.

Stigler, S. M. (1999). *Statistics on the table: The history of statistical concepts and methods.* Cambridge, MA: Harvard University Press.

Thompson, B. (2006). *Foundations of behavioral statistics: An insight-based approach.* New York: Guilford.

Tufte, E. R. (1997). *Visual explanations: Images and quantities, evidence and narrative.* Cheshire, CT: Graphics Press.

Tufte, E. R. (2001). *The visual display of quantitative information* (2nd ed.). Cheshire, CT: Graphics Press.

Walters, G. D. (1992). *Foundations of criminal sciences. Vol. 2: The uses of knowledge.* New York: Praeger.

Wolfgang, M. F., Figlio, R. M., & Sellin, T. (1972). *Delinquency in a birth cohort.* Chicago: University of Chicago Press.

Index

Note: figure (*f*), glossary (*g*), table (*t*)

A, in logistic regression, 440, 443–444.
    See *Y* intercept 545*g*
a, in linear regression. *See y*
    intercept 545*g*
a and *b*:
    best fitting constants in linear
        regression, 368–370, 390–393
A and β
    estimating constants, in logistic
        regression, 440, 443–444
Academy of Criminal Justice Sciences
    (ACJS), 39
Additive components, dividing total
    variation in *y* into two, 332–336
Alpha:
    α symbol, 230, 266, 545*g*
Alpha level, 230. *See* significance level
Alternative hypothesis, 229 *See*
    research hypothesis
American Psychological Association
    (APA), 39
American Society of Criminology
    (ASC), 39
Analysis:
    chi-square, 258–270. *See also*
        Chi-square analysis
    correlation, 379
    elaboration, 245–258. *See also*
        Elaboration analysis
    partial, 246. *See also* partial
        correlation analysis and
        partial regression analysis
    regression. *See* Regression analysis
    of variance. *See* ANOVA
Analysis of variance, 545*g*. *See also*
    ANOVA
Anchorage (AK) Coordinated Agency
    Network (CAN) project,
    448–454
ANOVA, defined, 326

ANOVA (one way):
    assumptions and hypotheses,
        327–331
    basic ideas underlying, 331–337
    dividing total variation in *y* into
        two additive components,
        332–336
    F statistic. *See F* statistic
    null hypothesis, testing in, 336–337
    presenting results, 347–348
    relationship between *F* and *t*, 352
    summary, 348*t*
    symbols and meaning in analysis
        of, 330*t*
    theoretical test statistic *F*, 337
    Tukey's HSD test, 349–350
Appropriate time sequence, 31, 545*g*
Areas under the normal curve, 149*f*,
    152–159:
    defined, 545*g*
    means, standard deviations and,
        curve, 141–144
Arneklev, B. J., 508
Arrestee Drug Abuse Monitoring
    program (ADAM), 9
Average deviation, as measure of
    dispersion, 112–113, 545*g*

b, 363–365, 368–370. *See also*
    slope and linear regression
    coefficient, 545*g*
β, 545*g*
    as logistic regression coefficient,
        440–444
    as probability of type II error, 230
Backward stepwise regression,
    422, 545*g*
Bar graphs, 545*g*
    caution with, 80–84
    creating, 55–58

cumulative frequency
    distribution, 69
cumulative percent distribution,
    69–71
frequency distribution, 55–58
proportional area, 134–140
segmented, 73–75
Barnard, George, 437
Baseline model calculations, 446
Before-after research design,
    34–35, 545*g*
Before-after with control group
    design, 35–38, 545*g*
Bell-shaped distribution, 94–95,
    109–110, 140 546*g*
Berkson, Joseph, 437
Best fitting linear regression line, 366,
    368–372, 546*g*, 370–372
Best fitting (linear regression) line
    constants *a* and *b*,
    368–370, 390–393
Beta (β), 230–231, 443–448, 545*g*
    standardized, 446
Beta (b) 368–370, 545*g*
    standardized, 378–379
Beta weights, 359*t*, 378, 545*g*
Between-group sum of squares,
    335, 545*g*
Between-group variance,
    337, 545*g*
Biased estimates, 208–209, 545*g*
Bimodal distributions, 103, 104*ft*
Binomial distributions, 177–184, 545*g*
    defined, 546*g*
    as sampling distribution,
        197–202, 545*g*
Binomial probability distributions,
    177–180, 545*g*
    conclusions, 184
    correction for continuity, 181–183

normal curve approximations of, 180–183
probabilities and random sampling, 184–185
Bivariate analysis, 545g
Bivariate statistical analysis, 46
Bliss, Chester, 437
Blue Crush initiative, 11
Bratton, William, 10, 11

Campus Crime Statistics Act, 520–521
Careers, professionalization of in criminal justice, 12
Carlson, Bonnie, 308–309
Casewise deletion, 412
Categorizing, 545g
statistics and, 5
Causal chain, 28, 545g
Causal inference, 35, 400, 401, 546g
Causality, conditions for:
about, 30
appropriate time sequence, 31
concomitant variation, 31
elimination of other possible causes of, 31
Causal variable, 27–29
Cause/causality/causal relationship, 546g
Cell frequencies, 237, 546g
calculating expected, chi-square analysis, 261–264
converting to percents, 242–243
Cell(s):
defined, 546g
in tables, 237
Census, 32, 546g
Central limit theorem, 205, 207–208, 546g
Central tendency, measures of, 127t
collapsing variable values, 103–105
mean, 97–99
median, 99–102
mode, 102–103
mode/median/mean distributions, 105–108
select appropriate, 108–111
Chi-square analysis, 546g
about, 258
assumptions, 258–259
basic ideas underlying, contingency tables and, 259–261
calculating expected cell frequencies, 261–264
calculating x^2, 264–265

results, presenting, 268–272
as univariate of goodness-of-fit test, 268
using chi-square table, 265–266
Chi square (χ^2) statistic, 259, 264–265
Classic experimental design, 35–38, 546g
Clery Act, 520–521
Coefficient of correlation, 546g
Coefficient of determination (r^2), 388–390, 546g
Coefficient of multiple correlation (See multiple correlation coefficient) (R^2), 411t, 546g
Coefficient of multiple determination, 422–423
Collapsing categories, 240–242, 546g
Collapsing variable values, 103–105
Column marginal frequencies, 238, 546g
Columns in contingency tables, 236–239
defined, 546g
COMPSTAT, 11
Concomitant variation, 31, 246, 546g
Confidence intervals, 447, 546g
limits, for difference between means, 316–318
inferential statistics and, 209–216
Confidence level:
defined, 546g
inferential statistics and, 209–216
Confidence limits, 546g
inferential statistics and, 209–216
intervals and, for difference between means, 316–318
Contingency tables, 257, 546g
chi-square analysis and, 259–261
collapsing categories, 240–242
constructing, cross-tabulation and, 236–239
diagonals, reading in, 243–245
titling and labeling, 239–240
using percents in, 242–243
Continuous variable, 546g
Continuous variable values, 23–24
Control group, 546g
before-after research with, 35–38
Control variable, 246. See also test factor
Conversion of the raw data to ranks, 467–468, 546g
Coordinates, of data points, 360, 546g

Correction for continuity, 181–183, 546g
Correlation, 546g
cross-tabulation and, 393–396
defined, 31
symbols, 359t
Correlation analysis, 379, 546g
assumptions of, 413
dummy variables in, 423–425
linear partial regression and, 397–398
reporting results of, 430–436
Correlation and regression, symbols and their meaning in, 411t
Correlation coefficient (Pearson's r), 380, 386–387, 546g
Correlation matrix, 383, 546g
Correlation of variables, 380
Correlation statistics, tests of statistical significance for, 430
Counting, 5, 546g
Covariance, 546g
Covariance of variables, 380
Cox & Snell R square, 447
Crime mapping, 14
Crime rate, calculate, 51–53
Criminal justice:
careers in, professionalization of, 12
statistics-based initiatives for improving, 13–15
Criminal justice, statistics use in:
description, 6–7
estimation, 7
explanation, 7
prediction, 8
sources of data, 8–9
Critical region, 267, 546g
Critical value, 265
Cronbach, L.J., 507
Cross-product of x and y, 369, 380–381, 546g
Cross-tabulation, 546g
contingency table, constructing, 236–239
correlation and, 393–396
defined, 236
Cumulative frequency distribution:
bar graph, 546g
bar/line graphs, 69
line graph, 546g
tables, 67–69, 546g
Cumulative percent distribution, tables/bar line graphs, 69–71
tables/bar/line graphs, 69–71

Cumulative percent distribution:
  bar graphs, 546g
  line graphs, 546g
  table, 546g
Curvilinear relationship, 244, 245f, 376–377, 547g

D: *See* difference score
  estimating standard error of sampling distributions for, 311–312
  mean and shape of sampling distributions for, 311
Data, 547g
  dealing with missing, 124–125
  defined, 2
  sources of, criminal justice, 8–9
Data analysis, ethics in:
  about, 38–39
  due diligence, in data management and, 39–40
  plagiarism, 39
Data array, 547g
Databases, 8–9, 547g
Data distribution:
  cumulative, 67–71. *See also* Cumulative distribution
  frequency distribution bar graphs, 55–58
  frequency distribution line graphs, 58–63
  frequency distribution tables, 53–55
  graphs, 73–86. *See also* Graphs
  percent distribution tables/graphs, 63–67
  trend graph, 62–63
Data distributions, creating, 53
Data mining, 533
Data point, 547g
  defined, 360
  in scattergram, 361f
Data set, 547g
Datum, 2, 547g
D_ρ (difference) score, Spearman's rho, 310–314, 547g
Decile(s):
  defined, 547g
  analysis, measure of location, 120–123
Decimal(s):
  defined, 547g
  statistical analysis and, 48–49
Decimal percent, 50

Degrees of freedom:
  calculating, 299–301, 313–314
  defined, 547g
Degrees of freedom, determining, 264–265
de la Place, Marquis, 141
Demographic variables, controlling for, 434–435
De Moivre, Abraham, 141
Dependence between random samples, 282–283, 547g
Dependence within a random sample, 282, 547g
Dependent events, 172, 547g
Dependent random samples, 283, 310, 547g
Dependent variable, 27–29, 547g
Description, 6–7, 547g
Descriptive analysis:
  assumptions and cautions, 398–400
  univariate, 47–48
Descriptive statistics, 47, 547g
Diagonals, of tables, 243–245, 547g
Difference score, 310, 548g, 547g
Directional hypothesis, 287, 547g
Discrete variable values, 23–24, 547g
Dispersion, measures of:
  average deviation, 112–113
  range, 112
  selecting appropriate, 117–118
  variance/standard deviation and, 113–117
Distribution:
  bell-shaped, 94–95, 110f
  binomial, binomal probability and, 177–180
  constructing sampling mathematically, 197–202
  creating data, 53–71. *See also* Data distribution, creating
  kurtosis, 97
  measures of central tendency, 97–111. *See also* Central tendency, measures of
  normal, 95, 140–149
  probability, 176–177
  sampling, inferential statistics and, 191–192
  skewed, 96
  theoretical normal curve, 140–141
  for t showing critical values, 305f
D_ρ, 547g
Drug Use Forecasting, 9
Due diligence, data management/analysis, ethics, 39–40, 547g
Dummy variables, 423–425, 547g

Effect (in ANOVA), 335, 547g
Effect component, 335
Effect variable, 27–29
Elaboration analysis, 547g
  about, 245–246
  examples of, 251–257
  explanation, 249
  interpretation, 249–250
  no apparent relationship in zero-order table, 251
  replication, 248–249
  specification, 250–251
Eliminate other possible causes, 31, 547g
Empirical construction, of sampling distribution, 193–196
Empirically falsifiable, 229–230
Empirically falsifiable hypotheses, 547g
Error, 547g
Error (in ANOVA), 335
Error component, of total sum of squares, 335
Error of estimate, 367, 418, 440, 547g
Estimation:
  biased and unbiased, 208–209
  defined, 547g
  population means, 202–216
  population proportions, 217–221
  population variances, 338–345
  statistics and, 7
Ethical integrity, in data analysis, 38–40. *See also* Data analysis, ethics in
Event, 168, 172, 547
Evidence-based best practices, 13, 547g
Exhaustive categories (or variable values), 547g
Exhaustive list of possible outcomes, 170, 547g
Exhaustive variable values, 23
Exp (β), 445–446, 547g
Expected frequencies, 259, 547g
Experimental design, 35–38, 547g
Experimental group, 35, 547g
Experimental research design, 35–38, 284–285
Explained sum of squares, 335, 547g
Explained variance, 337, 547g
Explanation:
  defined, 547g
  elaboration analysis and, 249
  statistics and, 7

F and *t*, relationship between, 352
F distribution(s), 346, 547*g*
Federal Bureau of Investigation (UCR), 520–521
Fifth rule of probability theory, 171
First-order partial relationships, 247, 547*g*
First-order partial tables, 247, 547*g*
First rule of probability theory, 170
Fisher, R. A., 141, 326
Fitzgerald, Jerry (Statistics: A Researcher's View), 529–538
Forward stepwise regression, 422, 548*g*
Fourth rule of probability theory, 171
Fractions:
  defined, 548*g*
  statistical analysis and, 48–49
Frequency counts
  defined, 3, 548*g*
  statistical analysis, 48
Frequency distribution:
  bar graphs, 55–58, 143*f*, 201*f*, 202*f*, 232*f*, 548*g*
  comparing, 231–236, 270
  curve, 211*f*
  defined, 548*g*
  line graph, 58–60, 548*g*
  line graph, *z*-scores, 148*f*
  tables, 53–55, 548*g*
Frequency polygons, 58–63, 548*g*
Friedman two-way ANOVA, 495
F statistic, 337, 548*g*
  calculating, 345–346
  follow-up analysis after significant, 348–349
F tables, 347
F tables, using, 347
  representations of sampling distributions for, 346*f*
  sampling distributions for, 346

Gaines, Larry K., 269–270
Garbage in-garbage out, 40, 398, 548*g*
Gauss, Karl Frederich, 141
Generalizing, to populations, 542
General linear multiple regression equation, 418–420
Giblin, Mather J., 448–454
Goodness-of-fit:
  defined, 427, 548*g*
  test, chi-square as univariate, 268
  test, *r* as, 382
Gosset, W. S., 281
Gottfredson, M.R., 505–510
Grand mean, 332, 548*g*

Graphs:
  about, 71–72
  bar, frequency distribution, 55–58
  bar/line cumulative frequency distribution, 69
  bar/line cumulative percent distribution, 69–73
  caution with, 80–86
  line, frequency distribution and, 58–63
  percent distribution tables and, 63–67
  pictographs, 78–80
  pie, 75–78
  potentially misleading aspects of, 80–87
  power of, 72–73
  proportional area, 134–140
  scattergrams. *See* Scattergrams
  segmented bar, 73–75
  titling and labeling, 80
  trend, 62–63
Grasmick, H.G., 507
Grouped scores, 103–108, 548*g*
Guassian curve or distribution, 141, 548*g*

H, 551*g*
Herman L. Toulson Correctional Boot Camp (TBC), 506
Heteroscedasticity, 287–288, 548*g*
Higher Education Opportunity Act, 520–521
Hirschi, Travis., 505–510
Histograms, 57, 548*g*
Homant, Robert J., 432–436
Homoscedasticity, 287–288, 548*g*
Hosmer-Lemeshow Goodness-of-Fit Test, 447
Hypothesis, 548*g*
  ANOVA (one way), 327–331
  bivariate, 258
  directional/nondirectional, 287
  as proposed causal explanations, 27–29
  research/null, 29–30
  univariate, 258
Hypothesis testing, 548*g*
  basics of, 228–230
  both variables at ordinal level, 236
  defined, 228
  one variable at nominal level/one variable at ordinal level, 234–236
  significance level, 265
  type I and type II errors, 230–231

Icon pictograph, 84–85
Illinois State Department of Corrections (DOC), 521–523
Imputing, missing variables, 125
Independence, within/between a random sampling, 282–285
Independence between random samples, 282–283, 548*g*
Independence within a random sample, 282, 548*g*
Independent events, 172, 548*g*
Independent random sample:
  defined, 282, 548*g*
  means, sampling distributions for difference between, 293–297
  version of the *t* test, 285–305
  version of *t* test, theoretical formulas for, 291–293
  version, of *t* test, calculating *t* for, 298
Independent variable, 549*g*
  designating *y* as, 372–373
  hypothesis and, 27–29
Inferential statistics, 549*g*
  assumptions/cautions, 221–222
  defined, 47, 168, 190
  parametric and nonparametric, 221
  sampling distributions and role in, 191–192
Interaction effects, 427–429, 549*g*
Interpretation:
  defined, 549*g*
  elaboration analysis and, 249–250
Inter-University Consortium for Political and Social Research, 9
Interval estimates, of population means, 202–204, 206
  biased/unbiased, 208–209
  confidence intervals, confidence limits, confidence levels, 209–216
  defined, 549*g*
  estimating standard error of sampling, for distribution means, 206–207
  third provision, of central limit theorem, 207–208
Interval-level measurements, 25, 549*g*
Interval (level) variable, 549*g*
Intervening variable, 28, 549*g*

Jeanne Clery Disclosure of Campus Security Policy, 520–521
Jensen, Carl J., 14

Kelling, G.L., 11
Kendall, Patricia, 246
Kendall coefficient of
  concordance, 495
Kruskal-Wallace *H* (K-W *H*) test, 549*g*
  about, 479
  assumptions of, 488
  basic ideas underlying, 488–489
  calculating, 492–493
  concluding remarks, 495
  defined, 462
  preparing data for analysis in,
    489–492
  reporting results of analysis, 495
  sample study, 480–488, 496–498
  testing for statistical significance,
    494–495
Kurtosis:
  defined, 549*g*
  distributions and, 97
K-W BSS_{obs}, 549*g*

Labeling, tables and graphs, 80
Lazarsfeld, Paul, 246
Least (sum of) squares, 368, 549*g*
Lenz, Nygel, 496–498
Leptokurtic distributions, 97, 549*g*
Likelihood ratio test, 447
Linear least squares bivariate
  correlation analysis, 379–383
  assumptions and cautions, 398–400
  calculating r^2, and the constants (*a*
    and *b*), 390–393
  coefficient of determination r^2,
    388–390
  comparing *r* and *b*, 386–387
  correlation matrixes, 383
  outliers, problem of, 383–386
  statistical measures, strength of
    relationship, 393
Linear least squares bivariate
  regression analysis,
    365–368
  assumptions and cautions, 398–400
  best fitting lines and means of *x*
    and *y*, 370–372
  calculating the best fitting
    (regression) line constants *a*
    and *b*, 368–370
  cautions with predictions from
    linear regression lines, 379
  designating *y* as the independent
    variable, 372–373
  linear nonlinear relationships,
    376–377

positive/negative/ no relationship,
  373–376
standardized betas, 378–379
Linear least squares correlation
  analysis, regression analysis and,
    359–360
Linear least squares multiple
  correlation, 422–423
Linear least squares multiple
  regression:
  assumptions of, 413
  tests of statistical significance
    for, 430
Linear least squares multiple
  regression analysis:
  about, 413–414
  general linear multiple regression
    equation,
    418–420
  linear multiple correlation,
    422–423
  standardized betas, 420–421
  stepwise regression, 421–422
  trivariate best fitting plane,
    414–418
Linear least squares partial regression,
  correlation analysis and,
    397–398
Linear least squares regression
  lines, 379
Linear least squares relationship, 244,
  376–377, 549*g*
Line graphs:
  caution with, 84–85
  cumulative distribution, 69
  cumulative percent distribution,
    69–71
  frequency distribution and, 58–63
  proportional area, 134–140
Listwise deletion, 412, 549*g*
Location, in distribution, measures of,
  120–124
Log_e, see natural log
Logan, J.R., 11
Logarithm-based analyses, 436–437
Logistic regression, 437–448, 549*g*
  analysis, 437–438
  assumptions and cautions, 454–455
  assumptions of, 438
  deriving logits, 441–443
  equation, 440
  estimating constants *A* and *B* in,
    443–444
  interpreting results of, 444–448
  natural log, 439

odds, 438–439
reporting results of, 448–454
symbols and their meaning in, 411*t*
Logits, 438, 441–443, 549*g*
Log likelihood, 446, 549*g*
Los Angeles Police Department, 10
Low-income housing, study, 523–524

Mackenzie, D.L., 505–510
Main effects, 427–429, 549*g*
Mann, H.B., 465
Mann-Whitney *U* test, 549*g*
  assumptions of, 465
  basic ideas underlying, 465–466
  calculating, 471–475
  concluding remarks, 479
  defined, 462
  preparing data for analysis,
    466–470
  reporting results of, 479
  sampling distribution for *U*,
    475–476
  symbols and meanings in, 472
  testing *U* for statistical significance,
    476–478
Mann-Whitney-Wilcoxon Test, 465
Marginal frequency, 238, 549*g*
Margin of error, 219, 549*g*
Marquis de la Place, 141
Matching, 283, 549*g*
Math anxiety, 15–16
Mathematical calculations, results of
  as statistics, 4
Maximum likelihood estimation,
  443–444, 446, 549*g*
Mean
  confidence limits and intervals for
    the difference between,
    316–318
  defined, 549*g*
  estimating standard error sampling
    distributions for, 206–207
  group scores, 105–108
  measure of central tendency, 97–99
  special property of, 118–119
  standard deviations, area, under
    normal curve, 141–144
  and standard errors, sampling
    distributions,
    196–197
  of *x* and *y* best fitting lines and,
    370–372
  and *z*-score, 152–153
Mean and Shape of the Sampling
  Distributions for *D*, 311

Mean and shapes, of sampling distributions for difference between two means, 293–294
Mean squares:
  defined, 338, 549g
  between, 338, 549g
  within, 339, 549g
Measurement, of central tendency, 97–111. *See also* Central tendency, measures of
Measurement levels:
  additional considerations, 26–27
  interval-level of, 25
  nominal-level, 24
  ordinal-level, 24–25
  ratio-level, 26
Measures of association, 549g
Measures of central tendency, 97–111, 549g
Measures of dispersion, 112–119, 549g
Measures of location (of a score in a distribution), 120–124, 549g
Measuring, 5, 549g
Median:
  defined, 549g
  grouped scores and, 105–108
  measure of central tendency, 99–102
Memphis Police website, 11
Mesokurtic distribution, 97, 549g
Missing data, 549g
  analysis and, 411–413
  dealing with, 124–125
Mitchell, O., 505–510
Mode:
  defined, 549g
  distribution of, as measure of central tendency, 102–103
  group scores, 105–108
Models, 425–427, 446, 550g
Morrison, Gregory B., 384–385
Mulford, Harold A., 529
Multicollinearity, 429–430, 550g
Multimodal distributions, 103, 104t, 550g
Multiple causation, 28, 550g
Multiple correlation
  analysis, 422–423, 550g
  coefficient, 422–423, 550g
Multiple regression, symbols and their meaning in, 411t
Multiple regression analysis, 413–432, 550g
  aim of, 414
  dummy variables in, 423–425
  reporting results of, 430–436

Multivariate statistical analysis, 46, 550g
Mutually exclusive
  categories (variable values), 23, 550g
  possible outcomes, 170

Nagelkerke R Square, 447
National Archive of Criminal Justice Data (NACJD), 9
National Crime Victimization Survey (NCVS), 8
National Incident-Based Reporting System (NIBRS), 8, 520–521
National Youth Survey-Family Study (NYSFS), 8
Natural log, 439, 550g
Negative linear relationship, 244, 550g
Negatively skewed distributions, 96
Negative relationship, 373–376
Negative skew, 550g
Nominal level measurement, 24, 232–236, 550g
Nondirectional hypothesis, 287, 550g
Nonlinear relationships, 244–245, 376–377
Nonparametric inferential statistics, 221, 550g
  assumptions of, 464–465
  cautions about, 510–511
  choosing between parametric and, 462–464
Nonquantitative raw data compilations, as statistics, 3–4
No relationship between variables, 373–376
Normal curves, 550g
  approximations, of binomial probability distributions, 180–183
  definition, 142
  means, standard deviations and areas under, 141–144
  tests for, 160–161
  theoretical, 140–141
  theoretical standard, z scores and, 144–149
Normal distribution, 94–95, 550g
Normality, tests for, 160–161
Null hypothesis, 29–30, 230t, 550g
  ANOVA (one way), 327–331
  calculating expected cell frequencies, 261–264
  chi-square analysis, for contingency tables, 259–265

chi-square analysis, testing, 258
  defined, 229
  mean and shapes of sampling distributions difference between two means, 293–294
  statistical significance, rejection regions, 266–268
  testing in ANOVA, 336–337
  using chi-square table, 265–266
Number of ranks, 472, 550g

Observed between-group (sample) mean rank sum of squares, 491–492, 550g
Observed frequencies, 259, 550g
Odds:
  calculate, 53
  define, 550g
  logistic regression and, 438–439
Odds ratio:
  defined, 446, 550g
  logistic regression and, 446
OLS, 554g
One-tailed significance test, 303–304, 550g
One-tailed test of significance, 301–304
One-tailed t test, 303–304
One variable at nominal level, one variable at ordinal level, 234–236
One-way analysis of variance, 348, 550g
One-way statistic, 268
Operational definition, 22–23, 550g
Ordinal level:
  both variables at, 236
  one variable at, nominal level, one variable at, 234–236
Ordinal-level measurements, 24–25, 550g
Ordinary least squares (OLS), 368, 550g
Outcome, 550g
  defined, 168
  in elaboration analysis, 252t
  of multiple trials, 173–176
  possible outcomes (36 sets), 174t
  single trial, rules for, 170–172
Outliers, 379, 383–386, 550g

Pair matching, 283, 550g
Pairwise deletion, 412, 550g
Parameter, 168, 202, 550g

Parameter estimation:
    defined, 190–209, 550g
    symbols and formulas for, 222t
Parametric inferential statistics:
    defined, 221, 550g
    choosing between nonparametric and, 462–464
Partial analysis, 246, 397–400, 550g
Partial betas, 417, 550g
Partial correlation, symbols, 551
Partial correlation analysis, 397–400
Partial correlation coefficient, 423, 551g
Partial regression, symbols, 359t
Partial regression analysis, 397–400, 551g
Partial regression coefficients, 417, 551g
Partial slopes, 417, 551g
Pearsall, Beth, 13
Pearson, Karl, 258, 281, 380
Percent(s), 551g
    statistical analysis, 49–51
    using in contingency tables, 242–243
Percentaging in the direction of the independent variable, 243, 551g
Percent distribution:
    cumulative, tables/bar/line graphs, 63–71
    tables, 64–67
Percentile analysis, measures of location, 120–123
Percentiles, 120–123, 551g
Physical control of variables, 409, 551g
Pictographs, 78–80, 84–85, 551g
Pie graphs, 75–78, 551g
Piquero, A.R., 508
Plagiarism, 39, 551g
Platykurtic distribution, 97, 551g
Point estimate, 551g
    defined, 202
    of population means, 202–206
PoliceOne.com, 10
Population, 32, 551g
Population means, point and interval estimates of, 202–204
    interval estimates of, 206–216. See also Interval estimates, of population means
    point estimates of, 205–206
    sampling distributions for sample means, 204–205
    two provisions, of central limit theorem, 205

Population parameters, 168, 551g
Population proportions, estimating, 217–221
Population variance estimates, calculating, 338–345
Positive linear relationship, 244, 551g
Positively skewed, distributions, 96
Positive relationship, 373–376
Positive skew, 95, 551g
Postmeasurements, 284–285, 551g
Power, of inferential statistic test, 231
Power (of a statistical set), 551g
Practical significance, 272, 551g
Prediction, 8, 551g
Predictive analysis, 13–15
    defined, 551g
Predictor blueprint, 441, 551g
Predictor variables, 440, 551g
Premeasurements, 284–285, 551g
Prison study, 521–523
Probabilities, 174–184
    binomial distributions, 184–185
    defined, 168, 551g
    random sampling and, 184–185
Probability distributions, 551g
    about, 176–184
    sampling of outcomes, 100t
Probability theory
    about, 168–169
    applying, 6
    defined, 551g
    fifth rule of, 171
    first rule of, 170
    fourth rule of, 171
    independent/dependent events, 172
    outcomes of multiple trials, rules for, 173–176
    rules of, 169–170
    second rule of, 170
    seventh rule of, 174
    single trial, rules for outcomes, 170–172
    sixth rule of, 174
    as statistics, 4–5
    third rule of, 171
Proportion, 48–49, 551g
Proportional area bar graph, 134–140, 551g
Proportional area graphs, 138–159
Proportions, statistical analysis and, 48–49
Pseudo R^2, 444

Q, 349–350, 551g
Quantile:
    analysis, measures of location and, 120–123
    defined, 551g
Quantitative raw data, as statistics, 3–4
Quantitative research, contrasting views, researchers/practitioners, 9–12
Quartile, 551g
Quartile analysis, measure of location, 120–123
Quasi-experimental research design, 38, 551g

r Pearsons's correlation coefficient, 380–383, 552g. See also Coefficient of determination
R^2, 422–423, 552g
r^2, 390, 392, 552g
r and b:
    comparing, 386–387
    test of statistical significance for, 395–397
Random experiment, 168, 552g
Random numbers, 34, 552g
Random sample:
    binomial distributions and, 184–185
    calculating t for, 313
    defined, 34, 552g
    independent, 282–285. See also Independent random sampling
    means, t test for difference between two dependent, 306–309
    version, of t test, 309–310
Range:
    defined, 552g
    as measurement of dispersion, 112
Rates, statistical analysis:
    about, 51
    crime rate, calculate, 51–53
    defined, 552g
    odds, 53
Ratio, 48, 552g
Ratio-level measurements, 26, 552g
Rations, statistical analysis and, 48–49
Raw data, 3–4, 552g
Regression analysis:
    linear bivariate, 365–368
    linear correlation, basic ideas underlying, 359–360
    linear, defined, 365, 552g
    logistic, 437–448
    symbols, 359t

Regression coefficient
    linear, 368–369, 372–373
    logistic, 440, 443–446
Regression equation
    linear, 367
    logistic, 440
Regression line, 365, 366, 552g
    best fitting constants *a* and *b*, 368–370
Regression of *y* on *x*, linear, 368, 552g
Regression plane, 415–416, 552g
Rejection regions:
    defined, 267, 552g
    statistical significance, 266–268
Relationships between variables, 229–230
    illustration, 245f, 307f
    linear/nonlinear/curvilinear, 376–377
    positive/negative/no, 373–376
Relative frequencies, 50, 552g
Repeat measurement matching, 283, 552g
Repeat measurement samples, 307
Replication:
    defined, 552g
    elaboration analysis, 248–249
Research:
    contrasting views, 9–12
    defined, 2
Research design, 552g
    about, 34
    before-after, 34–35
    before-after with control group, 35–38
    experimental, 284–285
    quasi-experimental, 38
Research hypothesis, 27–29, 229, 552g
Residual, 367, 552g
Rho (ρ), 498–504, 552g
Row marginal frequencies, 238
Rows in contingency tables, 236–239
    defined, 552g
Rules of probability theory, 169–172
$r_{xy \, T}$, calculating, 398–400

Sample, 32, 552g
Sample means, sampling distribution for, 204–206
Sample statistics, 168, 552g
Sampling 32–34, 552g
Sampling distribution, 552g
    binomial, 197–202
    constructing empirical, 193–196

constructing mathematically, 197–202
    defined, 192
    means and standard errors, 196–197
    role in inferential statistics, 191–193
Sampling error, 32, 192, 552g
Sampling frame, 33, 552g
Sandifer, Jacqueline, 314–315
Scale (of a graph), 55, 552g
Scattergrams, 367f, 552g
    about, 360–361
    data points in, 361f
    outliers and, 383–386
    straight lines in, 361–365
    trivariate, 414–418, 415f, 416f, 418f
Schlaf, John H. (Statistics, A Practitioner's View), 517–529
SCIPs. *See* Size changing icon pictographs
Second-order partial analysis, 257
Second rule of probability theory, 170
Segmented bar graphs, 73–75, 552g
Set of outcomes, 174, 552g
Seventh rule of probability theory, 174
Sherman, L.W., 10–11
Significance level, 265, 266, 553g
Simple random sampling, 33–34, 553g
Single trial, rules for outcome, 170–172
Sixth rule of probability theory, 174
Size changing icon pictograph (SCIP), 84–85, 553g
Skewed distributions, 96, 144f, 553g
Skewed to the left, 553g
Skewed to the right, 553g
Slope, 363–365, 553g. *See b*, β and regression coefficient
Smith, Brad, 350–351
Spearman, Charles, 499
Spearman's rank order correlation, 462
Spearman's rho (ρ) analysis, 498–504
    assumptions of, 499
    basic ideas underlying, 499–500
    calculating, 502–503
    concluding remarks, 504–505
    defined, 498–499, 553g
    preparing data for, 500–502
    reporting results of, 504
    testing for statistical significance, 503–504
Specification:
    defined, 553g
    elaboration analysis and, 250–251
Spurious relationship, 31, 249, 553g

SSMIPs. *See* Standardized size multiple icon pictograph
Standard deviation, 113–117, 553g
    means, areas, under normal curve, 141–144
Standard error:
    defined, 553g
    describing sampling distributions, 196–197
    of estimate of population mean, 206–207, 553g
    of the sampling distributions, difference between two means, 294–295
Standardized beta (β*), 420–421, 446, 553g
Standardized beta (*b**), 378–379
Standardized size multiple icon pictograph (SSMIPs), 79–80, 80–83, 553g
Standard normal curve, 214f, 553g
Standard scores, 149, 553g
Statistical analysis:
    descriptive/inferential, 47
    frequency counts, 48
    percents, 49–51
    rates, 51–53. *See also* Rates, statistical analysis
    ratios/fractions/proportions/decimals, 48–49
    univariate, bivariate, multivariate, 46
Statistical controls, 410, 553g
Statistically significant, 266
Statistical Package for the Social Sciences (SPSS), 531–534
Statistical significance:
    and critical values and, 261
    and practical significance, 272
    defined, 272, 553g
    tests, reflections on, 305–306. *See also t* test entries
    rejection regions and, 266–268
Statistics:
    categorizing and counting, 5
    data sources, 8–9
    defined, 2–3, 553g
    description, 6–7
    estimation, 7
    explanation, 7
    mathematical calculations as, 4
    measuring and, 5
    nonquantitative raw data compilations as, 3–4
    prediction and, 8

probability theory as, 4–5
quantitative raw data as, 3–4
sources of, 5
study, why?, 9
succeed in study of, 15–17
use, in criminal justice, 6–8.
 See also Criminal justice, statistics use in
Statistics: A Practitioner's View (Schlaf)
 background, 517–519
 low-income housing, 523–524
 luck as seat-of-the-pants statistics, 524–525
 prison study, 521–523
 rapist story, 525–529
 Uniform Crime Reports/Clery Reports, 520–521
Statistics: A Researcher's View (Fitzgerald)
 background, 529–530
 Cornell College years, 530
 graduate school statistics course years, 530–531
 graduate student research years, 531–534
 reflections on a research center, 538
 research practitioner years, 534–538
Statistics-based initiatives, 13–15
Stepwise regression, 421–422, 553g
Straight lines, in scattergrams, 361–365
Student's t test, 553g See t and t test
Sum of ranks, 472, 553g
Sum of squared deviations from the mean, 113–117, 553g
Sum of squares, 113–117, 553g
Symbols and their meaning:
 in analysis of variance, 330t
 correlation regression, 411t
 logistic regression, 411t
 in multiple regression, 411t
 M-W U calculations, 472t
 partial correlation, 359t
 partial regression, 359t
 in t tests, 286t
Symmetric distribution, 94–95, 553g

t:
 calculating for independent samples version of t test, 298
 calculating for the dependent random samples version of t test, 313
 relationship between z and, 316
 sampling distributions, 281, 299f

Table:
 contingency, constructing, 236–239, 257
 contingency, tilting and labeling, 239–240
 cumulative frequency distribution, 67–69
 cumulative percent distribution, 69–71
 defined, 3–4t, 553g
 F, 347
 frequency. See Frequency tables
 percent distribution, graphs and, 63–67
 Q distribution, 349–350
 titling/labeling, 80
 using chi-square, 265–266
 zero order/first order partial, 247
Tails of the distribution, 94–95t, 553g
Test factor, 246, 553g
Test of independence, 259, 553g
Theoretical normal curve, 140–141, 553g
Theoretical standard normal curve, z scores and, 144–149
Theory, 27, 553g
Third rule of probability theory, 171
Titling, labeling tables/graphs, 80
Total sum of squares, 334–335, 553g
Total variance, 337, 563g
Trend grap, 62–63h, 563g
Trial, 168, 554g
Trivariate best fitting plane, 414–418
t sampling distributions, 281, 553g
t statistic, 281, 554g
t test:
 assumptions and cautions, 308, 317–320
 basic ideas underlying random sample version of, 309–310
 calculating results, 314
 defined, 281, 554g
 for difference between two dependent random sample means, 306–309
 for difference between two independent random sample means, 285–288
 independent random samples version of, 289–291
 one-tailed, 303–304
 presenting results for, 314–316
 statistical significance. calculating degrees of freedom, 299–301

 statistical significance, sampling distributions for t, 298–299
 theoretical formula for dependent random sampling version of, 310
 theoretical formula for independent random samples version of, 291–293
 two-tailed, 304–305
Tukey's HSD test, 349–350, 554g
Turner, S., 508
Two-tailed significance tests, 304–305, 554g
Two-tailed t test, 304–305
Two-way analysis of variance, 348, 554g
Two-way statistic, 268
Type I error, 554g
 defined, 30
 hypothesis testing and, 230–231
Type II error, 554g
 defined, 30
 hypothesis testing and, 230–231

U:
 defined, 554g
 sampling distribution for (M-W U) test, 475–476
 testing for statistical significance, 476–478
Unbiased estimates, 208–209, 209–216, 554g
Unexplained sum of squares, 335, 554g
Unexplained variance, 337, 554g
Uniform Crime Reporting System (UCR), 8, 520–521
Unimodal distribution, 103, 104t, 554g
Units of analysis, 27t
 defined, 554g
 variables and, 22–23
Univariate analysis, 189–223, 554g
Univariate descriptive analysis, 47–48
Univariate descriptive statistics, 125–127, 554g
Univariate goodness-of-fit test, 268
Univariate hypothesis, testing for, 258
Univariate statistical analysis, 46
University of Michigan, crime databases, 9
U.S. Department of Education, 520–521

Variable, 554g
  both at nominal level, 232–233
  both at ordinal-level, 236
  continuous and discrete, 23–24
  defined, 3–4
  dummy, 423–425
  independent/dependent, 27–29
  nominal level/ordinal level, 234–236
  units of analysis and, 22–23
Variable deletion, 412, 554g
Variable interactions, 250–251, 554g
Variable values, 3–4t, 554g
  continuous/discrete, 23–24
  exhaustive/mutually exclusive, 23
Variance, 113, 554g
Variance deviation, 113–117

Wald test, 447
Weisburd, D., 11
Whitney, D.R., 465
Within-group sum of squares, 335, 554g
Within-group variance, 337, 554g

x,y, 360–361, 554g
$x.y$, 372–373, 554g
x and y best fitting lines, means of and, 370–372, 554g
x axis, 360, 554g
$\bar{X}_{K\text{-}W\ BSS}$, 494, 554g

Y, 439–440, 445, 554g
y, 372–373, 554g
$y.x$, 368, 554g

y axis, 360, 554g
Y intercept, 440–445, 554g
y intercept, 363, 417, 554g

Zanderbergen, Paul A., 480–488
Zero-order relationship, 246–247, 554g
Zero-order tables, 247, 251
z-scores, 152–159, 554g
  relationship between t and, 316
  theoretical standard, normal curves and, 144–149
z-scores table:
  about, 150
  areas and proportions under the curve, 153
  defined, 554g
  using, 150–159

LIST OF KEY FORMULAS

MEAN $$\bar{x} = \frac{\Sigma x}{n}$$

VARIANCE $$s^2 = \frac{\Sigma(x-\bar{x})^2}{n}$$

STANDARD DEVIATION $$s = \sqrt{\frac{\Sigma(x-\bar{x})^2}{n}}$$

Z SCORE $$z = \frac{x-\bar{x}}{s}$$

CONVERSION OF BINOMIAL OUTCOMES TO Z SCORES $$z = \frac{x-np}{\sqrt{npq}}$$

CONVERSION OF BINOMIAL OUTCOMES TO Z SCORES (CORRECTION FOR CONTINUITY FOR SAMPLES < 100) $$z = \frac{(x \pm .5) - np}{\sqrt{npq}}$$

EXACT PROBABILITY OF A SPECIFIC BINOMIAL OUTCOME $$p(K) = \frac{T!}{K!(T-K)!} p(S)^K p(F)^{T-K}$$

RELATIONSHIP BETWEEN THE STANDARD ERROR OF THE SAMPLING DISTRIBUTION FOR A MEAN AND THE STANDARD DEVIATION OF SCORES IN THE POPULATION FROM WHICH THE SAMPLE WAS DRAWN $$\sigma_{\bar{x}} = \frac{\sigma}{\sqrt{n}}$$

BIASED ESITIMATE OF THE STANDARD ERROR OF THE MEAN $$\hat{\sigma}_{\bar{x}} = \frac{s}{\sqrt{n}}$$

UNBIASED ESITIMATE OF THE STANDARD ERROR OF THE MEAN $$\hat{\sigma}_{\bar{x}} = \frac{s}{\sqrt{n-1}}$$

CONFIDENCE LIMITS FOR ESTIMATING A POPULATION MEAN $$cl = \bar{x} \pm z(\hat{\sigma}_{\bar{x}})$$

ESTIMATE OF THE STANDARD ERROR OF THE SAMPLING DISTRIBUTION FOR PROPORTIONS $$\hat{\sigma}_p = \sqrt{\frac{p(1-p)}{n}}$$

CONFIDENCE LIMITS FOR A POPULATION PROPORTION $$cl = p \pm z\sqrt{\frac{p(1-p)}{n}}$$

CHI SQUARE $$\chi^2 = \Sigma \frac{(O-E)^2}{E}$$

t TEST FOR INDEPENDENT SAMPLES $$t = \frac{\bar{y}_2 - \bar{y}_1}{\hat{\sigma}_{\bar{y}-\bar{y}}}$$

ESTIMATE OF THE STANDARD ERROR OF THE DIFFERECE BETWEEN MEANS $$\hat{\sigma}_{\bar{y}-\bar{y}} = \sqrt{\frac{\frac{\Sigma(y_1-\bar{y}_1)^2}{n_1-1}}{n_1} + \frac{\frac{\Sigma(y_2-\bar{y}_2)^2}{n_2-1}}{n_2}}$$

t TEST FOR DEPENDENT SAMPLES	$t = \dfrac{\bar{D}}{\hat{\sigma}_D / \sqrt{n}}$
ESTIMATE OF THE STANDARD ERROR OF D	$\hat{\sigma}_D = \sqrt{\dfrac{\Sigma(D-\bar{D})^2}{n-1}}$
CONFIDENCE LIMITS FOR THE DIFFERENCE BETWEEN MEANS	$cl = \bar{y}_2 - \bar{y}_1 \pm z(\hat{\sigma}_{\bar{y}-\bar{y}})$
ANOVA TOTAL SUM OF SQUARES	$TSS = \Sigma y_i^2 - \dfrac{(\Sigma y_i)^2}{N}$
ANOVA BETWEEN SUM OF SQUARES	$BSS = \Sigma \left[\dfrac{(\Sigma y_{ik})^2}{n_k} \right] - \dfrac{(\Sigma y_i)^2}{N}$
ANOVA WITHIN SUM OF SQUARES	$WSS = \Sigma y_i^2 - \Sigma \left[\dfrac{(\Sigma y_{ik})^2}{n_k} \right]$
ANOVA F	$F = \dfrac{BSS/(k-1)}{WSS/(N-k)}$
TUKEY'S HSD	$HSD = Q \sqrt{\dfrac{WSS}{n_{PS}}}$
GENERAL BIVARIATE LINEAR EQUATION	$y = a + bx +$ error of estimate
SLOPE OF THE BEST FITTING REGRESSION LINE (BETA)	$b_{y \cdot x} = \dfrac{\Sigma xy - \dfrac{(\Sigma x)(\Sigma y)}{n}}{\Sigma x^2 - \dfrac{(\Sigma x)^2}{n}}$
y INTERCEPT OF BEST FITTING BIVARIATE REGRESSION LINE	$a = \bar{y} - b\bar{x}$
PEARSON'S CORRELATION COEFFICIENT	$r = \dfrac{\Sigma xy - \dfrac{(\Sigma x)(\Sigma y)}{n}}{\sqrt{\left[\Sigma x^2 - \dfrac{(\Sigma x)^2}{n}\right]\left[\Sigma y^2 - \dfrac{(\Sigma y)^2}{n}\right]}}$
PEARSON'S COEFFICIENT OF DETERMINATION	r^2
TEST OF STATISTICAL SIGNIFICANCE FOR r USING THE t DISTRIBUTION AS THE SAMPLING DISTRIBUTION	$t = \sqrt{\dfrac{r^2}{1-r^2}(n-2)}$
PARTIAL CORRELATION	$r_{xy \cdot T} = \dfrac{r_{xy} - (r_{xT})(r_{yT})}{\sqrt{(1-r_{xT}^2)(1-r_{yT}^2)}}$
COEFFICIENT OF MULTIPLE DETERMINATION (TRIVARIATE)	$R^2 = r_{yx_1}^2 + r_{yx_2 \cdot x_1}^2 (1 - r_{yx_1}^2)$
GENERAL TRIVARIATE LINEAR EQUATION	$y = a + b_1 x_1 + b_2 x_2 +$ error of estimate

List of Key Formulas ❖ 585

PARTIAL SLOPE (TRIVARIATE)	$b_1 = b_{yx_1 \cdot x_2} = \left(\dfrac{r_{yx_1} - (r_{yx_2})(r_{x_1 x_2})}{1 - r_{x_1 x_2}^2} \right) \left(\dfrac{S_y}{S_{x_1}} \right)$
y INTERCEPT (TRIVARIATE)	$a = \bar{y} - (b_{yx_1 \cdot x_2})(\bar{x}_1) - (b_{yx_2 \cdot x_1})(\bar{x}_2)$
STANDARDIZED PARTIAL BETA (TRIVARIATE)	$b_1^* = b_{x_1}\left(\dfrac{S_{x_1}}{S_y} \right) = b_{yx_1 \cdot x_2}^* = \dfrac{r_{yx_1} - (r_{yx_2})(r_{x_1 x_2})}{1 - r_{x_1 x_2}^2}$
ODDS OF SUCCESS	$\text{Odds}_{\text{success}} = \left[\dfrac{p_{\text{success}}}{1 - p_{\text{success}}} \right]$
LOGIT	$\text{logit}(Y) = \log_e \left[\dfrac{p}{1-p} \right] = \log_e(\text{odds})$
GENERAL LOGSTIC REGRESSION EQUATION	$\text{logit}(Y) = A + \beta_1 X_1 + \beta_2 X_2 + \beta_3 X_3 + \ldots + \beta_j X_j + \text{error}$
MANN-WHITNEY U_1	$U_1 = n_1 n_2 + \dfrac{n_1(n_1 + 1)}{2} - \Sigma R_1$
MANN-WHITNEY U_2	$U_2 = n_1 n_2 + \dfrac{n_2(n_2 + 1)}{2} - \Sigma R_2$
MEAN OF THE SAMPLING DISTRIBUTION FOR MANN-WHITNEY U	$U_{\text{pop}} = \mu_{\text{pop}} = \dfrac{n_1 n_2}{2}$
STANDARD ERROR OF THE SAMPLING DISTRIBUTION FOR MANN-WHITNEY U	$\sigma_u = \sqrt{\dfrac{n_1 n_2 (n_1 + n_2 + 1)}{12}}$
TEST OF SIGNIFICANCE FOR MANN-WHITNEY FOR U USING THE Z-SCORE DISTRIBUTION AS THE SAMPLING DISTRIBUTION	$z = \dfrac{U_{\text{obs}} - \mu_{\text{pop}}}{\sigma_u}$
KRUSKAL-WALLIS BETWEEN GROUP SUM OF SQUARES (THREE SAMPLES)	$K\text{-W } BSS_{\text{obs}} = \left[\dfrac{(\Sigma R_1)^2}{n_1} + \dfrac{(\Sigma R_2)^2}{n_2} + \dfrac{(\Sigma R_3)^2}{n_3} \right] - \left[\dfrac{(\Sigma R_T)^2}{N_T} \right]$
KRUSKAL-WALLIS H	$H = \dfrac{K\text{-W } BSS_{\text{obs}}}{\dfrac{N_T(N_T + 1)}{12}}$
KRUSKAL-WALLIS H (Three Samples)	$H = \left[\dfrac{12}{N_T(N_T + 1)} \right] \left[\dfrac{(\Sigma R_1)^2}{n_1} + \dfrac{(\Sigma R_2)^2}{n_2} + \dfrac{(\Sigma R_3)^2}{n_3} \right] - 3(N_T + 1)$
GENERAL FORMULA FOR THE MEAN TEST OF SIGNIFICANCE FOR SPEARM FORK-WBSS	$\bar{X}_{K\text{-W BSS}} = (k - 1)\left[\dfrac{N_T(N_T + 1)}{12} \right]$
SPEARMAN'S rho	$\rho = 1 - \dfrac{6 \Sigma D_P^2}{N_T(N_T^2 - 1)}$
TEST OF SIGNIFICANCE FOR SPEARMAN'S rho USING t AS THE SAMPLING DISTRIBUTION	$t = \sqrt{\left(\dfrac{\rho^2}{1 - \rho^2} \right)(n - 2)}$

About the Authors

Jack Fitzgerald received his BA from Harvard College and MA and PhD from the University of Iowa. His professional interests include research methods, statistics, deviance and criminology. He taught sociology, including research methods and statistics, at Knox College. He is co-author (with Steven M. Cox) of *Research Methods and Statistics in Criminal Justice: An Introduction* and *Police in Community Relations*, as well as several research reports and articles in the professional literature.

Jerry Fitzgerald received his BA from Cornell College and his MA from the University of Iowa. He worked as a research associate in alcoholism studies in the Department of Psychiatry at the University of Iowa. He is author or co-author of over 40 research reports on alcohol and drug abuse published in peer-reviewed professional journals.

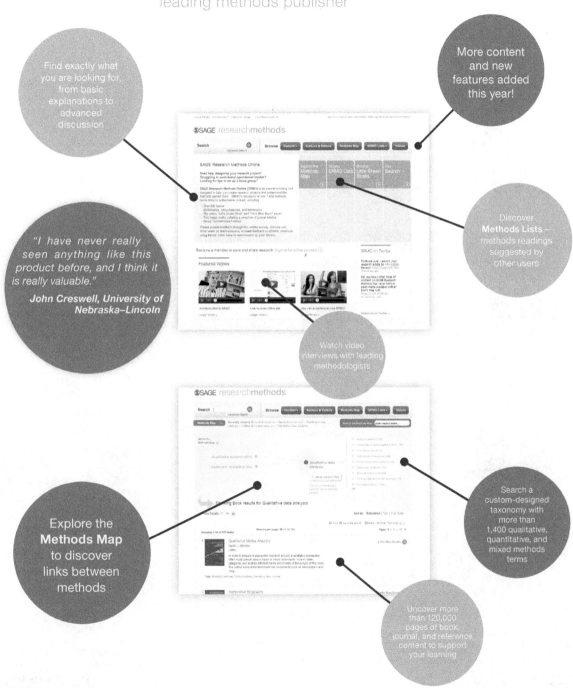

CPSIA information can be obtained
at www.ICGtesting.com
Printed in the USA
LVHW101302140821
695318LV00022B/714